Integrative Approaches to
Crop
Potential

Integrative Approaches to
Crop
Potential

Mohammad Mazid MSc, M Phil, PhD (AMU Aligarh)

Faculty of Applied Sciences and Humanities

Invertis University

Bareilly, UP

CBS

CBS Publishers & Distributors Pvt Ltd

New Delhi • Bengaluru • Chennai • Kochi • Kolkata • Mumbai

Bhubaneswar • Hyderabad • Jharkhand • Nagpur • Patna • Pune • Uttarakhand

Integrative Approaches to
Crop
Potential

ISBN: 978-93-86827-84-5

Copyright © Author and Publisher

First Edition: 2018

Published by Satish Kumar Jain and produced by Varun Jain for

CBS Publishers & Distributors Pvt Ltd

4819/XI Prahlad Street, 24 Ansari Road, Daryaganj, New Delhi 110 002, India.
Ph: 23289259, 23266861, 23266867   Website: www.cbspd.com
Fax: 011-23243014   e-mail: delhi@cbspd.com; cbspubs@airtelmail.in.
Corporate Office: 204 FIE, Industrial Area, Patparganj, Delhi 110 092

Ph: 4934 4934   Fax: 4934 4935   e-mail: publishing@cbspd.com; publicity@cbspd.com

Branches

- **Bengaluru:** Seema House 2975, 17th Cross, K.R. Road,
  Banasankari 2nd Stage, Bengaluru 560 070, Karnataka
  Ph: +91-80-26771678/79   Fax: +91-80-26771680   e-mail: bangalore@cbspd.com
- **Chennai:** 7, Subbaraya Street, Shenoy Nagar, Chennai 600 030, Tamil Nadu
  Ph: +91-44-26680620, 26681266   Fax: +91-44-42032115   e-mail: chennai@cbspd.com
- **Kochi:** 42/1325, 1326, Power House Road, Opposite KSEB Power House,
  Ernakulam 682 018, Kochi, Kerala
  Ph: +91-484-4059061-65   Fax: +91-484-4059065   e-mail: kochi@cbspd.com
- **Kolkata:** 6/B, Ground Floor, Rameswar Shaw Road, Kolkata-700 014, West Bengal
  Ph: +91-33-22891126, 22891127, 22891128   e-mail: kolkata@cbspd.com
- **Mumbai:** 83-C, Dr E Moses Road, Worli, Mumbai-400018, Maharashtra
  Ph: +91-22-24902340/41   Fax: +91-22-24902342   e-mail: mumbai@cbspd.com

Representatives

- **Bhubaneswar** 0-9911037372 • **Hyderabad** 0-9885175004 • **Jharkhand** 0-9811541605 • **Nagpur** 0-9021734563
- **Patna** 0-9334159340 • **Pune** 0-9623451994 • **Uttarakhand** 0-9716462459

Printed at Mudrak, Delhi, India

Contributors

Dildar Hussain
Assistant Professor, Department of Botany
Subhash Chandra Bose Institute of Higher
Education, Prabandh Nagar (Mubarakpur)
IIM Road Lucknow-226021
Phone-0522-6542555
EmailID: scbihe2012@gmail.com

EME Sayed
Department of Horticulture Sciences
Al-Sins University, Egypt

Farah Naz
Department of Plant Science
MJPRU, Bareilly 233122, UP India

Gulnaz Sabri
Microbiology Department
Gitam University, Visakapatnam

Khalil Khan
KVK Chandra Sekhar Azad University of
Agriculture and Technology, Kanpur
Khankhalil64@gmail.com

Mohammad Bagher
Department of Botany Science
Al-Azher University, Iran

Mohammad Mazid
Faculty of Applied Sciences and Humanities
Invertis University, Bareilly 243123,
UP, India

Nooris Naqvi
Department of Botany Science
Bareilly College Bareilly
MJP Rohilkhand University

DK Saxena
Professor
Department of Environmental Science
Bareilly College Bareilly
MJP Rohilkhand University

Taqi A Khan
Higher College of Education
AlKuwair, Oman

Foreword

In the last few years several books about nearly all aspects of plant physiology including the growth and stress mitigation aspects related the plant hormones and photosynthetic importance have appeared ranging in sophistication from the introductory level of plant physiology of Khana and Khana to the very broad and in some way overflowing edition of the recent manual of plant physiology by Bhagbat and Tomar. Whether a new book is need is an emerging question and issue of thinking. 'Need', I think not an authentic word to explain this that a new book should be published. Sufficient justification will be to collect the all published data regarding a particular topic under diverse points of view so as to give new or at least different views into the completeness of data scattered throughout the literature. If we consider the Chapter 1 of the book, easily we can identify that this subject made the theme of this book. Each critical point of development of physiology, biochemistry and molecular biology of each hormone, occurrence, forms, structure, functioning in normal circumstances as well as under drastic environments, relation to productivity is elaborated in a logic style which gives a realistic framework for understanding how the different processes of development are integrated into the whole view of a particular cytoplasmic hormone functioning.

This book is written in a clear language avoiding complicated argumentation and will be useful to all students integrated in this field and those who need a comprehensive summary for this own research. I thank the authors that they have grounded this basis, and I wish him a good response for his work and the book a wide distribution.

ZH Zaidi
Ex-Vice Chancellor
MJPRU, Bareilly, UP, India
Director Development
Invertis University, Bareilly, UP, India

Today, abiotic stress induced signaling is a new and advanced area of research in plant physiology and plant biochemistry. The most familiar signaling molecules that described in this book along with five classical plant hormones (GA, auxin, cytokinin, salicylic acid, triacontanol) and two recent evolving signaling molecules (NO and H_2O_2). In addition, role of plant hormones based signaling molecules including H_2O_2 and NO and nutrients (e.g. sulphur and phosphorus) signaling is still not fully explored in context to plant productivity, also explained here in the detail. The authors also attempted to illustrate a crosstalk between the plant hormones and these signaling molecules to enhance the productivity of plants in future climatic scenario. The multifarious contributions of the plant physiology and plant biochemistry are being increasingly recognized on a global basis. However, information about their diversified role in the welfare of mankind is meagre and scanty. Now, several important developments have emerged in the science of plant physiology. As with the aim to provide the degree (graduate) students, postgraduate students and researchers in plant science with a more elaborative account of physiology and biochemistry of these basic hormones and signaling molecules of plant system with highly updated information.

India is a fascinating country in its productivity or yield wealth where almost all agricultural crops that are consumable to human beings are grown. Quite a considerable number of crops have now been existent in this country as inmates of the man-made (plantations crops) but these apart, a large number are still there which are not cropped in organized plantations.

It is believed that plant physiology should be studied together with biochemistry and molecular biology which have provided new tools for investigating problems related with physiology and biochemistry and molecular biology of enzymes during plant growth and development. This is my fifth book [(1) *Salicylic acid and Environmental Stress*; (2) *Vigna radiata L. and Synthetic auxins*; (3) *Signaling Molecules and Abiotic Stress, LAP, Germany*; (4) *Plant Growth Regulators and Productivity*] and this has been written primarily with a view to provide a standard and balanced textbook on plant physiology and biochemistry of major hormone systems related to productivity under stressful circumstances, and ultimately associated with the productivity and yield of crops. These topics are related with the students of graduate and postgraduate studies in Indian Universities. It deals with both the physiological and biotechnological aspects of plant life processes including stress mitigation and photosynthesis, and thereby helps the readers gain a fundamental understanding to recent knowledge of N-fixation and photosynthesis in its entirety.

The text encompasses those phases of physiology and biochemistry of three most significant hormones (auxin, cytokinin, gibberellic acid, salicylic acid and triacontanol) and their aspects associated with productivity of grain (food) crops in near future with genetic modification. These hormones are witnessed the most rapid advances in recent years. An attempt has been made to present the detailed technical information in a simple and logic style. This book contains total nine chapters. Chapter 1 is introductory in nature and familiarizes readers with the general aspects of signaling (H_2O_2 and NO) and photosynthesis in plant physiology.

Chapters 3, 4, 5, 6 and 7 includes all possible physiological and biochemical changes happened during abiotic and abiotic stresses in plants like production of hormones. Chapter 2 includes the complete elaborative and comprehensive view of proline including its molecular aspects, general aspects, structural and biochemical aspects and factors affecting the proper function. Similarly, the Chapter 8 including the explanation of integrative role of nutrients (sulphur and phosphorus) and plant hormones and a significant photosynthetic fixation of carbon, with recent molecular advances. Also, Chapters 6, 8 and 9 through light on conclusion with productivity and yield prospective in turn with all possible approaches to enhancing yield and productivity of modern-day crops.

I strongly believe that the book for graduate and postgraduate students as well as research students should be of a slightly higher level and this aspect has been kept in mind throughout all the chapters of book. The treatments of chapters are simple, lucid, absorbing, and interesting to make the book readable and enjoyable.

I have tried to present the information on uses of these hormones in sufficiently interesting style that students can read it and get an overview of large areas related to possible uses of these three enzymes in enhancing productivity as well as yield.

Lastly, while gratefully acknowledging everybody who has assisted in this task, the author welcomes valued suggestions from the readers for improvement of the title in future.

Mohammad Mazid

Acknowledgements

First and foremost I praise and acknowledge Allah, the most beneficent and the most merciful, the Great Artisan, the Sustainer, the Omnipresent, the Creater of this universe, Who enshowered His benevolence on me and provided me the strength that made this book.

It is a great privilege to express my profound regard and deep sense of gratitude to my generous and most sympathetic Chancellor Sir, Dr Umesh Gautam, Vice Chancellor, Professor Jagdish Rai, Professor Vice-Chancellor, Professor YSD Arya, and Director Development, Professor ZH Zaidi, Registrar, Mr Santosh Kumar, Invertis University, Bareilly.

Thanks are also due to Professor PP Singh, DSW and Dean, Faculty of Science, for encouragement that I received from him. I shall remain indebted to Professor RK Shukla, Dean Engineering, Dr SP Sharma, Faculty of Science.

I express my heartfelt gratitude to Dr DK Saxena (Department of Botany, Bareilly College, Bareilly) and Professor LN Sharma (Former Vice-Principal, Government Post Graduate College, Bisalpur, Pilibhit), for his meticulous suggestions, constructive criticism, candour discussion and ebullient encouragement throughout the accomplishment of this research work. I have a great pleasure in expressing my sense of gratitude to him who has been very liberal in giving me his most valuable time and attention. They have suggested me many new lines of social and moral studies and gave me invaluable guidance on a large number of complex problems and helped me to overcome my weaknesses. I also acknowledge with thanks the assistance given by Dr Dildar Hussain, Fiza Khan, Nooris Naqvi, and Ms Saima Quddusi from time to time.

My humble gratitude must also be reserved for my students BSc (ZBC) and BSc, BEd II and IV semesters, for being the source of inspiration. They have always stood by my side in all ups and downs of my working style. Their blessings, support, encouragement, and caring attitude have really helped me complete this project.

Special mention must be made of my grandparents (late), parents, uncle, sisters, brothers and friends for their constant moral support at every stage of my work. I wish to express my heartfelt gratitude to all of them for their dedication and forbearance without which this work would have not existed. Last but not least, I am thankful to the Late Dr SS Ali, Principal Scientist (Nematology), IIPR, Kanpur.

Mohammad Mazid

Contents

Potentiality of Signalling Molecules in Crop Productivity Under Harsh Environment

Abiotic stresses are major constraint to agricultural production worldwide. The plants have an inbuilt mechanism to respond to fluctuations in circadian and seasonal environmental conditions. Abiotic stresses disrupt the cellular redox homeostasis which leads to the oxidative stress or generation of ROS. H_2O_2 is the two-electron reduction product of O_2. It is potentially reactive oxygen, but not a free radical, generated as a result of oxidative stress via superoxide (O_2), presumably in a non-controlled manner during electron transport processes such as photosynthesis and mitochondrial respiration. H_2O_2 generation via electron transport is increased in response to environmental stresses such as excess excitation energy, drought and cold and also induced in plants following exposure to a wide variety of abiotic and biotic stimuli. Although, in the last two decades, the potential of H_2O_2 as a stress induced signal to abiotic stress in plants has positioned for much attention. H_2O_2 is produced in response to various stimuli and mediates crosstalk between signalling pathways and is an attractive signalling molecule contributing to the phenomenon of cross-tolerance in which exposure of plants to one stress offers protection towards another. As it is well cleared in present review, recent studies on H_2O_2 functionality to induce tolerance in plants to abiotic stresses have been unravelled and very impressive.

Keywords: *Antioxidant, hydrogen peroxide, nitric oxide, signalling molecules, UV-radiation.*

INTRODUCTION

H_2O_2 has been implicated as a key factor mediating programmed cell death. Plants exposed to abiotic stresses can produce a systemic signal, a component of which may be H_2O_2 which sets up an acclamatory response in unstressed regions of plants. Also, H_2O_2 is an ancient signalling molecule that not only played a key role in inducing evolution of oxygenic photosynthesis but also modulates many physiological events such as stomatal movement, hypersensitive responses and programmed cell death. Increasing evidence now indicates that H_2O_2 acts as a local and systemic signal that directly regulates expression of numerous genes. During normal metabolism in a plant cell, H_2O_2 is generated in chloroplast, mitochondria and peroxisome and is kept in homeostasis by complicated and effective scavenging systems that have developed over the course of evolution. H_2O_2 has a long lifespan, is able to cross biological membranes, and rapidly diffuses from cell to cell or can be transported long distances from its sites of origin in plants. Also, its production quickly responds to various environment stimuli. Thus H_2O_2 has all of the characteristic features of an intercellular signalling molecule, and for this reason, has received increasing attention in recent years (Mazid *et al.*, 2011a; b). Several recent reviews have described the biological activities of ROS, placing special emphasis on the signalling role of H_2O_2. In particular, H_2O_2 that is produced by cytosolic membrane-bound NADPH oxidases has been implicated as a signal in a wide range of biotic and abiotic stress responses. These responses include defence reactions against pathogens and herbivores, the closure of stomata and the regulation of cell expansion and plant development.

Moreover, understanding the role of H_2O_2 in plant growth requires models that accommodate a large number of ways in which it can be formed and degraded at any given time, and that ROS produced by one source may be the drivers or substrates for a second. Whatever the source of ROS, it is now apparent that H_2O_2 acts as a signal to induce a range of molecular and biochemical responses within cells and plants. In addition, exposure to low levels of one stress can induce tolerance towards subsequent higher levels of exposure to the same stress, a phenomenon termed acclimation tolerance. The cellular responses of H_2O_2 differ according to its site of synthesis or perception for example, whether the H_2O_2 is synthesized in plastids or at the plasma membrane.

ENVIRONMENTAL STRESS

The generation of ROS in different location of the plant cell causes injury and cell death (Mano, 2002). On the other hand, ROS plays a vital role in intracellular redox signalling, activating antioxidant resistance mechanisms. It is now well-established that virtually all stresses induce or involve oxidative stress to some degree and the ability of plants to control oxidant levels is highly correlated with stress tolerance. For this purpose, they are equipped with complex processes such as perception, transduction and transmission of stress stimuli. Since all parts of plant body use oxygen to produce energy. Oxidative stress

is mediated by excess ROS which includes OH^-, O_2^- and H_2O_2 can lead to destruction of cellular components including lipid, protein and DNA. H_2O_2 can induce the expression of genes potentially involved in its synthesis such as NADPH oxidase and also of those encoding proteins involved in its degradation, implying a complex mechanism for cellular regulation of oxidative status. H_2O_2 induced the expres-sion of genes encoding ascorbate peroxidase in germinating rice embryos and in Arabidopsis leaves, and wounding induced the expression of gene encoding a catalase via H_2O_2 in embryos and leaves of maize (Abogadallah, 2010). Induction of peroxisome biogenesis genes by various abiotic stresses like temperature, UV and mechanical injury (also generates H_2O_2) and exogenous H_2O_2, place H_2O_2 as a key signal molecule mediating various cellular responses to biotic and abiotic stresses. Further studies is needed to understand the actual function of GPX in chilling stress during H_2O_2 pretreatment as observed during the chilling resistance (Desikan *et al.*, 1998). However, the fact that oxidative stress is a common facet of many cellular stress responses means that elucidating those intracellular signalling processes mediating H_2O_2 signalling.

SIGNALLING MOLECULES AND STRESSES RESPONSE

H_2O_2 is an important signal molecule that induces stomatal closure. To cope with increased levels of ROS, plants have evolved at least four kinds of ROS scavenging enzymes including CAT, SOD, APX and GPX (Gechev and Hille, 2005). It has been shown that H_2O_2 is scavenged by GPX in the guard cells. Recently, Arabidopsis mutants lacking either or both a cytosolic and chloroplatic APX, which are responsible for H_2O_2 removal, are found to be more tolerant to salinity stress. So far, the genes that regulate the expression of H_2O_2 scavenger's enzymes have not been identified and the mechanism of regulation of H_2O_2 levels especially in the stomata is largely unknown. Since H_2O_2 induces leaf stomatal closure. Results of Bienert *et al.* (2006) suggested that accumulation of H_2O_2 in guard cells probably underlies the increased stomatal closure in *dst* mutants and also proposes that accumulation of H_2O_2 in the *dst* mutant may be the result of downregulation of the genes related to H_2O_2 homeostasis.

The ABA is a vital signal that modulates a variety of growth and developmental processes and responses to environmental stress such as drought, salt and cold. When plants are drought-stressed, ABA acts as a key regulator of stomatal apertures to restrict transcription and reduces water loss. H_2O_2 is an essential signal in ABA induced stomatal closure. Exogenous ABA stimulated apoplast CuAo activity, increased H_2O_2 production and [Ca^{2+}] cyt levels in *vicia faba* guard cells and induced stomatal closure. ABA-induced H_2O_2 production and the H_2O_2 activated Ca^{2+} channels in the plasma membrane is important mechanism for ABA-induced stomatal closing (Halliwell *et al.*, 2000). Molecular genetic evidence shows that in Arabidopsis, the plasma membrane-associated NADPH oxidase catalytic subunits AtrobohD and AtrbohF are implicated in the ROS-dependent activation of Ca^{2+} channels and cytosolic Ca^{2+} increase. The results of An *et al.* (2008) suggests that CuAO in *vicia faba* guard cells is an essential enzymatic sources for H_2O_2 production in ABA-induced stomatal closure via the degradation of putrescine. The products from putrescine oxidation by CuAO include pyrroline that CuAo and PAO participate in plant development and defence responses via their reaction products.

SALINITY STRESS AND H_2O_2

In sodic soils, Na^+ binds to negatively charged clay particles, causing swelling and dispersal, thus making the soil less unfit for crop growth.

High salt concentration causes osmotic and ionic stresses in plants. It limits growth and development of plants by affecting several key metabolic processes. Further, salinity alters the activities of many enzymes involve in nitrate and sulphate assimilation pathways in plants which lower their energy status and increases the demand for nitrogen and sulphur. Exogenous H_2O_2 possibly functioned directly or may have induced intracellular H_2O_2 generation to act as a signalling molecule under abotic stresses. Pretreatment of wheat seeds with H_2O_2 has been shown to improve the subsequent salt tolerance of the seedlings (Wahid *et al.*, 2007). The control of Na^+ involvement across the PM and tonoplast to maintain a low Na^+ concentration in adaptation to salt stress (Rausch *et al.* 1996). Further results indicated that H_2O_2 content increased greatly under salt stress. The results suggested that H_2O_2 inducing an increased K to Na ratio. Therefore, it is clear from summing up this new assay that NO may be regulate the H_2O_2 generation (Wang *et al.*, 2007).

METAL POLLUTION AND H_2O_2

Because of their high reactivity they can directly influence growth, senescence and energy synthesizing processes. Tolerance to heavy metals in plants may be defined as the ability to survive in a soil that is toxic to other plants, and is manifested by an interaction between a genotype and its environment. The effects of their toxic influence on plants is largely a strong and fast inhibition of growth processes of the above and underground parts, as well as the active decrease of the photosynthetic apparatus, often correlated with progressing senescence processes (Mazid *et al.*, 2010). High H_2O_2 and O_2^- have been reported earlier in the case of various other plants under Cr, Zn, Pb, etc. (Panda *et al.*, 2003). The increase in SOD activity indicated higher H_2O_2 level seen by the increase in total H_2O_2 content in leaves, which tallies with those observed in the case of *Brassica juncea* and *Vigna radiata* under Zn and Al treatment. However, in barley plants only Mn increased the H_2O_2 content after 5 days but not Cu. This difference may indicate that H_2O_2 accumulation developed differently during a larger stress action. After a long time of Cd action, decrease in SOD activity observed. More recently, Lin *et al.* (2005) have shown that Cu can act through changes in H_2O_2-dependent peroxidase activity followed by cell wall stiffening due to the formation of cross-linking among the cell wall polymers. Also, Cd enhances H_2O_2 accumulation. NADPH oxidase is involved in plant growth and plant response to Cu. In fact, accumulation of H_2O_2 has been observed in Cd-exposed roots and in Cd exposed tobacco suspension cultures. Taking all these observations together, a hypothetical framework may be suggested that Cd induces a transient loss in antioxidative capacity perhaps accompanied by a stimulation of oxidant producing enzymes, which result in intrinsic H_2O_2 accumulation. H_2O_2, then, would act as a signalling molecule triggering secondary defences. These, in turn, would cause an ultimately cell wall rigidification and lignifications, thereby, decreasing cellular viability and finally resulting in cell death (Yeh *et al.*, 2003).

DROUGHT AND H_2O_2

Lipid peroxidation and membrane deterioration in plants lead to an imbalance between antioxidant defences and the amount of ROS resulting in oxidative stress. Apart from morphological structures contributing to drought stress tolerance, plants have evolved a variety of physiological and biochemical processes, which act as components of drought tolerance. The accumulation of H_2O_2 observed at the onset of drought in the mesophyll cell walls of *C. albidus* and *C. clusii* may be associated with its function in cellular

signalling at the first stage of drought or with drought-induced changes in cell wall structure or both. Accumulation of H_2O_2 in mesophyll cell walls occurred as the first symptom of drought in both species, indicating that H_2O_2 may play a role in inter- or intra-cellular signalling or both. Moreover, diurnal variations in H_2O_2 suggest a particular role for H_2O_2 in the response of plants to a combination of stresses. After a general introduction to the concept of drought and oxidative stress and its relationship, Jubany *et al.* (2010) describe the role of H_2O_2 in drought stress responses, emphasizing the importance of studies in H_2O_2 subcellular localization, needed for a better understanding of its role in plant responses to stress. The role of H_2O_2 in intracellular signalling in drought-stressed plants and in the putative regulation of antioxidant synthesis needs to be investigated also. Furthermore, during drought stress, ABA-mediated stomatal closure is a mechanism that plants use to adapt to water deficiency. H_2O_2 that widely generated under abiotic stress has been proposed to function as second messenger in ABA signalling. Early work has shown that H_2O_2 can induce stomata closure. In guard cells, ABA-stimulated ROS accumulation activates plasma membrane.

HEAT STRESS AND H_2O_2

High temperature induces oxidative stress, lipid peroxidation, membrane injury, protein degradation, enzyme inactivation, pigment bleaching and DNA strands disruption in plants. Similarly, low temperature (cold stress) caused many changes in biochemical and physiological processes and ROS-homeostasis in plants. The initial perturbations in plant metabolism are followed by alteration in plant development and morphology with a final result achievement of maximum freezing tolerance. Studies of Apostolova *et al.* (2008) reported that levels of endogenous H_2O_2 strongly increased in the spring wheat cultivar in response to cold hardening, and to a lesser extent in the winter wheat. Results of Wang *et al.* (2010) showed that pretreatment with H_2O_2 at appropriate concentration may improve the tolerance of warm-season Zoysia grasses to chilling stress and that manilagrass had better tolerance to chilling, as evaluated by lower MDA and EL, and better turfgrass quality, regardless of the pretreatment applied. Pretreatment with H_2O_2 has been shown to induce chilling tolerance in normally chill-sensitive maize seedlings (Neto *et al.*, 2005). Similarly, regenerated potato nodal explants treated with H_2O_2 became significantly more thermotolerant compared with untreated control (Lopez-Delgodo *et al.*, 1998). However, if the phenolic substrates are replaced by NADPH or related reduced compounds, a chain reaction starts that provides the basis for the H_2O_2 producing NADPH-oxidase activity of peroxidases. Because H_2O_2 is a mild oxidant that can oxidize thiol residues, it has been speculated that H_2O_2 is sensed via modification of thiol groups in certain proteins. So, therefore, H_2O_2 activates several MAPK cascades have important functions in plant stress responses and development and are key players in ROS signalling and in innate immunity. In Arabidopsis, the transmission of ROS signalling by MAPKs involves the coordinated activation of MPK6 and MPK3. Moreover, in Arabidopsis, H_2O_2 activates the MAPKs, MAK3 and MAK6 via MAPKKKANP1. Overexpression of ANP1 in transgenic plants resulted in increased tolerance to heat shock, freezing and oxidative stress. It is also exhibited that pretreatment of H_2O_2 induces not only ROS-scavenging enzyme activities but also expression of transcripts for oxidative stress related gene encoding sucrose phosphate synthase, D-pyrroline-5-carboxylate synthase and small heat shock protein 26 (HSP26). Microarray analysis of H_2O_2-induced gene expression in Arabidopsis indicates potential H_2O_2-responsive *cis*-elements in genes regulated by H_2O_2. One of these

elements, the as-1 promoter element, also has high homology with redox-sensitive mammalian AP-1 *cis*-element. However, recent analysis of transgenic plants indicates that ROS other than H_2O_2 activates this as-1 element. Further analysis will reveal whether similarity exists among plant, animal and fungal regulatory *cis*-elements of ROS-responsive genes. In contrast to O_2^-, H_2O_2 can diffuse into cells and activate many of the plant defences, including PCD. The suppression of ROS detoxifying mechanisms is crucial for the onset of PCD. Furthermore, recent work shows that H_2O_2 function as a second messenger mediating the systematic expression of various defence related genes in tomato plants. A transient increase in H_2O_2 is suggested to signal activation of protective mechanism for acclimation to chilling. Exogenous application of H_2O_2 can induce tolerance to chilling, high temperature and various other abiotic stresses, all of which cause elevated endogenous H_2O_2 production.

UV STRESS AND H_2O_2

Most types of protein oxidations are especially irreversible whereas a few involving sulphur-containing amino acids are reversible. Protein oxidation is widespread and often used as a diagnostic marker for oxidative stress. Concerns about potential impacts of stratospheric ozone depletion contributed to spark-interest in studies of plant responses to enhanced UV-B levels during the last two decades. The direct effects of UV radiation are mostly damaging, because UV photons have enough energy to create lesions in important UV-absorbing biomolecules such as nucleic acids and proteins. In addition, many of the effects of UV-B involve the differential regulation of gene expression. Responses to UV-B are mediated by both non-specific signalling pathways, involving DNA damage, ROS (e.g. H_2O_2) and various other defensive signalling molecules, and UV-B specific pathways that mediate photomorphogenic responses to low levels of UV-B (Jenkins, 2009). In the leaves of tropical tress, the ambient UV-B radiation might contribute to the reversible decline in potential PS-II efficiency observed upon exposure to full and direct sunlight. Progress in the understanding of the mechanism that mediates these effects of UV-B has been slow for various reasons. Moreover, UV-B may activate a variety of molecular sensitizers and give rise to enhanced H_2O_2 levels, which may lead to convergence with the wound induced cascade downstream of NADPH-oxidase. Arabidopsis leaves pretreated with H_2O_2 have been shown to develop increased tolerance to excess light.

STRESS INDUCTION OF SIGNALLING MOLECULES

Previous studies have shown that H_2O_2 function as stress signal in plants, mediating a range of resistance mechanisms in plants under stress conditions. The plasma membrane is an important protective barrier against extracellular H_2O_2. In higher plant plasma membranes are known for their high sterol content, which suggests that native plant membranes are relatively impermeable to non-electrolytes. The work of Phillips et al. (2005) has suggested that algal plasma membrane may contain pores for H_2O_2 signalling and defence-related small neutral solute like H_2O_2. Gradient of H_2O_2 have been reported across the membranes from mammalian cell lines, bacteria and yeast, suggesting that native biological membranes generally prevent the free diffusion of H_2O_2. The physiological role of H_2O_2 permeability across the tonoplast remains somewhat unclear. Although H_2O_2 diffusion across membranes is often considered as a passive property of lipid bilayers native membranes represent significant barriers for H_2O_2. H_2O_2 is detected by DAB (diamoinobenzidine) staining. The calculative identity differences

in the conduction between the substrates and reveal channel residues critically involved in H_2O_2 conductions. The results of Dynowski et al. (2008) strongly suggest that plasma membrane aquaporin pores determine the efficiency of H_2O_2 signalling between cells. Cellular H_2O_2 redox chemistry is mainly restricted to compartments surrounded by membranes such as peroxisome and mitochondria and may also be found in other endomembrane compartment. Among the ROS, H_2O_2 seems best suited to play the role of signalling molecule due to its higher stability and longer half-life. For example, in winter wheat (Triticum aestivum) leaf, chilling at $4\,°C$ caused the H_2O_2 level to increase to three-fold that of control within 1 min. Recently, PCD triggered in barley aleurone by the phytohormone gibberellins also found to be mediated by H_2O_2, implying a role for H_2O_2 in developmental PCD in addition to that induced by a stress factor. Specific H_2O_2 generation in plants involves plasma membrane NADPH oxidases that produce the O_2^- by enabling the transfer of electrons from the cytosolic NADPH across the membrane to external molecular oxygen. The spontaneous dismutation of the short-lived O_2^- produces external H_2O_2 followed by H_2O_2 influx and the subsequent activation of Ca^{2+} channels. Such NADPH-dependent processes have been identified in the plant defence against oxide burst in the regulation of ABA signalling and stomatal movements (Hancock et al. 2001). Under normal conditions, H_2O_2 can be generated in normal metabolism via the Mehler reaction in chloroplasts electron transport system in mitochondria and photorespiration in peroxisomes (Neill et al. 2002). Furthermore, studies of Wi et al. (2010) suggest that H_2O_2 is important signalling molecule involves in response to and abiotic stresses and developmental and physiological processes and stress tolerance of H_2O_2 treated transgenic plants resulted from reduced ethylene biosynthesis, which decreased ROS accumulation via increased gene expression and activity of ROS-detoxifying enzymes. Different stimuli activate specific H_2O_2-generating pathways and produce the signal leading to specific physiological processes (Neil *et al.*, 2002).

Although it is hypothesized that H_2O_2 produced intracellularly diffuses to other cells for use by POX and other defensive enzymes, it non appearance more probable that intracellularly produced H_2O_2 is consumed quickly and locally, and that extracellular metabolism uses H_2O_2 produced extracellularly. H_2O_2 localization with in tissues, sometimes to portions of cell wall in root hairs, or in epidermal cells in association with wounding or stomatal movements, indicates as does compartmentation at the tissue level within the leaves, in vascular tissues, and in areas of regulation (Naves *et al.*, 1998). During oxidative stress H_2O_2 is shown to induce stomatal closure (McAnish *et al.*, 1996) showed that elicitors could induce H_2O_2 production and Lee *et al.* (1999), demonstrated that both these responses are linked: elicitors caused H_2O_2 production which in turn, caused stomatal closure. For H_2O_2 to really to be a specific signalling molecule, a mechanism must exist to perceive the elevation of H_2O_2 in cells. H_2O_2 can interact with cysteine residues within proteins and this redox modulation of protein can potentially alter protein conformation, affecting protein activity and, therefore, initiating subsequently cellular responses. In the last five years, this response network has been repeatedly extended and summarized, not only for stomatal responses but also for responses to other abiotic stresses, and the signalling cascade has been shown to have many similarities. Furthermore, recent work has shown that H_2O_2 induces the expression of genes encoding proteins required for peroxisome are important sources of ROS as well as antioxidant and NO, and are thus important regulators of the cellular redox state. Calmodulin regulates NAD kinase

activity, which generates NADPH for NADPH oxidase activity. Thus cross-talk between H_2O_2 and calcium can regulate specificity and/or cross-tolerance towards various abiotic stresses. To date, though, no calcium-dependent protein kinases have been shown to be regulated by H_2O_2, although H_2O_2-regulated genes encoding protein kinases and phosphatases have been discovered. More lines of evidence concerning the relationship between H_2O_2 and Ca^{2+} signals is provided by the study of H_2O_2 homeostasis in Arabidopsis. In last, a protein phosphorylation cascade that has been shown to be activated by H_2O_2 in a MAPK cascade. This kinase then phosphorylated a MAPKK which in turn activates a MAPK by dual phosphorylation on both threonine and tyrosine residues in a conserved T-X-Y motif. Different previous observations indicate that H_2O_2 activating of a MAPK cascade is a central response mediating tolerance of various stresses: (1) that H_2O_2 generation occurs in response to diverse abiotic stresses, (2) that exposure to one stress offers cross-tolerance towards another, (3) that there exist commonalities in defence responses to various stresses, and (4) that activation of a H_2O_2-regualed MAPK pathway mediates multiple stress tolerance.

Future Challenges

The intracellular signalling cascades that transduce H_2O_2 perception into cellular responses have so far been characterized only superficially. Finally, they raise the question of how H_2O_2 is detected by cells. Such perception can conceivably involve direct interaction of H_2O_2 and other signalling molecule with cellular proteins such as transcription factors, ion channels or enzymes. H_2O_2 is a strong toxic oxidant causing cell damage or even cell death. At the same time, it serves conversely as a signalling molecule to activate a defence system for restoring the redox homeostasis in plant cells. The data available to date show that H_2O_2 is a key factor involved in responses to a number of abiotic stimuli. They indicate that endogenous H_2O_2 is a key factor in the tolerance of cells to the oxidative stress induced by a range of abiotic conditions, and that this probably involves the enhanced expression of genes encoding anti-oxidant enzymes. Of course, authors expect that numerous unanswered questions and important areas for further research will be open in future. The mechanisms by which H_2O_2 is generated are still largely unresolved and elucidation of how it is made by different plant cells in different situations is clearly a research priority.

REFERENCES

Abogadallah GM (2010). Antioxidative defence under salt stress. *Plant Signalling & Behaviour* , 5 (4): 369–374.

An Z, Jing W, Liu Y and Zhang W (2008). Hydrogen peroxide generated by copper amine oxidase is involved in abscisic acid-induced stomatal closure in Viciafaba. *Journal of Experimental Botany*, 59 (4): 815–825.

Apostolova P, Yordanova R and Popova L (2008). Response of antioxidative defence system to low temperature stress in two wheat cultivars. *General and Applied Plant Physiology*, 34: 281–294.

Bienert GP, Schjoerring JK and Jahn TP (2006). Membrane transport of hydrogen peroxide. *Biochimica Biophysica Acta*, 1758: 994–1003.

Cominelli E, Galbiati M, Vavasseur A, Conti L, Sala T, Vuylsteke M, Leonhardt N, Dellaporta SL and Tonelli C (2005). A guard-cell specific MYB transcription factor regulates stomatal movements and plant drought tolerance. *Current Biology*, 15: 1196–1200.

Desikan R, Reynolds A, Hancock JT and Neill SJ (1998). Harpin and hydrogen peroxide both initiate programmed cell death but have differential effects on gene expression in Arabidopsis suspension cultures. *Biochemical Journal*, 330: 115–120.

Dynowski M, Schaff G, Loque D, Moran O and Ludewig U (2008). Plant plasma membrane water channels conduct the signalling molecule H_2O_2. *Biochemical Journal*, 414: 53–61.

Gechev TS and Hille J (2005). Hydrogen peroxide as a signal controlling plant programmed cell death. *Journal of Cell Biology*, 168: 17–20.

Halliwell B, Clement M and Long L (2000). Hydrogen peroxide in the human body. *FEBS Letters*, 486: 10–13.

Hancock JT, Desikan R and Neill SJ (2001). Role of reactive oxygen species in cell signalling pathways. *Biochemical Society Transactions*, 29: 345–350.

Jenkins (2009). Signal transduction in responses to UV-B radiation. *Annual Reviews of Plant Biology*, 60: 407–431.

Jubany MT, Munne BS and Alegre L (2010). Redox regulation of water stress responses in field-grown plants. Role of hydrogen peroxide and ascorbate. *Plant Physiology and Biochemistry*, 48 (5): 351–358.

Lee S, Choi H, Suh S, Doo IS, Oh KY, Choi EJ, Taylor ATS, Low PS and Lee Y (1999). Oligogalacturonic acid and chitosan reduce stomatal aperature by inducing the evolution of reactive oxygen species from guard cells of tomato and Commelina-communis. *Plant Physiology*, 121: 147–152.

Li F, Liu P, Wang T, Bian P, Wu Y, Wu L and Yu Z (2010). The induction of bystander mutagenic effects *in vivo* by alpha-particle irradiation in whole *Arabidopsis thaliana* plants. *Radiation Research*, 174 (2): 228–237.

Lopez-delgado H, Dat JF, Foyer CH and Scott IM (1998). Induction of thermotolerance in potato microplants by acetylsalicylic acid and H_2O_2. *Journal of Experimental Botany*, 49: 713–720.

Mano J (2002). Early events in environmental stresses in plants. Induction mechanisms of oxidative stress (Ed.) Oxidative stress in plants. Taylor and Francis, London, pp. 217–246.

Mazid M, Ali B, Hayat S and Ahmad A (2010). The effect of 4-chloroindole-3-acetic acid on some growth parameters in mung bean under cadmium stress. *Turkey journal of Biology*, 34: 9–13.

Mazid M, Khan TA and Mohammad F (2011a). Potential of NO and H_2O_2 as signalling molecules in tolerance to abiotic stress in plants. *Journal of Industrial Research and Technology* , 1(1): 56–68.

Mazid M, Khan TA and Mohammad F (2011b). Role of Nitric oxide in regulation of H_2O_2 mediating tolerance of plants to abiotic stress: A synergistic signalling approach. *Journal of Stress Physiology and Biochemistry*, **7(2)**: 34–74.

McAinsh MR, Clayton H, Mansfield TA and Hetherington AM (1996). Changes in stomatal behaviour and guard cell cytosolic free calcium in response to oxidative stress. *Plant Physiology*, **111**: 1031–1042.

Muller HE (1985). Detection of hydrogen peroxide produced by microorganism on ABTS-peroxidase medium. *Zentralbl Bakteriol Mikrobiol Hyg*, **259**: 151–158.

Neill SJ, Desikan R, Clarke A and Hancock JT (2002). Nitric oxide is a novel component of abscisic acid signalling in stomatal guard cells. *Plant Physiology*, **128**: 13–16.

Neto ADA, Prisco JT, Eneas-Filho J, Jand-Venes R and Gomes-Filho E (2005). Hydrogen peroxide pretreatment induces salt stress acclimation in maize plants. *Journal of Plant Physiology*, **162**: 1114–1122.

Neves C, Sa MC and Amancio S (1998). Histochemical detection of H_2O_2 by tissue printing as a precocious marker of rhizogenesis in grapevine. *Plant Physiology and Biochemistry*, **36**: 817–824.

Panda SK, Chaudhury I and Khan MH (2003). Heavy metal induced lipid peroxidation and affects antioxidant in wheat leaves. *Biologia Plantarum*, **46**: 289–294.

Phillips JC, Braun R, Wang W, Gumbart J, Tajkhorshid E, Villa E, Chipot C, Skeel RD, Kale L and Schulten K (2005). Scalable molecular dynamics with NAMD. *Journal of Computational Chemistry*, **26**: 1781–1802.

Rausch T, Kirsch M, Low R, Lehr A, Vierck R and Zhigang A (1996). Salt stress response of higher plants: the role of proton pumps and Na^+/H^+ antiporters. *Journal of Plant Physiology*, **148**: 425–433.

Wahid A, Perveen M, Geelani S and Basra SMA (2007). Pretreatment of seed with H_2O_2 improves salt tolerance of wheat seedlings by alleviation of oxidative damage and expression of stress proteins. *Journal of Plant Physiology*, **164 (30)**: 283–294.

Wang L, Yang L, Yang F, Li X, Song Y, Wang X and Hu X (2010). Involvements of H_2O_2 and metallo-thionein in NO-mediated tomato tolerance to copper toxicity. *Journal of Plant Physiology*, **167 (15)**: 1298–1306.

Wang T, Zhang X and Li C (2007). Growth abscisic acid content and carbon isotope composition in wheat cultivars grown under different soil moisture. *Biologia Plantarum*, **51**: 181–184.

Wi SJ, Jang SJ and Park KY (2010). Inhibition of biphasic ethylene production enhances tolerance to abiotic stress by reducing the accumulation of reactive oxygen species in *Nicotiana tabacum*. *Molecules and Cells*, **30 (1)**: 37–49.

Wolfe SA, Nekludova L and Pabo CO (2000). DNA recognition by Cys(2) His(2) zinc finger proteins. *Annual Reviews of Biophysics and Biomolecular Structure*, **29**: 183–212.

YehCh-M, Hung W-Ch and Huang H-J (2003). Copper treatment activates mitogen-activated protein kinase signalling in rice. *Physiologia Plantarum*, **119**: 392–399.

Metabolic Implications of Proline in Plants Against Abiotic Environmental Stresses

2

ABSTRACT

Proline is a non-essential α-amino acid, one of the twenty DNA-encoded amino acids. It is unique among the 20 protein-forming amino acids in that the α-amino acid group is secondary. Biosynthetically, it is derived from the amino acid L-glutamate and its immediate precursor is the imino acid (S)-1-pyrroline-5-carboxylate. Proline may function also as protein-compatible hydrotrope and as a hydroxyl radical scavenger. Proline considered under a class of small molecules, compatible osmolytes, also including other amino acids, quaternary ammonium compounds and the tertiary sulfonium compounds 3-dimethylsulphoniopropionate. It acts as a signalling molecule to modulate mitochondrial functions, influences cell proliferation or cell death and triggers specific gene expression essential for plant recovery against various types of environmental stresses including drought, salinity, extreme temperatures, chemical toxicity and oxidative stress. In many plants, free proline accumulates in response to the imposition of a wide range of biotic and abiotic stresses. Proline is one of the most important compounds of plants defensive mixed action to environmental stresses. Although not all plants accumulate proline in sufficient amounts to help averting adverse effects of abiotic stresses. Further studies required for identification of multiple genes to enhance proline flux that could lead to new opportunities to improve plant tolerance.

Keywords: Drought, gene expression, proline, resistance, response, stress.

Introduction

Proline considered under a class of small molecules, compatible osmolytes, also including other amino acids, quaternary ammonium compounds (e.g. glycine betaine, proline betaine, β-alanine betaine, and choline-o-sulphate), and the tertiary sulfinium compounds 3-dimethylsulphoniopropionate (DMSP) (Miller *et al.*, 2009). Osmolytes or compatible solutes (e.g. proline) are groups of low molecular weight organic compounds that accumulate in organisms in response to osmotic stress. Abiotic stress evolves multiple responses that involve a series of physiological, biochemical and molecular events. In many plants, free proline accumulates in response to the imposition of a wide range of biotic and abiotic stresses. Efficiency of proline production considered as a major stress-induced diversion of N metabolism. Although less proline accumulated in the oldest leaves, a significant amount transported from senescing to emerging leaves (Abbaspour *et al.*, 2012). Moreover, during rehydration, proline readily recycled. Proline plays a significant role in leaf N remobilization and in N use efficiency in oilseed rape also (Albert *et al.*,

2012). The purpose of this chapter is to outline recent advances and new approaches to the investigation of proline biosynthesis, accumulation and function, which are not yet completely understood.

GENERALIZATION

Proline (abbreviated as Pro) is a non-essential α-amino acid, one of the twenty DNA-encoded amino acids. It is unique among the 20 protein-forming amino acids in that the α-amino acid group is secondary (Atkinson, 1977). Biosynthetically, it is derived from the amino acid L-glutamate and its immediate precursor is the imino acid (S)-1-pyrroline-5-carboxylate (P5C). Proline may function also as protein-compatible hydrotrope and as a hydroxyl radical scavenger (Ashraf and Fooland, 2007). Proline is an important osmoprotectant, and proposed to act as a compatible solute composition from dehydration injury and adjusts the osmotic potential in the cytoplasm. Proline has been shown to protect plants against damages caused by free radicals (ROS/AOS, *viz.* OH, H_2O_2) by scavenging the radicals and stabilizing of macromolecules. Therefore, it have been seen that the more tolerant plants store more proline. In addition, proline acts as a source of energy C and N which enhance tissues recovery, and the relief of stress effects.

If the proline confined to the cytoplasm, however, the concentration of proline could exceed 200 mM in these cells and, therefore, contribute substantially to cytoplasmic osmotic adjustment. Similarly, the cytosolic proline concentration of salt stressed *Distichlis spicata* cells is estimated to be ≥ 230 mM when it is treated with 200 mM NaCl. Under abiotic stress proline is accumulated in cells at concentrations of a few mM, depending on the species and the extent of stresses imposed. Therefore, proline accumulation is a common biochemical indicator for assessing environmental stress in plants. Moreover, results of Dhawi and Al-Khayri (2008) showed significant two-way intervals between static magnetic field intensity and exposure duration. They studied the proline accumulation in response to magnetic fields in date palm and finally suggest that at least lowest intensity (10 mM) of proline concentration increased in response to longer exposure durations reacting a maximum at 240 minutes (Chen and Kao, 1995).

Physiological and Biological Processes

The sensitivity of photosynthesis to all of the adverse abiotic environmental conditions capable of accusing proline accumulation is well-documented. It has been seen that all of the stresses capable of eliciting proline accumulation are also likely to increase levels of the generated stress hormone ABA which is known to cause stomatal closure. However, it appears that the concentrations of proline accumulated by resistant mutant may be an order of magnitude smaller than required to produce a significant physiological effect on osmotic stress tolerance. In winter wheat the hydroxyl-proline resistant lines are significantly more frost tolerant than wild type (Mazid *et al.*, 2010; 2011). Moreover, salt tolerant and PEG (polyethylene glycol) resistant mutants of *Nicotiana plumbaginifolia* have been derived from protoplast culture and appear to have enhanced proline accumulation in comparison to wild type. Moreover, the biocompatible feature of proline suggests that the accumulation of the end products of the biosynthetic pathway to high levels can be tolerated without deleterious effects on the stressed cell (Chinnusamy *et al.*, 2005).

A role for proline in stress recovery is consistent with the observation that the extensive accumulation of proline in stressed tissues is usually followed by its rapid disappearance when the stresses are removed. Proline differs from glycine betaine which is apparently maintained at stable levels long after relief from stress (Naidu *et al.*, 1990). A number of observations in different biochemical systems support a role for proline as a primer for TCA cycle (tricarboxylic acid cycle/Krebs cycle) and activity in plants recovering from osmotic stress (Delauney and Verma, 1993). The mitochondrial location of proline degradation and presence of glutamate dehydrogenase (GDH) in the mitochondrial matrix suggest that this process may contribute C to the TCA cycle. In soya bean nodules, PDH detected in the cytosol suggesting that proline oxidation provides energy for bacteroides during N fixation. When P5CDH activity is limited, the P5C-proline cycle can transfer more electrons to the mitochondrial electron transport chain (ETC) and generates reactive oxygen species (ROS).

High levels of proline oxidation in the bacteriodes of N-fixating root nodules of ureides-producing legumes suggests that proline may be the primary energy source used in the energy insensitive process of N-fixation (Kohl *et al.*, 1988). During stress conditions, the rate of the Calvin cycle (C3 cycle) is diminished, which prevents oxidation of NADPH and restoration of NADP$^+$. When combined with high light, electron flow in the electron transport chain is suppressed by the insufficient electron acceptor NADP$^+$ pool, leading to singlet oxygen production in the PS1 reaction centre and accumulation of ROS. Besides this, members of the small proline-rich protein family are major components of the cornified cell envelope are efficient ROS quenchers involved not only in the establishment of the skin's barrier function but also in cell migration and wound healing. In mitochondria, proline has distinct protective functions. After stress, proline pools supply a reducing potential for mitochondria through the oxidation of proline by PDH and P5CDH, provide electrons for the respiratory chain and, therefore, contribute to energy supply for resumed growth. An enhanced rate of proline

biosynthesis in chloroplasts during stress can maintain the low NADPH: NADP$^+$ ratio, contribute to sustaining the electron flow between photosynthetic excitation centres, stabilize the redox balance, reduce photoinhibition and damage of the photosynthetic apparatus. Therefore, proline catabolism is an important regulator of cellular ROS balance and can influence numerous additional regulatory pathways (Ghanate *et al.*, 2007).

Furthermore, proline biosynthesis is a reductive pathway and requires NADPH for the reduction of glutamate to P5C and P5C to proline, and generates NADP$^+$ that can be used further as electron acceptor. The phosphorylation of glutamate consumes ATP and produces ADP, which is a substrate for ATP biosynthesis during photosynthesis. Increasing amounts of data suggest that proline has certain regulatory function, controls plant development and acts as a signal molecule (Hare and Cress, 1997). A connection between photosynthesis and proline metabolism is supported by light-dependent proline accumulation, which is regulated by the light-controlled reciprocal P5CS and PDH gene activation. Moreover, contributing C to the TCA cycle, the mitochondrial degradation of proline to 2-oxyglutarate may also provide reducing equivalents needed to support mitochondrial electron transport and the generation of ATP for recovery from stress and repair of stress-induced degree under stress conditions altered flux through certain pathway is likely to be an important mechanism used to stabilize metabolism and ensures survival when conditions are suboptimal.

Effect of Proline on Sucrose Metabolism

Proline metabolism can also influence programmed cell death (PCD) in plants. Externally added proline is more toxic to transgenic plants expressing antisense PDH as well as to *pdh* Arabidopsis mutants than to wild type plants. Proline accumulates in plant tumours and functions as competitive antagonists of GABA-dependent plant defence, interfering with the GABA-induced degradation of quorum-sensing signal. Uncoupled induction of PDH and P5CDH in P5CDH mutants leads to P5C and ROS accumulation which can function as stress signal and cause PCD (Miller *et al.*, 2009). Besides contributing C to the TCA cycle, the mitochondrial oxidation of proline to 2-oxoglutarate may also directly provide reducing equivalents needed to support mitochondrial electron transport and the generation of ATP for recovery from stress and for their repair of stress-induced damage. Expression of genes encoding glycolytic enzymes is upregulated in response to several environmental perturbations capable of eliciting proline accumulation (Krishnamurthy and Bhagat, 1993).

Proline catabolism in the mitochondria is connected to oxidative respiration and administers energy to resumed growth after stress. Since proline degradation generates reducing equivalents needed during TCA cycle activity. Proline metabolism might transfer metabolic information between tissues with different metabolic requirements in the form of redox potential and activates metabolic pathways that do not involve any of the intermediates of metabolism (Kumar and Sharma, 1989). Tolerance to abiotic stresses is very complex at the whole plant and cellular levels. From a metabolic perspective, the plant is a highly integrated system, which is demonstrated by the capture of energy by photosynthesis and its use in C and N assimilation.

Proline and Abiotic Stress

In many plants, free proline accumulates in response to the imposition of a wide range of biotic and abiotic stresses. Proline accumulation may reduce stress-induced cellular acidification or proline oxidative respiration to provide energy needed for recovery. High levels of proline synthesis during stress may

maintain NAD $(P)^+$/NADP(H) ratios at value compatible with metabolism under normal conditions. Although, the regulation and function of proline accumulation are not yet completely understood, the engineering of proline metabolism could lead to new opportunities to improve plant tolerance to environmental stresses. In plants, proline is synthesized mainly from glutamate which is regulated to GSA by the P5CS enzyme, and spontaneously converted to P5C. P5C reductase (P5CR) further reduces the P5C intermediate to proline. In most plant species, P5CS is encoded by two genes and P5CR is encoded by one (Kurkdjian and Guern, 1989).

Moreover, a loss of feedback inhibition of P5CS leads to elevated proline accumulation. In Arabidopsis, P5CS splice variants have been annotated but not characterized. Conversion of P5CS to proline is not a rate limiting step in proline biosynthesis, yet the control of P5CR activity implies a complex regulation of transcription, which is shown to be under the developmental and osmotic regulation (Lee *et al.*, 1995). Overexpression of P5CS1 and enhanced proline content led to the early flowering of transgenic Arabidopsis plants. The accumulation of proline under abiotic stress conditions has been studied in numerous plant species for half a century. Nevertheless, controversy has arisen as to whether an increase in free proline has any real adoptive value. Clearly, a better appreciation of the extent to which proline accumulation is of protective value to plants exposed to several different environmental extremes and an understanding of the mechanism(s) whereby proline accumulation may exert a beneficial effect under stressful conditions, are likely to be critical prerequisites for the success of such endeavours. These observations provide convincing evidence of a cause and effect relationship between proline levels and abiotic stress tolerance. Important consideration in various attempts to account for a beneficial role for proline accumulation in tolerance of different stresses include whether several of the different stresses capable of eliciting the response have common negative physiological effects and assessment of whether alternations in proline metabolism may ameliorate these consequences (Llops-Tous et al., 2011).

As an alternative pathway, proline can be synthesized from ornithine, which is transmitted first by ornithine-delta-aminotransferase (OAT) providing GSA and P5C, which are then converted to proline. Proline catabolism occurs in mitochondria via the sequential action of proline dehydrogenase or proline oxidase (PDH/POX) producing P5C from proline, and P5C dehydrogenase (P5CDH), which converts P5C to glutamate. PDH is encoded by the two genes, whereas a single P5CDH gene has been identified in Arabidopsis and tobacco (Ribarits et al., 2007). Proline accumulation induced by stress conditions is mediated both by increased synthesis and reduced oxidation of the imino acid. Metabolic labelling studies also mediate that most of the proline accumulated in plants in response to stress is the results of enhanced synthesis from glutamate. The soluble protein and free amino acid in barley organs (root and bud) increased with NaCl increasing. Central role in cellular homeostasis against environmental stress (salinity and drought stress). One mechanism utilized by the plants for overcoming the salt stress effects might be via accumulation of compatible osmolytes, such as proline and soluble sugar. Production and accumulation of free amino acids, especially proline by plants tissue during drought, salt and water stress is an adoptive response.

Moreover, marked changes in the content of proline are observed, with some specific variations associated with the different organs of L. albus concerning the effects of boron deficiency in the metabolism indicate that various aspects of metabolism implicated in the amino acid accumulation affected by boron deficiency (Marin et al., 2010). Also,

proline increase in many other kinds of stresses and accumulated in petioles, apexes and hypocotyls. The increase in the proline concentration observed in all organs, suggests the involvement of boron with the cytoskeleton, whereas glycine decrease in leaf-blades and active growing organs like apexes and roots could be associated with the proposed role of glycine in plant signalling in processes that might be associated with the decreased growth rates observed in boron deficiency. The salt stress conditions could have effect on different stages of N metabolism, such as absorption, ionic reduction and protein synthesis. Proline content also higher in tolerant variety as compared to their lower accumulation in sensitive variety. The improved performance of the tolerant variety under high salinity accompanied by an increase in ascorbate peroxidase and catalase, though no salt-dependent increase in the activity of superoxide dismutase observed. Increased photoinhibition in sensitive variety observed by its reduced thylakoid membrane protein, D1 probably results from the greater photosynthetic damage caused by salt stress than tolerant variety (Mishra and Dubey, 2006). However, the correlation between proline accumulation and abiotic stress tolerance in plants not always apparent. For an instance, high proline levels can be characteristics of salt and cold hypersensitive Arabidopsis mutants (Chen et al., 2007). During adaptation to various types of environmental stress, plants accumulate cellular solutes which include quaternary amino acid derivatives such as proline, glycine betaine alanine, betaine and proline betaine (Patakas et al., 2002). Still however, the relationship between this trait and stress tolerance is not clear among species. As a case, members of solanacese family, can increase their proline pool by more than two orders of magnitude and others exhibits only a moderate increase in proline content under stress. Moreover, other researchers have challenged the value of proline accumulating potential as a positive index for resistance to osmotic stress (Heuer, 1994). It has been reported that elevated levels of proline biosynthesis in transgenic tobacco plants confer increased tolerance to hyperosmotic stress. Proline accumulations have been extensively studied as a common metabolic response of higher plants to drought and salinity stress. It is generally accepted that under conditions of drought or salinity, proline accumulation serves as a defence against osmotic challenge by acting as compatible solutes. Leaf osmotic potentials of the transgenic plants unaffected by drought and the plants displayed even less capacity for osmotic adjustment than compatible wild type tobacco. Proline appears to be the preferred organic osmoticum in many plants. Several findings highlight the need for further investigations of the mechanism whereby proline accumulation alleviates the effects of osmotic stress on plant growth (Mittal *et al.*, 2012). A number of researchers suggesting as increase in proline levels accompanying osmotic stress may be misleading since this increase is often based on an initially small proline content. This is not always found in many glycophytes in which proline accumulation has been reported under conditions of osmotic stress. In rice plants subjected to water stress, the concentration of proline was increased in the leaves. Transgenic tobacco plants, overexpressing P5Cs have shown increased concentration of proline and resistance to both drought and salinity stresses (Kavi-Kishor *et al.*, 1995).

GENETIC RECOMBINATION AND PROLINE

Globally, approximately 22% of the agricultural land is saline (FAO 2004), and areas under drought are already expanding and this is expected to increase further rapidly (Bhatnagar *et al.*, 2008). Success in breeding for better adopted varieties to abiotic stresses

depends upon the concentrated efforts by various research domains including plant and cell physiology, molecular biology, genetics and breeding. Use of modern molecular biology tools for elucidating the control mechanisms of abiotic stress tolerance and for engineering stress-tolerant crops is based on the expression of specific stress-related genes. Hence, genetic engineering for developing stress-tolerant lands based on the genes that are known to be involved in stress response and putative tolerance might prove to be a faster track towards improving crop varieties. For beyond the initial attempts to insert single action genes engineering of the regulatory machinery involving transcription factors has emerged as a new response genes (Pardo *et al.*, 1998). Evaluation of the transgenic plants under stress conditions and understanding the physiological effect of the inserted genes at the whole plant level remains as major challenges to overcome. In addition, the transgenic plants also showed increased expression of some drought-responding genes, and enhanced activity of antioxidant enzymes such as superoxide dismutase, peroxidase, and ascorbate peroxidase. Their membrane integrity considerably improved under water stress, as indicated by reduced MDA content and electrolyte leakage relative to control plants. These results suggest that the AtLOS5 transgenic cotton plants acquired a better drought tolerance through enhanced ABA production and ABA-induced physiological regulations (Pei *et al.*, 1998).

Transgenic approaches to improve plant stress tolerance via overproducing proline have some success. When a plant is subjected to abiotic stress a number of genes are turned on resulting in increased levels of several metabolites and proteins, some of which may be responsible for conferring a certain degree of protection to these stresses. Besides this, a key progress towards breeding better crops under stress has been to understand the changes in cellular, biochemical and molecular machineries that occur in response to stress. Moreover, modern molecular technologies involve the identification and use of molecular markers that can enhance breeding programmes (Poonlaphdecha *et al.*, 2012). Besides this, metabolic traits have been characterized genetically and appear more amenable to manipulations than structural and developmental traits. Further, genetic engineering allows controlling the timing, tissue specificity, and expression level of the introduced genes for their optimal function. The basic findings on stress promoters have led to a major shift in the paradigm for genetically engineering stress-tolerant crops (Katiyar *et al.*, 1999). The most widely used promoters in generating transgenic plants are constitutively expressed, i.e. they are turned on all the time and throughout the plant life cycle. With an increasing number of stress genes become available and genetic transformation becoming more or less a routine procedure, characterization of stress-induced promoters.

MODULATION OF PROLINE SYNTHESIS IN PLANT SYSTEM

The transcription factors activate cascades of genes that act together in enhancing tolerance towards multiple stresses. Dozens of transcription factors are involved in the plant response to abiotic stress tolerance. Most of these fall into several large transcription factor families, such as AP2/ERF, bZIP, NAC, MYB, MYC, Cys2His2 zinc-finger WRKY. Individual members of the same family often respond differently to various stress stimuli. On the other hand, some stress responsive genes may share the same transcription factors, as indicated by the significant overlap of the gene expression profiles that are induced in response to different stresses. Two families, bZIP and MYB, are involved in ABA signalling and its gene activation. Many ABA inducible genes share the (C/T) ACGTGGC consensus, *cis*-acting ABA-responsive element (ABRE) in

their promoter regions. The use of stress inducible rd29A promoter minimized the negative effects on plant growth in these crop species. However, overexpression of DREB2 in transgenic plants do not improve stress tolerance, suggesting involvement of post-translational activation of DREB2 proteins. The DREB2 protein is expressed under normal growth conditions and activated by osmotic stress through post-translational modification in the early stages of the osmotic stress response (Smirnoff, 1993). The overexpression of some drought-responsive transcription factors can lead to the expression of downstream genes and the enhancement of abiotic stress tolerance in plants. The regulatory genes/factors reported so far not only play a significant role in drought and salinity stresses, but also in submergence tolerance. Moreover, genes involved in stress signal sensing and a cascade of stress-signalling in *A. thaliana* have been of recent research interest. In addition, some gene products are needed in large amounts, such as LEA3, thereby necessitating the need for a very strong promoter. An ideal inducible promoter should not only be devoid of any basal level of gene expression in the absence of inducing agents, but the expression should be reversible and dose-dependent. Besides this, these promoters being constitutive in nature, by and large express the downstream transgenes in all organs and at all the stages (Verbruggen, 1993). Most of the stress promoter's conditions array of stress-specific *cis*-acting elements that are recognized by the requisite transcription cofactor; for example, the transcriptional regulation of *hsp* genes is mediated by the core heat shock element (HSE) located in the promoter region of these genes 5' of the TATA box. With other gene products, such as enzymes for polyamine biosynthesis, it may be better to use an inducible promoter of moderate strength.

The promoters that have been most commonly used in the production of abiotic stress-tolerant plants so far, include the CaMV 35S, ubiquitin 1 and actin promoters. Mostly promoters being constitutive in nature, by and large expression the downstream transgenes in all organs and at all the stages. An ideal inducible promoter should not only be devoid of any base at level of gene expression in the absence of inducing agents but the expression should be reversible and dose-dependent. The transcriptional regulatory region of the drought-induced and cold-induced genes have been analyzed to identify several in the gene expression that is induced by abiotic stress.

Two major issues that typically need to be addressed in stress response evaluation of transgenics include: (1) means of stress imposition and (2) hard data on the response of tested material to support conclusions. An important aspect of transgenic technology is the regulated expression of transgenic. Tissues specificity of transgenes expression is also an important consideration while declining on the choice of the promoter so as to increase the level of expression of the gene. All the plant *hsp* genes sequenced so far have been shown to certain partly overlapping multiple

HSEs proximal to TATA motif. The Arabidopsis *rd29A* and *rd29B* are stress responsive genes, but are differentially induced under abiotic stress conditions. The *rd29A* promoter includes both DRE and ABRE elements, where dehydration, high salinity and low temperature induce the genes, while the *rd29B* promoter include only ABREs and the induction is ABA-dependent. Although recent findings have convincingly demonstrated that proline overproduction in transgenic tobacco ameliorates the effects of hyperosmotic stress, it remains to be seen whether this phenotype alteration also increases tolerance of other commonly-encountered biotic and abiotic stresses. Despite the remarkable advances in our understanding of proline biosynthesis in plants genes over the past a few years, the isolation of plant genes encoding enzymes involved in proline degradation has yet to be reported (Wang *et al.*, 2011). Proline itself may act not only as an osmoticum but also as a substrate for the TCA cycle during recovery from stresses, while the interconversions between proline and its precursors may be involved in the regulation of cellular pH and redox potential.

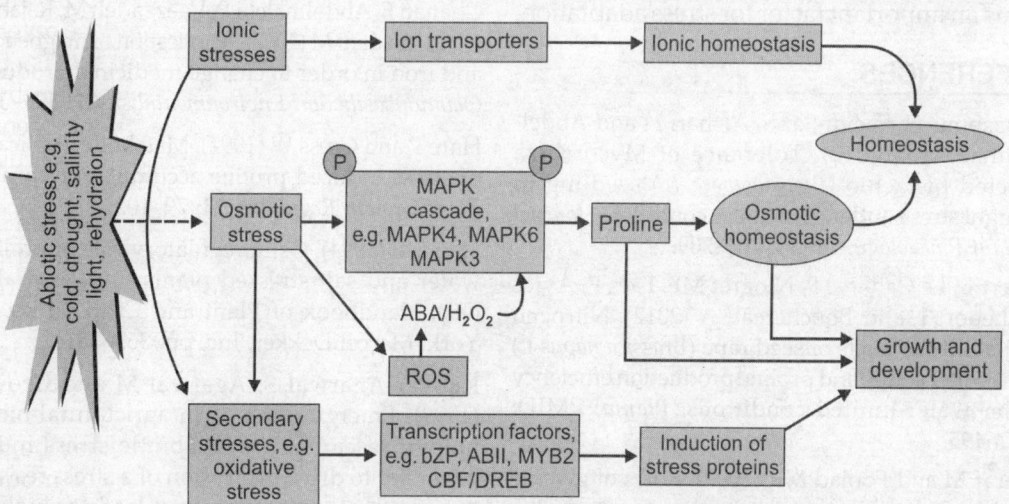

Fig. 2.1: Functional details of proline with interacting ROS, MAPK cascade and ion transporters in plants cell during influence against abiotic stress tolerance

Concluding Remarks

Some progress has been made in introducing genes for the production of these compounds in naturally non-accumulating or low-accumulating plant species; levels of accumulation in transgenic plants have often been low or insufficient to improve plant stress tolerance. Today's research to determine specific roles of proline in plant stress tolerance is expected to help improving their application as exogenous treatments to improve growth of plants and productivity under stress conditions. The application of system biology approaches might help to understand regulation of proline-dependent and proline-mediated signalling in plants. Using a similar strategy, feedback insensitive bacterial ProBA genes were overexpressed in transgenic Arabidopsis, leading to proline hyper-accumulation and enhanced osmotolerance. Also, several other studies suggested an unchanged stress tolerance, accompanied by abnormal seed and plant development and increased proline hypersensitivity of the transgenic lines and mutants suggest that proline might not be the actual proline content but the enhanced rate of proline biosynthesis that is an important factor for stress adaptation.

REFERENCES

Abbaspour H, Saeidi-Sar S, Afshari H and Abdel-Wahhab MA (2012). Tolerance of Mycorrhiza infected pistachio (*Pista ciavera L.*) seedling to drought stress under glasshouse conditions. *Journal of Plant Physiology*, **169(7)**: 704–709.

Albert B, Le Cahérec F, Niogret MF, Faes P, Avice JC, Leport L and Bouchereau A (2012). Nitrogen availability impacts oilseed rape (*Brassica napus L*) plant water status and proline production efficiency under water-limited conditions. *Planta*, PMID: 22526495.

Ashraf M and Foolad MR (2007). Roles of glycine betaine and proline in improving plant abiotic stress resistance. *Environmental and Experimental Botany*, **59**: 206–216.

Atkinson DE (1977). Cellular Energy Metabolism and Its Regulation. New York: Academic Press.

Bhatnagar P, Vadez MV and Sharma KK (2008). Transgenic approaches for abiotic stress tolerance in plants: retrospect and prospects. *Plant Cell Reproductio*, **27**: 411–424.

Chen SL, and Kao CH (1995). Cd induced changes in proline level and peroxidase activity in roots of rice seedlings. *Plant Growth Regulation*.**17**: 67–71.

Chen Z (2007). Compatible solute accumulation and stress mitigating effects in barley genotypes contrasting in their salt tolerance. *Journal of Experimental Botany*, **58**: 4245–4255.

Chinnusamy V, Jagendorf A and Zhu JK (2005). Understanding and improving salt tolerance in plants. *Crop Science*, **45**: 437–448.

Delauney AJ and Verma DPS (1993). Proline biosynthesis and osmoregulation in plants. *Plant Journal*, **4**: 215–223.

Dhawi F and Al-Khayri JM (2008). Proline Accumulation in Response to Magnetic Fields in Date Palm (*Phoenix dactylifera L.*). *The Open Agriculture Journal*, **2**: 80–83.

FAO (Food, Agriculture Organization of the United Nations) (2004). FAO production year book. FAO, Rome.

Ghanati F, Abdolmaleki P, Vaezzadeh M, Rajabbeigi E and Yazdani M (2007). Application of magnetic field and iron in order to change medicinal products of *Ocimumbasilicum*. *Environmentalist*, **27**: 429–34.

Hare P and Cress W (1997). Metabolic implications of stress induced proline accumulation in plants. *Plant Growth Regulator*, **21**: 79–102.

Heuer B (1994). Osmoregulatory role of proline in water and salt-stressed plants. In: Pessarakli M (ed). Handbook of Plant and Crop Stress, New York: Marcel Dekker, Inc, pp. 363–381.

Katiyar-Agarwal S, Agarwal M and Grover A (1999). Emerging trends in agricultural biotechnology research: use of abiotic stress induced promoter to drive expression of a stress resistance gene in the transgenic system leads to high level stress tolerance associated with minimal negative effects on growth. *Current Science*, **77**: 1577–1579.

Kavi-Kishor PB, Hong Z, Miao G-H, Hu C-AA and Verma DPS (1995). Overexpression of 1-pyrroline-5-carboxylate synthetase increases proline production and confers osmotolerance in transgenic plants. *Plant Physiology*, **108**: 1387–1394.

Kohl DH, Schubert KR, Carter MB, Hagedorn CH and Shearer G (1988). Proline metabolism in N2-fixing root nodules: Energy transfer and regulation of purine synthesis. *Proceedings of the National Academy of Sciences of USA*, **85**: 2036–2040.

Krishnamurthy R and Bhagwat KA (1993). Effect of foliar application of proline on the salt stressed rice seedlings. *ActaAgronomica Hungarica*, **42**: 267–272.

Kumar V and Sharma DR (1989). Effect of exogenous proline on growth and ion content in NaCl stressed and nonstressed cells of mungbean, *Vigna radiate* var. radiata. *Indian Journal of Experimental Biology*, **27**: 813–815.

Kurkdjian A and Guern J (1989). Intracellular pH: Measurement and importance in cell activity. *Annual Reviews of Plant Physiology*, **40**: 271–303.

Lee JH, Hubel A and Schoffl F (1995). Derepression of activity of genetically engineered heat-shock factor causes constitutive synthesis of heat shock proteins and increased thermotolerance in transgenic Arabidopsis. *Plant Journal*, **8**: 603–612.

Llop-Tous I, Ortiz M, Torrent M and Ludevid MD (2011). The expression of a xylanase targeted to ER-protein bodies provides a simple strategy to produce active insoluble enzyme polymers in tobacco plants. *PLoS One*, **6(4)**: e19474.

Marin JA, Andreu P, Carrasco A and Arbeloa A (2010). Determination of proline concentration, an abiotic stress marker, in root exudates of excised root cultures of fruit tree rootstocks under salt stress. *Revue des Régions Arides–Numérospécial–24 (2/2010) Actes du 3ème Meeting International "Aridocultureet Cultures Oasisennes: Gestion et Valorisation des Ressources et Applications Biotechnologiquesdans les AgrosystèmesArides et Sahariens" Jerba (Tunisie)*, **1**: 16–17.

Mazid M, Ali B, Hayat S and Ahmad A (2010). The effect of 4-chloroindole-3-acetic acid on some growth parameters in mung bean under cadmium stress. *Turkey Journal of Biology*, **34**: 9–13.

Mazid M, Khan TA and Mohammad F (2011). Potential of NO and H_2O_2 as signalling molecules in tolerance to abiotic stress in plants. *Journal of Industrial Research and Technology*, **1(1)**: 56–68.

Miller G (2009). Unraveling delta1-pyrroline-5-carboxylateproline cycle in plants by uncoupled expression of proline oxidation enzymes. *Journal of Biological Chemistry*, **284**: 26482–26492.

Mishra S and Dubey RS (2006) Inhibition of ribonuclease and protease activities in arsenic exposed rice seedlings: role of proline as enzyme protectant. *Journal of Plant Physiology*, **163**: 927–936.

Mittal S, Kumari N and Sharma V (2012). Differential response of salt stress on *Brassica juncea*: Photosynthetic performance, pigment, proline, D1 and antioxidant enzymes. *Plant Physiology and Biochemistry*, **54**: 17–26.

Naidu BP, Paleg LG, Aspinall D, Jennings AC and Jones GP (1990) Rate of imposition of water stress alters the accumulation of nitrogen-containing solutes by wheat seedlings. *Australian Journal of Plant Physiology*, **17**: 653–664.

Pardo JM, Reddy MP and Yang S (1998). Stress signalling through Ca^{2+}/Calmodulin dependent protein phosphatase calcineurin mediates salt adaptation in plants. *Proceedings of the National Academy of Sciences of USA*, **95**: 9681–9683.

Patakas A, Nikolaou N, Zioziuo E, Radogluo K and Notisakis B (2002). The role of organic solute and ion accumulation in osmotic adjustment in drought-stressed grape veins. *Plant Science*, **163**: 361–367.

Pei ZM, Ghassemian M, Kwak CM, McCourt P and Schroeder JI (1998). Role of farnesyltransferase in ABA regulation of guard cell anion channels and plant water loss. *Science*, **282**: 287–290.

Poonlaphdecha J, Maraval I, Roques S, Audebert A, Boulanger R, Bry X and Gunata Z (2012). Effect of Timing and Duration of Salt Treatment during Growth of a Fragrant Rice Variety on Yield and 2-Acetyl-1-pyrroline, Proline, and GABA Levels. *Journal ofAgriculture & Food Chemistr,*. **60 (15)**: 3824–3830.

Ribarits A (2007). Two tobacco proline dehydrogenases are differentially regulated and play a role in early plant development. *Planta,* **225:** 1313–1324.

Smirnoff N (1993). The role of active oxygen in the response of plants to water deficit and desiccation. *New Phytology,* **125:** 27–58.

Verbruggen N, (1993). Osmoregulation of a pyrroline-5-carboxylate reductase gene in *Arabidopsis thaliana. Plant Physiology,* **103:** 771–781.

Wang R, Huang W, Chen L, Ma L, Guo C and Liu X (2011). Anatomical and physiological plasticity in *Leymus chinensis* (Poaceae) along large-scale longitudinal gradient in northeast China. *PLoS One,* **6(11):** 254–267.

Molecular Approach of Auxin Functionality to Enhance Yield Potential of Crops

3

ABSTRACT

The auxin is a molecule similar to tryptophan, yet it elicits a diverse array of responses and is involved in the regulation of growth and development throughout the plant life cycle. The versatile functionality and physiological importance of the auxin is a major focus of attention in contemporary areas of advanced plant physiology. This ability to bring about such diverse responses appears to result partly from the existence of several independent mechanisms for its perception and signal transduction that involves the intentional degradation of various members of transcriptional regulator family, participating the complex and competing dimerization networks to modulate the expression of a wide range of genes targeted for physiological responses in plant. Forward and reverse genetic advances resulted in the identification of some of the underlying regulatory mechanisms as well as the emergence of functional frameworks for auxin action. In this review, we also shade a small beam of light on homeostatic regulation of auxin levels embraces various other endogenous auxins and described mechanism of auxin action including processes of downstream stress signal perception and transduction as well.

Keywords: Hormone, signal transduction, auxin, plant growth regulators and receptor.

INTRODUCTION

Phytohormones are important plant growth regulators that control many developmental processes such as cell division, cell differentiation, organogenesis and morphogenesis. They regulate a multitude of apparently unrelated physiological processes, often with overlapping roles, and they mutually modulate their effects. These features imply important synergistic and antagonistic interactions between the various plant hormones (Bielach *et al.*, 2012). Among them, Auxin is identified as a plant growth hormone because of its ability to stimulate differential growth in response to light stimuli. Studies of auxins originated in investigations of bending responses of coleoptiles towards a light source. The signal perceived by the coleoptiles top is shown to be transported asymmetrically from the tip downward, where it induced growth response due to differential elongation of one side of the coleoptiles (Went *et al.*, 1928). Much of our knowledge of the physiological role of auxin in plants is delivered from studies on how plants respond to excess exogenous auxin. However, an equally important aspect of auxin biology is to characterize the developmental defects caused by auxin deficiency, which cannot be achieved without a clear grasp of auxin biosynthetic pathways (**Fig. 3.1**).

Auxin is probably the most investigated plant hormone and is known to be involved

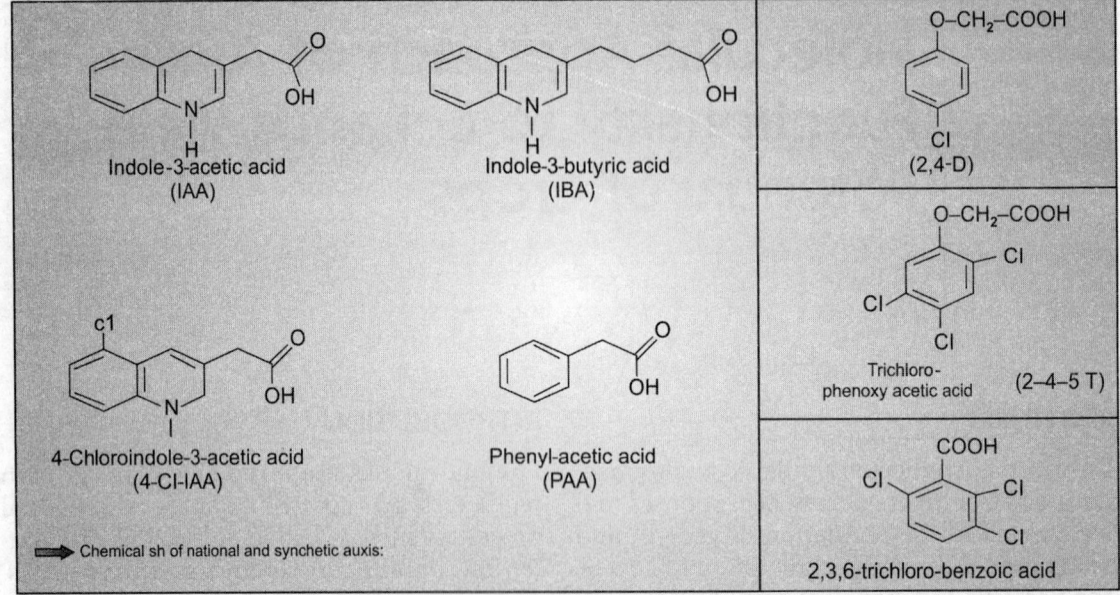

Fig. 3.1: Chemical structures of natural and synthetic auxin.

in virtually every aspect of plant growth and development. Reviews about auxin traditionally start with a sentence about how very important auxins is to plant growth and development, followed by a despairing comment about how, despite more than a century of research, we know very little about how it works/actions (Gray and Estelle, 2000). Later, researches demonstrated that auxin is required together with other plant hormones (e.g. most cases cytokinins) for both cell division and oriented cell expansion, influencing all aspects of plant development. In addition, Zhang *et al.* (2012) reported that cytokinins, and IAA levels also high, and their contents in attached haustoria increased than in non-attached haustoria. A high auxin-to-cytokinin ratio contributed to haustorial development of *Santalum album*. Endogenous hormones are involved in the haustorial development and in water and nutrient transport in the host-parasite association. Consequently, it has become difficult to unambiguously define typical "auxin activity". In contrast to the great progress made in

understanding auxin signalling is known about how auxin is produced in plants (Zhao, 2010).

The major naturally occurring auxin IAA. It has been implicated in virtually every aspect of plant growth and development, as well as defence responses (Zhao, 2010). At least in *Arabidopsis thaliana* studies indicate that biosynthetic, transport and signalling pathways have overlapping functions because plant deficient in either pathways have similar growth defects. Once synthesized, auxin is distributed throughout the plant via sophisticated cell to cell transport system. Cellular auxin influx and efflux carriers promote the formation of local auxin maxima and gradients that inform diverse growth and developmental processes. These complexes processes require communication systems that can operate over relatively long distances among different plant organs as well as different organelles within a single cell. In much systems, cells of different tissues and organs are not only able of detecting signals they receive for other parts of the plants, but also of responding and transmitting those signals in their own characteristics way.

There is numerous evidence for both genome and non-genomic auxin responses, but the mechanism of auxin-regulated transcription is much better characterized (Badescu and Napier 2006). The Auxins are short lived and their degradation requires the ubiquitin-proteosome pathway. Ubiquitin is covalently conjugated to protein substrates by the sequential activity of three enzymes: the ubiquitin-activity enzyme (E1), the ubiquitin-conjugating enzyme (E2) and the ubiquitin protein ligase (E3) (Pickart 2001). For example, the initiation of leaves on the flank of the shoot apical meristems (SAM) requires local accumulation of auxin at the site of organs primordium formation. The cellular localization of auxin is highly dynamic and responsive to both developmental and environmental cues. Because of the importance of the processes to plant development, this is an extremely active and exciting area of investigation. In this review we first report the current knowledge on auxin biosynthesis, degradation (stage and homeostasis) and perception and later this will focus on recent progress made in Arabidopsis in defining the role of auxin in phytotaxis, vascular development, root growth and embryology and on our current understanding of auxin perception and signal transduction.

In last, auxin is a major growth hormone in plants, and recent studies have elucidated many of the molecular mechanisms underlying its action, including transport, perception and signal transduction. However, major gaps remain in our knowledge of auxin biosynthetic control, partly due to the complexity and probable redundancy of multiple pathways that involve the YUCCA family of flavin-dependent mono-oxygenases.

Biosynthesis: A Survey of Historical Background

The long shoot believed to be the only source of an auxin biosynthesis. *De novo* auxin pro-duction is highly localized and local auxin biosynthesis plays a key role in shaping local auxin gradients. A well-recognized caveat of auxin biosynthesis may not be directly involved in the biosynthesis of auxin but may rather influence auxin levels through modification in related pathways. A second complication is that most of the synthesized IAA are not present in any free, active form, but an inactive conjugate plays important role as storage form for active plant hormone, IAA. In its free form, IAA comprises only up to 25% of the total species studied. Since, the discovery of genes and enzymes involved in synthesis and hydrolysis of auxin conjugates, much knowledge has been gained on the biochemistry and function of these compounds, but there are still much to discover (Muller 2011) (**Fig. 3.1, 2**).

Moreover, free IAA comprises only approximately 1% of the total auxin pool in plants, whereas the remaining part is conjugated to amino acids and sugars. The function of auxin conjugates has been mainly elucidated by mutant analysis in genes for synthesis or hydrolysis and a possible function for conjugates inferred from results of Muller (2011). In the evolution of local plants, auxin conjugates seen to be connected with the development of certain traits such as embryo, shoot and vasculature, etc. In most leaves, the synthesis of auxin is developed first, since it has been already detected in moss, whereas sequence of typical auxin conjugates hydrolases found according to database entries first in mosses and ferns (Muller 2011).

Although the physiological function of most of these auxins has been studied for decades, the last 10 to 15 years have been seen dramatic progress in our understanding of the molecular mechanisms of auxin biosynthesis, transport and response (Santner *et al.*, 2009). The biosynthetic pathways for most of the hormones are not well-characterized but are emerging (Santner *et al.*, 2009). Local and long-distance transport of auxin has an essential role in many aspects of plant growth and development (Santner *et al.*, 2009). Recent progress in auxin biosynthesis opens a new line of research into the mechanisms whereby auxin controls plant development. The plant growth regulator auxin has been implicated in the control of all of the stages of leaf development. In addition, Atta *et al.*, (2012) report a novel technique for controlled release of PGRs by sunlight using photoremovable protecting group (PRPG) as a delivery device. Carboxyl-containing PGRs of the auxin chemically caged using PRPGs of coumarin derivatives which exhibited good fluorescence properties. Bioactivity experiments indicated that caged PGRs showed better enhancement in the root and shoot length growth of *Cicer arietinum* compared to PGRs after sunlight exposure. The use of PRPG as a delivery device for controlled release of PGRs by sunlight in soil holds great interest for field application since it can overcome the rapid loss of PGRs in environmental conditions. What we are learning is that auxin levels are highly regulated and responsive to a changing environment.

Moreover, auxin displays morphogenic properties that are modulated by the environment and defined by dynamic changes in its perception and signal transduction. This machinery has been intensively studied during the post decade and includes effects that are either dependent or independent of gene expression. Thus "auxin action" may be understood the sum of all these responses. Today, many heterogeneous synthetic substances have auxin activity complicating studies of structural activity and the search for a common mode of action (Ferro *et al.*, 2010). Even the most frequently used synthetic auxins, 2,4-dichloroacetic acid (2,4-D) and naphthalene acetic acid (NAA), do not completely share their mechanism of action with native IAA, is widely used as herbicides. Unlike IAA, 2,4-D is not a good substrate for

the auxin-binding protein *ABP1* and is poorly transported by auxin efflux carriers. Only IBA, PAA and 4-Cl-IAA are synthesized by plants and, therefore, qualify as "endogenous auxins" but their role and mechanism of action have not been described satisfactorily (Zimmerman and Wilcoxon, 2009).

Auxin, predominantly represented by IAA is involved in the regulation of plant growth and development. Although IAA is the first plant hormone identified, the biosynthetic pathway at the genetic level has remained unclear. Two major pathways for IAA biosynthesis have been proposed: the tryptophan (Trp)-independent and Trp-dependent pathways. In Trp-dependent IAA biosynthesis, four pathways have been postulated in plants: (i) the indole-3-acetamide (IAM) pathway; (ii) the indole-3-pyruvic acid (IPA) pathway; (iii) the tryptamine (TAM) pathway; and (iv) the indole-3-acetaldoxime (IAOX) pathway. Although different plant species may have unique strategies and modifications to optimize their metabolic pathways, plants would be expected to share evolutionarily conserved core mechanisms for auxin biosynthesis because IAA is a fundamental substance in the plant life cycle. The genes known to be involved in auxin biosynthesis are summarized and the major IAA biosynthetic pathway distributed widely in the plant kingdom is discussed on the basis of biochemical and molecular biological findings and bioinformatics studies. Based on evolutionarily conserved core mechanisms, it is thought that the pathway via IAM or IPA is the major routes to IAA in plants (Mano *et al.* 2012).

Auxin is synthesized from tryptophan via at least two pathways: the tryptomine (TAM) and indole-3-pyruvic acid (IPA) pathways. In addition, studies in Arabidopsis and maize indicate that IAA can also be synthesized from indole, by passing tryptophan (Simon and Petrasek, 2011). At least in *Arabidopsis thalaiana*, studies indicate that bisosynthetic pathways have overlapping functions because plants deficient in either pathway have similar growth defects. All of this suggest that auxin levels are highly regulated which is consistent with its central role in plant growth. The exact sites of auxin biosynthesis are unknown but the identification of molecular components of auxin biosynthesis revealed the existence of at least two separate biosynthetic pathways. Transport of auxin is unique because it displays directionality, which is provided through the specific subcellular localization of auxin efflux and auxin influx mechanisms (Benjamins and Scheres 2008). Auxin is perceived by auxin receptors, represented by members of the transport inhibitors response 1 (*TIR1*) family, which results in the proteolysis of auxin/indole-3-acetic acid (Aux/IAA) protein, thereby releasing their inhibitory effects in auxin response factors (ARFs) transcription factors that regulate auxin responsive gene expression.

An important aspect of auxin is ARFs, which activate or repress the auxin response genes by binding to auxin response elements (AuxREs) on their promoters. Liu *et al.* (2012) focused on molecular biological advances of plant ARF families, and discussed ARF structures, regulation of ARF gene expression, the roles of ARFs in regulating the development of plants and in signal transduction and the mechanisms involved in the target gene regulation by ARFs. The phylogenetic relationships of ARFs in plants are close and most of them have 4 domains. ARFs are expressed in various tissues. Their expressions are regulated at both transcriptional and post-transcriptional levels. They play important roles in the interactions between auxin and other hormones. Auxin plays an essential role in embryonic root initiation, in part through the action of the ARF5/MP transcription factor and its auxin-labile inhibitor IAA12/BDL. MP and BDL function in embryonic cells but promote auxin transport to adjacent extra-embryonic suspensor cells, including the quiescent center (QC) precursor (hypophysis).

Also, Rademacher *et al.* (2012) showed that a cell-autonomous auxin response within this cell is required for root meristem initiation. ARF9 and redundant ARFs, and their inhibitor IAA10, act in suspensor cells to mediate hypophysis specification and, surprisingly, also to prevent transformation to embryo identity. ARF misexpression, and analysis of the short suspensor mutant, demonstrates that lineage-specific expression of these ARFs is required for normal embryo development. These results imply the existence of a pre-pattern for a cell-type-specific auxin response that underlies the auxin-dependent speci-fication of embryonic cell types.

After the discovery of IAA in the 1930s, auxin has been virtually synomous with IAA more than 70 years. Several studies demons-trated that IAA directly interacts with the F-box proteins *TIR1* and promotes the degradation of the *Aux/IAA* transcriptional repressors to activate diverse auxin responsive genes (Tan *et al.*, 2007). The *TIR1* gene encodes an F-box protein that interacts directly with *Aux/IAA* proteins. Importantly, this binding is enhanced by auxins. The discovery that *TIR1* functions as an auxin receptor was a landmark event. This discovery indicates those F-box proteins, and perhaps other E3S, can functions as receptor from small molecules. Beyond the *TIR1*-AUX/IAA-ARF pathway, the knowledge of the auxin-regulated translational networks is limited (Santner *et al.*, 2009). Moreover, structural studies demonstrated that auxin forms a complex with *TIR1* and the *Aux/IAA* proteins, thus stabilizes this interaction (Tan *et al.*, 2007). One important implication of the structure is that both *TIR1* and the *Aux/IAA* appear to contribute to high-affinity binding of auxin.

Auxin plays a central role in the regulation of plant growth and development, as well as in responses to environmental stimuli. Narciclasine (NCS), an alkaloid, isolated from *Narcissus tazetta* bulbs has a broad range of inhibitory effects on plants. Hu *et al.* (2012) demonstrated the inhibitory effects of NCS on auxin-inducible lateral root formation, root hair formation, primary root growth, and the expression of primary auxin-inducible genes in Arabidopsis roots using DR5::GUS reporter gene, native auxin promoters (IAA12::GUS, IAA13::GUS), and quantitative reverse transcription PCR analysis. Results also showed that NCS do not affect the expression of cytokinin-inducible ARR5::GUS reporter gene. NCS relieved the auxin-enhanced degradation of the Aux/IAA repressor modulated by the SCF (TIR1) ubiquitin-proteasome pathway. In addition, NCS do not alter the auxin-stimulated interaction between IAA7/AXR2 (Aux/IAA proteins) and the F-box protein TIR1 activity of the proteasome. These results suggest that NCS acts on the auxin signalling pathway upstream of TIR1, which modulates Aux/IAA protein degradation, and thereby affects the auxin-mediated responses in Arabidopsis roots.

Once again, auxin biosynthesis in plants is extremely complex. Multiple pathways likely contribute to *de novo* auxin production. IAA can also be released from IAA conjugates but hydrolytic cleavage for IAA-amino acids, IAA-sugar and IAA-methyl ester. Furthermore, although plants share evolutionary conserved core mechanisms for auxin biosynthesis, different plant species may also have unique strategies and modifications to optimize their IAA biosynthesis. Genetic and biochemical studies indicated that Trp is the main precursor of IAA in plants (Zhao, 2010). Despite the importance of IAA in plants, IAA biosynthesis is not fully understood most likely because of the existence of multiple pathways and functional redundancy of enzymes within the pathway (Zhao, 2010). Alternatively, the Trp-independent pathway has been proposed from IAA biosynthesis but a genetic basis for this pathway has not been defined (Zhao, 2010).

AUXIN CONJUGATES TRANSPORT AND HOMEOSTASIS

Auxin acts as a prominent signal providing by its local accumulation or depletion in selected cells, a spatial and temporal reference for changes in the developmental programme. The distribution of auxin depends on both auxin metabolism (biosynthesis, conjugation and degradation) and cellular auxin transport. Barbez *et al.* (2012) identified a novel putative auxin transport facilitator family, called Pinlikes (PILS), and illustrate that PILS proteins are required for auxin-dependent regulation of plant growth by determining the cellular sensitivity to auxin. PILS proteins regulate intracellular auxin accumulation at the endoplasmic reticulum and thus auxin availability for nuclear auxin signalling. PILS activity affects the level of endogenous auxin IAA, presumably via intracellular accumulation and metabolism.

It is generally accepted that IAA regulates plant morphogenesis through tissue-specific concentration gradients that are formed by the processes of auxin biosynthesis, conjugation and degradation as well as its intercellular and intracellular distribution. In plants, formation of local gradients of auxin is critical for plant developmental processes exhibiting polarity. The auxin efflux carriers, PINs, localize asymmetrically in the plasma membrane and cause the formation of local auxin gradients throughout the plant and a role in phosphorylation is important for polar PIN trafficking. The asymmetry of PIN distribution in the plasma membrane is determined by phosphorylation mediated polar trafficking of PIN proteins (Ganguly *et al.*, 2012). The complicated metabolism of IAA, which encompasses many enzyme systems involved in its activation and deactivation. Nevertheless, it is clear that homeostasis of free auxin pools in the plant plays a vital part in regulating auxin action in development and plant responses to environmental change. The endogenous auxin IBA contributes significantly to this free and hence active pool of IAA. It remains to be tested whether this applies also for the other two endogenous auxins. The fast auxin effects that are transduced through the activation of *ABP1* at the plasma membrane may be expected for IAA and 4-Cl-IAA, but are less likely in case of IBA. Importantly, IBA is actively transported in plants utilizing transport machinery parallel to the well-characterized IAA carrier-mediated transport machinery. Moreover, Barbez *et al.* (2012) findings reveal that the transport machinery to compartmentalize auxin within the cell is of an unexpected molecular complexity and demonstrate this compartmentalization to be functionally important for a number of developmental processes (**Fig. 3.3**).

The molecular basis of cellular auxin transport is still not fully understood. Although a number of carriers have been identified and proved to be involved in auxin transport, their regulation and possible activity of as yet unknown transporters remain unclear. Nevertheless, using single-cell-based systems it is possible to track the course of auxin accumulation inside cells and to specify and quantify some auxin transport parameters. The synthetic auxins 2,4-D and NAA are generally considered to be suitable tools for auxin transport studies because they are transported specifically via either auxin influx or efflux carriers respectively. Research indicates that NAA can be metabolized rapidly in tobacco BY-2 cells. This implies that the transport efficiency of auxin efflux transporters is higher than previously assumed. Moreover, using data on the accumulation of 2,4-D measured in the presence of auxin transport inhibitors, it is shown that 2,4-D is also transported by efflux carriers. Based on the accumulation data, a mathematical model of 2,4-D transport at a single-cell level is proposed. Optimization of the model provides estimates of crucial transport parameters, and

together with its validation by successfully predicting the course of 2,4-D accumulation; it confirms the consistency of the present concept of cellular auxin transport.

On the other hand, auxin is a mobile signal which affects nuclear transcription by regulating the stability of Aux/IAA repressor proteins. Auxin is polarly transported from cell to cell by auxin efflux proteins of the PIN family, but it is not as yet clear how auxin levels are regulated within cells and how auxin access to the nucleus may be controlled. The Arabidopsis genome contains eight PINs, encoding proteins with a similar membrane topology. While five of the PINs are typically targeted polarly to the plasma membranes, the smallest members of the family, PIN5 and PIN8, seem to be located not at the plasma membrane, but in endomembranes. Bosco *et al.* (2012) demonstrated by electron microscopy analysis that PIN8, which is specifically expressed in pollen, resides in the endoplasmic reticulum and that it remains internally localized during pollen tube growth shows a functional role for endoplasmic reticulum-localized PIN8 and suggests a mechanism whereby PIN8 controls auxin thresholds and auxin access to the nucleus, thereby regulating auxin-dependent transcriptional activity. Transgenic Arabidopsis and tobacco plants generated overexpressing or ectopically expressing functional PIN8 and its role in control of auxin homeostasis studied. PIN8 ectopic expression resulted in strong auxin related phenotypes. The severity of phenotypes depended on PIN8 protein levels, suggesting a rate-limiting activity for PIN8. The observed phenotypes correlated with elevated levels of free IAA and ester-conjugated IAA. Activation of the auxin-regulated synthetic DR5 promoter and of auxin response genes strongly repressed in seedlings overexpressing PIN8 when exposed to 1-NAA (**Fig. 3.4**).

Ester conjugates have been identified from a variety of plant species, mainly by mild alkaline hydrolysis. The presence of

IAA-glucose and IAA-myoinositol has been confirmed for monocots as well as dicots. Auxin conjugates can be divided into three main groups: (1) low molecular weight ester conjugates with sugar moieties; (2) low molecular weight amide conjugates with amino acids; and (3) high molecular weight conjugates with peptides and proteins also via an amide bond. These do not occur in all tissues at the same time, but up to now only little is known about the spectrum of auxin conjugates present in a given tissue. The regulation of auxin homeostasis likely depends on the hydrolysis of auxin conjugates. Both the amide- and sugar-linked IAA conjugates can be hydrolyzed and resulting in the release of free IAA. Different amide conjugates hydrolysis with their own specificities likely exists in Arabidopsis. Therefore, although the availability of mutants and molecule tools has provided information on auxin biosynthesis and homeostasis.

Moreover, amide conjugates occur in most plant species so far investigated. Individual IAA amide conjugates have been identified, e.g. IAA-Asp in Scots pine (Anderson and Sandberg, 1982) and Douglas fir (Chiwocha and von Aderkas, 2002), IAA-Glu and IAA-Asp in cucumber and soya bean and IAA-Ala in spruce. Ester conjugates are also present in seeds of other plant species in high amounts, such as Scots pine seeds and contribute to the increase in free IAA during germination. In addition, there is evidence that IAA-glucose is present in Arabidopsis and tomato. Also, IAA found to be attached to this protein called PvIAP1. Interestingly, the attachment of IAA to PvIAP1 is plant species specific, because heterologous expression of the gene PvIAP1 in Arabidopsis and *Medicago truncatula* does not result in the attachment of IAA to the protein (**Fig. 3.2**).

Meanwhile IAA conjugates with proteins are tentatively identified in Arabidopsis, but the nature of these proteins is still under investigation. It seems from an increasing number of experiments that: (1) these IAA proteins occur in a variety of plant species and (ii) different tissues might contain different proteins bound to IAA. Percival and Bandurski (1976) described an IAA ester glycoprotein fraction isolated from oat seeds. IAA-glucose may also be used to modify higher molecular weight conjugates in legume. In addition, due to the emerging sequences for complete genomes, the occurrence of putative hydrolases in land plants can be assumed. The higher free IAA in the tissue when a certain hydrolase is either present or mutated is used for mutant screens: mutants are more resistant to an amino acid conjugate of IAA if the hydrolase involved in the metabolism is not functional. This assay can be also used to test for the *in vivo* hydrolysis of IAA amino acid conjugates (Savic´ *et al*., 2009).

It is shown that the family in Arabidopsis has distinct, yet overlapping substrate specificity for different IAA conjugates tested. Auxin conjugate hydrolases from other plant species revealed that some are more specific for longer-chain auxin conjugates. From *M. truncatula,* a family of amidohydrolases is cloned that converted a rather broad substrate spectrum of IAA amino acid conjugates to free IAA, but some also hydrolyzed IBA conjugates. The synthesis of IAA-glucose is in equilibrium, it is thought that with low IAA-glucose synthesis the equilibrium would be on the side of the non-specific hydrolysis reaction. However, this would not fit into the concept of controlled auxin levels. However, molecular data are still missing on ester conjugate hydrolysis. In addition, Kowalczyk *et al*. (2003) described a bifunctional system for the synthesis and hydrolysis of IAA-myoinositol from immature endosperm of maize kernels. The synthesis of auxin conjugates has remained an enigma for a long time. Although the enzymatic synthesis of ester conjugates is described several decades ago. First gene for an IAA glucose synthase cloned in a pioneering work by Szerszen *et al.* (1994)

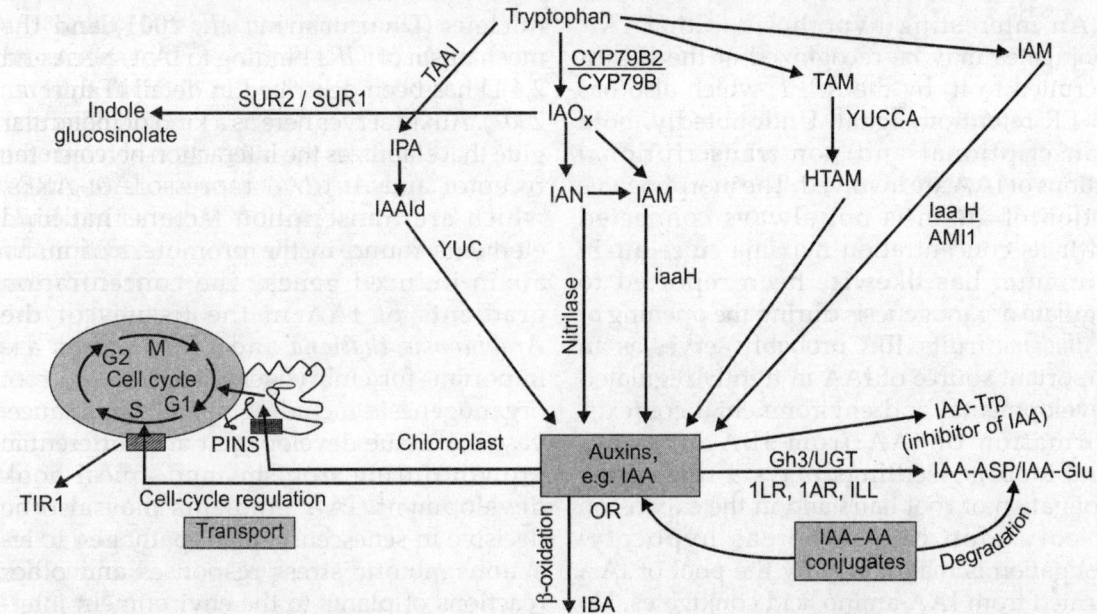

Fig. 3.2: Auxin-cytokinin signalling in plants and role of conjugates in signalling. Both these hormones exist in cell as free or conjugates form and regulate cell division by controlling the expression of cdc2 and cycD3. The amounts of both are regulated by conjugates degradation by enzyme-Ck-oxidase

from maize, understanding of the enzymatic synthesis of amide conjugates remained unclear until the work of Paul Staswick's group. An enzyme for the transfer of IAA from IAA-glucose to myoinositol from maize kernels is described by this group.

Amino acid sequencing of the protein (hormone) showed similarity to serine carboxypeptidase-like acyltransferases. Amide conjugates are thought to be synthesized upon treatment of plant tissue with high IAA concentrations. It should be noted that the synthesis of the IAA conjugate with Trp has a special role, since it is not an inactive auxin conjugate but rather has activity as a growth inhibitor. There is evidence that some of the auxin conjugates, i.e. those formed with Asp and glutamate might not be storage conjugates, but rather a form of IAA that is subject to degradation. In legumes (*Vicia faba* and *Dalbergia dolichopetala*), the main oxidative

metabolites of IAA-Asp and IAA-Glu are DiOx-IAA-Asp and DiOx-IAA-Glu. Induction of catabolism to yield 2-oxindole-3-acetic acid and irreversible conjugation to indole-3-acetyl-N-aspartic acid is noticed at the same time as *de novo* synthesis of IAA is first detected in Scots pine seeds (Ljung *et al.*, 2001). Therefore, it is not possible to strictly separate between IAA amino acid conjugates destined for catabolism or hydrolysis. Based on the result obtained so far, the synthesis of auxin amino acid conjugates most likely takes place in the cytosol. Most of the auxin conjugate hydrolases have endoplasmic reticulum (ER) retention sequences attached, but not all of them. The ER retention signal is not a prerequisite for activity, because two out of the five amidohydrolases characterized so far from *M. truncatula* lack such a tetrapeptide, but show activity and TaIAR3 has the unusual sequence motif RDEL.

An interesting hypothesis is that IAA conjugates may be recognized at the ER (or recruited to it) by the *ABP1*, which also has an ER retention signal. Undoubtedly, both transcriptional and non-transcriptional actions of IAA are involved. The morphogenic action of auxin is not always connected with its concentration maxima since auxin minimum has likewise been reported to regulate organogenesis during the opening of *A. thaliana* fruits. IBA probably serves as an important source of IAA in tightly regulated developmental and environmental contexts. Formation of IAA from IBA in young Arabidopsis seedlings plays a role in the elongation of root hairs and in the expansion of cotyledon cells, whereas hypocotyl elongation is maintained by the pool of IAA formed from IAA-amino acid conjugates. No IAA-independent biosynthetic pathway for IBA has yet been found, it seems that IBA levels depend on the levels of IAA. Because of the presence of IAA and IBA in the model plant *A. thaliana*, we know much more about these two compounds than do about the two other endogenous auxins, 4-Cl-IAA and PAA, which have not been detected in Arabidopsis. The endogenous auxin IBA contributes significantly to this free and hence active pool of IAA. It remains to be tested whether this applies also for the other two endogenous auxins.

GENETICS OF PERCEPTION AND SIGNAL TRANSDUCTION

During the past few years, remarkable progress has been made on our basic under-standing of the mechanisms, genes and proteins, and regulation of auxin action, profited from the development of molecular tools particularly in Arabidopsis. IAA plays a role in wide variety of growth, developmental and physiological processes. Transport inhibitor response 1/auxin signalling F-box (*TIR1/AFB*) proteins are localized in the nucleus (Dharmasiri *et al.*, 2005) and the mechanism of *TIR1* binding to IAA, NAA and 2,4-D has been described in detail (Tan *et al.*, 2007). Auxin serves here as a kind of molecular glue that stabilizes the interaction between the receptor and *Aux/IAA* repressors of ARFs, which are transcription factors that bind elements found in the promoters of many auxin-induced genes. The concentration gradients of IAA in the tissues of the *Arabidopsis thaliana* and other plants are important for embryogenesis shoot and root organogenesis including apical dominance, vascular tissue development and differential growth during tropisms and apical hook development. IAA gradients may also be decisive in senescence, plant-pathogen inter-actions, abiotic stress responses and other reactions of plants to the environment inter-action (Wang *et al.*, 2010) (**Fig. 3.3**).

Auxin signalling is assumed to start with the perception of auxin by its interaction with some kind of receptors. Evidence suggests that there are multiple sites for auxin perception, and in this sense, auxin can be considered to be multifunctional in that the auxin signal appears to be transduced through various signalling pathways. The auxin conjugates can then be hydrolyzed by the enzymes also localized in the ER. However, the subcellular localization cannot be demonstrated for any of the known proteins. The co-localization of an auxin receptor, auxin amino acid conjugate hydrolases, and a protein with IAA attached suggest a possible, not yet identified function of the ER in auxin homeostasis/biology (**Fig. 3.4**).

Moreover, the best-characterized auxin binding protein is *ABP1* (Napier, 1995), which first described in maize. Excitement about the role of *ABP1* in auxin perception is driven the high specificity and affinity of its auxin binding, with a KD for the synthetic auxin NAA of 5×10^{-8} M. Some *ABP1* apparently escape to the plasma membrane, where it mediates several cellular responses to applied auxin, including tobacco mesophyll protoplast

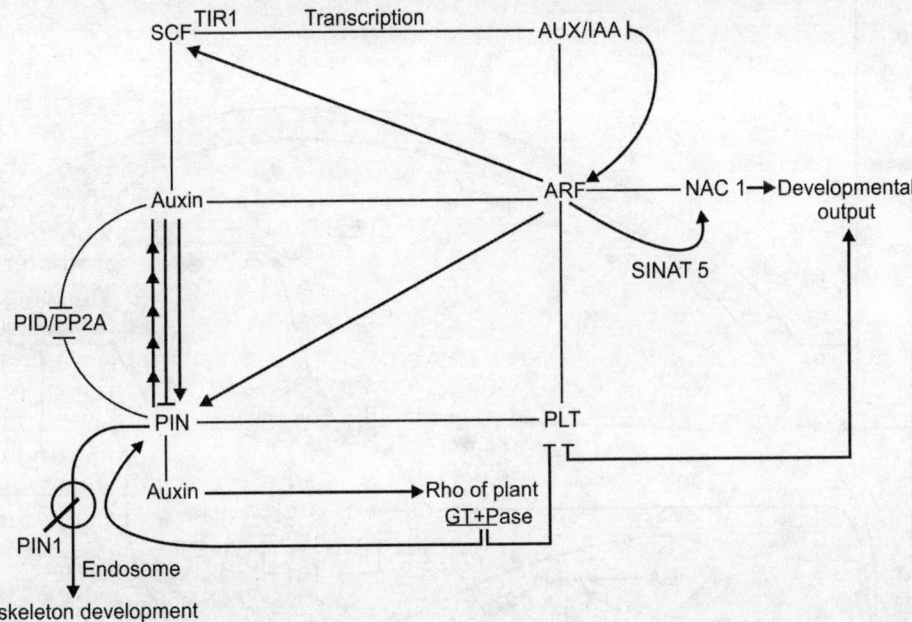

Fig. 3.3: A pathway of IAA (Auxin) synthesis in plant system along with showing the role of TAA1 and YUC respectively. IAA-Asp and IAA-Glu are conjugates form of Auxin (IAA) generally found in plant system play role the stable and specific functionality of auxin and interaction of auxin with other plant hormone during growth and development

hyperpolarization, the expansion of tobacco and maize cells in culture, tobacco mesophyll protoplast division, and stomatal closure. A role of *ABP1* has been suggested for some of the fast auxin responses connected with the activity of plasma membrane ion channels, cell expansion and endocytosis, as exhaustively reviewed recently. Besides this, there is still no convincing information about the downstream signalling pathway that is triggered following auxin binding to *ABP1*, but it appears likely that this protein is crucial for plant development, since *abp1* knockout mutants of Arabidopsis are embryo-lethal.

Interestingly, this mutation exhibits auxin transport-dependent phenol types when maintained in heterozygous state and also shows changes in the expression of auxin-regulated genes (Effendi *et al.*, 2011). In general, phenotypes are limited to effects on the balance between cell division and cell

expansion. For example, overexpression of *ABP1* in tobacco plants results in increase in leaf mesophyll cell size, without affecting final leaf size. Homologous of *ABP1* and IBR5, which are important for various fast auxin responses appeared early with the evolution of algae. Nevertheless, it is clear that homeostasis of free auxin pools in the plant plays a vital role in regulating auxin action in development and plant responses to environmental fluctuations.

The phenotype of plants homozygous for the mutation is embryo lethality early in the globular stage. This demonstrates the essential role that *ABP1* plays in plant growth, but it makes analysis of the postembryonic role of *ABP1* difficult, requiring conditional mutations. The second major advance is the solving of the crystalline structure of *ABP1* to a resolution of 1.9 Angstroms. Homologous of *ABP1* and IBR5, which are important for

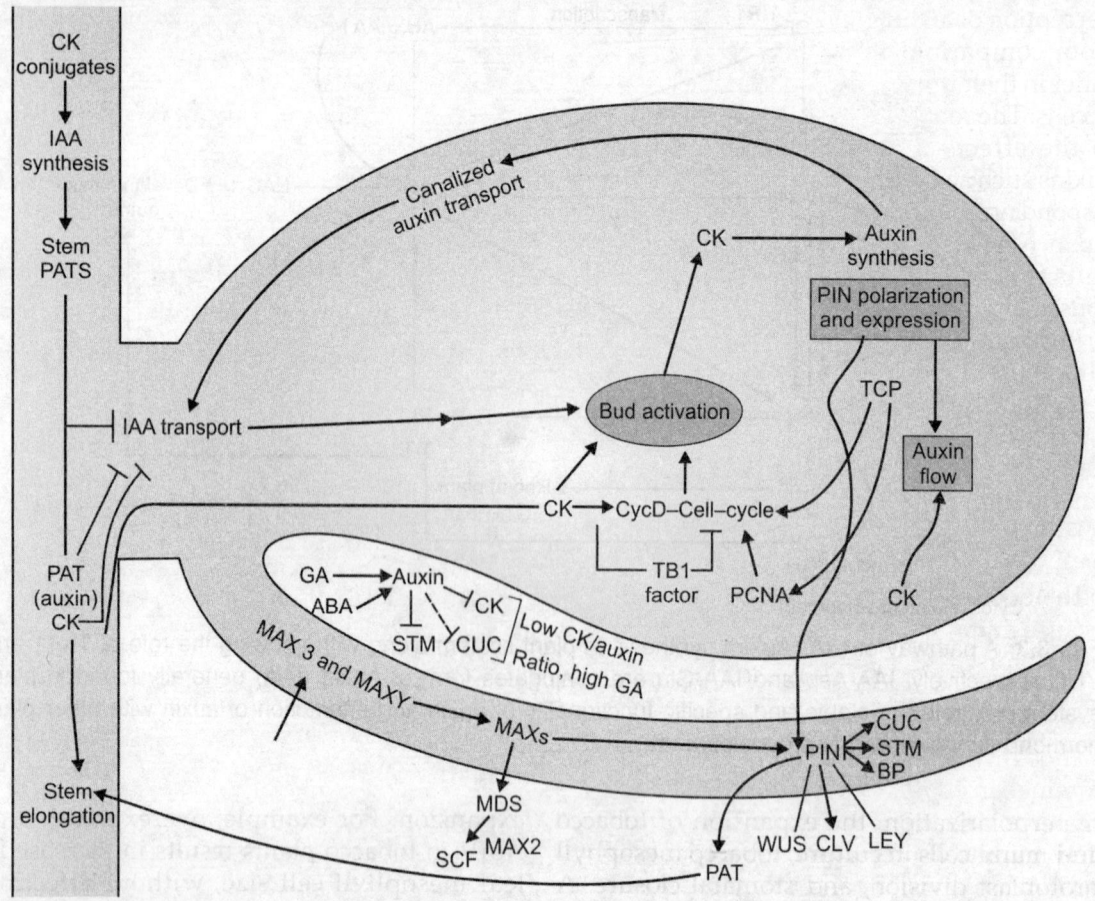

Fig. 3.4: Diagrammatic representation of regulatory systems participates to mediate auxin action in plant system. Such regulatory systems including AUX/IAA, ARF SCF^TIR1 (e.g. SKP1 and F-box, etc.), PP2A, PLT/NAC1, SINAT5, PIN proteins. The NAC1 and PLT proteins mediate the developmental outputs in response to auxin. High auxin levels will lead to the degradation of AUX/IAA proteins, resulting in the depression of ARF proteins, including the expression of auxin-responsive genes

various fast auxin responses, appeared early with the evolution of algae (Lau *et al.*, 2009). In comparison, the *TIR1/AFBs*-mediated pathway evolved later along with plant multicellularity and has become an important coordinating system in multicellular plants (Lau *et al.*, 2009). The combination of these new genetic and biochemical tools will allow better analysis of the events immediately up- and downstreams of *ABP1*, so that its role in auxin signalling can be clarified. *ABP1* is

expected to answer only part of the question of how the auxin signal is perceived.

In addition, the importance of *ABP1* in the general auxin response is also strongly supported by the fact that the levels of Aux/IAAs dynamically reflect the downregulation or overexpression of *ABP1*, providing evidence for the functional coupling of *ABP1* and *SCF-TIR1/AFBs* mechanisms. For example, although *ABP1* appears to act at the cell surface, there is a good evidence for intracellular perception of auxin, much of which is derived from comparing the effects of auxins that differ in their transport properties into and out of cells. The roots of *aux1* mutants are resistant to the effects of membrane-impermeable auxins such as 2,4-D. However, *Aux1* mutants respond normally to the membrane-permeable auxin NAA, and addition of NAA to *Aux1* mutant roots can restore gravitational response. This suggests that intracellular auxin is important for root growth inhibition. Although there is currently little to link auxin perception with downstream events, rapid progress in the area of auxin signal transduction has been made through the use of genetic approaches in Arabidopsis (Leyser, 1997). Among the loci defined by these screens are *AXR1*, *AXR2*, *AXR3*, *AXR4* and *AXR6*. A sixth locus, *TIR1*, is originally identified because mutations in it result in the resistance to inhibitors of polar auxin transport, but these mutations are subsequently found also to confer auxin resistance (Ruegger *et al.*, 1998).

Those *Aux/IAA* proteins that have been examined in detail are localized in the nucleus and have very short half-lives, ranging from a few minutes to a few hours. The fusion of *Aux/IAA* proteins to entirely unrelated reporter proteins, such as luciferase or β-glucuronase (GUS), results in the destabilization of the reporter proteins. This indicates that the Aux/IAAs contain a transferable destabilization sequence, a so-called degron. A second line of evidence for the importance of domain II in regulating *Aux/IAA* stability comes from the analysis of the molecular basis for the phenotypes conferred by *axr3-1*, *axr2-1*, and similar *Aux/IAA* mutants. Auxin signalling requires *SCF-TIR1*-mediated turnover of *Aux/IAA* proteins. In order to transduce auxin responses, this process must be in some way regulated by auxin. Auxin can act at a variety of levels by influencing the recognition of the Aux/IAAs by SCF-TIR1 or the overall activity of SCF-TIR1 in ubiquitinating the Aux/IAAs. Evidence to till date is limited but in general,

supports a role for auxin in regulating the SCF-TIR1-*Aux/IAA* interaction because the auxin-induced destabilization of Aux/IAAs correlates with an increase in the abundance of Aux/IAA-SCF-TIR1 complexes in the pull-down assay, without affecting the amount of *TIR1* (Gray *et al.*, 2001).

Moreover, the auxin binding activity of *TIR1/AFBs* may be under the control of an important intermediate of plant phospholipid metabolism, inositol-hexakisphosphate, which has its binding site located close to the pocket for IAA in *TIR1* (Tan *et al.*, 2007). The auxin-regulated degradation of *Aux/IAA* proteins is an essential part of the auxin response. *Aux/IAA* proteins appear to act as transcriptional regulators through the formation of a variety of dimers. First, they can dimerize with other members of the *Aux/IAA* family (Kim *et al.*, 1997). These interactions require domains III and IV, and possibly domain I (Kim *et al.*, 1997). In Arabidopsis, there are at least 24 different Aux/IAAs. Although only a subset of Aux/IAAs are expressed in any one tissue and not all *Aux/IAA* family members may dimerize with high affinity.

Over the past few decades several auxin responsive genes and gene families involved in the signalling of auxin have been identified as the *Aux/IAAs* and ARFs. The expression of most *Aux/IAAs* is rapidly upregulated by auxin; *Aux/IAAs* are primary response genes. The *Arabidopsis* genome contains 29 different *Aux/IAA* genes and the encoded proteins contain four conserved domains. In general, specific pairs of *Aux/IAA* and ARF proteins are suggested to determine auxin-dependent developmental processes. Proteins able to bind auxin have been identified, but none of those is generally accepted to be the elusive auxin receptor.

LEAF ARRANGEMENT ON STEM

In 1400s, Leonardo da Vinci postulated that proper arrangement of plant organs is crucial for plant growth and survival. Understanding auxin biosynthesis provides tools to manipulate auxin levels in plants with temporal and spatial precision. The available auxin biosynthetic mutants also provide sensitized backgrounds for genetically isolating key components that are responsible for auxin-mediated development. The importance of auxin transport in organ initiation is suggested by experiments in which plants are grown on polar auxin transport inhibitors, which strongly resemble *PIN1* mutant plants. Moreover, recent progress in auxin biosynthesis makes it possible to isolate mutants that can overcome or becomes exciting opportunity to identify new components responsible for auxin action in plant development. Leaf form and vascular patterns provide some of the most impressive examples of the complexity of biological shapes in nature. Application experiments suggested that an auxin accumulation mechanism could account for organ initiation (Reinhart *et al.*, 2003).

A common feature of the development of the leaf lamina and vein networks is the repeated use of basic modules. There is also congruence of leaf shape and vein layouts at least superficially; the pattern of vasculature formation is well-aligned with the final geometry of the leaf lamina. Over the past 15 years, genetic approaches have led to substantial increase in our understanding of leaf and vascular development, and have provided good evidence that regulated activity of auxin provides important spatial cues for both processes. The new primordial subsequently functions as auxin sinks, draining auxin from the surrounding tissue and thereby preventing growth of adjacent cells. This mechanism determines the position of the next primordium, thus guaranteeing outgrowth of lateral organs in a regular phyllotactic pattern. Leaves are lateral organs that derive post embryonically from a pluripotent cell population at the tip of the plant, termed the shoot apical meristem

(SAM). At very early stages of leaf development the growth of the leaf is largely attributable to cell division (Efroni *et al.*, 2008).

A key event in the development of leaves is the correct differentiation of the several specialized cell types that underpin the physiological functions of the leaf such as stomata for gas exchange, vascular cells for the transport of water and nutrients across the leaf, and mesophyll cells for photosynthesis. Loss of function in the *Arabidopsis thaliana* Pinformed1 (*PIN1*) efflux facilitator compromises organogenesis at the SAM, as does pharmacological inhibition of auxin transport (Galweiler *et al.*, 1998), and molecular work confirmed that leaf founder cells are characterized by elevated auxin activity that is largely generated by the delivery of auxin to the meristem via *PIN1*. Interestingly, the *PIN1* protein co-localizes with patches of high auxin; *PIN1* polarizes towards new primordia (Smith *et al.*, 2006).

In addition, leaf initials act as sinks of auxin and deplete it from their proximity, thus inhibiting the initiation of additional leaf primordia at the periphery of the SAM. The underlying *PIN1*-dependent mechanism that controls auxin distribution in the meristem has been proposed to be sufficient to explain the maintenance of the correct leaf initiation pattern termed phyllotaxis, and quantitative modelling approaches based on auxin concentration, flow, and *PIN1* polarization are successful to generate both the wild-type Arabidopsis leaf arrangements and the development of the midvein. Finally, the action of auxin in leaf initiation is likely to be mediated by Monopteros (MP), a transcription factor member of the ARF family, as *mp* mutants show organ initiation defects similar to *pin1* (Przemeck *et al.*, 1996). In addition, the repression of KNOX expression in the leaf is mediated by the ARP (Asymmetric leaves 1 (*AS1*) in Arabidopsis/Rough Sheath 2 (*RS2*) in maize/Phantastica (PHAN) in snapdragon) MYB proteins which act as dimers with

Asymmetric Leaves 2-type LOB domain proteins (Semiarti *et al.*, 2001). The complementary expression patterns of KNOX and auxin activity reporters during early organ specification at the SAM suggested that auxin may also contribute to KNOX repression in leaves. Ectopic KNOX expression in leaves decreases auxin transport and alters auxin activity distribution, suggesting antagonistic interactions between KNOX and auxin action.

Moreover, it is important to note that because adaxial/abaxial juxtaposition is fundamental for driving leaf growth (Waites *et al.* 1998), the involvement of auxin in axial patterning pathways is to indirectly influence leaf growth. Such more direct effects of auxin on cellular growth in the leaf are mediated by two distinct signalling pathways: (1) a well-characterized TIR1-Auxin/indole-3-acetic acid (AUX/IAA)-ARF dependent pathway and (2) a much less well-understood pathway involving the ER-localized protein auxin binding protein 1 (*ABP1*), which can act as an auxin receptor in parallel to TIRs. In addition, AUX1 is co-expressed with *PIN1* in the epidermal layer of the shoot meristem, although AUX1 localization is less polar compared with *PIN1*. These findings resulted in the proposition of a model in which *PIN1* together with AUX1 determines the localization of auxin maxima that are important for organ primordia initiation. Correct auxin transport is not only required for the formation of leaves, but it is also pivotal for the development of marginal outgrowths that sculpt the final leaf shape. In Arabidopsis, perturbations of auxin transport result in leaves that fail to initiate the characteristic marginal projections, called serration. Absence of marginal configurations on inhibition of auxin transport is similarly observed in leaves that normally produce deep lobes in response to ectopic KNOX expression. Epidermal *PIN1* convergence points define local auxin activity maxima at

the tips of forming serrations (Scarpella *et al.*, 2006) (**Fig. 3.5**).

Auxin modulates CUC expression in the Arabidopsis embryo (Furutani *et al.*, 2004); thus it is possible that the effects of auxin on leaflet delimitation occur through regulation of CUC expression. The CUC proteins modulate *PIN1* expression or auxin response to facilitate leaflet formation. Because the mechanisms regulating auxin levels and auxin-mediated responses present in early land plants, the finding that *PIN1* is required for both serrations and the generation of the dissected leaf form suggests that the evolution of multiple types of tissue outgrowths may have been constrained or canalized by the ability to regulate marginal auxin activity gradients. The distribution of *PIN1*, although quite complex and dynamic, represents the most crucial parameter in the model. A pivotal issue is how *PIN1* localization is regulated during primordium initiation. Besides this, a variant of the principle that auxin regulates its own efflux is used as the basis of models that predict *PIN1* localization during primordium initiation. Expression profiling identifies *PIN1* as the most relevant member of the *PIN* gene family in leaf vein formation.

Moreover, during normal and experimentally altered leaf vein formation, *PIN1* expression in subepidermal cells precedes and converges towards sites of procambial strand formation, and at the *PIN1* expression level; all veins appear to be generated through two basic ontogenies. The important assumption in these models is that in a given cell of the L1 layer *PIN1* is always polar localized towards the neighbouring cell that has the highest auxin concentration through a regulatory loop involving auxin and auxin transport. These models are able to generate the expected phyllotactic pattern. Several models can explain different phyllotactic patterns when parameters are changed to an extent. In addition, elevated auxin levels, occurring naturally in association with serration tips or

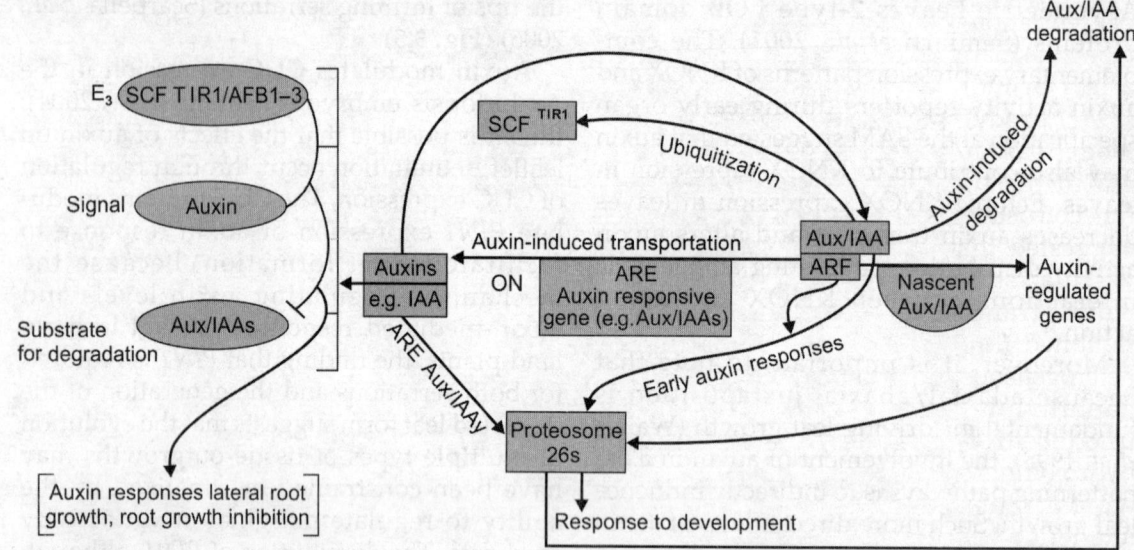

Fig. 3.5: A model for auxin signalling during development; Auxin/IAA protein able to form a variety of dimers both within the AUX/IAA family and with members of the ARF family

experimentally as a consequence of either direct auxin application or auxin transport inhibition, lead to the expansion of *PIN1* expression domains (Wenzel *et al.*, 2007). Within narrow *PIN1* domains, subcellular localization indicates auxin transport towards pre-existing veins: In free-ending domains a single polarity exists, whereas in connected domains two opposite polarities are connected by a bipolar cell (Wenzel *et al.*, 2007).

LEAF VASCULAR DEVELOPMENT

The vascular system of higher plants constitutes a continuous cellular network essential for solute transport and mechanic stability in plants. A vascular inducing signal from young leaf primordia can be replaced by auxin application, suggesting that endogenous auxin promotes vascular development basal to its site of synthesis. Regularities in vascular regeneration patterns and the possibility to induce the formation of vascular strands by local auxin application have implicated auxin in the formation of vascular strands. Vascular

tissue patterning needs to be precisely regulated, because the conducting functions of vascular tissues require not only proper integration into the context of nonvascular tissues, but also perfect cell alignment and tissue continuity within vascular strands.

A classical model proposed by Sachs (1981), suggests that vasculature is formed by a feedback mechanism in which auxin transport through cells increases the capacity of cells for polar transport of auxin, which in turn triggers their differentiation into vascular cells. The polarity of auxin transport is generally attributed to the restriction of auxin efflux carriers to the basal side of each cell. Auxin has been implicated in vascular differentiation under experimental conditions, but the distribution of auxin in naturally developing organs is unknown. The ontogeny of the Arabidopsis leaf vascular system has previously been described. The formation of continuous and ordered vascular networks in leaves has been connected to the transport of auxin. Further suggested that free auxin concentrations shift from the tip downward along the margins during the development of a leaf primordium. Moreover, Mitchison (1981) produced a mathematical transport model based on a feedback mechanism in which the transport of auxin varies as a function of the flux of auxin and various models suggested that in the young primordium, vascular strand formation is sink driven. Auxin transport can experimentally be inhibited through a number of chemically heterogeneous compounds, among them 1-*N*-naphthylphthalamic acid (NPA); 2,3,5-triiodobenzoic acid (TIBA) and 2-chloro-9-hydroxyfluorene-9-carboxylic acid (HFCA), which inhibit polar auxin transport by interfering with auxin efflux.

Next in this trend, Rolland-Lagan and Prusinkiewicz (2005) showed that multiple auxin sources as well as a high auxin flux from both source and sink exist in the leaf. The studies of Mattsson *et al.*, (2003) connect general auxin signalling with controls of vascular differentiation and suggest molecular mechanisms for auxin signalling in patterned cell differentiation. The formation of primary and secondary veins is tightly associated with the major growth directions of the primordium. Throughout leaf development, DR5 expression was restricted to subepidermal cell layers. Moreover, various observations have implicated the role of auxin in the formation of vascular tissues in plant organs and such as vascular strand formation in response to local auxin application, the effects of impaired auxin transport on vascular patterns and suggestive phenotypes of Arabidopsis auxin response mutants. Potential vascular patterning genes have been identified by mutant phenotypes. Although many of the identified gene products remain to be determined, available evidence suggests sterols, small peptides, cytokinin, and auxin in promoting vascular differentiation. Cytokinin is a multifaceted plant hormone and involved in various physiological processes in plant

system along with auxin (Mazid *et al.*, 2011c). Mattsson *et al.*, (2003) have used molecular markers to visualize auxin response patterns in developing Arabidopsis leaves as well as Arabidopsis mutants and transgenic plants to trace pathways of auxin signal transduction controlling the expression of early procambial genes. In addition, they suggest that in young Arabidopsis, leaf primordia, molecular auxin response patterns presage sites of procambial differentiation. Moreover, if IAA is compartmentalized within cells, biochemical assays cannot distinguish between pools of biologically perceived and inaccessible auxin. Therefore, auxin response reporter gene expression remains another necessary tool in the study of developmental functions of auxin because it can reveal correlated patterns of auxin response and cell differentiation, even in highly dynamic developmental processes.

In addition, Mattsson *et al.* (2003) further found that the activity of the Arabidopsis gene *Monopteros*, required for proper vascular differentiation, is also essential in a spectrum of auxin responses, which include the regulation of rapidly auxin-inducible *Aux/IAA* genes, and discovered the tissue-specific vascular expression profile of the class I homeodomain-leucine zipper gene, *AtHB20*. *Monopteros* activity is a limiting factor in the expression of *AtHB8* and *AtHB20*, two genes encoding transcriptional regulators expressed early in procambial development. ARF proteins bind to DNA and seem to act as homo- or heterodimers, whereas *Aux/IAA* proteins may regulate ARF function by interfering with ARF dimerization. Many *Aux/IAA* genes are themselves rapidly induced by auxin and are widely used as reporters of local auxin responses. The activity of ARF transcription factors is believed to be constrained by interaction with *Aux/IAA* proteins. Mattsson *et al.* (2003) show that the auxin signal transduction functions of MP include controlling the expression of auxin-inducible genes and that the expression of two transcriptional regulators expressed early in vascular development, *AtHB8* and *AtHB20*, is positively correlated with the amount of *MP* gene activity.

In summary, the expression of *AtHB8* and of two typical primary auxin response genes turned out to be auxin inducible and regulated by *MP* gene activity in a suitable genetic background, and the expression of *AtHB20* shows strict dependence on *MP* gene activity and likely dependence on auxin signals. Genetic screens in Arabidopsis and other species have identified a number of loci with potential functions in vascular differentiation, some of which suggest a role of auxin in vascular development. Mattsson *et al.* (2003) have explored the spatial relationship between the distribution of perceived auxin and vascular differentiation zones as well as pathways of auxin signalling in vascular differentiation during normal organogenesis. *PIN1* is the major auxin transport component in vascular development, because it is the only family member expressed during early stages of procambium formation (Scarpella *et al.*, 2006). A distinct *PIN1* localization suggests that auxin is transported towards so-called convergence points at the leaf margin, which guide the positioning of new veins. Application experiments using auxin and auxin transport inhibitors provided an excellent correlation between the accumulation of auxin in convergence points and *PIN1* expression determining the site of vein formation. This is remarkably similar to the relation between auxin fluxes and PIN1 expression as well as *PIN1* localization as proposed for the formation of lateral roots and phyllotaxis (**Fig. 3.2**).

Each primordium enlarges to become a nearly cylindrical protrusion, slightly flattened on the adaxial side. At very early stages of primordium development, a subset of the most distal subepidermal cells expressed DR5. Interestingly, the position of this distal focus of DR5 expression is found to be variable and could be either central or shifted to one side.

As reported previously, secondary veins form continuous lobes and emerge in a basipetal sequence. DR5 expression preceded this emergence for each secondary vein lobe and each lobe is composed of a long stretch of DR5-expressing cells parallel to the leaf margin and of a number of cells connecting the basal end of the lobe with the midvein. These lobes became first recognizable as heterogeneous DR5 expression domains parallel to the margin that subsequently became basally connected to the midvein and then differentiated into continuous lobes of elongated cell files. The distinct domains of high DR5 expression can be due to: (a) local accumulation of auxin that is derived from remote sources through polar auxin transport, (b) locally enhanced auxin synthesis or response within the incipient veins and (c) a patterned signal unrelated to auxin, spuriously activating the DR5 marker. Moreover, broadening of the DR5 expression domain along the leaf margin is associated with the multiplication of midveins, suggesting that a sharp distal expression focus in normal development promotes the formation of a single midvein.

ROOT DEVELOPMENTS

Auxin is the main regulator of root apical meristem (RAM) functioning, and auxin maxima coincides with the sites of RAM initiation and maintenance. Auxin gradients are formed due to local auxin biosynthesis and polar auxin transport. The PIN family of auxin transporters plays a critical role in polar auxin transport, and two mechanisms of auxin maxima formation in the RAM based on PIN-mediated auxin transport, have been proposed to date: the reverse fountain and the reflected flow mechanisms. Regeneration of the RAM in decapitated roots is provided by the reflected flow mechanism. The dual-mechanism model proposed can be a powerful tool for the study of several different aspects of auxin function in root.

Moreover, auxin along with cytokinin considered as central hormones involved in the regulation of plant growth and development, including processes determining root architecture, such as root pole establishment during early embryogenesis, root meristem maintenance and lateral root organogenesis. Thus to control root development both pathways put special demands on the mechanisms that balance their activities and mediate their interactions. Bielach *et al.*, (2012) also summarize recent knowledge on the role of auxin and cytokinin in the regulation of root architecture with special focus on lateral root organogenesis, molecular mechanisms of their interactions, and proposed forward genetic screen as a tool to identify novel molecular components of the auxin and cytokinin crosstalk.

Moreover, particularly auxin distribution is known to play a crucial role in the patterning and growth of roots, which represents the first case where an auxin maxima is demonstrated to be instructive for patterning. The early characterization of auxins as "root forming hormones of plants" established a long-standing link between this class of small molecules and root development. Auxin can be synthesized in young leaves and cotyledons (Ljung *et al.*, 2001). Since auxins are first described, there has been a tight connection between this class of hormones and root development. Some of the latest genetic, molecular, and cellular experiments that demonstrate the importance of generating and maintaining auxin gradients during root development. Auxins orchestrate almost every aspect of plant growth and development. In roots, the most well-characterized auxin-associated phenotypes are the dose-dependent increase in the length of epidermal-derived root hairs, the bimodal effect of auxin concentration on primary root length, the dose-dependent increase in

number of lateral root primordia, and the response to gravity (Peret *et al.*, 2009).

The local control of auxin levels generates regional concentration gradients and local maxima that are crucial for establishing and maintaining a root primordium (Benjamins and Scheres, 2008). A plant's roots system determines both the capacity of a sessile organism to acquire nutrient sand water, as well as providing a means to monitor the soil for a range of environmental conditions. The final root architecture remains at the heart of many active research programmes from very long times. The same long-distance pathway that carries carbohydrates from "source" to "sink" also facilitates the bulk flow of auxin and other hormones such as ABA and cytokinins as well as mRNA and proteins. A single root contains a number of cell types, which can be discerned by visual and molecular markers. A long proximal-distal axis of a root is characterized by a series of developmental zones. The quiescent centre (QC) promotes its neighbouring cells to continuously produce initial cells that give rise to cell files. Subsequently, cells become part of the elongation zone and then the differentiation zone. As such, the longitudinal axis of a root represents a constantly renewing gradient of cell differentiation. Although many of the developmental events that regulate patterning and the capacity to form lateral roots are not observable, the epidermal root surface bears easy detectable markers of the transition between these distinct zones: an increased length of epidermal cells demarcates the transition between the meristematic and elongation zones.

Moreover, Grieneisen and colleagues (2007) used multilevel computational modelling of diffusion and permeability to demonstrate that a robust auxin maxima and auxin gradient can be maintained in the root meristem that spans the meristem and can have an instructive function in patterning and meristem zonation. Importantly, many predictions of the model are validated experimentally or explained by previous observations. In the model, setting up the auxin maxima is fast, which is in line with earlier experimental data in which the auxin maxima is rapidly re-established after laser ablation of the QC. The projected instructive auxin gradient should depend on readout by molecular components. The family of PLT genes, which are also present in a gradient that nicely overlaps with the anticipated auxin gradient, are good candidates for performing the readout.

Many molecular components have been identified and their biological function is at least partly understood. Members of the TIR1 family of proteins are able to bind auxin, and therefore, represent auxin receptors for which the downstream signalling pathway is known. TIR1 proteins are involved in the regulation of the stability of Aux/IAA proteins, which transcriptional regulators are acting in concert with ARF proteins. High auxin is reported to retain PIN proteins at the membrane, whereas in the model low intracellular auxin correlates with the position of PIN proteins at the membrane. The interdependence of PIN and PLT genes, this model implies the existence of a regulatory loop that sets up an auxin gradient, which is self-regulating because PLT transcription factors subsequently regulate the expression of PINs. Moreover, gravity profoundly influences plant growth and development. Plants respond to changes in orientation by using gravitropic responses to modify their growth. Cholodny and Went hypothesized over 80 years ago that plants bend in response to a gravity stimulus by generating a lateral gradient of a growth regulator at an organ's apex, later found to be auxin. Auxin regulates root growth by targeting Aux/IAA repressor proteins for degradation. Band *et al.* (2012) used an Aux/IAA-based reporter, domain II (DII)-VENUS, in conjunction with a mathematical model to quantify auxin redistribution following

a gravity stimulus. Multidisciplinary approach revealed that auxin is rapidly redistributed to the lower side of the root within minutes of a 90° gravity stimulus. Unexpectedly, auxin asymmetry is rapidly lost as bending root tips reached an angle of 40° to the horizontal **(Fig. 3.5)**.

In addition, the family of *PLT* genes which are also present in a gradient that nicely overlaps with the anticipated auxin gradient are good candidates for performing the readout. The currently known regulatory mechanisms stress the importance of feedback loops in auxin action. At least two such regulatory loops exist: a transcriptional loop and a polarity loop. The transcriptional loop involves auxin regulation of the activity of *SCF-TIR1* (SKP1, Cullin, and F-box protein, in this case transport inhibitor response 1), thereby regulating the transcriptional activity of ARF proteins via the proteolysis rate of *Aux/IAA* proteins. Plethora (PLT) proteins directly or indirectly regulate the transcription of *PIN* genes that feedback on auxin by regulating the distribution of auxin, thereby completing the loop. The relative timing and balance between auxin-mediated expression of *Aux/IAA* genes and the auxin-dependent degradation of the *Aux/IAA* proteins balance the auxin response and auxin transport. The polarity loop involves the regulation of the subcellular localization of PIN efflux facilitators by affecting the phosphorylation status through the activity of Pinoid (PID) (or PID-like) kinases and protein phosphatase 2A (PP2A) phosphatases. GTPases likely also perform a regulatory function in polarity.

In this trend, Overvoorde *et al.* (2010) identified molecular components that convert auxin gradients into local differentiation events, which ultimately define the root architecture. The protonation of auxin in the acidic environment of the cell wall facilitates its movement by diffusion across cell membranes, referred to as "polar auxin transport" (PAT). PAT is the outcome of the coordinated activities of several membrane transport protein families that facilitate auxin influx (e.g. AUX1 and LIKE-AUX1 (LAX) and efflux (e.g. members of the P-glycoprotein ABC transporter family and the PIN proteins).

Moreover, the PAT-installed auxin maxima in the QC creates an organizing centre that organizes the root tip through contact with neighbouring stem cell initials. The maintenance of stems cells ensures the continued contribution of new cells to the apical meristem and underlies the indeterminate growth of the root. The Plethora (PLT1-4) genes represent a subclade of AP2 transcription factors that are required to define the root-stem cell niche. These genes are differentially expressed in a graded fashion in the root tip, their overlapping expression patterns lead to maximal PLT protein levels in the stem cell zone.

Moreover, many of the genes involved in the synthesis of auxin are expressed in roots and that root-generated auxin contributes to the maintenance of the gradients and maxima required for normal root development (Petersson *et al.*, 2009). Many auxin biosynthesis genes are expressed in the root tip and high-resolution auxin measurements in specific cell types after fluorescent activated cell sorting revealed the sites of auxin biosynthesis in the root apex (Petersson *et al.*, 2009). First, evidence for the role of auxin biosynthesis routes in roots came from the characterization of the weak ethylene insensitive (*wei2* and *wei7*) and transport inhibitor response 7 (*tir7-1*) mutants. These mutants suppress the high auxin phenotypes of the auxin-overproducing Superroot (*sur1* or *sur2*) and disrupt one of the two subunits of anthranilate synthase, an enzyme that catalyzes the rate limiting formation of anthranilate from chorismate during tryptophan synthesis. Second, a mutation in the protein kinase domain of the Raf-like kinase, Constitutive triple response 1 (CTR1) leads to increased IAA synthesis in roots, indicates that it is likely a negative regulator of auxin

formation. These examples clearly establish the importance of root-derived auxin pools and future studies will have to deal with this extra level of complexity to obtain a more realistic view on root development. The roles of multiple plant hormones and the effects of environmental signals demonstrate that auxin is the dominant regulator of lateral root development. In addition, Band *et al.* (2012) hypothesize roots use a "tipping point" mechanism that operates to reverse the asymmetric auxin flow at the midpoint of root bending. These mechanistic insights illustrate the scientific value of developing quantitative reporters such as DII-VENUS in conjunction with parameterized mathematical models to provide high-resolution kinetics of hormone redistribution.

Auxin Research: An Opportunity to Dissect the Genetics of Fundamental Mechanisms of Growth and Developments

Auxin has a fundamental role throughout the life cycle of land plants. Lavy *et al.* (2012) sequenced candidate genes in auxin-insensitive mutants of *Physcomitrella patens* and identified mutations in highly conserved regions of the moss ortholog of tomato DGT and did not observe a clear effect of the Ppdgt mutation on the degradation of Aux/IAA proteins. However, the induction of several auxin-regulated genes is reduced. Genetic analysis revealed that dgt can suppress the phenotype conferred by overexpression of an AFB auxin receptor as well as and DGT protein affects auxin-induced transcription and has a conserved function in auxin regulation in land plants.

Plant hormone mutants can be classified into two main groups: (1) those that influence hormone levels by altering biosynthesis called biosynthesis mutants including auxotroph and overaccumulation mutants and (2) those that influence the response to hormones, called response mutants including insensitive and hypersensitive mutants (Reid, 1993). Difference between a hormone response (insensitive or hypersensitive) mutant and a hormone biosynthesis mutant is that the response mutant phenotype cannot be restored to the wild type by exogenous hormone application. Several studies have shown that novel genes functioning in the hormone signalling pathway in plants (Hsieh et al., 2000). Not all hormone mutant genes determined in hormone screenings are necessarily directly involved in hormone signal transduction pathways. It is possible that mutations identified in a screen mark genes whose functions are necessary for a signalling event to occur, but which are not in the regulation of the signal transduction pathway **(Fig. 3.6)**.

Mutants directly involved in hormone signalling genes can modulate: (i) the level of receptors, (ii) the affinity of the receptor protein for the hormone and (iii) the magnitude of the response. The availability of the whole Arabidopsis genome sequence may provide an opportunity to use reverse genetics, such as insertional mutagenesis to resolve complex signalling pathways in plants. Reverse genetics begins with a mutant gene sequence and tries to identify the resulting change in the phenotype. Each organ appears to be self-sufficient in terms of controlling auxin gradients for development. Moreover, analyses of Arabidopsis mutants defective in auxin signalling or transport are instrumental in elucidating the molecular mechanisms of auxin action in plant growth and development (Santner and Estelle 2009). Feedback and feed forward loops represent essential mechanisms in developmental biology and there are strong indications that such loops play a crucial role in auxin biology. Good examples of auxin biology including are phyllotaxis, vascular patterning, and root patterning.

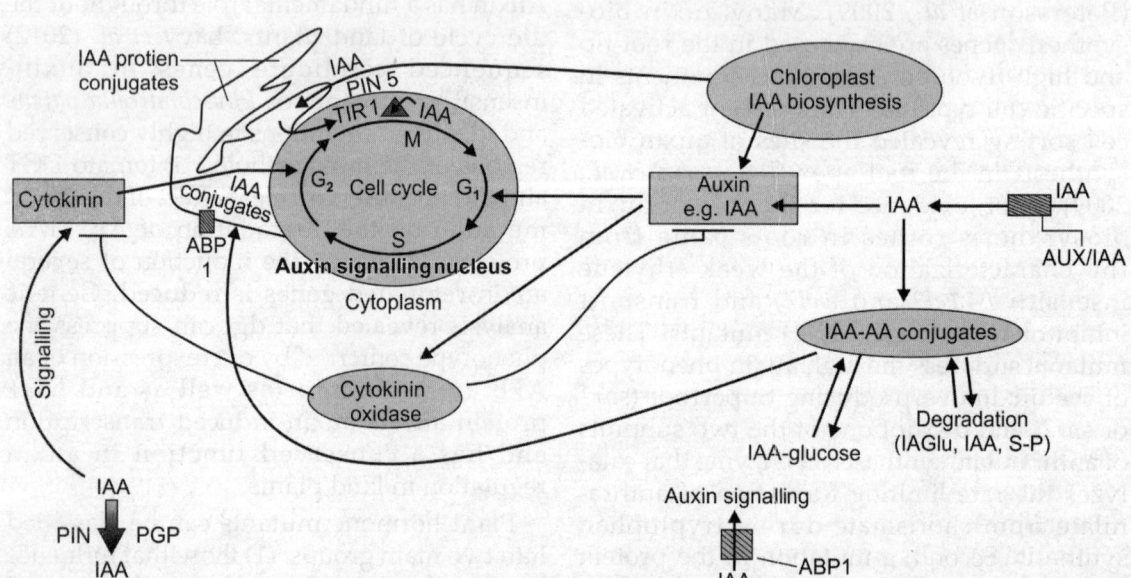

Fig. 3.6: The ubiquitin-mediated proteolysis of AUX/IAA proteins regulates auxin response. Among the ARF targets are the AUX/IAA genes themselves which produce nascent AUX/IAA proteins that restore repression upon the pathway in a negative feedback loop

In most traditional screens, since seeds and seedlings are exposed to higher concentrations of hormone than those plants experience, gene mutations that are homozygous lethal are usually missed, but can be maintained in the heterozygous plant population with insertional mutagenesis. Disruption of either pathway can potentially lower the IAA levels between the thresholds to cause similar phenotypes. TAA1 is expected in both shoot and root. In addition, YUC genes are also expressed in all organs including flowers, leaves and roots in Arabiodopsis. The mechanisms of auxin mediated organogenesis, particularly flower formation, appear to be analogous to those of phototropic responses. NPY1 is homologous to NPH3 and inactivation of NPY1 and its close homologues NPY3 and NPY5 lead, to pin-like inflorescences. Furthermore, the developmental defects of YUC mutants cannot be rescued by exogenous auxin treatments but are instead rescued by producing IAA from the gene under the control of a corresponding YUC promoter. Therefore, the auxin biosynthetic mutants provide a different angle for genetically dissecting auxin action in plant development. The successful identification of the YUC1 YUC4 enhancer, NPY1, clearly demonstrates the power of using auxin biosynthesis mutants as starting materials for isolating new auxin components. The YUC1 YUC4 double mutants produce abnormal flowers. When the NPY1 gene is inactivated in the YUC1 YUC4 background, the resulting YUC1 YUC4 NPY1 triple mutants develop pin-like inflorescences, a phenotype that is also observed in known auxin mutant's PIN1, PID and MP.

Moreover, genetic screens for auxin signalling mutants in Arabidopsis have taken advantage of the observation that primary root elongation is greatly inhibited in the presence of exogenous auxin. Mutants defective in auxin uptake and signalling are less sensitive to exogenous auxin, and thus have longer primary roots than wild type auxin-containing media. For example, MP and BDL, two key components of auxin signalling in specifying root meristem during embryogenesis, would not be isolated from a root-based auxin-resistant screen. Some other known auxin mutants, including PIN1 and PID, mainly affect shoot development and do not display auxin resistance in a root elongation assay. Recent progress in auxin biosynthesis makes it possible to isolate mutants that can overcome or become oversensitive to partial auxin deficiency.

All known auxin overproduction mutants have long hypocotyls, whereas the main phenotypic readout of IAA treatment is the inhibition of primary root elongation. Formation of pin-like inflorescences is a hallmark of defective auxin related processes. The NPY1 mutant is allelic to ENP1/MAB4 that is isolated as an enhancer of PID. The NPY1/ENP1 and PID double mutants do not make cotyledons, indicating that NPY1/ENP1/MAB4 plays a general role in organogenesis. Genetic analyses have put YUC, PID and NPY1 in a linear developmental pathway. NPY1 is a novel protein, but it shares significant homology with non-phototropichypocotyl 3 (NPH3) (Motchoulski and Liscum, 1999). Both NPY1 and NPH3 belong to a plant-specific super family with 32 members in the Arabidopsis genome. Identification of NPY1 in a genetic screen for YUC1 YUC4 enhancers demonstrates that genetic screens for modifiers of auxin biosynthesis mutants will probably lead to the discovery of additional components in the pathway. Another similarity between these two pathways is that both require the auxin response factor ARF5/Monopteros. Disruption of ARF5 causes the formation of pin-like inflorescences, whereas inactivation of ARF7 abolishes phototropic responses. This approach is beginning to provide valuable insights into the dynamics of auxin transport and its role in regulating organogenesis. Auxin transport models for three developmental systems that address regulatory loops are discussed feedback and feed forward loops represent essential mechanisms in developmental biology and there are strong indications that such loops play a crucial role in auxin biology.

PIN1, although quite complex and dynamic, represents the most crucial parameter in the model. A pivotal issue is how PIN1 localization is regulated during primordial initiation. A variant of the principle that auxin regulates its own efflux is used as the basis of models that predict PIN1 localization during primordial initiation. The important assumption in these models is that in a given cell of the L1 layer PIN1 is always polarly localized towards the neighbouring cell that has the highest auxin concentration through a regulatory loop involving auxin and auxin transport. The auxin transport fluxes that are important for initiating organ primordia are also suggested to determine later events in the differentiating primordium, such as boundary formation and organ polarity, by influencing the expression pattern of genes such as CUC2 and STM (Hibara *et al.*, 2006).

CONCLUSION AND FUTURE GUIDELINES

During the last ten years, our understanding of the molecular mechanisms of auxin biosynthesis, perception and response has improved dramatically. Knowledge of auxin metabolism and transport pathway will lead to new opportunities to manipulate auxin levels and thus regulate plant growth. Receptors for various auxins (e.g. IAA) have been identified, thus leading to exciting new models of auxin perception. Detailed knowledge of receptors functions may stimulate the development of new plant growth regulators. Also, next in this trend, many downstream signalling components have been identified. However, several outstanding questions remain to be answered before we can fully understand the mechanisms that determine

auxin homeostasis. The specificity of TIR1/AFBs receptors towards IAA, IBA needs to be experimentally determined to exclude or confirm the binding of these auxins and their role in downstream proteosome-mediated gene expression. Auxin promotes cell elongation in the plant stem. However, the relative contribution of signalling pathway to growth regulators in response to changes in the environment is uncertain. There are robust models of auxin-dependent regulations of shoot and root growth has been developed (Santner *et al.*, 2009).

HOW TO MOVE AHEAD?

While great strides have been made in recent years in understanding the molecular basis of auxin action, but however, a lot of fundamental questions remain answered. It is necessary to determine how the fast non-transcriptional responses and those involving transcriptional regulation are coupled and how the signalling cascade triggered by *ABP1* is constituted. To understand the molecular mechanisms by which auxin regulates plant growth and developments, findings from auxin biosynthesis, conjugation, transport and signalling must be integrated. Moreover, till date, current understanding of biosynthesis is still fragmented and no single complete *de novo* biosynthesis pathway has been defined. Also not clear is how the expression pattern of auxin biosynthesis genes is generated and how they are regulated.

To refine the current computers models, additional regulatory mechanisms and links as well as molecular mechanisms and links as well as molecular players must be identified. Such as transcriptional control of PIN genes in relation to auxin would provide important information and identifying direct targets of the ARF transcription factors. The specificity of auxin transporters towards individual auxin-like compounds has been largely overlooked and requires further investigation, possibly by means of chemical or genomic approaches. Moreover, the key challenges remaining unopened till date about the understanding about auxin signalling such as: exact manner in which complexity coded to produce specific auxin response and determination of mechanisms by which the resulting changes in gene expression mediates specific auxin responses and why some specific auxin responses to be of SCF systems independent. An analysis of regulatory elements in the promoter regions of individual genes involved in auxin metabolism, signalling and transport may also yield valuable information. Intensive studies with auxin mutants have indicated that plant hormone signalling pathways are not linear but rather a networks interacting with each other to make a coordinated plant responding growth and development, forward and reverse genetic approaches, gene knockouts or null mutations provide direct opportunities to determine the function of a gene product *in situ*.

REFERENCES

Abel S, Nguyen MD and Theologis A. (1995). The PS-IAA4/5-like family of early auxin-inducible mRNAs in *Arabidopsis thaliana*. *Journal of Molecular Biology*, **25**: 533–549.

Andersson B and Sandberg G (1982). Identification of endogenous N-(3-indolacetyl)aspartic acid in Scots pine (*Pinus sylvestris* L.) by combined gas chromatography–mass spectrometry, using high performance liquid chromatography for quantification. *Journal of Chromatography*, **238**: 151–156.

Atta S, Ikbal M, Kumar A and Pradeep Singh ND (2012). Application of photoremovable protecting group for controlled release of plant growth regulators by sunlight. *Journal of Photochemistry and Photobiology B*, **111**: 39–49.

Badescu GO and Napier RM (2006). Receptors for auxin: will it all end in TIRs? *Trends in Plant Science*, **11**: 217–223.

Bainbridge K, Guyomarch S, Bayer E, Swarup R, Bennett M, Mandel T and Kuhlemeier C (2008).

Auxin influx carriers stabilize phyllotactic patterning. *Genes and Development*, **22**: 810–823.

Bajguz A and Piotrowska A (2009). Conjugates of auxin and cytokinin. *Phytochemistry*, **70**: 957–969.

Benjamins R and Scheres B (2008). Auxin: The Looping Star in Plant Development. *Annual Reviews of Plant Biology*, **59**: 443–465.

Bhalerao RP, Eklof J, Ljung K, Marchant A, Bennett M and Sandberg G (2002). Shoot-derived auxin is essential for early lateral root emergence in Arabidopsis seedlings. *Plant Journal*, **29**: 325–332.

Bielach A, Duclercq J, Marhavy P and Benková E (2012). Genetic approach towards the identification of auxin-cytokinin crosstalk components involved in root development.

Brady SM, Orlando DA, Lee JY, Wang JY, Koch J, Dinneny JR, Mace D, Ohler U and Benfey PN (2007). A high-resolution root spatiotemporal map reveals dominant expression patterns. *Science*, **318**: 801–806.

Cheng Y, Dai X, and Zhao Y (2007). Auxin synthesized by the YUCCA flavin monooxygenases is essential for embryogenesis and leaf formation in *Arabidopsis*. *Plant Cell*. **19**: 2430–2439.

Dharmasiri N, Dharmasiri S and Estelle M (2005). The F-box protein TIR1 is an auxin receptor. *Nature*, **435**: 441–445.

Ferro N, Bredow T, Jacobsen HJ, and Reinard T (2010). Route to novel auxin: auxin chemical space toward biological correlation carriers. *Chemical Reviews*, **110**: 4690–4708.

Furutani M, Vernoux T, Traas J, Kato T, Tasaka M, and Aida M (2004). PIN-Formed1 and Pinoid regulate boundary formation and cotyledon development in Arabidopsis embryogenesis. *Development*, **131**, 5021–5030.

Gray WM, and Estelle M (2000). Function of the ubiquitin-proteasome pathway in auxin response. *Trends in Biochemical Science*, **25**: 133–138.

Grieneisen VA, Xu J, Maree AF, Hogeweg P, and Scheres B (2007). Auxin transport is sufficient to generate a maximum and gradient guiding root growth. *Nature*, **449**: 1008–1013.

Heisler MG, Ohno C, Das P, Sieber P, Reddy GV, Long JA and Meyerowitz EM (2005). Patterns of auxin transport and gene expression during primordium development revealed by live imaging of the Arabidopsis inflorescence meristem. *Current Biology*, **15**: 1899–1911.

Hibara K, Karim MR, Takada S, Taoka K, Furutani M, Aida M and Tasaka M (2006). Arabidopsis CUP-SHAPED COTYLEDON3 regulates postembryonic shoot meristem and organ boundary formation. *Plant Cell*, **18**: 2946–2957.

Kowalczyk S, Jakubowska A, Zielinska E and Bandurski RS (2003). Bifunctional indole-3-acetyltransferase catalyses synthesis and hydrolysis of indole-3-myoinositol in immature endosperm of *Zea mays*. *Physiologia Plantarum*, **119**: 165–174.

Mano Y and Nemoto K (2012). The pathway of auxin biosynthesis in plants. *Journal of Experimental Botany* PMID: 22447967.

Mattsson J, Ckurshumova W and Berleth T (2003). Auxin signalling in Arabidopsis leaf vascular development. *Plant Physiology*, **131**: 1327–1339.

Mazid M, Ali B, Hayat S and Ahmad A (2010). The effect of 4-chloroindole-3-acetic acid on some growth parameters in mung bean under cadmium stress. *Turkey Journal of Biology*, **34**: 9–13.

Motchoulski A and Liscum E (1999). *Arabidopsis* NPH3: A NPH1 photoreceptor-interacting protein essential for phototropism. *Science*, **286**: 961–964.

Overvoorde P, Fukaki H and Beeckman T (2010). Auxin control of root development. *Cold Spring Harbour Perspectives in Biology* **2**, a001537.

Percival FW and Bandurski RS (1976). Esters of indole-3-acetic acid from Avena seeds. *Plant Physiology*, **58**: 60–67.

Peret B, De Rybel B, Casimiro I, Benkova E, Swarup R, Laplaze L, Beeckman T and Bennett MJ (2009) Arabidopsis lateral root development: An emerging story. *Trends in Plant Science*, **14**: 399–408.

Petersson SV, Johansson AI, Kowalczyk M, Makoveychuk A, Wang JY, Moritz T, Grebe M, Benfey PN, Sandberg G and Ljung K (2009). An auxin gradient and maximum in the Arabidopsis root apex shown by high-resolution cell-specific analysis of IAA distribution and synthesis. *Plant Cell*, **21**: 1659–1668.

Pickart CM (2001). Mechanisms underlying ubiquitination. *Annual Reviews in Biochemistry*, **70**: 503–533.

Przemeck GK, Mattsson J, Hardtke CS, Sung ZR and Berleth T (1996). Studies on the role of the Arabidopsis gene MONOPTEROS in vascular development and plant cell axialization. *Planta*, **200**: 229–237.

Reinhardt D, Frenz M, Mandel T and Kuhlemeier C (2003a). Microsurgical and laser ablation analysis of interactions between the zones and layers of the tomato shoot apical meristem. *Development*, **130**: 4073–4083.

Rogg LE, Lasswell J and Bartel B (2001). A gain-of-function mutation in *IAA28* suppresses lateral root development. *Plant Cell*, **13**: 465–480.

Rubery PH and Sheldrake AR (1974). Carrier-mediated auxin transport. *Planta*, **188**: 101–121.

Sachs T (1981). The control of the patterned differentiation of vascular tissues. *Advances in Botany Research*, **9**: 151–262.

Sachs T (1991). Cell polarity and tissue patterning in plants. *Development Supplement*, **91**: 83–93.

Santner A, Calderon-Villalobos LIA and Estelle M (2009). Plant hormones are versatile chemical regulators of plant growth. *Nature chemical biology*, **5**: 301–307.

Santner A and Estelle M (2009). Recent advances and emerging trends in plant hormone signalling. *Nature*, **459**: 1071–1078.

Savic´ B, Tomic´ S, Magnus V, Gruden K, Barle K, Grenkovic´ R, Ludwig-Müller J and Salopek-Sondi B (2009). Auxin amidohydrolases from *Brassica rapa* cleave the alanine conjugate of indolepropionic acid as a preferable substrate: a biochemical and modeling approach. *Plant and Cell Physiology*, **50**: 1587–1599.

Scarpella E, Marcos D, Friml J and Berleth T (2006). Control of leaf vascular patterning by polar auxin transport. *Genes Development*, **20**: 1015–1027.

Scherer GFE, Zahn M, Callis J and Jones AM (2007). A role for phospholipase A in auxin-regulated gene expression. *FEBS Letters*, **581**: 4205–4211.

Simon S and Petrasek J (2011). Why plants need more than one type of auxin. *Plant Science*, **180**: 454–460.

Smith RS, Guyomarch S, Mandel T, Reinhardt D, Kuhlemeier C and Prusinkiewicz P (2006). A plausible model of phyllotaxis. *Proceedings of the National Academy of Sciences*, **103**: 1301–1306.

Sun J, Qi L, Li Y, Chu J and Li C (2012). PIF4-Mediated Activation of YUCCA8 Expression Integrates Temperature into the Auxin Pathway in Regulating Arabidopsis Hypocotyl Growth. *PLoS Genetics*, **8 (3)**: e1002594.

Szerszen JD, Szczyglowski K and Bandurski RS (1994). Iaglu, a gene from *Zea mays* involved in conjugation of growth hormone indole-3-acetic acid. *Science*, **265**: 1699–1701.

Tromas A, Paponov I and Perrot-Rechenmann C (2010). Auxin Binding Protein 1 functional and evolutionary aspects. *Trends in Plant Science*, **15**: 436–446.

Uehara T, Okushima Y, Mimura T, Tasaka M and Fukaki H (2008). Domain II mutations in Crane/IAA18 suppress lateral root formation and affect shoot development in *Arabidopsis thaliana*. *Plant Cell Physiology*, **49**: 1025–1038.

Waites R, Selvadurai HR, Oliver IR and Hudson A (1998). The Phantastica gene encodes a MYB transcription factor involved in growth and dorsoventrality of lateral organs in Antirrhinum. *Cell*, **93**: 779–789.

Wang S, Bai Y, Shen C, Wu Y, Zhang S, Jiang D, Guilfoyle TJ, Chen M and Qi Y (2010). Auxin-related gene families in abiotic stress response in Sorghum bicolour. *Functional Integration of Genomics*, **10**: 533–546.

Wenzel CL, Schuetz M, Yu Q and Mattsson J (2007). Dynamics of Monopteros and PIN-Formed1 expression during leaf vein pattern formation in *Arabidopsis thaliana*. *Plant Journal*, **49**: 387–398.

Wu G, Lewis DR and Spalding EP (2007). Mutations in Arabidopsis multidrug resistance-like ABC transporters separate the roles of acropetal and basipetal auxin transport in lateral root development. *Plant Cell*, **19**: 1826–1837.

Zazimalova E and Napier RM (2003). Points of regulation for auxin action. *Plant Cell Reproduction*, **21**: 625–634.

Zhao Y (2010). Auxin biosynthesis and its role in plant development. *Annual Reviews on Plant Biology*, **61**: 49–64.

Ziegler DM (1988). Flavin-containing mono-oxygenases: catalytic mechanism and substrate specificities. *Drug Metabolism Reviews*, **19**: 1–32.

Zimmerman PW and Wilcoxon F (2009). Several chemical growth substances which cause initiation of root and other responses in plants. *Contre of Boyce Thompson Institution*, **7**: 209.

QUESTIONS

Q. 1. Term hormone comes originally from the:
(1) Greek
(2) Latin
(3) English
(4) German

Q. 2. Plant hormone can be defined as:
(1) A naturally organic substance other than nutrient
(2) A naturally organic substance like nutrient
(3) A naturally organic substance provide energy to plants
(4) A naturally inorganic substance other than nutrient

Q. 3. In which of the following is a plant growth regulator/s?
(1) Nitric oxide
(2) Polyamines
(3) Triacontanol
(4) All of the above

Q. 4. This research is concerned with which scientists—placed agar blocks containing hormone diffused from coleoptiles tips asymmetrically on decapitated coleoptiles and found curvature growth of these coleoptiles resembling phototrophic curvature even when kept in the dark?
(1) Starling
(2) Bislay
(3) Went
(4) Both 1 and 2 are correct

Q. 5. In above experiment which of the hormone was discovered?
(1) IAA (Auxin)
(2) GA$_3$
(3) MCPA (Auxin)
(4) Zeatin (Cytokinin)

Q. 6. Hormones may be termed first messenger because:
(1) Chemical messenger for a specific function
(2) Chemical messenger for a number of function
(3) Secreted in very minute amount
(4) Acting in a sequential way

Q. 7. What is second messenger principle?
(1) Hormone mechanism discovered by E.W. Southerland and co-workers (1960)
(2) A mechanism in living system in which hormone transduce extracellular signals
(3) Both
(4) None

Q. 8. Who indicated that a diffusible substance originated in the coleoptiles tip and transported basipetally to cause a asymmetrical growth in the underlying tissue leading to phototrophic curvature?
(1) Boysen-Jensen
(2) Starling
(3) Went
(4) T. Stephan

Q. 9. Which is correct about cAMP?
(1) Cyclic adenosine-3,5-mono-phosphate
(2) Mononucleotide of adenylic acid where phosphate is esterified at both carbons 3 and 5 of ribose
(3) Hormone action modified by cAMP in animals
(4) Cell is excited by extracellular signal the its conc. increase
(5) All is correct

Q. 10. What is correct about cAMP?
(1) Stimulates a potein-kinase
(2) Phosphorylates a number of enzymes

(3) calcium also act as cAMP

(4) all is correct

Q. 11. Julius von sach (1832–1897) was a:

(1) German Botanist

(2) Frech Biochemist

(3) Sweidish Botanist

(4) Italian Anatomist

Q. 12. Who proposed first that chemical messenger is responsible for the formation and growth of different plant organs?

(1) J.V. Sach   (2) C. Darwin

(3) W. Starling   (4) H. Crab

Q. 13. Who suggested that external factors such as a gravity could affect the distribution of these substances within a plant?

(1) J.V. Sach   (2) C. Darwin

(3) W. Starling   (4) H. Crab

Q. 14. In animals particularly the chemical messengers that mediate intercellular communication are called?

(1) Hormones

(2) Enzymes

(3) Secondary messengers

(4) Both 1 and 2

Q.15. Hormones interact with specific cellular proteins called:

(1) Receptors

(2) Acceptors

(3) Protein kinases

(4) Protein phosphatases

Q. 16. What is correct about animal hormone?

(1) Mostly synthesized and secreted in one part and specific to function at other sites

(2) Belong to four categories protein small peptides, amino acids derivatives and steroids

(3) Both 1 and 2 are correct

(4) Secreted by the exocrine system

Q. 17. Odd one among them is:

(1) Protein systemin

(2) Jasmonic acid

(3) Salicylic acid

(4) GA_3

Q. 18. Growth in higher plants takes place:

(1) By growing points confined to certain regions of plant

(2) By growing points scattered all over the plant

(3) In the complete plant body

(4) In aerial parts only

Q. 19. The primitive scientists who suspected the presence of some growth substances was?

(1) Darwin

(2) Lamark

(3) Linnaeus

(4) De-veries

Q. 20. Auxin may cause:

(1) Develop adventitious roots in a cutting

(2) Promote stem growth and inhibit roots

(3) May not promote growth or may be detrimental

(4) All are correct

Q. 21. Most attractive auxin for botanists is:

(1) IAA   (2) IBA

(3) MCPA   (4) 2, 4-D

Q. 22. Which of the following is correct?

(1) For some plants day period is immaterial for flowering and these are called DNA

(2) Some plants require longer day light period for flowering and called LDP

(3) Some plants require shorter day light period for flowering and are called SDP

(4) All are collect

Q. 23. Indole-3-acetic acid at high concentration generally inhibits the growth of:

(1) Roots
(2) Leaves
(3) Shoots
(4) Plants in particular

Q. 24. In organs of plants there is a variation in rate of growth. It is first slow, the accelerates up to maximum and slows down to stand still. This whole period is known as:

(1) Grand period of growth
(2) Growth
(3) Period of growth
(4) Maximum period of growth

Q. 25. Geotropic responses shown by the root are because of

(1) More growth on the upper side of the root
(2) Auxin concentration in the stem
(3) Uniform growth of root on all sides
(4) More growth of stem than root

Q. 26. Native auxin is transported in the plant:

(1) From shoot tip in the downward direction by special transport mechanism
(2) From the tip in the upward direction
(3) Through vascular system of plants
(4) From xylem to phloem

Q. 27. If a planter is interested in obtaining a good crop of tea leaves from a single plant he should:

(1) Remove the apical bud of the main shoot and the branches
(2) Cut-off the tip of the plants and then apply auxins to the cut end
(3) Supply auxin from tip of plant as well as through roots
(4) Feed auxin to plants through soil

Q. 28. Apical dominance in higher plants is due to:

(1) Balance between auxins and cytokinins
(2) N to carbohydrate ratio
(3) Activity of enzymes
(4) Photoperiodism

Q. 29. Most classical experiments on growth were performed by:

(1) Darwin and Boysen Jensen
(2) DeVeries and Paal
(3) Larmark and Boysen Jensen
(4) None

Q. 30. Avena curvature test is associated with:

(1) Auxin   (2) GA_3
(3) ABA   (4) ET

Q. 31. After unidirectional light is received auxin is moved to the shady side of a stem and then the stem bends towards the light. Which step in this sequence represents transduction?

(1) Curving of stem towards light
(2) Auxin movement towards the shady side
(3) Both 1 and 2 are correct
(4) Sensitivity of a receptor to light

Q. 32. Which synthetic auxin used as herbicide/s?

(1) 2,4-D   (2) 2,4,5-T
(3) MCPA   (4) All of the above

Q. 33. The chemical structure of naturally occurring auxin is very similar to structure of:

(1) Tryptophan   (2) AMP
(3) ATP   (4) ADP

Q. 34. Which have ability to stimulate stem elongation?

(1) GA   (2) BRs
(3) Auxins   (4) All

Q. 35. Synthetic INDIGO dye obtained by:

(1) Tryptophan (2) 2,4-D
(3) IAA (4) GA_3

Q. 36. Minimum dry weight is present in:

(1) Germinating seeds
(2) Dry seeds
(3) Wet seeds
(4) Young seedlings

Q. 37. Growth without differentiation is best seen in:

(1) Callus (2) Gall
(3) Fruit (4) Seedlings

Q. 38. Cocus nucifera possessing the:

(1) Cytokinins (2) GA_3
(3) ABA (4) ET

Q. 39. In cucurbitaceae, femaleness is promoted by:

(1) IAA (2) Cks
(3) GA (4) ABA

Q. 40. The natural form of active auxin produced by plants is:

(1) Cotyledauxin
(2) Apical bud
(3) IAA
(4) Coleptauxin

Q. 41. Which promote flowering in the members of the family Bromeliaceae?

(1) NAA (2) IAA
(3) Both 1 and 2 (4) IBA

Q. 42. Normally, the effect of auxin to flowering is:

(1) Inhibitory (2) Stimulatory
(3) Both 1 and 2 (4) None

Q. 43. Regulatory (promoting and inhibitory) effects of auxin on flowering is concern with the:

(1) Regulating the ethylene concentration
(2) Regulating the CK concentration
(3) Regulating the GA concentration
(4) Regulation the ABA concentration

Q. 44. 4-CPA or 4-cholorophenoxyacetic acid used to:

(1) Increase fruit set and growth of tomato
(2) Increase the number of female flowers
(3) Increase the number of male flowers
(4) Both 2 and 3

Q. 45. Common among the auxins like 2,4-TP, 2,4-DP, NAA, 2,4-D

(1) Prevent the abscission of mature fruits (apple, pear, lemon and grape)
(2) Reduce the leaf fall
(3) Enhance the flowering time
(4) Both 2 and 3

Q. 46. Application of auxin to flower buds at the bisexual stage leads to the formation of:

(1) Male flowers
(2) Female flowers
(3) Both 1 and 2
(4) No effect on this

Q. 47. Direct inhibition theory (inhibition of growth of axillary bud directly) is concerned with the:

(1) Auxin
(2) GA
(3) CK
(4) ET

Q. 48. Apical dominance means:

(1) Suppression of growth of apical buds by the axiallry buds
(2) Suppression of growth of axillary buds by the presence of apical buds
(3) Stimulation of a growth of apical buds by the removal of axillary buds

(4) Inhibition of growth of axillary buds by the removal of axillary buds

Q. 49. Which of the following made pineapple to flower in off season?

(1) Zeatin   (2) Short-days

(3) ET   (4) Temperature

Q. 50. Which one of the following hormone is involved in phototropism?

(1) GA_3 (2) 2, 4-D

(3) Kinetin   (4) IAA

Q. 51. Induction of cell division and delay in senescence is done by:

(1) Ck   (2) GA_3

(3) Kinetin   (4) Auxin

Q. 52. Which one of the following is an agent orange?

(1) Weedicides with dioxin

(2) Chemical used in luminous paint

(3) Biodegradable insecticide

(4) Colour used in fluorescent lamp

Q. 53. A hormone used for inducing morphogenesis in plant tissue culture:

(1) ABA   (2) CK

(3) GA_3 (4) ET

Q. 54. Highest concentration of auxin exists

(1) At the base of various plant organs

(2) In growing tips of organs

(3) In leaves

(4) In xylem and phloem cells only

Q. 55. Which of the following is the commercial use of auxin?

(1) Apical dominance

(2) Root formation

(3) Enhancement of RNA

(4) Protein synthesis

Q. 56. Which of the following is an auxin?

(1) Maleic acid

(2) ABA

(3) Pyruvic acid

(4) IAA

Q. 57. The plant substances which become inhibitory on accumulation are?

(1) ABA

(2) Phenolic inhibitors

(3) Auxins

(4) CK

Q. 58. Which one is the test for gibberellin?

(1) Bolting of cabbage

(2) Elongation of oat coleoptile

(3) Morphogenesis in tobacco callus

(4) Rapid divisions in carrot cells

Q. 59. The phenomenon of growth is immediately followed by:

(1) Senescence

(2) Development

(3) Maturation

(4) Differentiation

Q. 60. Vernalization is applicable to plants like:

(1) Eucalyptus

(2) Gladiolus

(3) Narcissus

(4) Chrysanthemum

Q. 61. Dwarfness can be controlled by treating plants with?

(1) CK

(2) GA

(3) Anti-gibberellin

(4) ET

Q. 62. Which one of the following growth regulator is used for rooting the leaves of bryophyllum?

(1) Lycopene   (2) Carotene

(3) IAA   (4) GA_3

Q. 63. IAA, called auxin, was first isolated from:

(1) Human urine

(2) Corn germ oil

(3) Fusarium

(4) Rhizopus

Q. 64. Sprouting of potato in storage can be prevented by:

(1) MH
(2) 2,4-D
(3) IAA
(4) NAA

Q. 65. Which of the following physiological effect is caused by gibberellins in plants?

(1) Shortening of internodes
(2) Maleness in plant
(3) Femaleness in plants
(4) Chlorophyll preservation

Q. 66. ABA is primarily synthesized in:

(1) Lysosome
(2) Chloroplast
(3) Golgi complex
(4) Ribosomes

Q. 67. Who first suggested the presence of growth regulatory chemicals in plants?

(1) Darwin
(2) Went
(3) Sachs
(4) Paal

Q. 68. Seed dormancy occurs due to the presence of:

(1) ABA
(2) ET
(3) IAA
(4) Starch

Q. 69. Gibberellins causes:

(1) Curvature of coleoptiles
(2) Elongation of internodes
(3) Initiation of lateral roots
(4) Cell division

Q. 70. Increased availability of ABA stimulates:

(1) Lipid formation
(2) Protein formation in cell
(3) Starch synthesis in guard cell
(4) Cellulose synthesis

Q. 71. Negative geotropism in horizontal stems is caused by:

(1) Accumulation of auxins on the lower side
(2) Accumulation of auxins on the upper side
(3) Cell shrinkage on the lower side
(4) Cell enlargement on the upper side

Q. 72. Seedless fruits can be made by treating the unpollinated ovaries with?

(1) Auxins
(2) Colchicine
(3) Sucrose solution
(4) Pure lanolin

Q. 73. Cut or excised leaves remain green for long if induced to root or dipped in:

(1) CK   (2) ET
(3) GA   (4) Auxin

Q. 74. Which of the following phytohormone does not occur naturally in plants?

(1) 2,4-D
(2) GA
(3) IAA
(4) 6-furfuryl amino purine

Q. 75. Growth rhytham are set in a plant when it is exposed to:

(1) CO_2 environment
(2) Low temperature
(3) UV radiations
(4) Light

Q. 76. Etiolation of plants is caused when they?

(1) Are grown in intense light
(2) Are grown in blue light
(3) Have mineral deficiency
(4) Are grown in dark

Q. 77. In SDP, flowering is inhibited by

(1) Dark interruption by far-red light
(2) Interruption of dark by white or red light

(3) Dark-interruption red light followed by far-red light

(4) Not possible

Q. 78. Method of Donor-Receiver Agar Block used for:

(1) Polar transport of auxin

(2) Both polar and nonpolar transport of GA

(3) Transport of ABA

(4) Transport of ET

Q. 79. Phytotropins (NPA and TIBA) are anti-auxins are also called:

(1) Auxin transport inhibitors

(2) Phytotropins

(3) Both 1 and 2

(4) Auxin

Q. 80. TIBA is a:

(1) Non-phytotropic ATIs

(2) Phytotropic ATIs

(3) Gravitropic ATIs

(4) Nongravitropic ATIs

Q. 81. Most widely accepted model of polar xin transport is:

(1) Chemiosmotic model

(2) Gravitropical model

(3) Phototropical model

(4) None of the above

Q. 82. Auxin transport inhibitor/s is/are:

(1) NPA

(2) TIBA and difluenzopyr

(3) Curcumin

(4) Genistein

(5) All of the above

Q. 83. Most common thing among the Inasmuch (GA action inhibitor) and NPA (auxin transport inhibitor) is:

(1) Both absent in plants

(2) Both present in plants

(3) NPA present but Inasmuch absent in plants

(4) Inasmuch is present in plants but NPA is absent

Q. 84. Tansport of auxin in phloem is:

(1) Nonpolar

(2) Polar

(3) Both

(4) Localized

Q. 85. Transport of auxin from the phloem to other parts of plants (mainly in immature seeds) as a:

(1) Polar movement

(2) Nonpolar movement

(3) Both 1 and 2

(4) Localized

Q. 86. Two subcellular pools of auxins are:

(1) Cytosol and chloroplast

(2) Mitochondria and chloroplast

(3) Vacuoles and chloroplast

(4) ER and vacuoles

Q. 87. In wild type cells, principle pool of IAA is/are:

(1) Chloroplast

(2) Mitochondria

(3) Vacuoles

(4) ER

Q. 88. Exclusive location of IAA conjugates are/is:

(1) Cytosol

(2) Mitochondria

(3) Vacoles

(4) ER

Q. 89. 2,4-D cannot used to kill the:

(1) Mature dicot weeds

(2) Yong dicot weeds

(3) Young monocot weeds

(4) Mature monocot weeds

Q. 90. Name of a synthetic auxin with chloro-phenoxy ring is:

(1) 2,4-D

(2) 2,4, 5-T

(3) MCPA

(4) Picloram

Q. 91. Which chemical prolongs the growth response to auxin mainly by providing osmotically active solute that can be taken up for maintenance of turgor pressure during cell elongation?

(1) Fructose   (2) Sucrose/KCl

(3) Alcohol   (4) Indole

Q. 92. What is wrong about auxin is?

(1) Promote growth in the stems

(2) Promote growth in the coleoptiles

(3) Inhibits the growth in roots

(4) None of the above

Q. 93. Typical optimal auxin concentration for elongation growth is:

(1) 10^{-6} to 10^{-5}

(2) $10-8$ to 10^{-7}

(3) 10^{-12} to 10^{-23}

(4) 10^{-4} to 10^{-8}

Q. 94. An root growth inhibitor is:

(1) ET   (2) IAA

(3) Ck   (4) ABA

Q. 95. What is incorrect about indole auxin?

(1) Indole ring is benzopyrrole

(2) Side chain is fatty acid attached to carbon-3 of pyrole part of indole

(3) If side chain is acetic acid then auxin is IAA

(4) None of the above

Q. 96. Naturally occurring auxins are:

(1) IAA, indole pyruvic acid (IPyA), endole-3-ethanol (IEtOH), indole-acetaldehyde (IAAid),

(2) IAN (indole-3-acetonitrile)

(3) IBA

(4) Both 1 and 2

Q. 97. PESIGS rules is concerned with whose activity in organisms:

(1) Enzymes

(2) Hormones

(3) Secondary messengers

(4) Calcium signalling in plants particularly

Q. 98. PESIGS stands for:

(1) Parallel variation, excision, substitution, isolation, generality, specificity

(2) Parallel variation, excision, substitution, isobilateral, generality, specificity

(3) Pre-reticulate variation, excision, substitution, isolation, generality, specificity

(4) Parallel variation, excision, substitution, isolation, generality, specialty

Q. 99. Naphthoxy-2-acetic acid (NOXA) is:

(1) Synthetic auxin

(2) Natural auxin

(3) Natural cytokinin

(4) Modified base of ABA

Q. 100. Primary response genes or early genes are whose expression is stimulated by activation of?

(1) Preexisting transcription factors

(2) Postforming transcription factors

(3) Both

(4) Pre-existing translational factor

4 Role of Cytokinin Diversity in Plant Developmental Programme

ABSTRACT

Today, owing to the versatile functionality and physiological importance of phytohormones, cytokinin (CK) has become a major focus of attention in many areas of plant science, especially in plant physiology. The mechanism of CK action includes both fast responses not involving gene expression, possibly mediated by DNA-binding transcriptional activators, *viz.* AARs (ARR6::LUC) and slower responses requiring CK-regulated gene expression mediated by His kinases-CRE1/WOL/AHK4, AHK2 and AHK3. These two separate modes of action have been described to varying degrees for the major endogenous CKs and for synthetic compounds that possess CK-like activity. Although a complex spectrum of CK effects has been identified for all these as well as for several other endogenous compounds, we remain largely ignorant of many aspects of their mechanisms of action and the extent to which they contribute to CK-regulated plant growth and development. Here, we briefly summarize the action of 6-benzyladenine (BA) and discuss the extent to which its action overlaps with that of other CKs or results from metabolic conversion of BA to other bioactive CKs like zeatin or N^6-($\ddot{A}^2$-isopentenyl)-adenine (i^6Ade). Other possible pathways for CK action are considered. We also present a scheme for homeostatic regulation of CK levels that embraces other endogenous CKs in terms of the described mechanism of CK action including its receptors and steps involved in regulation of gene expression at the post-transcriptional level. In addition, this review also covers the effect of CK in whole plants as well as in cell division.

Keywords: Arabidopsis, His kinase, homeostasis, kinetin, plant hormone, response regulator.

THE ELUSIVE DEFINITIONS OF "CYTOKININS" AND CYTOKININ ACTION: HISTORICAL PERSPECTIVES

In the 1940s and 1950s, Folke Skoog at the University of Wisconsin tested many substances for their ability to initiate and sustain the proliferation of cultured tobacco pith tissue. After a difficult and time-consuming fractionation of heat-treated DNA, Skoog and coworker, Carlos Miller, identified a small molecule that in the presence of an auxin, would stimulate tobacco pith parenchyma tissue to proliferate in culture. They named this biologically active molecule as kinetin (Kin) and demonstrated it to be an adenine (or aminopurine) derivative, 6-furfurylaminopurine (Miller *et al.*, 1955). The discovery of Kin is important because it demonstrated that cell division can be induced by a simple chemical substance. Moreover, the discovery of Kin suggested that naturally occurring molecules with structures similar to that of Kin regulate cell division activity within plant. This hypothesis provided to be correct. Later, research convincingly demonstrated that cytokinins (CKs) are required together with other plant hormones for both cell division and oriented cell expansion (Sakamoto *et al.*, 2001), influencing all aspects of plant development. Consequently, it has become difficult to unambiguously define typical "CK activity". CK displays morphogenic properties that are modulated by the environment and defined by dynamic changes in its perception and signal transduction. This machinery has intensively been studied during the past decade and includes effects that are either dependent or independent of gene expression. Thus CK action may be understood as the sum of all these processes.

CKs are discovered in the course of studies aimed at identifying factors that stimulate plant cells to divide (i.e. undergo cytokinesis). Since their discovery, CKs have been shown to have effects on many other physiological and developmental processes as well, including leaf senescence, nutrient mobilization, apical dominance, the formation and activity of shoot apical meristem, floral development, the breaking of bud dormancy and seed germination. CKs also appear to mediate many aspects of light-regulated development, including chloroplast differentiation the development of autotrophic metabolism and leaf and cotyledon expansion (Ma *et al.*, 1998). Although, CK regulates many cellular processes, the control of cell division is of considerable significance for plant growth and development and is considered to be diagnostic for this class of plant growth regulators (PGRs). Other such functions liked to cell division are wounding, gall formation and tissue culture while other functions are not directly related to cell division such as chloroplast differentiation, the repression of leaf senescence, and nutrient mobilization. Chloroplasts are among the main targets of CK action in the plant cell. CKs (Kin) enhanced

the transcription of several chloroplast genes above the initial level measured before 6-benzyladenine (BA; syn. benzylaminopurine) treatment. Positive and differential effects of CK on the transcription of chloroplast genes that are dependent on light and on the age (developmental stage) of cells and leaves. Northern-blot analysis also detected a BA-induced increase in the accumulation of chloroplast mRNAs (Zubo *et al.*, 2008). The regulatory systems of CK-induced retardation of senescence differ in these two cases (Kim *et al.*, 2006). Zubo *et al.*, (2008) concluding that CK substantially and differentially enhanced the transcription of certain, but not all, chloroplast genes compared with the activities of these genes before CK treatment.

Some synthetic substances have CK-like activity complicating studies of structural activity and the search for a common mode of action. CKs are defined as compounds that have biological activities similar to those of *trans*-zeatin (Zea), while Kin is not a naturally occurring PGR, and it does not occur as a base in the DNA of any species. It is a by-product of the heat-induced degradation of DNA, in which the deoxyribose sugar of adenosine is converted to a furfuryl ring and shifted from the 9th position of the adenosine ring. Some molecules that act as CK antagonists are able to block the action of CK, and their effects may be overcome by adding more CK. Even the most frequent used synthetic CKs, BA, tetrahydro-pyranylbenzyladenine (THPBA) and NN1-diphenlyurea (non-amino purine with weak activity) do not completely share their mechanism of action with native CK.

Unlike native CK (e.g. Zea) these are not good substrates for the CK-binding protein-CK receptor 1 (CREi)/wooden leg (WOL)/*Arabidopsis thaliana kinase 4* (*AHK4*), *Arabidopsis thaliana kinase 2* (AHK2) and *Arabidopsis thaliana kinase 3* (AHK3) which initiate intracellular phosphotransfer and is poorly transported by CK efflux carriers. These are putative CK receptors that imply that the two-component signalling pathway initially detected in prokaroytes is a likely important element in CK signal transduction by phosphoryl group transfer, alternatively between His and Asp residues. The objective of this chapter is to summarize the present state of knowledge of the role of endogenous CKs in plants and to highlight some of the uncertainties and unresolved questions related to their mechanism of action (**Figs 4.1 and 4.2**).

In 2001, the Czech Republic hosted the 17th International Conference on "Plant Growth Substances" and invited many brilliant scientists of plant biology. This conference appears, to date, to be the highest and most valuable event in area of CK research. Also, 2001 saw an amazing progressive year in the field of CK studies. The groundbreaking study by Kakimoto *et al.,* (2001) evolving from the Kakimoto (1996) paper in which, unfortunately, CKI1 (CK independent 1) is devoid

of the properties essential for the receptor-elucidated CK receptor genes and genes encoding CK biosynthetic enzymes together with the corresponding proteins in plants and also the molecular mechanism of CK effects on the expression of CK-responsive genes and finally established the endogenous synthesis of CK in plant cells and justified its membership among the PGRs. In addition, in 2001 the nature of CK receptors is clarified and the pathway for intracellular signal transduction to primary response genes is elucidated. Moreover, also in 2001, CK synthesis in plants is ultimately substantiated based on the discovery of the enzymes and respective genes providing for their biosynthesis. Kakimoto (1996) reported the isolation of five *Arabidopsis* mutants which showed typical CK phenotypes such as rapid cell division and shoot formation in tissue culture in the absence of exogenous CK. Of these genes,

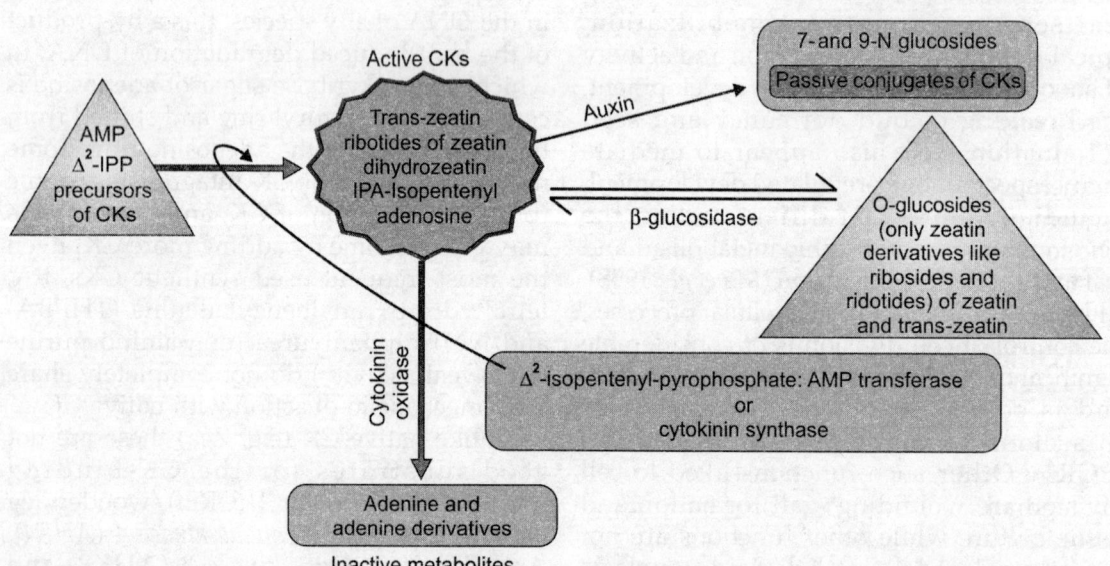

Fig. 4.1: A model of CK signal transduction in *Arabidopsis*. The three CK receptors, *viz.* CRE/WOL/ AHK4, AHK2 and AHK3, bind to CK and initiate phosphotransfer and type-A ARRs act as molecular switch of type-B ARR activity. Here, phosphorylation regulates transcriptional activity of type-B ARRs is an open question

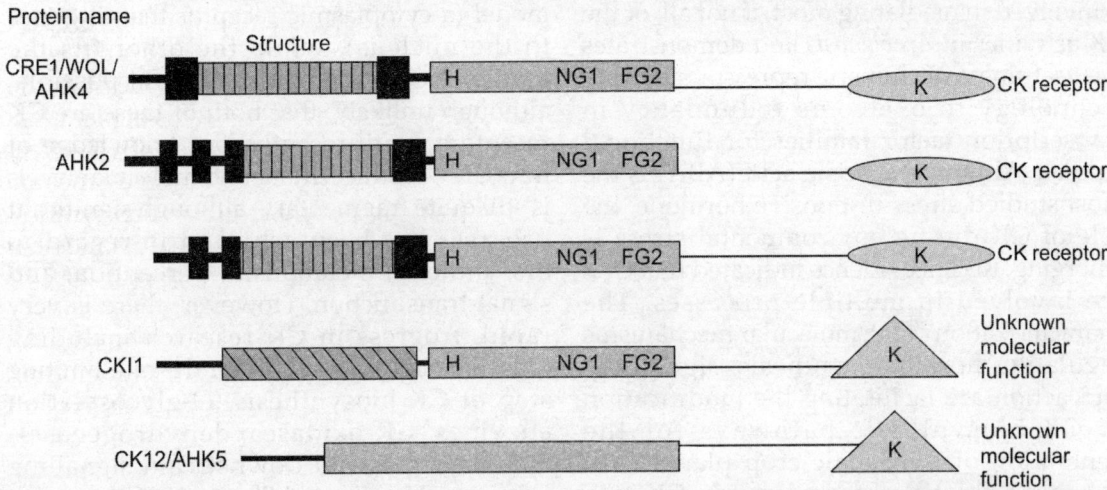

Fig. 4.2: Structural characteristics of histidine kinases and CK receptors. Black rectangle, striped rectangle, checker boxes, and open rectangle indicate the extracellular CHASE domain, transmembrane segments between the CKI1, At Ak1, extracellular domain and transmitter domain respectively. All these are characteristics of fundamental histidine kinases represented by H, N, G1, F, G2 respectively

CKI1 can induce typical CK phenotypes when overexpressed in plants encoding a two-component regulator like protein. The overexpression of CKI1 results in CK-independent callus growth and greening, suggesting that CKI1 might be a putative CK receptor. The CKI1 protein has drawn the attention of numerous CK researchers to the two-component system of signal transduction, while many of those working with the two-component system focused, in their turn, on plant CKs.

CYTOKININ PERCEPTION AND SIGNAL TRANSDUCTION

Plant hormones play central roles in the ability of plants to adapt to changing environments by mediating growth, development, nutrient allocation, and source/sink transitions. The signal transduction of CKs is mediated by a multistep His-to-Asp phosphorelay system. One component of this system is B-type response regulators (RRs), transcription factors mediating at least part of the response to CK. A link in the signal transduction chain to modulation of gene expression is believed to be provided by a class of proteins called ARRs that interact with, or function as transcription factors. ARRs have been classified into types A and B depending on their sequences and domain structure. Types A ARRs are CK primary response proteins while type B ARRs are a class of transcription factors. The 10 type A ARRs identified in *Arabidopsis* contain a receiver domain and short-N and C-terminal extensions. The amino acid sequences of the receiver domain are very similar but the sequences of their C-terminal extensions are quite different. On the other hand, the 11 type B ARRs are composed of receiver domains and a closely extended C-terminal region that is a putative output domain. In addition, the type A members can be further classified into two subgroups, depending on their responsiveness to stress treatment. The suppression of pleiotropic CK activities by a dominant repressor version of a B-type ARR indicates that this protein family is involved in mediating most, if not all, of the CK activities in *Arabidopsis* and demonstrates the usefulness of chimeric repressor silencing technology to overcome redundancy in transcription factor families for functional studies. Although abscisic acid (ABA) is the most studied stress-responsive hormone, the role of CK during environmental stress is emerging. Recent evidence indicated that CKs are involved in multiple processes. The characterization of the molecular mechanisms regulating hormone synthesis, signalling, and action are facilitating the modification of CK biosynthetic pathways for the generation of transgenic crop plants with enhanced abiotic stress tolerance. CKs are important regulators of developmental and environmental responses of plants that execute their action via the molecular machinery of signal perception and transduction (Frébort et al., 2011).

The limiting step of the whole process is the availability of the hormone in suitable concentrations in the right place and at the right time to interact with the specific receptor. Hence, the PGR concentrations in individual tissues, cells and organelles must be properly maintained by the biosynthetic and metabolic enzymes. Although there are merely two active CKs, isopentenyladenine and its hydroxylated derivative Zea, a variety of conjugates they may form and the number of enzymes/isozymes with varying substrate specificity involved in their biosynthesis and conversion gives the plant a variety of tools for fine tuning the hormone level. Recent genome-wide studies revealed the existence of the respective coding genes and gene families in plants and in some bacteria (Frébort et al., 2011) (**Fig. 4.3**).

Plant hormones are generally assumed to interact with specific receptors that reside either on the cell surface or within the cytoplasm. Two candidates for a CK receptor have recently been identified, one of which tends to fit the steroid hormone receptor model (a cytoplasmic receptor that migrates to the nucleus), while the other fits the membrane receptor model. It is possible, although unlikely, that both of these are CK receptors. Until recently, our knowledge of how CK works at cellular and molecular levels is still quite fragmentary, although significant progress has been achieved in regard to biosynthesis, metabolism, perception, and signal transduction. However, there is very rapid progress in CK research including identification of enzymes for the rate-limiting step of CK biosynthesis, *O*-glycosylation enzymes, CK-oxidases/dehydrogenases, cyto-receptors and downstream signalling elements (Hwang and Sheen, 2001).

Moreover, CKs are plant hormones involved in the regulation of diverse developmental and physiological processes in plants whose molecular mechanisms of action are being intensely researched (**Fig. 4.3**). Zubo et al. (2008) noted that differential response of chloroplast genes to CKs cannot be explained by an overall transcriptional activation of the whole chloroplast genome by CKs (e.g. due to changes in DNA topology, plastome copy numbers, or general activation of nucleus- and plastid-encoded plastid RNA polymerases). It seems likely that CK regulates the transcription of certain plastid genes via CK-dependent *trans*-factors (Zubo et al., 2008).

CKs are also implicated in diverse and essential processes of plant growth and development, and key genes for the metabolism and actions of CK have recently been identified. CKs are perceived by three His kinases—CRE1/WOL/AHK4, AHK2 and AHK3, which initiate intracellular phosphotransfer. The final destination of the transferred phosphoryl groups are RRs. It is now evident that CKs are perceived by His kinases and transduced by a two-component signalling system. Signal-induced phosphorylation of proteins is an often used regulatory mechanism to transduce

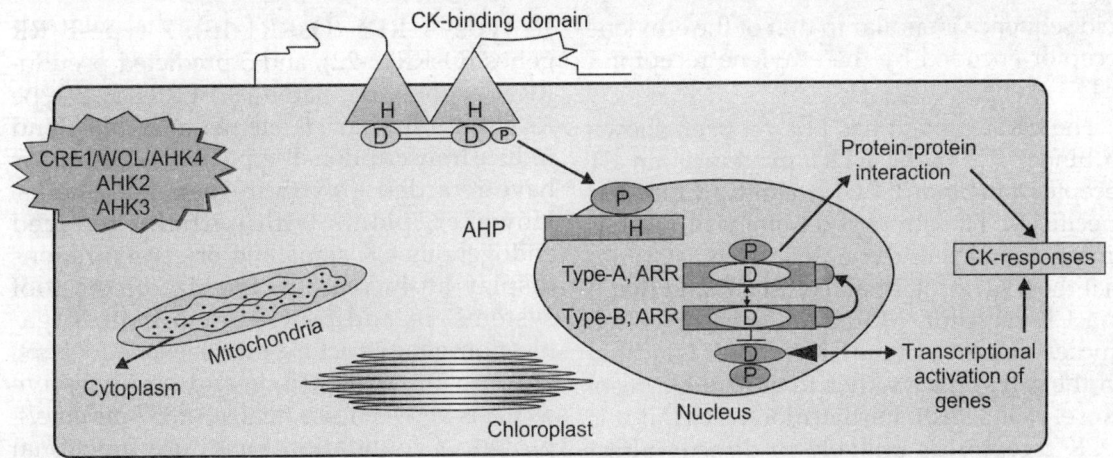

Fig. 4.3: Potential points of control of active CK pools by auxin. Usually auxin conjugates regulate enzyme activity and consequently changes in metabolite levels

intracellular or extracellular signals. In plants or bacteria, phosphorylation on a nitrogen (N) atom of an amino acid, His (a basic amino acid) residue, is predominantly used. This mode of signalling that uses this kind of phosphorylation has been referred to as the two-component system.

It is well-known that besides bacteria, archea, fungi and plants also have the two-component system, consisting of two proteins, the His kinase and the RR. RRs are characterized by the presence of a receiver domain only. When His kinase senses a signal, the conserved His residue in the transmitter domain is phosphorylated. The phosphoryl group is then transferred to the conserved Asp residue of the receiver domain. In these systems, the sensor is usually a hybrid His kinase that additionally carries a receiver domain. Another domain, HPt which contains a phosphorylated His residue, also takes part in the phosphotransfer. The phosphoryl group is relayed alternatively between conserved His residues and conserved Aspartate (Asp) residues. The phosphoryl group is linked by a high-energy bond, and the phosphotransfer is bidirectional. Many His kinases also have phosphatase activity

and the kinase/phosphatase ratio is regulated by an input signal that influences phosphatase while the His kinase may serve as a drain of the phosphoryl group.

HISTIDINE KINASES ACT AS CYTOKININ RECEPTORS

A 67-Kd protein, designated as Zea-binding protein (ZBP), is isolated from the cytosol of young barley plants. ZBP has a high affinity for Zea and Zea binding is highly specific. A molecular genetics approach to identifying a probable receptor is used by Kakimoto (1996) to generate dominant, gain-of function mutations in *Arabidopsis* that caused the mutants to be more sensitive than the wild type (WT) to endogenous CK levels. In addition, Kakimoto also screened *Arabidopsis* callus tissue for its ability to form green, growing callus tissue when cultured on medium lacking CK, after the tissue had been transferred with a T-DNA construct containing the 35S promoter. After screening 50,000 callus tissue samples, he obtained six mutants; the T-DNA tagged the same gene, which he designated as CKI1 (CK independent 1), which encodes a 125-Kd protein whose amino acid sequence is similar to that of the ethylene receptor encoded by the ethylene receptor 1 (ETR1) gene.

The CKI1 protein has not yet been shown to bind CK but the ETR1 protein is an ET receptor and binds ET with a high affinity and specificity. The strong homology in the His kinase domains of these two proteins argues that the CKI1 protein will bind CK and that it is a CK receptor. Moreover, microinjection studies suggest that the CK receptor is located on the cell surface rather than in the cytosol (Kosel et al., 2010). Furthermore, CKI1, if it is a CK receptor, is unlikely to directly affect either transcriptional elongation or initiation. By analogy with other two-component receptors, it is more likely to initiate a signal transduction pathway (**Fig. 4.4**).

In recent years, major breakthroughs have been achieved in elucidating the metabolism, signal perception and transduction, as well as biological functions of CKs. Thirty-seven genes have been identified in rice (*Oryza sativa* L.), including 5 HKs (OsHK1-4, OsHKL1), 5 HPs (His phosphotransfer proteins) (OsHP1-5),

15 type-A RRs (OsRR1-15), 7 type-B RR genes (OsRR16-22), and 5 predicted pseudo-RRs (response regulators) (OsPRR1-5). B-type *RRs* bind similar *cis* elements *in vitro* and induce transcription. B-type RR triple mutants have retarded growth in roots and shoots. However, plants with partially reduced endogenous CK signalling or concentrations display an increase in the size of the root systems. In addition, protein motif organization, gene structure, phylogenetic analysis, chromosomal location, and comparative analysis between rice, maize, and *Arabidopsis*, provide a foundation for future functional dissection of the rice CK two-component signalling pathway.

The two-step (His-Asp) phosphorelay system, composed of the LtnB, LtnA, and LtnC proteins, is distinct from the known phosphorelay systems, namely the typical two-component system (His-Asp) and the multistep phosphorelay system (His-Asp-His-Asp), because the HisKA domain of LtnC is the terminal phosphoacceptor that determines the signal output. LtnC is a new class of signal

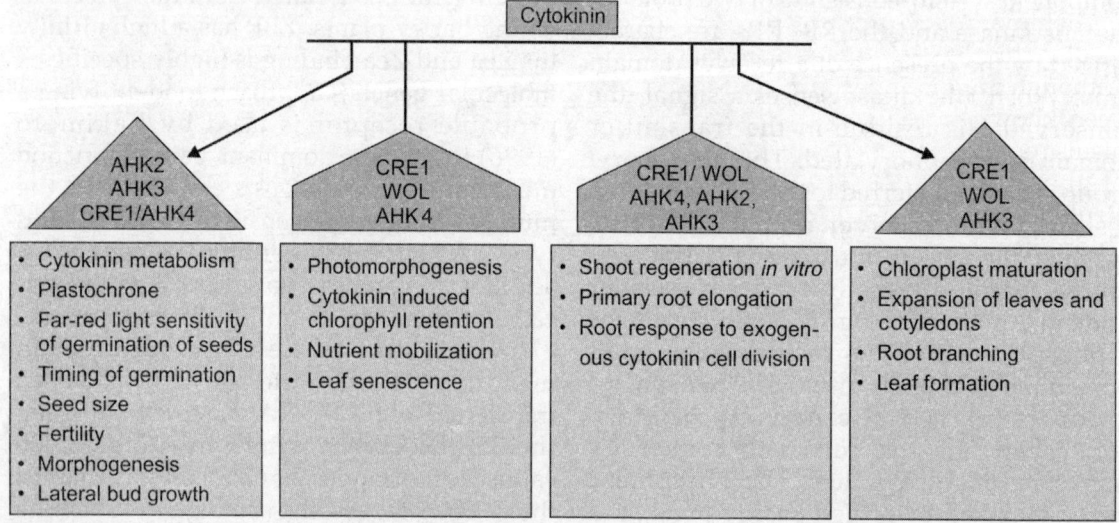

Fig. 4.4: Nutrient (e.g. NO_3^-) stimulates the fluxes of CK in the shoot and triggering gene expression for RRs

transducer in the His-Asp phosphorelay systems that contain a HisKA domain and an effector domain. LtnA, a response regulator without an effector domain, is phosphorylated by LtnB, a hybrid His kinase. Maeda *et al.* (2006) identified a protein LtnC that is required for activation of LtnT. LtnC consists of an N-terminal His-containing phosphoacceptor (HisKA) domain, a receiver domain, and a unique C-terminal domain found in some cyanobacterial proteins. Since LtnC lacks an ATP-binding kinase domain of a His kinase, it is incapable of autophosphorylation, but LtnC is phosphorylated by LtnA. The His residue in the HisKA domain, but not the Asp residue in the receiver domain, is essential for phosphorylation of LtnC and activation of LtnT. LtnC phosphorylation leads to oligomerization of the protein. Fusion of the C-terminal domain of LtnC to glutathione *S*-transferase, which forms oligomers, also activates LtnT, suggesting that oligomerization of the LtnC C-terminal domain causes LtnT activation. This study indicates that the C-terminal domain of LtnC acts as an effector domain that directs the output of the signal from the phosphorelay system (Maeda *et al.*, 2006).

An important activity of CKs is the involvement in chloroplast development and function. Although this biological function has already been known for 50 years, the exact mechanisms remain elusive. To elucidate the effects of altered endogenous CK content on the structure and function of the chloroplasts, chloroplast subfractions (stroma and thylakoids) from transgenic Pssu-ipt and 35S:CKX1 tobacco (*Nicotiana tabacum*) plants with, respectively, elevated and reduced endogenous CK content are analyzed using two different 2-DE approaches: Firstly, thykaloids are analyzed by blue-native polyacrylamide gel electrophoresis followed by SDS-Page (BN/SDS-Page) and secondly, a quantitative DIGE analysis of CHAPS-soluble proteins derived from chloroplast subfractions indicated

significant gel spot abundance differences in the stroma fraction. Proteomic studies of Cortleven *et al.* (2011) revealed that the constitutively altered CK status of transgenic plants do not result in any qualitative changes in either stroma proteins or protein complexes of thylakoid membranes of fully developed chloroplasts, while a few but significant quantitative differences are observed in stroma proteins.

The overexpression of CKI1 in plants induced typical CK responses independently of CK (Hwang and Sheen, 2001). CKI1 is a candidate CK receptor because it is a His kinase and its overexpression caused CK responses. In addition, CKI1 is constitutively active as a His kinase when expressed in *Escherichia coli*, which contrasts with the activation of CRE1/WOL/AHK3 by CK in these organisms. CKI1 is normally expressed in the female gametophyte only and the endosperm of immature seeds and CKI1-disruptants of *Arabidopsis* are lethal to final gametophyte. Therefore, CKI1 is essential for developing gametophytes, but its molecular function is unclear.

Similarly, CRE1/WOL/AHK4 functioned, in a CK-dependent manner, as a His kinase in mutants of *Saccharomyces pombe* or *Escherichia coli*, in which a particular His kinase gene had been disrupted (Suzuki *et al.*, 2001). Similar CK-dependent activity is also observed for two close relatives of CRE1/WOL/AHK4, AHK2 and AHK3 (Yamada *et al.*, 2001), indicating that the three proteins (CRE1/WOL/AHK4, AHK2 and AHK3) are CK receptors in *Arabidopsis*. The AHK4 gene is involved in the CK-signalling pathway as a direct receptor molecule in *A. thaliana* while AHK2, AHK3 and AHK4 genes each encoding a sensor His kinase in *A. thaliana*. To determine the relevant biological functions, Ueguchi *et al.* (2001) identified a loss-of-function mutation of the AHK4 gene. The mutant exhibited the CK-resistant phenotype not only in inhibition of root growth by CK but also in greening and shoot induction of calli. Moreover, AHK4 expressed in budding yeast showed His kinase activity in a manner dependent on the presence of CK. They also suggested that AHK4 is involved in the CK-signalling pathway, as a direct receptor molecule, in *Arabidopsis*. The vasculature of a *wol* mutant root consists of a reduced number of cell files and is composed exclusively of primary xylem. Cell divisions produce root vascular initial cells files after germination is impaired and are considered as the primary defect in this mutant.

CYTOKININ HOMOEOSTASIS: INTERPLAY BETWEEN DIFFERENT CYTOKININS

In 1955, Kin was isolated from DNA as an artifactual rearrangement product of the autoclaving processes (Miller *et al.*, 1956). Subsequently, its CK activity has been established, demonstrating a wide variety of biological effects, including those on gene expression, inhibition of auxin action, stimulating of calcium flux in the cell cycle, and as an antistress and antiageing compound. Recently, there are new data which show that it occurs in cellular DNA as the product of oxidative, secondary modification and a secondary reaction of DNA. Also, new results on the biochemical function of Kin have been reported. Various biological effects produced by this hormone *in vitro* and *in vivo* have made Kin even more scientifically interesting and commercially attractive as an ingredient of many beauty cosmetics.

Besides this, phytohormones, including auxins, ABA, brassinosteroids, CK, ET, GA, and jasmonates, are involved in all aspects of plant growth, and developmental processes as well as environmental responses. However, our understanding of hormonal homeostasis is far from complete. Phytohormone conjugation is considered as a part of the mechanism to control cellular levels of these compounds. Active phytohormones are changed into multiple forms by acylation, esterification or glycosylation, for example. It seems that conjugated compounds could serve as a pool of inactive phytohormones that can be converted to active forms by deconjugation reactions. Frébort *et al.*, (2011) summarizes the knowledge on enzymes that synthesize CK, form CK conjugates, and carry out irreversible elimination of the hormones, including their phylogenetic analysis and possible variations in different organisms. The complicated metabolism of CK, which encompasses many enzymes involved in its activation and deactivation, has not been discussed in this review.

Nevertheless, it is clear that homoeostasis of free CK pools in the plant plays a vital role in regulating CK action in development and plant responses to environmental stresses. The endogenous CK, *trans*-Zea contributes significantly to this free and hence, active pool of other Kins. It remains to be tested whether this applies also for the various endogenous CKs. Alternatively, BA and Kin seem to play a specialized role during the development of seeds and fruits in a wide range of species whilst naturally occurring endogenous possibly acts in coordination with Kin and BA during plant interactions with soil microorganisms. It is likely that with more studies of Kin, BA and other *trans*-Zea, perhaps some other specific responses will be linked to each of these compounds and that their targets receptors will be identified (**Fig. 4.5**).

Moreover, purine salvage enzymes have been implicated, but not proven, to be involved in the interconversion of CK bases, ribosides and nucleotides. Schoor *et al.*, (2011) used *Arabidopsis* lines silenced in adenosine kinase (ADK) expression to understand the contributions of this enzyme activity to *in vivo* CK metabolism. Both siRNA- and amiRNA-mediated silencing of ADK led to impaired root growth, small, crinkled rosette leaves and reduced apical dominance. Expression patterns of the cycB1; 1::GUS and ARR5::GUS

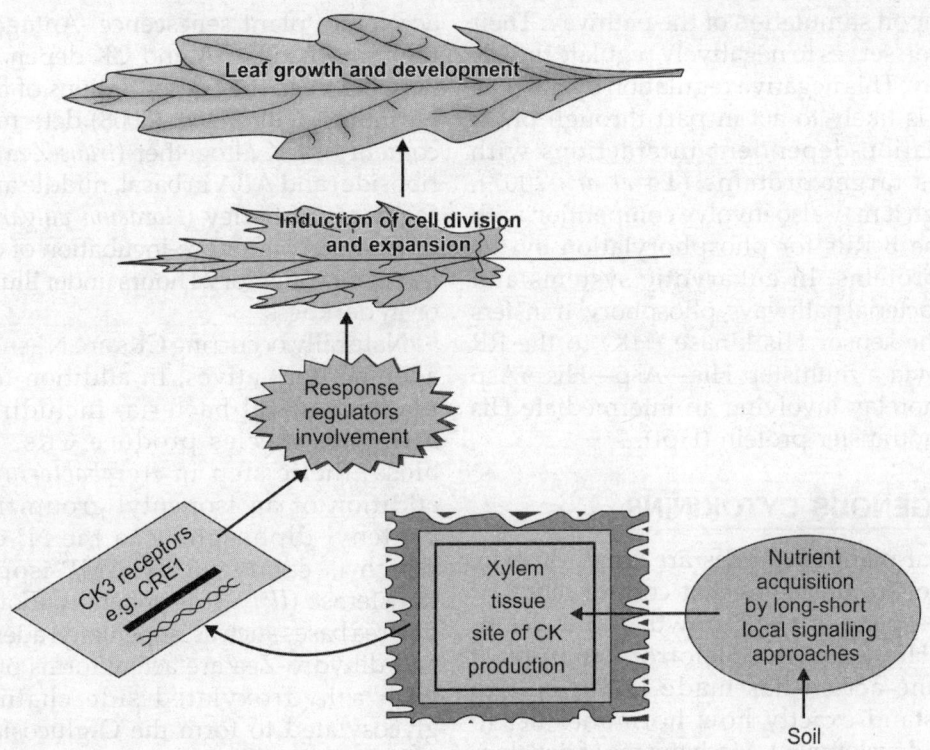

Fig. 4.5: Role of various CK receptors in the CK regulated developmental processes

reporters in the ADK-deficient background were consistent with altered cell division and an increase in CK activity respectively. *In vivo* feeding of ADK-deficient leaves with radio-labeled CK ribosides of isopentenyladenosine and Zea showed a decreased flux into the corresponding CK nucleotides. Comprehensive HPLC-MS/MS analysis detected significantly higher levels of active CK ribosides in both sADK and amiADK. These metabolic and phenotypic analyses of ADK-deficient lines indicate that ADK contributes to CK homeostasis *in vivo*. An electrochemical biosensor for detection of the plant hormone CK is introduced.

Until recently, CKs are the least understood plant hormones concerned with biosynthesis, metabolism, perception and signal transduction. CKs are perceived by three His kinases (CRE1/WOL/AHK4 AHK2 and AHK3)

which initiate intracellular phosphotransfer, but there are some rare data indicating that the action of other endogenous CKs operate through this mode of action. The available evidence suggests that the final destination of the transferred phosphoryl group is ARRs. In case of *A. thaliana*, there are two different kinds of RRs. Type A ARRs act as repressors of CK-activated transcription whereas type B ARRs are DNA-binding transcriptional activators that are required for responses to CKs. Unchanged red light sensitivity of mutant hypocotyl elongation suggests that previously reported modulation of red light signalling by type A RRs may not depend on CKs. Furthermore, the type A RR proteins are in general stabilized by CK induced phosphorylation, which acts synergistically with their transcriptional induction to affect a large increase in type A response regulator protein levels upon stimulation of the pathway. Their induction serves to negatively regulate the CK pathway. This negative regulation by the type A RRs is likely to act in part through phosphorylation-dependent interactions with various target proteins (To *et al.*, 2007), although it may also involve competition with the type B RRs for phosphorylation by the AHP proteins. In eukaryotic systems and some bacterial pathways, phosphoryl transfers from the sensor His kinase (HK) to the RR occurs via a multistep His→Asp→His→Asp phosphorelay involving an intermediate His phosphotransfer protein (Hpt).

ENDOGENOUS CYTOKININS

Classical plant hormones are small diverse, non-protein molecules that control many, if not all aspects of plant growth and development. However, the pleiotropic nature of hormone action has made it difficult to understand exactly how hormones act to pattern development. Mechanisms of developmental patterning require specificity, accuracy and the ability to unambiguously specify and maintain developmental identities. In contrast, to these conceptually elegant and economical models of developmental patterning, hormonal actions in plants have traditionally been considered much more complicated and confusing because the same molecule may have very different effects depending on concentration (Skoog and Miller, 1957) or may have diametrically opposite effects on the same process in different species.

Last, but not the least, different hormonal biosynthesis and sensitivity pathways are intertwined such that one hormone can regulate the activity of a different one, thus creating a maze of possible connections where it is very difficult to distinguish primary from secondary effects. The effect of CK treatment may depend on both the content of endogenous CK and the ratio between CK and ABA. ABA is one of the hormones known to accelerate plant senescence. Antagonism in the impacts of ABA and CK depends on the ratio between the concentrations of these two hormones. Zubo *et al.* (2008) determined the content of CK altogether (*trans*-Zea and Zea riboside) and ABA in basal, middle and apical segments of barley (*Hordeum vulgare*) leaves immediately after pre-incubation of detached leaves on water for 24 hours under illumination or in darkness.

Naturally occurring CKs are N^6-substituted adenine derivatives. In addition to higher plants, several bacteria, including *Agrobacterium* species produce CKs. The key biosynthetic step in *Agrobacterium* is the addition of an isopentyl group from isopentenyl diphosphate to the N^6 of AMP, which is catalyzed by AMP-isopentenyl transferase (*IPT*). It is generally thought that the free bases such as isopentenyl adenine, Zea and dihydro-Zea are active forms of CK. CK with a hydroxylated side chain can be glycosylated to form the O-glucoside or O-xyloside. These reactions are reversible because O-glycosylated CK has biological activity. Zea O-xylosyl transferase has been isolated from zygotic embryos. The enzyme is predominantly localized in the endosperm.

Moreover, Werner *et al.* (2001) suggested that analysis of the consequences of reduced endogenous CK content strongly indicated in which plant processes CKs are limiting and might, therefore, have a regulatory function. They are required to maintain the cell division cycle but might also be involved in promoting the transition of the cell division cycle from undifferentiated stem cells to differentiation. Earlier work showed that in unorganized growing cells, CKs induce the formation of SAMs, demonstrating that they have a function beyond maintaining the cell cycle (Skoog and Miller, 1957). CKs function as a regulatory factor in leaf cell formation, supported by the fact that transgenic *Arabidopsis* plants with an enhanced CK content produced more leaf cells than control plants.

Further, CK (Kin) appears to restrict leaf cell size as the cells of transgenic leaves are larger than in control plants. Alternatively, a compensatory mechanism may be activated in transgenic plants to reach a genetically determined organ size, as has been reported for plants expressing dominant-negative forms of CDC2 (cell division cycle 2). Interestingly, the flower phenotype of the transgenic plants was unaltered (Werner *et al.*, 2001). This suggests that the role of CK in the regulation of development of reproductive organs might be less important than it is during the vegetative phase. It may be that once the plant has entered the reproductive cycle, a more stringent mechanism operates in the meristem to ensure the proper course of the developmental programme (Werner *et al.* 2001). The mechanism of different types of CK remains enigmatic, probably due to its random presence or absence or random distribution in *Arabidopsis* and other plant kinds. There are also partially lack of evidence whether ribo-Zea and Kin has binding affinity for His kinases—CRE/WOL/AHK4, AHK2 and AHK3 which initiate intracellular phosphotransfer.

CYTOKININS IN PLANT DEVELOPMENT: REGULATING MORPHOGENESIS AND CELL DIVISION

CKs are plant growth-promoting hormones involved in the specification of embryonic cells, maintenance of meristematic cells, shoot formation and development of vasculature. CKs have also emerged as a major factor in plant-microbe interactions during nodule organogenesis and pathogenesis. Microbe-originated CKs confer abnormal hypersensitivity of CKs to plants, augmenting the sink activity of infected regions. However, recent findings of Choi *et al.* (2011) have shed light on a distinct role of CK in plant immune responses. They suggest that plant-borne CKs systemically induce resistance against pathogen infection which is orchestrated by endogenous CKs and SA signalling. They also consider the molecular mechanisms underlying plant-derived CK action in plant immunity.

Plant growth is based on the production of cells in the meristem and the ensuing elongation of these newly formed cells. As is well-documented, plant hormones affect both cell division and cell elongation. CK is involved in many developmental processes and plays a critical role in numerous physiological responses to changes in the environment (Mok and Mok, 2001). Numerous reports ascribe a stimulatory or inhibitory function to CK in different developmental processes such as root growth and branching, control of apical dominance in the shoot, chloroplast development, and leaf senescence. CKs act in regulating root growth by influencing cell-to-cell auxin transport through modification of expression of several auxin transport components, and thus modulate auxin distribution important for regulation of activity and size of the root meristem. Auxin inhibits the activation of axillary buds, and hence shoot branching, while CK has the opposite effect. Various hypotheses have been put forward to explain how auxin and CK influence axillary bud activity. Müller and Leyser (2011) discussed the roles of auxin and CK in regulating each other's synthesis, the cell cycle, meristem function and auxin transport, each of which could affect branching. Buds can subsequently remain dormant or grow out to produce a branch. In this way, new axes of growth can be added to the initial apical-basal axis of the plant. The branches can of course themselves branch, and so on, allowing ever higher orders of branching to be achieved. Furthermore, the number of axillary meristems in a phytomer can vary. Thus the formation of axillary meristems and the subsequent regulation of their activation contribute greatly to variation in shoot architecture.

Studies of Gan and Amasino (1995) demonstrated that endogenously produced

CK can regulate senescence and provides a system to specifically manipulate the senescence programme. The interaction between CK and IPT expression is a well-known part of plant developmental biology. Controlling expression of IPT, a gene encoding isopentenyl transferase (the enzyme that catalyzes the rate-limiting step in CK biosynthesis), with a senescence-specific promoter results in the suppression of leaf senescence. Transgenic tobacco plants expressing this chimeric gene do not exhibit the developmental abnormalities usually associated with IPT expression because the system is autoregulatory. Because sufficient CK is produced to retard senescence, the activity of the senescence-specific promoter is attenuated. Senescence-retarded leaves exhibit a prolonged, photosynthetically active life span. The development and function of the chloroplast are particularly regulated by CK. Nakano *et al.*, (2001) clarified the molecular mechanism of chloroplast development regulated by CK, and also attempted to clarify the mechanism using molecular biology and molecular genetics. The fundamental nature of CK effects suggests that changes in gene expression may be required in mediating the response of chloroplast development and that most photosynthetic genes are induced by CK. However, key genes upstream of CK signal transduction can affect chloroplast development and functions. In addition, based on the developed fluorescent differential display using cultured green tobacco cells, Cortleven *et al.*, (2011) identified the expression of three CK-inducible genes (*cig*) during the earliest stages of chloroplast development. Conclusions about the biological functions of CK have mainly been derived from studies on the consequences of exogenous CK application or endogenously enhanced CK levels, and up to now, it has not been possible to address the reverse question: what are the consequences for plant growth and

development if the endogenous CK concentration is decreased. Plants with reduced CK content are expected to yield more precise information about these processes. CKs limit and, therefore, might regulate. Unlike other plant hormones such as ABA, GAs and ET, number of CK biosynthetic mutants have been isolated. In addition, CK stimulates the formation and activity of root apical meristems (RAMs) firstly and later SAMs are able to establish sink tissues, retard leaf senescence, inhibit root growth and branching and play a role in seed germination and stress responses (**Figs 4.6 and 4.7**).

Development of Meristem Versus CK, Auxins and Gibberellins

Crop plant architecture determines planting density in the field and thus influences, to a large degree, the light harvest, disease resistance, and lodging. Rice is one of the most important staples and feeds more than half of the world population of world. And therefore rice attracts tremendous attention in crop breeding. Therefore, rice plant architecture is regarded as one of the most important factors that affect rice yield. CK and auxins are signalling hormonal molecules that may play an essential role in regulating cytokinesis, growth and development in plants. Although, both CK and IAA can be produced in roots and shoots, but however, the young shoot organs are the major sites of IAA production while root tips are the major sites of CK productions. The production of both CK and IAA does not occur randomly but is regulated by the locations of the synthesizing cells in the plant body and their developmental stages and is influenced by environmental conditions that although their signal move in specific structural pathways and by different mechanisms to regulate plant development and differentiation. CK and IAA are key hormones that regulate the root development; its vascular differentiation and

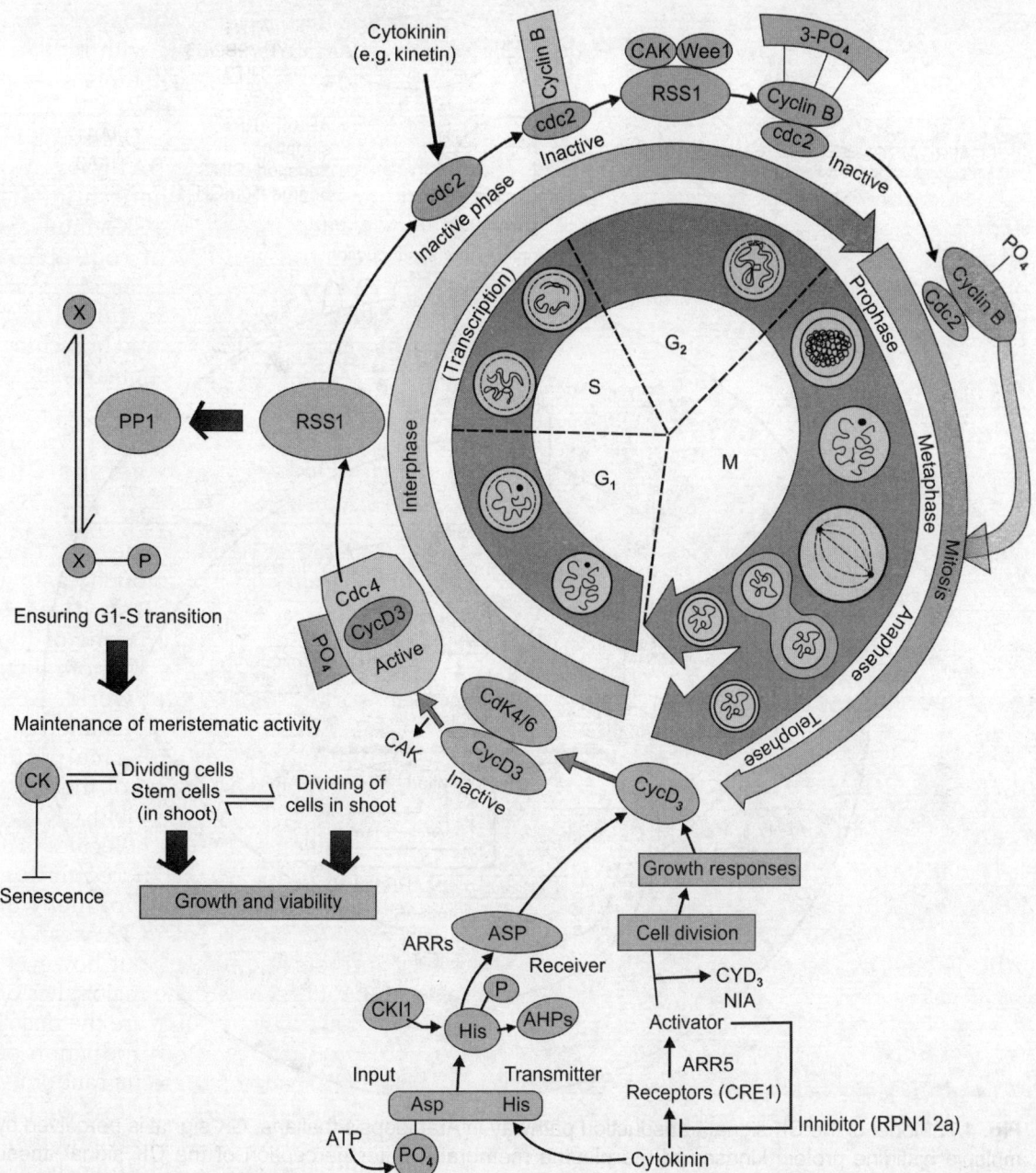

Fig. 4.6: Role of CK signalling components during the phases of cell cycle. Progression of cell division cycle occurs principally by the successive activation of a series of two sets of protein kinases. In addition, figure also demonstrates the possible role of RPN1 2a in CK signalling. The phosphate is transferred to a conserved His present in an AHP protein. Phosphorylation causes the AHP protein to move into the nucleus, where it transfers the phosphate to an aspirate residue located within the cell

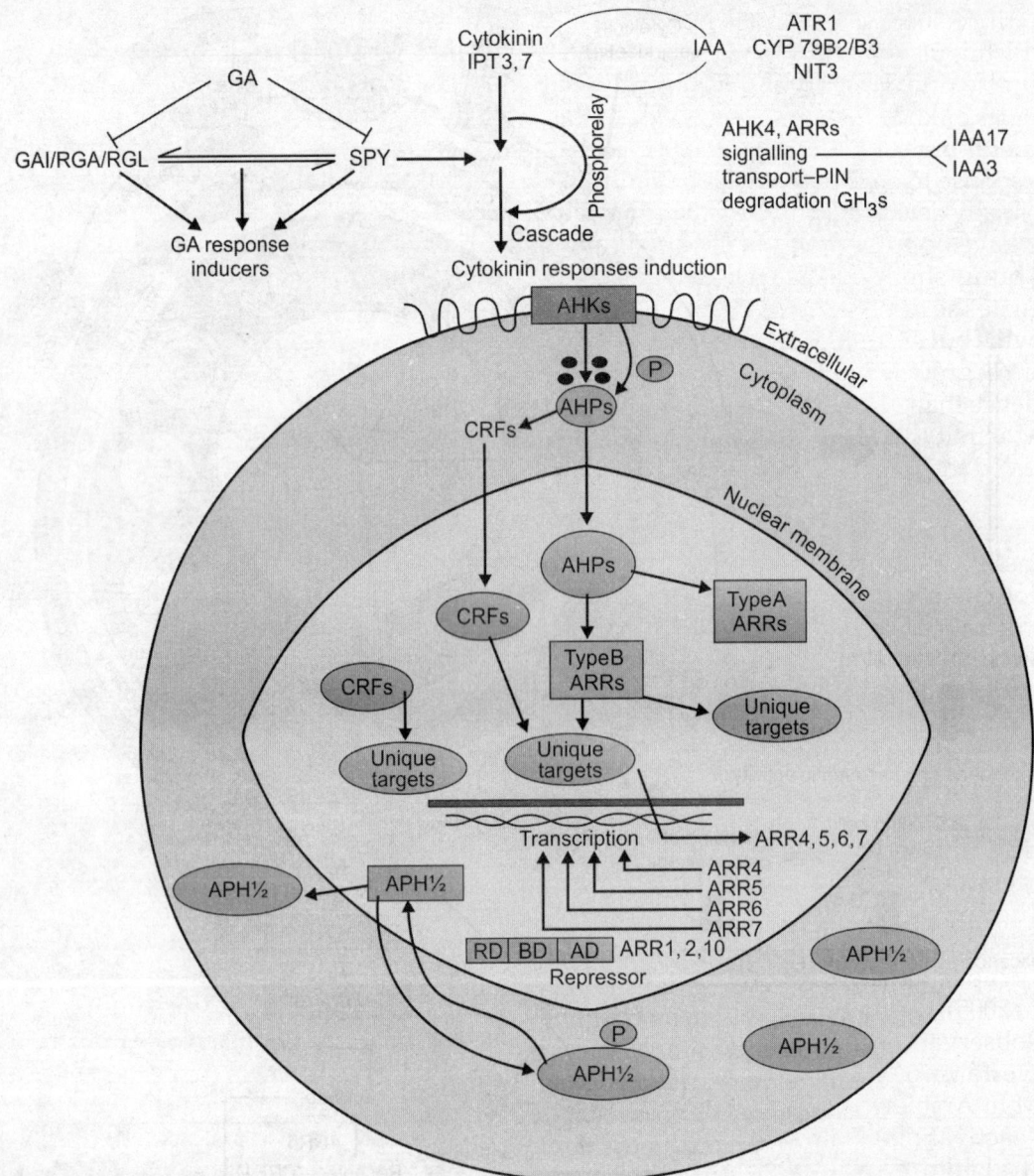

Fig. 4.7: Model of the CK signal transduction pathway in Arabidopsis thaliana. CK signal is perceived by multiple histidine protein kinases at the plasma membrane. After perception of the CK signal, these histidine protein kinases initiate a signal cascade through the phosphorelay that results in the nuclear translocation of AHPs from the cytosol. The activation of the transcription repressor ARRs as CK primary response genes provide a negative feedback mechanism

root gravitropism and along with enzyme ethylene, they maintain a regulate lateral root initiation.

Axiallary meristems are major determinants of plant architecture. A key component of architectural variations in the degree and pattern of shoot later organs by which man can distinguish different kinds of plants in the natural world even without advanced technologies or knowledge. Although, the pattern of lateral organs is flexible, to some extents, in response to environmental conditions, it is essentially determined by the genetic makeup. CKs have opposing roles in shoot and roots; in young shoot organs the CK positively regulate the development and promote shoot growth, but in root they are negative regulators of growth and development. The direct evidence that CK are involved in maintaining SAM activity comes from the experiments that revealed the relationship between CK and the home box gene STM. Besides CK, other PGRS phytohormones have been regarded as indispensible players in plant developmental biology. Among, CK and auxins are plant specific hormones that regulate cell division and are the best known hormones involved in maintaining meristem activity. CK also controls the SAM size by participating in the CLV-WUS loop sustains the dynamic balance of SAM activities; there should be some other molecules that determine the position and timing of a primordium. These findings suggest that ARR genes might negatively influence meristem size and that their repression by WUS might be necessary for the proper function of meristems (Leibfried et al., 2005). Consistent with this hypothesis is the observation that overexpresssion of an active form of ARR7 produces an aborting SAM in Arabidopsis (Leibfried et al., 2005).

Reactivation of dormant meristems is of central importance for plant fitness and survival. CK and GA play important roles in releasing potato tuber dormancy and promoting sprouting, but their mode of action in these processes is still obscure. Hartmann et al., (2011) established an in vitro assay using excised tuber buds to study the dormancy-releasing capacity of GA and CK and showed that the application of GA_3 is sufficient to induce sprouting. In contrast, treatment with 6-benzylaminopurine induced bud break but did not support further sprout growth unless GA_3 is administered additionally. The IPT from Agrobacterium tumefaciens and the Arabidopsis CK oxidase/dehydrogenase1 (CKX) are exploited to modify the amounts of CK in transgenic potato plants. IPT expression promoted earlier sprouting in vitro (Figs 4.6–4.8). Another positive regulator of SAM maintenance is STM, which encodes a homeodomin protein of the KN1 family. It has been shown that STM acts as an antagonist of CLV but synergistically sustain the balance of stem cell regeneration and differentiation. Consistent with its central position, the WUS promoter contain distinct regulatory region that control tissue specificity and levels of transcription in a combinatorial manner. CKs are synthesized in roots and transported through xylem into axillary buds to break the dormancy of arrested buds, whereas auxin modulates the CK concentration, this repressing AM outgrowth. However, auxin has been found incapable of a accumulation in the inhibited AMs, suggesting an indirect suppression effect of auxin on AM outgrowth. Dicotyledon roots have a few primary xylem strands and their lateral roots initiation typically occurs in pericycle cells located immediately outside the protoxylem point.

Auxin antagonizes CK signalling during formation of stem cell niche of the root meristem early embryogenesis. The core of the PR meristem consists of highly organized, etc. cells termed the stem cell niche. Formation of local auxin gradients and the activity of genes regulating auxin efflux are shown to be critical for its proper formation. Similarly, it has shown that endogenous CK levels change during early stages of the PR (plant root) development and that there is a developmental window specifying the increased sensitivity of the root towards endogenous CK. All these above findings suggest spatio-temporal specificity of the CK and auxin interaction during post-embryonic maturation of PR meristem. In addition, Laplaze et al. (2007) have further shown that endogenous CK inhibits LR formation by directly affecting LR initiation and that application of exogenous CK correlation with miss expression of genes of auxin-efflux carriers for the PIN finally in initiating and develops LRP.

CK and Gravitropism

CK and IAA are two key hormones that regulate root development, its vascular differentiation and root gravitropism; these two hormones, together with ET, regulate lateral root initiation (Aloni et al., 2006). The auxin hormone and its polar movement originating in young shoot organs (Aloni et al., 2006), play a crucial role in many aspects of root growth, development and differentiation. IAA regulates the development of the primary and lateral roots (Taiz and Zeiger, 2002), the quiescent centre, root apical meristem, root cap and root vascular differentiation (Aloni et al., 2004). In CK-deficient transgenic Arabidopsis plants, which overexpress the CKX genes and have only 30–45% of the wild-type CK content (Werner et al., 2003), indicating that CK retards root elongation in wild-type plants. CKs produced in the shoot are not involved in the regulation of root gravitropism. This is evident in horizontally orientated roots of young. Arabidopsis plants, in which the CK in the vascular cylinder is retained by the endodermis and, therefore, is not involved in regulating root gravitropism (Aloni et al., 2004). In summary, the extreme developmental plasticity of roots is regulated by complexes of diverse external and internal signals, in which hormones may mediate the external stimulation and adapt the root to changing environment, e.g. response to gravity.

Also, CK appears to participate in a number of light-regulated processes, such as de-etiolating and chloroplast differentiation (Mok, 1994). Analysis of CK-deficient plants has shown that CK plays opposite roles in shoot and root meristem and has suggested that the hormone has an essential function in quantitative control of organ growth. Root and shoot growth appear to be less tightly linked and it seems likely that the effect of CK on cell proliferation and/or expansion are superimposed to changes in the sink-source balance in the whole plant, at least under optimal conditions. Functionally distinct A. thaliana genes are combined that positively affect root or shoot growth when ectopically expressed to explore the feasibility of enhanced biomass production. Vercruyssen et al., (2011) suggested that enhanced root growth resulting from CK deficiency is obtained by overexpressing CK oxidase/dehydrogenase (CKX3) under the control of the root-specific PYK10 promoter. Root and shoot growth appear to be less tightly linked, and it seems likely that the effects on cell proliferation and/or expansion are superimposed to changes in the sink/source balance in the whole plant, at least under optimal conditions. Enhancing root growth can provide several advantages, such as a better exploitation of soil nutrients and water when environmental conditions are less favourable, and are becoming a key feature of ameliorating crop productivity. Simultaneously increasing the size of leaves, which provide the major energy for the plant, might alter the photosynthetic efficiency and create the potential for further biomass improvement under diverse environmental conditions. Plants harbouring the PYK10-CKX3 construct are crossed with four different transgenic lines showing enhanced leaf growth. Both leaf and root growth are synergistically enhanced in plants ectopically expressing CKX3 and brassinosteroid insensitive 1, indicating crosstalk between CK and brassinosteroid.

In addition, Su et al. (2011) helped in delay senescence or the ageing of tissues are responsible for mediating auxin transport throughout the plant and affect internodal length and leaf growth. They have a highly synergistic effect in concert with auxins and the ratios of the two groups of plant hormones affect most major growth periods during a plant's life time. In addition, CK along with auxin regulate many aspects of plant growth and development. Both have been known for a long time to act either synergistically or antagonistically to control several significant developmental processes, such as the formation and maintenance of SAM over the past few years, exciting progress has been made to reveal the molecular mechanisms underlying the auxin-CK action and interaction. Moreover, Su *et al.*, (2011) also briefly discussed the major progress made in CK transport and signalling. Both auxin and CK have been known for a long time to act either synergistically or antagonistically to control several significant developmental processes, such as the formation and maintenance of meristem (SAMs and RAMs). Over the past few years, exciting progress has been made to reveal the molecular mechanisms underlying the auxin-CK action and interaction. Further, this study also suggests the complicated interaction of these two hormones in the control of SAM and root apical meristem formation as well as their roles *in vitro* organ regeneration. It has been known for many decades that auxin inhibits the activation of axillary buds, and hence shoot branching, while CK has the opposite effect.

Müller and Leyser (2011) reviewed the evidence for various hypotheses that have been put forward to explain how auxin and CK influence axillary bud activity and discuss the activity of the roles of auxin and CK in regulating each other's synthesis, the cell cycle, meristem function and auxin transport, each of which could affect branching. CK positively regulates meristem function and is necessary for its maintenance. High levels of CK in the central zones of the meristem are connected to the maintenance of undifferentiated cells. There is potential to

provide tools to produce CK at various sites in lateral buds, including the stem cell niche as well as the whole bud. Branching analyses of various mutants might help to elucidate whether changes of CK concentration in the meristem contribute to the transition from arrested to active buds. Moreover, synthetic CK analogues may be informative. For example, different CK analogues have different impacts on lateral shoot growth in pea, suggesting that a subset of CK receptors is involved. SAM can be divided into different zones with specific functions. The central zone at the tip of the SAM contains the stem cells and the organizing centre of the meristem. It is characterized by a low rate of cell division. All aboveground plant cells are ultimately derived from these stem cells. The peripheral as well as the rib zone beneath the organizing centre show a higher rate of cell division, and cells from these domains are released to be incorporated into growing lateral organs and the stem.

Plant root development is mediated by the concerted action of the auxin and CK phytohormones, with CK serving as an antagonist of auxin transport. Similarly, Zheng *et al.* (2011) identify the Auxin UP-Regulated F-Box Protein 1 (AUF1) and its potential paralog AUF2 as important positive modifiers of root elongation that tether auxin movements to CK signalling in *A. thaliana*. AUF1 roots are also hypersensitive to CK and have increased expression of several components of CK signalling. Kushwah *et al.* (2011) results show that asymmetrical exposure of CK at the root tip in *A. thaliana* promotes cell elongation that is potentiated by glucose in a hexokinase-influenced, G-protein-independent manner.

Heyl *et al.* (2008) generated a dominant repressor version of the Arabidopsis RR ARR1 (ARR1-SRDX) using chimeric repressor silencing technology in order to study the extent of the contribution of B-type RRs to CK activities. Negative and positive feedback loops are reinforced facilitated by

PIN-Formed2 as well as auxin signalling through control of the steady state level of transcriptional repressors indole-3-acetic acid 7 (IAA7), IAA14, and IAA17 via transport inhibitor response 1/auxin signalling F-Box protein are involved in CK-induced root cell elongation. This root growth response may have adaptive significance, since CK responsiveness is inversely related to root coiling and waving, two root behaviors known to be important for fitness. The correlation of auxins and CK in the plant is constant (A/C = constant) (**Fig. 4.6**).

In fact, CKs are considered the most important senescence-retarding hormones (Faiss *et al.*, 1997), and their exogenous application has been demonstrated to prevent the degradation of chlorophyll and photosynthetic proteins, to cause induction of flower or pod set, to reverse leaf and fruit abscission, to release dormancy, and to modify substantially plant responses to a variety of environmental stresses (Aldesuquy and Gaber, 1992), anthocyanin production and maintenance of source-sink relationship, leaf area expansion, dry matter production and have a direct effect on determining photosynthetic parameters. The relationship between auxin and CK has long been recognized as central to normal plant growth and development.

CKs are important signalling molecules in plants, and recent studies have begun to shed light on the molecular mechanisms underlying their biosynthesis and response pathways. A discussion of CK crosstalk, its induction of ET biosynthesis in etiolated Arabidopsis seedlings, and studied that have begun to elucidate the mechanism underlying this regulation. Rashotte *et al.*, (2005) suggestsed that the synergistic effects of CK and auxin occur by some mechanisms other than the crosstalk of the primary signalling pathways. One point of crosstalk between these two hormones occurs via regulation of each other's level. A second paradigm for the interaction of these two hormones is the regulation of ET

biosynthesis, in which the regulation of a common process occurs via two distinct mechanisms, rather than through the interaction of the primary signal transduction events. In the case of light signalling, there may be crosstalk directly with CK signalling elements, although the interaction is complex.

Plants sense and respond to endogenous signals and environmental cues to ensure optimal growth and development. Studies of Swarup *et al.* (2002) concluded that auxin and CK control tobacco cell proliferation by regulating the expression of interacting cell cycle components. In common with other eukaryotes, the cell cycle in plants is controlled by serine-threonine kinases whose function is controlled by their association with regulatory cyclin subunits. The expression of proteins related to the class of CDC2 class of cyclin-dependent kinases in tobacco pith explants is upregulated by auxin. Although the expression of these genes is elevated by auxin, the catalytic activity of the CDC2 kinase is only increased when tobacco explants are also treated with CK.

Moreover, Jones *et al.* (2010) suggested that together, auxin and CK regulate many of the processes that are critical to plant growth, development, and environmental responsiveness. They have previously shown that exogenous auxin regulates CK biosynthesis in *A. thaliana* as well as they also suggest that application or induced ectopic biosynthesis of CK leads to a rapid increase in auxin biosynthesis in young, developing root and shoot tissues. Auxin and CK levels are regulated through the auxin-induced downregulation of CK biosynthesis. Conversely, CK induces auxin biosynthesis and increases steady state auxin levels in young, developing tissues in the root and shoot of Arabidopsis. Combined, the data suggest that a feedback homeostasis loop exists to regulate the relative levels of auxin and CK in plants. Results of Moubayidin *et al.* (2009) have shown that CK can also modulate auxin transport in the root via the regulation of PIN gene expression. Fundamental multicellular plant processes, such as embryogenesis, meristem development and maintenance, shoot branching and lateral root initiation and development, dependend on both hormones and both act as long-distance signalling substances and as paracrine signals during complete development. Genetic analysis indicated a CK-dependent endospermal and/or maternal control of embryo size. Some studies attested to the necessity of CK for the induction of SE (somatic embryogenesis). BA and zeatin (0.01 to 0.1 mg/L) in particular significantly inhibited SE. The inhibitory effect on SE increased in the order of 0.01 to 0.1 mg/L). Reasons for these activity differences are not known, but in some cases such differences are related to differential inactivation of CK through CK oxidase. Moreover, CK oxidase activity and its potential modulation by auxins (IAA) and interaction with phenolic PGRs of the phenylopropanoid pathway could elucidate the mechanisms of embryogenesis in pepper and contribute to development of a method for clonal regeneration of pepper (*Capsicum annuum* L.).

Arata *et al.* (2010) identified two phenylquinazoline compounds in a large-scale screening for CK antagonists in yeast expressing the *Arabidopsis* CK receptor CK response 1/His kinase 4 (*CRE1*) and obtained compound S-4893, which non-competitively inhibited binding of the natural ligand 2-isopentenyladenine to *CRE1*. S-4893 antagonized CK-induced activation of the *Arabidopsis* RR 5 promoters in *Arabidopsis*. Importantly, S-4893 has no detectable intrinsic CK agonist activity in *Arabidopsis* or in the transformed yeast system. S-4893 also promoted seminal, crown and lateral root growth in rice, suggesting that S-4893 can potentially promote root growth in a variety of agronomically important plants. No phenylquinazolines have been reported as a CK or a CK antagonist to date. The results of the target-based assay using transformed yeast and the ligand-binding assay demonstrated that S-4893 acts directly on CK receptor CRE1, inhibits CK receptor binding, and inhibits CK signal transduction. The antagonistic action of S-4893 during the early steps of CK signal transduction is confirmed *in planta* by the ARR5 promoter-GUS assay. Their experimental study demonstrated that CK-induced gene expression is reduced by S-4893, indicating that antagonistic interaction of S-4893 with CK receptors can block the early steps of CK signal transduction in *Arabidopsis*. Further, they believe S-4893 will be a useful tool in functional studies of CK action in a wide range of plants and a lead compound for the development of useful root growth promoters in agriculture.

CK as Systematic Mediators

Another interesting issue concerning the role of CK is whether they are systematic mediators or local mediators. Plant tissues exhibit high but transient levels of CKs (e.g. iP, [9R]iP, Z and [9R]Z) during specific periods of development. The decline in CK levels appears to be mainly due to the increased activity of CK oxidase, an enzyme which irreversibly cleaves the side chains of such CKs, leading to a complete loss of activity. Since CK oxidase is the only plant enzyme known to catalyze the degradation of these specific CKs, it appears to be an important point of control of CK levels, species or rate of turnover in specific plant tissues. Although evidence from studies using undifferentiated tissues clearly shows that CK levels and CK oxidase activity are tightly regulated, little work has been done to characterize this regulation in a plant system where CK action may play a major role in plant development. How CK oxidase is regulated, when, and in what organs and tissues it is expressed are not well-understood. However, the recent purification and production of polyclonal antibodies to CK oxidase should facilitate the cloning of the gene(s) encoding CK oxidase and the eventual elucidation of its role in regulation of levels of active CK in specific tissues of developing plants.

The interpretation by Sakakibara *et al.* (2006) that expression of transporter genes is tightly regulated by CK translocated from phloem tissue, and that nitrate levels around the phloem are important for determining macronutrient uptake capacity. The contact point between CK and macronutrients is apparently not limited to nitrate. Phosphorus deficiency leads to decreased CK content suggesting that phosphorus nutrient status also affects CK metabolism. Although knowledge of the interactive and hierarchical regulation of macronutrient acquisition and distribution is still limited, CK is a likely candidate for a key role in communicating nutrient use. It is well-known that CK is translocated via xylem vessels, whereas nitrate-responsive IPT3 is expressed in the phloem of roots and shoots. In several plant species, tZ riboside is the major form of xylem CK, and iP-type CK is the predominant form in phloem exudate. The CK translocation system is not well-understood, but the biased distribution of CK species in xylem and phloem implies the action of a selective loading system because the CK contents are distinct from normal tissues. Several studies have provided evidence that some members of the purine permease and equilibrative nucleoside transporter families can mediate the translocation of CK nucleotide bases and nucleosides respectively. The transporters also mediate the movement of purine derivatives and nucleosides. Characterization of the CK transport systems should provide clues about the compartmentalization of the two types of CK species in long-range translocation. A possible cross point in the transcriptional regulation of nitrogen and carbon metabolism is a GATA transcription factor, GNC (At5g56860). GNC expression is induced by nitrate, and the GNC mutant is sensitive to exogenous glucose, but the overexpressor is resistant. GNC expression is also induced by CK suggesting that a function of GNC is regulation of carbon and nitrogen metabolism via cellular nitrate and CK levels.

Inorganic nitrogen is a substrate for nitrogen assimilation and also functions as a signal triggering widespread changes in gene expression that modulate metabolism and development. To integrate the actions of the nitrogen signal at the whole plant level, plants use multiple signalling routes that communicate internal and external nitrogen status. One route depends on nitrate itself and one uses CK as a messenger. Recent genome-wide research has shown that the nitrate-specific signal regulates a wide variety of metabolic processes including nitrogen and carbon metabolisms, and CK biosynthesis. CK-mediated signalling is related to the control of development, protein synthesis and acquisition of macronutrients. The coordination and interaction of both regulatory pathways is important for normal plant growth under variable nitrogen supply conditions.

Some experimental results supporting the role of CK as systemic mediators is the presence of CK in the sap of the xylem and the phloem. CK levels in plants and in the xylem sap are positively correlated with soil minerals, especially mineral nitrogen, which suggests that CK mediate information on nutrient status. Results against the systemic role were also obtained from transgenic tobacco carrying the IPT gene from *A. tumefaciens*. Bohner and Gatz (2001) used a glucocorticoid-inducible and tetracycline-repressible promoter to express IPT from *A. tumefaciens* and showed that in systematically induced plants only buds receiving tetracycline did not exhibit outgrowths, suggesting further a paracrine action of CK. Therefore, the role and mechanism of long-distance, short-distance and transmembrane transport of CK are important issues for further research to solve in future perspectives.

Roots have traditionally been considered a primary site of CK biosynthesis, supplying the shoot within CK via the xylem sap. However, evidence for CK synthesis in shoots is now unequivocal. Nevertheless, studies by Bangerth (1994) with decapitated broad bean (*Phaseolus vulgaris*) plants led to the hypothesis that CK in the xylem sap from roots (X-CK = xylem sap CK) plays an important role in regulating auxiliary shoot branching. It is one of the most important determinants of plant architecture and is highly responsive to environmental and endogenous cues. CK, a mobile plant hormone, can influence shoot branching but its precise role is unclear. In several species, direct application of CK to axillary buds promotes outgrowth and endogenous CK leaves has been found to rise in and around auxiliary buds during growth initiation. In addition, transgenic plants expressing the bacterial *ipt* gene which catalyzes CK biosynthesis, exhibit elevated levels often accompanied by an increased-branching phenotype.

As already stated that CKs, are a class of plant specific hormones that play a central role during the cell cycle and influence numerous developmental programmes. CK-deficient plants developed stunted shoots with smaller apical meristem. Studies of Werner *et al.* (2001) suggest that CK is an important regulatory factor of plant meristem activity and morphogenesis, with opposing roles in shoots and roots. In addition, the hypothesis predicted that CK, together with auxin, plays an essential role in plant morphogenesis, having a profound influence on the formation of roots and shoots and their relative growth. Cell division activity is also important factor in determining sink strength.

CK is known to have regulatory roles during different phases of cell cycle including the G1/S transition, S-phase, and the G2/M transition. Their involvement in G1-S regulation is supported by the observation that CK increases the G1 cyclin, cyclin D3 and that constitutive expression of cyclin D3 caused CK-independent growth of *Arabidopsis* calli. Interestingly, overexpressed calli are green while the WT calli are not suggesting the surprising possibility that cyclin D3 may also regulate chloroplast development. Chloroplast harbour enzymes for the biosynthesis of CK and contain a set of natural CKs, including free bases, ribosides, ribitides and N-glucosides. Moreover, the activation of cyclin-dependent kinases (CDC2, CDK4 and CDK6) achieved by association with specific cyclins and then phosphorylation mediated by ATP involvement. Use of exogenous CK promotes the equilibrium level of CDC2 and CYCD3 and activation of CYCD3 obviates the CK requirement for division in tissue culture. In case of CDK4 and CDK6, a cyclin activating kinase (CAK) catalyzes this reaction while CDC2 demands an extra phosphorylation by WEE1 protein kinase. However, most of these results have been obtained in cell culture systems and it is unclear till date that at which of the cell cycle stages CK exerts its regulatory functions during different developmental process in different tissues (**Fig. 4.9**).

Furthermore, in *Arabidopsis*, CK stimulates the expression of the gene that encodes δ_3-cyclin (a G1-type cyclin). The stimulation of δ_3-cyclin expression is probably not the only way in which CK regulates the cell cycle. When cultured tobacco cells are specifically deprived of CK, they stop dividing and arrest in the G2 phase of the cell cycle, rather than at G1 or at the boundary between G1 and S as would be predicted if the only role for CK in regulating the cell cycle are to provide δ_3-cyclin. Similarly, CKs are also important for the regulation of the G2-M transition. When CK is grown to the G2-arrested cells, they re-enter the cell cycle and initiate mitosis. In tobacco BY-2 cells, which are CK-autonomous, endogenous Zea-type CK peaked around the S and M phases.

Although CK-induced mitosis is perceived by increased activity of the CDK-CDC2 complex; instead, its activity is controlled by a change in CDK phosphorylation, apparently by the removal of the phosphate group from the inhibitory phosphorylation site (Lipavská et al., 2011). This observation suggests that CK controls the activities of a phosphatase whose substrate is the CDC2 kinase with an inhibitory phosphate group. The removal of the inhibitory phosphoryl group acitivates the CDK-cyclin complex, permitting it to phosphorylate other proteins to initiate mitosis. The regulation of G2-M transition is probably mediated by activation of CDK (Kakimoto, 2003). The data suggests the direct involvement of CK in cell cycle regulation. However, these results are only indications of how CK might act to control cell cycle progression and there are many gaps in our understanding. Presently, the missing link between RRs and control of cell cycle remains as important and interesting question or how CK regulates the transcription of δ_3 cyclin or the phosphorylation of CDKs and, therefore, requires future research.

PRECURSORS OF BIOACTIVE KIN/BA AND STORAGE FORMS

Many chemical compounds have been synthesized and tested for CK activity. Analysis of these compounds provides insight into the structural requirements for activity. Nearly all compounds active as CK are N^6-substituted aminopurines and all the naturally occurring CKs are aminopurine derivatives. The CK, BA is an example of a synthetic N^6-substituted aminopurine CK as in Kin. The only exception to this generalization is certain diphenylurea derivatives are not N^6-substituted aminopurines, but they appear to be active as CK by affecting the metabolism of endogenous CK. In several species, direct application of CK to axillary buds promotes outgrowth and endogenous CK levels have been found to rise in and around axillary buds during growth initiation. In addition, transgenic plants expressing the bacterial ipt gene, which

catalyzes CK biosynthesis, exhibit elevated CK levels often accompanied by an increased-branching phenotype. Foo et al. (2007) experiments with grafted pea plants bearing two shoots of the same or different genotype revealed that regulation of root CK export is probably mediated by an inhibitory signal. The startling disconnection between CK content of xylem sap and shoot tissues of various rms (Pisum sativum; ramosus) mutants indicates that shoots possess powerful homeostatic mechanisms for regulation of CK levels. Increased-branching mutants of garden pea (Pisum sativum; ramosus) and Arabidopsis (Arabidopsis thaliana; more auxillary branches) are used to investigate control of CK export from roots in relation to shoot branching. In particular, the hypothesis that regulation of xylem sap CK is dependent on a long-distance feedback signal moving from shoot to root (Foo et al., 2007).

Moreover, Widespread, unmodified CK bases are isopentenyladenine and trans-zetin-ribose or ribose-5-phosphate may be attached at the N^9 atom of the adenine ring to form CK ribosides or ribotides and these also generally show CK activity when applied to plants (**Fig. 4.1**). CK can be modified by the conjugation of GLC to nitrogen at various positions of the adenine ring. They also can be modified by the conjugation of Glc and to a lesser extent, Xyl to the hydroxyl group of the N^6 side chain. These modifications generally inactivate the CK and in some cases are reversible. A subset of CK can be degraded irreversibly by cleavage of the N^6 side chain by the enzyme CK oxidase. The existence of pathways for the degradation and conjugation of CK suggests that the level of this signalling compound is tightly regulated.

However, because applied CK undergoes interconversion, the actual active forms are not known until recently. Recent receptor-binding assays have shown that the active forms are the free base CK isopentenyladenine and trans-Zea. CKs are inactivated by

O-glycosylation at the terminal hydroxyl group of the Zea-type CK or by N-glycosylation at the N3 or N7 positions of the adenine ring. O-glycosylation is reversible and O-glycosylated CK are regarded as a storage form. The CK ribosides and *cis*-Zea, sometimes found in abundance in plants, may also be important as stored or transportable forms. Because CK exists in the apoplasm as well as in the cytoplasm, specific transmembrane transporters for CK may exist. CK oxidase/dehydrogenase degrades CK by cleaving the side chain. CK metabolism has been reviewed in detail. CK occurs in both free or conjugated forms (not covalently attached to any macromolecules) in plants and bacteria but also occur as modified bases in certain transfer RNA molecules of all organisms. Some conjugates are thought to be temporary storage forms, from which free active hormones can be released after hydrolysis. It is also believed that conjugation serves functions, such as irreversible inactivation, transport, compartmentalization, and protection against degradation.

Nevertheless, CK can be stably or transiently inactivated by glycosylation of the purine ring or of the side chain. The purine ring can be glycosylated at the N3, N7 and N9 positions. In addition, the N6-side chain group can form O-glycosyl conjugates if it bears a hydroxyl group. Most often, glucose is the conjugated sugar molecule, more rarely xylose is attached. N7- and N9-conjugates are biologically inactive and extremely stable. Thus they are irreversibly inactivated CK. N3-and O-conjugates are biologically inactive but can be readily hydrolyzed. They are believed to be transient storage forms of CK. Glycosyl conjugation is considered to be important in the regulation of CK activity levels, at least in some tissues and species. Several genes coding for CK glycosyl transferases and glycosidases have been identified. Some conjugates of CK and amino acids (alanine) have been described as well. A characteristic feature of CK metabolism is the rapid metabolic interconversion of base, ribosides and ribotides (Schmülling, 2004). The biologically most active form of CK is the base. Attachment of ribose or ribose-5´-phosphate to the N9 atom of the adenine ring leads to the formation of ribosides and ribotides respectively. Interconversion of CK is presumably an important mechanism to regulate the concentration of active compounds. The interconversions may be catalyzed by the same enzymes that metabolize adenine, adenosine and AMP. The conversion between the *cis*- and *trans*-isomers of zeatin is catalyzed by the enzyme *cistranszeatin isomerise* (Schmülling, 2004).

Moreover, free CKs have been found in a wide spectrum of angiosperms and probably are universal in this group of plants. They have also been found in algae, diatoms, mosses, ferns and conifers. Their regulatory role has been demonstrated only in angiosperms, conifers and mosses but they may function to regulate the growth, development and metabolism of all plants. Usually Zea is the most abundant naturally occurring free CK, but dehydroZea and isopentenyladenine (i6 Ade) are also commonly found in higher plants and bacteria. Numerous derivatives of these three CKs have been identified in plant extracts: *trans*-Zea, 6-(4-hydroxy-3-methylbut-2-enylamino) purine, *cis*-zatin, dihydroZea, N^6-(Δ-isopentenyl)-adenine (I6 Ade), Zea ribotide (RibosylZea-5-monophosphate), RibosylZea (Zea riboside), *cis*-RibosylZea, I6Ado, N^6-(Δ2-isopentenyl)-adenosine (plants) and 2-methylthio-*cis*-ribosyl Zea (bacteria). Transfer RNA (t-RNA) contains not only the four nucleotides used to construct all other forms of RNA but also some unusual nucleotides in which the base has been modified. Some of these hypermodified bases act as CK when the t-RNA is hydrolyzed and tested in one of the CK bioassays. Some plant t-RNA contain Zea as a hypermodified base, although, it is present only in the *cis*-isomer form, not the active *trans* configuration (**Fig. 4.2**).

However, CK are not confined to plant t-RNAs. They are part of certain t-RNAs from all organisms, from bacteria to humans. Because the effect of CK treatment may be depend on both the content of endogenous CK and the ratio between CK and ABA, its antagonist in the regulation of chloroplast biosynthesis in the leaf tissues, (trans-Zea and Zea riboside), and ABA in the basal, middle, and apical segments of barley leaves, immediately after detachment from 9-day-old plants and after preincubation of detached leaves on water for 24 hours under illumination or in darkness. The content of ABA changed dramatically during the 24-hour preincubation of the leaf in the light. In the apical and middle leaf parts, the ABA levels increased approximately 7-fold and in the basal part, they increased up to 12-fold. The ABA level also rose during preincubation in darkness, but this increase is much less pronounced than in the light. This preincubation of the leaf on water in the light enhanced the content of CK and ABA and sharply increased the ratio of ABA to CK in detached leaves.

Moreover, most of the different chemical forms of CK are rapidly interconverted by plant tissues (Letham and Palni, 1983). CK bases, when given to many plants tissues, are converted of their respective nucleotides: Zea to Zea ribonucleotide, I6Ade ribonucleotide and so forth. They also may be converted to their glucosides. However, glucosides sometimes are not readily converted to free CK. CK glucosides have been considered to be a storage form, or metabolically inactive state of these compounds. Nevertheless, glucosides have been identified that will release the CK base from CK glucoside conjugates. For example, the *rol C* gene of *Agrobacterium rhizogenes* T-DNA encodes a glucosidase that can relase free CK. The activity of the *rol C* gene, along with the products of the other *Agrobacterium rhizogenes* T-DNA genes, *rol A* and *rol B* is responsible for the abnormal proliferation of roots induced by this bacterium (**Fig. 4.5**).

Furthermore, the free base is the hormonally active form of CK. Other compounds are active as CK, either, because they are readily converted to *trans*-Zea, dihydroZea or isopentenyl adenine or because they release these compounds from other molecules, such as CK glucosides. For example, excised radish cotyledons grow when they are cultured in a solution containing the synthetic CK base BA. The cultured cotyledons readily take up the hormone and convert it to various BA glucosides, BA ribonucleoside and BA ribonucleotide. When the cotyledons are transferred back to a medium lacking a CK, their growth rate declines, as do the concentrations of BA, BA ribonucleoside and BA ribonucleotide in the tisues. However, the level of the BA glucosides remains constant. This finding suggests that the glucosides cannot be the active form of the hormone. Tobacco cells in culture do not give unless CK ribosides supplied in the culture medium are converted to the free base (Frébort *et al.*, 2011). Thus, this free base is the most likely candidate for the active form of the hormone.

A gene encoding another glucosidase that can release CK from sugar conjugates has been cloned from maize and its expression can play an important role in the germination of maize seeds. Dormant seeds often have high levels of CK glucosides but very low levels of hormonally active, free CK levels of free CK increase rapidly, however, as germination is initiated and this increases in free CK is accompanied by a corresponding decrease in CK glucosides. Many plant tissues contain the enzyme CK oxidase, which converts Zea, Zea riboside and I6Ade to adenine or its derivatives. This enzyme inactivates the hormone and could be important in regulating or limiting CK effects. The activity of the enzyme is induced by high CK concentrations but its role in regulating the level of CK in tissues is still not completely clear and needs further investigations in future.

RESPONSE REGULATORS AND THEIR ROLE IN CK SIGNALLING IN *ARABIDOPSIS*

CK is a plant hormone that plays positive and negative regulatory roles in many aspects of plant growth and development, including cell division, shoots initiation, apical meristem function, and vascular formation. CK rapidly alters the steady state transcript levels of a number of transcription factor genes suggesting that these might have a function in mediating CK effects. Kollmer *et al.* (2011) report the analysis of *A. thaliana* plants with an altered expression level of four different CK-regulated transcription factor genes. These include GATA22 (also known as CGA1/GNL), two genes coding for members of the homeodomain zip (HD zip) class II transcription factor family (HAT4, HAT22), and bHLH64. Overexpression of HAT22 lowered the seedlings chlorophyll content and caused an earlier onset of leaf senescence. Enhanced expression of the HAT4 gene led to severe defects in inflorescence stem development and to a decrease in root growth and branching, while HAT4 insertional mutants developed a larger root system. Also, the results of Kollmer *et al.* (2011) are consistent with specific functions of these transcription factor genes in regulating part of the CK activities and suggest their action as convergence point with other signalling pathways, particularly those of GA and light.

In addition, CK organizes plant development and environmental adaptation through cell-to-cell signal transduction, and their action involves transcriptional activation. Recent international efforts to establish and maintain public databases of *Arabidopsis* microarray data have enabled the utilization of this data in the analysis of various phytohormone responses, providing genome-wide identification of promoters targeted by phytohormones. Yamamoto *et al.* (2011) utilized such microarray data for prediction of *cis*-regulatory elements with an octamer-based approach. The test prediction of a drought-responsive RD29A promoter with the aid of microarray data for response to drought, ABA and overexpression of DREB1A, a key regulator of cold and drought response provided reasonable results that fit with the experimentally identified regulatory elements group (REG) that have been extracted as position-dependent *cis*-regulatory elements with the aid of their feature of preferential appearance in the promoter region (**Figs 4.3 and 4.4**).

Progress has been made in our understanding of CK signalling and perception. Essential steps in their metabolism and signal transduction have been elucidated recently. The genes encoding several important CK metabolic enzymes have been identified in plants (Kakimoto, 2003). Overexpression of genes that code for CK-degrading CK-oxidase/dehydrogenase (CKX) enzymes is used to produce tobacco and *Arabidopsis* plants with reduced CK content. These plants show a compound phenotype called the CK deficiency syndrome. The main features of this syndrome are the formation of slow-growing, stunted shoot with small leaves and an enhanced root system. The phenotypic consequence of CK deficiency has largely been confirmed in loop-of-function mutants of CK receptors. It is known from previous work that CK regulates several parameters, which determined the source or sink strength of tissues, for example, carbon fixation, assimilation and portioning of primary metabolites and cell cycle activity and which could thus be causally involved in the establishment of the CK deficiency syndrome. The analysis of CK-deficient plants has shown that CK is a positive regulator of shoot growth and a negative regulator of root growth. However, it is still unknown which cellular process in growing tissues limit growth in the shoot or enhance growth in the root under conditions of CK-deficiency.

A model of CK perception and signalling has emerged that is similar to bacterial two components phosphorylation. Generally, a well-known two-component signalling systems are used to prokaryotic and eukaryotic organisms to sense and respond to changes in the environment. In a canonical two-component system, a stimulus is perceived by a sensor kinase, which autophosphorylates on a conserved His residue in the kinase domain. The signal is transmitted by transfer of the phosphoryl group to a conserved Asp residue on the receiver domain of a RR. Variations of the simple two-component system involve intermediate elements in the phosphotransfer from the sensor kinase to the RR. Receiver domain phosphorylation induces conformational changes, which in most RRs release represses of the output domain to allow the activation of down stress processes, often transcriptional regulation. In some RRs, these conformational changes allow specific interactions with target proteins (**Figs 4.3 and 4.8**).

Studies of To *et al.* (2007) shed light on the mechanism by which type-A ARRs act to negatively regulate CK signalling and reveal a novel mechanism by which CK controls type-A ARR function. This pathway of CK transcriptionally regulates the several closely related members of the *Arabidopsis* AP2 gene family of unknown function, called CRFs. In response to CK binding, these receptors autophosphorylate on a conserved His residue and relay His phosphoryl group to ARRs via an intermediate set of Hpt proteins called the AHPs. Similarly, studies of CK signalling components have been characterized in other plant species. The *Arabidopsis* RRs fall into four classes based on phylogenetic analysis and domain structure: type-A ARRs, type-B ARRs, type-C ARRs and the *Arabidopsis* pseudo-RRs (APRRs). The ARRs all contain the conserved Asp required for receiver domain phosphorylation in bacterial response regulators and phosphotransfer from an AHP to representative members of all three ARR groups has been demonstrated *in vitro*. The APRRs lack the conserved Asp phosphorylation site, and some play a role in modulating circadian rhythms. The type-C ARRs are more distantly related to type-A and type-B ARR receiver domain sequences. They do not contain the output domain of type-B ARRs and are not transcriptionally regulated by CK, although their overexpression results in reduced sensitivity to CK. The pair of type-C ARRs are less similar in sequence to the two other groups of ARRs, are not transcriptionally regulated by CK and do not have transcriptional activity. The ten type-A ARRs are primary transcriptional targets of CK signalling and contain short C-terminal extensions beyond the conserved receiver domain. The type-B ARRs contain C-terminal output domains that have DNA binding and *trans*-activating activity. Type-B ARRs are positive regulators of CK signalling that controls the transcription of a subset of CK-regulated targets, including the type-A ARRs. The type-C ARRs are more distantly related to type-A and type-B ARR receiver domain sequences. The all ARRs contain the conserved Asp required for receiver domain phosphotransfer from an AHP to representative members of all three ARR groups has been demonstrated *in vitro*. The APRRs act as the conserved Asp phosphorylation site, and play a role in modulating circadian rhythms (McClung, 2006).

At least eight of the ten type A ARRs act as partially redundant negative regulators of CK signalling (Zhang *et al.*, 2011). The type A ARR proteins are not stabilized by CK, ARR4 and ARR9, are less similar to ARR5, ARR6 and ARR7 receiver domain sequences and contain longer C-terminal regions (D'Agostino *et al.*, 2000). In, ARR4 and ARR9 are also less transcriptionally upregulated CK (D'Agostino *et al.*, 2000) and play a CK in dependent in modulating the circadian clock. The terminal regions of type A ARR proteins may impart specificity in protein regulation. CK of protein turnover of a subset of type A ARRs may reflect another for modulating their function specific processes, such as meristem activity. The ARRs lack the conserved Asp phosphorylation site, and some play a role in modulating circadian rhythms. Moreover, ARR4 interacts directly with the red light receptor phytochrome B and along with other type A ARRs, modulates the response to red light. A subset of type A ARRs is direct targets of the transcription factor Wuschel and regulates SAM function (Leibfried *et al.*, 2005). While, it is clear that type A ARRs play a role in multiple signalling pathways, little is known with regard to their mechanism of action and requires further investigation in future.

In addition to their transcriptional regulation by CK, the CRF proteins rapidly accumulate in the nucleus in response to CK, and this relocalization depends on the His kinases and the downstream His-containing phosphotransfer proteins, but is independent of the ARRs. Analysis of loss-of-function mutations results that the CRFs function redundantly regulate the development of embryos, cotyledons, and the leaves. Riefler *et al.* (2006) used loss-of-function mutants to study three *A. thaliana* sensor His kinases, AHK2, AHK3 and CRE1/AHK4, known to be CK receptors. Mutant's seeds had more rapid germination, reduced requirement for light, and decreased far-red light sensitivity, unravelling CK functions in seed germination control. Furthermore, the CRFs mediate a large fraction of the transcriptional response to CK, affecting a set of CK-response genes that largely overlap with type B ARR targets. The results of Rashotte *et al.* (2006) indicate that the CRF proteins function in tandem with the type B ARRs to mediate the initial CK responses. Thus, the evolutionary, ancient two-component system that is used by CK branches to incorporate unique functions of plant-specific transfer factors.

Furthermore, the current model of CK signalling predicts that the receptors feed into the two-component signalling system, which transfers the signal via phosphorelay to the nucleus (Ferreira and kieber, 2005). In addition, gene expression in response to CK has been extensively studied, and numerous genes have been identified that are transcriptionally up-regulated in response to CK including two members of the AP2/ERF superfamily of transcription factors within the ethylene response factor (ERF) family. Further studies of Rashotte *et al.*, (2006) demonstrated that this subgroup of AP2 transcription factors move into the nucleus in response to CK, and that they mediate, together with the type B ARRs, the transcriptional response to CK. mRNA of all three receptor genes is found in all organs, although with different abundance. CRE1/AHK4 is predominantly expressed in the root, where its mRNA is mainly localized to the vascular cylinder and the pericycle of the root. The AHK2 and in particular the AHK3 gene show greater expression in the aerial parts of *Arabidopsis* plants.

CONCLUDING REMARKS

It is clear from the observation reviewed here that defining "CKs" simply in terms of their ability to stimulate plant is no longer tenable. It is now apparent that CK (Isopentenyladenine (IPA), Zea (ZA), and dihydriZea (DZ), etc.) itself has wide ranging and pleiotropic effects encompassing the regulation of almost every aspect of plant growth and development including cell growth, cell division, cell differentiation, flowering, fruiting, histogenesis, organogenesis and responses to various kinds of environmental stresses (e.g. abiotic and biotic). A plethora of evidences indicates clear correlation between CK concentration in a given tissue and the nature and magnitude of the responses it stimulates. These displacements emerge the focus of investigations of CK action towards mechanisms that regulate homeostasis of endogenous CK pools in which processes such as biosynthesis, degradation, conjugation and specific transport play crucial roles, and towards mechanism of action of CK at the cellular, molecular and genomic levels.

From the point of view of terminology used, it may be desirable to redefine the group of compounds termed endogenous CK because their mechanisms of action may vary for each particular attribute of growth and development in plants. However, several outstanding questions remain to be answered before we can fully understand the mechanisms that determine CK homeostasis.

REFERENCES

Aldesuquy HS and Gaber AM (1992). Effect of growth regulating substances on *Vicia faba* plants irrigated by sea-water. 1. Leaf area, pigment content and photosynthetic activity. *Journal of Environmental Science*, **4**: 291–09.

Aloni R, Aloni E, Langhans M and Ullrich CI (2006). Role of cytokinin and auxin in shaping root architecture: regulating vascular differentiation, lateral root initiation, root apical dominance and root gravitropism. *Annals of Botany*, **97 (5)**: 883–893.

Aloni R, Langhans M, Aloni E and Ullrich CI (2004) Role of cytokinin in the regulation of root gravitropism. *Planta*, **220**: 177–182.

Arata Y, Nagasawa-Iida A, Uneme H, Nakajima H, Kakimoto T and Sato R (2010). The phenylquinazoline compound S-4893 is a non-competitive cytokinin antagonist that targets *Arabidopsis* cytokinin receptor CRE1 and promotes root growth in *Arabidopsis* and rice. *Plant and Cell Physiology*, **51: (12)**, 2047–2059.

Argueso CT, Ferreira FJ, Epple P, To JP, Hutchison CE, Schaller GE, Dangl JL and Kieber JJ (2012). Two-component elements mediate interactions between cytokinin and salicylic acid in plant immunity. *PLoS Genetics*, **8 (1)**: e1002448.

Bangerth F (1994). Response of cytokinin concentration in the xylem exudate of bean (*Phaseolus vulgaris* L.) plants to decapitation and auxin treatment, and relationship to apical dominance. *Planta*, **194**: 439–442.

Bohner S and Gatz C (2001). Characterization of novel target promoters for the dexamethasone-inducible/tetracycline-repressible regulator TGV using luciferase and isopentenyl transferase as sensitive reporter genes. *Molecular amd General Genetics*, **264**: 860–870.

Choi J, Choi D, Lee S, Ryu CM and Hwang I (2011). Cytokinins and plant immunity: old foes or new friends? *Trends in Plant Science*, **16 (7)**: 388–394.

Cortleven A, Noben JP and Valcke R (2011). Analysis of the photosynthetic apparatus in transgenic tobacco plants with altered endogenous cytokinin content: a proteomic study. *Proteome Science*, **9**: 33–37.

D'Agostino I, Deruere J and Kieber JJ (2000). Characterization of the response of the *Arabidopsis* ARR gene family to cytokinin. *Plant Physiology*, **124**: 1706–1717.

Faiss M, Zalubýlova J, Strnad M and Schmulling T (1997). Conditional transgenic expression of the IPT gene indicates a function for cytokinins in paracrine signalling in whole tobacco plants. *Plant Journal*, **12**: 401–415.

Ferreira FJ and Kieber JJ (2005). Cytokinin signalling. *Current Opinion in Plant Biology*, **8**: 518–525.

Frébort I, Kowalska M, Hluska T, Frébortová J and Galuszka P (2011). Evolution of cytokinin biosynthesis and degradation. *Journal of Experimental Botany*, **62 (8)**: 2431–2452.

Gan S and Amasino RM (1995). Inhibition of leaf senescence by autoregulated production of cytokinin. *Science*, **270 (5244)**: 1986–1988.

Hartmann A, Senning M, Hedden P, Sonnewald U and Sonnewald S (2010). Reactivation of meristem activity and sprout growth in potato tubers require both cytokinin and gibberellin. *Plant Physiology*, **155 (2)** 776–796.

Heyl A, Ramireddy E, Brenner WG, Riefler M, Allemeersch J and Schmulling T (2008). The Transcriptional repressor ARR1-SRDX suppresses pleiotropic cytokinin activities in Arabidopsis. *Plant Physiology*, **147**: 1380–1395.

Hwang I and Sheen J (2001). Two-component circuitry in *Arabidopsis* cytokinin signal transduction. *Nature*, **413**: 383–389.

Jones B, Gunnera SA, Petersson SV, Tarkowski P, Graham N, May S, Dolezal K, Sandberg G and Ljung K (2010), Cytokinin regulation of auxin synthesis in *Arabidopsis* involves a homeostatic feedback loop regulated via auxin and cytokinin signal transduction. *The Plant Cell*, **22**: 2956–2969.

Kakimoto T (2001). Identification of plant cytokinin biosynthetic enzymes as dimethylallyl diphosphate: ATP/ADP isopentenyltransferases. *Plant and Cell Physiology*, **42**: 677–685.

Kakimoto T (2003). Perception and signal transduction of cytokinins. *Annual Reviews of Plant Biology*, **54**: 605–627.

Kakimoto T, Miyawaki K, Inoue T, Higuchi M and Matsumoto M (2001). Biosynthesis and perception of cytokinins, Abst. 17th Int. Conf. Plant Growth substances, Brno: Mendel Univesity of Agriculture and Forest, pp 141–146.

Kim HJ, Ryu H, Hong SH, Woo HR, Lim PO, Lee IC, Sheen J, Nam HG and Hwang I (2006). Cytokinin-mediated control of leaf longevity by AHK3 through phosphorylation of ARR2 in Arabidopsis. *Proceedings of the National Academy of Sciences of USA*, **103**: 814–819.

Köllmer I, Werner T and Schmülling T (2011). Ectopic expression of different cytokinin-regulated transcription factor genes of *Arabidopsis thaliana* alters plant growth and development. *Journal of Plant Physiology*, **168 (12)**: 1320–1327.

Kosel D, Heiker JT, Juhl C, Wottawah CM, Blüher M, Mörl K and Beck-Sickinger AG (2010). Dimerization of adiponectin receptor 1 is inhibited by adiponectin. *Journal of Cell Science*, **123 (8)**: 1320–1328.

Kushwah S, Jones AM and Laxmi A (2011). Cytokinin interplay with ethylene, auxin, and glucose signalling controls *Arabidopsis* seedling root directional growth. *Plant Physiology*, **156 (4)**: 1851–1866.

Laplaze L, Benkova E, Casimiro I, Maes L, Vanneste S, Swarup R, Weijers D, Calvo V, Parizot B, Herrera-Rodriguez MB, Offringa R, Graham N, Doumas P, Friml J, Bogusz D, Beeckman T and Bennett M (2007). Cytokinins act directly on lateral root founder cells to inhibit root initiation. *Plant Cell*, **19**: 3889–3900.

Leibfried A, To JPC, Busch W, Stehling SK, Kehle A, Demar M, Kieber JJ and Lohmann JU (2005). WUSCHEL controls meristem size by direct transcriptional regulation of cytokinin inducible RRs. *Nature*, **438**: 1172–1175.

Letham DS and Palni LMS (1983). The biosynthesis and metabolism of cytokinin. *Annual Review of Plant Physiology*, **34**: 163–197.

Ma Q, Longnecker N and Atkins C (1998). Exogenous cytokinin and nitrogen do not increase grain yield in narrow-leafed lupins. *Crop Science*, **38**: 717–721.

Maeda S, Sugita C, Sugita M, and Omata T (2006). A new class of signal transducer in His-Asp phosphorelay systems. *Journal of Biological Chemistry*, **281 (49)**, 37868–37876.

McClung CR (2006). Plant circadian rhythms. *Plant Cell*, **18**: 792–803.

Miller CO, Skoog F, Okumura FS, Von Saltza MH and Strong FM (1956). Isolation, structure and synthesis of kinetin, a substrate promoting cell division. *Journal of American Chemical Society*, **78**: 1375–1380.

Miller CO, Skoog F, Von Saltza MH and Strong FM (1955). Kinetin, a cell division factor from deoxyribonucleic acid. *Journal of American Chemical Society*, **77**: 1388–1392.

Mok DW and Mok MC (2001). Cytokinin Metabolism and Action. *Annual Reviews of Plant Physiology and Plant Molecular Biology*, **52**: 89–118.

Mok MC (1994). Cytokinins and plant development—an overview. In: Mok MC (Eds). *Cytokinins—Chemistry, Activity, and Function*, CRC Press, Boca Raton, pp 155–166.

Moubayidin L, Di Mambro R and Sabatini S (2009). Cytokinin auxin crosstalk. *Trends in Plant Science*, **14**: 557–562.

Müller D and Leyser O (2011). Auxin, cytokinin and the control of shoot branching. *Annals of Botany*, **107 (7)**: 1203–1212.

Nakano T, Kimura T, Kaneko I, Nagata N, Matsuyama T, Asami T and Yoshida S (2001). Molecular mechanism of chloroplast development regulated by plant hormones. *RIKEN Review Focused on Bioarchitect Research*, **41**: 86–87.

Rashotte AM, Chae HS, Maxwell BM and Kieber JJ (2005). The interaction of cytokinin with other signals. *Physiologia Plantarum*, **123**: 184–194.

Rashotte AM, Mason MG, Hutchison CE, Ferreira FJ, Schaller GE and Kieber JJ (2006). A subset of *Arabidopsis* AP2 transcription factors mediates cytokinin responses in concert with a two-component pathway. *Proceedings of the National Academy of Sciences of USA*, **103**: 11081–11085.

Riefler M, Novak O, Strnad M and Schmulling T (2006). *Arabidopsis* cytokinin receptor mutants reveal functions in shoot growth, leaf senescence, seed size, germination, root development, and cytokinin metabolism. *The Plant Cell*, **18**: 40–54.

Sakakibara H, Takei K and Hirose N (2006). Interactions between nitrogen and cytokinin in the regulation of metabolism and development. *Trends in Plant Science*, **11**: 440–448.

Sakamoto T, Kamiya N, Ueguchi-Tanaka M, Iwahori S and Matsuoka M (2001). KNOX homeodomain protein directly suppresses the expression of a gibberellin biosynthetic gene in the tobacco shoot apical meristem. *Genes Development*, **15**: 581–590.

Schmülling T (2002). New insights into the functions of cytokinins in plant development. *Journal of Plant Growth Regulations*, **21**: 40–49.

Schoor S, Farrow S, Blaschke H, Lee S, Perry G, von Schwartzenberg K, Emery N and Moffatt B (2011). Adenosine kinase contributes to cytokinin interconversion in *Arabidopsis*. *Plant Physiology*, PMID: 21803861.

Skoog F and Miller CO (1957). Chemical regulation of growth and organ formation in plant tissues cultured *in vitro*. *Symposia of the Society of Experimental Biology*, **11**: 118–131.

Su YH, Liu YB and Zhang XS (2011). Auxin-cytokinin interaction regulates meristem development. *Molecular Plant*, **4 (4)**: 616–625.

Swarup R, Parry G, Graham N, Allen T and Bennett M (2002). Auxin crosstalk: Integration of signalling pathways to control plant development. *Plant Molecular Biology*, **49**: 411–426.

Taiz L and Zeiger E (2002). Plant physiology, 3rd edn. Sunderland, MA: Sinauer.

Tanaka Y, Sano T, Tamaoki M, Nakajima N, Kondo and Hasezawa S (2006). Cytokinin and auxin inhibit abscisic acid-induced stomatal closure by enhancing ethylene production in Arabidopsis. *Journal of Experimental Botany*, **57 (10)**: 2259–2266.

To JPC, Deruere J, Maxwell BB, Morris VF, Hutchison CE, Ferreira FJ, Schaller GE and Kiebera JJ (2007). Cytokinin regulates type-A *Arabidopsis* RR activity and protein stability via two-component phosphorelay. *The Plant Cell*, **19**: 3901–3914.

Vercruyssen L, Gonzalez N, Werner T, Schmülling T and Inzé D (2011). Combining enhanced root and shoot growth reveals crosstalk between pathways that control plant organ size in *Arabidopsis*. *Plant Physiology*, **155 (3)**: 1339–1352.

Werner T, Holst K, Pors Y, Guivarch A, Mustroph A, Chriqui D, Grimm B and Schmulling T (2008). Cytokinin deficiency causes distinct changes of sink and source parameters in tobacco shoots and roots. *Journal of Experimental Botany*, **59 (10)**: 2659–2672.

Werner T, Motyka V, Laucou V, Smets R, Van Onckelen H and Schmulling T (2003). Cytokinin-deficient transgenic *Arabidopsis* plants show multiple developmental alterations indicating opposite functions of cytokinins in the regulation of shoot and root meristem activity. *The Plant Cell* **15**: 2532–2550.

QUESTIONS

Q. 1. Cytokinin induced cell division related function which is/are?

(1) Nutrient mobilization
(2) Apical dominance
(3) Formation and activity of shoot apical meristems
(4) All of the above

Q. 2. Cytokinin induce light regulated development the related function which is/are?

(1) Chl differentiation
(2) Leaf and cotyledons expansion
(3) Development of autotrophic development
(4) All of the above

Q. 3. What is true about abscission zone?

(1) Consists of mature parenchyma cells
(2) It present at base of leaf petiole
(3) It is layer of cells with relatively weak cell walls
(4) All of the above are correct

Q. 4. Principle cytokinin of higher plants is:

(1) Kinetin
(2) BAP
(3) Triacanthene
(4) Zeatin

Q. 5. Cytokinins are:

(1) N^3-substituted aminopurine
(2) N^7-substituted aminopurine
(3) N^4-substituted aminopurine
(4) N^6-substituted aminopurine

Q. 6. A synthetic auxin, kinetin, absent in higher plants, chemically is:

(1) N^5-substituted aminopurine
(2) N^9-substituted aminopurine
(3) N^4-substituted aminopurine
(4) N^6-furfuryl-aminopurine

Q. 7. A natural auxin, zeatin, present in higher plants in abundant amount, chemically is:

(1) 3-(4 hydroxy-3-methyl-trans-2-butenyl aminopurine
(2) 1-(5 hydroxy-3-methyl-trans-3-butenyl aminopurine
(3) 4-(7 hydroxy-3-methyl-trans-8-butenyl aminopurine
(4) 6-(4 hydroxy-3-methyl-trans-2-butenyl aminopurine

Q. 8. Crown gall (neoplastic growth) is an infectious response of:

(1) *Agrobacterium rhizogenes*
(2) *Nitrosomonas spp.*
(3) *Corynebacterium faciens*
(4) *Agrobacterium tumifaciens*

Q. 9. Wiches Broom is a disease condition caused by:

(1) *Agrobacterium rhizogenes*
(2) *Nitrosomonas spp.*
(3) *Agrobacterium tumifaciens*
(4) *Corynebacterium faciens*

Q. 10. T-DNA can expressed in:

(1) Bacteria   (2) Animals
(3) Fungi   (4) Plants

Q. 11. Opines are source of which substance or nutrient for bacteria?

(1) S   (2) C
(3) P   (4) N

Q. 12. T-DNA expression in plants can produce

(1) Auxins   (2) Cytokinins
(3) Opines   (4) All

Q. 13. What is true for crown gall?

(1) A neoplastic growth
(2) Can be cured at temperature at 42°C

(3) Produce only when infection occurs at juncture between shoot and root

(4) All are correct

Q. 14. Root tumors is results of irregulation of which hormone:

(1) GA

(2) Auxin

(3) Both

(4) CK

Q. 15. Naturally occurring molecules with CKs activities can be detected by?

(1) Bioassays

(2) Physical methods

(3) Immunological methods

(4) All are correct

Q. 16. Naturally occurring CKs activities can be best detected by?

(1) Bioassays

(2) Physical methods

(3) HPLC

(4) Immunological methods

Q. 17. Naturally occurring CKs activities can be best detected by immunological methods because:

(1) Use enzmyes

(2) Use lusozymes

(3) Use lectins

(4) Use specific and sensitive antibodies

Q. 18. Isolation and measure of CK done by:

(1) MS and RIA

(2) CDS and MS

(3) TLC and ELISA

(4) HPLC and RIA

Q. 19. Mature plant cells generally do not divide in intact plant, but they can be stimulated to divide by

(1) Wounding

(2) Infection with certain bacteria

(3) Plant hormones like CKs

(4) All are correct

Q. 20. Agrobacterium tumifaciens transferred a small part of its plasmid to host organism called:

(1) C-DNA   (2) B-DNA

(3) Z-DNA   (4) T-DNA

Q. 21. Which ion used in induction of cell cycle promotion of G2 to M phase?

(1) Ca^{+2} (2) Na^+

(3) Cl^- (4) PO_4^{-2}

Q. 22. Which plant used in construction process of caves of Ajanta and Allora in Aurangabad, Maharashtra?

(1) *Allium sativum*

(2) *Oryza sativa*

(3) *Lettuce sativa*

(4) *Cannabis sativa*

Q. 23. World environment day celebrated at:

(1) 4 July   (2) 5 July

(3) 3 June   (4) 5 June

Q. 24. World ozone day celebrated at:

(1) 13 October

(2) 16 June

(3) 16 November

(4) 16 September

Q. 25. Botanical name of Myrtle herb or Periwinkle (5-petaloid flower):

(1) *Cicer arietinum*

(2) *Cathranthus roseus*

(3) *Littoria littorea*

(4) *Vinca rosea*

Q. 26. Zoological name of Periwinkle (a gastropod molluscan invertebrate)

(1) *Cicer arietinum*

(2) *Cathranthus roseus*

(3) *Vinca rosea*

(4) *Littoria littorea*

Q. 27. Botanical name of Medagascar Periwinkle or Rose Periwinkle or Old maid or Bright Eyes:

(1) *Cicer arietinum*
(2) *Littoria littorea*
(3) *Vinca rosea*
(4) *Cathranthus roseus*

Q. 28. Neelmi Kumar is:

(1) Indian Orthinologist
(2) Indian Taxonomist
(3) Indian Palentologist
(4) Indian Herpatologist

Q. 29. Headquarter of IKVK in India:

(1) Delhi   (2) Bareilly
(3) Bengaluru   (4) Mubbai

Q. 30. Most reliable organism to convert solar energy to chemical energy is:

(1) Earthworm   (2) Lion
(3) Cuscutta   (4) Chlorella

Q. 31. E. Coli is resistant against to:

(1) Endonuclease V
(2) Endonuclease I
(3) Endonuclease III
(4) Endonuclease II

Q. 32. Which disease caused due to water pollution:

(1) Joundice   (2) Cholera
(3) Typhoid   (4) All

Q. 33. MAB started in:

(1) 1972   (2) 1973
(3) 1974   (4) 1975

Q. 34. Golden Rice (GM) contain gene for:

(1) Carbohydrate
(2) Lipid
(3) Protein
(4) Carotene

Q. 35. CK overproducing plants tend to be:

(1) Dwarf
(2) Tall

(3) Medium sized
(4) Busy

Q. 36. Teratomas caused due to irregular production of CK: auxin also like gall and crown but is different from other two:

(1) Have clear root and shoot
(2) Un-differentiated
(3) Fully differentiated
(4) Partially differentiated

Q. 37. In which of the following plant shows strong apical dominance:

(1) Barley   (2) Rice
(3) Wheat   (4) Maize

Q. 38. Cigarette tobacco (Nicotiana tobaccum) produce:

(1) Intraspecific hybrids
(2) Pure hybrids
(3) Both 1 and 2
(4) Interspecific hybrids

Q. 39. Biological roles of CK a include:

(1) Senescence and AD
(2) Regulation of cell cycle
(3) Differentiation
(4) All

Q. 40. Importance of Agrobacterium tumifaciens lies in

(1) In killing of fungi at mass level
(1) Introducing foreign genes in the plants
(3) Study the developmental regulation
(4) Both 2 and 3

Q. 41. Habituation is concerned with:

(1) ET   (2) ABA
(3) GA   (4) CK

Q. 42. BAP (a synthetic CK base; Benzyl amino purine) exist as:

(1) BAP glucoside
(2) BAP ribonucleoside
(3) BAP ribonucleotide
(4) All of the above

Q. 43. Major site of free CK production is:

(1) Leaves
(2) Fruit
(3) SAM
(4) RAM

Q. 44. CK produces in:

(1) RAM
(2) Young maize embryo
(3) Young developing leaves
(4) All of the above

Q. 45. Richmond Mond effect is concerned with the CK along with its property to:

(1) Retention of protein-Chl
(2) Retarding senescence
(3) Both 1 and 2
(4) Promoting the leaf expansion

Q. 46. CK promotes cotyledon growth in the:

(1) Etiolated seedlings
(2) Non-etiolated seedling
(3) Both 1 and 2
(4) None

Q. 47. In which of the following is a odd one:

(1) 2,4-D
(2) 2,4,5-T
(3) MCPA
(4) None

Q. 48. Features of an etiolated seedlings are:

(1) Hypocotyls and internodes elongated
(2) Cotyledons and leaves do not expand
(3) Chloroplast do not mature
(4) All

Q. 49. Etioplasts are:

(1) Chlorophyll of tall seedlings
(2) Chloroplast of light grown seedlings
(3) Proplastids of dark grown seedling
(4) Amyloplasts of dark grown seedlings

Q. 50. Prolamellar bodies, a highly regular lattice, is a characteristic feature of thylakoids inner membrane of etiolated protoplasts, is due to deficiency of which plant hormone:

(1) GA_3 (2) IBA
(3) IAA   (4) CK

Q. 51. Etioplasts contain:

(2) Xanthophylls
(2) Chlorophyll
(3) Carotenes
(4) Carotenoids

Q. 52. Etiolated seedlings appear as:

(1) Red   (2) Green
(3) Blue   (4) Yellow

Q. 53. If in a etiolated seedlings we treat the leaves of plants with the CK we will noticed:

(1) Chloroplast formation with more extensive grana
(2) Chloroplast and photosynthetic enzymes synthesized at a extensive rate
(3) Both 1 and 2
(4) None

Q. 54. Effect of CK on cell enlargement is:

(1) Always promote
(2) Always inhibit
(3) Both 1 and 2
(4) Not concern

Q. 55. Leafy cotyledons are not present in:

(1) Mustard (dicot)
(2) Sunflower (dicot)
(3) Cucumber (dicot)
(4) Wheat (monocot)

Q. 56. Usually CK promote cell expansion or cell enlargement in:

(1) Root
(2) Stem
(3) Both 1 and 2
(4) Leaves

Q. 57. Usually CK inhibit cell expansion or cell enlargement in:

(1) Leaves
(2) Root
(3) Stem
(4) Both 2 and 3

Q. 58. Cotyledons of dicot spp. expanding during seedling growth as a result of the:

(1) Cell division
(2) Cell fusion
(3) Both 1 and 2
(4) Cell enlargement

Q. 59. CK act antagonistically in regulating the light induced development against

(1) ABA
(2) ET
(3) GA3
(4) Brassinosteroids

Q. 60. Nitrate reductase (NR) is a enzyme of:

(1) Mitochondrial
(2) Chloroplastic
(3) Nucleonic
(4) Cytosolic

Q. 61. Nitrite reductase (NiR) is a enzyme of:

(1) Mitochondrial
(2) Cytosolic
(3) Nucleonic
(4) Chloroplastic

Q. 62. Cauli Mosaic virus contain:

(1) 40 S promoter
(2) 39 S promoter
(3) 23 S promoter
(4) 35 S promoter

Q. 63. Plant with strong apical dominance is:

(1) Wheat   (2) Rice
(3) Barley   (4) Maize

Q. 64. Protonema is a feature of Moss (*Funaria hygrometrica*), a product of:

(1) Gamete   (2) Ova
(3) Zygote   (4) Spore

Q. 65. Protonemata or Protonema pass through two distinct stages during their developmental stages. These are:

(1) Hygrospore and caulonema
(2) Archegoniophore and chloronema
(3) Hygrospore and chloronema
(4) Chloronema and caulonema

Q. 66. What is true about 'Bud' in Moss?

(1) A stage between the initial stage and leafy gametophyte
(2) It formed after mitosis in initial cell
(3) Red light is needed for formation in Moss
(4) All are correct

Q. 67. What is true about cyclins?

(1) Enzymes regulates eukaryotic cell cycle
(2) Regulatory units of CDKs (Cyclin-dependent protein Kinases)
(3) Major CDKs is CDC_2, regulated by auxin
(4) All are correct

Q. 68. What is true about cells culturing under the plant tissue culture techniques?

(1) Not photosynthetically active
(2) Require sucrose as C-source
(3) Sucrose stimulate gene (G_1–cyclin) code a protein (γ_2)
(4) All are correct

Q. 69. In which of the following a quiescent tissue is?

(1) Wheat glumes
(2) Maize inflorescence
(3) Mango cotyledons
(4) Tobacco pith

Q. 70. In which of the following is showing a synergistic function in inducing the dividation of cells with CK, auxin and sucrose?

(1) ABA (2) Ethylene
(3) Lysozyme (4) Tobacco pith

Q. 71. Programmed aging process involves:

(1) Loss of chlorophyll
(2) Loss of RNA and proteins
(3) Loss of lipids
(4) All are correct

Q. 72. Programmed aging process will be fast during:

(1) Far-red light (2) Blue light
(3) Red light (4) Dark

Q. 73. Monocarpic senescence is reported in:

(1) Maize (2) Rice
(3) Wheat (4) Soya bean

Q. 74. Monocarpic senescence is:

(1) Senescence initiated in flowers by seed maturation
(2) Senescence initiated in bud by seed maturation
(3) Senescence initiated in roots by seed maturation
(4) Senescence initiated in leaves by seed maturation

Q. 75. CDK triggers entry of the cells into the:

(1) G1-phase
(2) G_0-phase
(3) M-phase
(4) S-phase

Q. 76. Cytokinin involved in delaying senescence are primarily zeatin riboside and dihydrozeatin riboside, transported into leaves from roots by:

(1) Phloem
(2) Xylem
(3) Transpiration stream
(4) Both 2 and 3

Q. 77. What is calcium spike?

(1) A rapid decrease in the calcium level
(2) A moderate increase in calcium level
(3) Both 1 and 2
(4) Rapid and transient increase in Ca^{+2} level

Q. 78. Plant protein kinases phosphorylates the cellular proteins primarily at which residue?

(1) Serine and arginine
(2) Cysteine and methionine
(3) Methionine and serine
(4) Serine and threonine

Q. 79. Rapid and transient increase in Ca^{+2} is a characteristic feature of:

(1) Leaf senescence
(2) Root senescence
(3) Mesophyll parenchyma degradation
(4) Stomatal closure by ABA

Q. 80. Pico-molar amount of cytokinin is used for:

(1) Bud development
(2) Root development
(3) Both 1 and 2
(4) Formation of initial cells

Q. 81. A dominant mutation causes a gene to be expressed at a time or place in which it would be silent in:

(1) Culture in media
(2) Domestic type
(3) Both 1 and 2
(4) Wild type

Q. 82. Principle aim of bacteria (*Agrobacterium tumifaciens*) to infect the plant is:

(1) To create space for living
(2) To meet the demand of lipid
(3) To meet the demand of carbohydrate
(4) To meet the nitrogen demand

Q. 83. Which acid used for preservation of juices of fruits?

(1) Acetic acid   (2) Alcohol

(3) Lactate   (4) Formic acid

Q. 84. Which chemical used to dilate the retina of eyes?

(1) Formic acid   (2) Acetic acid

(3) Ergot   (4) Atropine

Q. 85. Crown gall tissue contain:

(1) More auxin

(2) More CK

(3) Substantial amount of both

(4) All are correct

Q. 86. Synthetic cytokinins are:

(1) BAP or benzyladenine

(2) Tetrahydropyranyl-benzyladenine

(3) N-N-di-phenyl-urea

(4) All of the above

Q. 87. t-RNA contains:

(1) Two nucleotide

(2) Three nucleotides

(3) One nucleotides

(4) Four nucleotides

Q. 88. Cytokinins stimulate cell:

(1) Elongation

(2) Division

(3) Turgor

(4) Wall thickening

Q. 89. The chemical structure of naturally occurring auxin is very similar to the structure of:

(1) Tryptophan

(2) AMP

(3) Cellulose

(4) Glucose

Q. 90. When a plant is not reproducing, most of its CK are produced in its?

(1) Roots

(2) Shoot apex

(3) Lateral buds

(4) Leaves

Q. 91. Gibberelline, produced in the apical portions of both stem and root, cause:

(1) Stem elongation

(2) Phototropism

(3) Abscission of leaf and fruits growth of lateral branches

(4) Growth of lateral branches

Q. 92. In an intact plant, roots are the organs where CKs are synthesized and are major sources of CKs:

(1) Stem

(2) Root caps

(3) Roots

(4) Root hairs

Q. 93. In which of the following is a CKs?

(1) Kinetin, BA, isopentenyl adenosine (i^6A)

(2) Zeatin, zeatin riboside, isopentenyl adenine (i^6Ade)

(3) Tricanthene

(4) All of the above

Q. 94. In which of the following is not found in the higher plants?

(1) 6 (4-hydroxy-3-methyl)

(2) Zeatin

(3) Dihydrozeatin

(4) $ms^2 i^6$A

Q. 95. In which of the following is a native auxin?

(1) IAA

(2) IBA

(3) 2, 4-D

(4) Both 2 and 3

Q. 96. Zeatin like cytokinins in plant t-RNA have:

(1) cis-configuration

(2) trans-configuration

(3) Both 1 and 2

(4) None

Q. 97. Majority of active cytokinins have .... configuration:

(1) Trans   (2) Cis
(3) Both 1 and 2   (4) None

Q. 98. Cultural filtrates of mycorrhizal fungus Rhizopogon roseolus contain:

(1) Zeatin and zeatin ribosudes
(2) Kinetin
(3) i^6A
(4) i^6Ade

Q. 99. Transport mode of the cytokinin from the roots to the shoot is:

(1) Polar
(2) Nonpolar

(3) Both 1 and 2
(4) None of the above

Q. 100. Name of hormone whose absence prevent the differentiation of plastid?

(1) GA
(2) ABA
(3) Ck
(4) ET

Q. 101. 'i⁶ADE', produced by which pathogenic microorganisms?

(1) *Agrobacterium tumifaciens*
(2) *Corynebacterium fasciens*
(3) *Aspergillus niger*
(4) *Saccharomyces cerevisae*

Triacontanol: An Emerging Plant Hormone for Crop Yield Improvement

ABSTRACT

Triacontanol (TRIA) has gained a considerable attention during past decades due to its efficient role in advanced plant physiology. TRIA is an active growth substance at nano-molar concentrations and affects growth and yield attributes of crops by modulating the basic metabolic processes including photo-synthesis, respiration, enzyme metabolism and anion/cation uptake, etc. TRIA has shown both traditional and non-traditional plant hor-mones like activities but although, chemically it is totally different from commonly used plant hormones. A number of biological happenings are induced or enhanced in cells by TRIA, but however, the initial site of action has not been elucidated till date, but fastly induced a second messenger (TRIM) in rice. TRIM also like the TRIA at nano-molar concentrations effectively responses to TRIA like manner. In addition, several mechanisms are revealed by researchers showing how morphogenic events are induced by appli-cation of TRIA. Several investigations also revealed that TRIA may modify endogenous PGRS, either directly or indirectly and produce reactions in cell/tissue, necessary for its division/regulation. In this review, recent advancements in TRIA roles in plant phy-siology are discussed.

Keywords: Plant hormone, Triacontanol, L (+)-adenosine, Yield, Photorespiration.

INTRODUCTION: AN ELUSIVE VIEW

Plant hormones are chemicals that regulate plant growth. Plant hormones are signal molecules produced at specific location in the plant and in extremely low concentrations. Hormones are naturally produced within plants, though very similar chemicals are produced by fungi and bacteria that can affect plant growth (Srivastava, 2002). Also, a large number of related chemical compounds synthesized in the laboratory that function as hormones are called plant growth regulators (PGRs). The biosynthesis of plant hormones within plant tissues (especially sieve tubes) is often diffused and not always localized, and unlike animals which have two or more hearts that move fluids around the body, plants utilize simple chemical hormones that move more easily through the plants tissues. The concentration of hormones required for plant responses are very low (10^{-6} to 10^{-5} mol/L). Because of these low concentrations, it has been very difficult to study plant hormones (Srivastava, 2002).

Plant hormones affect gene expression and transcription levels, cellular division and growth. It is generally accepted that there are five major classes of plant hormones, some of which are made up of different chemicals that can vary in structure from one plant to the other. Each class has positive and inhibitory functions, and they often work in tandem with each other, with varying ratios of one or more interplaying to affect growth regulators. Hormones like cytokinins and auxins are chemicals that regulate plant growth. As such, they shape the plant and affect seed growth, time of flowering, sex of flowers and the senescence of leaves and fruits. Also, they affect the tissues that grow upward and downward, the formation of the leaf and the growth of the stem (Helgiopik and Stephen, 2005). Plants need hormones at very specific times during plant growth and at specific locations; they also need to disengage the effects when they are no longer needed (Helgiopik and Stephen, 2005).

OCTA inhibits the activity of TRIA at equimolar concentrations (Ries, 1985) and both compounds elicit the second messengers, OCTAM (octacosanol second messenger) and TRIM (triacontanol second messenger) respectively in rice seedlings (Ries and Wert, 1988). TRIM has been identified as L(+)-adenosine and is found very soluble in water and can be applied in solution at the desired concentration (Ries *et al.*, 1991).

OCTAM inhibits the activity of TRIA but not that of TRIM (Ries and Wert, 1988). It is the second messenger and works as a plant growth substance. During the process of isolating and identifying 9-β-L (+)-adenosine, it is shown that this enantiomer, which previously has not been reported as occurring in nature, made up about 1% of the total adenosine pool in roots from untreated rice seedlings (Ries, 1991). It has great stimulatory effect on various processes including growth (Ries *et al.*, 1977; Ries and Wert, 1982; Ries and Wert, 1990) (**Fig. 5.1b**). It appeared that TRIA extracted from alfalfa and applied to plants showed properties of growth regulator. Since then, the interests for application as growth substance. TRIA have widely increased and many experiments conducted proved that it has positive effects on the growth and yield of plants, chlorophyll content and photosynthesis activity in plants. Also, presence of TRIA is also reported first time in aerial parts of *Sida glutinosa* (Das *et al.*, 2011) and *Cichorium intybus* L. (Saied *et al.*, 2011).

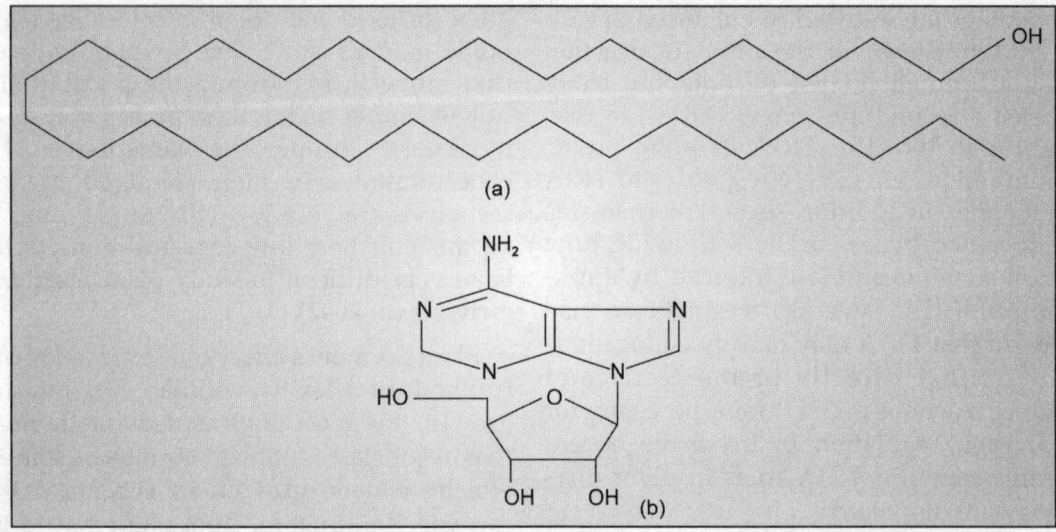

(a)

(b)

Fig. 5.1: (a) Structural formula of Triacontanol; (b) Molecular representation of secondary messenger responsible for growth stimulating properties of triacontanol through signal transduction approach

TRIA also found during bioassay guided isolation of methanolic extract of the leaves of *Origanum vulgare* L. There are no previous reports in the literature on the chemical composition of the *Phoradendron brachystachyum*, a potential source of hypoglycaemic and anti-hypersensitive compounds. There are 19 hypoglycaemic and anti-hypersensitive compounds extracted from this herb in which TRIA is one and other including β-sitosteryl and stigmasteryllinoleates, β-sitosterol, stigmasterol, TRIA, squalene, α- and β-amyrin, lupeol, lupenone, betulin aldehyde, betulon aldehyde, oleanolic aldehyde, betulinic acid, betulonic acid, moronic acid, morolic acid, oleanolic acid, flavonoids acacetin and acacetin 7-methyl ether.

TRIA having therapeutic activities, *viz.* anti-inflammatory and anti-ulcer properties and can used as active biomarker for the identification and standardization of stereospectrum suaveolens extract in the method of high performance thin layer chromatography. Klick *et al.* (2010) assessing the potentialities of *Lemna minor* (L.) for the treatment of reactive dyes polluted wastewaters and investigating the possibility of bioremoval performance stimulation by adding TRIA to the cultures. It has been well-documented that excess concentrations of boron causes toxic effects on many of the environmental systems. TRIA and BG11 media can increase the removal efficiency of Chlorella species to excess concentration of boron by increasing biomass.

Mode of Application and Applied Concentrations

The application method is an important factor in TRIA effectiveness. TRIA, both the natural and synthetic forms, applied as a foliar spray has been shown to increase the yield of several field crops. Foliage spray application of TRIA in nutrient medium increased the dry weight of rice seedlings, corn, barley and tomato

plants. However, it has been found that TRIA increased the height of corn shoots, but not the weight. Eriksen *et al.*, (1981) observed that TRIA applied in the nutrient solution in which tomato plants are grown enhanced their vegetative growth, photosynthetic rate and decreased the rate of photorespiration. However, TRIA showed no effect on the vegetative growth, and photosynthesis in maize. Also, its foliar spray to tomato plants increased the total yield and the number of fruits from all plants as compared to the control group. However, TRIA added to the growth medium increased total yield, and the number of fruits. The percent dry matter of the fruits is not significantly different, which indicates that the increase in fresh weight is not due to an increase in water uptake.

Moreover, TRIA-stimulated increase in tobacco callus is shown to be an increase in cell number and not simply caused by after uptake and cell enlargement. The difference in TRIA effects may be due to differences in the availability to the plants. When TRIA is applied in the growth substrate, it can have formed complex bindings with the rock wool or leaching caused by watering can have reduced its availability. Relative to the mode of action of exogenously applied TRIA to acidic mist seedlings, it is postulated that TRIA may quickly absorbed into the plant and probably is active in an unaltered form.

TRIA may act on the membrane in such a way that an enzyme(s), or secondary messengers L(+)-adenosine are triggered causing in cascading effect resulting in increased metabolism and the accumulation of various critical intermediary metabolic compounds, which result in an increase in dry weight and growth. The other possible recognized modes of action explain the synthesized unsaturated fatty acids in TRIA-treated leaves partially protect the cellular systems against acidic mist or due to the significant increase in MDDG and DGDG involved in the packing of photosystem against acidic mist. Previous observations in crop plants such as cucumber, tomato and maize plants following a foliar application of TRIA suggest that L(+)-adenosine triggered by TRIA acts by eliciting a rapidly propagated signal that increases the concentration of several ions in the apoplast. It postulated that modulations in apoplastic ion concentration, especially increase in Ca^{2+}, Mg^{2+} and K^+, constitute a mechanism by which plant regulates metabolic activity and growth in response to certain stimuli (Ries *et al.*, 1992). The effectiveness of foliage spraying of TRIA is supported by the observation that it resulted in an increase in nitrogen content of sweet potato leaves and yield of other crops. Studies have shown that TRIA applied either to the root medium or to the leaves as a foliar spray, enhanced both the growth and the yield of vegetables and cereals crops (Ries *et al.*, 1977; Ries *et al.*, 1982). In some cases, when treating rice seedlings with TRIA, a growth response is noticeable as early as three to six hours after treatment (Ries and Wert, 1977).

Exogenous application of TRIA has earlier been found beneficial in improving the herbage yield as well as leaf-artemisinin content in *Artemisia annua*. Srivastava and Sharma (1991) investigated the effect of various levels of TRIA on *Mentha arvensis* L. under control conditions in the greenhouse. They reported that TRIA application at 0.1 gm⁻³ increased the herb yield, essential oil yield as well as fresh and dry matter production of *Mentha arvensis*. They also reported the inhibitory effect of high dose of TRIA (4 gm⁻³) on the oil yield is largely due to its negative effect on biomass production and that there was no direct effect of TRIA on biomass and oil quality. Further, the inhibitory effect of high TRIA dose on photosynthetic rate is largely due to the toxic effect of Cu and Zn, unlike Fe and Mn, continued to increase in the mint leaves even at higher doses of TRIA. Such as negative effect of higher dose of TRIA (10^{-5} M) in comparison to that of 10^{-6} M TRIA might

have also possibly lowered the values of various parameters in *M. arvensis*.

The spray of 10^{-6} M TRIA proved the best and increased the values of all the growth attributes like plant height, leaf area, leaf-yield, plant fresh weight and plant dry weight. In contrast, 10^{-5} M TRIA caused an adverse effect on all the growth attributes at different growth stages and gave significantly lower values in comparison to 10^{-6} M TRIA, but it proved significantly better than the control in case of *M. arvensis*. Also, among the four TRIA concentration applied (10^{-3}, 10^{-4}, 10^{-5}, and 10^{-6} M), foliar application of TRIA at 10^{-6} M maximally accelerated the rate of photosynthesis and stomatal conductance over control *M. arvensis* L. The TRIA, applied at 10^{-6} M concentration, caused a significant increase in the total chlorophyll and carotenoids content, leaf phenolic contents, N-P-K contents, herbage yield, essential oil content, menthol, L-menthone, isomenthone and menthyl acetate compared to that of control at 10^{-6} M TRIA, values of the chlorophyll pigments decreased at 10^{-5} M TRIA, however, the TRIA (10^{-6} M) concentration gave significantly higher values of the photosynthetic pigments in comparison to the control.

The effects of TRIA on metabolic pools that have been measured in the laboratory may have some interesting practical aspects (Ries, 1985). Foliar studies of TRIA are applied in florida groves at 1 to 5 µg/L 2 to 3 weeks prior to harvest and stimulated sugar concentration and/or reducing acid concentrations. The growth of two weeks old rice seedlings is stimulated by foliar application of TRIA at a very low concentration (10 µg/L). This concentration increased dry weight, protein and chlorophyll content and leaf photo-synthetic rate significantly over control. Moreover, spray of aqueous 0.1% Tween 20 containing TRIA solution increased chloro-phyll and carotenoid contents of radish seedlings as well as also maintained the overall polypeptide level in a relatively high state in senescing cotyledons chloroplast than control and thus helps provide structural integrity to the chloroplast membrane in the cotyledons in radish seedlings (Duck Jin and Hong, 1988). Spray of TRIA concentration 100 µg/L may stimulate a change in chemical composition of the rice seedlings by altering plant metabolism (Knowles and Ries, 1981). Khan *et al*. (2006) reported that soaking of seeds of tomato (*Lycopersicon esculentum* L) with TRIA at 1.00 ppm enhanced most parameters of growth, yield and quality.

However, non-photochemical quenching coefficient (Φn) and non-radiative dissipation (NPQ) are decreased. When rice seedlings are treated by foliar spray of TRIA (2.3×10^{-8} M), an enhancement in growth is observed as early as 3 hours after treatment (Ries and Wert, 1977). The studies of Eriksen *et al*. (1981) reported that this concentration does not produce a rapid growth response, so they increased the concentration (5.7×10^{-8} M) which also failed to produce the desired response in same plant. In foregoing studies further they using a higher concentration (2.3×10^{-7} M), but even again their attempt is unsuccessful. They also taken TRIA concentration (2.3×10^{-7} M) for tomato and reported the significant increase in the dry weight. Therefore, they concluded the difference in the response of C3 and C4 plants to TRIA application indicates that it regulates processes related to photosynthesis. Moreover, 10 mM TRIA (50 mL/pot) is sprayed once in every two days interval for a period of 20 hours on salt stressed soya bean plants and showed an increase in vegetative growth, chlorophyll content and dry weight. Srivastava and Sharma (1991) mentioned that inhibitory effect of high dose of TRIA (4 gm^{-3}) on the oil yield is largely due to its negative effect on biomass production and that there was no direct effect of TRIA on biomass of oil or its quality. Further, they added that inhibitory effect of high TRIA dose on photosynthetic rate is largely due to the toxic effect of Cu and Zn,

unlike Fe and Mn, continued to increase in the mint leaves even at higher doses of TRIA. Such as negative effect of higher dose of TRIA (10^{-5} M) in comparison to that of 10^{-6} M TRIA might have also possibly lowered the values of various parameters in Naeem *et al*. (2011) study.

Evidences for Growth Promoting Properties

Evidence of the growth promoting effect of long chain alcohols can be traced back to 1959, when Crosby and Vlitos demonstrated enhanced elongation of Avena coleoptiles sections, Jones *et al*. (1979) observed no effects by fatty alcohols other than TRIA. Jones *et al*. (1979) demonstrated that a chain length of 30 C with a terminal –OH is specific for TRIA's growth promoting activity. Tests of the growth-promoting activity of TRIA analyses, varying in chain length from 16–32 C proved negative. Favourable effects of TRIA on plants are discovered for the first time by Ries *et al*. (1977). Rice, maize and tomato plants are treated with a range of alcohols (C-16 to C-32), all of which failed to stimulate growth. TRIA is a slow plant growth hormone (Ries *et al*., 1989). Because of this slow response, TRIA is added twice a week throughout the study of Eriksen *et al*., (1981). It is evident that the response to TRIA treatment is greater in young leaves. Favourable effect of TRIA on plants is discovered for the first time by Ries *et al*. (1977). It appeared then that TRIA extracted from alfalfa and applied to plants showed properties of growth regulator. Since then, the interests of TRIA have widely increased and many experiments conducted proved it has positively affected the growth and yield of plants, chlorophyll content and photosynthesis activity in plants.

However, although the plant received TRIA for four weeks, the oldest leaf has already stopped growing at the onset of TRIA treatment. Thus TRIA does not induce a new growth period in fully developed leaves. The middle leaf hads already emerged and started to grow by the time the TRIA treatment is begun, while the youngest leaf is exposed to TRIA throughout its development. This difference in the response of leaves at different stages of development could explain why a fast response is not observed, since the whole plant is analyzed and not only the youngest, most actively growing parts.

The study of growth stimulating effect of the TRIA is first observed by Ries et al. (1977). In this trend, further studies have shown that TRIA applied either to the root medium or to the leaves as a foliar spray, enhanced both the growth and the yield of vegetables and cereals crops (Ries et al., 1977). Moreover, octacosanol (C-28) caused inhibition even in trace amounts. Thus fatty alcohols, especially TRIA seem to enhance the growth and yield of many crops. Therefore, one can assume that TRIA in some way regulates process related to production. In some cases, when treating rice seedlings with TRIA, a growth response is noticeable as early as three to six hours after treatment (Ries and Wert, 1977). Furthermore, addition of the TRIA to the root medium of tomato plants increased the growth after about 3 weeks of treatment. TRIA induced growth enhancement and increase of yield have been described for several different plant species, including tomato (Ries et al., 1997; Bittenbender et al., 1978). In studies of Eriksen et al. (1981), TRIA appears as an impressive growth regulator, since growth stimulation can be observed after only one or a few applications (Srivastava and Sharma, 1990).

Several years later, TRIA is shown to increase the dry weight, leaf area. TRIA-induced growth increase in rice proved to be independent of light conditions, and CO_2 concentration appeared to play a regulatory rather than a substrate role (Bittenbender et al., 1978). Recent researches on a variety of plant species have provided convincing for this property. TRIA $[CH_3(CH_2)_{28} CH_2OH]$ and

its second messenger L(+)-adenosine possess a growth stimulating activity in many agricultural and horticultural crops (Ries, 1991). In ornamental plants, it can be used to activate the micropropagation. It has great stimulating effect on various processes including growth, protein content, improved the rate and extent of plants growth and also stimulates photosynthesis and several enzyme activities.

Past decades have witnessed much success in increasing the yields of food crops and vegetables with TRIA. Most profound effect of TRIA is increase in growth, biomass, free amino acids, reducing sugars, increase in photosynthetic activities and soluble proteins (Muthuchelian et al., 1995). Exogenous application of TRIA to barley roots results in a rapid stimulation of membrane associated Ca^{+2}/Mg^{2+} dependent ATPase activity in a calmodulin-dependent manner. Besides this, activity of NADH oxidase of the plasma membrane is potentiated by TRIA application. Moreover, dynamic membrane studies reveal an increase in the fluidity of membranes in vitro. Plants respond very rapidly to TRIA application. Whole rice and maize plants respond to TRIA application within 10 minutes. The response of whole plants has been characterized by increases in dry weight, leaf area and level of reducing sugars, amino acids, soluble protein, and total nitrogen content (Ries, 1985). An increase in dry weight has been assumed as the result of the increased photosynthetic activity and the accumulation of photosynthates.

Furthermore, TRIA is used to increase crop yields on millions of hectares, particularly in Asia. Many researchers have reported the enhanced growth and yield of plants with application of TRIA. When applied in field conditions, TRIA also showed an increase in vegetative growth, chlorophyll content and dry weight of various plants (Ries, 1985). However, TRIA showed no effect on the vegetative growth, or photosynthesis of maize.

Earlier studies using tomato (Borowski 2000) showed that TRIA introduced into roots increased this yield of fruits. However, it has no significant influence on the plant's association surface, which can suggest that TRIA mostly affected the elevated photosynthesis efficiency per leaf's surface unit. Such action of TRIA can result from its effect on leaf stomata, transpiration, carboxylase RuBP activity or activity of primary photochemical reactions. TRIA increased fresh and dry weight and total reducible nitrogen of rice seedlings. Increase in total nitrogen in the seedlings is shown to be independent of methods of nitrogen analysis and the presence of nitrate in the plants. TRIA does not alter the nitrate uptake or endogenous level of nitrate in corn and rice seedlings. TRIA increased the soluble nitrate pools of the plants, specifically the free amino acid and soluble protein fractions. TRIA may stimulate a change in the chemical composition of the seedlings, resulting in interference with standard methods of nitrogen analyses.

With regards with medicinal plants, TRIA improves the plant growth as well as yield and quality characteristics of various crops and increases the rate of several biochemical and physiological processes (Ries, 1985; Ries, 1991). However, there are rare information regarding the effect of TRIA on medicinally important crops till date except that of work of Srivastava and Sharma (1991) who reported that TRIA possibly increased fresh and dry weight production, photosynthetic characteristics as well as essential oil yield of Japanese mint. Recently Naeem *et al.* (2011) also reported that TRIA might presumably be considered applicable for maximizing the productivity and quality of mint that is used as an important crop drug in the modern and as well as alternative systems of medicine. Since these parameters reflect the overall growth of the plant TRIA might help to boost up the overall growth yield and quality of the plant. The positive role of TRIA in increasing growth,

yield and quality as well as physiological processes of various medicinal plants including *Mentha arvensis, Artesemia annua, Ocimum carnosum, Papaver sominiferum* and Pelargonium species has been reported by various researchers (Srivasata and Sharama, 1990).

TRIA characteristically increases growth (dry weight) and apparent detectable nitrogen content. Both total nitrogen (mg/plant) and concentration of nitrogen (mg/g) may be increased. The concentration of nitrogen never decreased in plants treated with TRIA, even though the dry weight increased. Eriksen *et al.* (1981) reported the differential response of C3 and C4 plants for the application of TRIA. They suggested that TRIA treatment caused a significant increase in dry weight and leaf area of tomato leaves at different stages of development as well as TRIA showed largest increase in growth when TRIA treatment is initiated before bud formation in tomato. In maize (C4), no effect of the TRIA treatment on dry weight is observed. *In vivo* and *in vitro* ^{15}N depletion studies established that the apparent increase in total nitrogen from TRIA treatment does not come from the environment. TRIA-induced redistribution of ^{15}N within the seedling could not be detected in studies with differentially enriched nitrogen fractions of rice. The apparent increase in nitrogen appears to be interference by TRIA to systems for nitrogen analysis. TRIA probably alters plant metabolism leading to compositional or chemical changes which interfere with the methods for detecting total nitrogen studied in research.

Rice: A Model Plant for Studying the Growth Promoting Properties of TRIA

Plants respond very rapidly to TRIA application. Whole rice and maize plants respond to TRIA application within 10 minutes (Ries and Wert, 1982). The response of whole plants has been characterized by increase in dry weight, leaf area, and level of reducing sugars, amino acids soluble proteins and total nitrogen content (Ries, 1985). An increase in dry weight has been assumed as the result of the increased photosynthetic activity and the accumulation of photosynthates. However, a little is known about the molecular mechanism for these responses. Isolation and characterization of TRIA action since it can give clues to the biochemical pathways and physiological process that TRIA regulates, and reveals the components involved in TRIA signalling. Many methods have been developed to study differentially expressed genes. Notable among these is suppression subtractive hybridization. It is an improved method based on representational difference analysis (RDA), and it has provided new insights into many old stories about TRIA application. The TRIA-regulated genes in rice were isolated from cDNA library by differential screening with probes generated from the forward and reverse-suppression subtractive hybridization populations and confirmed by Northern blot.

Sequence analysis revealed that most of the upregulated genes encoded the photosynthetic and photorespiratory proteins. Two downregulated genes are identified as those encoding an ABA- and stress-related proteins and a wounding-related protein. TRIA increased photosynthesis activity at a wide range of photosynthetic photon flux densities (PFDs). Chen et al., (2002) isolated and characterized TRIA-regulated genes by a combination of SSH and differential screening of cDNA library in the rice. A large number of TRIA-responsive genes are photosynthesis associated ones. The photosynthesis-associated genes are upregulated, and the stressrelated genes are downregulated by TRIA. The work of Chen et al., (2002) providing a number of molecular markers for TRIA action as well as considered as a critical step towards a better understanding of the physiological processes that TRIA regulates at the molecular level in plants. The growth of two weeks old rice seedlings is stimulated by foliar application of TRIA at a very low concentration. A higher level of dry weight is observed in TRIA treated plants as compared to the controls after TRIA treatment. The protein and chlorophyll contents increased significantly in TRIA treated plants. Moreover, results of Chen et al. (2002) are consistent with previous reports where a growth response of rice seedlings is noticeable as early as after TRIA treatment. Leaf net photosynthetic rate (Pn) is higher in TRIA treated plants as compared to the controls. Leaf Pn did not exhibit a notable time course difference for both groups, and it remained a higher level among time courses in TRIA treated plants as compared to the controls.

Data of Chen et al. (2002) also suggested that TRIA increased photosynthesis persistently. In order to construct leaf Pn curves in TRIA treated and the control plants, leaf Pn was recorded at different photosynthetic PFDs. It increased rapidly with the increasing PFD until a plateau was reached regardless of treatment. They also support previous findings of other researchers about TRIA effects on the photosynthetic process. Total protein and chlorophyll contents and dry weight were increased significantly. Straightforwardness was seen with leaf Pn. At a given PFD, TRIA increased leaf Pn very quickly and persistent. However, it exhibited a higher level in TRIA treated plants. The increased level of leaf Pn by TRIA is more than TRIA controls. Leaf Pn reached to its highest at about 1,400 μmol m^{-2} s^{-1} in control plants, while it reached to its highest level at about 1,600 μmol m^{-2} s^{-1} in TRIA treated plants. Such all observations demonstrated that TRIA increased leaf Pn and light saturation point of rice plants. Pn reached to its highest level at about 1,400 μmol m^{-2} s^{-1} in control plants, while it reached to its highest level at about 1,600 μmol m^{-2} s^{-1} in TRIA treated plants.

Also such observations demonstrated that TRIA increased leaf Pn and light saturation point of rice plants. An ubiquitin cDNA is first confirmed by Northern blot not to be regulated by TRIA and is then used to normalize the signal difference on the membranes. Total of thirty clones are found to be upregulated and three are downregulated. Many fewer downregulated clones are obtained relative to the upregulated ones, possibly because their abundance in the TRIA-treated cDNA library is low. Sequences are determined from the putative 5′ end of the cDNA in order to enhance the profitability of obtaining a coding sequence. Northern blot analysis is employed to verify whether those candidate genes are really regulated by TRIA. Furthermore, dot blot analysis is performed to reveal the quantitative level to which the photosynthesis-associated genes are regulated by TRIA. The regulated levels of genes for photosynthetic carbon fixation and PS^{22} proteins are higher than those of genes for photorespiratory proteins. The regulated levels varied among different members of rbcS.

Mechanism of Action

Recent researches are needed about protocols that will ensure consistent results with both TRIA and L(+)-adenosine in growth chamber, greenhouse and diverse field studies. One hypothesis is that it may partially explain the increase dry weight is that water is incorporated into products of starch and protein hydrolysis in response to TRIA. Moreover, TRIA application caused simultaneous increase in soluble protein, reducing sugars and free amino acids (Ries, 1985). These changes are due to TRIA causing an increase in total dry weight and/or percent composition. Similar increases in the same metabolic constituents occurred in cell-free extracts of maize leaves treated with TRIA although the response is less rapid (Ries, 1985). There is evidence for very rapid movement of other compounds within the plants. Zucconi et al., (1980) showed that 14C-and H3-labeled sucrose moved 28 to 56 cm/S in bean leaves.

Efforts have been made to elucidate the mechanisms of TRIA action. Assumption of a cascade effect leads to the identification of 9-β-L(+)-adenosine as a second messenger of TRIA (Ries, 1991; Ries and Wert, 1982). Exogenous application of TRIA to barley roots results in a rapid stimulation of membrane-associated Ca^+/Mg^{2+} dependent ATPase activity (Lesniak et al., 1986) in a calmodulin-dependent manner (Lesniak et al., 1989). Besides that, activity of NADH oxidase of the plasma membrane is potentiated by TRIA application. Moreover, dynamic membrane studies also reveal an increase in the fluidity of membranes in vitro (Shripathi et al., 1997). All these seem to suggest a hormonal mode of action. However, how plants sense TRIA is not understood nor is it known how the signal is transduced to elicit an appropriate response. The discovery that TRIA elicited the formation or release of L(+)-adenosine in the root tissue of rice seedlings within one minute of application to the shoots (Ries et al., 1990). It is suggested that influence of TRIA rapidly increases the ratio of L(+)- to D(+)-adenosine at the surface of tonoplast. Moreover, TRIA may act on the membrane in such a way that an enzyme(s) or secondary messengers L(+)-adenosine are triggered causing in cascading effect resulting in increased metabolism and the accumulation of various critical intermediary metabolic compounds, which result in an increase in dry weight and growth. Many factors reduce the effectiveness of TRIA as a growth stimulator. This notation is supported by the fact that TRIA application increased ATPase activity of plasma membrane-enriched vesicles from barley in the presence of calmodulin (Lesniak et al., 1989). The most probable source of adenosine is AMP derived from ADP and ATP. A small enhancement in concentration of L(+)-adenosine may be result of the action of a specific enzyme on L(+)-AMP or L(+)-ADP or L(+)-ATP.

It seems that TRIA might enhance the intrinsic genetic potential of the plants to produce additional quantity of secondary metabolites like essential oil and proteins. The enhanced yield in TRIA-treated leaves might also be ascribed to the increased uptake of leaf-nutrients (N, P and K) that could have been subsequently used to enhance the formation of photosynthates and other metabolites. In fact, TRIA induces the activation of a number of membrane bound enzymes (Ries and Wert, 1982). The stimulation of these enzymes leads to dephosphorylation of forms of AMP, ADP and ATP, resulting in the formation of adenosine, which triggers the cascade of events leading to rapid physiological responses (Ries *et al.*, 1990; Ries, 1991). Ries and Wert (1982) suggested that TRIA, like other plant hormones, might activate enzymes or alter the function of cell membranes, which could trigger cascading effects resulting in increased metabolism and enhanced accumulation of various critical intermediate compounds. Thus, TRIA enhanced plant growth, photosynthesis and the overall plant metabolism might have accounted significantly for secondary metabolites production. Srivastava and Sharma (1991) maintained that inhibitory effect of high dose of TRIA on the yield is largely due to its negative effect on biomass production and that there is no direct effect of TRIA on biosynthesis of secondary products or its quality. Further, they added that inhibitory effect of high TRIA dose on photosynthetic rate, the content of defensive proteins and yield attributes are largely due to the toxic effect of Cu and Zn that, unlike Fe and Mn, continued to increase in the leaves of plants even at higher doses of TRIA. Such a negative effect of higher dose of TRIA, in comparison to that of lower doses TRIA, might have also possibly lowered the values of various characteristics. Thus, application of TRIA as spray could be used to enhance the crop productivity as well as the production of secondary products and other active defensive proteins (**Fig. 5.2**).

Therefore, now, it will be necessary to prove that one or more of those phosphorylated adenosines exist as the L(+)-enantiomers. In present time, remaining problems are of how TRIA induced adenosine and other source of L(+)-adenosine in plants rather AMP, ADP and ATP. Furthermore, now it is also a significant challenge to discover how TRIA and L-(+)-adenosine rapidly increase plant metabolism and how TRIA elicit L(+)-adenosine. Also, researches along with adenosine deaminase indicate that it is possible in untreated plants that the L(+)-adenosine may exist as an inactive racemic mixture with D-adenosine and the remaining adenosine exists as the D(−)-isomer. It is seen that when plants treated with TRIA, the non-racemic L(+)-adenosine is released to affect plant metabolic processes. There are precedents for specific activities of such chemical enantiomers. The various evidences are overwhelming that TRIA applied at nano-molar combinations may increase the yield or improve the quality of a diverse group of crop species. Identification of OCTAM and determining how it inhibits the activity of TRIA may lead to discovery of the site of TRIA and/or L(+)-adenosine action. The lack of consistency may be due to many factors such as many times, crop yield are not improved by using the recommended doses of the major plant nutrients (Ries, 1991). Moreover, Jones *et al,* (1979) demonstrated that a chain length of 30-C with a terminal −OH was specific for TRIA's growth activity or TRIA analogs, varying in chain length from 16 to 32-C, proved negative. In fact, these compounds restricted in inhibition of the TRIA response when applied simultaneously. Thus, the primary alcohols, octocosanol (28-C) and tetracosanol (24-C) are excellent inhibitors of the TRIA response at equimolar rates. The enhancement of growth by TRIA might result from an increase in effective leaf area, stimulation of photosynthesis, RuBPCase and NRA, modification in partitioning of

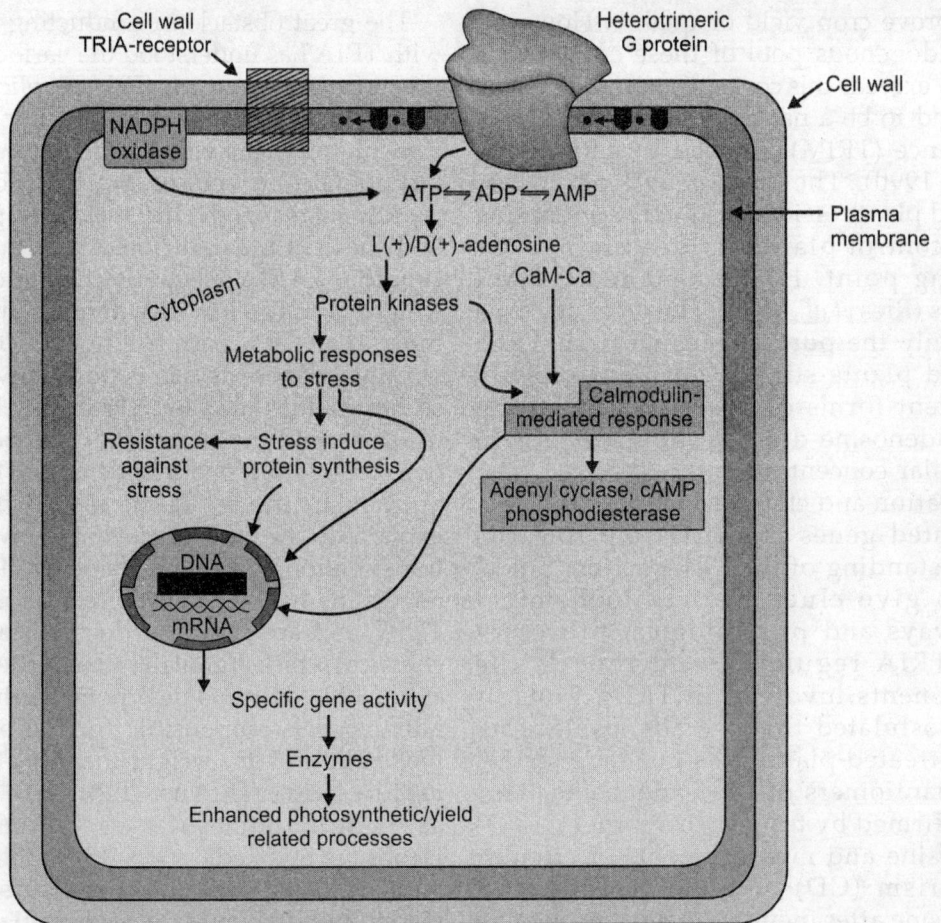

Fig. 5.2: Model representing the mode of signalling cascade modulated by triacontanol associated secondary messenger in plant system

photosynthesis, or from their cooperative effects. However, little is known about the molecular mechanisms for those responses. signalling. It is postulated that TRIA quickly observed into the plant and probably is active in an unaltered form. Inhibitory compounds, which have been reviewed in detail (Ries, 1985), include long chain alcohols, morpholine commonly found in distilled water from stem condensates and phthalate esters, particularly from polyvinyl chloride tubing.

What TRIA Stimulate L (+)-adenosine: Are L (+)-adenosine Act as Messenger of TRIA Action in Plant

TRIM is a second messenger in rice seedlings (Ries and Wert, 1988). Now, it has been identified as L(+)-adenosine. OCTAM (octacosanol) is also another second messenger which inhibits the activity of TRIA but not that of TRIM (Ries and Wert, 1988). It is also environment friendly or has no effect because its 0.1 to 1.0 mg amount applied per hectare to improve crop yield or quality. However, the endogenous pool of these compounds greatly exceeds this concentration. Adenosine is found to be a naturally occurring growth substance (TRIM) induced by TRIA (Ries et al., 1990). The adenosine from TRIA-treated plants is identical to the adenosine from control plants as determined by melting point, H^+ (proton) and C NMR studies (Ries et al., 1990). However, it is true that only the pure adenosine from TRIA treated plants stimulated plant growth. Different forms of adenosine including D(+)-adenosine did not stimulate growth at similar concentration.

Isolation and characterization of TRIA-regulated genes is a first step towards understanding of the TRIA action. Since, it can give clues to the biochemical pathways and physiological processes that TRIA regulates, and reveals the components involved in TRIA. Thus, it was postulated that the adenosine from TRIA-treated plants was L(+)-adenosine, the enantiomers of D(+)-adenosine. This is confirmed by tests with synthetic L(+)-adenosine and measurements of circular dichorism (CD) of the TRIA induced adenosine after incubation with adenosine deaminase (EC 3.5.4.4) which is specific for D(+)-adenosine.

Moreover, Oryza sativa L. seedlings treated with 1 µg/L of the L(+)-adenosine remaining after deamination of the D(−)-adenosine accumulated more dry weight than untreated plants in 24 hours (Ries, 1990). This adenosine is active as the L(+)-adenosine that is synthesized or obtained from TRIA after deamination. The L(+)-enantiomer of adenosine has not been reported previously as occurring in nature. 12% of the total adenosine in the roots of rice seedlings whose shoots had been sprayed with TRIA was found to be L(+)-adenosine compared to 1% L(+)-adenosine in the roots from control seedlings (Ries, 1990) **(Fig. 5.1b)**.

The great obstacle in conducting research with TRIA has understood the various responses of plants towards TRIA application. A few of the response plethora elicited are difficult to explain with current knowledge of physiological processes. For instance, TRIA rapidly increases the dry weight of plants in both the light and dark (Ries, 1985). In the light conditions, TRIA effectively enhanced the dry weight of maize shoots within 1 minute and more than 20% within 1 hour. Moreover, similar responses are reported with rice seedlings (Ries and Wert, 1988). The elicitation of the second messenger [L(+)-adenosine] in the roots within one minute after TRIA was applied to the foliage is also difficult to explain on the basis of current knowledge of translocation and enzyme kinetics. The L(+)-adenosine had the same effect on plants as TRIA, and apparently it does not elicit any chemical which stimulates plant growth (Ries et al., 1990). One logical point is that L(+)-adenosine is responsible for the observed metabolic and dry weight changes attributed to TRIA. Neither TRIA nor TRIM can be classified as plant hormones if the requirements of Jacobs are invoked (Jacobs, 1979). Since TRIA and TRIM are both endogenous ubiquitous compounds in plants and thus no plant organ can be removed leading to the cessation of the response? Although many specific responses have been demonstrated for TRIA, none has been shown to be directly responsible for the increase in growth caused by TRIM. A hypothesis is that plant metabolism is altered by TRIA or its second messenger L(+)-adenosine leading to compositional alterations which artificially alter the nitrogen determinants. Furthermore, supporting the idea that TRIA and/or L(+) adenosine eventually may be designated as hormones is the fact that both are active at picomolar concentrations which is well below the optimum concentration used for other plant hormones. In addition, L (+)-adenosine moves rapidly throughout plants (Ries et al., 1990).

Effects of TRIA on Various Parameters

Protein/Amino Acids

The trends of enhancement in protein and amino acid contents almost parallel with the activity of NRA (Kumaravelu et al., 2000). Such a positive correlation between NRA and leaf protein content after TRIA spray was also reported in Pennisetum (Muthuchelian et al., 1995). TRIA increased the protein content of tobacco cell cultures. The response involved an increase in cell number, indicating a stimulatory effect on the rate of protein synthesis. Metabolic profiling of extracts from rice seedlings grown in nutrient media containing D_2O showed that TRIA increased the incorporation of D_2O into several α-amino acids and organic acids. TRIA significantly increased the contents of sugar, starch, proteins and amino acids in the leaves at 20–30 DAS stages (Kumaravelu, 2000). Increase in the contents of leaf soluble proteins, starch, sugars and free amino acids in Erythrina, Oryza, Zea and Acacia leaves are also reported after TRIA treatment (Muthuchelian et al., 1995). Most profound effect of TRIA is increase in growth, biomass, free amino acids, reducing sugars, increase in photosynthetic activities and soluble proteins (Muthuchelian et al., 1995).

Chlorophyll

Increased chlorophyll content is reported after the foliar spray of TRIA at 3 weeks after sowing (Muthechelian et al., 1995; Kumaravelu et al. 2000). Perhaps the synthesis of Chl may be stimulated by low concentration of TRIA. Reduction of chlorophyll content observed at 30 DAS may be due to prevention of synthesis of Chl or due to increase in the breakdown of pigments or their precursors (Muthechelian et al., 1995). The carotenoid content is not significantly affected at 20 DAS, whereas at 30 DAS, increased dose of TRIA decreased the content of carotenoids (Kumaravelu et al., 2000). Enhanced content of photosynthetic pigments and other photosynthetic parameters may be the reasons for the increased biomass and saccharides and starch content. The optical density and total phenol contents are higher in both the stages compared to their respective contents (Kumaravelu et al., 2000). Moreover, the optical densities of phenols are known to increase whenever a stress is imposed on the plant.

Photosynthesis

TRIA is known to have a growth promoting activity when exogenously supplied to a number of plants. Earlier studies using tomato show that TRIA increased the yield of tomato fruits. However, it had no significant influence on the plant's assimilatory surface, which can suggest that TRIA mostly affected the elevated photosynthesis efficiency per leaf surface unit. Such action of TRIA can result from its effect on leaf stomata, transpiration, carboxylase RuBPCase activity or activity of primary photochemical reactions. Dry weight, protein and chlorophyll contents of rice seedlings are increased by foliar applications of TRIA. Leaf Pn is increased very quickly and persistently at a given PFD. Time course profiles of expression of rbcS isogenes suggested the complex mechanism involved in the regulation of photosynthesis promoted by TRIA. TRIA upregulated the photosynthesis process and suppressed stresses in rice plants (Chen et al., 2002). The study of Chen et al., (2002) also represented the first report on isolation and characterization of TRIA regulated genes in plants. As an important plant growth regulator, TRIA has attracted much attention in characterizing the physiological effects in a number of plants. However, the molecular mechanisms for TRIA action remain to be elucidated. Borowski et al. (2000) studied the effect of TRIA on chlorophyll fluorescence and tomato yield and have shown that TRIA regardless of the dose applied, significantly increased the maximum efficiency of PS-[22] photochemistry in the dark and consequently the actual quantum yield of PS-[22]. TRIA does not show univocal effects on dry matter content in fruits. (Kumaravelu *et al.*, 2000). PGRs such as TRIA which increase dry matter production may influence the inter-relationship between primary and secondary metabolisms leading to increased biosynthesis of secondary products. It has been also reported that the changes in essential oil synthesis due to PGRs is owing to the effect of these chemicals on enzymes of biosynthetic pathways. No effect of TRIA treatment could be observed in the oldest leaf (Eriksen *et al.*, 1981). The TRIA treated plants had a significantly higher rate of photosynthesis than the control plant. However, a significant difference is not found when comparing the TRIA treated plants with the control treatment because it did not affect the rate of photosynthesis in air.

Moreover, higher rbcS levels were associated with improved photosynthetic activity in TRIA treated plants. Most of the rbcS genes are induced rapidly and so are increased leaf Pn. Higher psbO transcript levels indicated an increase in photosystem efficiency in TRIA treated plants. GDC and SHMT are involved in the glycine cleavage of the photorespiratoty process. These enzymes catalyze the interaction of two molecules of glycine to form a molecule of serine, CO_2, NH_3 and to reduce NAD^+ to NADH concomitantly. Increase in the transcript levels of the gene for the P protein of GDC and SHMT indicate a higher photorespiration activity in TRIA treated plants. Interestingly, the extent to which the transcripts regulated by TRIA differed among different members of rbcS. In addition, time-course expression of rbcS isogenes revealed five different profiles. Except for Rtr4, others are induced as quickly after treatment, suggesting that Rtr3, others expressed at a high level after treatment, indicating rbcS isogenes are induced persistently rather than transiently. rbcS belongs to a gene family that consists of many members.

Previously, it has been shown that the expression pattern varies among different members. Chen *et al.* (2002) did not know exactly the evolutionary significance for various regulated patterns of rbcS. However, their study demonstrated the complex regulation mode for rbcS expression. Further studies on the regulation mechanism are needed to deepen our understanding of photosynthetic assimilation and TRIA application. The study of Chen *et al.* (2002) would also contribute to a better understanding of the molecular response of plants to TRIA. If TRIA merely reduces the time, it takes for a leaf to reach maturity; the difference in size would be temporary. Whether temporary or permanent, an enhanced growth rate is the result of an increase in net production which could be caused by, among other things, an increase in the rate of net photosynthesis in air. It is well-known that the photosynthetic rate increases as the leaf develops, passes a maximum and declines during senescence. It is thus important to compare leaves in a similar stage of development, but if TRIA enhances the growth rate, these leaves will be somewhat older than the control leaves. The inhibitory effect of O_2 on photosynthesis can be calculated by comparing the rate of photosynthesis at different O_2 concentrations and this inhibition is an expression of photorespiration. However, it should be taken into consideration that O_2 has been shown to inhibit photosynthesis directly.

Carbonic Anhydrase, Net Photosynthetic Rate and Stomatal Conductance

TRIA reported to accelerate the rate of photosynthesis and stomatal conductance (gs). Since the gs showed considerable importance in the TRIA treated plants, a significant increase in the rate of photosynthesis could obviously be expected. Such an increase in photosynthesis has presumably been reported as an important plant response to

TRIA, which in turn, might be associated with the increase in leaf chlorophyll content. Several earlier researches have also revealed a TRIA mediated increase in the rate of both CO_2 fixation and photosynthesis in *M. arvensis* L. as well as in other plants (Srivastava and Sharma, 1991; Chen *et al.*, 2002). In case of *Mentha arvensis* L. the increase in the gs and CA by TRIA application first reported by Naeem *et al.* (2011) also. They suggest that the increase in carbonic anhydrase (CA) by TRIA treatment is expected because TRIA increased the gs significantly that might have facilitated a comparatively higher diffusion of CO_2. In fact, CA catalyzes the reversible hydration of CO_2, thereby making available the ribulose-1, 5-biphosphate carboxylase/oxygenase (RuBis CO) in the chloroplast stoma. The enhancement of CA activity due to TRIA application might also be associated to the *de novo* synthesis of CA, which might involve the genes associated with its transcription and translocation in the cells. The enhancement of CA activity in the treated plants might have, presumably, been responsible for the enhanced rate of CO_2 fixation that accordingly could have resulted insignificant increase in the fresh and dry weight of TRIA treated plants (Kumaravelu *et al.*, 2000; Muthuchelian *et al.*, 2003).

RuBPCase Activity

Debata and Murty (1981) showed that TRIA enhanced ^{14}C-photosyntheis and mobilization of photosynthates to the panicle of rice cultivars. Houtz *et al.*, (1985a) reported that the increase in photosynthetic CO_2 assimilation in Chlamydomonas cells treated with TRIA could be measured after 1 hour of treatment, before any change in cell density is demonstrable. Especially, Erikson *et al.*, (1981) also observed that TRIA reduced oxygen inhibition of photosynthesis in tomato plants and Haugstad *et al.*, (1983) also found the same result in Chlamydomonas. These results indicate that

TRIA regulates profound effects on plants is an increase in dry weight (Ries and Wert, 1977). It follows that photosynthetic CO_2 assimilation may be a factor involved in the response of plants to TRIA. Therefore, changes in the total activity of RuBPCase in relation of TRIA treatment in radish cotyledons with age were investigated.

The features of TRIA effect on RuBPCase activity are divided into two phases with respect to cotyledon age. As compared with controls at the early development stage increase in total RuBP-Case activity is obtained in TRIA treated cotyledons. In senescencing cotyledons the value of RuBP-Case activity of TRIA treated cotyledons is higher than control. Houtz *et al.*, (1985b) showed that increase in photosynthetic CO_2 assimilation of TRIA treated Chlamydomonas cells is a result of an increase in RuBPCase activity. Such results indicate that TRIA can promote a growth and a mechanism for increasing photosynthetic CO_2 fixation via RuBPCase activity regulation. Moreover, Makino *et al.*, (1983) reported that RuBPCase activity is highly correlated with the Pn from leaf development through senescence.

CO_2 fixation via RuBPCase activity regulation may be a factor involved in the response of plants to TRIA (Duck Jin and Nam-Hong, 1988). Exogenously applied TRIA have specific regulation effects on chloroplast development within growing radish seedling with respect to chlorophyll content, CP (chloroplast-protein)-complexes, thylakoid polypeptides, ribosomal RNA and RuBPCase activity. Treharne *et al.* (1970) already showed that application of hormones such as cytokinin and gibberellin to fully expanded leaves of dwarf bean stimulated the RuBPCase activity. At the same time, however, they found that the increase in enzyme activity is not parallel by synthesis of chloroplast r-RNNA and fraction protein. In relation to TRIA treatment, the increase in RuBPCase activity is primarily associated with altered activation state or with the change of RuBPCase protein level. Some investigations have reported that loss of RuBPCase activity during senescence is caused by loss of enzyme protein. Thus, the mechanism to maintain RuBPCase activity in a relatively high state in a few days old cotyledon with TRIA treatment presumably the result of senescence retardation effect of TRIA. However, the reason for increasing in RuBPCase activity in TRIA treatment young cotyledons remains to be answered, too. Indeed, the chloroplast is one of the suitable organelles systems in both structure and function during cotyledons development. Thus, the chloroplast development as a useful assay system in a growth response to TRIA (Duck Jin and Nam-Hong, 1988).

Senescence and Chloroplast Development

The chloroplast development after application of TRIA in germinating radish seedling showed differential response on chlorophyll content, chlorophyll-protein (CP) complexes, thylakoid polypeptides, chloroplast and cytoplasmic ribosomal RNAs and RuBPCase activity. In the chloroplast isolated from young cotyledons, TRIA is efficient in promotion of all the above traits in contrast with non-treated control. Especially, total activity of RuBPCase which is a marker enzyme in photosynthesis, is increased by TRIA over non-treated control. Also, in senescencing cotyledons chloroplast, however, TRIA showed favourable influence on stabilization of structure and function of chloroplast with respect to these characters. These findings suggest the chloroplast acts as a useful assay system to study the plant growth response of TRIA (Duck Jin and Nam-Hong, 1988).

Application of TRIA has been shown to reduce the photorespiration, expressed as the O_2 inhibition of photosynthesis, in tomato and corn (Eriksen *et al.*, 1981), and in chlamydomonas (Haugstad *et al.*, 1983). TRIA also

enhanced photosynthesis and mobilization of photosynthates in rice (Debata and Murty, 1981) and increased the photosynthetic CO_2 assimilation as well as RuBPCase activity in chlamydomonas (Houtz *et al.*, 1985a; b). Because, the chloroplast is a well-defined plant subsystem in which developmental processes have been characterized. Therefore, chloroplast will be a good target to clarify the biochemical nature of TRIA response in plant growth. The chloroplast content of cotyledons in both the control and the TRIA treatment increased during early cotyledons growth and reached maximum values after germination. Thereafter, Duck Jin and Nam-Hong (1988) showed a decline through cotyledon senescence.

As compared with control, chlorophyll accumulation in TRIA-treated cotyledon in early development stage increased rapidly and degradation of chlorophyll in the late stage by the cotyledons senescence was remarkably retargeted. The result of study of Duck Jin and Nam-Hong (1988) is well consistent with the reports of TRIA-induced chlorophyll retention in oat and rice leaf senescence and the observation of TRIA-promoting chlorophyll increase in corn and rice (Ries *et al.*, 1981). On the chlorophyll degradation in senescencing cotyledon, three possible enzymatic degradative processes as well as a photo-oxidation of pigment have been reported. Among three enzymes, *viz.* chlorophyllase, lipoxygenase and peroxidase predominantly found in plant materials, bleaches chlorophyll in the presence of H_2O_2 and certain phenolics. Therefore, the role of TRIA in peroxidase activity for controlling the chlorophyll degradation ought to be elucidated in future studies. Foliar senescence is characterized by a major change in the chloroplast structure and function. Growth regulator like benzyl adenine may induce mRNA synthesis directing chlorophyll synthesis in the etioplast in the dark and increases the amount of proteins necessary for chlorophyll synthesis in the light. Therefore, the chloroplast can be used to determine the mechanism of action of TRIA.

Generally, two major CO_2-complexes are associated with the chloroplast thylakoid membranes of higher plants. These two complexes, commonly referred to as P700 chlorophyll, a protein complex (CPI) and light-harvesting chlorophyll a/b protein complex (LHCP or CP22), differ in total amount of bound pigment, in relative content of chlorophyll and carotenoids, in their amino acid compositions and apparent molecular weight as well as in their postulated roles in the photosynthetic process. Additionally, numerous CP-complex band patterns as presented in five pigment bands of some higher plants, six pigments bands of lettuce, six pigments bands of mustard have been described. As compared with controls, the increase of quantities in both CP2 and CP22 are detected under the TRIA treatment. It means that this increase may be coupled with a concomitant increase in the biological action of CP2 and CP22 in TRIA treated radish chloroplasts. Furthermore, this relation to the chlorophyll content and the increased thylakoid polypeptides of TRIA-treated cotyledons seem to be significant.

Also, TRIA induced some changes in the CP-complexes pattern in chloroplasts from one-week-old cotyledons as compared with non-treated cotyledons. The degradation of CPI and CPII due to the cotyledon senescence was retarded by TRIA treatment. Because TRIA is known as a senescence retardant, this result may be probably due to a stabilization of membrane integrity of chloroplasts induced by TRIA treatment. The protein subunit of CPII, in turn, is the single largest component of the chloroplast membrane protein. Because the two CP-complexes account for the majority of the chloroplast thylakoid mass, the characterization of their protein moiety and its relationship to individual polypeptides are obvious interest. Moreover, Ries *et al.* (1977) postulated that such a lipoidal substance with terminal polar groups as TRIA may have specific effects on membrane. Axelos and Peaud-Lenoel (1980) have found the apo-protein of the light-harvesting chlorophyll complex serves as a molecular marker of cytokinin activity using tobacco cells. Therefore, developmental changes of chloroplast thylakoid polypeptides in radish cotyledons from one-week and two-week-old seedlings and the effects of TRIA thereon are examined by SDS-PAGE. When comparing with controls and TRIA treated cotyledons from 4-day-old seedlings, accumulation of 2S and 25S RNAs are promoted in a relatively high level in the TRIA-treated cotyledon. In senescencing cotyledons from one-week-old seedlings, however, the phenomenon of maintaining 23-S chloroplast rRNA is conspicuous under the TRIA treatment. In addition, TRIA is effective in causing the retention of cytoplasmic rRNAs (25S + 18S) during senescence. The results of Duck Jin and Nam-Hong (1988) are interesting in relation to the effect of TRIA on the developments of CP-complexes and thylakoid polypeptides. However, the precise mechanism of TRIA action on rRNA accumulation remains to be ascertained, up-to-date.

Photorespiration

It is also known that photorespiration increases with age. The observed difference in sensitivity to O_2 could be even larger if leaves in exactly the same stage of development are compared, and this decrease in the sensitivity to O_2 could explain the increase in growth. Although it is evident that photosynthesis of young leaves from TRIA treated plants is less sensitive to changes in the O_2 concentration than the control plants (Eriksen *et al.*, 1981). TRIA treatment increases the yield of tomato plants. If the TRIA induced growth enhancement is merely temporary and does not give a larger plant, then the increase in yield could be explained if the decreased sensitivity to O_2 persists in older leaves. Even though the rate of photosynthesis of tomato plants treated with TRIA are less sensitive to O_2, other processes related to production such as an increased ion uptake, may have contributed to the enhanced growth rate. The rate of net photosynthesis of maize (a C4 plant) that is insensitive to changes in O_2 levels, offered a system where the effect of TRIA on processes other than the effect of oxygen on photosynthesis could be studied.

However, when treating maize with TRIA during the vegetative growth period, no effect of TRIA is found. Prolonged treatment did not affect the vegetative growth, or the rate of photosynthesis and dark respiration. This difference found in the response of C4 plants and C3 plants to TRIA treatment indicates that TRIA in some way regulates processes related to photosynthesis, especially that part of photosynthesis which is affected by the CO_2/O_2 ratio. In maize, no change in photosynthesis could be observed, neither after altered oxygen concentration nor after TRIA treatment. The difference in the response of C3 and C4 plants to TRIA indicates that it regulates processes related to photosynthesis.

Moreover, Eriksen et al. (1981) studies also deal with the effect of TRIA on vegetative growth and especially its effect on photosynthesis, photorespiration and dark respiration. The C3 and C4 plants are studied and reported that net production in C3 plants is affected by the rate of respiration while net production of maize is relatively unaffected. Since in C3 plants, the rate of photorespiration is important for net production. Moreover, the rate of photorespiration is affected by the CO_2/O_2, a high CO_2/O_2 ratio favouring photosynthesis. Therefore, the rate of photosynthesis is also studied in O_2 and this low O_2 concentration increased the rate of photosynthesis. While the TRIA treated plants are less sensitive to O_2, only decreasing photosynthesis. Furthermore, TRIA treatment did not affect the chlorophyll content or the chlorophyll a/b ratio. Addition of the TRIA to the root medium of tomato plants increased the growth after about three weeks of treatment.

Yield Attributes

TRIA, both the natural and synthetic forms applied as a foliar spray has been shown to increase in the yield of several field crops. Foliage spray and application of TRIA in nutrient medium increased the dry weight of rice seedlings, corn, and barley and tomato plants. However, it has been also found that TRIA increased the height of corn shoot, but not the weight. Most previous studies on TRIA have concentrated on physiological aspects of crops leading to effects on components of yield. Improved yield by TRIA application of several important food crops is shown by many researchers (Ries et al., 1977). Recent researches on a variety of plant species have provided convincing evidence for this property (Muthuchelian et al., 1996; Kumaravelu et al., 2000). In ornamental plants, it can be used to activate the micropropagation. Past decades have witnessed much success in increasing the yields of food crops and vegetables with TRIA (Eriksen et al., 1981; Ries, 1985). TRIA also speed up the flowering and improved the yield.

In addition, investigations of Srivastava and Sharma (1990) reveal that TRIA significantly enhances various processes related to production physiology as well as significantly maximize plant height, capsule number and weight, morphine content, CO_2 exchange rate, total chlorophyll and fresh and dry weights of the shoot in opium poppy. The primary processes, in turn, contribute significantly in increasing overall yield of straw, capsule and morphine content.

Since, TRIA has been reported to increase dry matter production and it possibly affects the inter-relationship between primary and secondary metabolisms of the plant. The effect of TRIA on alkaloids biosynthesis in medicinal plants including poppy and the relationship between alkaloid production (capsule and constituents) and physiological parameters related to productivity including CO_2 exchange rate, chlorophyll production, leaf area ratio, biomass production and ion uptake (Srivastava and Sharma, 1990). They also reported that TRIA has differential effect on uptake and distribution of micronutrients including Mn, Cu, Zn in poppy. Besides this, growth promoting effects of TRIA on vegetables (Ries *et al.*, 1977), cereals (Ries and Wert, 1977; Bittenbender *et al.*, 1978) and horticultural crops (Erikson *et al.*, 1981) are well documented. These are associated with increased protein content, water uptake (Hangarter *et al.*, 1978), uptake of elements (Ramani and Kanan, 1980) and photosynthetic CO_2 fixation (Erikson *et al.*, 1981). TRIA applied to tomato as a foliar spray caused a significant increase in total yield per plant. TRIA is added to the growth medium only a temporary increase in yield and a number of fruits are observed also. On the other hand, the yield of maize as unaffected by TRIA either applied to the leaves or to the growth substrate (Eriksen *et al.*, 1982). These findings result that a reduction in photorespiration is involved in the regulatory function of TRIA.

Seedlings of green gram (*Vigna radiata* L.) Wilczek cultivar KM-2 is sprayed with different concentrations of TRIA at 15 and 25 DAS and noticed the increase in the plant height, soluble proteins, amino acids and phenols (Kumaravelu *et al.*, 2000). Moreover, TRIA stimulated the onset of flowering, pod production and retention, but a less number of pods and seeds, leaf nitrate content are reduced with a parallel increase in NRA (Kumaravelu *et al.*, 2000). Increased uptake of nutrients, enhanced photosynthesis and improved translocation of photosynthates and other metabolites to the reproductive parts may have contributed to the production of more pods. Yield reduction by TRIA is due to reduced pod number and mass or seed number and mass per pod (Kumaravelu *et al.*,

2000). Furthermore, TRIA increased the root fresh mass more than the shoot fresh mass which may be due to an increased water absorption seen as an immediate response to low concentrations of TRIA or due to promotion of GA activation in the dark (Ries, 1985).

Artemisin yield is substantially influenced by the growth regulating substances (Shukla *et al.*, 1992). TRIA produced a statistically significant positive effect on artemisin level as well as on plant height, leaf and herbage yield. TRIA application enhanced GA-like activity but ABA levels decreased while Chloromequat increased ABA but reduced GA like substances. The effect of TRIA on artemisin yield seems to be mediated through its effect on plant growth. Plant height is affected significantly when TRIA and chloromequat were applied to the plants. Moreover, herbage and leaf yield per plant are affected substantially by the growth substances. TRIA significantly increased the herbage yield. However, effects of higher and lower concentrations are not statistically significant. Because herbage yield is affected by the same treatment, the artemisin yield per plant is affected in the same direction. Substantial effects of TRIA and Chloromequat on leaf and herbage yield have been demonstrated. These growth promoting effects of TRIA are consistent with the effects of TRIA and TRIA based formulations on certain cereals, horticultural oil crops and medicinal as well as aromatic plants (Ries and Wert, 1977; Ries *et al.*, 1977; Srivastava and Sharma, 1990). A substantial effect of TRIA and Chloromequat on artemisin yield was found like several other PGRs, e.g. GA3, kinetin, and NAA (Shukla *et al.*, 1992).

The model showed that the balance between production and utilization of photosynthates is an important determinant of oil accumulation and major components of the oil. As per the model, the rates of photosynthesis as well as the factors affecting photosynthesis were suggested to be the determining factors regarding oil accumulation (Srivastava and

Sharma, 1991). Since photosynthesis leads to the increase in total biomass of the plant, Srivastava and Sharma (1991) revealed a positive correlation between PN and the fresh and dry weights of the plant and argued that significant increase in the oil yield is due to the increase of biomass in TRIA-treated plants of *Mentha arvensis* L. They further claimed that the oil quality is practically not affected by TRIA application except at 0.1 and 4 gm^{-3} TRIA, where the change is due to increase and decrease in menthol content respectively. They maintained that increase in PN of the mint resulted in the increase in oil percentage and menthol content, whereas the decrease in PN is accompanied by lower menthol and higher menthone content that led to the positive correlation of PN with oil content and yield. However, in TRIA-treated plants, Naeem *et al.*, (2011) found a progressive increase in content and yield of active components of *Mentha arvensis* as compared to the control that might be ascribed to the TRIA mediated improvement in overall growth of the plants as revealed by TRIA-enhanced leaf-N, P and K contents, photosynthesis and growth and other physiological attributes. However, a positive effect of TRIA on mint oil components such as content and yield of isomenthone and menthyl acetate have been reported for the first time. TRIA application significantly increased the menthol and menthone contents of the mint have also been reported (Srivastava and Sharma, 1991). In fact, it has been reported that the composition of the essential oil of *Mentha arvensis* L. might be altered using plant growth regulators. The positive effect of TRIA on essential oil yield might be attributed to the TRIA-improved plant growth and metabolism as revealed by studies by Naeem *et al.* (2011).

Quality Parameters

The TRIA application also improved the leaf phenolic content in *M. arvensis* L. (Naeem *et*

al., 2011). The leaf phenolic contents reflect the free radical scavenging capability of the plant that may help the plant to maintain the normal growth at later growth stages, at which frequent production of free radicals takes place including bad effects of aging. The significant effect of TRIA application on phenol content also has been reported in green gram (*Vigna radiata* L.) (Kumaravelu *et al.*, 2000). Naeem *et al.*, (2011) also reported that application of TRIA improved the leaf-N, P and K contents at various stages of growth in *M. arvensis* L. Enhancement in leaf-nutreints contents, particularly the nitrogen due to the TRIA application could be attributed to the compositional or chemical change in plants leading to alterations in nitrogen concentration (Knowles and Ries, 1981; Kumaravelu *et al.*, 2000). The effect of TRIA is also prominent on content and yield of essential oil in *M. arvensis* L. In fact, the RI is a physical constant can be used against the adulteration of drugs as it is helpful to check the identity and purity of a compound. The improved content and yield of essential oil in TRIA treated plants could perhaps be ascribed to the enhanced rates of photosynthesis as pointed out by Srivastava and Sharma (1991) in the case of *Mentha arvensis* L. The growth and essential oil production of aromatic plants may be altered using several plant growth regulators. Being a potent PGR, TRIA is expected to augment the growth, yield and quality of *M. arvennsis* L. like other PGRs.

TRIA Application and Tissue Culture

Since plant cells can be maintained for extended periods in the apparent absence of all known plant hormones, it seems safe to conclude that no hormone is essential just to maintain the viability of plant cells (Davies, 1995). About 50 years ago, Skoog and Miller (1957) described the controlled organ regeneration in plants; however, developmental biologists are surprised by the unbelievable capacity of plant tissues to regenerate the whole plants. During the last few decades, several compounds have been synthesized to induce regeneration potential in plant cell. It is proved that TRIA, unlike traditional phytohormones, individually fulfilled the requirements of various regenerative responses of many different plant species (Pullman *et al.*, 2011). TRIA emerged as an effective bioregulant in cell and tissue cultures in wide array of plant species. These findings raised many tantalizing questions in plant morphogenesis, most obviously, how could one single compound induce such different results in different species and yet induce the same response in such a wide range of species. Somatic embryogenesis has the potential to be the lowest-cost method to rapidly produce a large number of high-value somatic seedlings with desired characteristics for plantation forestry. Successful initiation depends heavily on explant type, embryo developmental stage, and medium salt base. Most first reports of initiation used 2,4-D and BAP or a combination of cytokinins. Pullman *et al.*, (2011) reported that initiation can be stimulated with medium supplements including TRIA along with other substances like abscisic acid, brassinosteroids, ethylene inhibitors, gibberellin inhibitors, organic acids, putrescine, specific sugar types and D-xylose, vitamins. Moreover, the seeming contradiction provided the foundation for more than a decade of work to understand plant morphogenesis in TRIA regulated systems. The complex nature of the biochemical and morphological responses that have been reported for plant tissues exposed to TRIA has provided some indication of the cascade of physiological reactions within the plant tissues, but there have been relatively a few investigations that have utilized radio-labelled TRIA for characterization of the fate of the TRIA molecule.

In spite of intensive efforts over the last decade, the precise determination of the mode of action of TRIA in the induction of plant regeneration has remained elusive. TRIA is widely applied in plant *in vitro* or *in vivo* that influences a number of parameters in plants. A miscellaneous range of responses with a high grade of efficacy is induced via TRIA application. Some examples of the diversity of physiological effects mediated by TRIA include efficient seed germination, expedited bud break, induction and stimulation of sprouting, cotyledonary growth and development, formation of trichomes and stomata appearance on floral parts and cluster and berry weight of grapes. More recently, the morphoregulatory potential of the chemical has led to its application in plant cell, tissue and organ culture for the betterment of regeneration protocols. The exogenous application of TRIA affects concentration of endogenous plant growth regulators in some members of dicots. However, TRIA is involved in modification of cell membranes, energy levels, nutrient uptake and nutrient assimilation. In depth study of the physiological responses of plant cells to TRIA will lead to an insight of the process of morphogenesis. Plant cells have the potential to reproduce intact plant via organogenesis or embryogenesis. TRIA has the greatest influence on actively growing tissue has been also observed by Hangarter *et al.*, (1978) in callus tissue of tomato and tobacco.

Plant growth regulators play a role of backbone in process potentials, dedifferentiation and redifferentiation. These regenerative processes in cell and tissue cultures may be provoked by TRIA alone and in collaboration with other plant growth regulators. An array of complex physiological mechanisms like functions of an intact molecule in both/alone and in engaged system are involved in TRIA-treated somatic embryogenesis (Pullman *et al.*, 2011) and also, TRIA-treated tissues maintain and enhance the accumulation and transport of auxin. All these results suggest that TRIA has a keen role in the induction of growth regulator processes and physiological maintenance of plant tissues during culture process. The undifferentiated mass of cells is called callus and the process of callus formation is called callogenesis, which is the primary step in the stimulation of shoot reproduction via indirect mode and adventitious organs regeneration, where auxin is the best choice. In different plant culture systems, TRIA induced callogenesis, in some cases higher cell proliferation rate is achieved at comparable levels to other growth substances. TRIA indicates high intrinsic activity when compared with other plant growth substances due to low absorbance in callus. Protoplast technology has been used as a significant tool to produce new genotypes through para-sexual hybridization, genetic engineering, etc. It also provides opportunity to improve biologically active constituents in elite medicinal plant species. It is beneficial to understand the biosynthesis of secondary metabolites related to particular medicinal contents from combination of medicinal plants with altered metabolites and could contribute efficiently in rapid and steady production of unique secondary metabolites.

Protoplast technology is exploited to isolate plant derived secondary metabolites, where protoplast is isolated, cell division is induced and plant is regenerated. Rooting is difficult and a key step in plant micropropagation System. However, rooting reticence and several small plantlets regeneration resulted due to high values of suppression of cytokinin cessation and/or the consistent biosynthesis of purine cytokinin. Extensive progress has been made in many disciplines of plant organogenesis once the phytohormones are innovated and hormonal regulation is postulated (Skoog and Miller, 1957). Studies showed that TRIA is frequently associated with the metabolism of plant growth regulators. The two clusters of growth regulators, purine based cytokinin and phenylurea induce biotic response recommended a common location in the presence of competitive inhibitors. Even though TRIA have proved to be the best option for adventitious shoot organogenesis from carnation petals, but still, it is a mystery that whether phenylurea derivatives effect endogenous cytokinin metabolism directly or indirectly. It is proposed that TRIA stimulate auxin-like response as auxin application enhanced ethylene production. So it is likely to perceive that TRIA treatment may not cause leaf abscission directly, but as a result of TRIA mediated auxin response. Thus it is inferred that application of TRIA enhanced accumulation of minerals or other metabolites and predisposes the explant to stress. To get rid of this physiological constrain, the plant tissues reformed their metabolic pathways, the alternate result of which is the synthesis and storage of different metabolites and favouring the production of regenerates. In last few years, calcium signal response to TRIA has been made a point of doing. Calcium, a ubiquitous second messenger, plays the role of a facilitator of stimulus response pairing in the regulation of miscellaneous cellular activities. A calcium ion prickle produces when the calcium ion level in plants is getting to its peak due to maximum calcium ion influx and swift to basal level via calcium ion efflux, various stimuli responsible are: light, gravity, physicochemical and biological stresses and hormones. Response of plant cells to different hormones is due to external calcium concentration or rise in the level of this cation in the tissue. Thus TRIA was classified as plant growth regulator.

The mechanism of TRIA in the response of plant cells, especially in the plant tissue and organ culture is conjectured in relation with the balance of calcium concentration in plant tissue. This is substantiated by the effectiveness of TRIA at concentration of externally supplied calcium which is insufficient for shoot formation. In certain procedures, a two-fold culture system is conducted with pronounced success, where TRIA fortified initial medium induces shoot multiplication which is followed by secondary medium containing low level of TRIA or other phytohormones to enhance shoot organogenesis. However, in spite of the popularity of TRIA as a phyto-hormone and more than thirty years of research work, the exact biological role of TRIA is still a mystery.

TRIA and Abiotic Stress

High soil salinity or drought is the major environmental factor, which reduces the crop yield in the cultivated lands. The excess amount of soluble inorganic salts could alter the nature of soil through soil aeration, water and texture, and also affect the living organisms. Nearly 20% of the world's cultivated area is affected by soil salinity. Salinity leads to various metabolic disturbances resulting in general suppression of seed germination, plant growth and yield (Sharma and Saran, 1994). High concentration of ions in the external solution (Na^+, Cl^- or Ca^{2+}) that are taken up by roots at high rates may lead to excessive accumulation in the tissue. These ions may inhibit the uptake of other ions into the root (such as K^+) and their transport to the shoot through the xylem, eventually leading to a deficiency in the tissue. Thus, there is the potential for many nutrient interactions in salt stressed plants which may lead to important consequences for growth. Application of abiotic stresses resulted in an altered level of plant growth hormones that decreased plant growth. The yield of soyabean is reduced due to high salinity in the soil. Therefore, reduction in plant growth under stress conditions could be an outcome of altered hormonal balance, and hence their exogenous application provides an alternative approach to counter the stress conditions.

One of the downregulated clones is identified as a gene for the ABA-induced protein OsAsr. The OsAsr1 transcript has been reported to be upregulated by exogenous ABA, salt stress and mannitol stress in the shoot, the other downregulated clone is a gene for

wounding inducible protein WIP1, which shows significant homology to Bowman-Birk proteinase inhibitors. It has been reported that plant hormones regulate expression of proteinase inhibitors. Finding of stress-related genes in the study of Chen *et al.*, (2002) not only revealed the crosstalk between TRIA signal and others but also helped to understand the role that TRIA play role in stress responses. It has been found that TRIA extenuates the unfavourable effects of stress on proliferation of woody plants *in vitro*.

Moreover, Rajasekaran and Blake (1999) also find that TRIA can reverse the damaging effects of drought and enhance drought tolerance of pine seedlings. It has been found that TRIA inhibits lipid peroxidation (Chen *et al.*, 2002) know the breakdown products of lipid peroxidation have been implicated in triggering stress-related responses. All the data suggest that TRIA serves as an alleviant of stresses. An ABA and stress-related gene was downregulated by TRIA, and so is a wounding related gene. These observations provided an excellent explanation at the molecular level for the findings obtained elsewhere and also deepened our under-standing of the relationships between TRIA and stresses and confirmed the stimulating effects of TRIA on plant growth as well as increased photosynthesis activity at a wide range of PFD. In addition, TRIA is sprayed on the plants grown under the 20 mM NaCl added soil and reported the increase in specific leaf area, leaf weight ratio, and relative water content and decreased in leaf osmotic potential in plants treated with TRIA than salt stressed untreated plants (Krishnan and Kumari, 2008). Moreover, they also found that chlorophyll pigments, nucleic acids, total soluble sugars and proteins also found to be increased in the TRIA treated plants. The accumulation of proline is decreased in salt-stressed plants that have been treated with TRIA.

The exogenous application of TRIA increased the plant growth and yield (Chen *et al.*, 2002).

When applied in field conditions, TRIA also showed an increase in vegetative growth, chlorophyll content and dry weight of various plants (Ries, 1985). Application of TRIA considerably restored the stem height, leaf weight ratio, leaf osmotic potential and relative water contents in plants grown in saline medium. Salt stress, which increased the osmotic potential of leaves of plants, compared to the control plants; the TRIA is found to decrease the leaf osmotic potential. TRIA is found to be more effective in increasing the relative water content in salt stressed plants compared to salt stressed plants without TRIA treatment. The application of TRIA considerably restored the pigment level in plants grown in saline soil. The salt treated plants produced a decreased content of chlorophyll a, b and total chlorophyll compared to the control plants. The level of chlorophyll a, b and total chlorophyll are found to increase in salinity affected plants treated with TRIA.

An increase in total soluble sugar was observed in salt induced plant that had been treated with TRIA when compared to salt induced untreated plant. In NaCl stressed (without TRIA treated) plants, the soluble proteins decreased compared to control plants, while foliar spray of TRIA increased the soluble proteins in plants under the salt stress. Moreover, nucleic acids (DNA and RNA) decreased in plants grown in saline soil than that of in normal soil. The application of TRIA increased the contents of DNA and RNA in NaCl stressed plants. The proline content was increased in stress affected plants than control plants; while the proline content in the salt stressed plants subjected to TRIA treatment was reduced. The salt stress could adversely affect the cell division and enlargement of leaves resulting in reduced leaf area. Foliar application of TRIA increased the stem length and this could be due to acceleration of cell division and enlargement. As reported by Darra and Saxena (1971), the ameliorative role of growth regulators (GA3) on leaf size

enlargement might be attributed to accelerate cell division and enlargement. The presence of TRIA could be enhancing the nutrient uptake of salt stressed plants. The high uptake of essential nutrients such as K^+ and Ca^{2+} reduce the low uptake of Na^+ ions might also be responsible for the enhanced leaf growth. The TRIA treated salt stressed plants; osmotic potential was reduced than salt stressed plants. The TRIA might be increase the K^+ and Ca^{2+} contents of the leaves.

Whereas, Nandini and Subhendu (2002) observed the K^+ and Ca^{2+} contents of the hormone treated mung bean plants under salt stress are almost like control plants. Salt stress induced a reduction in the relative water content of the leaves, which indicates a loss of turgor that resulted in limited water availability for cell extension process. The growth regulator TRIA is able to overcome the stress effect. Moreover, decreased in chlorophyll levels is observed in salt stressed plants (Chen et al., 2002). Similarly, the effect of salt stressed plants on reduction of chlorophyll contents has been reported in several plants, such as rice and tomato. Salinity decreased nitrogen availability which could be one of the reasons for decreased chlorophyll content. The reduction of total chlorophyll content is probably related to the enhanced activity of the enzyme chlorophyllase. The TRIA is found to increase chlorophyll levels in salt stressed plants. Qasim et al. (2003) observed the reduction in total soluble sugar in Brassica nappa L. grown under NaCl added soil. The total soluble sugar content increased in TRIA applied salt stressed plants.

Salinity decreases the soluble protein and increases the protease activity. When the TRIA is sprayed on the leaves, there is an increased in accumulation of soluble proteins in salinized plants. GA3 has been reported to increase the soluble proteins in the leaves of a tree legume Parkiajavanica. The promotion of growth in rice seedlings by TRIA under saline conditions is associated with enhanced levels of nucleic acids and soluble proteins. The NaCl treatment suppressed the synthesis of DNA and RNA contents and this effect is significantly alleviated by the foliar application of TRIA (Chen *et al.*, 2002). These results are supported by Anuradha and Seeta Ram Rao (2001) and they reported that the DNA and RNA contents decreased in rice seedlings due to the effect of salt stress, and the application of brassinosteroids to the stressed plants overcame the stress effect. Study of Krishnan and Kumari (2008) showed that stem length, leaf weight ratio, relative water content, chlorophyll pigments, nucleic acids, soluble sugars and soluble proteins are reduced in plants grown in saline substratum. The growth regulator TRIA is able to reduce the effect of salt stress and increased plant growth and other biochemical parameters. Even though the leaf osmotic potential and proline accumulation are increased by the effect of salt stress and decreased when the salt stressed plants are treated with foliar spray of TRIA.

Acidic-mist Stress

Acidic mist (pH 4.0 and 2.0) is a kind of abiotic stress. Acidic mist greatly retarded the root and shoot elongation. Muthuchelian *et al.* (2003) studies indicated the role of TRIA in alleviating the effect of acidic mist on the seedlings of *Erythrina variegata* . This is a first report in this field. When the seedlings of *E. variegata* L. are sprayed with TRIA, the acidic mist effect is partially or completely reversed indicating that TRIA can protect from acidic mist treatment and the artificial electron donors (DPC and NH_2OH) markedly restored to the loss of PS-[2] activity in acidic mist treated leaves. They also targeted to elucidate whether TRIA can protect from acidic mists by assessing the concentrated effect of TRIA and acidic mist on seedlings with particular reference on growth and photosynthesis. Leaf density and leaf area were also affected. Besides this, overall stunting of the plant leaves is small, thin, and leathery in texture

with less cuticular waxes on their upper surfaces. Morphological symptoms, such as curling of leaves, deterioration of the cuticular barriers, and cracking of the thin waxy plugs which cover the stomata, are observed. Similar reductions in leaf size and cracking of the thin waxy plugs have been reported in tree seedlings that are exposed to acidic mist (Muthuchelian *et al.*, 1994; Muthuchelian *et al.*, 1995). The fact that acidic mist retards root and shoot elongation indicates that acidic mist controls the growth through auxin.

Moreover, the result of various previously published researches (Muthuchelian *et al.*, 1992; Muthuchelian *et al.* 1995; Muthuchelian *et al.*, 1994; Muthuchelian *et al.*, 1990; Muthuchelian *et al.*, 1996; Muthuchelian *et al.*, 2001), suggested that the lipophilic TRIA may act on cell membranes to produce 9-(+)-adenosine (Ries and Wert, 1992), which is rapidly translocate throughout the plant causing a cascade of metabolic events and resulting in increases in growth and dry matter. An explanation for increased growth and dry weight in Erythrina may come from all possibilities except water absorption. It is possible that water is metabolically incorporated via carbohydrate and/or fat hydrolysis (Ries and Wert, 1982), and there may also be an increase in hydroscopicity (physically bound water) of the TRIA-treated plants, because of the large increase in free amino acids and reducing sugar, which constitute about 30% of the dry weight of the plants. Any growth attribute to TRIA may not be simply caused by increased water uptake and cell elongation but also may be due to an increase in the cell number (Hungarter and Ries, 1978). TRIA treatment resulted in significantly higher root, shoot elongations, leaf density, leaf area, fresh and dry biomass accumulation in salt, drought, flooding and cadmium stressed Erythrina seedlings (Muthuchelian *et al.*, 1995; Muthuchelian *et al.*, 1996; Muthuchelian *et al.*, 2000). These results suggest that, the above-mentioned growth retardation by acidic mist was ameliorated by TRIA application (Muthuchelian *et al.*, 1995; Muthuchelian *et al.*, 1996).

In addition, total soluble protein was reduced appreciably at pH 2.0. As the PS-II activity loss due to acidic mist action must be prior to PQ in the electron transport. To locate the possible site(s) of inhibition in the PS-II reaction, they followed the DCPIP photo-reduction supported by various exogenous electron donors in thylakoids isolated from control and acidic mist-treated with or without TRIA-treated leaves. TRIA application reduced the inhibition by acidic mist in both whole chain and PS-II activities. TRIA enhances monogalactosyl diacylglycerol (MGDG) and digalactosyl diacylglycerol (DGDG) levels (Shripathy and Swamy, 1994). It is worth mentioning that MGDG appears to be involved in the protection of photosystem activities. The extensive change in thylakoid membrane fatty acid composition correlating with electron transport activities is an essential part of the process by which cells control membrane function and stability (Muthuchelian *et al.*, 1996). Significant decrease in the ratio of unsaturated to saturated fatty acids in acidic-mist treated seedlings perhaps reflects depletion of unsaturated fatty acid by lipid peroxidation due to acidic mist. TRIA application rapidly increases the unsaturated fatty acid contents (oleic acid 18:1; linoleic acid 18:2; linolenic acid 18:3) which would help to maintain the thylakoid membrane in an appropriate state. This could be the possible mode of action that the synthesized unsaturated fatty acids in TRIA-treated Erythrina seedlings partially protect the cellular systems against acidic mists.

Besides this, the effects on PS-I activity are much smaller in size but of a similar character. Similar trend is also observed in *E. variegata* seedlings by the application of TRIA and cadmium stress (Muthuchelian *et al.*, 2001). RuBPC activity is reduced markedly in acidic mist-treated leaves, whereas TRIA treatment increased it. The relatively low level of soluble proteins in acidic mist-treated seedlings may have been due to decrease in the synthesis of RuBPC, the major soluble protein of leaf. A loss of protein in acidic mist-treated leaves would partially account for damaged chloroplasts or could be the result of inhibition of protein synthesis or proteolytic degradation of the enzyme (Swirshi and Gepstein, 1985) or to competitive inhibition of RuBPC by acidic ions. The reduction in the overall photosynthetic rate correlates well with the decreased RuBPC activity in acid-treated leaves. A marked reduction of RuBPC activity was observed in pH 2.0. Such reduction is due to inhibition of protein synthesis induced by acidic mist. The reduction in RuBPC activity in acidic mist-treated seedlings and improvement by TRIA treatment correlated with the $^{14}CO_2$ fixation. The reduction in $^{14}CO_2$ fixation of acidic mist-treated seedlings was probably an indirect effect due to the destruction of photosynthetic pigments or a consequence of stomata closure and reduced RuBPC. The increase in RuBPC activity by TRIA treatment may be due to an increase in the substrate supply, the molecule of which gets bound to the enzyme site and increases the rate of reaction.

Seedlings grown in the presence of acidic mist treatment had a relatively low NRA that was ameliorating by TRIA application. The reduction in NRA may reflect a balance between synthesis or inactivation on one hand, and degradation or inactivation on the other hand. The changes in intercellular pH values due to acidic stress might decrease the transfer of nitrate (substrate) from a storage pool to an active cytoplasmic pool accessible to the enzyme. The inhibition of NRA might also be due to the inhibition of protein synthesis or it might have stemmed out from decreased rate of photosynthetic supply in the acidic mist-treated leaves.

Conclusion

Crop improvement through conventional methods to provide food security for the ever-growing population has several limitations. Modern agricultural technologies have held promise over the years to improve outputs from plants. The use of TRIA as growth hormone is a recent way of improving plant yield through its pre-sowing seed treatment and/or foliar spray is the focus of present research on TRIA application. Improved and disease resistant crops could easily be made available to farmers if the use of TRIA for plantlet regeneration is vigorously pursued. Now TRIA have goes beyond the defence reaction in plant immunity and response to abiotic stresses including salinity, drought and acidic mist. In coordination with other PGRs, TRIA importantly contributes to growth and developmental regulation although the biochemical mechanisms that mediate most of these responses remain largely unknown.

Moreover, much has not been learned during the past few years regarding how the SA signal is generated, regulated, and transduced to result in increased yield and production of stress proteins against abiotic stress circumstances. Today, one of the biggest outstanding questions in TRIA biology concerns how TRIA is initially perceived and how TRIA event triggers L(+)-adenosine as a second messenger which later produce signalling responses against resistance circumstances. Our information implies that there are many biochemical events and many pathways which are responsible for growth and yield responses and there are also influences by different types of abiotic stimuli, which the plant encounters.

REFERENCES

Anuradha S and Seeta RRS (2001). Effect of brassinosteroids on salinity stress induced inhibition of seed germination and seedling growth of rice (*Oryza sativa* L.). *Plant Growth Regulation*, **33**: 151–153.

Axelos M and Peaud-Lenoel C (1980). The apoprotein of the light-harvesting chlorophyll ab complex of tobacco cells as a molecular marker of cytokinin activity. *Plant Science Letters*, **19**: 33–41.

Bittenbender HC, Dilley DR, Wert V and Ries SK (1978). Environmental parameters affecting dark response of rice seedling (*Oryza sativa* L.) to tricontanol. *Plant Physiology*, **61**: 851–854.

Borowki E, Balamowski ZK and Michalek W (2000). Effects of tomatex/Tricontanol on chlorophyll fluorescence and tomato (*Lycopersicon esculentum* L.) yields. *Acta Physiologia Plantarum*, **22**: 271–274.

Chen X, Yuan H, Chen R, Zhu L, Du B, Weng Q and He G (2002). Isolation and characterization of triacontanol regulated genes in rice (*Oryza sativa* L.): Possible role of triacontanol as a plant growth stimulator. *Plant Cell Physiology*, **43**: 869–876.

Daphne J, Michael O and McManus T (2005). Hormones, signals and target cells in plant development. Cambridge University press, pp 158.

Darra BL and Saxena SN (1971). Effect of gibberlic acid pre-soaking seed treatment at different salinity regimes on germination, growth and yield attributes of hybride maize (Ganga-3). *Indian Journal of Agronomy*, **16**: 46–49.

Das N, Achari B, Harigaya Y and Dinda B (2011). A new flavonol glucoside from the aerial parts of Sida glutinosa. *Journal of Asian Natural Products Research*, **13**: 965–971.

Datta SC (1980). A Text of Plant Physiology, 1st edition, Central Book Depot, Allahabad, pp 583–694.

Davies PJ (1995). The plant hormones: Their nature, occurrence, and functions. In Plant Hormones: Physiology, Biochemistry and Molecular Biology, Davies PJ, ed., Kluwer, Boston, pp 3–38.

Debata A and Murty KS (1981). Relation between leaf and panicle senescence in rice. *Indian Journal of Experimental Biology*, **19**: 986–989.

Duck Jin C and Hong YN (1988). The effect of tricontanol on chloroplast development of radish cotyledons. *Korean Biochemical Journal*, **21**: 68–76.

Eriksen AB, Sellden G, Skogen D and Nilsen S (1981). Comparative analysis of the effect of tricontanol on photosynthesis, photorespiration and growth of tomato (C3 plants) and maize (C4 plants). *Planta*, **152**: 44–49.

Hangarter R, Ries SK and Carlson P (1978). Effect of triacontanol on plant cell cultures *in vitro*. *Plant Physiology*, **61**: 855–858.

Haughstad M, Ulasker LK, Ruppel A and Nilson S (1983). The effect of tricontanol on growth, photosynthesis and photorespiration in *Chamydomonas reinharditi* and *Anacystis nidulans*. *Physiologia Plantarum*, **58**: 451–456.

Helgi O, Stephen A and Rolfe (2005). The physiology of flowering plants published, Cambridge University Press. Plant Physiology, pp 191.

Houtz RL, Ries SK and Tolbert NE (1985a). Effect of triacontanol on chlamydomonas: I. Stimulation of Growth and Photosynthetic CO_2 Assimilation. *Plant Physiology*, **79**: 357–364.

Houtz RL, Ries SK and Tolbert NE (1985b). Effect of Triacontanol on *Chlamydomonas*. *Plant Physiology*, **79**: 365–370.

Jacobs WP (1979). Plant Hormones and Plant Development. Cambridge University Press, New York.

Jones J, Wert V and Ries SK (1979). Specificity of l-triacontanol as a plant growth stimulator and inhibition of its effect by other long chain compounds. *Planta*, **144**: 277–282.

Khan MMA, Mujibur-Rahman M, Naeem M, Mohammad F, Siddiqui MH and Khan MN (2006). Triacontanol-induced changes in the growth yield and quality of tomato (*Lycopersicon esculentum* Mill.). *Electronic Journal of Environmental and Agriculture Chemistry*, **5**: 1492–1499.

Kiliç NK, Duygu E and Dönmez G (2010). Triacontanol hormone stimulates population, growth and Brilliant Blue R dye removal by common duckweed from culture media. *Journal of Hazardous Materials*, **182**: 525–530.

Knowles NR and Ries SK (1981). Rapid growth and apparent total nitrogen increase in rice and corn plants following application of triacontanol. *Plant Physiology*, **68**: 1279–1284.

Kolker LS (1978). Analytical procedures for 1-triacontanol and its presence in plants and the environment. MS thesis, Michigan State University, East Lansing, MI.

Krishnan RR and Kumari BDR (2008). Effect of N-triacontanol on the growth of salt stressed soyabean plants. *Journal of Bioscience*, **19**: 53–62.

Kumaravelu G, Livingstone VD and Ramanujan MP (2000). Triacontanol induced changes in the growth, photosynthetic pigments, cell metabolites, flowering and yield of green gram. *Biologia Plantarum*, **43**: 287–290.

Lesniak AP, Haug A and Ries SK (1989). Stimulation of ATPase activity in barley (*Hordeum vulgare*) root plasma membranes after treatment with triacontanol and calmodulin. *Physiologia Plantarum*, **75**: 75–80.

Makino A, Mae T and Ohira K (1983). Photosynthesis and Ribulose 1, 5-bisphosphate carboxylase in rice leaves: Changes in photosynthesis and enzymes involved in carbon assimilation from leaf development through senescence. *Plant Physiology*, **73**: 1002–1007.

Muthuchelian K, Bertamini M and Nedunchezhian N (2001). Triacontanol can protect *Erythrina variegata* from cadmium toxicity. *Journal of Plant Physiology*, **158**: 1487–1490.

Muthuchelian K, Murugan C, Harigovindan R, Nedunchezhian N and Kulandaivelu G (1995). Effect of triacontanol in flooded *Erythrina variegate* seedlings. 1. Changes in growth, photosynthetic pigments and biomass productivity. *Photosynthetica*, **31**: 269–275.

Muthuchelian K, Murugan C, Harigovindan R, Nedunchezhian N and Kulandaivelu G (1996). Ameliorating effect of triacontanol on salt stressed *Erythrina variegata* seedlings. Changes in growth, biomass, pigments and solute accumulation. *Biologia Plantarum*, **38**: 133–136.

Muthuchelian K, Nedunchezhian N and Kulandaivelu G (1992). Effects of stimulated acid rain on $^{14}CO_2$ fixation, ribulose-1, 5-bisphosphate carboxylase and nitrate and nitrite reductases in *Vigna sinensis* and *Phaseolus mungo*. *Photosynthetica*, **28**: 361–367.

Muthuchelian K, Nedunchezhian N and Kulandaivelu G (1994). Acid rain: Acidic mist- induced response in growth and photosynthetic activities on crop plants. *Achieves in Environmental Contamination and Toxicology*, **26**: 521–526.

Muthuchelian K, Velayutham M and Nedunchezhian N (2003). Ameliorating effect of triacontanol on acidic mist-treated *Erythrina variegata* seedlings changes in growth and photosynthetic activities. *Plant Science*, **165**: 1253–1257.

Naeem M, Masroor M, Khan A, Moinuddin, Idrees M and Aftab T (2011). Triacontanol-mediated regulation of growth and other physiological attributes, active constituents and yield of *Mentha arvensis* L. Plant Growth Regulation, **65**: 195–206.

Pullman GS and Bucalo K (2011). Pine somatic embryogenesis using zygotic embryos as explants. *Methods in Molecular Biology*, **710**: 267–291.

Qasim M, Ashraf M, Ashraf MY, Rehman SU and Rha ES (2003). Salt induced changes in two canola cultivars differing in salt tolerance. *Biologia Plantarum*, **46**: 629–632.

Rajasekaran LR and Blake TJ (1999). New plant growth regulators protect photosynthesis and enhance growth under drought of jack pine seedlings. *Journal of Plant Growth Regulation*, **18**: 175–181.

Ries S (1991). Triacontanol and its second messenger 9-L(+)-adenosine as plant growth substances. *Plant Physiology*, **95**: 986–989.

Ries S, Wert V, O'Leary D and Nair M (1990). 9-/3-L(+)-adenosine: A new naturally occurring plant growth substance elicited by triacontanol in rice. *Plant Growth Regulation*, **9**: 263–273.

Ries SK (1985). Regulation of plant growth with triacontanol. *CRC Critical Reviews in Plant Science*, **2**: 239–285.

Ries SK, Wert V, Sweeley CC and Leavitt RA (1977). Triacontanol: A new naturally occurring plant growth regulator. *Science*, **195**: 1339–1441.

Ries SK and Wert VF (1982). Rapid *in vivo* and *in vitro* effect of triacontanol. *Journal of Plant Growth Regulation*, **1**: 117–127.

Ries SK and Wert VF (1988). Rapid elicitation of second messengers by nanomolar doses of triacontanol and octacosanol. *Planta*, **173**: 79–84.

Ries SK and Wert VF (1992). Response of maize and rice to 9-(+)-adenosine applied under different environmental conditions. *Plant Growth Regulation*, **11**: 69–74.

Ries SK and Wert W (1977). Growth responses of rice seedlings to triacontanol in light and dark. *Planta*, **135**: 77–82.

Saied S, Shah S, Ali Z, Khan A, Marasini BP and Choudhary MI (2011). Chemical constituents of Cichorium intybus and their inhibitory effects against urease and alpha-chymotrypsin enzymes. *Natural Product Communications*, **6**: 1117–1120.

Shirpathi V, Swamy GS and Chandershekhar KS (1997). Microviscocity of cucumber (*Cucumis sativus* L.) fruit protoplast membranes is altered by triacontanol and abscissic acid. *Biochemica et Biophysica Acta*, **1323**: 263–271.

Shripathy V and Sivakumar Swamy G (1994). Effect of triacontanol on the lipid composition of cotton (*Gossypium hirsutum* L.) leaves and its interaction with indole-3-acetic acid and benzyladanine. *Plant Growth Regulation*, **14**: 45–50.

QUESTIONS

Q. 1. Precursor of ethylene, a PGR, in higher plants is:

(1) Glycine
(2) Methionine
(3) Proline
(4) Histidine

Q. 2. E. coli and yeast produce ethylene as a metabolic product act as a hormone from which?

(1) Hydroxyproline
(2) Methionine
(3) Arginine
(4) Cysteine

Q. 3. Ethylene content of soil is due to presence of:

(1) BGA
(2) Fungi
(3) Bacteria
(4) Both 2 and 3

Q. 4. In a culture the production of ethylene by microorganisms is depends on:

(1) Type of organisms
(2) Nature of media
(3) Both 1 and 2
(4) Condition of media

Q. 5. What is correct about ethylene?

(1) Healthy mammalian tissues produce it
(2) It is also a metabolic product of the invertebrates
(3) Brewing yeast produce ethylene fro cysteine
(4) None is correct

Q. 6. What is AdoMet?

(1) S-adenosyl-methionine is full name
(2) Derived from the methionine and ATP
(3) It is an intermediate of ET pathway
(4) All is correct

Q. 7. What is correct about ACC in ethylene biosynthesis?

(1) Intermediate precursor of ET synthesis
(2) Its exogenous application produce very little ET
(3) Its synthesis is a limiting step in ET biosynthesis
(4) Its name is 1-aminocyclopropane-1-carboxylic acid
(5) All are correct

Q. 8. 1 ppm is equal to:

(1) $1\ \mu L/L$
(2) $10\ \mu L/L$
(3) $100\ \mu L/L$
(4) $1000\ \mu L/L$

Q. 9. Highest concentration of ET is reported in:

(1) Wounded/mechanical perturbed non-senescent tissues
(2) Ripening fruits
(3) Senescence tissues
(4) Both 2 and 3

Q. 10. Usually ET is highest in:

(1) Senescence tissues
(2) Flowering
(3) Ripening fruits
(4) Meristematic fruits

Q. 11. In which of the following is incorrect about ET production?

(1) Mosses and liverworts produce ET
(2) Gymnosperms produce ET
(3) Ferns produce ET
(4) Certain BGA produce ET
(5) None of the above

Q. 12. What is incorrect about ET production in plants?

(1) Internal ET conc. In ripe fruits is $2500\ \mu l/L$

(2) Young leaves produce more leaves than fully expanded leaves

(3) It is biologically active at low conc.

(4) None of the above

Q. 13. What is correct about ET is?

(1) $KMnO_4$ is an ET absorbent

(2) $KMnO_4$ is used in apple storage to reduce ET concentration

(3) $KMnO_4$ is able to enhance the storage life of fruits

(4) All are correct

Q. 14. ET trapping system is used in storage of:

(1) Dry fruits

(2) Fruits and vegetables

(3) Fruits and flowers

(4) Fruits, vegetables and flowers

Q. 15. Biosynthesis of ET is depend on:

(1) Tissue type and developmental stage

(2) Meristematic regions and nodal regions are significant

(3) Leaf abscission, flowering senescence and fruit ripening increase ET synthesis

(4) Any kind of wounding can induce ET synthesis

(5) All are correct

Q. 16. In which of the following physiological stresses are responsible to enhance the ET production?

(1) Flooding and drought

(2) Chilling

(3) Disease and temperature

(4) All

Q. 17. About 25 years is a lag period in recognition of ET as PGR because:

(1) Believed of its effect is mediated by auxin

(2) Lack of quantification techniques

(3) It is diffusible nature

(4) Both 1 and 2

Q. 18. Which technique is signified for the recognition of ET as PGR?

(1) Gas chromatography

(2) Paper chromatography

(3) Thin layer chromatography

(4) None of the above

Q. 19. About ET what is correct?

(1) A simplest olefin

(2) It completely oxidized in CO_2 in tissues

(3) Ethylene glycol, oxalic acid and ethylene oxide are oxidative products

(4) All are correct

Q. 20. During 19th century, which gas was used to street lamp illumination:

(1) Ethylene

(2) Coal gas (CH_4)

(3) Acetylene

(4) Ethylene derivative

Q. 21. Dark grown pea seedlings in laboratory shows the:

(1) Reduced stem growth

(2) Increased lateral growth

(3) Abnormal horizontal growth

(4) All are correct

Q. 22. In Q. 21 mentioned three features are related to the exposure of ET are called:

(1) Tertiary response

(2) Triple response

(3) Triangle response

(4) Skotomorphogenesis

Q. 23. Organe produces ET when it affected by?

(1) Penicillium   (2) Aspergillus

(3) Bacteria   (4) Virus

Q. 24. In which of the following are concerned with ET research?

(1) HH Cousins

(2) R Gane

(3) Adamas and Yang

(4) All

Q. 25. Botanically zucchini are:

(1) Vegetables

(2) Fruits

(3) Both 1 and 2

(4) Nuts

Q. 26. Cofactor of ACC synthase is:

(1) Pyridoxal phosphate

(2) Hg ions

(3) Cu ions

(4) Cobalt chloride

Q. 27. What is correct about ACC synthase?

(1) A cytosolic enzyme

(2) Catalyze a committed step (ado-Met to ACC conversion)

(3) Less stable

(4) All are correct

Q. 28. Inducers of genes which regulates ET production in plants?

(1) Environmental factors

(2) Fruit ripening

(3) Wounding

(4) Auxin conc. In plant tissue

(5) All are correct

Q. 29. Cyclohexamide is:

(1) Protein synthesis inhibitor

(2) Inducer for mRNA of ACC synthase genes

(3) Prevents the synthesis of nuclease

(4) All are correct

Q. 30. Role of ET in fruit ripening and enhancing storage life like bio-technological functions can me made possible by which genetic approach/s?

(1) Use of Ti plasmid of *A. tumifaciens* to control ET production (antisense transcript)

(2) Reduce ET production by use of gene from *A. tumifaciens* that metabolize the ACC or *AdoMet*

(3) Both 1 and 2

(4) Cytoplasmic inheritance

Q. 31. Agent orange contain:

(1) 2,4-D (2) 2,4,5-T

(3) Both 1 and 2 (4) IAA

Q. 32. During second World War which used against Vietnam through America:

(1) Paramequat

(2) Defoliant

(3) Antibiotics

(4) Kinetin

Q. 33. Apoptosis of animals is equivalent to which process of plant cell:

(1) Gall formation

(2) Senescence

(3) Crown formation

(4) Abscission

Q. 34. DNA lodders of apoptosis is associated with?

(1) Gel electrophoresis

(2) Southern blotting

(3) Western blotting

(4) Gas chromatography

Q. 35. Trade name of ethylene producing compound (ethephon) is:

(1) Defoilant

(2) Etherel

(3) Paraquat

(4) None of the above

Q. 36. Senescence is a process of development which is controlled?

(1) Genetically

(2) Transcriptionally

(3) Translationally

(4) Both 2 and 3

Q. 37. Which PGR known to induce flowering in family of pine apple or *Bromeliaceae*?

(1) ET (2) ABA

(3) GA_3 (4) Kinetin

Q. 38. Which PGR known to initiate the flowering in mango?

(1) ET
(2) ABA
(3) GA3
(4) SA

Q. 39. Which PGR known to induce the number of female flowers in cucumber family/change the sex/change mono-ecious flower to dioecious flowers?

(1) ET
(2) ABA
(3) Cks
(4) IBA

Q. 40. The stimulatory effect (increasing internode elongation) in deepwater rice of ET is mediated through which hormone?

(1) ABA
(2) GA
(3) ET
(4) CK

Q. 41. In Arabidopsis root hairs located in:

(1) Epidermal cell
(2) Hypodermal cells
(3) Endodermal cells
(4) Both 1 and 2

Q. 42. Ethylene induce adventitious root formation in:

(1) Leaf
(2) Other root
(3) Stems
(4) Flower stem
(5) All are correct

Q. 43. Which plant ET induce petiole/stem elongation (opposite to its normal behaviour)?

(1) Regnellidium diphyllum
(2) Deep water rice
(3) Callitriche platycarpa
(4) Nymphea peltata
(5) All are correct

Q. 44. Epinasty is:

(1) CK induced stem elongation
(2) ET induced asymmetric growth
(3) ET induced symmetric growth
(4) ABA induced asysmmetirc growth

Q. 45. The trade name of chemical which secrete ethylene?

(1) Etherel
(2) Ethephon
(3) Ethone
(4) None of the above

Q. 46. The chemical name of etherel is:

(1) 2-chloro-ethyl-phosphonic acid
(2) 4-di-chloroethenic acid
(3) 2,4,5-T
(4) 2,4-D

Q. 47. Ethephone can increase yield in members of family through promotion of female sex organs and inducing cross pollination or preventing self-pollination:

(1) Cucumber
(2) Solaneous
(3) Rose
(4) Rapeseed

Q. 48. Inhibition of ripening in tomato and petunia induced by introducing the antisense technology. This is concerned with which hormone?

(1) ET
(2) ABA
(3) GA
(4) Ck

Q. 49. What is fertile crescent is?

(1) Remains of earliest settlements in regions of near east
(2) A region near Afganistan concerned with wheat cultivation
(3) A regions concerned with a war for water
(4) A regions is concerned with joint cultivation of barley and wheat

Q. 50. Number of fertile crescent at globe is:

(1) 4   (2) 3

(3) 5   (4) 7

Q. 51. In which of the following is not concerned with fertile crescent?

(1) Barley and Emmer wheat

(2) Einkorn wheat and sheep

(3) Goat, cattle and pigs

(4) Crow, rice and maize

Q. 52. Antisense DNA consists of a gene of interest in the reverse orientation with respect to the:

(1) Inducer   (2) Repressor

(3) Promoter   (4) All

Q. 53. Exogenous application of Ag⁺ in (biosynthetic inhibitor of ET) carnation causes an increase in:

(1) Longevity of cut flowers

(2) Stem growth

(3) Number of male flowers

(4) Number of female flowers

Q. 54. Before agriculture development Nomadic groups whose migration depends upon the seasonal availability of food obtained from?

(1) Domestic plants

(2) Domestic animals

(3) Wild plants and wild animals

(4) Domestic plants and wild animals

Q. 55. Epinasty occurs when?

(1) ACC/ET moves from root to stem

(2) ET moves from shoot to stem

(3) Both 1 and 2 are correct

(4) None of the above

Q. 56. Epinasty occurs when?

(1) Adaxial (upper) side of petiole grows more than abaxial (lower) side of petiole

(2) Abaxial side of petiole grows more than adaxial side of petiole

(3) ET and high concentration of Auxin in leaves

(4) Both 2 and 3 are correct

Q. 57. What is not true about ET?

(1) Anaerobic conditions induce ET production

(2) Aerobic conditions induce ET synthesis

(3) Conversion of ACC to ET need O_2

(4) ACC is higher in xylem sap and is the immediate precursor of ET

Q. 58. In which is the initiating signal for leaf senescence?

(1) ET   (2) ABA

(3) GA   (4) CK

Q. 59. In which is the initiating signal for leaf abscission?

(1) ET

(2) ABA

(3) GA

(4) Ck

Q. 60. Ethylene is an unusual hormone in that it is

(1) Transported by Xylem

(2) Transported by phloem

(3) None-movable

(4) A gas

Q. 61. What is product of reaction between the methionine and ATP?

(1) S-adenosylmethionine (SAM)

(2) Ethylene-ester

(3) Ethylene-glycol

(4) Ethylene phosphate

Q. 62. When leaves are subjected to water stress, ET production is increased which is caused primarily by an increase in?

(1) ACC synthesis

(2) SAM synthesis

(3) Both 1 and 2

(4) IAA synthesis

Q. 63. Auto-catalysis is concerned with which hormone?

(1) ET
(2) ABA
(3) GA
(4) Ck

Q. 64. What is auto-catalysis?

(1) ET can promote its own synthesis in intact ripening fruits
(2) ET can promote its own synthesis in intact fruits
(3) IAA can promote its own synthesis in intact ripening fruits
(4) Ck can promote its own synthesis in intact ripening fruits

Q. 65. Auto-inhibition is concerned with which hormone?

(1) ET
(2) ABA
(3) GA
(4) Ck

Q. 66. In excised fruit tissues, ET production can be inhibited by ET treatment, is known as:

(1) Auto-inhibition
(2) Auto-catalysis
(3) Self-inhibition
(4) All of the above

Q. 67. The stimulation of ripening by ET seems to be restricted to:

(1) Non-climacteric fruits
(2) Climacteric fruits
(3) Both 1 and 2
(4) Fruits of family apocyanaceae

Q. 68. Methionine cycle or Yang cycle is concerned with which plant hormone synthesis?

(1) GA
(2) Ck
(3) ET
(4) ABA

Q. 69. In climacteric fruits, ripening is associated with a sudden increase in:

(1) Respiration
(2) Ethylene production
(3) Sucrose content
(4) Both 1 and 2

Q. 70. In climacteric fruits, ripening is associated with?

(1) CO_2 released massively first and then decrease
(2) O_2 demand constant
(3) Both CO_2 and O_2 released
(4) Demand of O_2 decreases

Q. 71. In which of the following is a odd one in reference of ET production and respiratory rise?

(1) Bananas
(2) Melons
(3) Avocados
(4) Grapes (rise in respiratory rate, climacteric fruits)

Q. 72. In which of the following is a odd one in reference of ET production and respiratory rise?

(1) Oranges
(2) Lemons
(3) Grapes
(4) Tomatoes (no rise in respiration, non climacteric fruits)

Q. 73. Ethylene stimulates:

(1) Germination of dormant seeds
(2) Prolongs the seed longevity
(3) Break dormancy increase its production
(4) All of the above

Q. 74. Triple response of ethylene not includes:

(1) Reduction in elongation
(2) Swelling of hypocotyl
(3) Change in the direction of growth
(4) None of the above

Q. 75. Ethylene favoured the:

(1) Lateral growth (increase in stem diameter, i.e. secondary growth)
(2) Longitudinal growth
(3) Redirects the orientation of new cell wall micro-fibrils from longitudinal to radial direction
(4) Both 1 and 3

Q. 76. Downward growth of petiole is termed epinasty is a result of redistribution of auxin in response to:

(1) ET treatment
(2) CK treatment
(3) GA treatment
(4) ABA treatment

Q. 77. Epinasty is downward bending of the petiole due to:

(1) Increased growth in upper part of the petioles causes increased growth in that region
(2) Decreased growth in upper part of the petioles causes increased growth in that region
(3) Increased growth in lower part of the petioles causes increased growth in that region
(4) Increased growth in upper part of the petioles causes reduced growth in that region

Q. 78. The ability of plants to respond to a number of physical stimuli like gravity and light has been correlated with changes in the distribution of which hormone, ET has been shown to be an active agent in some cases?

(1) GA   (2) Auxin
(3) ABA   (4) CK

Q. 79. The response of the some plants to tactile stimuli appears to be mediated through an increased production of which hormone?

(1) CK
(2) GA

(3) ABA
(4) ET

Q. 80. Which plant hormone improves support through the stimulation of development of root hairs?

(1) ABA
(2) ET
(3) CK
(4) GA

Q. 81. The effect of ET on the growth of roots is:

(1) Low concentration stimulates and higher concentration inhibited
(2) Both low and high concentration inhibits the root growth
(3) Both low and high concentration stimulates the roots growth
(4) Low concentration inhibits the root growth and low concentration stimulates the root growth

Q. 82. The development of arenchymatous roots in flooded maize plants is an example of:

(1) Root anatomy affected by endogenous ET content
(2) Root anatomy affected by endogenous CK content
(3) Root anatomy affected by endogenous ABA content
(4) Root anatomy affected by exogenous ET content

Q. 83. In which of the following is a endogenous adoptive response of the ET production?

(1) Production of root hairs
(2) Development of arenchymatous roots in flooded maize plants
(3) Increased intracellular concentration and stimulates the formation of adventitious roots leaves, stem and pre-existing roots
(4) All of the above

Q. 84. **In which of the following is a function of ET?**

(1) Pollution cause a rapid rise in ET production

(2) Pollution act as a stimulus for ET precursor

(3) Ethylene act as a wound hormone

(4) All are correct

Q. 85. **When ABA causes abscission, it may do so either?**

(1) By stimulating ET formation

(2) By interfering with auxin synthesis

(3) Auxin transport from the leaf

(4) All of the above

Q. 86. **In which of the ideal model system for studying the flower senescence wherein the colour changes from pink to purplish-blue during senescence?**

(1) Bougainvillea Spp.

(2) Petunia hybrid

(3) Neurospora curcus

(4) Pseudomonas petunia

Q. 87. **Like climacteric fruits, senescence of aged flowers can be caused by less .... Because they become increasingly sensitive to........ as they as:**

(1) ET

(2) ABA

(3) GA

(4) CK

Q. 88. **One of the commercially important effects of ET is the induction of flowering in:**

(1) Pineapple

(2) Mango

(3) Apple

(4) All of the above

Q. 89. **Production of the fungal phyto-alexins in wounded plants induced by:**

(1) ET

(2) ABA

(3) GA

(4) CK

Q. 90. **An number of secretary processes like gum production and latex flow are stimulated by:**

(a) ET

(b) ABA

(c) CK

(d) GA

Q. 91. **Juvenility factors includes:**

(a) Auxin

(2) CK

(3) Light and good nutrition

(4) All of the above

Q. 92. **ET receptor site contains a metal, it may be:**

(1) Zn

(2) Cu

(3) Both 1 and 2

(4) Mg

Q. 93. **ET has been shown to increase the levels of m-RNA transcripts of several genes corresponding to the enzymes proteins like?**

(1) Cellulose

(2) Chitinase

(3) β-1,3-glucanase

(4) Peroxidase and chalcone synthase

(5) All of the above

Q. 94. **Which is the major components of the cell walls of higher fungi?**

(1) β-1, 3-glucanase

(2) Chitinase

(3) Both 1 and 2

(4) PR-proteins

Q. 95. **In which the following can exert ET-like biological activities in plants?**

(1) Olefins

(2) Unsaturated hydrocarbons

(3) Sucrose

(4) Both 1 and 2

Q. 96. In which of the following has a similarity among the two most important antagonists of ET action (CO$_2$ and Ag$^+$), this is

(1) Both compete to ET for their binding sites

(2) Both bind with ET substrates to modify its

(3) Both neutralize the binding efficiency of ET to their promoters

(4) All of the above

Q. 97. Cytokinins are structural components of .... specific for certain amino acids:

(1) t-RNA

(2) r-RNA

(3) m-RNA

(4) Both 1 and 2

Q. 98. In which of the following promote ET biosynthesis?

(1) Auxins

(2) CK

(3) Water stress

(4) All of the above

Q. 99. All plant hormones which regulate ET production, the most appropriate option will be:

(1) GA, IAA, ET, CK, ABA

(2) CK, 2, 4-D, GA, ABA, ET

(3) Kinetin, GA, Auxin, ABA

(4) GA, ABA, IBA, CK

Q. 100. ACC is an enzyme, termed EFE (ethylene forming enzyme), the chemical nature of this enzyme is?

(1) Hydrolase

(2) Reductase

(3) Oxidase

(4) Oxido-reductase

Q. 101. During ET synthesis, methionine first reacted with ATP and produce:

(1) SAM (S-adenosylmethionine)

(2) MTA (Methythioadenosine)

(3) MTR (Methylthioribose)

(4) Epo-oxide

6 Role of Salicylic Acid in Biotic and Abiotic Stress Tolerance in Plants

ABSTRACT

Salicylic acid (SA) is a true plant hormone that induces defence reaction in plant immunity and response to biotic and abiotic stress tolerances. Presently, it has been gained the attention of major research programmes around the globe owing to its function as an extensive signalling molecule during the plant responses to biotic stresses including defence against pathogens including local disease resistance mechanisms like host cell death, expression of defence genes and systemic acquired resistance (SAR). On the other hand, SA also considers a significant stress signal during abiotic stress such as salinity, drought, metals toxicity, heat and various other kind of secondary stresses. On the basis of co-ordination with other major plant hormones, it contributes to growth and developmental regulation by physicochemical pathways mediate most-responses remains largely unknown. The identification of the unresolved signalling targets and molecular modes responsible for inducing resistance to tolerance the harmful effects of biotic and abiotic stresses could satisfy the researchers to understand the complex SA signalling behaviour. Also, synergistic and antagonistic interactions of SA with other plant hormones and signalling molecules that only effective against stresses but also regulate developmental processes should unveil subtle mechanisms of plant to maximize yield by balancing developmental processes and stress tolerance.

Abbreviation: ROS, NPR1, HR, GPx, CAT, SOD.

INTRODUCTION

SA is a naturally existing phenolic compound. Evidence put forward that externally applied SA involved plant's tolerance to several abiotic stresses including osmotic stress, drought, salinity, and heavy metal stress (Moussa and El-Gamel, 2010). Exogenous SA reduced transcription and increased nitrate reductase activity (NRA), flower longevity as well as the yield of some plants, which overall suggest the SA may enhance the multiple types of stress tolerance in plants through which interactive effects on several functional molecules or other signalling molecules participating in more complex stress responses. SA appears to have innate potentiality for increasing antioxidants and influencing antioxidant enzyme activity in plants subjected to oxidative stress. Plants have developed a variety of sophisticated defence mechanisms to cope with an environment in which many different microbes live as well as environment also fluctuates to a greater extent by anthropogenic and as natural activities. Higher plants induce a variety of defence mechanisms (responses) when they are attacked by microbial pathogens, such as fungi, bacteria or viruses. Most microbes which colonize plant tissue are harmless. Some enter the plant but kill a few plant cells because the plants hypersensitive response (HR) prevents further damage.

SA at History Background

SA (from Latin Salix, Willow tree) is a mono-hydroxybenzoic acid, with formula $C_6H_4(OH)$ COOH. Where the OH group is ortho to the carboxyl group. Also, it is known as 2-hydroxy-benzenecarboxyl group acid and poorly soluble in water (0.2 g/100 mL H_2O at 2°C). SA is a phenolic phytohormone and is found in plants with roles in plant growth and development, photosynthesis, transpiration, ion uptake and transport. It is involved in the SAR. During SAR, the signal can also move to nearby plants by SA being converted to the volatile ester, methyl salicylate. In addition, it causes specific changes in leaf anatomy and chloroplast ultrastructure and mediating plants defence against pathogens by inducing PR proteins. Hippocrates (Greek physician) extracted a powder from willow bark that could ease aches and pains and reduce fever. The medicinal part of the plant is the inner bark and is used as a pain reliever for a variety of ailments. It is also isolated from the meadowsweet (*Filipendula ulmarial* or *Spiraea ulmaria*) and caused digestive problems such as gastric irritants bleeding, diarrhoea and ever death when consumed in high doses.

SA as a Signalling Molecule

For more than 200 years, SA, the plant hormone, has been studied for its medicinal use in humans. However, its extensive signalling role in plants, probably in defence against pathogens and abiotic stresses, have only become evident during the past 20 years. Vlot *et al.* (2009) surveys how SA in plants regulates both local disease resistance mechanisms and tolerance to abiotic stress including host cell death and defence gene expression and SAR. On the other hand, genetic studies

reveal an increasingly complex network of proteins required for SA-mediated defence signalling and this process is exemplified by several regulatory feedback loops. The interaction between the SA signalling pathway and those regulated by other plant hormones and/or defence signals as also have been studied. Although, in recent years, SA has been the focus of research to its role as signal of local and systemic plant defence response against pathogens and a stress signal molecules during the plants responses to abiotic stress such as drought, chilling, heavy metal toxicity, heat and osmotic stress. In this sense, SA appears to be an effective therapeutic agent for plants.

Besides this, function during biotic and abiotic stresses, SA plays a crucial role in the regulation of physiological and biochemical processes during the entire life span of the plant. Studies of Rivas-San Vicente and Plasencia (2011) support the role of SA during plant growth and development by comparing experiments performed by exogenous application of SA with analysis of genotypes affected by SA levels and/or perception. Also, SA is one of a wide variety of phenolic compounds bearing a hydroxyl group or its derivatives that are synthesized by plants. Traditionally, plant phonics is classified as secondary meta-bolites as they are thought to be relatively unimportant or waste produtcs. However, this concept changed drastically with the discovery that phenolic have many important functions. SA is considered one of the key endogenous signals involved in the activation of numerous signals involved in the activation of numerous plant defence responses.

Salicylic Acid: A Stress Induced Signal

SA is a naturally existing phenolic compound. Evidences put forward that externally applied SA increased plant's tolerance to several kind of environmental stresses. Phenylalanine-ammonia-lyase (PAL) plays a significant role in plant disease resistance. It catalyzes the committed step in the phenylpropanoid pathway that supplies intermediates in the synthesis of isoflavonoid and related phytoalexins, as well as various phenolic derivatives and the signal molecule, SA. Early evidences showed that SA is one of the key endogenous signals involved in the activation of numerous signals including plant defence responses, including response to pathogenic attack, expression of PR proteins in a variety of plants. These properties subsequently found to mimic the natural defence responses in tobacco and cucumber when elevated endogenous SA levels are correlated with induced resistance to the invading pathogens. SAR is a pathogen-inducible broad-spectrum resistance occurring in tissue distinct from the primary infection. Infected transgenic plants are unable to express SAR and also show reduced local resistance to pathogens (Delaney et al., 1994).

Flowering

SA was later identified as the phloem-transmissible factor secreted in the aphid honeydew responsible for inducing flowering in Lemna gibba plants kept under a non-photo-inductive light cycle. Since contribution of SA to flowering regulation has been well-known for a long time. In the short days species, Pharbitis nil, flowering is induced by poor-nutrition stress. However, flowering under this condition is prevented by treatment with amino-oxyacetic acid, a PAL inhibitor, but is restored by SA application. SA also stimulates flowering in various genera of the Lemnaceae family, including long day, short day and photo-period insensitive types. Subsequent studies provided conflicting evidence regarding SA's role in flowering. However, a demonstration that SIZ1, a Sumoe3 ligase, negatively regulates flowering via an SA-dependent pathway argue that SA plays some role in this process. It has been suggested that in long day-grown plants, SA

regulated flowering time through an FCA-independent pathway that may be the one mediated by FVE, whereas under long day conditions, SA could exert its regulation in parallel to both branches of the autonomous pathway in order to regulate integrator genes such as FT SOC1.

Senescence

Senescence is characterized by a decline in photosynthetic activity and increased ROS levels due to a loss of antioxidant capacity. After reviewing the important role of SA in cell redox homeostasis and photosynthesis, it is not surprising that SA is also involved in senescence regulation. NO, is another signalling molecule has been implicated as an activator in defence mechanism induced by SA and stimulates the accumulation of SA also. SA also induces the production of ROS such as H_2O_2 and NO (Durner and Klesssig, 1995), both H_2O_2 and NO are considered emerging signalling molecules acting against the abiotic stress including drought, salinity (Mazid et al., 2011a), heavy metal (Mazid et al., 2011b), temperature and ultraviolet radiation stress in plants (Mazid et al., 2012). The application of H_2O_2 to tobacco leaves is known to trigger the accumulation of SA (Leon et al., 1995). Thus these signals appear to be self-amplifying. One likely role for NO, SA and ROS is to promote the HR and pathogen killing. Both ROS and SA have been shown to synergize with NO to enhance host cell death in soya bean suspension cells. SA and NO may work synergistically to transduce the defence signal by targeting the same effectors proteins and/or their genes.

Senescence is accompanied by important changes in gene expression, and SA contributes greatly to this process. Consistent with this observation, Arabidopsis plants affected in SA biosynthesis such as the transgenic NahG and the mutant pad4, or with a disrupted SA signalling pathway, such as NPR1, exhibits altered senescence patterns that include delayed yellowing and reduced necrosis compared with wild type plants (Morris *et al.*, 2000). Transcripts of several SAGs such as SAG12, are considerably reduced or undetectable in SA-deficient Arabidopsis plants (Morris *et al.*, 2000).

The involvement of the SA signalling pathway in senescence is confirmed through a detailed gene expression analysis in Arabidopsis senescent leaves (Buchanan-Wollaston *et al.*, 2005). Most of the senescence-induced genes that are dependent on the SA pathway encode kinases, transferases and hydrolases, but their function in senescence progression remain to be elucidated. Autophagy (ATG) is an important process for plant development, especially during senescence and in the defence responses. The importance of the SA pathway in this developmental stage is highlighted by a comparative analysis of genes expressed during silique, leaf and petals senescence. Autophagy induced by SA is regulated by ACBP3, an acyl-CoA binding protein that binds phosphatidyl choline and phosphatidyl-ethanolamine, thus interfering with the formation of the ATG 5-phosphatidylethanolamine complex and disrupting autophagosome formation and subsequent degradation of ATG8.

Photosynthetic System

SA is an important regulator of photosynthesis because it affects leaf and chloroplast structure, chloroplast and carotenoids contents and the activity of enzymes such as Rubisco and carbonic anhydrase (Melotto *et al.*, 2006). Stomata closure is an important factor for photosynthesis and is subjected to control by several plant hormones. Several evidences link stomata closure to innate plant immunity, high lightens the role of SA in the function of the guard cells (Meltto *et al.*, 2006). In *Arabidopsis thaliana* the SA signalling pathway contributing to achieving optimal photosynthetic activity

through regulating light acclimation processes and redox homeostasis. The significant interplay between ROS and SA signalling was uncovered when applications of H_2O_2 and SA to tobacco and Arabidopsis plants induced each other, suggesting that they are involved in a self-amplifying feedback loop.

Moreover, several studies carried out under laboratory or field conditions strongly suggest that SA and other salicylates play an important role in many biological responses in plants. The effect of these substances on the physiology of the plants is variable, promoting some processes and inhibiting others. Larque-Saavedra (1978) used varying concentrations of SA to test its anti-transpirant effect on leaves of *Phaseolus vulgaris* and its inhibition of stomata opening in epidermal strips of *Commelina communis*. Significant reductions in transpiration and stomatal aperture were obtained, but SA has also been reported to reverse the stomatal closure induced by ABA. Exogenous applications of SA to different species of crops have been shown to elicit effects on yield and yield components. An increase in the number of pods and yield has been found in *Mung bean*, *P. vulgaris* (Lang, 1986) and wheat (*Triticum aestivum* L.).

Besides this, other effects of SA and its regulatory role in plant physiology include inhibiting ethylene biosynthesis, interfering with membrane depolarization, blocking wound responses, and an increase in photosynthetic rate and chlorophyll content in soya beans. More recently it has been recognized that SA is required in the signal transduction chain for inducing SAR. Shoot growth is increased with the three concentrations of SA used; an average increase of 23% and 20% in plant height is observed under greenhouse conditions and in field experiments respectively. A dramatic effect on root growth is observed for the SA concentrations under both greenhouse and field conditions. Various concentrations of SA significantly increased root length; for example, an increase of 45% in relation to control is found. Singh (1993) found that SA stimulated root formation in young shoots of ornamental plants and Li and Li (1995) reported the formation of adventitious roots on hypocotyl cuttings of mung beans.

However, there is not a clear dose-response relationship, nevertheless, the effect of SA on shoot and root growth is large. The mechanism by which shoot and root length is increased, is not known. It is possible that SA can be involved in the regulation of cell enlargement and division in synergy with other substances such as auxin, which is recognized to regulate cell enlargement and division during root formation. It is clear that more work needs to be done to begin to understand the mechanism by which SA is increasing root and shoot growth in soya bean and whether this effect can be reproduced in other plant species. It is clear from the results of this work that SA had a profound effect on root growth of *Glycine max*. The mechanism by which SA is causing such an effect is unknown; however, the mechanism controlling cell enlargement and division must be altered. The implications of the above finding may be of particular importance, especially in situations where the root has to explore deeper layers of soil to seek nutrients or water. An additional positive effect of SA on photosynthesis is the protection conferred to barley seedlings and maize plants against oxidative stress induced by paraquat and cadmium (Cd) respectively. SA inhibits the antioxidant enzymes catalase (CAT) and ascorbate peroxidase (APX), thus contributing to stabilizing H_2O_2 levels. H_2O_2 is a signalling molecule produces in response to abiotic stress (Mazid *et al.*, 2011a; 2011b; 2012).

Respiration

SA negatively and positively interacts with several other plant hormones and signalling molecules that not only affect defence but also regulated developmental processes like respiration, etc. An ongoing challenge is to unravel how these interactions affect different processes that are occurring in parallel way to each other. Heat production, known as thermogenesis occurs in the male reproductive structures of cycads and in the flowers of some angiosperms. SA is involved in the regulation of the alternative oxidase (AOX) pathway in thermogenic and non-thermogenic plants by inducing its gene expression (Kapulnik *et al.*, 1992). In Sauromatum guttatum schott (Voodoo lily), about 100-fold increase in SA proceeds the onset of thermogenesis in the spadix (central column of the inflorescence) (Raskin, 1992). In tobacco cell suspension culture, addition of 2–20 μM SA causes an increased cyanide-resistant O_2 uptake within 2 hours, which is accompanied by a 60% increase in the rate of heat evolution from cells, measured by calorimetry (Kapulink *et al.*, 1992).

Moreover, exogenous SA also induces thermogenesis, and this effect is very specific. SA stimulates thermogenesis primarily by increasing the activity of the alternative respiratory pathway in mitochondria. In Voodoo lily, SA enhances the capacity of the alternative respiratory pathway by inducing expression of AOX, the terminal electron acceptor of the alternative respiratory pathway. Interestingly, SA treatment also induces AOX expression and increased alternative respiration in Tobacco, a non-thermogenic plant (Norman *et al.*, 2004). AOX couple's ubiquinol oxidation with the reduction of molecular oxygen to yield water in a reaction that is insensitive to inhibitor of the cytochrome oxidase pathway. Because AOX is a non-proton driven carrier, it allows a flexible abol of ATP synthesis to maintain growth rate homeostasis (Moore *et al.*, 2002), and is a potential target of SA for plant growth regulation. Also, AOX is thought to limit AOS production in mitochondria, besides the induction of AOX, SA stimulates the inhibition of mitochondrial electron transport and is dependent on the expression of the AOX gene, SA might control electron transport and oxidative phosphorylation in plant mitochondria (Norman *et al.*, 2004). Low concentration of SA (1 mM) stimulates the respiration of whole cells and isolated mitochondria in the absence of added ADP by acting as an uncoupler.

Besides this, SA at concentration as low as 20 µM inhibits both ATP synthesis and respiratory O_2 uptake within minutes of incubation in tobacco cell cultures although a significant inhibition occurs only at SA concentration more than 50 µM. Furthermore, at higher concentration (1–5 mM), SA inhibits respiration apparently by preventing electron flow from the substrate dehydrogenases to the ubiquinol pool. In addition, treatment with 500 µM SA decreases ATP levels by 50% within the first 30 minutes of incubation after which the ATP levels continue to decrease to as low as 15% of control levels. The impact of SA on mitochondrial function is not unique to tobacco as similar uncoupling and inhibitory effects on soyabean mitochondria (Norman *et al.*, 2004), and SA uncoupling mammalian mitochondria have also been reported (Jorgensen *et al.*, 1976). Induction of alternative repression by SA is associated with *de novo* synthesis of AOX and requires hours to reach maximum levels (Kapulnik *et al.*, 1992). Combined uncoupling and inhibitory effects of SA in respiration would act to lower cell ATP levels in mutants of Arabidopsis.

Defensive role of SA in association with other signalling pathways: A crosstalk between SA, MAPK and ROS

MAPK cascades are important mediators of the interplay between SA, the phytohormones and ROS signalling in cell growth regulation. ROS produced by NADPH oxides are important regulators of polarized growth of root hairs and pollen tubes, by controlling cell wall rigidity and cell signalling events involving CA+2 and MAPK cascades. Besides this, MAPK cascades are involved in many signal transduction pathways in plants as well as in mammalians and fungi. In Arabidopsis stress signalling mainly depends on AtMAK3, MAK4 and MAK6 with SA signalling positively regulated via AtMPK3 and AtMPK6 and negatively regulated via AtMPK3 and AtMPK6 and negatively regulated via AtMPK4. This complex intricate association of SA, ROS and MAPK cascades, although this has been more thoroughly descriptive for case of defence. In addition, AtMPK4 along with its kinase substrates MKS1, WRKY25 and/or WRKT33 repressing SA signalling and activates JA signalling. AtMPK4 is activated in Arabidopsis by Pseudomonas infection or by treatment with the pseudomonas PAMP and may serve to fine-tune AtMPK3- and AtMPK6-mediated defence responses associated with PTI. The MPK4 mutants have a severely dwarf phenotype that might be due to SA accumulation. Two lines of evidences support this conclusion because mutation that disrupts SA biosynthesis (eds1 and pad4) or overexpression of the NahG transgene partially reverts the MPK4 phenotype. Because EDR1 encodes a MAPKKK with similarity to CTR1, a negative regulator of ethylene responses, EDR1 may function at the beginning of a cascade that negatively regulates SA-induced defences.

Further evidence linking SA to Arabidopsis growth comes from the characterization of the null MPK1 (map kinase phosphatase 1) and ptp1 (protein tyrosine phosphatase 1) mutants, which are negative regulators of MPK6 and MPK3. Subsequent stress of these primed plants resulted in enhanced accumulation of phosphorylated, active AtMPK3 and AtMPK6, which correlated with enhanced inducibility of PAL and PR-1 expression. Reduction of SA levels by the NahG PAD4 or eds1 genotypes largely suppresses the MKP1 and MKP1 PTP1 dwarf phenotypes and the constitutive PR gene expression. The MKP1 and MKP1 PTP1 mutants have growth defects, increased levels of endogenous SA, and constitutive defence responses including PR gene expression and resistance to the bacterial pathogens *Pseudomonas syringae*. Moreover, MPK6 and MPK3 null mutations partially and differentially suppress the MKP1 phenotype.

Crosstalk between SA and 'ABA-GAs-Auxin complex' to regulate the germination and vegetative growth

SA crosstalk with other hormones can be more direct. The growth hormone auxin enhances pathogen susceptibility; SA is shown to repress auxin signalling, thereby reducing susceptibility. The perception of the SA begins with the interaction of the hormone with the receptor molecule. There are indications that some sort of hormone recognition system on the plasma membrane may exist for some of the hormones. This is particularly true of the cereal aleurones system, which responds to low-level of GA3 with increased transcription of interalial α-amylase encoding genes. This increased rate of transcription is abolished by either ABA or the withdrawal of GA3 (Hooley et al., 1991). Various hormones involved in plant development communicate with SA. For example, gibberellic acid (GAs) may affect disease resistance by modelling the SA-JA equilibrium. The action of ABA and GA3 in signalling transduction has been extensively studied using the cereal aleurone layer.

Evidence suggests that these hormones are perceived at the plasma membrane and that phospholipases and G-proteins are involved in the early signalling events. By the interaction of Ca^{2+}, calmodulin and various ion channels, protein kinases and phosphatases, GA and ABA regulate the expression of a number of proteins in the aleurone layer, including α-amylase. However, GA can also promote cell death in this system, a process that involves AOS, notably H_2O_2, which is produced in glyoxysomes by the activity of a flavin-containing acyl CoA oxidase. Besides this, ABA can prevent cell death by promoting high activities of enzymes that destroy ROS. NO can also alleviate cell death, and in addition to its ability to react with certain ROS, may act as a signalling molecule. Fluctuations in the cytoplasmic Ca^{2+} concentrations in plant cells seem to play an important role in signalling. The use of fluorescent Ca^{2+} indicating dyes such as indo-1 and fluorescence ratio imaging allows intracellular Ca^{2+} concentration to be monitored on single cell impaled on micropipettes. This technique has been applied with good effect to both aleurone and guard cells, demonstrating that GA3 and ABA affect Ca^{2+} concentrations.

The fungal outcome of hormone perception and signal transduction is the regulation of gene expression. Some of the hormonally regulated genes are auxin inducible SAUR and GH genes and their analogues Gm AUX22 and Gm AUX28, ABA-inducible gene Em, and Rab, and the GA3/ABA-responsive α-amylase genes. It has also been shown that along with Ca^{2+} and JA, the activation of a protein kinase and putative GTP-binding proteins play a role in the signalling transduction pathway that mediates the induction of benzophenanthridine alkaloid biosynthesis by ABA and fungal elicitors. Furthermore, the finding that enzymes involved in auxin amino acid conjugation, and thus inactivation, affect SA-mediated defences provide another possible level of crosstalk between SA and auxin GH 3.5 conjugates. Both SA and IAA (auxin type) and altered expression of this enzyme affect disease resistance. In Arabidopsis, there is a strong relation between SA and H_2O_2 levels and lipid peroxidation and carbonyl groups suggesting that SA is capable of generating H_2O_2 *in vivo* and inflicting oxidative damage to membranes and proteins (Rao et al., 1997).

PAL plays a significant role in plant disease resistance (Dorey et al., 1997). It catalyzes the committed step in the phenypropanoid pathway that suppresses intermediates in the synthesis of isoflavonoid and related phyto-alexins, as well as various phenolic derivatives, and the signal molecule SA. Induction of Pal expression by H_2O_2 is, therefore, entirely consistent with H_2O_2 being part of the signal transduction chain that leads to activation of defence genes in response to a pathogen. H_2O_2 can stimulate a rapid influx of Ca^{2+} in soya bean cells. However, Ca^{2+} is required to activate cell death programme in soya bean cells. The effects of an elicitor prepared from liquid cultures of an isolate of *Verticillium alboatrum*, which is non-pathogenic to *Medicago sativa*, on accumulation of H_2O_2 medicarpin, deposition of phenolic polymers and PAL activity in cultured cells of *Medicago Sativa* L. cv. Kabul (Lucerne) has been studied. In tomato, it has been shown that H_2O_2 from oxidative burst is neither necessary nor sufficient for plant death, PAL activation, SA accumulation or scopoletin consumption (Dorey *et al.*, 1999).

Nonetheless, the generation of AOS, chiefly H_2O_2 and the anion superoxide O^{2-}, is one of the early responses that may be induced during interaction between plants and micro-organisms. The response in cell culture can be induced in plants by inoculation with micro-organisms, or with elicitors occurs in both specific and non-specific plant pathogen interactions (Lamb and Dixon, 1997). The apoplastic oxidative burst, a frequent plant response to invading pathogen has been induced internally in cultured cell wall, elicitor for this act derived from the fungus *Colleto-trichum lindemuthianum*. This system differs from others in that H_2O_2 is generated directly by the action of cell wall peroxidases following extracellular alkalization and the appearance of a reductant, rather than via production of superoxide. The relationship between SA and ROS is complicated.

ROS generated by chloroplasts and mito-chondria also appears to play an important role in the oxidative burst (OB) (Foyer and Noctor, 2005). In addition, H_2O_2 from the OB

is proposed to orchestrate HR-associated defence responses with high levels activating cell death and low levels signalling defence gene expression. Constitutively elevated ROS also appears to confer enhanced disease resistance based on analysis of transgenic tobacco and potato. To reconcile a considerable body of conflicting results concerning whether SA is upstream of ROS or vice versa, several researchers proposed that SA and H_2O_2 form a self-amplifying feedback loop. In addition, to regulate H_2O_2 production, low concentration of SA potentiates cell death in pathogen-related soyabean suspension cells. The inter-relationship between SA, cell death and H_2O_2 led to the hypothesis that defence responses are regulated via an oxidative cell death loop. Moreover, the initial H_2O_2 increases following pathogen infection activates SA synthesis; increased levels of SA then works with ROS generated during the second sustained phase of the OB, to potentiate cell death and defence gene expression. SA also potentiates H_2O_2 production, which in turn, activates the synthesis of more SA and cell death in a self-amplifying loop (Overmyer *et al.*, 2003).

Disease Resistance

Plants have developed a variety of sophi-sticated defence mechanisms to cope with an environment in which many different micro-bes live. Higher plants induce various defence responses when they are attacked by microbial pathogens such as fungi, bacteria or viruses. These different responses include suicide of the attacked host cell (HR); the production of anti-microbial proteins, of which many exert anti-microbial properties; and the production and oxidative crosstalk linking of cell wall polymers. For SAR to develop in systemic leaves, a signal generated in the inoculated leaf is transmitted via the phloem to the uninfected portions of the plant (Vlot *et al.*, 2008). Early evidence showed that application of SA induced resistance against several pathogens and the expression of PR-proteins in a variety of plants. Such properties subsequently are found to mimic the natural defence response in tobacco and cucumber when elevated endogenous SA levels are correlated with induced resistance to the invading pathogen.

SA is initially proposed already to serve this function because: (1) SA levels rise coincidently with or just prior to SAR development and systemic PR expression or peroxidase activation in pathogen-infected tobacco and cucumber; (2) SA is detected in the phloem of pathogen-infected cucumber and tobacco (Rasmussen *et al.*, 1991), and (3) radio-tracer studies suggested that a significant amount of SA in the systemic leaves of pathogen-infected tobacco and cucumber is transported from the inoculated leaf. Further studies have implicated SA as an essential component in the induction of SAR in several plant species. Moreover, leaf detachment assays suggested that the mobile SAR signal moved out of the infected leaf before increased SA levels are detected in petiole exudates from that leaf (Rasmussen *et al.*, 1991). Several families of serologically distinct, low molecular weight, PR proteins are associated with HR and SAR. The discovery of the protective function of SA is first shown in tobacco. SAR is abolished when MeSa accumulation is repressed in the SAR signal-generating leaves by either silencing SA methyltransferase 1, which generates MeSA from SA overexpressing amount of SABP2 whose MeSA esterase is not inhibited by SA. These results, together with the rise in MeSA levels in petiole exudates of TMV-infected leaves, indicate that MeSA is a phloem-mobile signal for SAR. MeSA also may function as an airborne disease signal; MeSA emitted from TMV-infected tobacco or *P. syringae* infected Arabidopsis expressing OsB-SMT1 (a SA/BA methyltransferase gene from rice), induced defence gene expression in neighbouring plants (Shulaev *et al.*, 1997).

SA Induced Constitutive Defence Response

Environmental factors like UV light ozone, and the repression/inappropriate expression of endogenous genes lead to constitutive activation of defence responses, and in some cases spontaneous cell death. The involvement of the SA signalling pathway in senescence is confirmed through a detailed gene expression analysis in Arabidopsis senescent leaves. Almost 205 of the upregulated genes during senescence show at least 2-fold reduced expression in SA-deficit NahG transgenic plants. Assortments of Arabidopsis mutants that display constitutive SA accumulation, PR gene expression, and SAR have been identified. The morphology of many constitutive defence mutants is altered as their growth is stunted and their leaves are curly and called lesion mimic mutants (Durrant and Dong, 2004).

Moreover, several constitutive defence mutants have been discussed previously including H2A.Z, the NPR1 suppressor SSI2, SSI4 and SNI1; the MAPK-associated mutants' MPK4, EDR1 and overexpression of MKK7 or MKS. Light intensity or duration also affects the phenotype of some constitutive defence mutants. High light intensity largely suppresses the dwarf phenotype of CPR1-1, CPR5-1, CPR6-1 and DND1-1 whereas continuous light induces the stunted phenotype of BAP1 (a member associated phospholipid-binding protein 1). These results are consistent with the fact that the SA signalling pathway is activated during light acclimation. In addition, foliar levels of conjugated SA, ascorbate and GSH increase 1.5, 1.8 and 2 folds respectively in Arabidopsis plants cultivated in low light (100 $\mu molm^{-2}s^{-1}$; Chang *et al.*, 2009). Several studies have indicated that environmental conditions regulate the phenotype displayed by certain constitutive defence mutants. High relative humidity growth conditions suppress both the dwarf morphology and enhanced disease resistance phenotype in LSD6, CPR22, SSI4, SLB1 and CPN1/BON1. Analyses of several defence mutants have led to the suggestion that an additional signal besides SA is required to promote disease resistance and HR development.

Supporting this possibility, nahG sid2–2 and eds5–1 suppressed the stunted, necrotic phenotype of ACD11 to different extents, although SA levels in acd 11/nahG and acd11/sid2–2 plants are comparable. Endogenous SA levels promote stomata closure upon pathogen attack. Both human (*E. coli*) and plant-pathogenic bacteria (*Pseudomonas syringae* pv. tomato DC 3000) can induce stomata closure within the first hour of contact with Arabidopsis leaves. This response is compromised in the SA-deficient NahG and eds 16–2 genotypes, and in the ABA-deficient mutant aba 3–1, suggesting that a positive crosstalk between SA and ABA is required to promote stomata closure upon pathogen perception (Melotto *et al.*, 2006). Also, LSD1 appears to condition runaway cell death because of a failure to acclimate to light conditions that promote excess elicitation energy (EEE).

SA inhibits acclimation to EEE promoting conditions, as it induces stomata closure, reduces photosynthetic electron transport and leads to photo bleaching and cell death (Mateo *et al.*, 2004). Because stomata closure is inversely proportional to relative humidity, the ability of low humidity or high intense light to induce cell death and or stunting in some constitutive defence mutants may have a common mechanism is the generation of EEE-associated redox stress. EEE is the amount of absorbed light energy in excess of what is needed for photosynthesis, is promoted in wild type plants by rapid changes in light intensity or quality. In Arabidopsis, EEE induces stomata closure, which, in turn, activates photo-respiration and this H_2O_2 production also induces cell death and expression of APX2 and PR-1 and stimulates SAR and PTI (Muhlenbock *et al.*, 2008).

SA-induced Signalling Versus Growth and Development

A complex genetic regulatory network that either affects signalling upstream of SA or is required to relay the disease resistance signal downstream of SA has been uncovered. The current knowledge of SA-mediated signalling, including upstream and downstream signals and pathways, as well as knowledge gained from constitutive defence response mutants. The role of SA in plant growth and development has been little studied compared with other plant hormones. Mostly recent articles not include SA or its role (Santner *et al.*, 2009). More direct evidences supporting the key role of endogenous SA in the regulation of plant cell growth come from the characterization of Arabidopsis mutant or transgenic plants affected in the SA signalling pathway. The effect of exogenous SA on growth depends on the plant species, developmental stage, and the SA concentrations tested. Growth-stimulating effects of SA have been reported in soyabean, wheat, maize and chamomile. The treatment of exogenous SA (100 µM and 1 mM) has a negative effect on trichome development because its application reduces trichome density and number. Moreover, 50 µM SA stimulates the growth of leaf rosettes and roots of chamomile plants by 32% and 65% respectively but higher concentration (250 µM) has the opposite effect. Arabidopsis plants that overexpress the SA-inducible DOF (DNA binding with one finger) transcription factor OBP3 show a decreased growth rate in both roots and aerial parts of the plants, which in the most severe cases led to death. Although the biochemical events involved in the regulation of cell division and growth by SA are still unknown, these results correlate well with the anti-proliferative properties in mammalian tumour cell lines of the acetylated derivatives. It has been suggested that the growth promoting effects of SA could be related to changes in the hormonal status, or by improvement of photosynthesis, transpiration and stomatal conductance. The effect of SA depletion on plant growth is more evident at low temperature. Arabidopsis NAhG transgenic plants grown faster at 4 °C than wild type plants that have increased CK levels (Xia et al., 2009).

NahG plants have approximately one additional end cycle compared with wild type plants resulting in DNA values as high as 32 °C. It has been suggested that the SA negatively regulates expression of cyclin-D3 (CYCD3; which drives the G1/S phase transcription) because an increased expression is found in NahG plants growth at 4 °C. The elevated CK levels or the decreased SA levels improve plant growth at low temperature through different mechanisms. These results suggest an unexpected crosstalk between SA, CK and BRs signalling pathways since the latter two are positive regulators of CYCD3 expression (Hu et al., 2000). Depletion of SA levels through NAhG transgene expression reverts the ACD6-1 phenotype, but leads to the appearance of abnormal tumor-like growth in the AGD2 mutants background. Although most of the evidences suggest that the SA is a negative regulator of cell division, its role is much more complex.

Upstream Mode of SA Signalling

The plant-signalling molecules SA and other molecules play an important role in the plant defence signalling network. Blocking the response of any of these signals can render the plants more susceptible to pathogens. Negative interactions have been reported as well: SA and its functional analogues 2,6-dichloro-isonicotinic acid and benzothiadiazole suppress JA-dependent defence gene expression, possibly through the inhibition of JA synthesis and action (Doares et al., 1995). JA and ethylene have been stimulating SA action although the antagonistic effects have been described as well. NPR1 is the key

regulator protein that functions downstream of SA in the SAR pathway. The transcriptional regulator NPR1 is the key transducer of the SA signal as NPR1 mutants are SA insensitive. Despite NPR1 is required for SA perception, it is not considered to be the SA receptor, which has not yet been identified. Zhang et al. (1999) provided evidence that, upon induction of SAR, NPR1 activates PR-1 gene expression by physically interacting with a subclass of basic leucine zipper protein transcription factors that bind to promoter sequences required for SA-inducible PR gene expression. There are five paralogues of NPR1 in the Arabidopsis genome; there is a partial redundancy in SA perception as determined by the insensitivity to BTH in a high-throughput mutant screening (Canet et al., 2010).

Moreover, rhizobia-mediated induced systemic resistance (ISR) is independent of pathogen-induced SAR. The NPR1 mutation in the ACD6 background causes a reduction and delay in the cell death phenotype and partially reverts the reduced stature of ACD6 mutants. The ACD-6 NPR1 double mutants develop abnormal growth that protrudes on the abaxial leaf surface. Elucidation of the sequence of ISR signalling events revealed that NPR1 also functions downstream of the JA and ethylene response in the ISR pathway. It would be interacting to determine whether NPR1 is involved in a crosstalk with other phytohormones which can help to explain the abnormal growth, and whether this interaction resembles those between NPR1 and the JA, ABA and ET pathways, to modulate plant defence response against pathogens (Spoel et al., 2003). A combination of SA-dependent systemic SAR pathway and JA-dependent ISR pathway provides an attractive tool for the improvement of disease control.

Crosstalk type interaction between SA and Aux during signalling

The lipase-like protein Enhanced Disease Susceptibility 1 (EDS1) and its sequence-related interacting partner Phytoalexin Deficient 4 (PAD4) act upstream of SA in basal resistance to host-adopted biotrophic pathogens as well as in ETI initiated by the TIR-NSB-LRR subset of R genes. The discovery that the SA-inducible DOF transcription factors OBP1, OBP2 and OBP3 are also responsive to Auxs provides a strong link between the SA and Aux signalling pathways. SA can rescue defence gene induction in EDS1 and POD4 mutants and induce expression of EDS1 and PAD4 in wild type plants arguing that EDS1 and PAD4 lie upstream of SA and are positively feedback regulated by SA. Disease-resistance genes have been cloned and sequenced. The first gene cloned, Pto, encodes a serine/threonine protein kinase, but all subsequently isolated genes encoded leucine-rich repeat (LRR) proteins. Pto is the only resistance gene for which experimental evidence suggests that its proteins product directly interacts with the cognate a virulence gene protein, Avr Pto.

Plant disease-resistance genes are often clustered on particular chromosomes and those regions may be highly recombinogenic. The L locus in flax contains 13 or more alternative alleles governing resistance to resist fungi carrying the complementary avirulence genes. Recombinant gene constructs further showed that phenotype specificity is controlled by the LRR domain. Recombination of the RP1 genes may lead to the recognition of rust races not perceived by either parent or to a degree of constitutive expression even in the absence of a pathogen. Such new genes are created largely by meiotic mispairing and likely amplifying the evolution of new resistance gene specificities. The increased cell division rate observed in wheat seedlings treated with 50 µM SA correlates with an increase in the endogenous levels of the Aux indole acetic acid (IAA) (Shakirova et al., 2003).

Interestingly, the reduced apical dominance and stunted growth phenotypes in the Arabidopsis CPR5, CPR6 and SNC1 mutants that contain increased endogenous SA levels are reminiscent of Aux-deficient or Aux-insensitive mutants. This association indicates that SA might interfere with the Aux-mediated responses. These SA-accumulating mutants contain lower endogenous levels of free IAA and reduced sensitivity to Auxs compared with wild type plants, although exogenous levels of free IAA and reduced sensitivity to Auxs compared with wild type plants although exogenous treatment of wild type plants with SA has little effect on free Aux levels. Potentialities of SA action may be regulated by different EDS1 complex, including cytosolic EDS1 homodimers interactions between EDS1 and the PAD4 heterodimers and nuclear interactions between EDS1 and the PAD4-related and partly redundant senescence-asoociated gene 101 (SAG101) protein (Feys et al., 2005). EDS1 is needed for PAD4 and SAG101 accumulation and analyses of mutant's combinations points to a cooperative signalling role of all three partners in host defence (Feys et al., 2005).

An additional interesting finding is that the inhibitory growth effect of high SA levels in several Arabidopsis cpr mutants is particularly overcome at high light intensities. The dwarf phenotype of CPR6-1, CPR5-1 and DND1-1 is partially reverted under high light conditions, whereas CPR1-1 reverts to almost normal growth. The cross of the Aux-overproducing mutant yucca with the SA-accumulating mutants, CPR6 or SNC1 suppresses most of the phenotypes associated with yucca. This suppression is due to a repression of the Aux response and not to a reduction in its synthesis. Growth retardation in (CPR6-1, CPR5-1 and DND1-1) mutants is due to impaired photosynthetic activity, and they are able to improve the operating efficiency of PS-[22] during acclamatory responses to high light (Mateo et al., 2006).

Moreover, Transcriptome analysis of Arabidopsis plants treated with the SA analogue BTH showed that 21 genes involved in Aux signal transduction are repressed, including Aux1 and PIN7 (encodes a Aux importer and exporter respectively), TIR1 and AFB1 (genes for AUX receptors), and Aux/IAA family genes (Wang *et al.*, 2007). Aux is not the only growth phytohormone targeted by SA because several Arabidopsis genes involved in the GA pathway are also down-regulated in response to BTH treatment (Wang *et al.*, 2006). Although the precise mechanism are still unknown.

Intricate association of SA with other signalling molecules in order to control growth and development of plants

Another signalling molecule that has been implicated in the activation of plant defence is nitric oxide (NO). This compound has previously been shown to serve as a key redox-active signal for activation of various mammalian defence responses. NO as well as other AOS have been shown to stimulate the accumulation of SA, and SA induces the production of ROS such as H_2O_2 and NO. Thus these signals appear to be self-amplifying. One likely role for NO, SA and ROS is to promote the HR and pathogen killing. Both ROS and SA have been shown to synergize with NO to enhance host cell death in soya bean suspension cells (Delledonne *et al.*, 1998). SA and NO may work synergistically to transduce the defence signal by targeting the same effector proteins and/or their genes. In addition to acting synergistically with NO to activate various defence responses, SA may also antagonize NO's ability to inhibit respiration (and thereby cause oxidative stress) by activating the NO insensitive alternative oxidase. In soya bean, the regulation of phytoalexin accumulation is contributed by a pathway independent of the oxidative burst. A variety of nitric oxide (NO) donors have been used to demonstrate that NO inhibits the activities of tobacco CAT and APX. This inhibition appears to be reversible because removal of the NO donor led to a

significant recovery of enzymatic activity (Clark *et al.*, 2000).

In plants, NO and SA appear to function in a positive feedback loop; NO donors induce SA accumulation, and NO signalling in defence requires SA. Supporting this hypothesis, nahG expression suppressed NO-inducible local and systemic resistance in TMV-infected tobacco, whereas SA-induced SAR is compromised by an NO scavenger or inhibitors of NO synthesis (Song *et al.*, 2008). Moreover, NO is involved locally in the induction of cell death in conjunction with SA, H_2O_2 and ethylene. Studies over the past ten years have revealed extensive crosstalk between hormonal signalling pathways. SA-JA crosstalk appears to be at least partially regulated by (transient) changes in the cellular redox status. SA antagonism of JA signalling is abolished by a glutathione biosynthesis inhibitor. Furthermore, glutaredoxin 480 (GRX480) represses PDF1.2 expression in Arabidopsis. Expression of GRX480 is induced by SA in an NPR1-dependent manner, and GRX480 interacts with TGA factors *in vivo*. Although antagonism between SA and JA is bidirectional, the main flow of regulation appears to be repression of JA signalling via SA-dependent cues.

On the other hand, the biological effects elicited in plants by oligosaccharides are diverse. Delayed responses are usually observed hours or days do not affect basal metabolism and protein synthesis. Of the two algal polysaccharides, only carrageenan efficiently induced signalling and defence gene expression in tobacco leaves, as observed with *Phytophthora parasitica* var. nicotianae (Ppn) elicitor. L-Carrageenan, with its high sulphate content, proved the most active. Defence genes encoding sesquiterpene cylase, chitinase and proteinase inhibitor are induced locally, and the signalling pathways mediated by ET, JA and SA, are triggered. Some effects lasted for at least a week. Carrageenans are a family of partly sulphated linear galactans found in the cell walls of many red algae.

Role of NPR1

Cytosolic NPR1 oligomers are held together by disulphide bridges and monomerizes upon SA-induced changes in the cellular redox state leading to reduction of two cysteine residues (CYS82 and CYS 216) by Thioredoxin-H5 (TRX-H5) and or TRX-H3. Although NPR1 is not a receptor itself, it is the only known gene at when mutated generates plants insensitive to SA (Canet *et al.*, 2010) and causes a clear phenotype on plant defence response and some effects on development. Moreover, a mutant form of NPR1 that is constitutively monomeric and present in the nucleus is recently shown to enhance resistance (Canet *et al.*, 2010). However, not all SA-induced genes depend on a functional NPR1, demonstrated by microarray analysis in wild type and NPR1 genotype. Characterization of NPR1 paralogues and alleles must reveal their functions both during defence response (Zhang *et al.*, 2006), as has been determined for NPR3 and NPR4 and during development (Canet *et al.*, 2010). However, plants expressing only mutant form of NPR1, are incapable of mounting an SA-dependent SAR response owing to rapid degradation of NPR1. In Arabidopsis, it is clear that NPR1 subcellular localization is regulated through a redox-sensitive mechanism mediated by conserved cysteine residues that form intermolecular disulphide bonds that upon SA accumulation are reduced and the monomerization and re-oligomerization of NPR1 are required for the full array of SA-mediated resistance mechanisms and provides a link between SA and redox signalling because re-oligomerization is facilitated by S-nitrosylation of Cys 156 of NPR1 (Canet *et al.*, 2010).

Future researchers modulate redox potential in the plant cell by discovering the genomics of NPR1 paralogues in various plant species. Although several studies have concluded that NPR1 and SA enhance binding of TGA2 to PR-1 promoter elements. Rochon *et al.* (2006) argued that NPR1 and TGA2 are independently recruited to the PR-1 promoter, but that SA enhances the interaction between NPR1 are TGA2 resulting in the formation of a so-called enhanceomer in which the C-terminus of NPR1 functions as a transcriptional trans-activator. However, the precise mechanism by which NPR1 cooperates with TGA2 to induce defence gene expression remains unclear. Johnson *et al.* (2008) suggested that transient binding of NPR1 to TGA2 acts to promote dimerization and DNA binding of TGA2, upon which NPR1 dissociates from the complex. The best studied late SA-inducible gene is PR-1. Its promoter contains one negative regulatory element and at least one positive element including the as-1 element that is bound by TGAs. Four of the TGA factors that interact with NPR1 differentially regulate PR-1 expression in Arabidopsis.

Biochemistry of Proteins of SA Signalling Transduction Pathway

A receptor for SA has long been sought, and four tobacco proteins that bind SA have been identified of which SABP2 has the highest affinity for SA. The transcription factor WRKY53 is a master regulator of senescence, and also a convergence node with the JA signalling pathway by interacting with the JA-inducible protein ESR (epithio specifier senescence regulator). Expression of WRKY53 and ESR genes is antagonistically regulated in response to JA and SA and each one negatively influences the other. ESR appears to have a dual function in Arabidopsis, one in senescence and the other in pathogen defence, most probably depending on its cellular localization.

In the presence of WRKY53, ESR is directed to the nucleus where it inhibits WRKY53 binding to DNA and affects the transcription of SAGs such as SAG12 and SAG101 (Miao *et al.*, 2004). These results indicate that SA inducible WRKY53 gene is expressed early during leaf senescence than the increase of JA levels during progression of leaf senescence induces ESR expression to modulate WRKY53 action in the nucleus, and WRKY53 expression is suppressed after the onset of senescence. ESR is localized in the cytoplasm in the absence of WRKY53 where it can function as a cofactor of myrosinase to drive the conversion of glucosinolates into nitriles which is important for resistance to fungal and bacterial pathogens.

Early/Late Induction of Genes by SA
Induced Expression of Genes

Genes regulated downstream of SA can be divided roughly into two classes: immediate-early genes, induced within 30 minutes of SA treatment and genes induced late including the SA marker gene PR-1. Gene expression profiling experiments conducted over the 15 years past have indicated complex patterns of regulation for a large number of genes that are induced or repressed relatively early or late after SA treatment or pathogen infection (Bartsch *et al.*, 2006). Additional evidence supporting SA involvement in light acclimation is that the Arabidopsis response to EEE is regulated by LSD1 (lesion simulating disease 1), PAD4 (phytoalexin deficient 4), and EDS1 (enhanced disease susceptibility 1), all genes of the SA signalling pathway leading to disease resistance (Mateo *et al.*, 2004). LSD1 is a negative regulator of SA-dependent pro-grammed cell death and plant disease resistance, whereas EDS1 and PAD4 exert a positive regulation on the SA pathway in plant immunity (Wiermer *et al.*, 2005). Both EDS1 and PAD4 modulate ET and ROS production in EEE stress signalling, while LSD1 limits the spread of cell death induced by EEE or virulent pathogens, by supporting ROS production through the regulation of SOD and CAT gene expression and activities. From these results, it is proposed that LSD1, EDS1 and PAD4 constitute a ROS/ET homeostatic switch to control acclamatory and pathogen defence mechanism (Muhlenbock *et al.*, 2008).

By comparing the transcript profiles of wild type plants with those of SA signalling or bio-synthesis mutants, including *ics1* and different clusters of genes whose expression is SA-mediated induction of the NPR1-independent, immediate early genes tested depends at least partially on TGA2 in Arabidopsis and tobacco. Moreover, TGA3 enhances SA-induced PR-1 expression, based on reduced levels of the transcription of PR-1 also is fully abolished in TGA2, TGA5, TGA6 triple mutants but not in any of the single or double mutants tested indicating that TGA2, 5 and 6 are functionally redundant positive regulators of SA dependent PR-1 expression (Durrant and Dong, 2004). However, because basal PR-1 levels are elevated in the TGA2, TGA5, TGA6 triple mutants in a TGA3-dependent manner, TGA2, 5 and 6 repress PR-1 transcription in the absence of SA (Durrant and Dong, 2004).

Genetics of NPR1 Suppressor Mutants

Transcription factors that affect SA signalling including ethylene's response factors (ERFs), and R2R3-MYB factors. Several SA- or pathogen-induced WRKY factors, including WRKY7, 11, 38 and 62 repress SA-mediated defence. WRKY38 and 62 induced by SA in an NPR1-dependent manner encoding negative regulators of PTI whose activities are regulated by histone deactylase 19 (HDA19). The ability of SA to induce gene expression via an NPR1-independnet pathway may require members of the Whirly (WHY) transcription factors family; these proteins bind single-stranded DNA in an NPR1-independnet fashion. DNA-binding activity of tWHY1 or AtWHY1 is induced by arachidonic acid or SA respectively, and St PR-10a expression correlates with stWHY1 DNA binding activity. Moreover, WRKY38 and WRKY62 physically interact with HDA19 in the nucleus and in plants transcription assay, WRKY38 and

WRKY62 act as transcriptional activators whose activity is repressed by HDA19. Thus, HDA19 may positively regulate PTI by repressing-WRKY38 and WRKY62, which indirectly suppress resistance by activating an unknown repressor (Kim *et al.*, 2008). Moreover, SA signalling coincident with or downstream from NPR1 has been further investigated using various suppressors and suppressor-of-suppressor mutants. NPR1 mutant phenotype, SSI2 (suppressor of SA insensitivity 2), occurs in a gene encoding a stearoyl-ACP desaturase. It accumulates SA and PR-1 transcripts and displays enhanced resistance to biotrophic pathogens. This phenotype partially requires SA, EDS1 and PAD4, but not NPR1. Because SSI2-mediated resistance also depends on genes affecting chloroplastic galactolipid metabolism, the combined data indicate that galactolipid metabolism affects SA-mediated defence via an NPR1-independent mechanism. Furthermore, two different NPR-1 suppressor mutants, SSI4 and SNC1 (suppressor of NPR-1 constitutive 1) display constitutive SA-dependent NPR1-independent resistance owing to mutations in the encoded R proteins. Both mutants constitutively accumulate SA and express PR-1. Several mutations supporting the constitutive resistance phenotype of SNC1 are identified modifier of SNC1 (MOS2) encodes a nuclear protein with putative RNA-binding motifs (Zhang *et al.*, 2005).

Mutations in MOS3 or 6 compromised SA-dependent resistance as well as SNC1 dependent SA accumulation reinforcing the importance of nucleocytoplasmic trafficking of proteins, such as NPR1, various R proteins and passively EDS1, in SA-mediated signalling. Durrant *et al.* (2007) hypothesized that SA regulates the accessibility of DNA for transcription by NPR1, SNI1, and/or RAD51D. NPR1-independent signalling downstream from SNC1 depends on a complex of at least three proteins that shows homology with mammalian protein complexes involved in RNA splicing.

SA and Abiotic Stresses

Several environmental factors adversely affect plant growth and development and final yield performance of a crop. Drought, salinity, nutrient imbalances (including mineral toxicities and deficiencies) and extremes of temperature are among the major environmental constraints to crop productivity worldwide. Development of crop plants with stress tolerance, however, requires, among others, knowledge of the physiological mechanisms and genetic controls of the contributing traits at different plant developmental stages. In the past two decades, biotechnology research has provided considerable insights into the mechanism of biotic stress tolerance in plants at the molecular level. Furthermore, different abiotic stress factors may provoke osmotic stress, oxidative stress and protein denaturation in plants, which lead to similar cellular adaptive responses such as accumulation of compatible solutes, induction of stress proteins, and acceleration of ROS scavenging systems. Several authors try to improve plant tolerance to salinity, heavy metals and cold stress through either chemical treatments (plant hormones, minerals, amino acids, quaternary ammonium compounds, polyamines and vitamins) or biofertilizers treatments (asymbiotic nitrogen-fixing bacteria, symbiotic nitrogen-fixing bacteria and mycorrhiza) or enhanced a process used naturally by plants to minimize the movement of Na^+ to the shoot, using genetic modification to amplify the process, helping plants to do what they already do, but to do it much better (Hamdia and Shaddad, 2010).

But on the other hand, SA is an endogenous growth regulator of phenolic nature, which participates in the regulation of physiological processes in plants. Present considerable interest has been aroused by the ability of SA to produce a protective effect on plants under the action of stress factors of different abiotic nature. Thus convincing data have been obtained concerning the SA induced increase in the resistance of wheat seedlings to salinity, and water deficit. Tari *et al.* (2002) studied long-term incubation of tomato plants in low concentration of SA enabled plants to tolerate salt stress caused by 100 mM NaCl. Na$^+$ ions accumulated in the leaf tissues of treated plants and functioned as osmolytes without the well-known detrimental effects of the excess Na$^+$. Sakhabutdinova *et al.*, (2003) investigated the effect of SA on plant resistance to environmental stress factors. Treatment of wheat plants with 0.05 mM SA increased the level of cell division within the apical meristem of seedling roots which caused an increase in plant growth. Phytohormones are known to play a key role in plant growth regulation. It is found that the SA treatment caused accumulation of both ABA and IAA in wheat seedlings. However, the SA treatment does not restoration of growth processes. Treatment with SA essentially diminished the alteration of phytohormone levels in wheat seedlings under salinity and water deficit.

The SA treatment prevented the decrease in IAA and cytokinin content completely which reduced stress-induced inhibition of plant growth. Also, high ABA levels are maintained in SA treated wheat seedlings which provided the development of anti-stress reactions, for example, maintenance of proline accumulation. Thus protective SA action includes the development of anti-stress programmes and acceleration of normalization of growth processes after removal of stress factors influence cytokinin content. The SA treatment reduced the damaging action of salinity and water deficit on seedling growth and accelerated a restoration of growth processes. Treatment with SA essentially diminished the alteration of phytohormone levels in wheat seedlings under salinity and water deficit. The SA treatment prevented the decrease in IAA and cytokinin content completely which reduced stress-induced inhibition of plant growth. Also, high ABA

levels are maintained in SA treated wheat seedlings which provided the development of anti-stress reactions, for example, maintenance of proline accumulation.

Antioxidant Enzymes, SA and Abiotic Stress

Drought stress is a major abiotic stress limiting agricultural crop production worldwide. Plants respond to drought stress and acclimatize through various physiological and biochemical changes (Patel *et al.*, 2011). Drought induces oxidative stress in plants, in which ROS such as O$_2^-$, OH, H$_2$O$_2$ and alkoxy-radical (RO) are produced. Oxidative damage in the plant tissue is alleviated by a concerted action of both enzymatic and non-enzymatic antioxidant metabolisms (Hasegava *et al.*, 2000). These mechanisms include β-carotenes, ascorbic acid (AA), α-tocopherol (α-Toc), reduced glutathione (GSH) and enzymes including SOD, POX, APX, CAT, polyphenol oxidase (PPO) and GR. Plants experience drought stress either when the water supply to roots is interrupted or when transpiration rate becomes very high. These two conditions often coincide under arid and semiarid climates. Drought stress tolerance has been seen in almost all plant species but its extent varies from species to species. Exogenous SA reduced transpiration and increased NRA, flower longevity as well as the yield of some plants (Raskin, 1992), which overall suggest that SA may enhance the multiple types of stress tolerance in plants through which interactive effects on several functional molecules or other signalling molecules participating in more complex stress responses (Wang *et al.*, 2010). SA appears to have innate potentiality for increasing antioxidants and influencing antioxidant enzyme activity in plants subjected to oxidative stress. RWC and Ψleaf are low at preanthesis drought stress compared to postanthesis in all the genotypes. Leaf water potential (Ψleaf) decreased with declining RWC when drought stress is imposed at pre- and postanthesis. As the drought progressed, Ψleaf repeatedly declined to lowest mean value of about –2.5 MP.

Farooq *et al.* (2009) indicated that there is a strong correlation between plant water content and accumulation of compatible solutes (proline and glycine betaine) under drought stress. SA treatment obviously improved RWC and Ψleaf with simultaneous and significant increase in proline resulted in osmotic adjustment to a great extent. The critical role of osmolytes accumulation under drought stress is well-documented that explicates plant tolerance for dehydration. Proline accumulation is the first response of plants exposed to water-deficit stress in order to reduce injury to cells. Both MDA and MP decreased in SA treated plants as compared to control plants and the reduction is highest with 1.5 mM SA at both the critical stages of drought induction, e.g. peroxides of poly-unsaturated fatty acids generate malon-dialdehyde (MDA) on decomposition, and in many cases MDA is the most abundant individual aldehydic lipid breakdown product and strikingly malondialdehyde (MDA) is a widely used marker of oxidative lipid injury whose concentration varies in response to biotic and abiotic stresses (Davey *et al.*, 2005).

Efficient nitrogen assimilation is said to be favoured by a high rate of CO_2 assimilation. SA induced conservation of water in stressed plants also resulted in the protection of NRA in SA treated stressed plants. The reduction in growth of many plants subjected to water stress at different growth stages has been shown to be more pronounced at the repro-ductive stage. Since SA increased water potential of stressed plants, it is expected that SA will reduce the damaging action of water deficit on growth. SA has been shown to reduce the damaging effect of water stress on seedling growth and accelerates a restoration of growth processes in wheat, bean and tomato. SA is also found to be more effective in protecting amaranth and tomato plants against the adverse effects of water stress when the stress is given at the vegetative stage than at the flowering stage.

The accumulation of osmolytes allows additional water to be taken up from the environment, thus reducing the immediate effect of water shortage within the plant and they help to stabilize protein tertiary structure and cells. Water potential is significantly reduced by water stress at the vegetative and flowering stages of amaranth and tomato plants. Generally, water deficit caused a decrease in NRA, plant height, shoot and root biomass of both plants. SA induced high proline content, an osmolyte that helps the plant to adapt to drought. The protective effect of SA is shown by the increase in water potential under water stress and enhanced nitrate reductase activity and growth of stressed amaranth and tomato plants. 3 M SA is more effective than 1 M SA in protecting both plants against the damaging effects of drought and the vegetative stage (EV and LV) is more receptive than the flowering stage. Both plants showed almost similar response to water deficit and SA treatments.

Abiotic Stress, SA and MAPK Interaction

In some ways, analyses of plant responses to abiotic stresses are simpler than studies of biotic or host-pathogen responses because it is relatively simple to apply an abiotic stress. Nonetheless, abiotic studies are often less mechanistically revealing because they lack the tools provided by an understanding of the genetics of the biotic stressor or pathogen. In addition, although responses to abiotic stresses such as heat versus cold or drought versus salinity are related, their mechanistic relationships to more general metabolic fluxes, which include redox potentials, ROS, and Ca^{2+} levels, can be difficult to disentangle. These strengths and caveats are apparent in studies that implicate MAPK cascades in regulating responses to environmental cues posed by abiotic stresses, water, salt, cold and osmotic stress. Stressor-specific induction of MAPK genes and increased MAPK kinase activity have been detected when plants are subjected to touch, cold, salinity, genotoxic agents, UV irradiation, ozone and oxidative stress. An *A. thaliana* cascade that responds to salt, drought, and cold may include the components MEKK1, MKK2, MPK4 and/or MPK6. Initially, MKK2 mutants had reduced tolerance to salinity; transgenic lines that overexpress MKK2 exhibited enhanced tolerance to salt and cold. Therefore, more rigorous data are needed to demonstrate that MEKK1 is the specific MAP3K upstream of the MPK4 and/or MPK6 cascade in response to cold and salt. Future studies should also assess if the activation of MPK4 and/or MPK6 is a response to dehydration or osmotic stress caused by elevated salinity and cold.

SA and JA

The role of SA as a defence signal molecule is widely recognized. More than a decade ago, researchers showed that SA induces the transient activation of MAPKs in tobacco suspension cells, a finding that coined the term SA-induced protein kinase (SIPK). Later experiments with *A. thaliana* roots confirmed that MAPK phosphorylation is directly correlated with SA application. The *A. thaliana* ortholog of SIPK is MPK6, which together with wound-induced protein kinase (WIPK) or its *A. thaliana* ortholog MPK3, appears to balance the accumulation of JA or SA in response to mechanical or herbivore induced wounding (Seo *et al.*, 2007). In turn, MPK1 and MPK2 are activated by ABA and H_2O_2, and their activation is also a late JA and wounding response. In addition, colocalization in vascular tissues implies that these MAPKs act in the vasculature specifically (Doczi *et al.*, 2007). Lower concentrations appear to incite synergistic effects, which become antagonistic at higher dosage differences, similar to

MEKK1 or MPK4 mutants with increased SA and the reduced expression of JA-inducible marker genes. Thus, the MEKK1-MPK4 module is currently considered a switch to balance SA/JA hormone signalling. The functions of MKKs accumulate to study the genetic interactions among available MAP2K mutants, especially between autoactive MKK9 and MKK7, and between MKK4 and MKK5 that share some of the same MAPK substrates. Modes of hormone signalling modulation are emerging and MAPK modules are recognized as nodal points in many instances. Further efforts should include systematic observations of MAPK signalling regulation at the organ and tissue level in specific environmental or developmental contexts.

Salinity

Plant growth is impressed by biotic and abiotic stress inversely. There are many reports about proteins change level in salinity stress. The abiotic stress causes loss of hundred million dollars annually, because of reduction and loss of products. Leaves fill up more soluble sugars such as glucose, fructose and proline with treatment of SA. The results demonstrated that increasing of proline and sugars due to osmotic slope in plants lead to increasing tolerance against dehydrations of leave content and acceleration of plant developments in stress conditions. Salinity is the most important limiting factor for crop production and it is becoming an increasingly severe problem in many regions of the world. Plant's behavioural response to salinity is complex, and different mechanisms are adopted by plants when they encounter salinity. The soil and water engineering methods increase farm production in the damaged soil by salinity, but achievement of higher purpose by these methods seems to be very difficult. The high salinity affected the soil penetration, decreased the soil water potential and finally caused physiological drought. The plants under salinity condition change their metabolisms to overcome the changed environmental condition. One mechanism utilized by the plants for overcoming the salt stress effects might be via accumulation of compatible osmolytes, such as proline and soluble sugar. Production and accumulation of free amino acids, especially proline by plant tissue during draught, salt and water stress is an adaptive response. Proline has been proposed to act as a compatible solute that adjusts the osmotic potential in the cytoplasm. Thus proline can be used as a metabolic marker in relation to stress.

SA is a plant phenol, and today it is in use as internal regulator hormone, because its role in the defensive mechanism against biotic and abiotic stresses has been confirmed. By high salinity concentrations, the level of sugar in leaf increases. Also SA increases the sugar salinity decreases the leaf protein level. SA increases protein concentration. The increasing of carbohydrate is a signal for drought tolerance. The high carbohydrate concentration with its role to reduce water potential helps to prevent oxidative losses and protein structure maintenance during water shortage. Also carbohydrates play a molecule role for sugar responsible genes that give different physiological response like defensive response and cellular expansion (Koch, 1996). Salt stress and salicylic acid increase leaf sugar. SA causes balance in the sugar level at salinity stress condition. The increasing of induced glucose storage by salt stress is possible, that is for storage demand reduction of carbon or starch decomposition. Sucrose breaks down to glucose and fructose, and starch decomposition to glucose increases its osmotic pressure cell. Marian and colleagues (2000) reported the increase in soluble sugar content of the root of tomato under salt stress. The use of SA can activate the consumption of soluble sugar metabolism by increasing osmotic pressure. It is supposed that SA treatment deranges the enzymatic system of polysaccharide hydrolysis. There are many reports about increasing and decreasing of protein level in salicylic stress. The soluble protein and free amino acid in barley organs (root and bud) increases with NaCl increasing. The increasing amino acid in the plant tissue under stress is related to protein fraction. Leaf protein level decreased by salt stress but SA can increase it.

The cause of protein reduction at salinity condition is the prevention of NRA. The salt stress induced some changes on the protein of rice leaf shoots and root but not effective on leaf blade. The level of some protein decreases because of protein synthesis reduction (Kong-Ngern et al., 2005). Under high water stress, some plants produce materials with low molecular weight such as amino acid and polyamines, which reduce water potential. The plants produce some proteins in response to biotic and abiotic stresses, that some of these proteins deduct by SA (Hussien et al., 2007). The salt stress decreases the protein level in leaf, but SA increases the protein levels. The proteins at salt stress condition accumulate and act as osmotic regulator. The salinity stress deducts special protein in root and leaves of barley. Salinity stress increases amino acid content in wheat varieties.

Cold Stress

Results of Szalai et al. (2011) suggested that an overlap may exist between the ABA-induced cold acclimation and the SA-related stress response. Under normal growth conditions increased levels of bound SA and ortho-hydroxycinamic acid (OHCA) are observed in the leaves during ABA treatment. In the roots, ABA does not affect the free and bound SA levels, but increased the amount of free and bound OHCA. SA is also shown to enhance the chilling tolerance of various species. This enhanced tolerance is accompanied by increased activities of certain antioxidant enzymes including glutathione reductase (GR) and guaiacol peroxidase. Cold acclimation also caused an increase in the level of OHCA. Crosstalk between ABA and SA has been recently discussed but the relationship has not yet been completely elucidated. In the leaves, ABA treatment and/or cold stress does not affect the free oHCA levels. In the leaves of control plants the bound oHCA content increased.

Moreover, ABA treatment increased the level of free and bound oHCA at normal temperature at both concentrations, but when ABA treatment is followed by cold treatment, the amount of free oHCA does not change, while the amount of bound oHCA showed a slight decrease. The activity of GR increased at low temperature and ABA pre-treatment does not affect this level. The GST activity increased after treatment with ABA, either alone or combined with cold, but is not affected by cold stress alone. Similar changes are observed in the case of APX. ABA treatment increased the level of bound SA in the leaves under normal growth conditions. This is in accordance with study of Li *et al.*, (2006) where they treated pea plants with an ABA biosynthesis inhibitor resulted in the disappearance of the SA peak during heat acclimation. When plants treated with ABA are exposed to chilling, the SA levels decreased, in contrast to their unchilled counterparts. A possible reason for this is that the treated plants do not require a further enhancement of the SA-related pathway. Although the exact mechanism of the cross-talk between the ABA and SA signalling pathways is unclear, it is also possible that ABA inhibits the activity of SA-glucosyl- transferase thus increasing the level of free SA (Li *et al.*, 2006). However, treatment with a high concentration of ABA without stress may induce general stress responses including SA synthesis and the rate of generation of bound SA from the newly synthesized SA is probably higher than the inhibitory effect of ABA on SA-glucosyltransferase. Furthermore, it is also found that ABA negatively regulates SA synthesis by the transcriptional regulation of at least isochorismate synthase. It is also found that cold treatment significantly increased the amount of free and bound oHCA in the roots upon ABA treatment, while ABA has very little effect on SA levels in the roots.

Heavy Metals

Presoaking of *Oryza sativa* L. seeds with SA resulted in partial protection against Cd as observed by minor changes in length, biomass and total chlorophyll and thus indicate that Cd-induced oxidative stress can be regulated by SA. SA priming resulted in low Cd accumulation. Under SA priming the extent of TBARS, H_2O_2 and O^{2-} increases significantly low, suggesting SA-regulated protection against oxidative stress. Under SA-priming conditions, the efficiency of the antioxidant enzymes is significantly elevated. GPx (guaiacol peroxidase) and SOD activity showed significant increase. The ascorbate activity increased after Cd treatment, followed by a decline in glutathione under SA-free condition. SA priming showed gradual increase in these non-enzymatic antioxidants also.

Conclusion

SA is a true plant hormone that goes beyond the defence reaction in plant immunity and response to biotic and abiotic stresses. In coordination with CKS, ET, AUXs, GAs, JA and ABA; SA importantly contribute to growth and developmental regulation although the biochemical mechanisms that mediate most of these responses remain largely unknown. However, much has been learned during the past two decades regarding how the SA signal is generated, regulated and transduced to result in HR cell death, defence gene expression, and/or SAR. One of the biggest outstanding questions in SA biology today concerns how SA is initially perceived and how SA event triggers resistance signalling. All these factors play role in gene regulation and trigger activation of the pathways leading to *in situ* production of a number of secondary plant products like SA which in turn offer protection to the plant. There seems to be necessity of in depth study on the response of the plants from the point of view of biosynthetic since a plant would always adopt less energy intensive pathways under the giving circumstances, which needs to be elucidated.

REFERENCES

Buchanan-Wollaston V, Page T, Harrison E, Breeze E, Lim PO, Nam HG, Lin JF, Wu SH, Swidzinski J, Ishizaki K and Leaver CJ (2005). Comparative transcriptome analysis reveals significant differences in gene expression and signalling pathways between developmental and dark/starvation-induced senescence in Arabidopsis. *The Plant Journal*, **42**: 567–585.

Canet JV, Dobon A, Ibanes F, Perales L and Tornero P (2010). Resistance and biomass in Arabidopsis: A new model for salicylic acid perception. *Plant Biotechnology Journal*, **8**: 126–141.

Chang C, Slesak I, Jordá L, Sotnikov A, Melzer M, Miszalski Z, Mullineaux PM, Parker JE, Karpinska B and Karpinski S (2009). Arabidopsis chloroplastic glutathione peroxidases play a role in crosstalk between photooxidative stress and immune responses. *Plant Physiology*, **150**: 670–683.

Clark D, Durner J, Navarre DA and Klessig DF (2000). Nitric oxide inhibition of tobacco catalase and ascorbate peroxidase. *Mol. Plant-Microb. Interact*, **13**: 1380–1384.

Delaney TP, Uknes S, Vernooij B, Friedrich L, Weymann K, Negrotto D, Gaffney T, Gut-Rella M, Kessmann H, Ward E and Ryals J (1994). A central role of salicylic acid in plant disease resistance. *Science*, **266**: 1247–1250.

Delledonne M, Xia Y, Dixon RA and Lamb C (1998). Nitric oxide functions as a signal in plant disease resistance. *Nature*, **394**: 585–588.

Doares SH, Narraez-Vasquez J, Conconi A and Ryan CA (1995). Salicylic acid inhibits synthesis of proteinase inhibitors in tomato leaves induced by systemin and jasmonic acid. *Plant Physiol*, **108**: 1741–1746.

Doczi R, Brader G, Pettko-Szandtner A, Rajh I, Djamei A *et al.* (2007). The Arabidopsis mitogen-activated protein kinase kinase MKK3 is upstream of group C mitogen-activated protein kinases and participates in pathogen signalling. *Plant Cell*, **19**: 3266–3279.

Dorey S, Kopp M, Geoffery P, Fritig B and Kauffmann S (1999). Hydrogen peroxide from the oxidative burst is neither necessary nor sufficient for hypersensitive cell death induction, phenylalanine ammonia lyase stimulation, salicylic acid accumulation, or scopoletin consumption in cultured tobacco cells treated with elicitin. *Plant Physiol*, **121**: 163–171.

Durner J and Klessig DF (1995). Inhibition of ascorbate peroxidase by salicylic acid and 2,6-dichloroisonicotinic acid, two inducers of plant defence responses. *Proceedings of the National Academy of Sciences*, USA, **92**: 11312–11316.

Durrant WE and Dong X (2004). Systemic acquired resistance. *Annu. Rev. Phytopathol*, **42**: 185–209.

Durrant WE, Wang S and Dong X (2007). Arabidopsis SNI1 and RAD51D regulate both gene transcription and DNA recombination during the defence response. *Proc. Natl. Acad. Sci*, USA, **104**: 4223–4227.

Farooq M, Wahid A, Kobayashi N, Fujita D and Basra SMA (2009a). Plant drought stress: effects, mechanisms and management. *Agron. Sust. Dev*, **29**: 185–212.

Feys BJ, Wiermer M, Bhat RA, Moisan LJ, Medina-Escobar N *et al.* (2005). *Arabidopsis* senescence-associated gene101 stabilizes and signals within an enhanced disease susceptibility 1 complex in plant innate immunity. *Plant Cell*, **17**: 2601–2613.

Group M, Ichimura K, Shinozaki K, Tena G, Sheen J *et al.* (2002). Mitogen-activated protein kinase cascades in plants: A new nomenclature. *Trends Plant Sci*, **7**: 301–308.

Hamdia, MA and Shaddad MAK (2010). Salt tolerance of crop plants. *Journal of Stress Physiology and Biochemistry*, **6**: 64–90.

Hooley R, Beale MH and Smith SJ (1991). Gibberellin perception at the plasma membrane of *Avena fatua* aleurone protoplasts. *Planta*, **183**, 274–280.

Hu Y, Bao F and Li J (2000). Promotive effect of brassinosteroids on cell division involves a distinct CycD3-induction pathway in Arabidopsis. *The Plant Journal*, **24**: 693–701.

Hussein MM, Balbaa LK and Gaballah MS (2007). Salicylic acid and salinity effects on growth of maize plant. *Research Journal of Agriculture and Biological Sciences*, **3(4)**: 321–328.

Jorgensen TG, Weis-Fogh US, Nielsen HH and Olesen HP (1976). Salicylate- and aspirin-induced uncoupling of oxidative phosphorylation in mitochondria isolated from the mucosal membrane of the stomach. *Scandinavian Journal of Clinical and Laboratory Investigation*, **36**: 649–654.

Kapulnik Y, Yalpani N and Raskin I (1992). Salicylic acid induces cyanide-resistant respiration in tobacco cell-suspension cultures. *Plant Physiology*, **100**: 1921–1926.

Koch K (1996). Carbohydrate-modulated gene expression in plants. *Annu. Rev. Plant Physiol. Plant Mol. Biol*, **47**: 509–540.

Lamb C and Dixon R (1997). The oxidative burst in plant disease resistance. *Annu. Rev. Plant Physiol. Plant Mol. Biol*, **48**: 251–271.

Larque-Saavedra A (1978). The antitranspirant effect of acetylsalicylic acid on *Phaseolus vulgaris*. *Physiol. Plant*, **43**: 126–128.

Leon J, Lawton MA and Raskin I (1995). Hydrogen peroxide stimulates salicylic acid biosynthesis in tobacco. *Plant Physiology*, **108**: 1673–1678.

Li J, Brader G, Kariola T and Palva ET (2006). WRKY70 modulates the selection of signalling pathways in plant defence. *Plant J*, **46**: 477–491.

Li L and Li L (1995). Effects of resorcinol and salicylic acid on the formation of adventitious roots on hypocotyl cutting of *Vigna radiate*. *J. Trop. Subtrop. Bot*, **3**: 67–71.

Marian EB, Jose DA and Francisco PA (2000). Carbon partitioning and sucrose metabolism in tomato plants growing under salinity. *Physiol Plant*, **110**: 503–511.

Mateo A, Funck D, Muhlenbock P, Kular B, Mullineaux PM *et al.* (2006). Controlled levels of salicylic acid are required for optimal photosynthesis and redox homeostasis. *J. Exp. Bot*, **57**: 1795–1807.

Mateo A, Muhlenbock P, Rusterucci C, Chang CC, Miszalski Z, Karpinska B, Parker JE, Mullineaux PM and Karpisnki S (2004). Lesion Simulating Disease 1 is required for acclimation to conditions that promote excess excitation energy. *Plant Physiology*, **136**: 2818–2830.

Mazid M, Khan TA and Mohammad F (2011a). Potential of NO and H_2O_2 as signalling molecules in tolerance to abiotic stress in plants. *Journal of Industrial Research and Technology*, **1(1)**: 56–68.

Mazid M, Khan TA and Mohammad F (2011b). Role of nitric oxide in regulation of H_2O_2 mediating tolerance of plants to abiotic stress: A synergistic signalling approach. *Journal of Stress Physiology and Biochemistry*, **7(2)**: 34–74.

Mazid M, Khan TA and Mohammad F (2012). Role of NO in H_2O_2 regulating responses against temperature and ultraviolet induced oxidative stress in plants. *Acta Biologica Indica*, **1(1)**: 1–16.

Melotto M, Underwood W, Koczan J, Nomura K and He SY (2006). Plant stomata function in innate immunity against bacterial invasion. *Cell*, **126**: 969–980.

Miao Y and Zentgraf U (2007). The antagonist function of Arabidopsis WRKY53 and ESR/ESP in leaf senescence is modulated by the jasmonic acid and salicylic acid equilibrium. *The Plant Cell*, **19**: 819–830.

Moore AL, Albury MS, Crichton PG and Affourtit C (2002). Function of the alternative oxidase: Is it still a scavenger? *Trends in Plant Science*, **7**: 478–481.

Morris K, Mackerness SAH, Page T, John CF, Murphy AM *et al.* (2000). Salicylic acid has a role in regulating gene expression during leaf senescence. *Plant J*, **23**: 677–685.

Moussa HR and El-Gamel SM (2010). Effect of salicylic acid pre-treatment on cadmium toxicity in wheat. *Biol. Plant*, **54**: 315–320.

Muhlenbock P, Szechynska-Hebda M, Plaszczyca M, Baudo M, Mullineaux PM *et al.* (2008). Chloroplast signalling and lesion simulating disease 1 regulate crosstalk between light acclimation and immunity in Arabidopsis. *Plant Cell*, **20**; 2339–2356.

Norman C, Howell KA, Millar H, Whelan JM and Day DA (2004). Salicylic acid is an uncoupler and inhibitor of mitochondrial electron transport. *Plant Physiology*, **134**: 492–501.

Omueti O (1990). The effects of age on different cultivars of Amaranthus. *Exp. Agric*, **16**: 279–286.

Overmyer K, Brosche M and Kangasjarvi J (2003). Reactive oxygen species and hormonal control of cell death. *Trends Plant Sci*, **8**: 335–342.

Patel PK, Hemantaranjan A, Sarma BK and Singh R (2011). Growth and antioxidant system under drought stress in chickpea (*Cicer arietinum* L.) as sustained by salicylic acid. *Journal of Stress Physiology and Biochemistry*, **7**: 130–144.

Rao MV, Paliyath G, Ormrod DP, Murr DP and Watkins CB (1997). Influence of salicylic acid on H_2O_2 production, oxidative stress, and H_2O_2 metabolizing enzymes. *Plant Physiology*, **115**: 137–149.

Raskin I (1992). Role of salicylic acid in plants. *Annu. Rev. Plant Physiol. Mol. Biol*, **43**: 439–463.

Raskin I (1992). Salicylate, a new plant hormone? *Plant Physiol*, **99**: 799–803.

Rasmussen JB, Hammerschmidt R and Zook MN (1991). Systemic induction of salicylic acid accumulation in cucumber after inoculation with *Pseudomonas syringae* pv. syringae. *Plant Physiol*, **97**: 1342–1347.

Rochon A, Boyle P, Wignes T, Fobert PR and Despres C (2006). The coactivator function of Arabidopsis NPR1 requires the core of its BTB/POZ domain and the oxidation of C-terminal cysteines. *Plant Cell*, **18**: 3670–3685.

Sakhabutdinova AR, Farkhutdinova DR, Bezrukova MV and Shakirova FV (2003). Salicylic acid prevents the damaging action of stress factors on wheat plants. *Bulg. J. Plant Physiol*, **1**: 314–319.

Santner A, Calderon-Villalobos LIA and Estelle M (2009). Plant hormones are versatile chemical regulators of plant growth. *Nature Chemical Biology*, **5**: 301–307.

Seo S, Katou S, Seto H, Gomi K and Ohashi Y (2007). The mitogen-activated protein kinases WIPK and SIPK regulate the levels of jasmonic and salicylic acids in wounded tobacco plants. *Plant J*, **49**: 899–909.

Shakirova FM and Sakhabutdinova DR (2003). Changes in the hormonal status of wheat seedlings induced by salicylic acid and salinity. *Plant Sci*. **164**: 317–322.

Shulaev V, Silverman P and Raskin I (1997). Airborne signalling by methyl salicylate in plant pathogen resistance. *Nature*, 385: 718–721.

Singh SP (1993). Effect of non-auxinic chemicals on root formation in some ornamental plant cuttings. *Adv. Hort. For*, **3**: 207–210.

Song JT, Koo YJ, Seo HS, Kim MC, Choi YD *et al.* (2008). Overexpression of AtSGT1, an Arabidopsis salicylic acid glucosyltransferase, leads to increased susceptibility to *Pseudomonas syringae*. *Phytochemistry*, **69**: 1128–1134.

T (2011). Abscisic acid may alter the salicylic acid-related abiotic stress response in maize. *Acta Biologica Szegediensis*, **55(1)**: 155–157.

Tari I, Csisaa1 J, Szalai G, Horath F, Kiss G, Szepesi G, Szabó 1 M and Erdei L (2002). Acclimation of tomato plants to salinity stress after a salicylic acid pre-treatment. *Acta Biologica Szegediensis*, **46**: 55–56.

Wang D, Pajerowska-Mukhtar K, Hendrickson Culler A and Dong X (2007). Salicylic acid inhibits pathogen growth in plants through repression of the auxin signalling pathway. *Curr. Biol*, **17**: 1784–1790.

Wang LJ, Fan L, Loescher W, Duan W, Liu GJ and Cheng JS (2010). Salicylic acid alleviates decrease in photosynthesis under heat stress and accelerates recovery in grapevine leaves. *BMC Plant Biol*, **10**: 34–39.

Zhang Y, Cheng YT, Bi D, Palma K and Li X (2005). MOS2, a protein containing G-patch and KOW motifs, is essential for innate immunity in *Arabidopsis thaliana*. *Curr. Biol*, **15**: 1936–1942.

Zhang Y, Cheng YT, Qu N, Zhao Q, Bi D and Li X (2006). Negative regulation of defence responses in Arabidopsis by two NPR1 paralogs. *The Plant Journal*, **48**: 647–656.

Zhang Y, Fan W, Kinkelma M, Li X and Dong X (1999). Interaction of NPR1 with basic leucine zipper protein transcription factors that bind sequences required for salicylic acid induction of the PR-1 gene. *Proc. Natl. Acad. Sci, USA*, **96**: 6523–6528.

QUESTIONS

Q. 1. Botanical name of sycamore (common name is occidental plane or Button wood) is:

(1) *Citrus officinalis*
(2) *Cicer arietinum*
(3) *Platanus occidentalis/Acer pseudo-planatus*
(4) *Arabidopsis thaliana*

Q. 2. American planetree belong to the family, plantanaceae, is botanical name is:

(1) *Cycas revoluta*
(2) *Ginkgo biloba*
(3) *Platanus occidentalis*
(4) *Centella asiatica*

Q. 3. Sycamore, a name of plant concerned with the discovery of which hormone?

(1) ET
(2) GA
(3) ABA
(4) CK

Q. 4. A growth inhibitor act as a negative regulator of growth and stomatal opening particularly when plant is under environmental stresses?

(1) Auxin   (2) ET
(3) ABA   (4) GA

Q. 5. Stress hormone is the common name of:

(1) Ethylene
(2) Kinetin
(3) ABA
(4) Salicylic acid

Q. 6. What is true about ABA?

(1) Ubiquitous in vascular plants
(2) Absent in liverworts
(3) Found root cap to apical bud and all cells contain chloroplast or amyloplasts
(4) All are correct

Q. 7. Lunularic acid found in liverworts, is a similar compound to which plant hormone found in higher plants?

(1) CK   (2) GA
(3) ABA   (4) ET

Q. 8. Chemical structure of ABA (15-C) confugurates:

(1) An aliphatic ring with one double bond
(2) Three methyl group
(3) An unsaturated chain, has—COOH group
(4) All are correct

Q. 9. Nearly all naturally occurring ABA is:

(1) Trans form
(2) Ester form
(3) Cis-form
(4) Salt form

Q. 10. Asymmetric C-atom is found in (at C-1), called enantiomers (S and R forms):

(1) GA   (2) ABA
(3) Both 1 and 2 (4) ET

Q. 11. During fast response, which form of ABA is involved?

(1) R   (2) S
(3) Both 1 and 2 (4) Trans-form

Q. 12. Protein synthesis, a slow process, which form of ABA is/are involved?

(1) R
(2) S
(3) Both 1 and 2
(4) Cis-form

Q. 13. ABA has/have:

(1) 4-trans-pentadienoic side chain
(2) 1-ketone
(3) one double bond in cyclohexene ring
(4) All are correct

Q. 14. Most widely used techniques in hormone (ABA) estimation are:

(1) Gas chromatography
(2) HPLC
(3) Thin-layer chromatography
(4) All are correct

Q. 15. ABA is synthesized from which and site of its synthesis is?

(1) Vitamin-P and mitochondria
(2) NADH and ER
(3) Xanthophylls intermediate and chloroplast and other plastids
(4) Alcohol and peroxisomes

Q. 16. Vivipary is a feature of plants (mutant) in which?

(1) ET deficient of barley
(2) GA deficient of rice
(3) ABA is deficient mutant of maize
(4) All are correct

Q. 17. Highest concentration of ABA is observed in the:

(1) Developing seeds
(2) Developing leaves
(3) Mature seeds
(4) Mature fruits

Q. 18. Concentration of free ABA in cytosol is regulated by:

(1) Degradation
(2) Compartmentation
(3) Transport and biosynthesis
(4) All of the above

Q. 19. ABA increase during water stress due to:

(1) Synthesis in leaf
(2) Re-distribution within mesophyll cell
(3) Import from roots
(4) All of the above

Q. 20. ABA decrease during re-watering due to:

(1) Degradation
(2) Export from leaf

(3) Decrease in biosynthesis rate
(4) All of the above

Q. 21. ABA can be inactivated by:

(1) Oxidation   (2) Conjugation
(3) Both   (4) Hydration

Q. 22. Phaseic acid (PA) and dihydro-phaseic acid (DPA) is a intermediate in synthesis of which plant hormone

(1) GA   (2) ET
(3) ABA   (4) CK

Q. 23. GA$_3$ induced α-amylase production in barley aleurone layer is inhibited by:

(1) CK   (2) ET
(3) ABA   (4) Auxin

Q. 24. A root signal, reduce the transpiration rate by closing the stomata is:

(1) GA   (2) ET
(3) ABA   (4) CK

Q. 25. Physiological functions of ABA includes:

(1) Promotion of desiccation tolerance of embryo
(2) Promotes accumulation of seed storage protein during embryogenesis
(3) Inhibits germination and vivipary
(4) All are correct

Q. 26. Seed dormancy is controlled by ratio of ABA with?

(1) CK   (2) ET
(3) GA   (4) All

Q. 27. Functions of ABA is:

(1) Maintenance of seeds in dormant conditions
(2) Increase hydraulic conductivity and ion flux of roots
(3) Mediates stomata closure to water stress
(4) All of the above

Q. 28. What is true about ABA action?

(a) Translocation of food materials and regulates turgor pressure

(b) Inhibits shoot growth under low water-potential

(c) Promotes root growth under water potential

(d) All of the above

Q. 29. Stages of seed development is/are:

(1) Cell division

(2) Embryogenesis

(3) Endosperm and tissue maturation and cessation of cell division

(4) All of the above

Q. 30. LEA (late embryogenesis abundant) protein is concerned with which hormone:

(1) ET   (2) GA

(3) ABA   (4) CK

Q. 31. Function of abscissic acid is not include:

(1) Reduce the destruction of cell membrane and cellular compartments

(2) Synthesis of desiccation tolerance protein

(3) Flower induction

(4) Affect the synthesis of reserve materials

Q. 32. Seed germination is:

(1) Resumption of growth of embryo of mature seed

(2) It depends on same environmental conditions a vegetative growth does

(3) Both 1 and 2

(4) Rapid increase in post-embryonic activities

Q. 33. Dormancy of Clover (*Trifolium spp.*) and alfalfa (*Medicago sativa*) is due to the prevention of water uptake. Reasons for this is/are:

(1) Waxy cuticle

(2) Suberized layers

(3) Lignified sclerids

(4) All of the above

Q. 34. First visible sign of germination is:

(1) Plumule breaking through the seed coat

(2) Separation of cotyledons

(3) Radicle breaking through the seed coat

(4) Mobilization of cotyledonary reserves

Q. 35. Reasons of dormancy in hard nut is due to:

(1) Interference with gas exchange

(2) Prevention of water uptake

(3) Mechanical constraints

(4) All of the above

Q. 36. Most common reason of seed dormancy is:

(1) Interference with gas exchange

(2) Prevention of water uptake

(3) Mechanical constraints

(4) All of the above

Q. 37. The most probable reasons of seed dormancy are:

(1) Interference with gas exchange

(2) Prevention of water uptake

(3) Mechanical constraints

(4) All of the above

Q. 38. Reason of dormancy in 'Cockle-bur (*Xanthium pennsylvanicum*)' is:

(1) Less permeable seed coat to CO_2

(2) Maximum permeability of CO_2

(3) Less permeable seed coat to O_2

(4) Both 2 and 3

Q. 39. Reason of dormancy in 'Xanthium Spp.' is:

(1) Less permeable seed coat to CO_2

(2) Maximum permeability of CO_2

(3) Retention of inhibitors in seed coat

(4) Mechanical constraints

Q. 40. Most common inhibitor of germination is:

(1) ABA   (2) ET
(3) ABA   (2) GA

Q. 41. Primary and secondary growth are inhibited by:

(1) CK
(2) Auxins
(3) Gibberellins
(4) ABA

Q. 42. An important effect of ethane (ethylene) is to cause maturation of:

(1) Fruits
(2) Leaf primordia
(3) Vascular cambium
(4) Root meristems from parenchyma cells

Q. 43. After unidirectional light is received, auxin moves to the shady side of a stem and then the stem bends towards the light. Which step in this sequence represents transduction?

(1) Auxin movement towards the shady side
(2) Curving of stem towards light
(3) A sensitivity of a receptor to light
(4) All of the above

Q. 44. Which of the following is/are correct statements?

(1) Only stem shows positive gravitropism
(2) Only root shows positive gravitropism
(3) Both stem and roots show negative gravitropism
(4) Both stem and roots show negative gravitropism

Q. 45. Almost all communication in a plant is done by chemical messengers called:

(1) Hormones
(2) Circadian rhythm
(3) Photo-periodism
(4) Electron transport system

Q. 46. Which of the following is not a synthetic auxin?

(1) IAA   (2) IBA
(3) 2,4-D   (4) IPA

Q. 47. Which is wrong in concern of GA_3?

(1) It has effect on apical dominance
(2) It does not affect root growth
(3) It promotes seed germination and breaking of dormancy
(4) All of the above

Q. 48. ABA causes

(1) Dormancy of tubers
(2) Faster leaf fall
(3) Retardation of growth
(4) All of the above

Q. 49. In which of the following is a correct match

Column A	Column B
a. European Hazel	(i) Xanthium pennsylvanicum
b. European Ash	(ii) Corylus avellana
c. Small flower scorpionweed	(iii) Fraxinus excelsior
d. Cockle-bur	(iv) Phacelia dubia

(1) a (ii), b (iii), c (iv), d (i)
(2) a (i), b (iii), c (iv), d (ii)
(3) a (iv), b (iii), c (i), d (i)
(4) a (ii), b (iii), c (iii), d (iv)

Q. 50. Embryo dormancy is a:

(1) Physiological feature
(2) Inherent feature
(3) Induced feature
(4) Due to retention of inhibitors

Q. 51. Lateral transport of auxin can seems during the:

(1) Phototropism
(2) Gravitropism
(3) Both 1 and 2
(4) None

Q. 52. SAUR early gene family related to:

(1) Tropic responses
(2) Root initiation
(3) Shoot growth inhibition
(4) All of the above

Q. 53. Optically active among these PGRs:

(1) ABA   (2) ET
(3) GA   (4) CK

Q. 54. In which of the following PGR synthesized as a chemically as racemic mixture (enantiomers):

(1) 1ABA
(2) ET
(3) GA
(4) IAA

Q. 55. Bioassays for ABA includes:

(1) Cell division test
(2) Chlorophyll preservation test
(3) Cell enlargement test
(4) Differentiation test
(5) All of the above

Q. 56. In which of the following accelerates the flower drop in lupins?

(1) ABA   (2) ET
(3) CK   (4) Auxins

Q. 57. Which plant hormone contain a trivial name?

(1) ABA   (2) ET
(3) CK   (4) GA

Q. 58. What is after ripening?

(1) A method of dormancy releasing or inducing germination from reducing the moisture content through drying
(2) A method of dormancy releasing or inducing germination from enhancing the moisture content through water application
(3) A method of inducing flowering from reducing the moisture content through drying

(4) A method of inducing germination from enhancing the moisture content through cold treatment

Q. 59. What is wrong about stratification is

(1) Release of dormancy of seeds with effect of low temperature/chilling
(2) It is a time honored practice in agriculture and forestry
(3) Farmers allowing seeds with a chilling requirements to over-winter outdoors in layered mound of moist soil
(4) None of the above

Q. 60. What is a factor responsible for causing release of seed dormancy or induce germination?

(1) Chilling temperature
(2) Drying
(3) Light
(4) All of the above are correct

Q. 61. All light requiring seeds exhibits:

(1) Seed coating dormancy
(2) Primary dormancy
(3) Secondary dormancy
(4) None of the above

Q. 62. Some times vivipary is a natural feature of plant's life cycle:

(1) Mangrove
(2) Angiosperms
(3) Gymnosperms
(4) Pteridophytes

Q. 63. What is true about the vivipary is?

(1) A varietal feature in grain crops
(2) Exhibits usually by siliques
(3) *Rhizophora mangle* shows vivipary
(4) All are correct

Q. 64. Role of ABA in bud dormancy mainly applied to:

(1) Monocotyledonous perennials
(2) Dicotyledonous annuals

(3) Woody perennials

(4) All of the above

Q. 65. Which inhibits the breakdown of the storage reserves?

(1) ABA

(2) GA

(3) CK

(4) ET

Q. 66. Bud growth inhibitory substance is:

(1) ABA   (2) ET

(3) GA   (4) CK

Q. 67. Bud growth inducing substance is:

(1) CK   (2) GA

(3) Both   (4) ET

Q. 68. Which hormone can exhibits a hihest change in concentration gradient against the environmental stimuli?

(1) ABA   (2) ET

(3) CK   (4) GA

Q. 69. Precursor of ABA biosynthesis in plant systems is a compound contain:

(1) C_{40} (2) C_{25}

(3) C_{30} (4) C_{10}

Q. 70. Precursor of ABA biosynthesis is a:

(1) Xanthophyll carotenoids (C_{40})

(2) Chlorophyll b

(3) Chlorophyll c

(4) Chlorophyll a

Q. 71. Farnesyl pyrophosphate, is also a precursor of ABA biosynthesis, contain number of carbon atoms:

(1) 12   (2) 19

(3) 15   (4) 20

Q. 72. Xanthoxin is similar to have the properties like neutral growth inhibitor:

(1) ABA

(2) GA

(3) CK

(4) ET

Q. 73. IpPP (isopentenyl pyrophosphate) is a C5 carbon unit, a biosynthetic intermediate in synthesis of:

(1) GA   (2) ABA

(3) ET   (4) CK

Q. 74. ABA biosynthesis pathway in higher plants termed a:

(1) Terpenoid pathway

(2) Aconitase pathway

(3) Carotenoid pathway

(4) Melavonic acid pathway

Q. 75. ABA can antagonize the response of plant materials to growth promoting hormone/s is/are:

(1) GA

(2) CK

(3) Auxins

(4) All of the above

Q. 76. Normal growth is attributed to its less than optimal concentrations to produce an inhibitory effect which is also thought to be:

(1) Masked by the presence of growth promoter GA

(2) Masked by the presence of growth promoter CK

(3) Masked by the presence of growth promoter IAA

(4) All of the above

Q. 77. Direct or Isoprenoid pathway is concerned with ABA synthesis, found in the:

(1) Fungi

(2) Plants

(3) Animals

(4) Liverworts

Q. 78. Free ABA can be inactivated by:

(1) Conjugation with monosaccharides

(2) Oxidation

(3) Both 1 and 2

(4) Reduction

Q. 79. **ABA-glucosyl ester (ABA-GE) is a conjugated form:**

(1) Active ABA

(2) Inactive form

(3) Transported form

(4) Untransported form

Q. 80. **Very low concentration (10^{-9} M) of ABA found to be promoting which growth process/es in presence of kinetin?**

(1) Parthenocarpic seed development

(2) Rooting of cuttings

(3) Soya bean callus growth

(4) All of the above

Q. 81. **Promotion of frond number of duckweed (*Lemna polyrizha*) is concerned with?**

(1) Kinetin   (2) IBA

(3) ABA   (4) ET

Q. 82. **What is true about 'Late-embryo-genesis abundant (LEA) proteins'?**

(1) Desiccation tolerance enhancement

(2) ABA promotes its synthesis

(3) It protects the membranes and other cellular organelles

(4) All of the above

Q. 83. **In which of the following is incorrect?**

(a) ABA synthesized in the root caps in response of gravity

(b) ABA produced in the root caps basipetally

(c) In roots, it causes a positive geotropic response

(d) None of the above

Q. 84. **The highest concentration of ABA in the embryo occurs in many seeds at a time when their dry weight is?**

(1) Increasing rapidly

(2) Decreasing rapidly

(3) Remain constant

(4) Increasing with increase in temperature

Q. 85. **High ABA levels during the late embryogenesis cause a accumulation of storage proteins in the developing seeds either by:**

(1) Regulating the translocation of sugars and amino acids to the seeds

(2) By promoting protein synthesis

(3) By inhibiting the protein synthesis

(4) Both 1 and 2

Q. 86. **Exogenous application of ABA regulates:**

(1) Inhibits the germination of most nondormant seeds

(2) Inhibits the induction of various enzymes which rises the during germination

(3) Inhibits the α-amylase and other hydrolyses in aleurone layer in grains

(4) All of the above correct

Q. 87. **Richest sources of ABA is:**

(1) Fruits

(2) Ripening fruits

(3) Abscised leaves

(4) Dormant shoots

Q. 88. **The site where ABA has the capacity to hasten the ripening and colouring of the fruits?**

(1) Ripening grape berry

(2) Ripening mango drupe

(3) Both 1 and 2

(4) Ripening pineapple

Q. 89. **What is true about ABA?**

(1) ABA application in very low concentration has a slight promoting effect on flower growth

(2) High ABA inhibits or delays flowering in a number of plants

(3) ABA as inhibitory effect on protein synthesis (ribonuclease and protease in barley aleurone layer)

(4) All of the above

Q. 90. ABA has regulatory effect at level of:

(1) Translational
(2) Transcriptional
(3) Both 1 and 2
(4) Post-transcriptional

Q. 91. ABA has been shown to stimulate the transcription of the genes, which encode DNA binding proteins termed?

(1) Transcription factors
(2) TATA boxs
(3) Exons
(4) Plosmone

Q. 92. ABA function for:

(1) Only transcription of genes
(2) Only repression of genes
(3) Both 1 and 2
(4) Only translation of genes

Q. 93. Turgour changes based on stomatal regulation is caused by the movement of:

(1) K^+ (2) H^+
(3) Cl^- (4) All of the above

Q. 94. During the stomatal regulation, exogenous addition of the ABA causes:

(1) Increases the rate of closure
(2) Increases the rate of malate leakage
(3) Inhibits the H^+/K^+ exchange
(4) All of the above

Q. 95. ABA functions for, during stomatal regulation?

(1) Inhibits K^+ uptake in the guard cells
(2) Inhibits H^+ release
(3) Affects the distribution of malalte
(4) All of the above

Q. 96. Fungal toxin fusicoccin (FC) overcomes the effect of ABA on the stomata by:

(1) Stimulating H^+/K^+ exchange
(2) Affecting distributing malate

(3) Both 1 and 2
(4) Increasing movement of Cl^- outside from the guard cells

Q. 97. ABA, during the stomatal regulation, would:

(1) Inhibit H^+/K^+ exchange
(2) Promote specific leakage of malate
(3) Inhibiting opening or promoting closure
(4) All are correct

Q. 98. During the stomatal regulation, ABA has been shown to lead the membrane depolarization (closure of stomata) by induce a:

(1) Decrease in cytosolic Ca^{2+} concentration
(2) Increase in cytosolic Ca^{2+} concentration
(3) A release of internal store like vacuole
(4) Both 2 and 3

Q. 99. ABA induced stomatal closure is mediated by the:

(1) Reduction in guard cell turgor pressure
(2) Massive outward movement of K^+ and anions (31^- and malate)
(3) Promotes a net influx of positive charge
(4) All of the above

Q. 100. Under normal conditions, xylem sap is:

(1) Basic slightly
(2) Acidic slightly
(3) Highly acidic
(4) Highly alkaline

Q. 101. ABA causes:

(1) Increasing cytosolic Ca^{+2} levels
(2) Alkanization of cytosol
(3) Inhibits the PM proton pump
(4) All of the above

7 | Why Plants Need a Rich Diversity of Gibberellins?

ABSTRACT

The versatile functionality and physiological importance of a separate class of phyto-hormone, gibberellins, presently gaining more attention in several areas of plant science, especially in contemporary plant physiology. Recent molecular and transgenic level researches have substantially contributed to our understanding of the physiological attributes about mechanism of gibberellin action, includes both fast responses, not involving gene expression, possibly mediated by KNOX and F-box proteins, and slower responses requiring gibberellin regulated gene expression mediated by DELLA, GAMYB, GID1, SLY1 and LFY proteins. These two separate modes of action have been described to varying degree for the major endogenous gibberellins and for the synthetic compounds possess the gibberellins like activities. Although a broad myriad of gibberellic acid (GA_3) effects has been identified for all these as well as several other endogenous compounds, we remain largely ignorant about various aspects of their mechanism of action and the extent to which they contribute to gibberellins regulated plant development. Here, we briefly summarize the action of GA_3 and discuss the extent to which their action overlaps with that of other gibberellin or conversion of GA_3 to other bioactive gibberellins like GA_1, GA_4, GA_7, etc. Other possible implications such as gibberellins act as a florigen agent and regulators of seed development. In addition, this review present a systematic scheme for homeostasis regulation of gibberellin levels on hormonal and environmental bases as well as we also shade a small beam of light on role of inhibitors on gibberellin biosynthesis.

Introduction: The Elusive Definition of Gibberellins and their Action

Gibberellins (GAs) are a group of tetracyclic diterpenes and consist of 19 or 20 carbon atoms that unlike the auxins are defined by their chemical structure rather than by their biological activity. They biosynthesized through relatively well-understood complex pathways and control diverse aspects of growth and development, but best known for its promotion of stem elongation. Thus GA deficient mutants have dwarf phenotypes. It is now clear that both GA biosynthesis and deactivation pathways are tightly regulated by developmental, hormonal and environmental signals, consistent with the role of GAS as key growth regulators. The subsequent steps involved in GAs metabolism have been studied by using cell-free enzymatic systems prepared, for example, from immature seeds of pumpkin or pea. Radiolabelled substrates are converted into their respective products under distinct conditions in the presence of suitable cofactors. These *in vitro* biosynthesis systems have, in conjugation with analyzing the GAs present in intact plant, also been used to identify the point of interaction of inhibitors in the biosynthetic sequence leading to GAs. More recently, further details of GA biosynthesis are elucidated by employing distinct plant mutants and by the cloning and characterization of genes coding for the GA biosynthetic enzymes.

At present, more than hundred (at least 136) GAs are known to occur in higher plants and/or GA producing fungi. A continuously updated list of structures and their occurrence may be found on the internet (MacMillan, 2002). Only a very small number of them (e.g. GA1, GA4, GA3 and GA7) possess biological activity *per se*, whereas the majority are precursors or catabolites. The concentration of bioactive GAs in a given plant tissue are determined by the rates of their synthesis and deactivation. Deactivation is important for effective regulation of the concentrations of bioactive hormones in plants. GAs are metabolically deactivated in several different ways. Methylation of GAs is a common deactivation reaction in various plant species has yet to be investigated. Several biochemical, genetic and genomic approaches have led to the identification of the majority of the genes that encode GA biosynthesis and deactivation enzymes. Recent studies have highlighted the occurrence of previously unrecognized deactivation mechanisms. Biologically active GAs control diverse aspects of plant growth and development, including seed germination, stem elongation, leaf expansion, and flower and seed development. But, however, the main hormonal functions of GAs are the promotion of longitudinal growth, the induction of hydrolytic enzymes in germinating seeds, then induction of bolting in long day plants and the promotion of fruit setting and development. However, some of the many GAs might have functions that are still unknown.

Later, researches convincingly demonstrated that several GAs are required together with other plant hormones like auxins for both cell division and oriented cell expansion (Perrot-Rechenmann, 2010) influencing all aspect of plant development. The GA metabolism pathway in plant has been studied for a long time, and a number of genes encoding the metabolic enzymes have been identified. Genes encoding these enzymes have been identified through conventional enzymes purification from rich sources of GAs enzymes, functional screening of a cDNA expression library, or molecular genetic approaches using dwarf mutants defective in GA biosynthesis (Hedden and Phillips, 2000). Moreover, recently the availability of genomics tools in model plant species has accelerated the identification of additional genes involved in the GA metabolism pathway.

Normally, it has been seen that only two kinds of responsive mutants have been useful in the identification of genes involved in the GA-signalling pathway: (1) GA-insensitive dwarf and (2) constitutive GA responders. Such studies have led to the identification of two responsors of the GA response: GA1 and SPY. The GA1 gene has been cloned and shown to encode a possible transcriptional regulator. Thus, GA appears to induce its effect by derepressing negatively regulated genes. The GA receptors are on the plasma membrane of aleurone cells, with a signal transduction pathway subsequently regulating the production of GA-MYB. The objective of this chapter is to summarize the present state of knowledge of the role of endogenous GAs and to unraveled some of the uncertainties and unresolved the questions about signal transduction pathway.

Gibberellin Homeostasis: An Interplay between Several forms of Gibberellins

The prominent bioactive GAs, including GA_1, GA_3, GA_4 and GA_7. In higher plants, GA_s are biosynthesiszed from geranylgeranyl diphosphate (GGDP)—a C20 precursor for diterpenoids. Three groups of enzymes required for GAs synthesis from GGDP are:

terpene synthases (TPSs), cytochrome P450 (P450s), and 2-oxoglutarate-dependent deoxygenases (2ODDs). Recent work with isotope-labeled precursors showed that the methylerythritol phosphate pathway in the plastid provides the majority of the isoprene units to GAs in Arabidopsis seedlings, whereas there are minor contributions from the cytosolic mevalonate pathway (Kasahara et al., 2002). Moreover, two TPSs ent-copalyl diphosphate synthase (CPS) and ent-kaurene synthase (KS), are involved in the conversion of GGDP to the tetracyclic hydrocarbon intermediate ent-kaurene. Both CPS and KS are located in the plastids (Sun et al., 1997). Ent-kaurene is then converted to GA_{12} by two P450. GA12 is converted to GA4, a bioactive form, through oxidations on C-20 and C-3 by GA20-oxidase ($GA20_{ox}$) and GA_3-oxidase ($GA3_{ox}$) respectively, both of which are soluble 2ODDs. $GA20_{ox}$ is responsible for the production of C_{19}-GAs using C_{20}-GAs as substrates. Some $GA3_{ox}$ enzymes possess minor catalytic activity to synthesize GA_3 and GA_6 from GA_{20} via GA5 (Ttoh et al., 2004). Although, the subcellular localization of these 2ODDs, has not been demonstrated experimentally, they are assumed to be cytosolic enzymes because of the lack of any apparent targeting sequence. GA_{12} is also a substrate for $GA12_{ox}$ for the production of GA_{53}, which is a precursor of GA1 in the 13-hydroxylated pathway.

The precise sites of GA biosynthesis and response must be determined to understand how this hormone controls plant growth and development. During the post-germinative growth of cereal grains, GAs are synthesized in the embryo and then transferred to be aleurone cells, where α-amylase gene expression is induced for the hydrolysis of endosperm starch. None of these GA biosynthesis genes are expressed in the aleurone, whereas expression of the SLR1 transcript is detectable (Kaneko et al., 2003). These results support the premise that the cereal aleurone is a non-GA producing tissue that responds to GAs transported from the embryo. Therefore, in these cases, GAs likely function as a paracrine signal. In germinating Arabidopsis seeds, transcripts of $AtGA3_{ox}1$ and $AtGA3_{ox}2$ are present predominantly in the cortex and endodermis of embryonic axes illustrating that those are the major sites of GA biosynthesis (Yamaguchi et al., 2001). However, in situ hybridization analysis of three GA-up-regulated transcripts indicates that GA-dependent transcriptional events are not restricted to the sites of bioactive GA synthesis (Ogawa et al., 2003). These results suggest the movement of bioactive GAs or a GAsignal, during indication of Arabidopsis seed germination. Studies in several plant sperm suggest that the tapetum of anthers is one of the major sites of bioactive GA synthesis during flower development (Kaneko et al., 2003). Weiss and Colleagues (1995) proposed that the anthers might be a source of GAs for other flower organs in petunia, because emasculation of anthers causes reduced growth of the corolla, which can be reduced by GA treatment.

The expression of GA biosynthesis genes in flowers is restricted to the tapetum cells in anthers, whereas GA signalling genes are expressed in additional organs, supporting the potential role of anthers in providing GAs to other floral organs (Kaneko et al., 2003). In Arabidopsis flowers, the expression of all four $AtGA3_{ox}$ genes is restricted to stamens and flower receptacles, whereas bioactive GAs are required for petal growth as well, suggesting the GAs originating from other floral organs are responsible for petal growth. The synthesis of bioactive GAs in this system would require an intercellular movement of a pathway intermediate, possibly, ent-kaurene, within the embryonic axis; biosynthesis pathway may ocean in separate cell types. In germinating Arabidopsis gene, AtCPS, is localized to the provasculature, whereas transcripts of AtKO, $AtGA3_{ox}1$ and $AtGA3_{ox}2$ are mainly present in the cortical and endodermal cell layers

(Yamaguchi *et al.*, 2001). A possible physical separation of early and late GA biosynthesis roots. The $AtGA3_{ox}1$ and $AtGA3_{ox}2$ genes are expressed in similar cell types along the vasculature of non-dividing, non-elongating regions of roots, but AtCPS expression is absent in these cells (Silverstone, 1997). Further research needs to determine the biological significance of the possible separations of early and late steps of GA biosynthesis **(Fig. 7.1)**.

The level of bioactive GAs in the plants are maintained via feedback and feed forward regulation of AGs metabolism (Hedden and Phillips, 2000). The identification of the majority of GAs metabolism enzymes has provided a clear view to the mechanism by which a large variety of GAs are produced in plants. Because of the multifunctionality of several enzymes are required for the 12-step conversion of GGDP to GA4. In addition, many GA-modifying enzymes, including the 2ODDs, 16α, 17-expoxidase and GAMTs, accept multiple GAs as substrates. The promiscuous nature of these enzymes creates a

number of branches in the pathway and contributes to the production of diverse GAs by a relatively small number of enzymes. For example, reverse genetic analysis indicates that, of the four genes encoding GA3 in Arabidopsis, $AtGA3_{ox}1$ and $AtGA3_{ox}2$ play distinct as well as overlapping roles in vegetative development, but they are dispensable for reproductive development (Mitchum *et al.*, 2006). Also, there is evidence that $AtGA3_{ox}1$ and $AtGA3_{ox}2$ are differentially regulated by environmental signals during seed germination (Yamaguchi *et al.*, 1998 and Yamauchi *et al.*, 2004). The key role of the 2ODDs in determining bioactive GA levels is also supported by the results of overexpression studies. Increased expression of GA levels and GA-overdose a $GA20_{ox}$ gene in Arabidopsis plants causes an increase in phenotypes. In contrast, although overexpression of AtCPS in Arabidopsis is effective in increasing the accumulation of ent-kaurene, ent-kaurenoic acids, and GA12, it does not affect the levels of bioactive GAs or the phenotype.

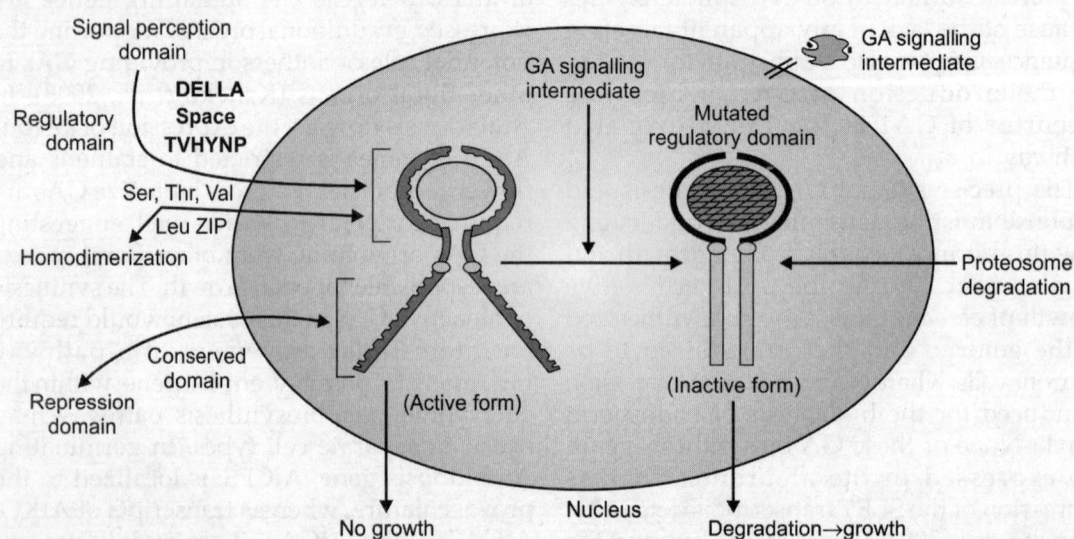

Fig. 7.1: Significance of gibberellic acid based degrative proteins in activation and deactivation of hormone

Role of 2ODDs in Regulation of Bioactive GAs

Transcript analysis shows that GA signalling is mainly targeted to 2ODDs in the GA metabolism pathway to establish homoeostasis; e.g. expression of the Arabidopsis GA biosynthesis genes, $AtGA2_{ox}1$ and $AtGA3_{ox}1$, is highly elevated in a GA-deficient background, whereas these genes are downregulated after application of bioactive GAs (Yamaguchi *et al.*, 1998). In contrast, expression of the GA deactivation genes, $AtGA2_{ox}1$ and $AtGA3_{ox}2$, is upregulated upon GA treatment. Although, the molecular mechanisms underlying this homeostatic regulation have yet to be elucidated, the central GA signalling components are soluble GA receptors GID1, the DELLA proteins, and the F-box proteins SLEEPY1 (SLY1) (Arabidopsis)/GID2 (rice). For example, in the rice GID1 and GID2 mutants, expression of the $OsGA2_{ox}2$ (SDI) gene is upregulated and the levels of bioactive GA1 are highly elevated (Ueguchi-Taneka *et al.*, 2005). Conversely, a DELLA loss-of-function mutant of Arabidopsis has reduced levels of $AtGA3_{ox}1$ transcripts even in a GA-deficient mutant background. Repression of shoot growth (RSG) is a tobacco transcriptional activator that contains a basic leucine zipper domain and binds to the promoter of the Arabidopsis AtKO gene. Importantly, RSG is translocated into the nucleus in response to a reduction in GA levels. 14-3-3 proteins might be involved in the feedback regulation of $GA20_{ox}$ expression. The probable role of RSG in GA homeostasis appears to be restricted to $GA20_{ox}$, because it does not affect the feedback regulation of the $GA3_{ox}$ gene (Ishida *et al.*, 2004).

Multiple hormones are often involved in the regulation of a given biological process. Therefore, how different hormones cooperatively regulate a common developmental process has been an important question. Both bioactive GAs and auxin positively regulate stem elongation. In pea, the auxin (IAA) is essential for the maintenance of GA1 levels in elongating internodes. The IAA induction of AG1 levels is correlated with an increase in $PsGA3_{ox}1$ transcript abundance and a decrease in $PsGA2_{ox}1$ transcript levels. In barley, auxin from the developing inflorescence plays a role in stem elongation by regulating GA3-oxidation and downregulating GA2-oxidation. Collectively, these results suggest that auxin regulation of GA metabolism in stems is a general mechanism. Studies using various auxin-response mutants revealed that the Aux/IAA and ARF-dependent signalling pathways are involved in these transcriptional changes, whereas they are independent of the feedback regulation mediated by DELLA proteins. Partial alleviation of the phenotype of several gain-of-function mutants of Aux/IAA genes by GA application suggests that changes in GA metabolism mediate part of auxin action during Arabidopsis seedlings development. Moreover, the role of brassinosteroid (BR) as a regulator of GA metabolism is less clear. On the basis of the effect of BR on bioactive GA levels, Jager and coworkers concluded that the BR growth response in pea is not mediated by changes in bioactive GA content. Moreover, previous studies have suggested that ethylene may increase the level of GAs during internode elongation of deep water rice upon submergence (Hoffmann-Benning and Kende, 1992). The levels of GA1 and GA4 are substantially reduced in the CTR1 mutant, suggesting that the ethylene signal is initially targeted to the GA metabolism pathway and then to DELLA proteins as a consequence of altered GA content **(Fig. 7.2)**.

Furthermore, antagonistic effects of ABA and GA on seed germination have been well-documented. However, evidence as to whether the endogenous GA levels are regulated by ABA, or vice versa, remains inconclusive. Recently, Seo and co-workers (2006) found that GA4 levels in dark-imbibed Arabidopsis seeds are elevated in the ABA-deficient

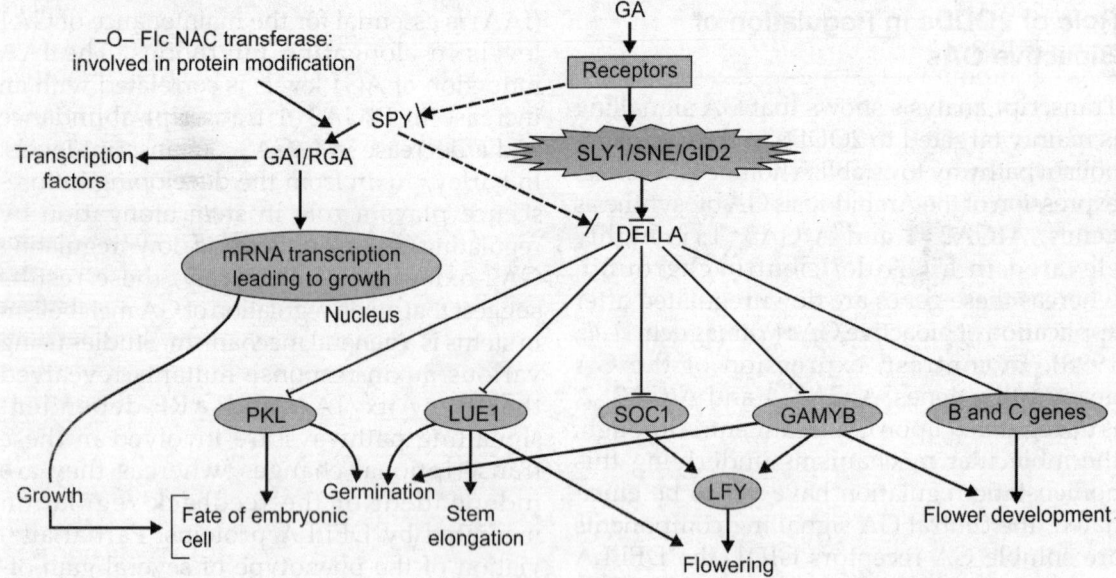

Fig. 7.2: This figure represents the association of gibberellic acid with an array of signalling genes and their responses in terms of plant development

ABA2-2 mutant as well as activation of GA biosynthesis genes in the ABA2-2 mutant is also observed during seed development. These findings suggest that ABA plays a role in the suppression of GA biosynthesis in both imbibed and developing Arabidopsis seeds (Seo *et al.*, 2006). Bioactive GAs function as key mediators between the perception of environmental signals and the resulting growth responses. Light is one of the major environmental factors that affect plant growth and development. Among light dependent processes, current evidence indicates that changes in GA concentrations are at least in part, responsible for light-regulated seed germination, photo-morphogenesis during de-etiolation, and photoperiod regulation of stem elongation and flowering. Extensive studies have established that photoperiodic control of stem elongation in long day (LD) rosette plants is mediated by GAs. This LD-induced stem elongation is inhibited by the application of GAs biosynthesis inhibitors and

this effect is reversed by GA3 treatment (Zeevaart *et al.*, 1993). The grass *L. temulentum* flowers in response to a single LD treatment and has been utilized for studies on GA-induced flowering. Interestingly, GA5 and GA6 are more effective in inducing flowering than GA1or GA4, both of which are active in inducing stem elongation in *L. temulentum*. Evidence suggests that GA5 and GA6 are synthesized in the leaf upon exposure to LD and transported to the shoot apex to induce floral initiation (King *et al.*, 2006).

A two-fold increase in the levels of GA5 and GA6 occurs in the shoot apex following an LD exposure, and this increase is preceded by a rapid increase in GAs content and a drastic increase in the levels of $LtGA20_{ox}1$ mRNA in the leaf after the LD treatment. GA2 and GA4 do not reach the shoot apex, presumably because of deactivation by $GA2_{ox}$; the corresponding gene in rice ($OsGA2_{ox}1$) is strongly expressed at the base of the vegetative shoot transition to the reproductive phase (Sakamota *et al.*, 2001). In contrast, GA5 and GA6 are resistant to deactivation by $GA2_{ox}$, so logically, these compound may act as floral stimuli. Thus, GA biosynthesis is regulated by the photoperiod signal, whereas it is independent of vernalization in *L. perenne*. In Arabidopsis, flowers initiation under SD conditions requires GA biosynthesis. The flower meristem identity gene LEAFY (LFY) is a key component downstream of the GA signal. Unlike in *L. temulentum* in Arabidopsis GA4 increases drastically in abundance shortly before floral transition in the shoot apex, and functions as the major bioactive GA for the induction of LFY expression in the shoot apex. This GA4 increase might be due to transport of GAs from other tissues, because the expression of the known GA metabolism genes in the shoot apex does not correlate with acute increase in GA4 content in this tissue. This suggests that endogenous GA4 made in the leafy may be transported to the shoot apex to induce flowering, although further studies are necessary to proof this hypothesis.

Overexpression of Dware and Delayed Flowering 1 (DDF1) causes a reduction in GA4 content and dwarfism in Arabidopsis (Magome *et al.*, 2004). DDF1 expression is strongly induced by high-salinity stress and encodes an AP2 transcription factor that is closely related to the dehydration responsive element-binding proteins (DREBs) involved in stress responses. In addition, transgenic plants over-expressing DDF1, as well as a GA-deficient GA1-3 mutant, exhibit a higher survival rate (Magome *et al.*, 2004). Similarly, there is a correlation between the survival of salt toxicity and the function of DELLA proteins (Achard *et al.*, 2006). These results suggest that the salt-inducible DDF1 gene is involved in growth responses under high salinity conditions in part through altering GA levels. In fact, salt-treated Arabidopsis plant contains reduced levels of bioactive GAs (Achard *et al.*, 2006), supporting the idea that salt shows growth by modulating the GA metabolism pathway.

Recent work has shown that $AtGA2_{ox}7$, which encodes a $GA2_{ox}$ that specifically deactivates C20-GAs, is a target of DDF1, suggesting that salt decreases bioactive GA levels through elevated deactivation.

Inhibitors of Gibberellins Biosynthesis

As we know that only a few of the GAs possess biological activity *per se*, whereas the majority are precursors or catabolites. The sequential steps involved in GAs metabolism have been studied by using cell-free enzymatic systems prepared, for example, from immature seeds of pumpkin or pea. Radiolabeled substrates are converted into their respective products under distinct condition in the presence of suitable cofactors. These *in vitro* biosynthesis systems have in conjugation with analyzing the GAs present in intact plants, also been used to identify the point of interaction of inhibitors in the biosynthetic sequence leading to GAs. More recently further details of GA biosynthesis are elucidated by employing distinct plant mutants and by the cloning and characterization of genes coding for the GA-biosynthetic enzymes. The biosynthesis of GAs can be separated into three stages according to the nature of the enzymes involved and the corresponding localization in the cell: terpene cyclases acting in proplastids, mono-oxygenases associated with the endoplasmic reticulum and dioxygenases located in the cytosol. Plant growth retardants are applied in agronomic and horticultural crops to reduce unwanted longitudinal shoot growth without lowering plant productivity. Most growth retardants act by inhibiting GA biosynthesis. To date, four different types of such inhibitors are known: (a) onium compounds, such as chlormequat chloride, mepiquat chloride, clorophonium and AMO-1618, which block the cyclases copalyl-diphosphate synthase and ent-kaurene synthase involved in the early steps of GA metabolism, (b) compounds with an

N-containing heterocycle, e.g. ancymidol, flurprimidol, tetecyclacis, paclobutrazol, uniconazole-P and inabenfide.

These retardants block cytochrome P450-dependent monooxygenases, thereby inhibiting oxidation of ent-kaurene into ent-kaurenoic acid, (c) structural mimics of 2-oxoglutaric acid, which is the cosubstrate of dioxygenases that catalyze late steps of GA formation. Acyclohexanediones, e.g. prohexadione-Ca and trinexapac-ethyl and daminozide, block particularly 3β-hydroxylation, thereby inhibiting the formation of highly active GAs from inactive precursors, and (d) 16,17-dihydro-GAs and related structures act most likely to mimicking the GA precursor substrate of the same dioxygenases. Enzymes similar to the ones involved in GA biosynthesis, are also of importance in the formation of ABA, ethylene, sterols, flavonoids and other plant constituents. Changes in the level of these compounds found after treatment with growth retardants can mostly be explained by side activities on such enzymes.

GA Perception and Signal Transduction: Transcriptional and Non-transcriptional Regulation

Little is known about GA receptors, although advances are beginning to be made. A surface localization of the GA receptor is suggested by studies with GA analogues that are unable to cross the plasma membrane. Such membrane-impermeant analogs of GA have been synthesized and shown to be active when added to aleurone protoplast preparations, indicating that entry into the cell is not required for activity. A more direct approach is taken by Gilory and Jones (1994), who microinjected GA3 into barley aleurone protoplasts. When the protoplasts are immersed in GA3 they produced α-amylase, whereas when GA3 is microinjected into the protoplasts it has no effect, suggesting that GA is perceived only on the outer face of the plasma membrane. A plethora of recent advancement evidenced that heterotrimeric G proteins may be involved in the early GA signalling events in aleurone cells. Treatment of wild oat aleurone protoplasts with the peptide Mas7, which stimulates GDP/GTP exchange by heterotrimeric G proteins, induced the synthesis and secretion of α-amylase gene expression.

In addition, treatment of aleurone protoplasts with GDP-β-S, a non-hydrolyzable analog of GTP which inhibits GDP/GTP exchange by heterotrimeric proteins, blocked α-amylase induction by GA. These findings, together with the evidence presented in the preceding paragraph, tend support to a model for GA action based on hormones binding to a plasma membrane receptor followed by interaction of the receptor with a hetero-trimeric G-protein. However, further research work is required to confirm this hypothesis. Genetic analysis of GA regulated growth has identified some genes and their respective gene products but not the specific biochemical pathways involved in the GA-signal transduction.

The biochemical and molecular mechanisms have been studied most extensively in relation to GA-stimulated synthesis and secretion of α-amylase in cereal aleurone layers. There are now definitive evidences that GA acts primarily by inducing the expression of the gene for α-amylase, belongs to multigene family. During germination and early seedling growth, the stored food reserves of the endosperm, chiefly starch and proteins, are brokendown by a variety of hydrolytic enzymes, and the solubilized sugars, amino acids and other products are transported to the growing embryo. It is soon discovered that GA3 can substitute for the embryo in stimulating starch degradation when half-seeds are incubated in buffered solutions in the presence of GA3; secretion of α-amylase into the medium is greatly stimulated.

Before molecular biological approaches are developed there is already indicaton that GA (GA3) might enhance α-amylase production at the level of transcription (Huttley and Phillips, 1995). In previous studies, it is demonstrated by both radioactive and heavy-isotope labeling studies (using ^{14}C-labelled amino acid and $H_2{}^{18}O$) that the stimulation of α-amylase activity by GA3 is due to *de novo* synthesis of the enzyme rather than to activation of pre-existing enzyme. GA3-stimulated α-amylase production is blocked by inhibitors of transcription and transduction. There is now definitive evidence that GAs act primarily by inducing the expression of the gene for α-amylase. This situation is very complex actually than this because α-amylase belongs to a multigene family, but for the sake of clarity they conserved as a single group. Firstly, It is shown that GA3 enhances the level of translatable mRNA is extracted from GA3-treated and central tissue and translated *in vitro* in the presence of the radioactively labeled amino acid [^{35}S] methionine. There are two mechanisms can increase the level of α-amylase mRNA: stimulation of transcription or decrease in mRNA turnover. To discriminate between these alternatives, investigators performed nuclear runoff experiment (Jacobsen and Beach, 1985). Isolated nuclei; although incapable of initiating transcription, can complete the transcripts already being synthesized at the time of their isolation if provided the appropriate conditions and substrates. The regulation of transcription by GAs is proved when such chimeric genes containing α-amylase promoters that are fused to reporter genes are introduced into aleurone protoplasts and the expression of the reporter genes is shown to be regulated by GA3.

The partial deletion of known sequences of bases from α-amylase promoters of several cereals indicates that the sequences conferring GA responsiveness to the α-amylase gene are within 200 to 300 bp upstream of the transcription start site. The placement, order and orientation of several sequences appear to be highly conserved in the different cereal species. One particular sequence (TAACAAA) can act alone to induce responsiveness to GA and has been called the gibberellin response element (GARE). In addition, mutagenesis of another specific sequence, TATCCAC, results in a loss of GA3-induced expression, but less so than for TAACAAA. These results indicate that both the TAACAAA and the TATCCAC boxes act cooperatively, and a third sequence (C/TCTTTTC/T), referred to as pyrimidine box, and may also be required for full GA responsiveness. Together these three sequences have been referred to as the gibberellins response complex (GARC). Transcription factors associated with the GARC are assumed to interact with the general transcription factors at the TATA box, although the precise mechanism is unknown.

The promotion of α-amylase gene expression by GA mediated by specific transcription factors. To identify the DNA sequences involved in the protein binding, the DNA containing the upstream sequence is incubated with an exonuclease in presence of the protein extract from GA3-treated aleurones. The GA induced protein is found to protect the region where it bound from digestion by the exonuclease. Analysis of the sequences of one of the barley α-amylase promoters provided a clue to the nature of the DNA-binding protein. The sequence is shown to have two possible MYB-binding sites. MYB are transcription factors that regulate growth and development. The synthesis of a MYB gene transcript is shown to be upregulated by GA3 within 3 hours of GA application, well before the synthesis of α-amylase m-RNA. Cycloheximide, a translational inhibitor, has no effect on the production of MYB mRNA, indicating that the MYB gene is a GA primary response gene. Recent preceeding results suggest that MYB represents one of the transcription factors that bind to the GA response complex of the α-amylase promoter. This hypothesis is confirmed by mobility shift assays in which it is shown that the GA induced MYB protein (GA-MYB) binds to the GARE, TAACAAA. GA-MYB is also shown to be able to activate the transcription of the gene for α-amylase in a double transformation experiment: (1) the GA-MYB gene fused to a constitutive promoter that caused the aleurone cells to synthesize GAMYB in the absence of applied GA and (2) the gene that encodes GUS fused to the α-amylase gene promoter. Since the doublly transformed aleurone cells are able to synthesize GUS in the absence of GA, and further addition of GA does not increase GUS activity, suggests that GA-MYB alone can induce the expression of amylase (Gubler *et al.*, 1995) **(Fig. 7.3)**.

Recent findings include that GA acts by causing the synthesis of the transcriptional activation factor GA-MYB and possibly other transcriptional factors as well. MYB-type transcription factors may play important roles in regulating gene expression during plant development. Since as we know that its expression is insensitive to cycloheximide, the gene that encodes GA-MYB is an early or primary response gene. The protein GA-MYB then binds to the GA response elements in the α-amylase gene promoter, stimulating the synthesis of α-amylase m-RNA, which is subsequently translated to the α-amylase enzyme during the germination of cereal grain. To summarize, GA stimulates the expression of the GA-MYB gene, and the MYB protein serve as a transcription regulator of the gene for α-amylase. Since, protein synthesis is not involved, GA may bring about the activation of one/more pre-existing transcription factors. The activation of

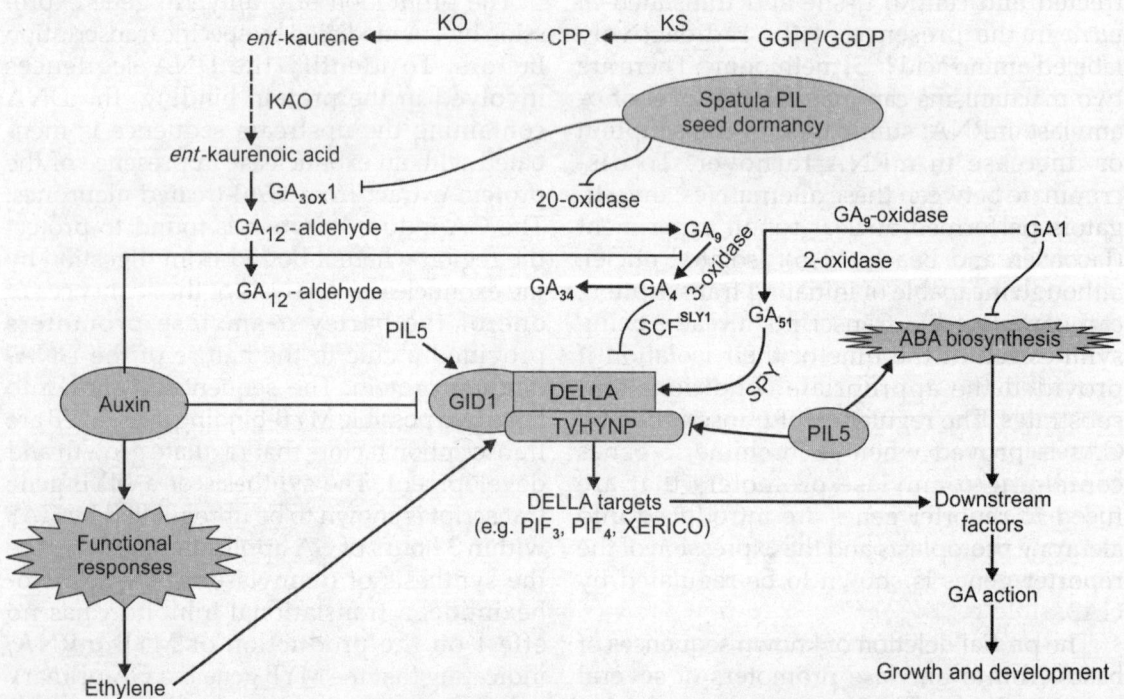

Fig. 7.3: Interaction of gibberellic acid with other hormones and signalling proteins to precede the functional responses

transcription factors is typically mediated by protein phosphorylation events occurring at the end of a single transduction pathway. The genetic approaches applied to the study of GA-stimulated growth led to the identification of the GAI-SPY negative regulatory pathway. The proteins GAI and SPY act as repressor of GA responses. GA acts by deactivating these repressors. Because the aleurone layers of GA-insensitive dwarf wheat are also insensitive to GA, the same signal transduction pathways regulate growth appear to regulate GA-induced α-amylase production. Barley aleurone protoplasts show a slow rise in cytosolic Ca^{2+} upon incubation with GA (Bethke *et al.*, 1995). This increase begins 1 to 4 hours after exposure to the hormone, and thus precedes the onset of α-amylase synthesis.

Consistent with the role for calcium in α-amylase production, GA, in the presence of calcium, increases the level of calmodulin in barley aleurone layers by two-fold and the effect begins as early as 2 hours after the start of incubation. Recall that calcium calmodulin complex is capable of activating specific enzymes, such as Ca^{2+}-calmodulin dependent protein kinases. Studies of Gilory (1996) have suggested that AG stimulates the secretion of α-amylase and other hydrolases via a calcium dependent pathway, whereas GA appears to stimulate expression of the α-amylase gene via a calcium independent pathway. The operation of difficult signal transduction pathways for enzymes secretion and gene expression is consistent with the observation of GA that stimulates both the secretion and the synthesis of some enzymes (e.g. α-amylase), but only the secretion of other enzymes (e.g. ribonuclease and β-1, 3-glucanase). cGMP is a possible candidate for a co-independent signalling intermediate involved in GA-induced α-amylase gene expression. cGMP has been implicated as a second messenger in phytochrome-regulated gene expression. GA causes a transient rise in cGMP levels in barley

aleurone layers after a lag prerid of only 1 hour.

An inhibitor of guanylyl cyclase, the enzyme that synthesizes cGMP from GTP, blocks GA-induced α-amylase synthesis and secretion, and the inhibition can be overcome by membrane-permeant analog of cGMP. These findings that cGMP is one of the compounds of the signal transduction pathway involved in the GA responses. Recently, a few of the genes and some of the biochemical components have now been identified which represent a composite of the factors that has been implicated in the GA control of growth and α-amylase gene transcription, and it is based on the assumption that the two or more than two responses share a common signal transduction pathway. In conclusion, GAs signal transduction seem to involve calcium ions as well as cGMP, but the detailed signalling pathway has not been worked out. α-amylase secretion is regulated by a calcium-dependent pathway, where α-amylase gene expression is regulated by a calcium-dependent pathway.

GAs in plant development: GAs gradients regulating morphogenesis in association with other plant hormones like cytokinins

The most dramatic phase change that flowering plants undergo is the transition from vegetative to reproductive growth. For this transition to be successful, plants must integrate a variety of environmental signals with endogenous cues, such as plant age. The GAs, a class a plant hormones play a role in many processes during plant development, including seed germination, cell elongation, and flowering. The major bioactive GAs, including GA1, GA3, GA4 and GA7 commonly have a –OH on C-3β, a–COOH on C-6, and a lactone between C-4 and C-10. GA1 has been identified frequently that it acts a widespread bioactive hormone. However, GAs also exist in most species and is thought to be the major bioactive GA in

Arabidopsis thaliana and some cucurbitaceae members.

The relative roles of GA1 versus GA4 (and GA3 and GA7) still remain to be clarified through the identification of genes encoding of a soluble GA receptor, GID1 (gibberellin insensitive dwarf 1) from rice (*Oryza sativa* L.) and its homologues in Arabidopsis has illustrated that these structural requirements for bioactive GAs are reflected in their affinity for receptor GID1, as well as their ability to form a complex consisting of GID1, GA and the DELLA protein (repressor of GA signals and degraded upon interaction with the GID1-GA complex), in yeast. Intriguingly, GA4, but not GA1, is the most favoured GA for the rice GID1 in terms of the ability to replace the binding of 16,17-dihydro-GA4 to GID1 *in vitro* (Ueguchi-Tanaka *et al.*, 2005), the complex formation in yeast, and the degradation of the DELLA protein in seedlings and calli (Veguchi-Tanaka, 2005) whereas GA1 is the major bioactive form in vegetative tissues of rice.

In the last decades, information has begun to accumulate on the molecular event involved in conveying the GA signal from an as yet unidentified receptor, through the cytoplasm to the nucleus (Sun and Gubler, 2004). Studies of the GA-signalling pathway in various plants, including *Arabidopsis thaliana*, led to the identification of several positively and negatively acting components (Sun and Gubler, 2004). Mutations at the Arabidopsis Spindly (SPY) locus result in phenotypes resembling that of wild-type treated with exogenous GA. SPY is a negative regulator of GA responses; however, SPY mutants exhibit various phenotypic alternations not found in GA-treated plants. GA also repressed the effects of cytokinin suggesting that there is crossstalk between the two hormone-response pathways, which may involve SPY function.

Two SPY alleles showing severe (SPY-4) and mild (SPY-3) GA-associated phenotypes exhibited similar resistance to CKs, suggesting that SPY enhances CK responses and inhibits GA signalling through distinct mechanisms. GA and SPY repressed numerous CK represses, from seedling development to senescence, indicating that crosstalk occurs early in the CK-signalling pathway. Because AG3 and SPY-4 inhibited induction of the CK primary-response gene, type-A Arabidopsis response regulators, SPY may interact with modify element from the phosphorrelay cascade the CK signal transduction pathway; CK, on the other hand, has no effect on GA biosynthesis or responses. Results of Weiss *et al.* (2005) demonstrate that SPY acts as both a repressor of GA responses and a positive regulators of CK-GA mediated signalling in plants. Hence, SPY may play a central-talk during plant development.

GAs interaction with CKs plays central physiological roles in the regulation of plant development; CKs act early during shoot ignition to control meristem activity, and GAs act at later stages, regulating cell division and expansion to control shoot elongation. Results of Weiss *et al.*, (2005) suggest that crosstalk between the two hormones, with GA inhibiting various CKs responses at different stages of plant development. Because the GA constitutive signalling mutants SPY and GA have similar inhibitory effects, SPY itself or a component downstream of SPY in the GA-signalling pathway may directly control CK signalling. Several pieces of evidence support a direct role for SPY in this interaction. SPY is negative regulator of GA-signal transduction, but mutants in SPY exhibit additional, GA-unrelated phenotypic alternations. Therefore, it is suggested that the protein is involved in other signalling pathway. Recently, Tseng et al. (2004) showed that SPY interacts with the nuclear protein GI and is involved in light–signal transduction controlling flowering, circadian cotyledon movements, and hypocotyls elongation.

Moreover, a plethora of recent evidences suggest that SPY is a positive regulator for the

CK-signal transduction. Several pieces of evidence support a direct role for SPY in this interaction. The strong SPY-4 and weak SPY-3 alleles with respect to GA-signalling showed similar resistance to exogenous CK and has similar round, non-seriated leaves, a phenotypes associated with the inhibition of CKs responses. Furthermore, SPY mutants exhibit deviant phyllotaxy (Swain et al., 2001) which is also associated with attend CK responses but is not found in GA-treated plants. Finally, for some responses, SPY mutants exhibited higher resistance to CK than GA-treated plants, even when GA is applied at high concentrations.

All of these observations suggest that SPY and not SPY-regulated elements in the GA signalling pathway, affects CK responses. They also propose that SPY promotes CK signalling through a distinct mechanism than that involved in the suppression of GA responses. Because GA and SPY displayed similar inhibitory effects on CK responses, GA may suppress CK signalling via inhibition of SPY, independently of SPY or both. It is shown previously that GA does not affect SPY mRNA level (Izhaki et al., 2001). In addition, treatments with Paclobutrazol or GA3 had no detectable effect on the abundance of a SPY-GFP fusion protein. However, GA may repress SPY activity. A GA effect on SPY function as supported by the findings that application of exogenous GA suppresses the inhibition of GA repress caused by ecotropic expression of SPY in transgenic petunia plants (Izhaki et al., 2001). Although mature SPY mutants exhibited greater resistance to exogenously applied CK than GA-treated plants, in seedlings, the effect of GA on CK responses is similar to that of SPY. Different domains of the SPY protein may be involved in the regulation of CK and GA signals.

The regulation of growth and development by GA is affected by other phytohormones and environmental signals. A negative interaction between ABA and GA activity in the regulation of seed germination and gene expression is well-established. ABA seems to act downstream of the GA-signalling repressors, the GA1/RGA DELLA proteins. More recently, a promotive effect of auxin and a repressive effect of ethylene on GA regulation of root elongation have been demonstrated. Both ethylene and auxin modulate the rate of DELLA protein degradation by GA; auxin decreases and ethylene increases the proteins stability. The interaction between GA and CK is less clear. GA and CK both promote the development in Arabidopsis and tobacco (Nicotiana tabacum L.). On the other hand, GA inhibits CK induced cell differentiation in culture. Further, Arabidopsis mutants with introduced GA levels or a block in GA signalling show an increased ability to regenerate shoot meristem from leaves in culture (Fig. 7.4).

Gibberellins as Regulators of Seed Development

It is unexpected that GA1 and GA4 would be undetectable in the vegetative and early floral apex although detected in leaves (Gocal et al., 1999). Deactivation is important for effective regulation of the concentrations of bioactive hormones in plants. Recent studies have linked the homeodomain proteins to GA metabolism and highlighted the role of bioactive GAs in promoting the shift from meristem identity to organ differentiation. KNOX proteins are key regulators in the establishment of meristem identity and leaf morphology. Ectopic expression of KNOX genes from several plant species results in dwarfism and a reduction in endogenous AG levels.

Bioactive GAs and abscisic acid (ABA) act antagonistically to control seed development, thus there should be a mechanism that tightly regulates the balance between these two hormones, LEC2 (leafy cotyledon 2) and FUS3 (fusca 3) are Arabidopsis B3 transcription

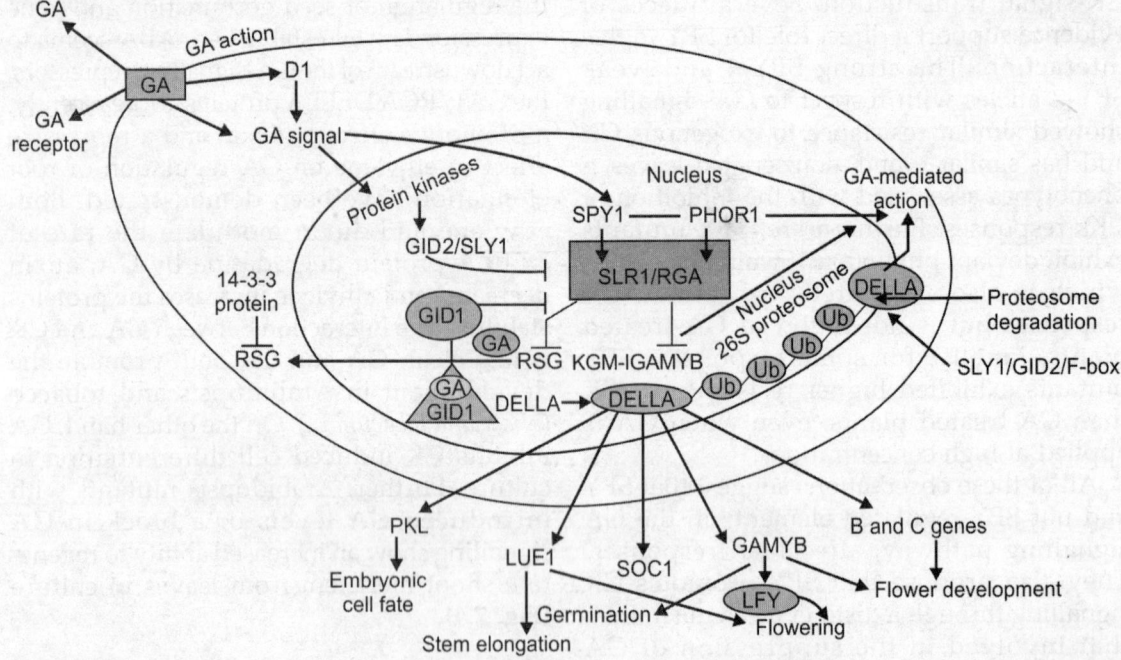

Fig. 7.4: Role of ubiquitin/proteosome pathway in gibberellic acid signalling in various developmental processes of plant

factors, and both are essential for seed maturation processes. In addition, FUS3 binds directly to two RY elements in the promotor of AtGA3$_{ox}$2 *in vitro*. Gazzarrini *et al.* (2004) demonstrated that a transient induction of FUS3 expression results in an increase in BA content and repression results of the GA biosynthesis genes, AtGA3$_{ox}$1 and AtGA20$_{ox}$1. These above results suggest that FUS3 functions as a positive and negative regulators of ABA and GA levels respectively. Further, this protein positively regulated by ABA and negatively by GA, suggesting that these regulatory mechanisms may play a role in the establishment of GA-ABA balance in the seed development (Gazzarrini *et al.*, 2004). AGL15 (Agamous-Like 15) is a member of the MADS (terms for MCM1 Agamous, Deficiens and SRF) domain family and accumulates during embryo development in Arabidopsis. Above outlined results indicate that AGL15 plays a role in lowering GA content during embryogenesis through upregulation of a GA-deactivation gene.

Gibberellins as Florigen

Since GAs are most often associated with the promotion of stem growth; however, its application can induce flowering in some plants especially grasses. Also GAs can substitute for the long-day or cold requirement for many plants, especially rosette species that require either long day or low temperatures to flowering. Thus GA may be a component of the flowering stimulus in some plants but apparently not in others. Comprehensive studies in greases show that GAs play a role as a florigen, for example, *Lolium temulentum*, flowers in response to a single long day (LD), GAs are transmitted signal, there are content increasing in the leaf early in the DL and then hours later, at the shoot apex.

There is a continous trail of eveidence of hormonal action of these GAs for *L. temulentum* and support for a similar role in the flowering of other LD-responsive temperate grasses and cereals. A characteristic of the initial flowering responses of grasses and cereals is their limited stem elongation. Interestingly, it is GAs with low effectiveness for stem elongation, GA5 and GA6 that reach the shoot apex, and structurally, are probably not degraded by 2-oxidase enzymes. By contrast, GA and GA4 cause stem elongation, may be inactive for floral evocation, and do not reach the vegetative shoot apex apparently because of susceptibility to degradation. However, GA4 can be florally active if protected against 2-oxidases either structurally or by using a 2-oxidase inhibitor. Later in inflorescence development, GA1 and GA4 can be detected at the shoot apex and are florally active if applied. The 2-oxiadase restrictly accessible to the apex has probably declined at this time so there is a second florigenic LD-regulated GA action (King and Evans, 2003).

Long days (LDs) increase shoot contents of highly bioactive GAs (e.g. GA1 and GA4), especially in rosette dicot species where the stem begins rapid elongation (bolting), but apparently, without a specific linkage to flowering. On the other hand, for grasses and cereals there is little early stem elongation in LD, a potentially adoptive response for survival of close grazing by herbivores. Thus, florigenic GAs of grasses and cereals should be weakly active for stem elongation. Some other prerequisites for florigenicity are as fallows:

1. Applied GAs replace the need for LD induction.

2. Florigenic GAs increase in leaves soon after LD induction.

3. These GAs more to the shoot apex by the time of floral evocation.

4. The concentration of GA at the apex is sufficient to cause flowering.

Endogenous GA5 and GA6 are presumably transported from the leaf blade through the leaf sheath and into shoot apex. Both GA5 and GA6 are florigenic when only 1 or 5 µg is applied to the leaf of plants held in non-inductive SD. Their lack of effect on stem elongation, except at high doses, also parallels the response to one LD and GA5 supplied via agar to apices excised from vegetative plants. The effective threshold concentration of GAs supplied via the agar matches very closely the maximum estimated endogenous GAs concentration in the apices. Most interestingly, when applied via agar, a three-to-five fold increase in GAs concentration over the threshold value is sufficient for a near maximal flowering responses. Thus doubling the endogenous GA content would have been florally effective. Results of Evans and King, 2003 suggest strongly that GA5 and GA6 are as sufficient LD stimuli for evocation in *L. temulentum*.

The implication that florigenic activity reflects the extent to which a GA is protected from 2-oxidation is further supported by the florigenicity for *L. temulentum* of applied GA3, GA5, GA6, GA32 and 2, 2-dimethyl GA4. For a GA to truly mimic LD-induced floral induction it must have a limited effect on stem elongation as with GA5 GA6, the 3α epimers of AG3 and 2,2-dimethyl GA4, and poly-hydroxylated GAs such as GA32. The natural occurrence of 3α-OH epimers of GA3 in *L. temulentum* is not known although they have been identified in some other species. Other GAs, including GA3, fail as candidate florigens because they promote both stem elongation and flowering. GA4 promotes elongation but not flowering, while GA8 is inactive.

Grasses have a unique inflorescence structure, although many of the genes involved in their floral morphogenesis appear to be homologous with those in Arabidopsis, Antirrhinum, and other dicots, the timing and order of their action may well be different. For instance, the LEAFY and GAMYB genes of Arabidopsis express both during floral evocation and later during floral development, but for *L. temulentum* they express only later during the establishment of floral meristem identity (Gocal *et al.*, 2001). Expression is also late in rice, with upregulation of RFL, the LEAFY homologue, at panicle branch initiation. In wheat, all the species are LD plants but they differ in their LD requirement for inflorescence formation. The GA-insensitivity of wheat dwarf lines is associated with a rise in levels of endogenous GA1 by 4-to 24-fold in leaf and stem tissue, and GA3 levels are also higher. Unexpectedly, the application of florigenic GAs, such as exposure to LD, accelerates inflorescence initiation for both tall and dwarf lines, while the growth retardants CCC delays it (Evans *et al.* 1995).

In rice, it is unclear if flowering time changes in the dwarf GA-biosynthetic mutants, but as for corn, a difficulty also evident when GA3 responses for grain α-amylase production and highest growth are compared across a number of dwarf growth and tall rice lines. In Sorghum, early flowering of a tall mutant with an elevated content of endogenous GA in its shoot also fits with this scenario of GAs promoting flowering. In last of this section, we also mention that, of all plant species, *L. temulentum* is a continous trail liking GA to the photoperiodic induction of leaves, to floral evocation, and to floral differentiation. Exposure of the leaf blade to one LD increases GA5 contents three-to four-fold and 8 to 16 hours later, GA5 and GA6 double in the shoot apex to a concentration known to be inductive for apices *in vitro*. Moreover, labeled GA5 can travel the whole pathway intact. Furthermore, at inflorescense differentiation, other LD-regulated GAs becomes more important, and in this instance, there is an associated up-regulated expression of a GAMYB gene at the spikelet sites. Thus it can be claimed with some confidence that GAs act as floral stimuli in the LD flowering response of *L. temulentum* and possibly of other LD-responseive grasses. With exposure to LD, petiole GAs may raise 3-to 10- fold and plants flower. In addition, shoot apex GAs are yet to be examined, expression at the shoot apex of GAMYB gene and of LFY is strongly up-regulated, and applied GA also activates expression of both genes and causes flowering. Whether LD might change shoot apex sensitivity to a hormone in addition to or rather than hormone content increasing is an issue raised initially and discussed in detail. For example, flowering of cultural shoot apices of *L. temulentum* shows an age-dependent increase insensitivity to GA3 (King *et al.*, 1993), but the change is small and unlikely to reflect a large, rapid change expected at floral evocation. At least for *L. temulentum*, GAs must be emphasized as both an initial signal triggering LD floral evocation and a secondary one regulating floral development. However, response to bioactive GAs may depend on tissue localization and control of GA metabolism by enzymes responsible for GA 2β-and 3β-hydroxylation and for desaturase activity. Therein may lay a key to understanding the relationship between GA and flowering in the grasses and cereals. All models of flowering include a role for day length perception in leaves, with unknown promoter accumulating and/or inhibitory disappearing from the shoot apex. The original concept of a single universal florigen is based on grafting experiments, appears to be unduly restrictive. Although, GAs are transmitted factors limiting to floral induction in the grasses and cereals. The possible role of GAs in the flowering of higher plants is comprehensively reviewed by Pharis and King (1985).

Conclusion and Future Prospects

It is clear from the observation reviewed here that defining "gibberellin" simply in terms of their ability to stimulate plant is no longer tenable. It is now apparent that GAs (GA1,

GA3, GA4 and GA7) itself have wide ranging and pleiotropic effects encompassing the regulation of almost every aspect of plant growth and development including cell growth, cell division, cell differentiation, flowering, fruiting, histogenesis, organogenesis and responses to various kinds of environmental stresses (e.g. abiotic and biotic). A plethora of evidences indicates clear correlation between GAs concentration in a given tissue and the nature and magnitude of the responses it stimulates. These displacements emerge the focus of investigations of GAs action towards mechanisms that regulate homeostasis of endogenous GAs pools in which processes such as biosynthesis, degradation, conjugation and specific transport play crucial roles, and towards mechanism of action of GAs at the cellular molecular and genomic levels. From the point of view of terminology used, it may be desirable to redefine the group of compounds termed endogenous gibberellin because their mechanisms of action may vary for each particular attribute of growth and development in plants.

However, several outstanding questions remain to be answered before we can fully understand the mechanisms that determine gibberellin GAs homeostasis. First of all, the specificity of GARE and GARC, and members of GARS family (GAI, RGA and SCR) receptors towards bioactive GAs needs to be experimentally determined to exclude or confirm the binding of these bioactive GAs and their role, if any, in downstream proteasome-mediated gene expression. It is also necessary to determine how the fast non-transcriptional responses and those involving transcriptional regulation are coupled and how the signalling cascade triggered by DELLA, GAMYB, SPY and LFY proteins are constituted. The specificity of GAS transporters towards individual GA-like compounds has been largely overlooked and requires further confirmation, possibly by means of chemical or genomic approaches. An analysis of regulatory elements in promoter regions of individual genes involved in GA metabolism, signalling and transport may also yield valuable information.

REFERENCES

Gilroy S (1996). Signal transduction in barley aleurone protoplasts is calcium dependent and independent. *Plant Cell*, **8**: 2193–2209.

Gubler F and Jacobsen JV (1992). Gibberellin-responsive elements in the promoter of barley high-pI α-amylase gene. *Plant cell*, **4**: 1435–1441.

Huttly AK and Philips AJ (1995). Gibberellin-regulated plant genes. *Physiologia Plantarum*, **95**: 310–317.

Jacobsen JV and Beach LR (1985). Control of transcription of α-amylase and ribosomal RNA genes in barley aleurone protoplasts prepared from mature barley aleurone layers. *Plant Molecular Biology*, **16**: 713–724.

Jacobsen JV and Close TJ (1991). Control of transient expression of chimeric genes by gibberellic acid and abscisic acid in protoplasts prepared from mature barley aleurone layers. *Plant Molecular Biology*, **16**: 713–724.

Jacobsen JV, Gubler F and Chandler PM (1995). Gibberellin and abscisic acid in germinating cereals. In: Davies PJ (Eds). *Plant Hormones: Physiology Biochemistry and Molecular Biology.* Kluwer Boston, pp 246–271.

Lones HD, Smith SJ, Desikan R, Plakidou-Dymock S, Love grove A and Hooley R (1998). Heterotrimeric G proteins are implicated in gibberellins induction of α-amylase gene expression in wild oat aleurone layer. *Plant Cell*, **10**: 245–253.

Lenton JR, Appleford NEJ and Croker SJ (1994). Gibberellins and α-amylase gene expression in germinating wheat grains. *Plant Growth Regulation*, **15**: 261–270.

Singh SP and Paleg LG (1986). Low temperature induced GA$_3$ sensitivity of wheat. VI. Effect of inhibitors of lipid biosynthesis on α-amylase production by dwarf (Rht3) and tall (Rht) wheat on lipid metabolism of tall wheat aleurone tissue. *Australian Journal of Plant Physiology*, **13**: 409–416.

Schuurink RC, Chan PV and Jones RL (1996). Modulation of calmodulin mRNA and protein levels in barley aleurone. *Plant Physiology*, 111: 371–380.

Skriver K, Olsen FL, Rogers JC and Mundy J (1991). *Cis*-acting DNA elements responsive to gibberellins and its antagonist abscisic acid. *Proceedings of the National Academy of Sciences of USA*, 88: 7266–7270.

MacMillan J (2002). Occurrence of gibberellins in vascular plants fungi and bacteria. *Journal of Plant Growth Regulation*, 20: 387–442.

Hedden P and Kamiya Y (1997). Gibberellin biosynthesis: Enzymes, genes and their regulation. *Annual Reviews of Plant Physiology and Plant Molecular Biology*, 48: 431–60.

Hedden P and Phillips AL (2000). Gibberellin metabolism: New insights revealed by the genes. *Trends in Plant Science*, 5: 523–530.

Sponsel VM and Hedden P (2004). Gibberellin biosynthesis and inactivation. In: Davies PJ (Eds). *Plant Hormones: Biosynthesis Signal Transduction Action*. Kluwer Academy, Dordrecht, pp 63–94.

Yamaguchi S and Kamiya Y (2000). Gibberellin biosynthesis: Its regulation by endogenous and environmental signals. *Plant Cell Physiology*, 41: 251–257.

Finkelstein RR and Zeevaart JAD (1994). Gibberellin and abscisic acid biosynthesis and response. In: Meyerowitz EM, Somerville CR (Eds). *Arabidopsis*. Cold Spring Harbor NY, pp 523–553.

Nakajima M, Shimada A, Takashi Y, Kim YC, Park SH, Ueguchi-Tanaka M, Suzuki H, Katoh E, Iuchi S, Kobayashi M, Maeda T, Ueguchi-Tanaka M, Nakajima M, Katoh E, Ohmiya H, Asano K, Saji S, Hongyu X, Ashikari M, Kitano H, Yamaguchi I and Matsuoka M (2007). Molecular interactions of a soluble gibberellin receptor GID1 with a rice DELLA protein SLR1 and gibberellin. *Plant Cell*, 19: 2140–2155.

Ueguchi-Tanaka M, Nakajima M, Motoyuki A and Matsuoka M (2007). Gibberellin receptor and its role in gibberellin signalling in plants. *Annual Reviews of Plant Biology*, 58: 183–189.

Yamaguchi S and Kamiya Y (2000). Gibberellin biosynthesis: Its regulation by endogenous and environmental signals. *Plant Cell Physiology*, 41: 251–257.

Ueguchi-Tanaka M, Ashikari M, Nakajima M, Itoh H, Katoh E, Kobayashi M, Chow TY, Hsing YC, Kitano H, Yamaguchi I and Matsuo M (2005). Gibberellin Insensitive Dwarf 1 encodes a soluble receptor for gibberellin. *Nature*, 437: 693–698.

Sun TP and Gubler F (2004). Molecular mechanism of gibberellin signalling in plants. *Annual Reviews of Plant Biology*, 55: 197–223.

Olszewski N, Sun TP and Gubler F (2002). Gibberellin signalling: Biosynthesis, catabolism and response pathways. *Plant Cell*, 14: 61–80.

Richards DE, King KE, Ait-ali T and Harberd NP (2001). How gibberellin regulates plant growth and development: A molecular genetic analysis of gibberellin signalling. *Annual Reviews of Plant Physiology and Plant Molecular Biology*, 52: 67–88.

Sakamoto T, Kobayashi M, Itoh H, Tagiri A, Kayano T, Tanaka H, Iwahori S and Matsuoka M (2001). Expression of a gibberellin 2-oxidase gene around the shoot apex is related to phase transition in rice. *Plant Physiology*, 125: 1508–1516.

Sun TP and Gubler F (2004). Molecular mechanism of gibberellin signalling in plants. *Annual Reviews of Plant Biology*, 55: 197–223.

Kasahara H, Hanada A, Kuzuyama T, Takagi M, Kamiya Y and Yamaguchi S (2002). Contribution of the mevalonate and methylerythritol phosphate pathways to the biosynthesis of gibberellins in *Arabidopsis*. *Journal of Biological Chemistry*, 277: 45188–45194.

Sun TP and Kamiya Y (1994). The *Arabidopsis GA1* locus encodes the cyclase *ent*-kaurene synthetase A of gibberellin biosynthesis. *Plant Cell*, 6: 1509–1518.

Sun TP and Kamiya Y (1997). Regulation and cellular localization of *ent*-kaurene synthesis. *Physiologia Plantarum*, 101: 701–708.

Appleford NE, Evans DJ, Lenton JR, Gaskin P, Croker SJ, Devos KM, Phillips AL and Hedden P (2006). Function and transcript analysis of gibberellin-biosynthetic enzymes in wheat. *Planta*, 223: 568–582.

Itoh H, Ueguchi-Tanaka M, Sentoku N, Kitano H, Matsuoka M and Kobayashi M (2001). Cloning and functional analysis of two gibberellin 3β-hydroxylase genes that are differently expressed during the growth of rice. *Proceedings of the National Academy of Sciences of USA*, **98**: 8909–8914.

Kaneko M, Itoh H, Inukai Y, Sakamoto T, Ueguchi-Tanaka M, Ashikari M and Matsuoka M (2003). Where do gibberellin biosynthesis and gibberellin signalling occur in rice plants? *Plant Journal*, **35**: 104–115.

Yamaguchi S, Kamiya Y and Sun T (2001). Distinct cell-specific expression patterns of early and late gibberellin biosynthetic genes during *Arabidopsis* seed germination. *Plant Journal*, **28**: 443–453.

Weiss D, Van Der Luit A, Knegt E, Vermeer E, Mol J and Kooter JM (1995). Identification of endogenous gibberellins in petunia flowers (induction of anthocyanin biosynthetic gene expression and the antagonistic effect of abscisic acid). *Plant Physiology*, **107**: 695–702.

Koornneef M and Van der Veen JH (1980). Induction and analysis of gibberellin-sensitive mutants in *Arabidopsis thaliana* (L.) Heynh. *Theoritical Application in Genetics*, **58**: 257–263.

Yamaguchi S, Kamiya Y and Sun T (2001). Distinct cell-specific expression patterns of early and late gibberellin biosynthetic genes during *Arabidopsis* seed germination. *Plant Journal*, **28**: 443–453.

Mitchum MG, Yamaguchi S, Hanada A, Kuwahara A, Yoshioka Y, Kato T, Tabata S, Kamiya Y and Sun TP (2006). Distinct and overlapping roles of two gibberellin 3-oxidases in *Arabidopsis* development. *Plant Journal*, **45**: 804–818.

Silverstone AL, Chang C, Krol E and Sun TP (1997). Developmental regulation of the gibberellins biosynthetic gene GA1 in *Arabidopsis thaliana*. *Plant Journal*, **12**: 9–19.

Hedden P and Phillips AL (2000). Gibberellin metabolism: New insights revealed by the genes. *Trends in Plant Science*, **5**: 523–530.

Olszewski N, Sun TP and Gubler F (2002). Gibberellin signalling: Biosynthesis, catabolism and response pathways. *Plant Cell*, **14**: 61–80.

Yamaguchi S, Sun T, Kawaide H and Kamiya Y (1998). The GA2 locus of *Arabidopsis thaliana* encodes *ent*-kaurene synthase of gibberellin biosynthesis. *Plant Physiology*, **116**: 1271–1278.

Yamauchi Y, Ogawa M, Kuwahara A, Hanada A, Kamiya Y and Yamaguchi S (2004). Activation of gibberellin biosynthesis and response pathways by low temperature during imbibition of *Arabidopsis thaliana* seeds. *Plant Cell*, **16**: 367–378.

Huang S, Raman AS, Ream JE, Fujiwara H, Cerny RE and Brown SM (1998). Overexpression of 20-oxidase confers a gibberellin-overproduction phenotype in *Arabidopsis*. *Plant Physiology*, **118**: 773–781.

Fleet CM, Yamaguchi S, Hanada A, Kawaide H, David CJ, Kamiya Y and Sun TP (2003). Overexpression of *AtCPS* and *AtKS* in *Arabidopsis* confers increased *ent*-kaurene production but no increase in bioactive gibberellins. *Plant Physiology*, **132**: 830–839.

Pharis RP and King RW (1985). Gibberellins and reproductive development in seed plants. *Annual Reviews of Plant Physiology*, **36**: 517–526.

Zeevaart JAD (1983). Gibberellins and flowering. In: Crozier A (Eds). *The Biochemistry and Physiology of Gibberellins*. Praeger, New York pp 333–373.

Cleland CF and Zeevaart JAD (1970). Gibberellins in relation to flowering and stem elongation in the long day plant *Silene armeria*. *Plant Physiology*, **46**: 392–400.

Evans LT, King RW, Chu A, Mander LN and Pharis RP (1990). Gibberellin structure and florigenic activity in *Lolium temulentum* a long day plant. *Planta*, **182**: 97–106.

King RW, Evans LT, Mander LM, Moritz T, Pharis RP and Twitchin B (2003). Synthesis of gibberellin GA6 and examination of its role in flowering of *Lolium temulentum Phytochemistry*, **62**: 77–82.

King RW, Moritz T, Evans LT, Junttila O and Herlt AJ (2001). Long-day induction of flowering in *Lolium temulentum* involves sequential increases in specific gibberellins at the shoot apex. *Plant Physiology*, **127**: 624–632.

Evans LT, King RW, Mander LN and Pharis RP (1994). The relative significance for stem elongation and flowering in *Lolium temulentum* of 3-hydroxylation of gibberellins. *Planta*, **192**: 130–136.

King RW, Blundell C and Evans LT (1993). The behaviour of shoot apices of *Lolium temulentum in vitro* as the basis of an assay system for florigenic extracts. *Australian Journal of Plant Physiology*, **20**: 337–348.

King RW, Moritz T, Evans LT, Junttila O and Herlt AJ (2001). Long-day induction of flowering in *Lolium temulentum* involves sequential increases in specific gibberellins at the shoot apex. *Plant Physiology*, **127**: 624–632.

King RW and Evans LT (2003). Gibberellins and flowering of grasses and cereals: Prizing open the lid of the "florigen" black box. *Annual Reviews of Plant Biology*, **54**: 307–328.

Evans LT, Blundell C and King RW (1995). Developmental responses by tall and dwarf isogenic lines of spring wheat to applied gibberellins. *Australian Journal of Plant Physiology*, **22**: 365–371.

Pharis RP, Evans LT, King RW and Mander LN (1987). Gibberellins endogenous and applied in relation to flower induction in the long-day plant *Lolium temulentum. Plant Physiology*, **84**: 1132–1138.

Fujioka S, Yamane H, Spray CR, Katsumi M, Phinney BO, Gaskin P, Macmillan J and Takahashi N (1988). The dominant non-gibberellin-responding dwarf mutant (*D8*) of maize accumulates native gibberellins. *Proceedings of the National Academy of Sciences of USA*, **85**: 9031–9035.

Gocal GFW, King RW, Blundell CA, Schwartz OM, Andersen CH and Weige D (2001). Evolution of floral meristem identity genes. Analysis of *Lolium temulentum* genes related to *APETALA1* and *LEAFY* of Arabidopsis. *Plant Physiology*, **125**: 1788–1801.

Kyozuka J, Konishi S, Nemoto K, Izawa T and Shimamoto K (1998). Downregulation of RFL the *FLO/LFY* homologue of rice accompanied with panicle branch initiation. *Proceedings of the National Academy of Sciences of USA*, **95**: 1979–1982.

Bodson M, King RW, Evans LT and Bernier G (1977). The role of photosynthesis in flowering of the long-day plant *Sinapis alba. Australian Journal of Plant Physiology*, **4**: 467–478.

Appleford NEJ and Lenton JR (1991). Gibberellins and leaf expansion in near-isogenic wheat lines containing *Rht1* and *Rht3* dwarfing alleles. *Planta*, **183**: 229–236.

Evans LT, Blundell C and King RW (1995). Developmental responses by tall and dwarf

isogenic lines of spring wheat to applied gibberellins. *Australian Journal of Plant Physiology*, **22**: 365–371.

Mitsunaga S, Tashiro T and Yamaguchi J (1994). Identification and characterization of gibberellin-insensitive mutants selected from among dwarf mutants of rice. *Theoritical Application of Genetics*, **87**: 705–712.

Beall FD, Morgan PW, Mander LN, Miller FR and Babb KH (1991). Genetic regulation of development in *Sorghum bicolor* V. The ma3 R allele results in gibberellin enrichment. *Plant Physiology*, **95**: 116–125.

Weyers JDB and Patterson NW (2001). Plant hormones and the control of physiological processes. *New Phytologist*, **152**: 375–407.

King RW, Blundell C and Evans LT (1993). The behaviour of shoot apices of *Lolium temulentum in vitro* as the basis of an assay system for florigenic extracts. *Australian Journal of Plant Physiology*, **20**: 337–348.

Lang A (1965). Physiology of flower initiation. In: Ruhland W (Eds). *Encyclopedia of Plant Physiology*. Berlin: Springer pp 1380–536.

Pharis RP and King RW (1985). Gibberellins and reproductive development in seed plants. *Annual Review of Plant Physiology*, **36**: 517–568.

Tanaka-Ueguchi M, Itoh H, Oyama N, Koshioka M and Matsuoka M (1998). Overexpression of a tobacco homeobox gene NTH15 decreases the expression of a gibberellin biosynthetic gene encoding GA20-oxidase. *Plant Journal*, **15**: 391–400.

Batge SL, Ross JJ and Reid JB (1999). Abscisic acid levels in seeds of the gibberellin-deficient mutant *lh-2* of pea (*Pisum sativum*). *Physiologia Plantarum*, **105**: 485–490.

White CN, Proebsting WM, Hedden P and Rivin CJ (2000). Gibberellins and seed development in maize. I. Evidence that gibberellin/abscisic acid balance governs germination vs maturation pathways. *Plant Physiology*, **122**: 1081–1088.

Gazzarrini S, Tsuchiya Y, Lumba S, Okamoto M and McCourt P (2004). The transcription factor FUSCA3 controls developmental timing in *Arabidopsis* through the hormones gibberellins and abscisic acid. *Developmental Cell*, **7**: 373–385.

Phillips AL, Ward DA, Uknes S, Appleford NE, Lange T, Huttly AK, Gaskin P, Graebe JE and Hedden P (1995). Isolation and expression of three gibberellin 20-oxidase cDNA clones from *Arabidopsis*. *Plant Physiology,* **108**: 1049–1057.

Yamaguchi S, Smith MW, Brown RG, Kamiya Y and Sun T (1998). Phytochrome regulation and differential expression of gibberellin 3β-hydroxylase genes in germinating *Arabidopsis* seeds. *Plant Cell,* **10**: 2115–2126.

Thomas SG, Phillips AL and Hedden P (1999). Molecular cloning and functional expression of gibberellin 2-oxidases multifunctional enzymes involved in gibberellin deactivation. *Proceedings of the National Academy of Sciences of USA,* **96**: 4698–4703.

Sun TP and Gubler F (2004). Molecular mechanism of gibberellin signalling in plants. *Annual Reviews of Plant Biology,* **55**: 197–223.

Ueguchi-Tanaka M, Nakajima M, Katoh E, Ohmiya H, Asano K, Saji S, Hongyu X, Ashikari M, Kitano H, Yamaguchi I and Matsuok M (2007). Molecular interactions of a soluble gibberellin receptor GID1 with a rice DELLA protein SLR1 and gibberellin. *Plant Cell,* **19**: 2140–2155.

Sasaki A, Itoh H, Gomi K, Ueguchi-Tanaka M, Ishiyama K, Kobayashi M, Jeong DH, An G, Kitano H, Ashikari M and Matsuoka M (2003). Accumulation of phosphorylated repressor for gibberellin signalling in an F-box mutant, *Science,* **299**: 1896– 1898.

Ueguchi-Tanaka M, Ashikari M, Nakajima M, Itoh H, Katoh E, Kobayashi M, Chow TY, Hsing YI, Kitano H, Yamaguchi I and Matsuoka M (2005).

Gibberellin Insensitive Dwarf 1 encodes a soluble receptor for gibberellin. *Nature,* **437**: 693–698.

Dill A and Sun T (2001). Synergistic derepression of gibberellin signalling by removing RGA and GAI function in *Arabidopsis thaliana*. *Genetics,* **159**: 777–785.

King KE, Moritz T and Harberd NP (2001). Gibberellins are not required for normal stem growth in *Arabidopsis thaliana* in the absence of GAI and RGA. *Genetics,* **159**: 767–776.

Fukazawa J, Sakai T, Ishida S, Yamaguchi I, Kamiya Y and Takahashi Y (2000). Repression of shoot growth a bZIP transcriptional activator regulates cell elongation by controlling the level of gibberellins. *Plant Cell,* **12**: 901–915.

Ishida S, Fukazawa J, Yuasa T and Takahashi Y (2004). Involvement of 14-3-3 signalling protein binding in the functional regulation of the transcriptional activator repression of shoot growth by gibberellins. *Plant Cell,* **16**: 2641–2651.

Frigerio M, Alabad D, Perez-Gomez J, Garcia-Carcel L, Phillips AL, Hedden P and Blázque MA (2006). Transcriptional regulation of gibberellin metabolism genes by auxin signalling in *Arabidopsis*. *Plant Physiology,* **142** 553–563.

Jager CE, Symons GM, Ross JJ, Smith JJ and Reid JB (2005). The brassinosteroid growth response in pea is not mediated by changes in gibberellin content. *Planta,* **221**: 141–148.

Hoffmann-Benning S and Kende H (1992). On the role of abscisic acid and gibberellin in the regulation of growth in rice. *Plant Physiology,* **99**: 1156–1161.

QUESTIONS

Q. 1. Second group of plant hormones or natural plant growth promoters or regulators is:

(1) Gibberellins
(2) Cytokinins
(3) Ethylene
(4) ABA

Q. 2. Cell organelles involved in the gibberellins synthesis are:

(1) Plastids/proplastids
(2) Endoplasmic reticulum
(3) Cytosol
(4) All

Q. 3. The chief site of action of gibberellins is:

(1) Intercalary meristems
(2) Cambium
(3) Medullary rays
(4) Vascular bandles

Q. 4. Which PGR synthesized under strict developmental control?

(1) GA (2) CK
(3) ABA (4) ET

Q. 5. Gibberellins can be defined by the:

(1) Biological activity
(2) Chemical structure
(3) Both 1 and 2
(4) None

Q. 6. Basic common structure of the gibberellins group of hormones:

(1) Steroid
(2) Catecholamines
(3) Ent-kaurane/Lactone ring
(4) Both 2 and 3

Q. 7. Mendel pure lines peas varities are the best example of the

(1) CK deficiency
(2) GA deficiency
(3) ABA deficiency
(4) ET deficiency

Q. 8. GA inhibitors are:

(1) CCC, tetcyclis, paclobutrazol
(2) BX-112
(3) AMO1618
(4) Phosphone-D and bonzil
(5) All

Q. 9. Bioassys for GA are:

(1) Intermodal elongation in deepwater rice
(2) Dwarfism in thaliana
(3) Alpha-amylase synthesis and secretion in barley aleurone layer
(4) Dwarf-rice leaf sheath bioassay and lettuce hypocotyls elongation
(5) All

Q. 10. *Gibberella fujukuroii*, a nectriaceae member, secrete GA as their:

(1) Metabolic product
(2) Excretory product
(3) Secretary product
(4) All

Q. 11. Fusarium moniliformi, is:

(1) Sexual stage of *Giberella fugukuroii*
(2) Asexual stage of *Giberella fugukuroii*
(3) Vegetative stage of *Giberella fugukuroii*
(4) Fruiting bodies of *Fusarium spp.*

Q. 12. Cabbage is a:

(1) LDP
(2) SDP
(3) DNP
(4) A Pteridophytes

Q. 13. Who written a wonderful personal account of history of discovery of GA?

(1) Phinney
(2) Darwin
(3) N. Takahashi
(4) S. Tamura

Q. 14. First higher plant where GA was identified?

(1) Runner bean (Phaseolus coccinus)
(2) Horse bean
(3) Munge bean
(4) Green bean

Q. 15. Two gibberellins, viz. GA1 and GA2 shows similarity in:

(1) Close chemical similarity
(2) Close metabolic similarity
(3) Order of discovery
(4) Physiological effect

Q. 16. Two gibberellins, viz. GA1 and GA2 shows dis-similarity in:

(1) Number of C-atoms
(2) Number and locations of –OH
(3) Locations and stereochemistry of the –OH groups
(4) Basic structure especially oxidation state
(5) All

Q. 17. Of the total discovered GA, just a few act as biologically active form. Rest act as:

(1) Precursors
(2) Represent inactivated forms
(3) Both 1 and 2
(4) Inhibitors for active GAs

Q. 18. Chemically GAs is:

(1) Lipids/tetracyclic diterpenoid acid
(2) Polysaccharides
(3) Proteins
(4) Minerals

Q. 19. What is correct about GAs?

(1) Do not absorb UV rays
(2) Do not give fluorescence
(3) No distinguishing chemical structure
(4) All

Q. 20. Point of identification for GAs is:

(1) Distinguishing chemical structure
(2) Fluorescence

(3) Absorption of UV rays
(4) Varying degree of purification

Q. 21. Most widely used method for Gibberellin analysis:

(1) HPLC
(2) GC-MS
(3) HPLC-MS
(4) Paper chromatography

Q. 22. Most recently developed, costly but used limitedly:

(1) HPLC
(2) GC-MS
(3) HPLC-MS
(4) Gas chromatography

Q. 23. Number of isoprene units involved in the synthesis of gibberellins:

(1) 2   (2) 3
(3) 4   (4) 5

Q. 24. Full name of IPP:

(1) Isopentenyl pyrophosphate
(2) Iso-pyrophosphate
(3) Both 1 and 2
(4) None

Q. 25. Precursor for biosynthesis of IPP is:

(1) Mevalonic acid
(2) Penta-endonic acid
(3) Tryptophan
(4) Phenylene

Q. 26. First gibberellin formed in all plants and precursor for all other gibberellins in plants:

(1) GA-12-aldehyde
(2) GA3
(3) GA19
(4) GA20

Q. 27. Mutations is leaky means is (it concerned with GA effect):

(1) Mutated gene is partly active
(2) Mutated gene is fully active
(3) Mutated gene is inactive
(4) All are correct

Q. 28. Which is only gibberellic controlling stem growth (a universal function) is?

(1) GA_1 (2) GA_7

(3) GA_3 (4) GA_4

Q. 29. Of which gibberellins is primarily active one in stem growth for most species?

(1) GA1   (2) GA2

(3) GA4   (4) GA7

Q. 30. GA_3 is different from GA_1 in which feature?

(1) Containing a single double bond

(2) Containing one $-CH_3$ group

(3) Containing one $-C_2H_5$ group

(4) Containing one more $-OH$ group

Q. 31. Which one is a substitute for GA_1 in most of the assay in higher plants?

(1) GA_3

(2) GA_4

(3) GA_7

(4) All of the above

Q. 32. As seeds near maturation, the amount of:

(1) All GAs decreases

(2) Particularly GA1 decreases

(3) Both GA1 and GA4 decreases

(4) Only GA3 decreases

Q. 33. What is correct about GAs?

(1) Present in root exudates

(2) Present in the root extract

(3) Both 1 and 2 are correct

(4) Synthesize in the roots

Q. 34. GAs cause:

(1) Delay in senescence in citrus

(2) Elongation and improves shape of apples

(3) Induce increase in stalk length of grapes

(4) Increase in yield of sugarcane

(5) All are correct

Q. 35. GA biosynthesis is regulated by:

(1) Light

(2) Temperature

(3) Feedback control

(4) All are correct

Q. 36. *d8*, is a GA insensitive mutant of:

(1) Arabidopsis   (2) Maize

(3) Brassica   (4) Chickpea

Q. 37. *gai*, is a GA insensitive mutant of:

(1) Arabidopsis   (2) Maize

(3) Brassica   (4) Chickpea

Q. 38. Below we mention 4 different approaches for regulation of concentration of GA1 in plants which is odd one is?

(1) Transport (reversible)

(2) Synthesis (reversible)

(3) Conjugation with sugars (reversible)

(4) Catabolic inactivation (irreversible)

Q. 39. Level of GA can be reduced by:

(1) Catabolism

(2) Glycosylation

(3) Cold treatment

(4) Temperature

(5) Both 1 and 2 are correct

Q. 40. Bakane disease is characterized by:

(1) A decrease in stem thickness

(2) A decrease in leaf size

(3) A light green colour of leaves

(4) Internode elongation

(5) All are right

Q. 41. Natural bolting is regulated by which PGR by inducing cell division?

(1) GA   (2) CK

(3) ABA   (4) ET

Q. 42. Botanical name of brookweed is:

(1) *Samolus parviflorus*

(2) *Cicer arietinum*

(3) *Phaseolus vulgaris*

(4) *Citrus reticulata*

Q. 43. Some LDP, rosette plants, have a cold requirement for stem elongation and flowering. This need can be overcome by the application of which phytohormone?

(1) GA   (2) ABA
(3) CK   (4) ET

Q. 44. Main areana or site of action of gibberellic acid is:

(1) Intercalary meristem
(2) Lateral meristems
(3) Both 1 and 2
(4) Vascular cambium

Q. 45. Botanical name of English ivy is:

(1) *Hedera helix*
(2) *Samolus parviflorus*
(3) *Cicer arietinum*
(4) *Phaseolus vulgaris*

Q. 46. Transition from juviles to adult phase in woody perennials (conifers) regulated by:

(1) GA   (2) ABA
(3) ET   (4) CK

Q. 47. Which is correct statement about below given pairs are?

(1) GA1, GA3-Polar
(2) GA4+ GA7-Nonpolar
(3) Both 1 and 2 are correct
(4) Botanical name of hemp is; *Raphanus sativus L.*

Q. 48. In which of the following group of plants GA are not effective?

(1) Mosses
(2) Cycadales
(3) Ferns
(4) Conifers

Q. 49. The name of process where unisexual flowers are produced (influence by GA)?

(1) Bisexuality
(2) Sex determination

(3) Emasculation
(4) Cleistropism

Q. 50. The effect of ET is antagonistic to GA in cucumber for which feature?

(1) Flower induction
(2) Fruit formation
(3) Seed germination
(4) Dormancy overcome

Q. 51. Which is dioecious plants?

(1) Spinach
(2) Maize
(3) Hemp
(4) Both 1 and 3

Q. 52. Process of sex determination in plants are influenced by:

(1) GA
(2) Photoperiod
(3) Nutritional status
(4) Genetics
(5) All are correct

Q. 53. Tassel in maize represents the:

(1) Male flower
(2) Female flower
(3) Both 1 and 2
(4) Calyx

Q. 54. Ear in maize represents the:

(1) Male flower
(2) Female flower
(3) Both 1 and 2
(4) Calyx

Q. 55. Most economical GA is:

(1) 90% alcohol dissolved
(2) 10% alcohol dissolved
(3) 30% alcohol dissolved
(4) 40% alcohol dissolved

Q. 56. GA stimulate 'fruits set' in:

(1) Apple
(2) Grape
(3) Pear
(4) Apricot

Q. 57. GA stimulate 'fruits set' in those places where?

(1) Auxin have no effect
(2) ABA have no effect
(3) ET have no effect
(4) CK have no effect

Q. 58. In which of the following is important for purpose of the GA role in Brewing Industry?

(1) It promotes fruit set
(2) It promotes seed development
(3) Influence floral initiation
(4) It promotes seed germination

Q. 59. In which of the following is concerned with seed germination?

(1) Loss of dormancy
(2) Mobilization of endosperm reserves
(3) Malt formation
(4) All are concerned

Q. 60. Seed germination require GA for which step/s:

(1) Activation of vegetative growth of embryo
(2) Weakening of a growth-constraining endosperm layer surrounding embryo
(3) Mobilization of stored food reserves of endosperm
(4) All are correct

Q. 61. α-amylase is:

(1) Hydrolase
(2) Carboxylase
(3) Oxygenase
(4) Aminotransferase

Q. 62. GA stimulates which category of enzymes in germinating seed aleurone layer:

(1) Carboxypeptidases
(2) Lipases
(3) Hydrolase
(4) Protease

Q. 63. Principle system in which GA signal transduction pathway has been analyzed:

(1) Brewing industry/malt production
(2) Fruit set formation
(3) Sex determination
(4) Floral initiation

Q. 64. 'Wort' is results of:

(1) Pulverization during malting
(2) Heating during malting
(3) Drying during malting
(4) Mashing during malting

Q. 65. Wort is concerned with which PGR?

(1) GA   (2) ET
(3) ABA   (4) CK

Q. 66. Apples (berry) are elongates and improved shape for better marketing purposes through which?

(1) GA + Benzyladenine
(2) CK + ET
(3) ET + GA
(4) ABA + ET

Q. 67. GA + Benzyladenine responsible for which characteristics in apple?

(1) Shape, elongation
(2) Yield, taste
(3) Chemical composition
(4) delay in ripening

Q. 68. Which is not a step involved in the brewing industry?

(1) Heating   (2) Drying
(3) Pulverized (4) Mashing
(5) All are correct

Q. 69. Which is a step involved in the brewing industry?

(1) Germination
(2) Malting
(3) Worting
(4) Fermentation
(5) All are correct

Q. 70. Which is intermediate in the brewing industry?

(1) Starch
(2) Maltose
(3) Glucose
(4) Ethanol
(5) All of the above

Q. 71. First step of brewing industry is:

(1) Malting   (2) Worting
(3) Hydrolysis   (4) Fermentation

Q. 72. In brewing industry, during malting, seeds of barley are allowed to germinate at low temperature to maximize:

(1) Production of hydrolytic enzymes
(2) The concentration of zymase
(3) Both 1 and 2
(4) The production of invertase

Q. 73. In brewing industry, GA is substitute for:

(1) High pressure
(2) Low temperature
(3) High temperature
(4) Low pressure

Q. 74. Role of GA in brewing industry is:

(1) Speed-up the rate of germination
(2) Enhance the concentration of hydrolytic enzymes
(3) Both 1 and 2
(4) Slow down the fermentation

Q. 75. The characteristic physiological responses (bioassay) elicited by GA is/are:

(1) Elongation of internodes or leaf sheaths of dwarf plants
(2) Hypocotyl elongation
(3) Induction of amylase and probably other hydrolases in germinating cereal seeds
(4) Flowering in some long-day plants
(5) All of the above

Q. 76. Typical bioassay methods used for GA are:

(1) Dwarf maize test and Amylase formation test
(2) Dwarf pea test and rumex leaf senescence test
(3) Hypocotyl elongation test and potato eye test
(4) All of the above

Q. 77. Most specific bioassay for GA are/is:

(1) Amylase formation test
(2) Potato eye test
(3) Rumex leaf senescence test
(4) Hypocotyl elongation test

Q. 78. Which plant hormone is the consistently enhance germination and are positively implicated in many seed processes?

(1) GA   (2) Auxin
(3) ET   (4) CK

Q. 79. Which plant hormone have been shown to effectively cause flower formation in a wide variety of plants?

(1) CK
(2) Auxin
(3) GA
(4) Both 1 and 3

Q. 80. In which of the following category of plants are responsive to exogenous GAs when they kept under non-inductive condition?

(1) LDP and cold requiring plants
(2) SDP and LDP
(3) SDP and DNP
(4) DNP and cold requiring plants

Q. 81. Role of bolting (on stem) phenomenon is in mediation of which GA regulated function?

(1) Flowering in rosette LDP
(2) Germination in SDP
(3) Hypocotyl elongation in DNP
(4) Vivipary

Q. 82. Silene dioica or Silene vulgaris is a angiosperm, is a:

(1) LDP
(2) SDP
(3) DNP
(4) LSDP

Q. 83. In which of the cold-requiring plant is?

(1) Chrysanthemum
(2) Silene
(3) Bryophyllum
(4) Pharbitis nil

Q. 84. In which of the short-day (SDP) plant is:

(1) Pharbitis nil
(2) Silene diocia
(3) Chrysanthemum
(4) Bryophyllum

Q. 85. Long-short day plants (LSDP) is:

(1) Bryophyllum
(2) Chrysanthemum
(3) Silene diocia
(4) Pharbitis nil

Q. 86. In general, GA movement is (opposite to auxin):

(1) Polar
(2) Nonpolar
(3) Both 1 and 2
(4) Along with sugar

Q. 87. Plant usually grows as rosette plants are:

(1) GA-sensitive LDP and cold requiring
(2) GA-insensitive LDP and cold requiring
(3) CK-sensitive and cold requiring
(4) ET-sensitive

Q. 88. CDKs along with cyclins, regulate the transition from:

(1) G_1 to S
(2) G_2 to M (mitosis)
(3) Both 1 and 2
(4) None

Q. 89. In which of the following is a potent inhibitor of root elongation in intact seedlings?

(1) Auxin   (2) CK
(3) ET   (4) GA

Q. 90. The inhibition of root growth by auxins is used as a:

(1) Quantitative
(2) Qualitative
(3) Both 1 and 2
(4) None of the above

Q. 91. When rice plant infected with ascomycetes fungus (gibberella fujikuroi, a sexual stage or imperfect stage is Fusarium moniliforme), shows:

(1) Excessively tall
(2) Chlorotic with reduced root growth
(3) Tillering
(4) All of the above

Q. 92. Bioassay method/s for auxin estimation is/are (a) Coleoptile curvature Test and root inhibition test:

(1) Coleoptile section straight growth test
(2) Split pea test and pea root test
(3) Oat mesocotyl straight growth test
(4) All are correct

Q. 93. Site of GA synthesis is:

(1) Entire vegetative organs of higher plants particularly the shoot tip portion
(2) Root tip portion
(3) Both 1 and 2
(4) None of the above

Q. 94. Abundant amount of GAs found at the:

(1) Immature seeds
(2) Vegetative parts
(3) Flowers, fruits and seeds
(4) All of the above

Q. 95. Which has been shown to cause a male-flowering plant to produce hermaphrodite flowers?

(1) CK   (2) GA

(3) ABA   (4) Auxins

Q. 96. Enhancement of fruit set and fruit size in *grape* varieties and induction of parthenocarpy in *fig* also been reported due to which hormone?

(1) CK   (2) ABA

(3) GA   (4) ET

Q. 97. Ca^{2+} acts as a second messenger in CK-induced bud formation in:

(1) Moss (*Funaria hygrometrica*)

(2) Bryophyllum

(3) Kalanchoe

(4) Baugainvellea

Q. 98. In which of the following is a lipid in nature:

(1) GA   (2) Auxin

(3) Cytokinins   (4) ET

Q. 99. In which of the following is a hydro-carbon in nature:

(1) GA   (2) Auxin

(3) Cytokinins   (4) ET

Q. 100.

Column A	Column B
Kind of nucleus	DNA amount
(A) Post-mitotic G_1 nucleus	(i) 1C
(B) Haploid nucleus	(ii) 2C
(C) G_2 nuclei	(iii) 4C
(D) S-phase nuclei	(iv) Intermediate DNA content

(1) A-ii, B-i, C-iii, D-iv

(2) A-i, B-ii, C-iii, D-iv

(3) A-ii, B-i, C-iv, D-iii

(4) A-i, B-iii, C-ii, D-iv

Q. 101. GA regulates cell cycle between the

(1) G_2 to mitosis

(2) G_1 to S

(3) G_2 to S

(4) G_0 to S

8

Biosynthesis and Homeostatic Environmental Regulation of Gibberellic Acid During Progressive Development

ABSTRACT

Gibberellic acid (GA_3) is a plant growth hormone that occurs in many plants naturally. It is also produced commercially to improve plant growth, flowering and fruiting. In this Chapter, we review the data on the structure (nature), homeostasis and growth stimulating properties accumulated during the last two decades. In the 1950s, a second group of plant hormones (after auxins), the gibberellins (GAs) are characterized. The GAs are a large group of related compounds defined by their chemical structure, opposite to other plant hormones, defined on the basis of their biological activities. Among GAs, GA_3 is a hydroxylated GA to be isolated and structurally characterized first of all among the other forms of GAs. Since it is readily extracted from fungal cultures, it is also the most common commercially available form, consequently, it is the most studied among the GAs perhaps. Subsequently, it's GA like activities, similar to other C_{19} and C_{20}-GAs have been established, demonstrating a wide variety of biological effects, including those on gene expression, synergism with cytokinin action, stimulation of calcium flux, regulation of cell cycle. Recently, our views on this very well-known and second most important plant hormone have changed. Today, there is a plethora of new data, which show that it occurs in more unsaturated form, thereby, more active than other GAs. It works with auxins to promote rapid elongation and diameter of stem and as anti-stress compound. Also new results on the biological function of GA_3 has been reported such as it relieves certain type of dormancy including physiological dormancy, phytodormancy and thermodormancy and to promote flowering in a variety of plant species under non-inductive conditions as well as role of inhibitors during GA_3 biosynthesis also described. Various biological effects produced by this hormone *in vitro* and *in vivo* have made GA_3 even more scientifically interesting and commercially attractive as an ingredient of various kinds of growth promoting and callus inducing solutions used in plant tissue and organ culture techniques.

Introduction

Gibberellins are the generic name used to designate the plant growth substances that play a major role in cell division and cell differentiaton. Among the hormones, GAs are diterpenoid plant hormones, have long been recognized as plant growth regulators that are biosynthesized through complex pathways and act as endogenous hormones controlling various aspect of plant growth and development including seed germination, stem elongation, leaf expansion, root and fruit growth, leaf shape, pollen maturation, floral induction, and de-etilation, flowering and flower development and the regulation of gene expression in cereal aleurone layer. Over the past two decades, excellent progress has been made in understanding these aspects of GA physiology. It is now clear that both GA biosynthesis and deactivation pathways are tightly regulated by developmental, hormonal and environmental signals, consistent with the role of GAs as key growth regulators (Yamaguchi, 2008).

As already stated that gibberellins are tetracyclic diterpene acids, which are themselves members of vast group of naturally occurring compounds in plants called terpenoids. Over 136 naturally occurring gibberellins are known now, in plants, fungi, and bacteria and additional numbers added every year. Gibberellins are produced in greater mass when the plant is exposed to cold temperature. They are involved in stimulation of natural process of breaking dormancy and budding and various other aspects of germination. They do the last by breaking the seed's dormancy and acting as a chemical messenger. These hormones bind to a receptor and resulting complex binds to DNA, producing an enzyme to stimulate growth in the embryo. A major effect of gibberellins is degradation of DELLA proteins, the absence of which then allows phytochrome interacting factors to bind to give promoters to regulate gene expression. It is speculated that gibberellins cause DELLA to become polyubiquitinated and thus destroyed by the 26S proteosome pathway (Daviere et $al.$, 2008).

All known gibberellins are synthesized by the terpenoid pathway in plastids and then modified in the endoplasmic reticulum and cytosol until they reach their biologically active forms such as GA_1, GA_2, GA_3, GA_4, GA_7, etc. All known gibberellins are derived via the ent-gibberellane skelton, but are synthesized via ent-kaurene. These are abbreviated as GA with a subscript such as GA_1, GA_2, GA_3, GA_4 and so on. These are named in order of discovery. Of which, GA_3 is commonly known as gibberellic acid. GA_1 and GA_{20}, both C19 GAs, are probably the most active, and consequently the most important gibberellins in higher plants (Marschner, 2002). Gibberellins and gibberellin-like substances have been found in almost all the representatives of the plant kingdom starting from bacteria through fungi (lower plants) to angiosperms (higher plants). In the later, they are synthesized in expanding leaves and shoot apex as seeds and presumably in roots.

Since all GAs are based on the ent-gibberellane skeleton, some gibberellane have the full complement of 20 carbons (C20-GAs), having one carbon lost during metabolism. In almost all C19-GAs, the carboxylic acid at carbon 19 bonds to carbon 10 to form a lactone bridge structure, especially the oxidation state of carbon 20 (in C20-GAs) and the number and position of hydroxyl groups and their stereochemistry are designated by special symbols (particularly for α and β bonds) behind or in front of the formula as viewed on a page, respectively have a strong bearing on their biological activity. For instance, hydroxylation in the β-configuration at C-2 always eliminates biological activity. There are two classes based on the presence of 19C or 20C. A little more than one-third of the gibberellins characterized to date have retained the full complement of 20 carbons in atoms and are known as C20-gibberellins. The others have one carbon atom less and are consequently known as C19-gibberellins. The 19-carbon gibberellins, such as gibberellic acid, have lost carbon-20 and in place, possess a 5-member lactone bridge that links carbons 4 and 10. The 19-carbon forms are in general, the biologically active forms of gibberellins. Hydroxylation also has a great effect on the biological activity of the gibberellins. In general, the most biologically active compounds are dehydroxylated gibberellin, which possess hydroxyl groups on both carbon 2 and carbon 13.

It is believed that GA_3 in seed embryo signal starch hydrolysis through inducing the synthesis of the enzyme α-amylase in the aleurone cells. In the model of GA_3 induced production of α-amylase, it is demonstrated that GA_3 produced in the scutellum diffuse to the aleurone cells where they stimulate the secretion of α-amylase. α-amylase then hydrolyzes starch which is utilized in cellular respiration to produce energy for the seed embryo. Studies of this process have indicated that GA_3 causes higher levels of transcription of the gene coding for the α-amylase enzyme in order to stimulate the synthesis of α-amylase. Exogenous application of GA_3 has been shown to relieve certain type of dormancy, and to promote flowering in a variety of plant species under non-inductive conditions. The influence of gibberellic acid includes parthenocarpic fruit development, senescence; promotes cell growth; increases cell wall plasticity, stem elongation and growth of whole plant, among others (Salisbury and Ross, 1992; Taiz and Zeiger, 2006). In addition, subsequent studies have proved their role in modulating the activity of many enzymes.

In this paper we discuss data on the biosynthesis, metabolism, its homeostatic environmental regulatory approaches, properties and mechanism of action of GA_3. We consider that there are at least three main reasons which make GA_3 a very interesting hormone (subject) of research: (1) recent identification of GA_3 in abiotic stress resistance, (2) new data on the recently discovered biological properties of GA_3, and (3) a few commercial applications like malt formation and role in enhancing the sugar cultivation to a greater extent.

History

GAs cause hyperelongation of intact stems and also predominantly involved in seed germination and mobilization of endosperm reserves during early embryo growth as well as flowers and fruit development. All the gibberellins that are demonstrated to be naturally occurring and that have been characterized are assigned as 'A' number (Macmillan and Takahashi, 1968). The discovery of gibberellins dates from 1898, when Korishi, for the first time described 'bakanae disease' (foolish seedlings) in rice with characteristics symptoms of tall spindy plants (Arteca, 1996). In 1926, Kurosawa, for the first time reported gibberellins from the cell culture of *Gibberella fujikuroi*. In 1938, Yabuta and Sumiki were successful in isolating a small quantity of high active crystalline material from sterile culture filtrates and was given the name 'gibberellin A' as it was isolated from gibberella. Subsequently, they isolated another compound of similar nature and named it 'gibberellin B'. The interest in gibberellins outside of Japan began after World War II. Besides this, in the United States, the first research is undertaken by a unit at Camp Detrick in Maryland, via studying seedlings of the bean *Vicia faba*. Interest in gibberellins spread around the world as the potential for its use on various commercially important plants became more obvious.

The concentration of hormones required for plant responses are very low (10^{-6} to 10^{-5} mol/L), because of these low concentrations, it has been very difficult to study plant hormones, and only since the late 1970s have scientists been able to start piercing together their effects and relationships to plant physiology. Much of the early work on PGRs involved studying plants that are genetically deficient in one or involved the use of tissue-cultured plants grown *in vitro* that are subjected to differing ratios of hormones, and the resultant growth compared. The earliest scientific observation and study dates to the 1880s; the determination and observation of PGRs and their identification are spread-out over the next 70 years (Fig. 8.1).

In 1954, British chemists Brian and others identified and chemically characterized a pure compound from culture filtrates of *gibberella fujikuroi*. They called this new substance

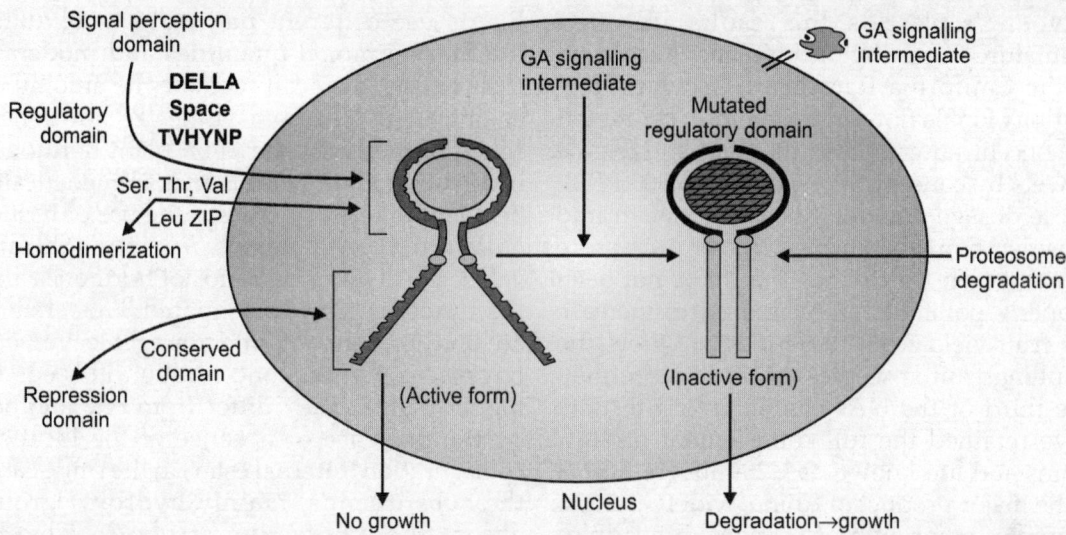

Fig. 8.1: Significance of gibberellic acid based degrative proteins in activation and deactivation of hormone

gibberellic acid. Two teams, Brian *et al.* in 1954 at the Imperical Chemical Institute (ICI) in England, and Stodola *et al.* in 1955 at the United States Department of agriculture (USDA) working on large scale preparation of gibberellins from fungus culture isolated entirely new compound. The ICI team gave the name 'gibberellic acid' while the USDA team, 'gibberellins X'. The former name has been universally accepted and gibberellic acid is now also known as GA_3. In most experiments, GA_3 has been applied to plant organs or cultured tissues where they activate the expression of specific genes responsible for growth, differentiation and finally development. In addition, they affect signal transduction and cell regulation. GA_3 enhances the resistance of plants to various forms of stress such as imposed by salinity, drought and high temperature, they regulate plant growth under drought conditions and delay senescence of intact plant parts. They also might be involved in coordinating certain metabolic activities, sink capacities and the mobilisation of storage products in different parts of leguminous and non-leguminous

plants during development. There are also data, which suggest that GA_3 enhanced the gene expression is not a result of GA_3 action, including other plant hormones, for which synergistic, antagonistic and additive interactions have been observed. GAs biosynthetic genes are found in many plants including *Agrobacterium tumifaciens*, *Pseudomonas savastanoi* and *Corynebacterium fasciens*. These pathogens possess encoded plasmids and their expression of which leads to the infectious transformation of plant tissue. Although, GAs binding proteins (DELLA and GID1, RGA, etc.) have been reported in plants, their functions till date not fully recognized and required further research in future.

GA_3 is isolated from the crystalline solid and in 1938 as a crystalline compound. Research on GA_3 in the US and England began on the late 1940s and increased rapidly as the potential benefits to the plant industry are realized. The effects of using even a small amount of GA_3 to encourage plant growth are often successful. It is frequently used as a substance to stimulate germination in seeds that have become dormant. If GA_3 is applied to young's plastids, the results are often premature flowering of the plant. According to the California Rare Fruit Growers' formation of male flowers is generally promoted by concentration of 10 to 200 PPM and female flowers by concentrations of 200 to 300 PPM. These dosage amounts should be taken into consideration when using GA_3 for premature flowering. In fruit plants that have not been properly pollinated, GA_3 is used to increase the fruit yield from these plants. Often, the resulting fruit is seedless. A little more than one-third of the GAs characterized to date have retained the full complement of 20-C atoms and are known as C20-gibberellins. It is the major product of China, widely used to promote the growth of oranges, pineapples and grapes, stimulates the growth of spinach and other leafy vegetables, break the dormancy of the seeds of ginseng and potatoes and keeps vegetables fresh longer, aiding their transportation to outlaying markets. Despite almost a half century of study, the mechanisms that mediate the many reported responses to GA_3 and their effects on plants and plant tissues have not been fully explained. More general reviews on GA_3 appeared recently (Ueguchi-Tanaka and Matsuoka, 2010).

Occurrence and General Properties of Gibberellic Acid

Plant growth regulators are not nutrients, but chemicals that in small amounts promote and influence the growth (Helgi opik and Stephen, 2005), development and differentiation of cells and tissues. Their role in development has been studied for nearly a century, yet the concept of hormones in plants is steeped in controversy. GA_3 generally occurs in matured seeds, germinating seedlings, cotyledons and leaves. Also, they are present within plant body either in bound state or in modified forms. The production of hormones occurs very often at sites of active growth within the meristem, before cells have fully differentiated.

Plants use different pathways to regulate internal hormonal quantities and moderate their effects; they can regulate the amount of chemicals used to biosynthesize hormones. Much of the early works on plant hormones involved studying plants that are genetically deficient in one or involved the use of tissue-cultured plants grown *in vitro* that are subjected to differing ratios of hormones and the resultant growth compared. Gibberellins are produced in roots and younger leaves, but have their highest concentration in seeds of higher plants. They differ from one another by the presence or absence of the location configuration (internal ester) in the ring A and the substituent's, mainly hydroxyl group absent the whole ring structure. Due to presence of an additional ethylenic double bond in ring A, GA_3 is more unsaturated, and thereby more active than other gibberellins (Salisbury and Ross, 1992). GA_3 is the first widely available active form of commercial gibberellins. GA_3 works with auxins in most cases reported to promote rapid elongation and diameter of stem tissues.

Moreover, it became evident that an entire family of GAs exists and that in each fungal culture different GAs predominant. Though, GA_3 is always a principal component. As we will see the structural feature that all GAs has in common, and that defines them as a family of molecules, is that they are derived from the *ent*-kaurene ring structure. As GA_3 became available, physiologists began testing it on a wide variety of plants. Spectacular responses are obtained in the elongation growth of dwarf and rosette plants, particularly in genetically dwarf peas (*Pisum sativum* L.) and dwarf maize (*Zea mays* L.) and in many rosette plants. The growth promoting potentiality of GA_3 described later in this Chapter. The biosynthesis of plant hormones within plant tissues is often diffused and not always localized. Plants lack glands to produce and store hormones, because unlike animals which have two circulatory systems powered by a heart that moves fluids around the body. Plants use more passive means to move chemicals around the plants. Plants utilize simple chemicals as hormones, which move more easily through the plant's tissues. They are often produced and used on a local basis within the plant body. Also, plant cells produce hormones that affect even different regions of the cell producing the hormones. Hormones are transported within the plant by utilizing four types of movement's, *viz.* localized movement, cytoplasm streaming within cells, slow diffusion of ions and molecules between cells are utilized.

GA_3 is used to treat seeds to force them from dormancy and germinate rapidly. It is also applied to force a plant to flower early and stop roots from forming. It can force pollination between self-incompatible clones and closely related species to help with hybridization. Applied to trees, it stimulates the rate of growth and as a spray can protect blossoms from frost. It is used on seedless grapes per cluster, and on many other fruits such as cherries, oranges and blueberries to manipulate the time fruit set occurs and to slow down aging. GA_3 is applied to plants to increase overall plant growth. GA_3 not only increases the number of grapes per bunch but also the average size of each grape. GA_3 is sometimes used in laboratory and greenhouse settings to trigger germination in seeds that would otherwise remain dormant. It is also widely used in the grape-growing industry as a hormone to induce the production of larger bundles and bigger grapes, especially Thompson seedless grapes, and in the Okanagan and Crestan Valley it is used in the Cherry industry as a growth regulator. GA_3, if sprayed on plants in full-bloom, can counteract the deadly effects of frost when the weather gets cold. GA_3 should be used with care as it can have an opposite effect if too much is used. Some flowers require light and appropriate temperature for bloom but under its influence such light and temperature are not required.

In addition, by applying appropriate amount of GA_3 the number of male flowers can be diminished and the number of female flowers can be increased. Similarly, dwarf plants with short internodes and rosette of leaves are develop elongated internodes and bear flowers, a process called bolting. In addition, application of GA_3 can induce bolting in winter. However, it appears that all tissues have the potential to produce only of the phytohormones, which are transported via vascular tissues from one part of the plant to another; these include sieve tubes that move sugars from leaves to the roots and flowers and xylem and phloem that move water, food materials (e.g. sucrose) and minerals solutes from the roots to the foliage (Weiler and Ziegher, 1981). The prevailing direction of transport depends on the type of phytohormones and developmental stage of plant.

Physical Properties

The chemical formula of GA_3 is $C_{19}H_{22}O_6$. When purified, it is a white-to-pale-yellow solid. It can be dissolved in ethanol but is only slightly soluble in water. It has a high MP at which it breaks down and is readily degraded by acids. It is most widely used of 136 different GAs that have been isolated since its discovery in 1898. GA_3 is a simple GA, promoting growth and elongation of cells. It affects composition of plants and helps plants grow if used in small amounts, but eventually plants develop tolerance for it. GA_3 stimulates the cells of germinating seeds to produce mRNA molecules that code for hydrolytic enzymes. GA_3 is very potent hormone whose natural occurrence in plants controls their development. Since GA regulates growth, application at very low concentrations can have a profound effect while too much will have the opposite effect. It is eventually used in concentrations between 0.01 and 10 mg/L. Because of these low concentrations, it has been very difficult to study them and only since the alter 1970s have scientists been able to start piercing together their effects and relationship to plant physiology.

Regardless of genotype (tall or small plants) more GA equals more lateral growth. GA_3 is first discussed in Japan in 1935 as a result of the study of a condition common in rice plants called *'foolish seedlings'* disease which caused the plants to grow much taller than normal. The effects of GAs are not widely understood until years later. GA_3 is not manufactured; it is a natural product extracted from the *Gibberella fujikuroi* fungus. Seeds of many plant species require exposure to low or high temperature within a period before they will germinate, and the process called thermal stratification. Alternatively, the GA_3 can be used to break seed dormancy. In addition, alcohol soluble GA_3 powder 90 percent is the most economical form of GA_3 and is soluble in 70 percent common rubbing alcohol; before it can be used is must be turned into a liquid. The amount of GA_3 that needs to be used is very small. Drop the correct amount of powered in a small bottle, then add a few drops of rubbing alcohol. The only reason to use alcohol is to dilute the GA_3 powder. Use just enough alcohol to wet the GA_3 powder. 90 percent GA_3 powder will not dissolve in water.

GA_3 is a (C-19) non-organic acid and metabolic by-product of the fungus *Gibberella fujikuroi*, which has lost C-20 and in place possesses a five-member lactone ring that links C-4 and C-10. In 1926s a Formosan plant pathologists Kurosawa observed that when a cell-free extract of the saccharomycetic fungus *Gibberella fujikuroi* is applied on healthy rice seedlings elongation of the seedlings take place, a symptoms characteristic of the disease. GA_3 is not a toxic substance it should be handled with care and kept out of reach of children. The quantity applied for best results is very important to know as well too much can actually have a negative effect. Do not ingest, but however, on ingestion it does not induce vomiting. So, therefore, protective clothing such as gloves and possibly a respirator should be worn out during application depending on the method. GA_3 is vital to plant growth and lacking them, plants would be mostly a mass of undifferentiated cells. GA_3 frequently regulates the concentrations of other plant hormones. The greatest effects occur at specific stages during the cells' lives with diminished effects occurring before or after this period. Plants need hormones at very specific times during plant growth and at specific locations.

Phytohormones act at genetic level (Marschner, 2002; Taiz and Zeiger, 20006). Not all plant cells respond to hormones, but those cells that are programmed to respond at specific points in their growth cycle. The greatest effects occur at specific stages during the cell's life with diminished affects occurring before or after this period. Plants feed hormones at very specific times during plant growth at specific locations. They also need to disengage the effects that hormones have when they are no longer needed. After production, they are sometimes moved to other parts of the plant, where they cause an immediate effect; or they can be stored in cells to be released later. Plants use different pathways to regulate internal hormone quantities and moderate their effects; they can regulate the amount of chemicals used to biosynthesize hormones. They can stir them in cells, inactivate them or cannibalize already formed hormones by conjugating them with carbohydrates, amino acids or peptides. Plants can also breakdown hormones chemically, effectively destroying them. Plant hormones frequently regulate the concentrations of other plant hormones (Swarup *et al.*, 2007).

Chemical Isolation

Although active GAs are free, a variety of GA glycosides are formed by a covalent linkage between GA_3 and a sugar and is partially prevalent in some seeds. The conjugating sugar is usually glucose, and it may be attached to the GA_3 by a carboxyl group forming a GA glucoside, or via a hydroxyl group forming a GA glucosyl-ether. When GA_3 is applied to a plant, a certain portion usually becomes glycosylated. Glycosylation, therefore, represents another form of inactivation. In some cases, applied glycosides are metabolized back to free GAs, so glucosides may also be a storage form of GA_3 (Schneider and Schmidt, 1990). As with all other plant hormones, the original means of detecting and assaying GAs are bioassays, because of their sensitivity and specificitiy. Measuring GA_3 physically or chemically is extremely difficult, since GA_3 does not absorb UV radiation, does not fluoresce, and has no distinguishing chemical characteristics that can form the basis of a specific chemical bioassay. Thus, except for the highly complex characterization of crystallized forms of GA_3 obtained from vast amount of plant material, almost all identifications in plants in the past consisted of varying degrees of purification followed by some forms of chromatography of the paper or thin layer chromatography (TLC).

Since, late 1980s HPLC (high performance liquid chromatography) followed by bioassay of the chromatographic fractions has been used. With the increasing availability of GC (gas chromatography) combined with GC-MS (mass spectrometry), or more recently, HPLC-MS. These highly sensitive and selective analytic methods or far the most widely used method for GA_3 analysis found to be more exact means of identifications today. Data produced by a mass spectrometer are as specific as fingerprint, and the intensity of the signal can be used to calculate the amount of the substance present. When a gas chromatography, which can separate up to dozens of compounds in a mixture, is placed in front of the mass spectrometry the purified compounds are fed one at a time to the mass spectrometer for analysis (Horgan, 1995). The more recent development of HPLC-MS enables the direct analysis of compounds in the HPLC effluent, with no chemical modification required for GC.

Chemistry of GA₃

GA_3 is like all other GAs which are tetracyclic diterpenoids made up of four isoprenoid units (Bramley, 1997), a terpenoid is a compound made up of five carbon (isoprene) building blocks. Terpenes are a functionally and chemically diverse group of molecules, probably the largest and most diverse class of organic compounds in plants. This large diversity arises from the number of basic units in the chain and the various ways in which they are assembled. The terpene family includes, in addition to the GA_3, other plant hormones also made by terpenes such as ABA and brassinosteroids. In addition, cytokinins although not a separate terpene *per se* but do contain terpenoid side chains. The biological isoprene unit is isopentenyl pyrophosphate (IPP). Moreover, recently, mevalonic acid is thought to be the immediate precursor of IPP for all terpenoid pathways: (1) a mevalonic acid dependent pathway and (2) a mevalonic acid independent pathway (Lichtenthaler *et al.*, 1997). The former occurs in the cytosol and is involved primarily in sterol biosynthesis; the latter is localized in the chloroplast and leads to the synthesis of carotenoids and related compounds. Since, the early step in GA_3 biosynthesis occurs in proplastids, the IPP used in GA_3 biosynthesis may not be derived from mevalonic acid. In the plastid terpenoid pathway, IPP is synthesized from glyceraldehyde-3 phosphate and pyrophosphate rather than from mevalonate (Lichtenthaler *et al.*, 1997). Thus far, the source of the IPP used in GA biosynthesis has not been definitely established.

Biosynthesis

Bioactive GAs are diterpene plant hormones that are biosynthesized through complex pathways and control diverse aspects of growth and development (Davies, 1995). It is now clear that both GA$_3$ biosynthesis and deactivation pathways are tightly regulated by developmental, hormonal and environmental signals, consistent with the role of GA$_3$ as a key growth regulator (Yamaguchi *et al.*, 2008). Regardless of the origin of the IPP, the next few steps are common to both the cytosolic and plastid pathways. The isoprene units are added successively to produce geranyl pyrophosphate (C19), farnesyl pyrophosphate (C15), and geranyl pyrophosphate (C20). At this stage all the intermediates have chains of C5 units. A series of genes encoding the enzymes involved in the GA$_3$ biosynthetic pathway has been cloned from a variety of species (Hedden and Phillips, 2000). Expression analysis has revealed that the developmental regulator of expression of these genes plays an important role in controlling the many aspects of GA$_3$ regulated plant growth such as stem elongation, flower development and seed germination (Yamaguchi *et al.*, 1998).

GAs are first isolated as metabolites of a fungal rice pathogen. It also occurs in other fungi and bacteria (MacMillan, 2002). Recent identifications of genes encoding GA$_3$ biosynthetic enzymes from *G. fujikuroi* and a species of Phaeosphaeria revealed remarkable differences in GA$_3$ biosynthesis pathways and enzymes between plants and fungi. In plants two separate terpene cyclases (CPS and KS) are involved in the synthesis of *ent*-Kaurene from GGDP, whereas in fungi these two reactions are catalyzed by a single bifunctional enzymes (CPS/KS). In *G. fujikuroi*, three multifunctional P450s, P450-4 and P450-1, play a similar role to that of KOS (CYP701As) and KAOs (CYP88As) in plants respectively. However, despite their similar catalytic activities, the fungal P450s are not closely related to the plant enzymes in amino acid sequence. Remarkably, P450-1 has 3β-hydroxylase activity in addition to KAO activity and produces GA14. Thus,

3β-hydroxylation is catalyzed by a P450 at an early step of the pathway in *G. fujikuroi*, in contrast to plant GA$_3$oxs that are soluble 2ODDs and act at the final step to produce bioactive GAs.

In GA$_3$ biosynthesis pathway, the most peculiar step is the conversion of GA$_{14}$ to GA$_4$ by P450, P450-2 (Tudzynski *et al.*, 2002). Similarly, oxidation of GA20ox proceeds in *G. fujikuroi* plant GA$_{20}$oxs. GA$_4$ is then converted to GA$_7$ by GA$_4$-desaturase and finally to GA$_3$ by P450-3 through 13-hydroxylation. Notably, these GA$_3$ biosynthetic genes are clustered on a single chromosome in fungi, whereas they are randomly located on multiple chromosomes in plants (Kawaide, 2000). Summation of all above-mentioned points, these substantial differences in genes and enzymes suggest that plants and fungi have evolved their complex GA$_3$ biosynthetic pathways separately. Moreover, GA$_3$ biosynthesis in case of lower plants can be studied generally in reference of the moss *Pyscomitrella patens* is a model organism of bryophytes group. Some other plant growth hormones like auxin, cytokinins and ABA are biosynthesized and function as growth regulators in *P. patens*. However, any kind of GA$_3$ as a growth regulator in moss is absent or unknown till date. Recently, a cDNA clone encoding *ent*-kaurene synthase is identified from *P. patens*. Curiously, *P. patens ent*-kaurene synthase is a bifunctional enzyme with both CPS and KS activities as is the case of fungal CPS/KSs. Although, both GA$_1$ and GA$_4$ are identified in saprophytes of some trees fern species. On the other hand, the pteridophytes, subgroup lycophyta member *Selaginella moellendorfii* and *S. kraussina* possess functional GID1 and DELLA homologues that are capable of forming a complex with GA. However, such functional GID1/DELLA proteins are not found in *P. patens*, suggesting that GA-stimulated GID1-DELLA interactions presumably arose in the land plant linage after the bryophyte divergence (Yasumura *et al.* 2007).

Sequential Steps in Gibberellic Acid Biosynthesis

In maize, researchers have demonstrated the entire GA_3 biosynthetic pathway in vegetative tissues by feeding them various radioactive intermediates (Kobayashi *et al.*, 1996). On the basis of these and numerous other studies, the GA biosynthetic pathway has been shown to be divided into three stages. Each stage residing in a different cellular compartment. This compartmentation occurs according to the nature of the enzymes involved and the corresponding localization in the cell: Terpene cyclases acting in proplastids, mono-oxygenases associated with the endoplasmic reticulum, and dioxygenases located in the cytosol. Only a brief outline is given here for orientation; for detailed information on different aspects of GA metabolism the readers are referred to several recent review articles (Sun *et al.* 2011).

Cyclization Reaction

GA_3 is biosynthesized from a common C20 precursor for diterpenoids called geranyl geranyl diphosphate (GGDP). Three different categories of required enzymes for the GA_3 biosynthesis from GGDP in plants are as follows: terpene synthase (TPSs), cytochrome P450 monooxygenases (P450s), and 2-oxoglutarate-dependent dioxygenases (2ODDs). In the cytosol MVA is phosphorylated via two steps into MVA-5-diphosphate, which after decarboxylation yields IPP. However, new results indicate that IPP can also be formed via a non-mevalonate pathway in plastids. In this pathway, D-glyceraldehyde-3-phosphate plus pyruvate yields 1-deoxy-D-xylulose-5-phosphate, converted to IPP. In addition, mevalonate pathway gives rise to sterols, sesquiterpenes and triterpenoids, whereas the pathway involving 1-deoxy-D-xylulose-5-phosphate yields carotenoids, phytol, plastoquinone-9, mono- and diterpenoids. Some interchange between the pathways

seems to exist. In general, it appears likely that GA precursors also are formed primarily via the 1-deoxy-D-xylulose-5-phospahte pathway in plastids of green tissues; although this has not yet been conclusively demonstrated. IPP is transformed via an isomerase catalyzed reaction into dimethylallyl-PP. The molecules of IPP are orderly joined to this compound to form geranyldiphosphate (GPP), fernesyl diphosphate (FPP), and finally the C20 compound geranyl geranyl diphosphate (GGPP), which is cyclised via copalyldi-phosphate (CPP) to *ent*-kaurene, catalyzed by two different enzymes called CPP synthase and *ent*-kaurene synthase by step cyclization reactions, located in proplastids of meristematic shoot tissues but they are not present in mature chloroplasts (Hedden and Kamiya, 1997). Higher activities of both are detected in shoots and leucoplasts from pumpkin endosperm. In contrast, mature chloroplasts are low in such activities and, therefore, it is proposed that *ent*-kaurene is primarily produced in rapidly dividing cells. Prefix 'ent' refers to the enantiomeric form of kurene. Oxidation of *ent*-kaurene to GA_{12}-aldehyde is catalyzed by monooxygenases located on the endoplasmic reticulum, which requires O_2 and NADPH for activity and involves cytochrome P450. The highly lipophilic *ent*-kaurene is oxidized stepwise at C19 via *ent*-kaurenol and *ent*-kaurenal to *ent*-kaurenoic acid. After an oxidative ring concentration with extrusion of C7 and GA_{12}-aldehyde is formed. GA_{12}-aldehyde can be seemed to be the first intermediate specific for GAs.

Oxidation Reactions

Further oxidation of GA_{12}-aldehyde to the different GAs takes place primarily in the cytosol. Most of the reactions of this conversion are enhanced by effects of soluble dioxygenases which require 2-oxoglutarate as a co-substrate and Fe $(^{22})$ and ascorbate as co-factor for their proper activity. However, depending on the plant species and the form of tissues, some primitive stages may still be catalyzed by monooxygenases. The specific steps in the modification of GA_{12} vary from species to species, and between organs of the same species. Two basic chemical changes occur in most plants: (1) hydroxylation of C13 or C3 or both; (2) a successive oxidation at C20 ($CH_2 \rightarrow CH_2OH \rightarrow CHO$), followed by loss of C20 as CO_2. In the pathway that is common in higher plants, the early-13 hydroxylation of C13. All the C20 oxidation steps are carried out by single multifunctional enzymes, GA_{20}-oxidase (Xu et al., 1995). GA_1 is then converted to the biologically active form by the enzyme 3β-hydroxylase.

Hydroxylation Reactions

Finally, 2β-hydroxylation reaction inactivates GA_1 by converting it to GA_8 or they remove GA_{20} from the pathway by converting it to GA_{29}. GA_{12}-aldehyde is oxidized by either a monooxygenase or a dioxygenase at position 7, thereby converting the aldehyde function into carboxylic acid group and leading to GA_{12}. This conversion is common to higher plants; GA_{53} would be the next intermediate after GA_{12}. Thereafter, a stepwise oxidation of C20 as CO_2 is catalyzed by the multifunctional GA_{20}-oxidase. The products of these reactions are GA_{14} GA_{19} to GA_{20}, a C19-GA group member. Considerable biological activities can be found only among C19-GAs are further hydroxylated at position 3β (e.g. GA_1 as a product of GA_3 and other). Its opposite, hydroxylation at position 2β (e.g. conversion of GA_1 to GA_8) drastically reduces biological activity. Besides this, numerous evidence is available that several related or isoenzymes of GA_{20}-oxidase, 3β-hydroxylase and 2β-hydroxylase exist that are relatively low in substrate specificity and that many have overlapping activities.

Gibberellic Acid Deactivation: Role of GA_3 Biosynthetic Inhibitors

Deactivation is important for effective regulation of the concentrations of bioactive hormones in plants. GA_3 can be metabolically deactivated in several ways.

Role of ODDs enzymes

The best characterized deactivation reaction is 2β-hydroxylation catalyzed by a class of 2ODDs, GA_2-oxidases. In addition, a new type of GA_2ox that accepts only C20-GAs is reported (Schomberg et al., 2003). These enzymes are likely to play a role in depleting pools of precursor GAs (e.g. GA_{12} and GA_{53}) that converted to bioactive forms.

Role of EUI

Recent work on a recessive tall rice mutant, elongated uppermost internode (EUI), revealed a new GA deactivation mechanism (Zhu et al., 2006), because it accumulates bioactive GAs at extremely high levels (Zhu et al., 2006). It is designated as CYP74D1 epoxidizes the 16,17-double bond of non-13-hydroxylated GAs, including GA_4, GA_9 and GA_{12}. 16α,17-dihydrodiols, hydrated products of the 16α,17-epoxides either in vivo or during purification are detected in transgenic rice plants that overexpresses the EUI genes. Thus, the discovery of this enzyme explains the occurrence of GA, 16α,17-dihydrodiols in many plant species (Zhu et al., 2006).

Methylation

A third approach for GA_3 deactivation has yet to be investigated recently is methylation. Some studies have shown that Arabidopsis GAMT1 and GAMT2 encode enzyme (GA methyltransferases) that catalyzes methylation of the C6 carboxyl group of the GAs using S-adenosine-L-methionine as a methyl donor (Varbanova et al., 2007). Both the above enzymes utilize a variety of GAs, including bioactive GAs and then precursors as substrates in vitro and produce the corresponding methyl esters. Also, ecotropic expression of GAMT1 or GAMT2 in Arabidopsis, tobacco and petunia results in dwarfed plants with GA-deficiency.

Both heavily expressed in developing and germinating seeds. Results of several studies suggest that the GAMT genes play a role in deactivating the GAs in Arabidopsis seeds.

Conjugation

All forms of GAs including GA_3 can be converted into conjugates in plants (Sasaki *et al.*, 2003). Conjugation of GA_3 to glucose occurs either through a hydroxyl group of GA_3 to give a GA-O-glucosyl either or via the 6-carboxyl group to give a GA-glucosyl ester. Although, formation of these conjugates may also serve to deactivate GA_3, it remains unclear whether GA_3 conjugation plays regulatory role in control of bioactive GA_3 levels.

Biosynthetic Inhibitors

There are four major groups exist: (1) nitrogen-containing heterocyclic compounds, (2) onium type compounds, (3) various structural modified form of 2-oxoglutaric acid, and (4) 16,17-dihydro-GAs. Each group prevents GA_3 biosynthesis at a specifically critical step rather than many step inhibition. An overview of the GA biosynthetic inhibitors is given below.

Nitrogen Containing Heterocyclic Compounds

Various kinds of N-containing growth retardants are as follows: pyrimidines, ancymidol, flurprimidol, norbornanodiazeatin, paclobutrazol, uniconazole-P, triapenthenol, BAS III...W, inabenfide, 1-n-decylimidazole, 1-geranyleimidazole, HOEO74784 possess plant growth retardants properties (Tschabold *et al.*, 1970). Among them, some are of commercial relevance, used as a dwarfing agent and have attached a relatively high degree of interest. Also, a few are found to have practical uses in rice, fruit trees and ornamentals. The structure of a few is described below:

All above-mentioned growth retardants act as inhibitors of monooxygenases catalyzing the oxidative steps from *ent*-kaurene to *ent*-kaurenoic acid. The structural feature common to all these inhibitors of *ent*-kaurene oxidation is a electro pair on the SP^2 hybridized nitrogen of their heterocyclic ring. Depending on the presence or absence of double bonds. Uniconazole-P and paclobutrazole possess one/two asymmetric C-atom respectively. Detailed experiments conducted with the optical enantiomers of paclobutrazol have shown that these forms exhibit more pronounced plant growth regulatory activity and block GA_3 biosynthesis more specifically, whereas the enantiomers are more active in inhibiting sterol biosynthesis (Hedden and Graebe, 1985). Now, there are well-cleared evidences available that reduction of shoot growth by pyrimidines, 4-pyrimidines, triazole, imidazoles and diazetines is caused by a lowered content of biosynthetically active GA_3.

16,17-Dihydro-Gibberellins

It represents the most recent group of growth retardants. They are mostly GA derivatives structurally and their growth retarding activity is due to an inhibition of dioxygenases, catalyses the late stages of GA_3 metabolism during 3β-hydroxylation particularly (Takagi *et al.*, 1994). Treating plants with 16, 17-dihydro-GAs results in changes of GAs levels similar to the ones caused by acylclohexane diones. Applying the compounds in conjuction with suitable adjuvants has significantly raised their biological activity. In addition, 16,17-dihydro derivatives of GA_{19}, GA_{20} and GA_1 do not cause growth retardation in Willow. It demonstrates that 16,17-dihydro derivatives interact very specifically with GA_3 formation only in graminous species. The endoform of 16,17-dihydro-GA_5-13-acetate is somewhat less active than its exo-counterpart. A number of substituents of 16,17-dihydro-GA_5 at C13 in particular esters and ethers of different chain length, have been assayed in wheat and barley. According to real knowledge, it appears that a double bond between C-2 and C-3 is of importance for high growth-retarding activity. In addition, several naturally occurring GAs also reduce the activity of 3β-hydroxylases obtained from immature *Phaseolus vulgaris* seeds. Inhibitors of GA metabolism have also been reported for other structural GA variants. Moreover, several 16,17-dihydro-GAs occur naturally in higher plants or in fungi. Also some synthetically produced 16,17-dihydro-GAs are dealt with a number of years (Brian *et al.*, 1967). At that time, testing is rather performed to determine GA-like activity and except for some dwarfing genotypes, graminous species are not employed in the assays. As a consequence the growth retarding properties of compounds such as 16, 17-dihydro-GAs do not show up.

Conformational Mimics of 2-oxoglutaric Acid

Stem stabilization in cereals crops, oilseed rape, growth control in turf grasses and reduction of vegetables growth in fruit trees are the main application of this group. Several examples are as follows: prohexadione-calcium, trinexapac-ethyl and the experimental compounds LAB198 (Nakayama *et al.*, 1990). Studies with cell-free preparations have revealed that most steps after GA_{12}-aldehyde are inhibited by acylcyclohexanediones (Nakayama *et al.*, 1991). Enzyme kinetics data also indicate that the retardants act largely competitively with respect to 2-oxoglutarate (Hedden, 1991). The hydroxylations at position 2β appear to be the primary targets of acylcyclohexanediones (Nakayama *et al.*, 1990). All above findings supported by fact that growth reduction is accompanied by lowered levels of biologically active GA_1 and its metabolites GA_8 but increased concentration of GA_{20} and earlier precursors of GA_1. A number of different acylcyclohexadiones and structurally related compounds have been evaluated for their ability to inhibit $GA_2\beta$ and

3β-hydrolases in cell-free systems. When the cyclohexane ring is replaced by benzene, an almost complete loss of activity resulted. In structures related to prohexadione, a free carboxylic acid function resulted in higher activity as compared to the corresponding methyl/ethyl ester, most likely due to a higher degree of similarity to 2-oxoglutaric acid. Moreover, esters may be easier to handle for preparing formulated products. The growth retardant daminozide has been used for many years to reduce excessive shoot growth. Its growth retardant activity is, however, restricted to relatively a few plant species. Due to toxicological concerns, the importance of daminozole has declined markedly in recent years, particularly for edible crops.

Onium Type Compounds

Chlormequat chloride is the most prominent representative of this group. Several others are piproctanyl bromide AMO-1618 and chlorphonium BTS-44584. All such compounds have a positively charged ammonium, phosphonium or sulphonium group and block the biosynthesis of GA_3 directly before *ent*-kaurene formulations. In addition, all such compounds have a quaternary ammonium group as anti-lodging agents in cereal production and reduce excessive vegetative growth. Several other representatives of such compounds are as chlormequat chloride and mepiquat chloride. Also, *ent*-kaurene synthase is also inhibited by these compounds, but mostly at a lower degree of activity. In addition, tertiary amine analogs of squalene are efficient inhibitors of oxidosqualene cyclase. All such compounds are positively charged at physiological PH and mimic the carbocationic and are expected to bind very tightly to the enzyme blocks the reaction. It appears also likely that inhibitors of CPP-synthase mimic cationic intermediates in the conversion of GGPP into CPP. More definite results with some of the onium type compounds (growth retardants) have also been obtained by studying their effects on GA levels in intact higher plants. Several older investigations exist in which levels of endogenous GAs have been detected by bioassays. In addition, GA levels are found to be decreased by the growth retardants, more or less parallel to reduction in shoot length (Rademacher, 1991). With regard to chlormequat chloride, these results can more recently be confirmed in employing modern techniques such as combined gas chromatography-mass-spectrometry.

Metabolism

GAs are diterpene synthesized from acetyl CoA via the mevalonic acid pathway (MVA). GAs are widespread and so far ubiquitous in both flowering (angiosperms) and non-flowering (gymnosperms) plants as well as ferns. GAs like other GAs are produced in greater mass when the plant is exposed to cold temperatures. GA_3 shows many physiological effects, each depending on the type of GA_3 present as well as species of plant. A large number of studies indicated that GAs cause higher levels of transcription of the gene coding for the α-amylase enzyme in order to stimulate the synthesis of α-amylase. It is also believed that GAs in the seed embryo stimulate signal to starch hydrolysis targets including the synthesis of α-amylase in the aleurone cells. Then α-amylase hydrolyzes starch, which is abundant in many seeds, into glucose that can be utilized in cellular respiration to produce energy for the embryo development in growing seeds.

All GAs have either 19 or 20 C units grouped into their 4 or 5 ring systems. The fifth ring is lactone ring and attached to ring A. Like other GAs, GA_3 is believed to be synthesized in young's tissues of the shoot and also the developing seeds. It is uncertain whether young root tissue also produces GAs. In addition, these are some evidence that leaves may be the source of some biosynthesis (Salisbury and Ross, 1995). GA_{12} is the first true GA ring system with C20. From the aldehyde form of GA_{12} arise both 20 and 19 carbon GAs but there are many mechanisms by which these other compounds arise. Certain commercial chemicals which are used to stunt growth do so in part because they block the synthesis of GAs. During the active growth the plant metabolizes most GAs by hydroxylation to inactive conjugates quickly with the exception of GA_3. GA_3, particularly, is degraded much slower which helps to explain why the symptoms initially associated with the hormones in the disease Bakane are present. Inactive conjugates might be stored or translocated via the phloem and xylem before their release (activation) at proper time and in the proper tissue (Arteca, 1996).

Moreover, application of GA_3 to dwarf plants made them grow tall, it is presumed that GAs must be the natural regulators of plant stem growth, but evidences are not available. Primitive proofs to demonstrate that tall plants have more or more active GA_3 and the other GAs than dwarf plants are unsuccessful. Jake MacMillan's group at the university of Bristol in England, finally demonstrated that tall stems do contain more bioactive GA that dwarf stems do contain more bioactive GA that dwarf stems have and that the levels of the endogenous GAs mediate the genetic control of tallness (Reid and Howell, 1995). The breakthrough can be attributed to several factors. First, tall and dwarf plants of unknown genetic makeup are compared. Genes regulating tallness are identified and the plants used are genetically identical except for the gene that is primarily responsible for tallness. Second, GA_3 chemically and instrumental analysis have advanced so that unequivocal identification can be made, and custom-tailored of GA_3 molecules, labelled with both stable and radioactive isotopes can be used in sophisticated studies of metabolism. Third, only the expanding internodes where the bioactive GAs is concentrated are compared rather than whole shoots including non-growing mature tissues.

The GA_3 of tall plants containing the Le allele are compared with biogenic dwarf plants (plants with the same genetic makeup except for the genes mentioned) containing the Le allele. These are the two alleles of the genes that regulate tallness in pea, which is first investigated by Greger Mendel in the pioneering study in genetics in 1866. The implications are that the Le gene conferred on the plants the ability to convert GA_{20} to GA_1. Thus, it is demonstrated by concluding that the Le gene, which regulates tallness (or stem length) in peas, does so by causing the synthesis of an enzyme that 3β-hydroxylates GA_{20} to produce GA_1 (Lester et al., 1970). Since, it has been concluded that GA_3 is the controlling gibberellins in the regulation of tallness in peas. Although GA_1 appears to be the primary active GA in stem growth for most species, the possibility still exists that a few other GAs have biological activity in other species or tallness. For example, GA_3 which differs from GA_1, only in having one double bond, is relatively rare in higher plants but appears to be able to substitute for GA_1 in most bioassays.

Genes for Gibberellic Acid Metabolism

In both Arabidopsis and rice, the enzymes that catalyze the early steps of GA biosynthesis are encoded by one or two genes. In Arabidopsis, CPS, KS and KO are each encoded by a single gene, and the null alleles of these genes (GA_1, GA_2 and GA_3) result in severe GA-deficient dwarves. Additional CPS-like enzymes (OsCys1 and OsCyc2) function as syn-copalyl diphosphate (CDP) synthases in the biosynthesis of phytoalexins. Several genetic studies indicate that KS and KO in GA biosynthesis are also encoded by single genes, although, multiple KS-like and KO-like sequences exist in the genome. In comparison

with the early biosynthesis of enzymes, the 2ODDs that catalyze the late steps in the pathway are each encoded by the multiple families. Accumulating evidence indicates also that members in each of these 2ODDs families are differentially regulated by developmental and environmental cues, and that they are the primary sites for the regulation of bioactive GA levels. The key role of the 2ODDs in determining bioactive GA level is also supported by the results of overexpression studies. Increased expression of a GA_{20}ox gene in transgenic Arabidopsis thaliana plants causes an increase in GA levels and GA-overdose phenotypes. In contrast, although overexpression of AtCPS in Arabidopsis is effective in increasing the accumulation of ent-kaurene, ent-kaurenoic acid and GA_{12}, it does not affect the levels of bioactive GAs or the phenotype (Fleet et al., 2003).

Homeostatic Environmental Regulation

Temperature

Cold temperatures are required for the germination of certain seeds (stratification) and for flowering in certain species (vernalization). Exposure of imbibed seeds to cold temperature (cold stratification) accelerates the release from seed dormancy and induces germination in many plant species. The best-studied case is the vernalization of Thalspi arvense (field pennycress). A prolonged cold treatment is required for both the stem elongation and flowering of T. arvense and the GAs can substitute for the cold treatment. In the absence of the cold treatment, ent-Kaurene acid accumulates to high levels in the shoot tip, which is also the site for perception of the cold stimulus. After the cold treatment and a return to high temperatures, the ent-kaurenoic acid is converted to GA_9 and later to GA_3, the two most active GAs for the stimulating and flowering responses. These results consistent with a cold-induced increase in the activity of ent-kaurenoic acid. Moreover, microarray analysis showed that approximately a quarter of cold-responsive genes corresponding to GA-regulated genes, suggesting an important role for GA in mediating the cold temperature signal in Arabidopsis seeds. Plants monitor day and night temperatures and alter their growth and development accordingly. The ability of plants to detect the diurnal temperature change is referred to as thermoperiodism. In pea, a day/night temperature combination of 13C/21C (and 17C/17C), and this response is correlated with a decrease in GA_1/GA_3 levels (Stavang *et al.*, 2005). Additional research work showed also that SPATULA (SPT), abHLH transcription factor closely related to PIL5, acts as a light-stable repressor of seed germination and controls responses to cold stratification in part through regulating the $AtGA_3ox2$ genes (Penfield *et al.*, 2005). In addition, *Pisum sativum* $PsGA_2ox2$ transcript abundance increases significantly in 13C/21C conditions compared with 21C/13C, suggesting that a higher rate of GA deactivation is involved in the thermoperiodic response in pea. Furthermore, a constitutive GA-response mutant, La crys, shows no or very poor thermoperiodic response in stem elongation, which suggests that GA_3/GA_1 ratio acts as a mediator of the thermoperiodic response (Stavang *et al.*, 2005).

Abiotic (Salt) Stress

Evidence has emerged that the GA metabolism pathway is altered in response to abiotic stresses. There is an intimate relationship has been suggested to exist between GA_3 levels and the acquisition of stress protection in barley (Vettakkorumakankav *et al.* 1999). The level of active GA_3 can be reduced by catabolism or by conjugation to sugars. In some cases, active GA_3 can be generated by release from the conjugated form. Finally, the transport of GA (or GA precursor) to or form a tissue can also affect the steady state level of active GA. In fact, salt-treated Arabidopsis plants contain reduced levels of bioactive GAs including GA_3, supporting the idea that salt stress shows

growth by modulating the GA_3 metabolism pathway. In addition, recent researches have shown that $AtGA_2ox7$, encodes a GA_2ox that specifically deactivates C20-GAs, is a target of DDF1 (dwarf and delayed flowering 1), suggesting that salt stress decreases bioactive GA levels through elevated deactivation. Overexpression of DDF1 causes a reduction in GA_3 content and dwarfism in Arabidopsis (Magome *et al.*, 2004). DDF1 encodes an AP2 transcription factor that is closely related to the dehydration responsive element-binding proteins (DREBs) involved in responses, and DDF1 expression is strongly induced by high salinity stress.

Thermoperiodism

Light is one of the major environmental factors that affects plant growth and development. Current evidence indicates that changes in GA concentration are at least in part, responsible for light-regulated seed germination, photoperiodism during de-etiolation, and photoperiod regulation of stem elongation and flowering. Bioactive GAs function as key mediators between the perception of environmental signals and the resulting growth responses. In model plant, Arabidopsis phytochrome B (phyB) is responsible for the low fluence response to red (R) light in a far-red (FR) light-reversible manner. Unlike phyB, phyA accumulates during dark-inhibition and promotes germination by sensing very low fluence light in a wide range of wave lengths. In both phyA and phyB-dependent germination conditions, light treatments that activate phytohormones elevate expression is suppressed; these changes in gene expression result in an increase in GA_4 levels in the seeds (Yamauchi *et al.*, 2007). In lettuce seeds, R light induces expression of the $LsGA_3ox1$ gene and suppresses $LsGA_2ox2$ expreession, whereas a subsequent FR light treatment cancels the effects of R light, under a light regime similar to the PhyB-dependent germination conditions (Nakaminami *et al.* 2003). Thus the phy signal is commonly targeted to GA_3ox and GA_3ox genes to alter bioactive GA content in lettuce and Arabidopsis seeds.

Moreover, a similar role of cryptochromes (CRY1 and CRY2) in response to blue light is shown during de-etiolating of Arabidopsis seedlings; blue light downregulated expression of $AtGA_{20}ox1$ and $AtGA_3ox1$ genes, whereas it induces $AtGA_2ox1$ expression. These transcriptional changes correlate with a *cry*-dependent transient decrease in GA_4 levels after exposure to blue light. These studies in pea and Arabidopsis suggest a general role of blue light in regulating bioactive GA levels during de-etiolation. This hormonal change is likely to contribute, at least in part, to a rapid inhibition of stem elongation during the establishment of photomorphogenesis. This hypothesis is supported by the essential role of GA in the repression of photo-morphogenesis. Numerous extensive studies have established that photoperiodic control of stem elongation in long-day (LD) rosette plants is mediated by GA_3. Transfer of spinach plants from SD to LD results in elevated levels of C19-GAs which is primarily attributable to up-regulation of $SOGA_{20}ox1$ transcript levels (Lee and Zeevaart, 2007). Furthermore, additional research work has shown that this transcriptional change is reflected in elevated accumulation of $SOGA_{20}ox1$ protein in LD (Lee and Zeevaart, 2007). When $14C-GA_{53}$ is fed to spinach plants more $14C-GA_{53}$ are metabolized to $14C-GA_{97}$ by 2β-hydroxylation in SD than in LD, and more $14C-GA_{20}$ are formed in LD than SD (Lee and Zeevaart, 2005). In Arabidopsis, flower initiation under SD conditions requires GA biosynthesis. The flower meristem identity gene LEAFY (LFY) is a key component downstream of the signal. In *Lolium perenne*, both vernalization and LD are required for flower initiation. In this species, exposure to two LDs upregulates expression of the $LDGA_{20}ox1$ gene and causes an increase in some GAs in the leaf and young

shoot tissues regardless of the vernalization status (MacMillan *et al.*, 2005). Thus, GA biosynthesis is regulated by the photoperiodic signal, whereas it is independent of vernalization in *L. perenne*.

Gibberellic Acid Alone or Combination with Other PGRs

Several latest researches provide evidences about the growth promoting properties of GA_3 which are as follows:

GA_3 along with different combination of benzyladenine, kinetin indole-butyric acid (IAB), indole acetic acid (IAA) enhanced multiple shoot induction, elongation of shoots and root induction in *Withania somnifera* L (Das *et al.*, 2011). Results of Hassanpouraghdam *et al.*, (2011) showed that the preferable foliar application levels for promoting the growth characteristics and essential oil production of a value-added multidisciplinary aromatic plant, *Lavandula officinalis* chaix. Similarly, studies of Barzali *et al.* (2011) revealed that the artificial control of fertilization by the GA_3 after crossing and hybrid embryo culture in the media will increase probability of hybrid plant production in cotton.

Also, Lipa-TsaKalidi *et al.* (2011) studied the effect of NaCl, chitin and GA_3 on seedlings growth of chervil (*Anthriscum cerefolium*) under controlled growth chamber combinations where NaCl reduced the hypocotyls and root length while GA_3 increased the hypocotyls and root length. In addition, Tiwari *et al.* (2011) studied the exogenous application of various PGRs including GA_3 significantly increases seed yield with a particular range and finally they concluded that treatment combination $(GA_3 + \text{urea} + \text{boric acid} + ZnSO_4 + K_2SO_4)$ gave best results and can be used to enhance hybrid rice seed production and substitute of GA_3 in India as well as other hybrid rice growing contribution.

Yang *et al.* (2011) study suggests that contents of IAA, zeatin, GA_3 and ABA are

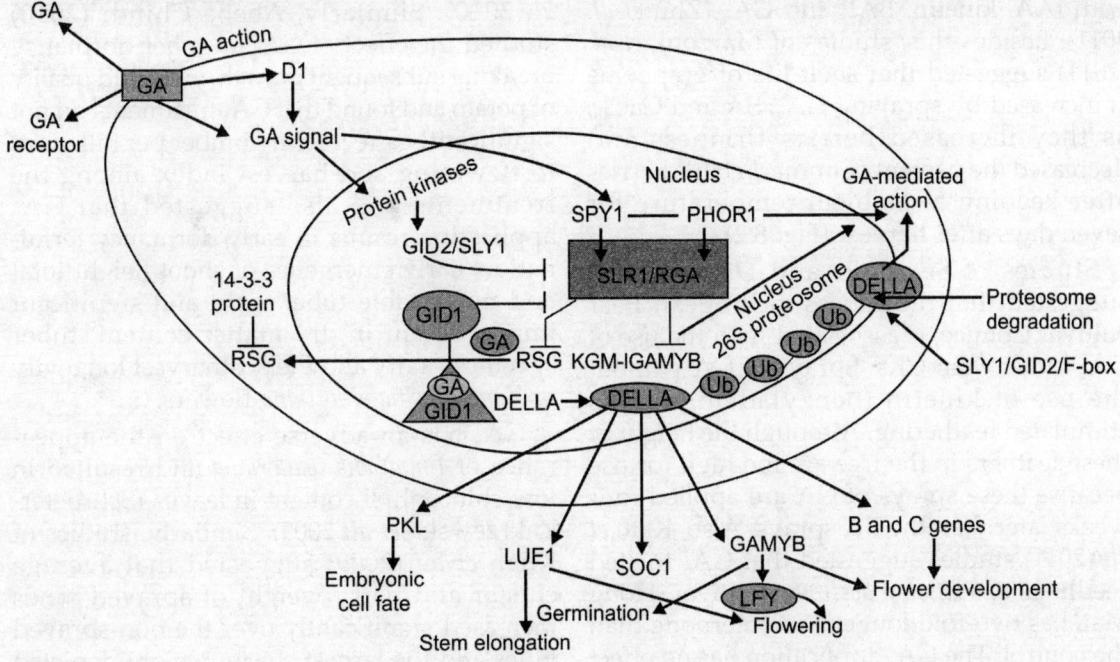

Fig. 8.2: Role of ubiquitin/proteosome pathway in gibberellic acid signalling in various developmental processes of plant

found higher many times during pathogenesis (malformed conditions) in mango plants than the health ones. They reported this disturbance as change in the anatomical structural characteristics; parenchyma cells in cortex and phloem fibre found more but vessel are less; branch and leaf trace also existed in internodes and the cells in marrow are a quarter than control. Chan *et al.* (2011) results indicate that IAA, GA_3 and KT have a little effect on germination viability, plant vegetative growth, inflorescence length, ratio of female inflorescence are increased greatly and germination rate, germination differentiation are impacted by IAA, GA_3 and KT significantly in castor beans. Similarly, Zhang *et al.* (2011) evaluated the potential of GA_3 and prohexadione-Ca (PCa) to affect sweet cherry (*Pronus avium*) fruit size, quality and demonstrate the ability of ostensibly counteracting PGRs to significantly improve sweet cherry fruit size,

quality and postharvest characteristics. In addition, they also concluded that preharvest foliar application of PCa + GA_3 at the onset of stage II of fruit development shows potential to affect canopy source-sink relations and improved quality and shelf-life of cherry. Also, by following the the above trends, studies of Chang *et al.* (2011) suggest that a correlation analysis showed that there is a synergies relationship between endogenous GA_3 + IAA content, but an antagonistic relationship between GA_3 + ABA during panicle differentiation in rice. The relationships of hormone contents or their ratios with panicle characteristics differ at different panicle developing stage. The regenerated shoots are detached from the calli and transferred to the elongation medium supported with IBA, BAP and GA_3. Besides this, the highest shoot forming rate in *Jatropa curcas* L is obtained on the medium supplemented with IAA, kinetin, BAP and GA$_3$ (Zhu *et al.* 2011). Besides this, studies of Marzouk *et al.* (2011) suggested that shelf-life of grapevine is increased by spraying GA$_3$, SA and CaCl$_2$, as they increased berries firmness and decreased the percent of unmarketable berries after keeping at ambient temperature for seven days after harvest (Fig. 8.2).

Studies of Seymour and Diack (2011) suggested that thorniness in Eropean Pear cultivar Comice, is associated with the use of GA$_3$ rather than CKs. Sprays of GA without the use of kinetin (benzyladenine) also stimulated feathering. Although the height of these feathers in the tree are too high for use because these sprays of GA are applied four weeks later than the BA sprays. Also, Kato *et al.* (2011) studies suggested that GA$_3$ treated seedlings of *Triticum aestivum* cultivar, Hong Mai, has two-fold longer first internode than the control. The GA$_3$ application has no effect on the vegetative growth and leafy green colour intensity of *Citrus latifolia* L (Pereira *et al.* 2010). Similarly, Abebe Chindi (2010) studied the effect of GA$_3$ on tuber dormancy breaking subsequent growth, yield and quality of potato and found that GA$_3$ treatments do not significantly affect stem number per hill, days to flowering and harvest index among the treatments and also suggested that GA$_3$ application results in early dormancy termination, early emergence of shoot height total and marketable tuber yield and significant improvement in dry matter content, tuber specific gravity and the postharvest longevity of *Zantedeschia elliottiana* flowers.

GA$_3$ has an adverse effect on the appearance of *Impatiens walleriana* and resulted in low chlorophyll content in leaves (Schroeter-Zakrzewska *et al.* 2009). Similarly, studies of Khan *et al.* (2009) suggested that average cluster and berry weight of sprayed vines increased significantly over the non-sprayed vines and the largest cluster weight depicted as fruit yield per vine is found in the treatment with highest concentration of GA$_3$. GA$_3$

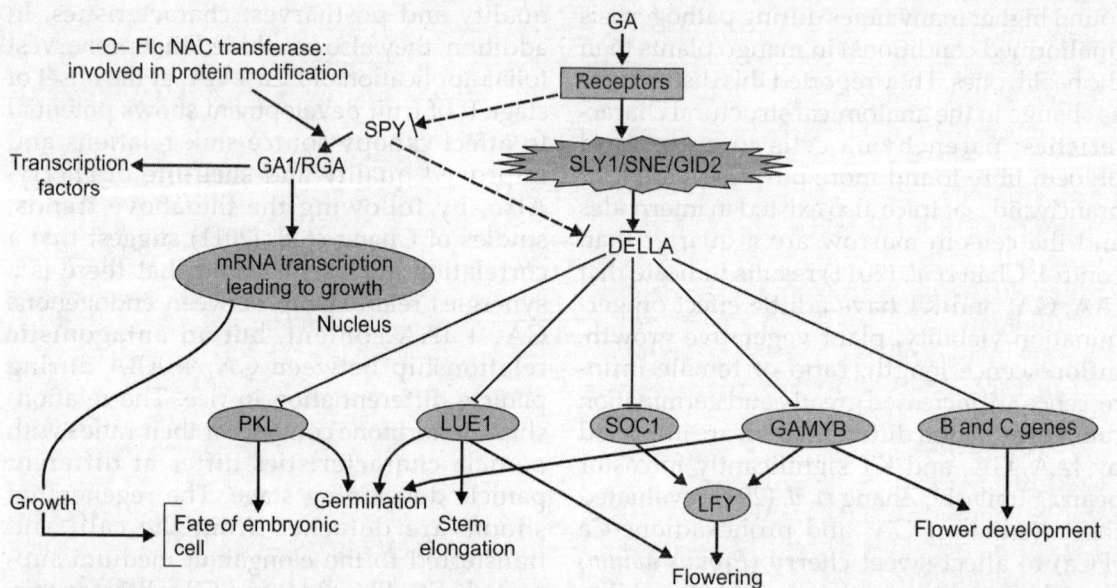

Fig. 8.3: This figure represents the association of gibberellic acid with an array of signalling genes and their responses in terms of plant development

increases berry size of seedless grape (Emperatriz), the response depending on the phonological stage of vine at treatment date and on the concentration applied, but GA_3 does not affect berry pericarp cell number but increases pericarp cell diameter (Moret and Agusti, 2009). Saleem *et al.* (2007) studied the effect of two exogenously applied plant growth regulators (GA_3 + 2,4-D) on fruit drop and fruit quality in *Citrus sinensis* and find that fruit diameter and seed health is not affected fruit weight but juice quantity, total sugars and reducing sugars are improved by most of the treatments compared with control but in case of acidity and vitamin C. Also, results of studies of Gonzalez *et al.* (2007) showed that GA_3 dose of 25 mg/L is the most appropriate one for floral induction and largest plant height, while the dose of 5 mg/L allowed accelerating the height and quantity of bio-mass in *Brassica oleraceae*. Similarly, Neelima *et al.* (2006) reported that all the yield con-tributing parameters increased over those of the control with GA_3 and cycocel treatments in chickpea. Cycocel enhanced the yield through ameliorative effects on flower reten-tion, pod setting percentage, pod number and seed weight in normal sown as compared to that of late-sown crop. In addition, Yadav and Bharud (2006) recorded the plant height, number of primary and secondary branches per plant, chlorophyll a and b, total chlorophyll content, seed protein content, number of pods per plant, seeds per plant, 100-grain weight, and grain yield per plant, gram yield per hectare and harvest index in *Cicer arietinum* L. All treatments are significantly superior to both water spray and absolute controls. Besides this GA_3 significantly improved stem length, internode length, root weight and top/root, and significantly improved leaf number. Growth acceleration by GA_3 is both inde-pendent and additive effect in root weight where reduction is observed (Dizon *et al.* 2005).

Gupta *et al.* (2005) treated the pedicels of pollinated buds with a mixture of growth regulators (120 PPM GA_3 + 30 PPM NAA + 15 PPM kinetin) in the morning (10.00 hours) or in the evening (16.00 hours) for three consecutive days in chickpea and found that application of growth regulators to pollinated buds once and twice daily increased bud retention. Charatnone Tachom *et al.* (2005) studied the effect of GA_3 along with BRs and NAA on Logan fruit sized and suggests that BRs and GA_3 + NAA tended to have the biggest fruit whereas NAA + BRs tended to have the heaviest fresh and dry fruit weight in Logan. Similarly, GA_3 increased plant height, fresh and dry weight of herb, number of seeds per capsule, seed yields as well as fixed and volatile oil yields in *Nigella sativa* (Mousa *et al.* 2003). Tripathi *et al.* (2003) also reported that chlorophyll content is highest with 20 PPM TIBA treatment at pre-and pot-anthesis respectively in *Cicer arietinum* L. Dry matter production, and protein and starch content are highest with the 20 PPM TIBA, 5 PPM cytokinins and 50 PPM IAA treatments respectively.

Moreover, studies of Arif (2002) suggestted that application of GA_3 has increased plumule length and dry weight of radical while GA_3 also has brought about an increase in fresh and dry weights of plumule in unsoaked seeds of *Vigna radiate* L. Similarly, pod length and yield per plant are only the yield parameters in which varieties and treatment interaction is non-significant in soaking and foliar appli-cation of GA_3. Application of 10-5M GA_3 increased seed yield, oil yield and seed yield merit of Indian mustard (Khan *et al.* 2002). Following the above trend, Iqbal *et al.* (2001) reported that fresh and dry weights of shoot increased by the application of GA_3 accom-panied by increased plant height and appli-cation of GA_3 at vegetative stage showed more reduction than at flower initiation stage. Czapla *et al.* (2000) found that the application of 3-indolebutyric acid caused a significant increase in grain mass yield, whereas the application of GA_3 resulted in a longer yield of vegetative mass of spring triticale.

Kaur et al. (2000) reported that underwater stress amylase activity in cotyledons is decreased by water stress, but increased by GA_3 and kinetin after sowing. Activity of acid and alkaline invertase is greatest in shoot and least in cotyledons, with acid invertase activity being higher in all the tissues. Stressed roots of *Tulip gesheriana* seedlings have increased alkaline invertase activity, while GA_3 and IAA reduced this. It is also possible that better penetration and uptake of GA_3 take place after removal of roots. It seems that GA_3 can substitute for cold requirement (Wegrzynowicz-Lesiak and Okido, 1999). In addition, studies of Pittaya Sruamsiri (1997) suggested that response of plants to GA_3 is applied by temperature and by application of ethephon under extreme temperature, plants developed only tiny leaves with very short petiole, no flowering and no fruit set in strawberry. Ahmad and Qasim (1996) studied the effect of GA_3 on two varieties of maize and suggests that GA_3 caused a significant increase in various parameters like internodes length, leaf area, size of cobs, number and weight of grain and total yield and finally concluded that foliar spray proved more useful than seed soaking method. Besides this, Oranutda Bulyalert (1991) suggested that size of corn (*Liatris spicata*) and the concentration of GA_3 have affected significantly the growth and flowering.

In last, primitive studies also have provided several evidences about the growth promoting properties of GA_3. Results of El-Quesni (1989) suggested that GA (soaking + spraying) inhibited the accumulation of Zn and Mn in spinach leaves. However, GA_3 promoted the acceleration of K in the leaves sprayed with 50 PPM while sowing of GA_3 at 50 PPM increased plant height, leaf area dry weight and CA content. In soaking treatment at 50 and 100 PPM, GA_3 favoured the acceleration of Fe and oxalic acid in spinach leaves. Generally, it can be concluded that the highest root, top and sugar yield of sugarbeet may achieved by planting a high yielding cultivar when sprayed with 200 PPM of GA_3 (El-Kassaby et al., 1988).

Similarly, Hamad et al. (1987) studied the effects of GA_3 and cycocel (CCC) on yield quality and quantity of tomato and observed that no significant effect of the growth regulators are observed on the total yield per unit area and per plant, fruit number per plant and average fruit weight.

Physiological and Biochemical Properties

Like the growth and morphological studies, GA_3 also reported to promote the physiological and biochemical characteristics of plants. In this context first of all, studies of Steffens et al. (2011) suggested that preharvest spraying with GA_3 and aminoethoxyvinylglycine (AVG) increased fresh firmness, and delayed the increased of solid contents of fruit quality attributes and also suggests that the treatment of GA_3 alone also caused high titratable acidity in *Laetitia plums*. Jha et al. (2011) studies suggested that exogenously applied GA_3 + JA acts as an elicitor, in variable concentrations and enhanced the biosynthesis of andrographolide. Also, the increment in the diterpene content has shown its association with the expression level of hmgr genes in the andrographolide accumulation regulatory cascade in *Andrographis paniculata*. Also, results of Shou et al. (2011) suggested that exogenous GA_3 promoted the seed germination rate, germination capacity, germination index and seed vigour index of *Salicornia europaea* L under salt stress and finally they also concluded that within a certain concentration range, exogenous GA_3 can alleviate the inhibition effects of salt stress on seed germination and seedlings growth.

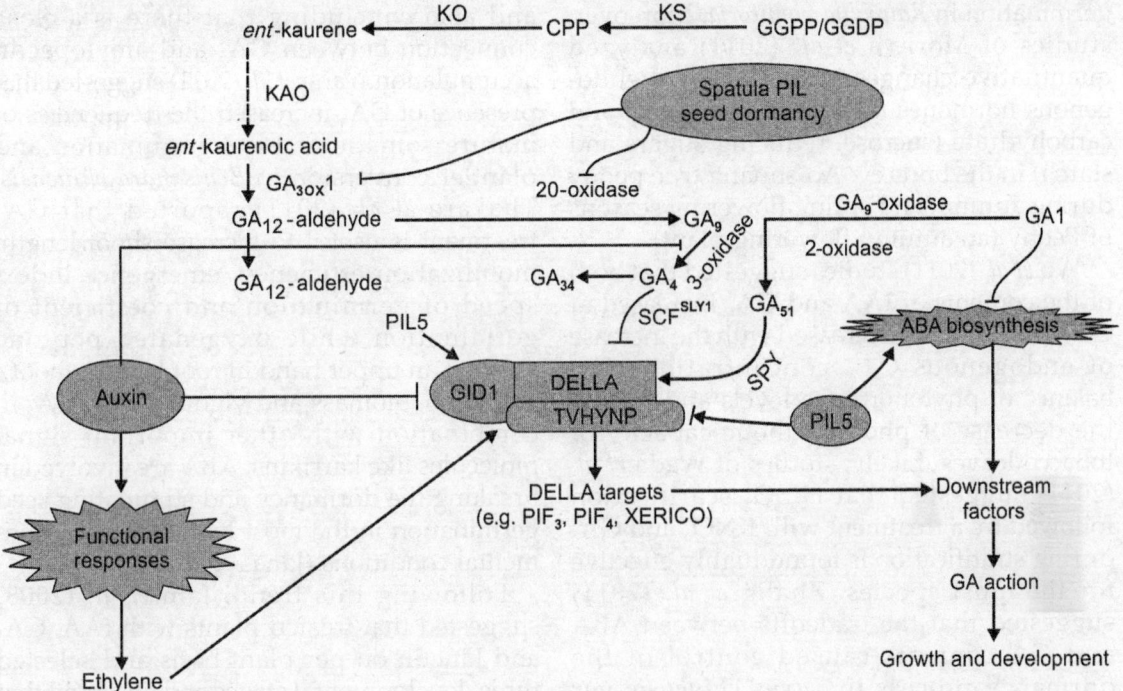

Fig. 8.4: Interaction of gibberellic acid with other hormones and signalling proteins to precede the functional responses

Similarly, the results of Che *et al.* (2011) showed that GA_3 + Cold stratification can also break seed dormancy in *Sorbus amabilis*, but less effective than treated with directly cold stratification.

Xue *et al.* (2011) suggested that GA_3 in range of 50 approximately 100 mg/L increased the germination energy, germination percent, germination index, radical length and hypocotyls length and MDA content. All parameters decreased gradually with the rise of GA_3 concentration in seed soaking with approximate concentration of GA_3 can promote the germination of tomato seeds under NaCl stress. The optimal effect can be obtained when the concentration of GA_3 reached 100 mg/L. In addition, GA_3 has the promotion effect to the germination of *Polygonum capitatum* (Hu *et al.* 2011). Besides this, Wei *et al.* (2011) investigated the effect of GA_3 on

flower formation of *Betula platphylla* and the possible mechanism in the process and showed that flowering induction is late in May and flowering transition is significantly inhibited by different concentration of GA_3. Therefore, they finally concluding that the exogenous GA_3 is distinctive during the flowering transition, plays a role in different gene expression of the multiple flowering pathways rather than individual one.

In addition, studies of Zhao *et al.* (2011) revealed that expression of heat, shock transcription factor HsfA1d in populus is induced not only heat-shock drought and high salt stress, but also upregulated by GA_3, ABA and glucose and sucrose signals. Also, studies of Guan *et al.* (2011) showed that warm water soaking and GA_3 solution treatment do not exert significant promoting effect on the seed germination in *Rauvolfia vomitoria*. Moreover, studies of Mornya *et al.* (2011) analyzed quantitative changes in the levels of endogenous hormones (IAA, ABA and GA_3) and carbohydrate (sucrose, reducing sugars and starch) in the buds cv. Ao-shuang true peony during autumn and spring flowering seasons of Peony (an autumn flowering plant).

Wu *et al.* (2011) studies suggested that both of the contents of IAA and GA_3 increased at Cd^{2+} (5 mg/L) but decreased with the increase of endogenous Ca^{2+} concentration. The balance of phytohormone levels and caused the decrease of photosynthetic capacity of tobacco leaves. Likely, studies of Wada *et al.* (2011) suggested that H_2SO_4 scarification followed by a treatment with KNO_3 and GA_3 during stratification is found highly effective for the most species. Zhang *et al.* (2011) suggested that the tradeoffs between ABA and GA contents caused control of the dormancy process in *Taxus chinensis* var marirei seed. Calculated ratio data of GA/ABA, IAA/ABA and zeatin/ABA exhibited gradually increasing trends within stratification time and dormancy is relieved accordingly with them. Similarly, Gisbert *et al.* (2011) studies suggested that the GA_3 pretreatment not only increased the final germination percentages but promoted germination also by reducing the germination time, and also showed that the seed treatments (GA_3 + ABA) can contribute to improve germination of Solanum accessions with low germination. Furthermore, Zhang *et al.* (2011) studies suggested that the chilling resistance cultivars of maize showed more endogenous GA_3 contents than chilling sensitive line. In addition, Liu *et al.* (2011) results showed that the fruit size and berry quality of seedless grape all have some changes by treatment (GA_3), can make fruit expression significantly.

Moreover, Li *et al.* (2011) results revealed that the sugar accumulate rate and the activity of sucrose synthase raised in grape fruits after treated by GA_3 treatment is the best significant

and also concluding that there is a close connection between GA_3 and amylopectin accumulation. Yang *et al.* (2011) suggested that presence of GA_3 increased the frequencies of mature somatic embryo germination and plantlet conversion in *Schisandra chinensis*. Thakare *et al.* (2011) reported that GA_3 treatment is useful to increase shoot length, mobilization efficiency, emergence index, speed of germination and coefficient of germination while oxygenated peptone showed an upper hand in root length, shoot/root ratio, biomass and vigour index. GA_3 in combination with other important signal molecules like karrikins, ABA are involved in breaking the dormancy and stimulating seed germination in the most favourable environmental conditions (Janas *et al.* 2010).

Following this trend, Jain *et al.* (2008) suggested that treated plants with IAA, GA_3 and kinetin on per plant basis and selected three developmental stages and observed that almost all growth regulators showed a general promotory effect on leghaemoglobin biosynthesis and protein content of nodules at lower concentrations *Cicer arietinum* L. Although, this enhancement is not observed after a particular concentration of growth regulators, which vary differently for different growth regulators. Similarly, studies of Kang *et al.* (2007) suggested that GA_3 treatment is more effective on the germination of Kentucky bluegrass than BAP single treatment or the combination treatment of GA_3 and BAP regardless of their treatment concentration. Also Rahman *et al.* (2004) reported that effect of planting dates and GA_3 concentration indicated that early plantings grown without GA_3 showed better performance than the late plantings grown with or without GA_3. Studies of Sarkar *et al.* (2002) on the effect of PGR for growth of soya bean in terms of enhancement of physiological characters, *viz.* leaf area index, crop growth rate, relative growth rate and net assimilation rate are influenced by the application of growth regulators. Their study also clearly shows that 100 PPM of GA_3 and IAA treated plants performed better than control and other treated plants.

Some primitive studies also reported the growth enhancing properties of GA_3 are as follows: Application of both GA_3 and NAA increased vegetative growth as measured by plant height, leaf length, number of leaves per plant, plant fresh weight and percent dry matter as compared with control plants. Total yield, average bulb weight and total soluble solid contents are also increased (Saleh and Abed, 1989). Besides this, Pain *et al.* (1985) studied the effect of GA_3 in different concentrations along with a control in distilled water on the growth and metabolism of rice (*Oryza sativa* L) seedlings and observed the growth in length of the shoot increased remarkably as well as they also finds that nucleic acid, total and soluble nitrogen and phosphorus contents in the shoot increased significantly with the increase in case of GA_3 throughout the growth period.

Conclusion

In conclusion we would like to underline that GA_3 a very well-known gibberellin for last 50 years has a potential to be used not only as a plant growth regulatory hormone but also has a few commercial applications and its presence in plant used as marker of the active growth and development of plant especially elongation of shoots. Further research needs on other regulatory factors of GA_3 action rather than environmental homeostasis, exact mechanism of activation pathways involved in the deactivation especially role of ODDs enzymes, conjugational mechanisms. Also a small study required for revealing the association between GA_3 biosynthetic genes and inhibitors in plant systems. Besides this, some open questions also need future investigations: (1) the identification of additional enzymes such as GA_{13}-oxidase and GA-conjugating enzymes, will be necessary to understand the whole picture of the GA metabolism pathway, (2) since GA_3 exists in tissues at very low concentration, requires improvements in analytical systems to understand the regulation of the GA metabolism pathway, and (4) to elucidate the molecular mechanisms of GA_3 transport in plant system under normal conditions of growth and development.

REFERENCES

Gilroy S and Jones RL (1994). Perception of gibberellins and abscisic acid at the external face of the plasma membrane of barley (*Hordeum vulgare* L) aleurone protoplasts. *Plant Physiology*, **104**: 1185–1192.

Gubler F and Jacobsen JV (1992). Gibberellin-responsive elements in the promoter of Barley high-pI α-amylase gene. *Plant cell*, **4**: 1435–1441.

Gubler F, Kalla R, Roberts JK and Jacobsen JV (1995). Gibberellin-regulated expression of a MYB gene in Barley aleurone cells: Evidence of MYB trans-activation of a high pI α-amylase gene promoter. *Plant Cell*, **7**: 1879–1891.

Lones HD, Smith SJ, Desikan R, Plakidou-Dymock S, Love grove A and Hooley R (1998). Heterotrimeric G proteins are implicated in gibberellins induction of α-amylase gene expression in wild oat aleurone layer. *Plant Cell*, **10**: 245–253.

Lenton JR, Appleford NEJ and Croker SJ (1994). Gibberellins and α-amylase gene expression in germinating wheat grains. *Plant Growth Regulation*, **15**: 261–270.

Penson SP, Schuurink RC, Fath A, Gubler F, Jacobsen JV and Jones RL (1996). cGMP is required for gibberellic acid induced gene expression in barley aleurone. *Plant Cell*, **8**: 2325–2333.

Ross JJ, Murfet IC and Reid JB (1997). Gibberellin mutants. *Physiologia Planataum*, **100**: 550–560.

Schuurink RC, Chan PV and Jones RL (1996). Modulation of calmodulin mRNA and protein levels in barley aleurone. *Plant Physiology*, **111**: 371–380.

Skriver K, Olsen FL, Rogers JC and Mundy J (1991). Cis-acting DNA elements responsive to gibberellins and its antagonist abscisic acid. *Proceedings of the National Academy of Sciences of USA*, **88**: 7266–7270.

Sponsel VM and Hedden P (2004). Gibberellin biosynthesis and inactivation. In: Davies PJ (Eds) *Plant Hormones: Biosynthesis Signal Transduction Action*. Kluwer Academy, Dordrecht, pp 63–94.

Bernier G (1988). The control of floral evocation and morphogenesis. *Annual Reviews of Plant Physiology and Plant Molecular Biology*, **39**: 175–219.

Finkelstein RR and Zeevaart JAD (1994). Gibberellin and abscisic acid biosynthesis and response. In: Meyerowitz EM, Somerville CR (Eds). *Arabidopsis*. Cold Spring Harbor NY, pp 523–553.

Ueguchi-Tanaka M, Nakajima M, Katoh E, Ohmiya H, Asano K, Saji S, Hongyu X, Ashikari M, Kitano H, Yamaguchi I and Matsuoka M (2007). Molecular interactions of a soluble gibberellin receptor GID1 with a rice DELLA protein SLR1 and gibberellin. *Plant Cell*, **19**: 2140–2155.

Richards DE, King KE, Ait-ali T and Harberd NP (2001). How gibberellin regulates plant growth and development: A molecular genetic analysis of gibberellin signalling. *Annual Reviews of Plant Physiology amd Plant Molecular Biology*, **52**: 67–88.

Hay A, Kaur H, Phillips A, Hedden P, Hake ST and Siantis M (2002). The gibberellin pathway mediates KNOTTED1-typehomeobox function in plants with different body plans. *Current Biology*, **12**: 1557–1565.

Sun TP and Gubler F (2004). Molecular mechanism of gibberellin signalling in plants. *Annual Reviews of Plant Biology*, **55**: 197–223.

Kasahara H, Hanada A, Kuzuyama T, Takagi M, Kamiya Y and Yamaguchi S (2002). Contribution of the mevalonate and methylerythritol phosphate pathways to the biosynthesis of gibberellins in *Arabidopsis*. *Journal of Biological Chemistry*, **277**: 45188–45194.

Aach H, Bode H, Robinson DG and Graebe JE (1997). *ent*-kaurene synthetase is located in proplastids of meristematic shoot tissues. *Planta*, **202**: 211–219.

Helliwell CA, Chandler PM, Poole A, Dennis ES and Peacock WJ (2001). The CYP88A cytochrome P450 *ent*-kaurenoic acid oxidase catalyzes three steps of the gibberellins biosynthesis pathway. *Proceedings of the National Academy of Sciences of USA*, **98**: 2065–2070.

Spray CR, Kobayashi M, Suzuki Y, Phinney BO, Gaskin P and MacMillan J (1996). The *dwarf-1* (*dt*) mutant of *Zea mays* blocks three steps in the gibberellin-biosynthetic pathway. *Proceedingds of the National Academy of Sciences of USA*, **93**: 10515–10518.

Yamaguchi S, Kamiya Y and Sun T (2001). Distinct cell-specific expression patterns of early and late gibberellin biosynthetic genes during *Arabidopsis* seed germination. *Plant Journal*, **28**: 443–453.

Ogawa M, Hanada A, Yamauchi Y, Kuwahara A, Kamiya Y and Yamaguchi S (2003). Gibberellin biosynthesis and response during *Arabidopsis* seed germination. *Plant Cell*, **15**: 1591–1604.

Weiss D, Van Der Luit A, Knegt E, Vermeer E, Mol J and Kooter JM (1995). Identification of endogenous gibberellins in petunia flowers (induction of anthocyanin biosynthetic gene expression and the antagonistic effect of abscisic acid). *Plant Physiology*, **107**: 695–702.

Koornneef M and Van der Veen JH (1980). Induction and analysis of gibberellin-sensitive mutants in *Arabidopsis thaliana* (L.) Heynh. *Theoritical Application in Genetics*, **58**: 257–263.

Silverstone AL, Chang C, Krol E and Sun TP (1997). Developmental regulation of the gibberellins biosynthetic gene *GA1* in *Arabidopsis thaliana*. *Plant Journal*, **12**: 9–19.

Olszewski N, Sun TP and Gubler F (2002). Gibberellin signalling: Biosynthesis catabolism and response pathways. *Plant Cell*, **14**: 61–80.

Yamauchi Y, Ogawa M, Kuwahara A, Hanada A, Kamiya Y and Yamaguchi S (2004). Activation of gibberellin biosynthesis and response pathways by low temperature during imbibition of *Arabidopsis thaliana* seeds. *Plant Cell*, **16**: 367–378.

Coles JP, Phillips AL, Croker SJ, Garcia-Lepe R, Lewis MJ and Hedden P (1999). Modification of gibberellin production and plant development in *Arabidopsis* by sense and antisense expressions of gibberellin 20-oxidase genes. *Plant Journal*, **17**: 547–556.

Huang S, Raman AS, Ream JE, Fujiwara H, Cerny RE and Brown SM (1998). Overexpression of 20-oxidase confers a gibberellin-overproduction phenotype in *Arabidopsis*. *Plant Physiology*, **118**: 773–781.

Fleet CM, Yamaguchi S, Hanada A, Kawaide H, David CJ, Kamiya Y and Sun TP (2003). Overexpression of *AtCPS* and *AtKS* in *Arabidopsis* confers increased *ent*-kaurene production but no increase in bioactive gibberellins. *Plant Physiology*, **132**: 830–839.

Rod W, King R and Lloyd T (2003). Gibberellins and flowering of grasses and cereals: Prizing open the Lid of the "Florigen" Black Box. *Annual Reviews of Plant Biology*, **54**: 307–328.

Pharis RP and King RW (1985). Gibberellins and reproductive development in seed plants. *Annual Reviews of Plant Physiology*, **36**: 517–526.

Cleland CF and Zeevaart JAD (1970). Gibberellins in relation to flowering and stem elongation in the long day plant *Silene armeria*. *Plant Physiology*, **46**: 392–400.

Evans LT, King RW, Chu A, Mander LN and Pharis RP (1990). Gibberellin structure and florigenic activity in *Lolium temulentum*, a long-day plant. *Planta*, **182**: 97–106.

King RW, Moritz T, Evans LT, Junttila O and Herlt AJ (2001). Long-day induction of flowering in *Lolium temulentum* involves sequential increases in specific gibberellins at the shoot apex. *Plant Physiology*, **127**: 624–632.

King RW and Evans LT (2003). Gibberellins and flowering of grasses and cereals: Prizing open the lid of the "florigen" black box. *Annual Reviews of Plant Biology*, **54**: 307–328.

QUESTIONS

Q. 1. The basic needs of all living organisms are essentially the:

(1) Same
(2) Different
(3) Usually different
(4) Almost different

Q. 2. Who demonstrated 'Plants could be grown to maturity in a defined nutrient solution in complete absence of soil'?

(1) Julius van Sachs
(2) Francis Dalton
(3) Charles Darwin
(4) Hungungton

Q. 3. Hydroponics (a technique in which plants growing in a nutrient medium without soil) devised by which scientist?

(1) Julius van Sachs
(2) Francis Dalton
(3) Charles Darwin
(4) Hungungton

Q. 4. Common need for all methods, employed to try and determine the mineral nutrients essential for plants:

(1) Soil free, defined mineral solution with pure water
(2) Soil aided, defined mineral solution with double distilled water
(3) Soil free, defined mineral solution with distilled water
(4) Soil aided, undefined mineral solution with fresh water

Q. 5. Significance of hydroponics includes:

(1) Identification of essential elements and their deficiency symptoms
(2) For commercial production of vegetables, seedless cucumber and lettuce
(3) Nutrient solutions must be adequately aerated to obtain the optimum growth
(4) All of the above

Q. 6. In which of the following is an incorrect statement?

(1) Most soil containing mineral enter the plants by roots only
(2) 60 out of 105 elements found in different plants
(3) Plants grow near nuclear test sites take up radioactive Srontium
(4) Available techniques can detect mineral at very low concentration (10^{-5} g/mL)

Q. 7. Techniques of soil biology are able to detect the mineral even at a very low concentration, this is:

(1) 10–5 g/mL
(2) 10^{-6} g/mL
(3) 10^{-4} g/mL
(4) 10^{-8} g/mL

Q. 8. The mineral element must be absolutely necessary for supporting:

(1) Normal growth
(2) Reproduction
(3) Complete their life cycle or set the seeds
(4) All of the above

Q. 9. In which of the following is incorrect statement:

(1) The requirement of element is specific
(2) The need of element cannot be meet by supplying some other element
(3) The element must be indirectly involved in the metabolism of the plant
(4) The need of element is replaceable

Q. 10. In hydroponics technology plants are grown in a tube placed on a:

(1) Full incline
(2) Slight incline
(3) Almost incline
(4) Usually incline

Q. 11. The solution flows down the tube in hydroponics method and returns to the reservoir due to:

(1) Gravity
(2) Phototrophic
(3) Antigravity
(4) Both 1 and 2

Q. 12. In hydroponics plants are bathed in nutrient solution which is:

(1) Un-aerated
(2) Continuously aerated
(3) Discontinuously aerated
(4) Both 1 and 3

Q. 13. Only a few elements have been found to be absolutely essential for plant growth and metabolism on basis of essentiality criteria. These few elements divided into macro- and micro nutrient on which basis:

(1) Quantitative
(2) Qualitative
(3) Both 1 and 2
(4) None

Q. 14. Macronutrients are generally present in plant tissues in large amounts in:

(1) Excess of 10 m mole/kg of dry matter
(2) Lesser of 10 m mole/kg of dry matter
(3) Excess of 15 m mole/kg of dry matter
(4) Excess of 8 m mole/kg of dry matter

Q. 15. In which of the following is an odd one:

(1) S   (2) Fe
(3) K   (4) Mg

Q. 16. In which of the following is an odd one:

(1) Cl   (2) Ni
(3) K   (4) Mo

Q. 17. In which of the following is a trace element?

(1) Fe   (2) Mn
(3) Cu   (4) All of the above

Q. 18. Elements is/are required by higher plants particularly is:

(1) Na and Si
(2) Ca and Na
(3) Se and Co
(4) All of the above

Q. 19. Essential elements can also be grouped into four broad categories on basis of diverse functions. These categories are:

(1) Structural elements, energy-related chemicals, enzyme-regulated and osmotic potential regulated elements
(2) Structural elements, energy-related chemicals, hormone-regulated and osmotic potential regulated elements
(3) Structural elements, ATP-related chemicals, enzyme-regulated and osmotic potential regulated elements
(4) Structural elements, energy-related chemicals, enzyme-regulated and reproductively used elements

Q. 20. Principle sites of N requirement in plants body is/are:

(1) Meristematic tissues and meta-bolically active cells
(1) Only metabolically active cells
(3) Only meristematic tissues
(4) Meristematic tissues and incipiently dividing cells

Q. 21. N absorbed in plant roots as:

(1) NO_2^-
(2) NH_4^+
(3) NO_3^{2-}
(4) All of the above

Q. 22. Most usual form in which N absorbed through plant roots is:

(1) NO_3^{2-} (2) NH_4^+

(3) NO (4) NO_2^-

Q. 23. P absorbed in plant roots as:

(1) $H_2PO_4^-$

(2) HPO_4^{2-}

(3) Both 1 and 2

(4) $PO4^-$

Q. 24. P is a constituent of which set:

(1) Cell membrane, all phosphorylation reactions, all proteins and all nucleotides

(2) Cell membrane, some phosphorylation reactions, certain proteins and some nucleotides

(3) Cell membrane, some phosphorylation reactions, all proteins and all nucleotides and nucleic acids

(4) Cell membranes, all phosphorylation reactions, certain proteins and all nucleotides and nucleotides

Q. 25. K^+ is required in:

(1) Meristematic tissues, buds, leaves, root caps

(2) Buds, leaves, meristematic tissues, root tips

(3) Leaves, root tips, intercalary meristems

(4) Shoot tips, buds, leaves, meristematic tissues

Q. 26. In which of the following, is not a function of K?

(1) Maintain anion-cation balance and turgidity

(2) Protein synthesis and enzymes activation

(3) Opening and closing of stomata, activation of enzymes

(4) Lipid synthesis and carbohydrates formation

Q. 27. Function of Ca^{2+} is/are:

(1) Meristematic and differentially tissues

(2) Cell wall (formation of middle lamella during cell division)

(3) Formation of mitotic spindle formation and normal functions of cell membranes

(4) All of the above

Q. 28. Mg^{2+} functionally includes:

(1) Activation of enzymes of respiration (pyruvate decarboxylases, keto-glutarate dehydrogenase, dihydro-lipoate-transsuccinylase and dihydrolipoate dehydrogenase) Photosynthesis (phosphor-glycerate kinase, Fructose-1,6-biphosphatase and Rubisco-activase)

(2) Synthesis of nucleic acids

(3) Synthesis of ring-structure of Chl and maintains of ribosome structure

(4) All of the above

Q. 29. S absorbed by plants as:

(1) S^- (2) SO_3^-

(3) SO_4^- (4) SO_2

Q. 30. Which vitamins contain S as a important constituent is/are?

(1) Thiamine

(2) Biotin

(3) Co-enzyme-A

(4) All of the above

Q. 31. S is a main constituent of:

(1) Some vitamins

(2) Ferredoxin

(3) Co-enzymes and few amino acids

(4) All of the above

Q. 32. Iron absorbed in which form through the application of roots:

(1) Fe^{+3}

(2) Fe^+

(3) Fe^{+2}

(4) All

Q. 33. **Among the macronutrient need in higher amount:**

(1) Cu   (2) I2
(3) Fe   (4) Cl

Q. 34. **In which of the following pair of elements used in synthesis of proteins responsible for the transfer of electron (ferredoxins):**

(1) Fe,S
(2) Fe,K
(3) S,Mg
(4) Se,Na

Q. 35. **Electron transfer proteins is/are:**

(1) Ferredoxin
(2) Cytochrome
(3) Pyrophosphate
(4) Both 1 and 2

Q. 36. **Elements responsible maximally in electron transferring processes:**

(1) Fe   (2) S
(3) Na   (4) Mg

Q. 37. **Which is correct about conversion of Fe during electron transfer reactions?**

(1) Fe^{3+} to Fe^{2+} (2) Fe^{2+} to Fe^{3+}
(3) Fe^{2+} to Fe^{+} (4) Fe^{3+} to Fe+

Q. 38. **During electron transferring processes in cells, Fe transform (oxidized) or in a manner which is:**

(1) Reversible   (2) Irreversible
(3) Both 1 and 2 (4) None

Q. 39. **Chrolrophyll synthesis requires:**

(1) Mg   (2) Fe
(3) Ca   (4) Both 1 and 2

Q. 40. **In which of the following enzyme required Fe as activator for their proper functioning?**

(1) Catalase
(2) Super-oxide-dismutase
(3) Per-oxidase
(4) Both 1 and 2

Q. 41. **In which of the following below mentioned, chemical conversion need Fe?**

(1) Hydrogen peroxide dissociation
(2) Hydrochloric acid synthesis
(3) Both 1 and 2
(4) Conversion of N_2 and H_2 into ammonia

Q. 42. **Mn catalyzes maximizes number of biochemical processes in plants:**

(1) Ca   (2) Mg
(3) Mn   (4) Cd

Q. 43. **Mn used to activate the enzymes for processes like:**

(1) Respiration, photosynthesis, N-fixation
(2) Respiration, N-fixation, urea cycle
(3) Protein synthesis, photosynthesis, lipid formation
(4) N-fixation, urea cycle, N-fixation

Q. 44. **Best defined function of Mn in plants biochemical processes**

(1) H_2O braking in to H_2 and O_2
(2) Association of N_2 to O_2 in nodules
(3) Reaction of NH_3 to H^+ during NH4+ synthesis
(4) All of the above

Q. 45. **In which of the following is correct about Zn?**

(1) Absorbed as Zn^{2+}
(2) Activates enzymes, carboxylase
(3) Promotes IAA synthesis
(4) All of the above

Q. 46. **Fe function is similar to which mineral element involved in redox reactions:**

(1) Zn   (2) Cd
(3) Cu   (4) Ni

Q. 47. **Functionss of Cu are:**

(1) Absorbed as Cu^{2+}
(2) Essential for overall metabolism

(3) Part of enzymes used in Redox reactions and reversibility oxidized from Cu^+ to Cu^{2+}

(4) All of the above

Q. 48. Incorrect about Boran is:

(1) Uptake and utilization of Ca^{2+}

(2) Membrane functioning, cell elongation, cell differentiation

(3) Carbohydrate translocation

(4) None of the above

Q. 49. Which pair is correct in reference of Boron?

(1) Absorbed as BO_3^{-3} and required for pollen germination

(2) Absorbed as $B_4O_7^{-3}$ and required for cell differnation

(3) Absorbed as $B_4O_7^{-3}$ and required for protein synthesis

(4) Both 1 and 2

Q. 50. Absorbed form of Mo is:

(1) Molybdate ions (MoO_2^{2+})

(2) Molydaeic acid (MoO_4^2)

(3) Both 1 and 2

(4) Absent in soil as mineral nutrient

Q. 51. Function of Mo is in:

(1) Nitrogen fixation

(2) Nitrogen metabolism

(3) Both 1 and 2

(4) Nitrogen absorption

Q. 52. Mo is an activator of enzymes used in N metabolism are:

(1) Nase   (2) NR

(3) NiR   (4) Both 1 and 2

Q. 53. In which of the following below mentioned sets of helpful in determining the solute concentration and the anion-cation balance in cells along with Cl?

(1) Na^+, Cl^-

(2) Na^+, NO_3^{2-}

(3) Ca^{2+}, Mg^{2+}

(4) K^+, Ca^{2+}

Q. 54. In photosynthesis, water splitting step is catalyzed by which mineral along wit Cl^-?

(1) Mg   (2) K^+

(3) Ca^{2+} (4) Mn^+

Q. 55. Match the Column A to Column B

(i) N metabolism	(A) Mo
(ii) N fixation	(B) Mn
(iii) Photolysis of water	(C) Cl
(iv) Anion-cation balance	(D) Na

(1) i(A), ii(B), iii(D), iv(C)

(2) i(B), ii(A), iii(C), iv(D)

(3) i(A), ii(D), iii(B), iv(C)

(4) i(D), ii(B), iii(A), iv(C)

Q. 56. When supply of an essential element becomes limited, plant growth is?

(1) Always retarded

(2) Induced

(3) Both 1 and 2

(4) Usually induced

Q. 57. Critical concentration of an animal is:

(1) Concentration of essential element below which plant growth is retarded

(2) Concentration of essential element above which plant growth is promoted

(3) Concentration of essential element at which plant growth is normal

(4) Concentration of essential element at which plant growth is diseased free

Q. 58. The element is said to be deficient when present:

(1) Above critical level

(2) Below critical level

(3) Both 1 and 2

(4) Equal to critical level

Q. 59. Deficiency symptoms generally are:

(1) Only physiological

(2) Only morphological

(3) Only biochemical

(4) All of the above type

Q. 60. **Which is incorrect about deficiency symptoms?**

(1) Morphological characterization

(2) Vary element to element

(3) Can disappear with aid of specific deficient element

(4) None of the above

Q. 61. **If deprivation of mineral element continues, it may eventually lead to:**

(1) Wilting

(2) Permanent wilting

(3) Death

(4) Delay in fruit set

Q. 62. **The part of the plants that show the deficiency also depend on the:**

(1) Ionic nature of mineral element

(2) Mobility of elements in plant

(3) Relative capacity to react with other element

(4) Both 1 and 3

Q. 63. **Why the deficiency symptoms tend to appear first in the older tissues?**

(1) Elements exported actively to young developing tissues

(2) Elements conjugated to proteins at young developing tissues

(3) Elements oxidized during metabolized during metabolism at young developing tissues

(4) Elements recharged rapidly to young developing tissues

Q. 64. **For which pair of elements, deficiency system appears first on senescent leaves?**

(1) N, K, Mg

(2) N, K, P

(3) N, P, Ca

(4) K, Mg, Ca

Q. 65. **Most common deficiency symptoms of mineral nutrients are:**

(1) Chlorosis, necrosis, stunted plant growth

(2) Premature fall of leaves, buds and stunted growth

(3) Inhibition of cell division and stunted plant growth

(4) All of the above

Q. 66. **In which of the following element is not easily released towards the mature and their different symptoms appear first at the growing tissue organs rather than usually older tissues?**

(1) Ca   (2) Mg

(3) K   (4) Na

Q. 67. **Last manifestation of chlorosis is:**

(1) Redness of older leaves

(2) Whiteness of mature living cells

(3) Yellowing in leaves

(4) Greenness in leaves

Q. 68. **Chlorosis caused by which set of elements?**

(1) N, K, Zn   (2) S, Fe, Mn, Mo

(3) K, N, Cl, P   (4) Both 1 and 2

Q. 69. **Necrosis (death of tissues) particularly leaf tissue is done due to deficiency of:**

(1) Ca

(2) Mg

(3) Cu

(4) K

(5) All of the above

Q. 70. **Which is the most common effect due to common lack or low level of N K S and Mo is?**

(1) Reduced rate of photosynthesis

(2) Reduced rate of respiration

(3) Reduced rate of N-fixation

(4) Inhibition of cell division

Q. 71. Which is the most common effect due to common lack or low level of N, S and Mo is?

(1) Delay in fruiting
(2) Delay in flowering
(3) Rapid rate of senescence
(4) Rapid rate of flowering

Q. 72. What is incorrect about mineral nutrition application to plants?

(1) Deficiency of any element can cause multiple symptoms
(2) Some symptoms may be caused by deficiency of one of several different elements
(3) Different plants also respond differently to deficiency of the same element
(4) For element that are actively mobilized within plants and exported to relatively mature tissues

Q. 73. Deficiency symptoms causes due to deficiency of a:

(1) Moderate decrease of micro-nutrients
(2) Moderate decrease of both micro-nutrients and macronutrient
(3) Moderate increase of micro-nutrients
(4) Moderate decrease of both micro and macronutrients

Q. 74. Toxicity causes due to:

(1) Usual decrease in micronutrients
(2) Moderate increased in micro-nutrients
(3) Rapid decrease in macronutrients
(4) Normal increase in micronutrients

Q. 75. Most of the plants can assimilate nitrate as well as NH_4^+, the latter cannot accumulate in the plant body?

(1) Toxicity
(2) High reactivity

(3) Used rapidly
(4) Easily consumpted

Q. 76. Reductive amination and trans-amination are two ways for synthesis of amino acids in plants through which substance?

(1) NH_3 (2) NH_4^+
(3) Both 1 and 2   (4) N_2

Q. 77. Reaction α-ketoglutarate acid + NH_4^+ + NADPH′→ → → Glutamate + H_2O + NADP show

(1) Transamination
(2) Reductive amination
(3) Ammonification
(4) De-ammonification

Q. 78. During transmination, most of amino acids are formed in which $-NH_2$ providing amino acid is:

(1) Glutamic acid
(2) Glycine
(3) Arginine
(4) Aspartic acid

Q. 79. Which pair represents a most important group of plant amides?

(1) Asparagine and glutamine
(2) Asparagine and arginine
(3) Proline and glutamine
(4) Lysine and isoleucine

Q. 80. Amides differ from the amino acids in:

(1) Contain less N
(2) Contain more N
(3) Contain more H
(4) Contain less N and H

Q. 81. Amides are transferred from one place to another place by which source?

(1) Companion cells
(2) Phloem fibres
(3) Xylem vessels
(4) Xylem tracheids

Q. 82. Ureides characterized by:

(1) Particulalry low N:C ratio
(2) Particulalry high N:C ratio
(3) Particulalry high H:C ratio
(4) Particulalry high C:O ratio

Q. 83. Ureides represents the:

(1) Temporary N-sources
(2) Fixed N-sources
(3) Temporary C-sources
(4) Fixed N-sources

Q. 84. Final reservoir, most appropriate set of mineral elements on earth is:

(1) Rock, oceans and atmosphere
(2) Soil, oceans and air
(3) Water atmosphere and air
(4) Air, water and ocean

Q. 85. Auto trophic or self-feeding organisms includes:

(1) Only green plants and certain microorganisms
(2) Some green plants and most organisms
(3) All green plants and microorganisms
(4) All green plants and all BGA

Q. 86. In which of the following is incorrect statement?

(1) De Saussure demonstrated that inorganic mineral nutrient contained in plant ash are obtained from the soil via root system
(2) N is not mineral element typically
(3) Sachs and Knop attempted to determine the mineral content of plants experimentally
(4) Sach and Knop experimentally showed that N and inorganic mineral elements supported by soil

Q. 87. An element is considered as essential if:

(i) Without it plants cannot complete its life cycle
(ii) It must not be replaceable by other element

(iii) It to be a necessary component of an essential metabolite
(iv) It tit be at least required as an activator of an essential enzyme

(1) (i), (ii), (iii) are correct and (iv) is incorrect
(2) All are correct
(3) (i), (ii) and (iv) are correct and (iii) is incorrect
(4) (i), (iv) are correct and (ii) and (iii) are incorrect

Q. 88. Who prepare a list of elements essential to plant life through the application of hydroponic culture:

(1) Charles Darwin
(2) de Saussure
(3) Sach and Knop
(4) Both 2 and 3

Q. 89. There are certain exceptions, for which criteria, necessary a mineral to be essential?

(1) Without it plant cannot complete its life cycle
(2) Cannot be replaceable
(3) Necessary component of an essential metabolite
(4) At least it should be required as an activatot of an essential enzme

Q. 90. I PPM is equal to:

(1) µg/gm
(2) µg/1L
(3) µg/10 gm
(4) µg/100 gm

Q. 91. Which element is present in highest % or ppm?

(1) O or C   (2) N
(3) S   (4) P

Q. 92. Which element is present in highest % or ppm?

(1) K   (2) Ca
(3) P   (4) S

Q. 93. Among the mineral nutrient (micronutrient) present in highest % or ppm:

(1) Fe or Cl   (2) B
(3) Mn   (4) Cu

Q. 94. Which set carry more than 90% part of dry matter of common plant materials:

(1) C, H, O   (2) H, O, N
(3) Mg, O, C   (4) C, H, N

Q. 95. Frame work elements are:

(1) C, H, O   (2) H, O, N
(3) Mg, O, Ca   (4) C H N

Q. 96. Which elements absorbed as anion?

(1) N   (2) P
(3) S   (4) All of the above

Q. 97. Balancing elelents are

(1) Mg, Ca, K, Na, Cl
(2) Mg, P, K, Ca, H
(3) Mg, C, P, Cl, Na
(4) Cl, Na, Mg, Zn

Q. 98. Infinitesimal nutrients are those which required comparatively small in quantities and assigned catalytic or enzyme forming. Of these correct set is:

(1) Mo, Cu, Zn   (2) Mg, Fe, P
(3) C, Na, Mg   (4) Cl, Zn, Na

Q. 99. What is incorrect statement in below mentioned?

(1) Required in 1000 µg/g of dry matter
(2) Required in equal or less than 100 µg/g of dry matter
(3) K and Mg act as balancing elements as well as inorganic catalysts
(4) All inorganic plant nutrients required except CHO are obtained directly or indirectly from oceans

Q. 100. In which of the following is the method of determination of mineral requirements of plants?

(1) Plant analysis
(2) Solution culture (hydroponics)

(3) Medium culture
(4) All of the above

Q. 101. Method of (plant analysis) determination of nutrient requirement involves a process for final analysis. It may be:

(1) Wet digestion
(2) Ash preparation
(3) Both 1 and 2
(4) Hydroponics

Q. 102. Ash content is highest in which type of plants:

(1) Halophytes and Xerophytes
(2) Hydrophytes and Sciophytes
(3) Xerophytes and Sciophytes
(4) Mangroves and Xerophytes

Q. 103. Least Ash content is represented in:

(1) Halophytes   (2) Xerophytes
(3) Hydrophytes (4) Heliotypes

Q. 104. The ash content of different plants and tissues varies from which % of fresh weight:

(1) 2–6%   (2) 1–4%
(3) 1–2%   (4) 1–8%

Q. 105. A method of plant analysis in which N cannot be detected and escape as NH_3 or N_2 is:

(1) Ash preparation
(2) Soild medium culture
(3) Wet method
(4) Hydroponics

Q. 106. Chemically ash consist of:

(1) Oxides of metals
(2) Sulphides of metals
(3) Both 1 and 2
(4) Nitrates of metals

Q. 107. Plant ash can be dissolved in:

(1) Warm dilute HCl and HNO_3
(2) Warm concentration H_2SO_4 and HCl

(3) Warm dilute alcohol and H_2SO_4

(4) Warm diluate HNO_3

Q. 108. Improved methods of detection and quantitification of elements are:

(1) Atomic absorption spectrometery

(2) Optical emission spectrometry

(3) Both 1 and 2

(4) None of the above

Q. 109. The application of spectrophotometer is:

(1) Measuring wavelength

(2) Quantitification of energy content

(3) Counting the emission of electrons

(4) Both 1 and 3

Q. 110. Invention of solution culture (hydroponics) is carried out:

(1) W. Pfeffler

(2) Julius Sachs

(3) W. Knop

(4) All of the above

Q. 111. Which provides an excellent means of controlling the quantity and relative proportions of minerals salts given to a plant in an experiment is/are

(1) Solution culture

(2) Plant analysis

(3) Solid culture

(4) Both 1 and 2

Q. 112. A advantages of hydroponics in mineral nutrition studies is/are:

(1) Water is excellent solvent for mineral salts

(2) Water can be easily freed from contaminations

(3) Both 1 and 2

(4) Water is conductor of electricity

Q. 113. In hydroponics mineral salts are dissolved in:

(1) DW   (2) DDW

(3) Fresh water (4) Shallow water

Q. 114. What is incorrect about solution culture?

(1) Every time only one element is left out from solution

(2) Best way to estimate the amount and relative quantity of mineral to a particular plant

(3) It best method than plant analysis and soild medium culture

(4) Solution is suited to meet the need of root aeration

Q. 115. Disadvantage of hydroponics are/is:

(1) Solution not meets the need of aeration of root

(2) Replacing of solution every or two days due to relative absorption power of each nutrient

(3) Differential uptake causes PH changes

(4) Root needs supporting devices

(5) All of the above

Q. 116. Solid medium culture is best/better than hydroponics:

(1) Roots do not need any outer support

(2) Silica quartz, sand or gravel is used to make substation contain least impurities

(3) Availability of various ways to apply solution

(4) All of the above

Q. 117. Slope culture, drip culture and sub-irrigation culture is a part (type) of which technique of culture:

(1) Hydroponics

(2) Plant analysis

(3) Soild medium culture

(4) Liquid solution culture

Q. 118. On which basis, solid medium culture, a method of culture divided into three different culture methods:

(1) Way of apply nutrient solution

(2) Way of apply solution particularly

(3) Way of apply solute partially

(4) All of the above

Q. 119. In slope culture, solution applied as:

(1) By pouring over solid medium

(2) By injecting onto solid medium continously

(3) By forming solution up from bottom of container

(4) By injecting onto solid medium at suitable intervals

Q. 120. In drip culture, solution apply:

(1) Dripping onto soild medium at suitable intervals

(2) By injecting onto solid medium continously

(3) By forming solution up from bottom of container

(4) By injecting onto solid medium at suitable interval

Q. 121. In subirrigation technique of culture, solution apply:

(1) By forming solution up from bottom of container

(2) By injecting onto solid medium continuously

(3) By forming solution up from bottom of container

(4) By injecting onto solid medium at suitable intervals

Q. 122. In which of the following methods re-circulating solutions that flow through solid medium around roots are used?

(1) Drip culture (2) Subirrigation

(3) Slope culture (4) Hydroponics

Q. 123. In hydroponic culture gas jar normally covered with which chemical substance to exclude light and thus algal growth:

(1) Al (2) Cu

(3) Zn (4) Fe

Q. 124. In which method, nutrient solution applied by hand?

(1) Slop culture (2) Subirrigation

(3) Drip culture (4) Liquid culture

Q. 125. Slope culture used:

(1) Sand (2) Soil

(3) Quartz (4) Clay

Q. 126. Which culture method is the easiest method to operate but exposure of roots to constant amount of essential elements and water cannot be controlled?

(1) Slop culture

(2) Drip culture

(3) Hydroponics

(4) All of the above

Q. 127. What is correct about subirrigation method?

(1) It is most automatically and desirable method among three methods

(2) More costly

(3) Need sophistication

(4) All of the above

Q. 128. What is true about drip irrigation?

(1) Amount of solution being added should be equal to amount of solution drained off

(2) Most costly

(3) It needs sophistication

(4) Both 2 and 3

Q. 129. What is correct statement?

(1) Nutrient solution developed and named after workers like Knop, Hoagland, Evans, Shive, Sachs

(2) Most important formulations Hoagland's solution and Shive's solution

(3) A solution ideal for one species may not be ideal for another species

(4) All of the above

Q. 130. In which of the following is incorrect statement?

(1) Ash is prepared keeping the dried plant materials to high temperature (about 600C) in a Muffle furnace

(2) A prussion blue colouration when Fe reacts with K

(3) A canary yellow PPt. of ammonium phosphomolybdate is formed when ash solution reacts with ammonium molybdate

(4) A chocolate-brown ppt. of cupric ferrocyanide is formed when Ash solution mixed with K-ferrocyanides solution

(5) None of above is incorrect

Q. 131. General functions of the essential elements are:

(1) Mon-ovalent cations increase hydration

(2) Divalent (usually polyvalent) cations decrease it

(3) They show antagonistic effect

(4) Plant tissues usually control the degree of acidity and buffer action primarily by organic acids

(5) All are correct

Q. 132. Framework elements are:

(1) C (2) H

(3) O (4) All of the above

Q. 133. Which are not mineral in true sense?

(1) C (2) C, H

(3) O, N (4) All of the above

Q. 134. Chief source of N is:

(1) Rock

(2) Soil

(3) Oceans

(4) All of the above

Q. 135. N is absorbed from the soil in two major ionic forms:

(1) NO_3 and NH_4

(2) NH_2 and NH_4

(3) NH_4 and NO_2

(4) NO_2 and NO_3

Q. 136. What is true about nitrogen?

(1) Soil generally remain deficient in N

(2) Soil fertility always depend on the added N

(3) Cytochrome, a nitrogenous product, is essential in respiration and photosynthesis

(4) N found in the coenzymes like NAD, NADP and FAD

(5) All of the above

Q. 137. During N deficiency induce the production and accumulation of anthocyanin pigment is found which result a purplis colouration appears on:

(1) Stem

(2) Petiole

(3) Lower leaf surface

(4) All of the above

Q. 138. The concentration range at which the elements are optimum is:

(1) Heavy

(2) Narrow

(3) Average

(4) Moderate

Q. 139. What is criteria/condition for a mineral element to be toxic in plant?

(1) Any concentration in tissue that reduces the dry weight of tissues by about 1%

(2) Any concentration in tissue that reduces the dry weight of tissues by exact 10%

(3) Any concentration in tissue that reduces the dry weight of tissues by about 15%

(4) Any concentration in tissue that reduces the dry weight of tissues by almost 7%

Q. 140. Critical concentration of elements to be toxic in plant tissues vary........ Among different microelements:

(1) Minimally (2) Widely
(3) Moderately (4) Both 1 and 3

Q. 141. Excess of Mn may induce deficiencies of:

(1) Fe, Mg, Ca (2) Fe, Mg, S
(3) Ca, K, Zn (4) Ca, Mg, C

Q. 142. Deficiency symptoms of Mn causes due to deficiency of

(1) Fe, Ca (2) Cd, S
(3) Hg, K (4) B, Zn

Q. 143. N deficiency symptoms appear first on older parts and later on younger leaves because

(1) They receive soluble forms of N transported from older leaves
(2) Younger leaves are less vascularized
(3) Younger leaves are less sensitive to deficiency symptoms
(4) Both 2 and 3 are correct

Q. 144. What is correct in reference of N deficiency symptoms:

(1) Starch content increased
(2) Protein content decreased
(3) Flowering delay and fruits and seeds are small and weak
(4) All of the above

Q. 145. Most recognized role of N in plants is:

(1) Presence in structure of protein molecule
(2) Constituent of DNA/RNA
(3) Presence in structure of porphyrins and Cytochromes
(4) Presence in structure of vitamins

Q. 146. What is correct about P?

(1) Second limiting nutrient
(2) Present in soil as organic and inorganic forms

(3) Primarliy absorbed as mon-ovalent inorganic anions ($H_2PO_4^-$) and slowly absorbed as divalent anions ($H_2PO_4^-$)
(4) All of the above

Q. 147. Substances where P present as organic P (non-utilizable forms):

(1) Nucleic acid
(2) Phospholipids
(3) Inositol phosphates
(4) All of the above

Q. 148. Most important factor controlling the availability of P are:

(1) pH of soil solution
(2) Dissolved Al and Fe and available Ca
(3) Anion exchange
(4) Presence of microorganisms in soil

Q. 149. P is a constituent of

(1) Phospholipids
(2) Phosphoglycerides
(3) Glycerol phosphatides along with protein
(4) All of the above

Q. 150. The most abundant phosphoglycerides in higher plants are:

(1) Phosphophatidyl ethanol amine
(2) Lecithin (phosphatidyl choline)
(3) Both 1 and 2
(4) Glycerol-phosphtides

Q. 151. Most widely used coenzymes in processes like photosynthesis respiration N metabolism carbohydrates metabolisms and fatty acid metabolisms is:

(1) NAD^+ (2) $NADP^+$
(3) FAD^+ (4) $FADP^+$

Q.152. In which of the following is correct?

(1) All the intermediates of GMP and are phosphorylated compounds
(2) P is part of all enzyme phosphorlyates in photosynthesis

(3) High content is present in meta-bolic regions

(4) All are correct

Q. 153. Reason behind high concentration of P is found in meristematic regions of actively growing plants:

(1) Involved in synthesis of nucle-oproteins

(2) Involved in activation of amino acids through ATP and GTP

(3) Involved in initiation and elongation of steps of polypeptide chain synthesis for protein moiety of nucleoprotein molecules

(4) All of the above

Q. 154. P deficiency symptoms are of thern compared with which mineral element?

(1) N   (2) Zn

(3) Cd   (4) S

Q. 155. Sometimes P deficiency causes distortion in shape of leaves, this deficiency symptoms may be confused with:

(1) Zn   (2) Mn

(3) B   (4) Si

Q. 156. In which of the following is not a P deficiency symptom:

(1) Accumulation of carbohydrates

(2) Large amount of Pith

(3) Small amount of UT in stems of tomato

(4) Light green colouration of leaves

Q. 157. Why commercial fertilizers usually contain NPK elements?

(1) Usually these three deficient in soil

(2) Plants need them in large amount

(3) These are less costly

(4) Easy in absorption

Q. 158. Most of K content of the soil is:

(1) Fixed (non-excangeable)

(2) Soluble form

(3) Exchangeable form

(4) Combined form

Q. 159. In which of the following element does not enter into composition of any organic compound in plants is?

(1) Na   (2) Mg

(3) K   (4) B

Q. 160. Physiological functions of K includes:

(1) Carbohydrates metabolism and sugar translocation

(2) Stomatal opening in hihjer plants

(3) Osmotic swelling of guard cells and stomtatal opening

(4) Regulation of water in plants cells

(5) All of the above

Q. 161. What is correct about K and enzymes

(1) Required by acetic thiokinase from spinach leaves for maximum activity, starch synthetase (sweet corn) and ATPase activity also

(2) Regulator of pyruvate kinase by enzyme repression

(3) Required by enzyme succinyl-Co.A synthetase in tobacco

(4) NR formation in rice seedlings

(5) All of the above

Q. 162. What is correct?

(1) K deficiency symptoms first appear on older leaves (due to easy mobility)

(2) P deficiency symptoms first appear on older leaves (like K)

(3) P deficiency symptoms first appear on younger leaves

(4) All are correct

Q. 163. Gama-glutamylcysteine synthesis especially requires

(1) Na

(2) Mg

(3) K

(4) Ca

Q. 164. A mottled chlorosis followed by development of dark necrotic lesions at tip and margins of leaf is generally found as a deficiency symptoms of:

(1) K (2) P
(3) Na (4) B

Q. 165. Deficiency symptoms of K includes:

(1) Easy lodging by wind/rain
(2) Stunted growth with shortened internodes
(3) Disintegration of pith cells
(4) Cereals roots susceptible to root rtting organisms
(5) All of the above

Q. 166. Which is usual form or source (non-exchangeable) of calcium present in soil is?

(1) Ca Al_2SiO_5 (anorthite)
(2) $CaCO_3$ (Lime stone)
(3) Dolomite (Mg $CO_3.CaCO_3$)
(4) Flore-apetite ($3Ca^3(PO_4)_2.Ca.Fe^2$)

Q. 167. Matches the columns:

Col. A	Col. B
A. Calcium carbonate and Ca-phosphate	(i) Alkaline soils
B. Anorthite	(ii) Growth of avena coleoptiles by increased plasticity by by removal of pectate bound calcium
C. Calcium salt of lecithin	(iii) Soils of arid and semiarid regions
D. EDTA	(iv) Cell membrane organization

(1) A (iii), B (i), C (iv), D (ii)
(2) A (iii), B (ii), C (iv), D (i)

(3) A (i), B (iii), C (iv), D (ii)
(4) A (iv), B (i), C (iii), D (ii)

Q. 168. Induced low pH is found to mimic .... induced cell elongation:

(1) IAA
(2) Ck
(3) IAA+GA
(4) ET

Q. 169. Cell wall extension induced by CO_2 and low pH is reduced when:

(1) K^+ is added
(2) Ca^{2+} is out
(3) Ca^{2+} is added
(4) Mg^{2+} is added

Q. 170. EDTA a chelating agent function as:

(1) stimulates Avena coleoptiles growth
(2) Increase in cell permeability by removal of Ca^{2+}
(3) Both 1 and 2
(4) Plactity

Q. 171. In which of the following is correct statement

(1) Most calcium remain in vacuoles as insoluble crystals of oxalate, carbonate, phosphate or sulphates
(2) Low concentration of crystals must be maintain partly to prevent formation of insoluble Ca^{2+} salts of ATP and are organic phosphates
(3) Ca ion protects plants from injurious effects of H^+
(4) All organic maintain low concentration of free Ca^{+2} in their cytosol
(5) All of the above

Q. 172. Phospholipase-D from cabbage and carrot is activated by:

(1) Mg^{2+} (2) Ca^{2+}
(3) Na^+ (4) K^+

Q. 173. Mitochondria number in what roots is reduced under:

(1) Ca deficiency
(2) Mg supplementation
(3) K$^+$ deficiency
(4) N deficiency

Q. 174. Incorrect levels of carbohydrate in the leaves and decreased levels in stems and roots of cotton plants results from Ca-deficiency. An effect similar to that found in:

(1) K deficiency (2) Ni deficiency
(3) B deficiency (4) Fe deficiency

Q. 175. Physiological and biochemical function of Ca includes:

(1) Relatively high concentration of calcium is required for nodulation and successful SNF
(2) Calmodulin, a small soluble protein in cytosol, activated by Ca binding
(3) Activate α-amylase in barley and arginine kinase, adenyl-kinase and potato apyrase
(4) All of the above

Q. 176. In which of the following is a cytological function of calcium?

(1) Normal mitosis
(2) Synthesis of microtubules of spindle
(3) Chromomatin organization
(4) All of the above

Q. 177. Symptoms 'appeaerence of brown spots surrounded by chrlorotic veins' is due to deficiency of which mineral?

(1) Zn (2) Mn
(3) B (4) Cl

Q. 178. What is true about Mn fertilizers in plants?

(1) It competes with Fe and Mg for uptake
(2) It competes with Fe and Ca for uptake

(3) It competes with Mg for binding with enzymes
(4) It inhibits calcium translocation in shoot apex
(5) 1 and 2 are correct and 2 and 4 are wrong
(6) 1, 2 and 4 are incorrect and 2 is wrong
(7) 1, 2 and 4 are incorrect and 3 is correct
(8) All are correct

Q. 179. Much of the studies on mechanism of absorption of elements by plants has been carried out in isolated:

(1) Cells
(2) Tissues
(3) Organisms
(4) All of the above

Q. 180. Process of absorption can be demonstrated into which phases?

(1) 1 (2) 2
(3) 3 (4) 4

Q. 181. Phases of absorption includes:

(1) A apoplastic (free/outer space) passive phase
(2) A symplastic (inner space) active phase
(3) Both 1 and 2
(4) None of the above

Q. 182. First process involved in absorption of elements is

(1) Passive
(2) Active
(3) Faciliated
(4) All of the above

Q. 183. The first process of mineral absorption (passive movement) into apoplast usually occurs through:

(1) Ion channels
(2) transmembrane proteins
(3) Selective pores
(4) All of the above

Q. 184. The entry or exit of ions to and from the symplast requires the expenditure of metabolic energy is an:

(1) Passive process
(2) Active process
(3) Faciliated process
(4) Osmosis type

Q. 185. Usually term Flux used for:

(1) Movement of ions into the cells
(2) Inward movement in the cells
(3) Outward movement from the cells
(4) All of the above

Q. 186. Mineral salts are translocated through which vascular tissues along with the ascending stream of water which is pulled up through the plant by transpirational pull:

(1) Xylem
(2) Phloem
(3) Both 1 and 2
(4) Cambium and medullary rays

Q. 187. Majority of the nutrients that are essential for the growth and development of plants become available to the roots due to:

(1) Weathering and breakdown of rocks
(2) Paedogenesis
(3) Action of bacteria and fungi
(4) Decomposition and chemical actions

Q. 188. What set is correct:

A. NH_3 .... Nitrite (NO_2^{2-}): Process .... oxidation Organism involved: Nitrosomonas

B. NO_2^{2-} .... Nitrate Process: reduction Organism involved: Nitrobacter

C. Both above process called nitrification

D. Both above bacteria are chemo-autotrophs

(1) A, B and C are correct and iv is incorrect
(2) A, C and D are correct and C is incorrect
(3) A and B are correct and C and D are correct
(4) All are correct

Q. 189. Denitrification is carried out by which bacteria?

(1) Nitrobacter (2) Nitrosomonas
(3) Thiobacillus (4) Both 2 and 3

Q. 190. Denitrification is carried out by which bacteria?

(1) Nitrosomonas
(2) Pseudomonas
(3) Thio-bacillus
(4) Both 2 and 3

Q. 191. Where nitrate is reduced to form ammonia that finally forms the amine group of amino acid

(1) Roots   (2) Shoot
(3) Leaves   (4) All of the above

Q. 192. Ammonification is a process which includes:

(1) Decomposition of organic N of dead plants and animals into NH_3
(2) Decomposition of organic N of dead plants and animals into NH_4
(3) Decomposition of organic N of dead animals into NH_4Cl
(4) Decomposition of organic N of dead microorganisms into NO_3

Q. 193. What is fate of NH_3 produced as results of ammonification is/are:

(1) Some volatilization and dissolved in water and rest changed into NO_2
(2) Some volatilization and reenter the atmosphere
(3) Most of NH_3 converts into NO_3 by soils bacteria
(4) Both 1 and 3

Q. 194. Correct reactions catalyzed by soil bacteria after ammonification is/are:

(i) $2NH_3 + 3O_2$ .... $2NO_2 + 2H + 2H_2O$

(ii) $2NO_2 + O_2$ .... $2NO_3$

(iii) $2NO_2 + O_2$ .... $2NO_2$

(iv) $2NH_3 + O_2$ .... $NH_4 + H_2O$

(1) i, ii are correct and iii, iv are incorrect

(2) i, iii and iv are correct and ii is wrong

(3) i, iv are correct and ii and iii are wrong

(4) iii and vi are correct and i and ii are wrong

Q. 195. Principle N pool is:

(1) Atmosphere

(2) Soil

(3) Biomass

(4) All of the above

Q. 196. Plant nutrition is referred to as mineral nutrition, derived from:

(1) Rock minerals

(2) Soil minerals

(3) Plant residues minerals

(4) All of the above

Q. 197. Processes of weathering and breakdown of rocks enrich the soil with:

(1) Dissolved inorganic salts

(2) Dissolved ions

(3) Dissolved both ions and inorganic salts

(4) Dissolved ions and inorganic salts

Q. 198. Soil significance lies particularly:

(1) Supply minerals air and hold water

(2) Supply minerals air hold water stabilizes the plant

(3) Harbour N-fixing bacteria, microbes supply minerals air ahold water and act as a matrix that stabilizes the plant

(4) Supply minerals and hold water

Q. 199. Components of fertilizers are .... which applied as per need?

(1) Micronutrients

(2) Macronutrients

(3) Both 1 and 2

(4) Only as N, P, S and Mg

Q. 200 Plant competes with microbes for limited:

(1) S

(2) N

(3) C

(4) P

Q. 201. N is a constituent of:

(1) Proteins hormones, chl, some vitamins

(2) Vitamins, proteins, lipid, carbohydrates

(3) Lipid protein minerals salts and vitamins

(4) Enzymes, hormones, carbohydrate vitamins

Q. 202. Which is a typical mineral element and also limiting for both natural and agricultural ecosystems?

(1) N

(2) Zn

(3) Ca

(4) P

Q. 203. N-fixation is the process of conversion of:

(1) N_2 to NH_3

(2) N_2 to NO_3^{2-}

(3) N_2 to NO_2^{2-}

(4) N_2 to NH_4

Q. 204. The source of energy for conversion of N to nitrogen oxides in nature is:

(1) Lightening

(2) UV rays

(3) Sun and sunlight

(4) Both 1 and 2

Q. 205. In which of the following is a correct set of sources for atmospheric N oxides production are?

(1) Industrial combustions, forest fires, smoking

(2) Smoking, domestic stoves, forest fires

(3) Industrial combustion, forest fires, automobiles exhaust and power generating stations

(4) All of the above

Q. 206. Which pair of bacteria responsible for denitrification?

(1) Nitrobacter and nitrosomonas

(2) Pseudomonas and thiobacillus

(3) Thiobacillus and nitrosomonas

(4) Pseudomonas and azotobacter

Q. 207. Among below mentioned minerals, one of which is most abundantly found in living system:

(1) S

(2) N

(3) P

(4) Ca

Q. 208. Who are capable of N-fixing?

(1) Only certain prokaryotic species

(2) Only certain eukaryotic species

(3) Usually most of the prokaryotes

(4) Few pro and few eukaoytes

Q. 209. BNF (biological N-fixation) is:

(1) Reduction of N to NH_3 by living organisms

(2) Oxidation of NO_2 to NO_3 by bacteria

(3) Conversion of N to NH_4 by plants

(4) All are correct

Q. 210. N_2-fixers are:

(1) Prokaryotes usually

(2) Some eukaryotes and few prokaryotes

(3) Exclusively prokaryotes contain N-ase

(4) Exclusively eukaryotes contain N-ase

Q. 211. N-fixing organisms may be:

(1) Free living

(2) Symbiotic

(3) Both 1 and 2

(4) Parasitic

Q. 212. Free living N-fixing aerobic organisms (microbes) as/are:

(1) Azotobacter

(2) Beijernickia

(3) Bacillus

(4) Anaebaena

(5) 1–3

Q. 213. BGA are:

(1) Symbiotic N fixers

(2) Free living N-fixers like Azoto bacter and Bejiernickia

(3) Parasitic N fixers

(4) Heterotrophic N fixers

Q. 214. Bacillus is:

(1) Free living N fixing usually aerobic but rarely anaerobic bacteria

(2) Free living N fixing usually anaerobic

(3) Free living N fixing always aerobic

(4) Gram +ve free living N fixation anaerobic bacteria

Q. 215. Most famous symbiotic biologically N fixing association is in which till date:

(1) Chickpea-Rhizobium

(2) Alnus-Frankia

(3) Azolla-Rice

(4) Pinus-Fungi

Q. 216. What is incorrect among below mentioned statements?

(1) The most common relation (association-symbiosis) on roots in reference of N-fixing is nodules

(2) Frankia, produce nodules on non-leguleminous plants (e.g. Alnus)

(3) Both Rhizobium and Frankia are free living in soil but as symbiotics can fix atmosphere N

(4) Most symbiotic BNF associations is Rice-Azolla relationship

Q. 217. Nodules are?

(1) Near spherical outgrowth on roots

(2) Round out growth on roots

(3) Circular outgrowth on roots

(4) Fully spherical outgrowth on roots

Q. 218. When we can see nodules on roots of a legume plant?

(1) During flowering

(2) Before flowering

(3) After flowering

(4) At time of fruit set

Q. 219. Pink colour of nodule appear in cortical region is due to presence of:

(1) Hemocyanin

(2) Hemoglobin

(3) Leghaemoglobin

(4) Phycoerythrin

Q. 220. Below mentioned the stages of nodules formation in a sequence. Identify the correct sequence:

(i) Rhizobia get attached to epidermal and root hairs

(ii) Rhizobia multiply in surrounding of roots

(iii) Rhizobia colonize the surroundings of roots

(iv) The root hair curl and bacteria invade the root hairs

(v) An infection thread produced carrying the bacteria into cortex of root

(1) (ii), (iii), (i) (iv) and (v)

(2) (ii), (i), (iii) (iv) and (v)

(3) (ii), (iii), (i) (v) and (iv)

(4) (iii), (ii), (i) (iv) and (v)

Q. 221. Nodule formation starts in which part of root:

(1) Cortex   (2) Pericycle

(3) Endodermis (4) Epidermis

Q. 222. Newly formed nodules on roots establishes a ...... vascular connection with the host for exchange of which substances?

(1) Direct and nutrient

(2) Indirect and water

(3) Both 1 and 2

(4) Direct for removal of metabolic waste

Q. 223. Nodule contains:

(1) N-ase (at N_2 to NH_3)

(2) Lb

(3) Mo-Fe protein

(4) All of the above

Q. 224. First stable product of N-fixation in chickpea plant is

(1) NH_4 (2) NO_3^{2-}

(3) NO_2^{2-} (4) NH_3

Q. 225. During development of root nodules in soya bean, Rhizobium bacterium divides:

(1) Inside vegetative cells of root

(2) Near susceptible root hairs

(3) Inside the susceptible root hairs

(4) In vacuoles of a normal root hairs

Q. 226. Successful infection of Rhizobium in root hair causes:

(1) Rapid division

(2) Curling

(3) Susceptibility to the soil fauna

(4) Uncontrolled growth and susceptibility tumour

Q. 227. Infected thread (root hairs) carries the bacteria to the:

(1) Endodermis

(2) Inner cortex

(3) Outer cortex

(4) Outer of stele and pericycle

Q. 228. After infection, bacterial get modified into bacteroids, the shape of wall be:

(1) Spherical   (2) Round

(3) Rod shaped (4) Oval

Q. 229. After successful invasion in root hair, bacteria cause:

(1) Division of inner cortical and pericycle cells

(2) Divions of outer cortical and stele

(3) Divisions of both inner and outer cortical only

(4) Inhibits the cell division in cortical, pericycle and stele

Q. 230. Nodule formation is product of:

(1) Division and growth of cortical and pericycle cells

(2) Divisions of cortical and stealer cells

(3) Division of epidermis and periderm

(4) Division of epidermis and endo-dermis

Q. 231. Enzyme N-ase is highly sensitive to:

(1) Molecular oxygen

(2) Oxygen of water

(3) Nascent oxygen

(4) Both 1 and 3

Q. 232. Action of N-ase during N-fixation requires

(1) Aerobic conditions

(2) Anaerobic conditions

(3) First anaerobic and then aerobic conditions

(4) Successive steps of process require aerobic and anaerobic atmosphere

Q. 233. Energy required during the N-fixation comes from:

(1) Photosynthesis

(2) Respiration

(3) N-fixation also a exergonic reactions

(4) No need of ATP during N-fixation

Q. 234. All N-fixing bacteria during N-fixation processes operates their activities under:

(1) Aerobic conditions also

(2) Anaerobic conditions always

(3) CO_2 rich atmosphere

(4) Weak CO_2 atmosphere

Q. 235. During N fixation, each NH_3 molecules need:

(1) 16 ATP molecules

(2) 14 ATP molecules

(3) 7 ATP molecules

(4) 8 ATP molecules

Q. 236. In which of the following enzymes operates their activities only under anaerobic conditions?

(1) N-ase

(2) RuBPcarboxylase oxygenase

(3) NiR

(4) NR

Q. 237. Work of O_2 scavenger or creating anaerobic atmosphere inside nodule is done through which substance:

(1) N-ase

(2) NR

(3) NiR

(4) Lb

Q. 238. In this reaction, $N_2 + 8e + 8H^+ + ATP$ .... $\rightarrow 2NH_3 + H_2 + ADP + Pi$ What is the number of ATP required to proceeds this reaction?

(1) 8   (2) 16

(3) 15   (4) 14

Q. 239. First symptoms of Mg^{2+} deficiency are:

(1) Extensive interveinal chlorosis of older leaves

(2) Chlorosis

(3) Necrotic spotting

(4) Extensive chloroenchyma develop-ment and scanty pith formation

(5) All of the above

Q. 240. Reduced S-compounds in plant tissues is/are:

(1) Sulphate esters

(2) Sulpholipids

(3) Both 1 and 2

(4) Sulphate

Q. 241. Ca deficiency symptoms includes:

(1) Abnormal mitosis

(2) Termination of growth in apical meristems regions at stem, leaf and root tips

(3) Chlorotic patches appear near margins of younger leaves

(4) Roots became short, study and brown

(5) All of the above

Q. 242. Mg present in soil as:

(1) Water soluble

(2) Exchangeable

(3) Fixed form

(4) All of the above

Q. 243. Zn which of the following, form is unavailable form:

(1) Magnesium silicate

(2) Magnesite ($MgCO_3$) and Livine (Mg Fe)$_2$ SiO_4)

(3) Dolomite ($MgCO_3.CaCO_3$)

(4) All of the above

Q. 244. Most popular and economical source of Mg fertilizer is:

(1) Magnesium silicate

(2) Magnesite ($MgCO_3$) and Livine (Mg Fe)$_2$ SiO_4)

(3) Dolomite ($MgCO_3.CaCO_3$)

(4) All of the above

Q. 245. Structural function of Mg includes:

(1) Chlorophyll structure

(2) Ribosome integrity

(3) Structural integrity of chromatin fibres

(4) All of the above

Q. 246. Coiling of 110 A thick DNA histone protein fibres into a 300 A thick chromatin fibre is carried out by action of:

(1) H^+ (2) Ca^{2+}

(3) Mg^{2+} (4) K^+

Q. 247. Almost all the phosphorylation enzymes involved in carbohydrate metabolism require a mineral (nutrient) as activator for maximal activity:

(1) Ca^{2+}

(2) K^+

(3) Mg^{2+}

(4) Fe^{2+}

Q. 248. Which is responsible for full activity of the two principal CO_2 fixation enzymes (PEP carboxylase and Rubisco)?

(1) Ca^{2+}

(2) K^+

(3) Mg^{2+}

(4) Fe^{2+}

Q. 249. Mg^{2+} helps in:

(1) Protein synthesis by activating enzymes of nucleic acid synthesis

(2) Forming complexes with mRNA

(3) Forming complexes with ribosomes and fMet initiator t-RNA

(4) All of the above

Crop (Pulses) Responses to Plant Growth Regulators and Nutrients

9

ABSTRACT

The practice of agriculture is several thousand years old and faces many challenges world-wide. Plethora of research investigations has been made to cover the various aspect of combined effect of plant growth regulators and nutrients in the growth, physiological, biochemical and yield characteristics of pulse crops which include length, fresh and dry weight of root, leaf number, leaf area, leaf area index, net assimilation rate, chlorophyll content, photosynthesis, nitrate reductase activity, carbonic anhydrase activity, nutrient accumulation, nitrogen, phosphorus and potassium contents, leghaemoglobin, protein and carbohydrate content and various other growth, yield and quality parameters. So the present review indicates that the process of growth and development, in addition to the yield of plants is highly affected by the plant growth regulators along with sulphur in stress and non-stressful circumstances.

Keywords: Plant growth regulators, Nutrients, Yield, Biological quality characteristics.

Introduction

The world food supplies are usually debated in terms of cereals, wheat, rice and maize being the dominant commodities, but there exists second group of crops, the pulse (legume grains), which make a major contribution to human diet (both in the peasant's hut and in the international hotels) in developing countries in tropical and subtropical areas, where their nutritional contribution is of paramount importance as a large segment of the populations in these areas have limited access to food of animal origin. On the pulse map of the world, India is largest producer, processor, consumer and importer of pulses with 25 percent share in global production (13.50 million tonnes). Pulses form an important part of Indian dietary, are essential adjuncts to a predominantly cereal-based diet and enhance the biological value of the protein consumed. The diverse agro-ecological conditions of the country are favourable for growing all the annual pulse crops including chickpea, pigeon pea, mung bean, urad bean, lentil and field pea, are important pulses crop contributing 39%, 21%, 10%, 7% and 5% to the total production of pulses in the country (Saxena *et al.*, 2010).

Further, it has been established that species of the genes (and even varieties of a species) differ, in their ability to fully utilize in puts, including nutrients, under the same environmental conditions (Mazid *et al.*, 2012a). India is the principal pulse producing country (83% share in the region). To achieve this goal, the Indian Council of Agricultural Research (ICAR) has established several research centres in different parts of the country to deal with various pulse crops, including two for chickpea improvement are the International

242

Centre for Agricultural Research in the Dry Areas (ICARDA) and the International Crops Research Institute for the Semi-arid Tropics (ICRISAT). Also, many research projects and national programmes have been launched by non-government organizations to boost the production of chickpea and the technology is being increasingly adopted by farmers.

Commercial cultivation of chickpea for both protein-rich supplement to cereal based diets, especially critical in developing countries where people either cannot afford animal protein or are vegetarian by choice and in sustaining soil fertility by fixing up to 140 kg N ha^{-1} year^{-1} (organic cropping systems). Thus, chickpea is clearly not cost effective and attempts have been made to produce a dual purpose chickpea crop with good yield and more N$_2$-fixation. However, little progress has been made in breeding dual purpose varieties synchronized for both seed yield and organic cropping. Under these circumstances, the best strategy for dual-purpose chickpea would be to increase the height (root + shoot length) or number of root nodules on root systems of the plant and to improve seed weight, a task which may prove simpler than achieving the synchronizing of seed organic cropping.

Also, increasing use of high analysis fertilizers results in a growing deficiency of secondary nutrients and micronutrients. Further, much of the fertilizers are rendered unavailable to the plants if applied as a single dose at sowing due to many factors. Seed filling is a critical stage for pulse crops. Seed yield and quality of storage protein are influenced by both sulphur and nitrogen nutrition during seed filling. Since pulse crops have the ability to fix nitrogen for the atmosphere, their nitrogen requirement from the soil is lower than that of other crops. However, studies have shown that nitrogen stress can result in decrease in seed yield and protein concentration. For example, up to 60% of total applied S may be lost through leaching and volatilization, and up to 70% of the phosphorous (P) by fixation. Thus, for achieving the desired productivity, the limiting nutrients need to be supplied judiciously using innovative methods of application.

Plant Growth Regulators

The PGRs are organic natural or synthetic compounds (other than nutrients). They are naturally produced within plants, though very similar chemicals are produced by fungi and bacteria that can also affect plant growth as well as human use them to control plant growth and development (Nickell, 1979). On the other hand, PGRs are chemicals produced by plant that alter growth pattern and/or maintenance of the plant. They can be found in many cells and tissues, although they seem to be concentrated in meristem and buds. They control cell activation by sending chemical signals or messenger to cells to do something or not to do something including activating the genes that code for specific enzymes. They inhibit as well as promote cellular activities. Most PGRs have multiple effects in plants and they work in very small concentrations. PGRs often work in conjunction with each other and have overlapping effects. There are several classes of PGRs, *viz.* gibberellins, auxins, cytokinins, abscisic acid and ethylene. Additionally, a number of recently "discovered" PGRs remotely related with the above PGRs have varied important roles in the regulation of plant activities. These include brassinosteroids, salicylates, jasmonates and triacontanols. Interestingly, the synthetic growth regulators bring about the more or less same plant responses when applied exogenously at very low concentrations. So the agrophysiologists are moving in a direction where the physiological efficiency of the plant including the photosynthetic rate and nitrogen fixation, water and mineral uptake, leaf senescence, better harvest index and stress resistance may be improved by using PGRs.

PGRs significantly influence agronomical, morphological and physiological traits in crops and it is observed that at limited concentration they stimulate rapid cell division resulting faster vegetative and reproductive growth (Tiwari *et al.*, 2011). They supply either carbon and energy or essential mineral elements and active in very small quantity (e.g. <1 mM, often 1 µM) which found in certain parts of the plant and usually translocated to other sites, where they evoke specific biochemical, physiological and/or morphological responses. Moreover, PGRs are important agents in the response of plants to the external physiological environment (Steudle, 2000). The increase in yield with the application of various PGRs might be due to increased yield attributes, which in turn resulted from effective translocation of photosynthates. The plant growth regulators also increase mobilization of reserve food materials to the developing sink through increase in hydrolyzing and oxidizing enzyme activities and lead to increase in yield. While, Zahir *et al.* (2007) observed that exogenously supplied PGRs may undergo several metabolic processes in the soil resulting in loss of their activity and reduced availability to plants and such type of behaviour is only seen with auxin (e.g. IAA) and GA$_3$ (Panday *et al.*, 1996).

In addition, remarkable accomplishments of PGRs such as manipulating plant developments, enhancing yield and quality have been actualized in recent years using new emerging and efficient PGRs. It has long been ascertained that plant hormones (e.g. auxin, cytokinin, gibberellins and ethylene) are involved in controlling developmental events such as cell division, cell elongation and protein synthesis. Plants have the ability to store excessive amounts of exogenously supplied hormones in the form of reversible conjugates which release active hormone when and where plant needs them during the growth period. PGRs are proved to improve effective

partitioning and translocation of accumulates from source to sink in the field crops (Senthil *et al.*, 2003).

Auxins

The word 'auxin' is derived from the Greek word 'auxein' meaning 'to grow'. These are organic compounds having a ring structure and a side chain. A number of auxins including indole 3-acetic acid (IAA), indole 3-butyric acid, phenyl acetic acid and 4-chloro-indole acetic acid have been isolated from different parts of plants. IAA (Fig. 9.1) has been recognized as the principal auxin in higher plants and is discovered by Kogl *et al.* (1934).

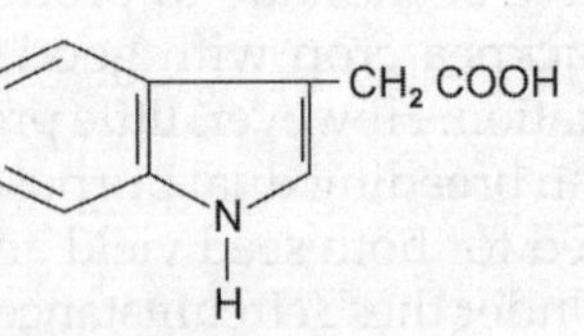

Fig. 9.1: Indole 3-acetic acid

They are generally produced by the growing apices of the stem and roots, from where they migrate polarly through phloem to the regions of their action. However, they may also be produced in young leaves, seeds and fruits of higher plants. Typical IAA concentration ranges from 0.01 to 3 mg per litre (l) (www. sigmaalder.com). Auxins enhance a number of physiological processes in plants, including abscission of older mature leaves and fruits, apical dominance, cell division, cell enlargement, distribution of growth between primary and lateral root and shoot meristems, flowering and parthenocarpy, loosening of cell wall, mediation of tropistic responses of shoot and root to light and gravity, patterning of embryos, root initiation, synthesis of ribonucleic acid (RNA), deoxyribonucleic acid (DNA) and protein and vascular tissue differentiation.

Gibberellins

The word 'gibberellin' is coined by Yabuta and Sumiki (1938) after the genus name of the fungus (*Gibberella fujikuroii*) from which the active factor is isolated. These are tetracyclic diterpenoid acids. Over 136 naturally occurring gibberellins have been isolated from plants, fungi and bacteria. These are abbreviated as GA with a subscript such as GA_1, GA_2, GA_3 and so on. These are numbered in order of their discovery. Of these, GA_3 (Fig. 9.2) also known as gibberellic acid (GA) is commonly available and most widely used in plant physiological research. It is isolated and characterized by two groups, one headed by Cross in England and one by Stodola in the USA (Stodola *et al.* 1955).

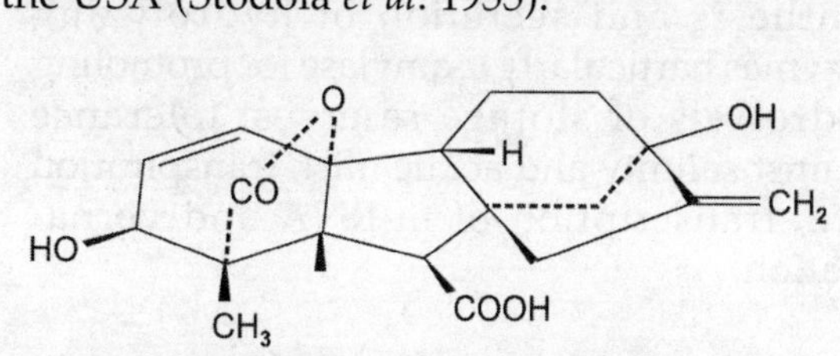

Fig. 9.2: Gibberellic acid

In plants, they are synthesized in expanding leaves and shoot apex as also in other parts of shoot, including fruits and seeds and presumably in roots. In general, GA movement is non-polar and occurs through the conducting tissue (Chin *et al.*, 1965). The typical GA concentration ranges from 0.01 to 5 mg/L (www.sigmaalder.com). Gibberellins inhibit the adventitious root formation but enhance a number of physiological processes including activity of ribulose-1, 5-bisphosphate carboxylase (RuBPcase), bunching of grapes, breaking of seed and bud dormancy, cell wall plasticity, cell elongation, flowering, growth and yield of sugarcane, PN, parthenocarpy, protein synthesis, phloem loading, relative growth rate (RGR), stomatal aperture, senescence, stem elongation, seed germination, synthesis and secretion of hydrolyzing enzymes particularly α-amylase for promoting hydrolysis of storage reserves, transpiration rate, transcription of messenger (m)-RNA and vernalization.

Cytokinins

The word 'cytokinin' is derived from the Greek word 'kineein' meaning 'to move'. These are the substances that regulate plant growth primarily by inducing cell division. All naturally occurring cytokinins are aminopurine derivatives while nearly all compounds active as cytokinins are N^6-substituted aminopurines. Zeatin, dihydrozeatin and isopentenyl adenine are the three most commonly detected and most physiologically active cytokinins in various plants. Kinetin (Kn) and benzyladenine are highly active but not formed by plants. Miller *et al.* (1955) for the first time isolated and identified kinetin as 6-furfurylaminopurine (Fig 9.3).

Cytokinins are produced by both lower and higher plants. In the latter, they are synthesized in growing areas such as roots and shoots, actively dividing tissues of seeds, fruits and leaves, root tips, germinating seeds as well as wounding tissues. Studies indicate that root tips are most likely the location of cytokinins production. Cytokinins are transported from the root to the shoot in the xylem in a polar fashion (Blackwell and Horgan, 1994). Kn is generally used at a concentration ranging from 0.01 to 10.0 mg/L (www.sigmaalder.com). Cytokinins enhance

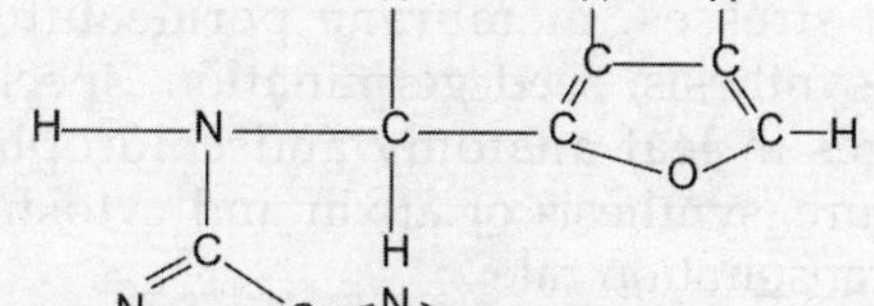

Fig. 9.3: Kinetin

a number of physiological processes in plants, including activation of cell growth in leaves, apical dominance, breaking of bud dormancy, cell cycling, chloroplast differentiation, floral development, leaf senescence, nutrient mobilization, N-dependent regulation of gene expression in photosynthesis, P_N, seed germination and source-sink balance.

Salicylates

The word 'salicylic acid' (salicylate) is coined by Raffaele Piria in 1838 from the Latin word *salix* meaning willow tree from bark of which he obtained the active principle, i.e. SA (Arteca, 1996). Salicylates are a class of compounds having activity similar to SA (orthohydroxybenzoic acid) which is a plant phenolic compound (Fig. 9.4).

Green leaves and reproductive organs are the main site of SA biosynthesis. However, the highest level of SA synthesis is reported in+ the inflorescence of thermogenic plants and plants infected by necrotizing pathogens. SA can be readily transported throughout the plant with the help of vascular tissues. SA reduces ethylene biosynthesis and enhances a number of physiological processes, including defence mechanism against abiotic and biotic stresses, membrane permeability, photosynthesis, seed germination, specific changes in leaf anatomy and chloroplast structure, synthesis of auxin and cytokinin and transpiration rate.

Triacontanol

It is a trivial name for a long, straight chain saturated primary alcohol, 1-hydroxytricontane.

It is a constituent of beeswax and the cuticle of many leaves and also a synthetic PGR (Noggle and Fritz, 1986). Tria reduces the level of abscisic acid but enhances a number of physiological processes including activity of RuBPcase and nitrate reductase (NR), bunching of grapes, breaking of seed and bud dormancy, chlorophyll content, cell wall plasticity, CO_2 fixation, cell elongation, dark respiration, dry weight, flowering, growth and yield, gibberellin-like activities, leaf-area ratio, nutrient uptake, photosynthesis and its related processes like photorespiration, parthenocarpy, protein synthesis, phloem loading, RGR, reducing sugars and free amino acids, stomatal aperture, senescence, stem-elongation, seed germination, shoot weight, synthesis and secretion of hydrolyzing enzymes particularly α-amylase for promoting hydrolysis of storage reserves, tolerance against salinity and acidic mist, transpiration rate, transcription of m-RNA and verna-lization.

Response to the Application of Plant Growth Regulators and Nutrients

Pulses (chickpea) like other crops, respond to exogenously applied inputs, including PGRs and mineral nutrients. In this concern, Jain *et al*. (1999) conducted a field experiment at Gwalior (MP), studied the effect of four levels of P at 0, 30, 45 and 60 kg P_2O_5/ha (0, 13.09, 19.64 and 26.19 kg P/ha) in the presence of 20 kg N + 20 kg potassium oxide (K_2O)/ha, i.e. 16.60 kg K/ha on the performance of chickpea cultivar JG-315. It is observed that each successive increase in P levels from 0 to 26.19 kg P/ha enhanced the number of nodules per plant, plant height, number of pods per plant, seed yield per plant, test weight and protein content. Guhey *et al*. (2000) undertaken a field trial at Jabalpur (MP), studied the effect of five levels of P at 0, 20, 40, 60 and 80 kg P_2O_5 (0, 8.74, 17.48, 26.22 and 34.96 kg P)/ha on protein content of chickpea cultivar JG-315.

Seed protein content is found to be improved with increasing levels of P. Iqbal *et al.*, (2001) performed a pot experiment at Faisalabad (Pakistan), studied the effect of foliar application of GA on the growth performance of two cultivars of chickpea, *viz.* C 727 and CM 72. They sprayed 10 and 20 mg GA/L at vegetative or flower initiation stage. They also included a no spray control. Foliar application of 20 mg GA/L at flowering stage proved best for plant height, root dry weight and shoot fresh and dry weight. Foliar treatments do not affect length and fresh weight of root. However, spray of GA decreased number of branches per plant. Cultivars do not differ with regard to root length. There is no mention of cultivar differences in respect of other parameters. Upadhyay (2002) undertaken a field experiment at Berthin (HP), reported the effect of foliar spray of naphthalene acetic acid (NAA), GA and Kn each at 10, 20 and 30 PPM on the performance of chickpea cultivar H 208 grown with a uniform dose of 20 kg N + 40 kg P_2O_5 + 40 kg K_2O/ha (20 kg N + 17.46 kg P + 33.19 kg K/ha). A no spray control is also included in the scheme of treatments. Among various treatments, NAA at 20 PPM gave the maximum value for buds per plant, number of flowers per plant, length of pod, circumference of pod, number of grains per pod, number of pods per plant, biological yield, test weight and grain yield of chickpea, however, NAA at 30 PPM showed early flowering and early maturity of crops. On the other hand, spray of 20 PPM Kn registered the maximum chlorophyll content with increasing levels of Kn delaying flowering and maturity of crop progressively. Kumar *et al.* (2003) performed a field experiment at Jobner (Rajasthan), studied the effect of four basal levels of S (0, 20, 40 and 60 kg S/ha) and four PGRs (water spray, 20 PPM NAA, 50 PPM cycocel (CCC) and 50 PPM maleic hydroxide) applied as foliar sprays twice, alone or in combination on yield and quality

of chickpea (cultivar not mentioned) grown with a uniform basal dose of 20 kg N + 40 kg P_2O_5 (17.46 kg P/ha). Application of S particularly at 60 kg S/ha enhanced grain yield, straw yield, protein content in grain and S content in straw and grains. Spray of maleic hydrazide followed by NAA proved best.

Inorganic Plant Mineral Nutrition

Low availability of plant nutrients limits yield in many crops. Inorganic ions obtained from the soil having specific and essential functions in plants are called mineral nutrients and their absorption, translocation and metabolism refer to as mineral nutrition. The contribution of plant nutrition as a science bloomed in the 20th century. In due course of time, the essentiality of using seven other elements, *viz.* boran (B), chlorine (Cl), copper (Cu), manganese (Mn), molybdenum (Mo), nickel (Ni) and zinc (Zn), has been established on the basis of sophisticated analytical techniques to purify salts and the water for hydrophonic cultures (Salisbury and Ross, 1992; Marschner, 2002). Among these, S represents the 9th and least abundant essential macroelements in plants, preceded by C, O, H, N, K, Ca, Mg and P. The dry matter of S in plants is only about 1/15th of that of N. Moreover, S plays critical roles in the catalytic or electrochemical fractions of the biomolecules in cells and also as signalling molecules for fundamental cellular functions (Matsubayashi *et al.*, 2002).

S is one of the essential nutrients and it contributes to yield and quality of crops. S occurs in a wide variety of organic and inorganic combinations. S is present in nature in both inorganic and organic forms. S is cycled in ecosystem in nature where conversion of sulphate to organic S compounds is primarily dependent on sulphate uptake and reduction pathways in photosynthetic organisms and microorganisms. The transfer of S between the organic and inorganic pools is entirely caused by the activity of the soil biota, particularly the soil microbial biomass, which has the greatest potential for both mineralization and also for subsequent transformation of the oxidation state of S. S oxidation is the most important step of S cycle, which improves soil fertility. It results in the formation of sulphate, which can be used by the plants, while the acidity produced by oxidation helps to solubilize plant nutrients and improves alkali soils. In addition, S is required at 0.1 to 1.0 (on a dry weight basis) for growth and development. S is mainly taken up by lands via the roots from the soil and translocated symplastically through endodermal cells to the stele for distribution to the various plant tissues (Khan and Mazid, 2011). Plant canopies are a strong sink for deposition of atmospheric sulphur dioxide, which enters mainly through the stomatal apertures (Khan *et al.*, 2011).

On the other hand, S is a part of every living cell and is a constituent of two of the 21 amino acids which form proteins. The benefits from S fertilization of crops can be traced to its role in protein development, to improvement of N use, etc. However, in recent years, S deficiency has become an increasing problem for agriculture resulting in decreased crops quality parameters and yield. Although, the availability of S needed for profitable crop production continues to decline. Reasons for the decline include the emphasis on improved air quality, the increasing amount of S removed from the soil by higher yielding crops and use of modern fertilizers containing less S. Up to 90% of the total S is present in most plants as cysteine and methionine that, in turn, are predominantly bound in protein. Because methionine is one of the ten amino acids essential for animal nutrition, there has been sustained interest increasing the concentration of methionine in plant material used for feed and food. Most reported attempts to increase seed S amino acid concentration by adding S-rich sink protein have methionine with success, but some of

these modified seeds have been reported to display alterations in endogenous protein composition similar to those triggered by S nutritional deficiency. Reduced S is required in the function of cofactors, such as acetyl coenzyme A, thiamine, biotin and lipoic acid. The S containing tripeptide glutathione is involved in the regulation of protein synthesis, and in the compensation of various forms of stress. Both functions of glutathione are highly significant for the survival of plants in a stressful environment. Moreover, S containing plant secondary compounds, like allicin and isothiocyanate derivatives can be important for phytomedical applications. There are many S-containing compounds, which have been limited, directly or indirectly, with the defence of plants against microbial pathogens; these include thionins, defensins glucosinolates, crucifer phytoalexins, alliin and glutathione (Hell *et al.*, 2002).

Appropriate applications of fertilizers can remedy deficiencies in many instances; however, they remain considerable uncertainties regarding timing and type of S-application which, in turn, influence the persistence of the S in the soil and the availability to the plant. A common situation is one in which there is a substantial seasonal variation in S available to the plant and ideally, crops will be engineered to maximize uptake when S is abundant and, therefore, be better able to tolerate periods of low-S availability. Modern agriculture requires adequate fertilization of S to achieve maximum crop yield and performances. Plants use sulphate, the oxidized form of S existing in the soil, as an S source. By contrast, animals including humans require S-containing amino acids and proteins as dietary S sources because of their inability to assimilate sulphate into Cys and Met. Significance of plant sulphate assimilatory pathway is manifested by its ability to fill this metabolic gap in the global S cycle in nature.

In addition to its basic nutritional importance, S is present in numbers of plant metabolites representing important biological activities as redox controller, vitamins, co-enzymes, flavones and defence chemicals and other secondary metabolites. S is probably the best-described nutrient with respect to correlated behaviour of metabolites and transcripts during the deficiency responses. S is necessary for proper growth and development of living organisms; however, it is attributed rather catalytic and regulatory than structural functions because it is much less abundant than other macroelements. The plant biomass as consumed as food and feed serves as the main sources of organic S for animals and humans (Hawkesford, 2003).

Interaction Effect on Growth and Yield Characteristics

Leaf area and other growth parameters are influenced by different growth regulators in pulse crops. The PGRs have greater influence on plants which showed comparable values of LAI (leaf area index), LAD (leaf area dry matter), CGR (crop growth rate), NAR (nitrate assimilation rate) and TDM over control plants. LAI, CGR, NAR and AGDM (average ground dry matter) have a significant linear relationship with seed yield. Kumar *et al.* (2003) studied the effect of S and PGRs on yield and quality parameters of chickpea and reported improved grain, straw yield, and protein content. The application of PGRs to pollinated buds once and twice daily increased bud retention many folds. Percent bud retention is significantly higher when the growth regulators are applied twice. Moreover, triacontanol singly or with potassium nitrate enhances pod setting, 100-seed weight, biomass, harvest index and seed yield at harvest as well as reduces flower abortion in chickpea. Nellima *et al.* (2006) reported that all the yield contributing parameters including flower retention, pod setting percentage, pod number and seed weight, increased by application of GA_3 and cycocel treatments.

Foliar application of GA_3 (10 ppm), NAA (20 ppm) cycocel (25 ppm) recorded the significant increase in the plant height, number of primary and secondary branches per plant, chlorophyll a and b, total chlorophyll content, seed protein content, number of pods per plant, seeds per plant, 100-grain weight, grain yield per plant per hectare and harvest index.

Increase in number of flowers per plant, percentage of pod set per plant, number of pods per plant, number of seeds per plant pods, 100-seed weight, seed-yield and productivity of chickpea cv. Avrodhi is reported by application of TIBA, AlAR triacontanol, IAA, cytokinin and NAA. The combined application of 50 kg P_2O_5 plus 20 kg/ha with FYM and PGR particularly triacontanol raised grain productivity grain protein, protein yield. Moreover, kinetin is found to be most effective in increasing growth parameters (*viz.* root/shoot biomass, growth yield) and N-fixation (*viz.* specific nitrogenase activity of nodules, and total N-fixed per plant) of chickpea. The kinetin seed soaking with (10^{-5} M) and ABA foliar spray (10^{-6} M) are more effective in increasing the grain weight as compared to control. The foliar application of PGRs increased the seeds yield components i.e. number of seeds per plant, number of pods per plant, and 100-grain weight. Besides this, Tripathi *et al.* (2003) studied the effect of PGRs on chickpea cv. Avorodhi reported that dry matter production, protein and starch content are highest with the 20 ppm TIBA, 5 ppm cytokinin and 50 ppm IAA treated respectively.

Moreover, Raut and Sabale (2003) studied the effect of fertilizers and PGRs under irrigated conditions and revealed that they increased plant height, branch number, dry matter, grain weight per plant, harvest index and grain and stover yields increased with increasing fertilizer rate. In this trend, other PGRs (CCC, paclobutrazol) and antitranspirants (calcium carbonate, kaolin and china clay) are found to be effective for enhancing the growth of chickpea cv. Phule G-5 when this sprayed during the flowering and days after the initial flowering and among PGRs CCC gave the highest number of pods per plant and grain yields and are either as effective as or less effective than the control plants. Namdeo *et al.* (2001) first reported that foliar application of 250 ml triacontanol produced the highest growth and yield components with an increase in grain yield compared to the control plants of chickpea cv. Secondly, foliar spray of 0.5 mg dm^{-3} TRIA significantly promoted the plant height, fresh mass and also stimulated the onset of flowering, pod production and retention, but less number of pods and seeds per plant. As next evidence, Fatima *et al.* (2008) compared the effect of three PGRs (kinetin, IAA and ABA) at single or integrated form on growth and yield parameters and N-fixation of chickpea under natural conditions and reported that kinetin found to be most effective in increasing growth parameters (*viz.* root/shoot length biomass, grain yield) and N-fixation (*viz.* specific nitrogenase activity of nodules and total N-fixed per plant.

Moreover, ABA significantly decreased nodule weight, nitrogenase activity of nodule, specific nitrogenase activity of nodules and total N-fixed per plant. LA, LAI, CGR, NAR and AGDM accumulation found to be enhanced with application of PGRs (potassium naphthenate (Knap) and naphthalene acetate acid (NAA) as foliar spray. The application of GA$_3$ at vegetative stage of chickpea cv. C727 showed more reduction than at flower initiation stage while length and fresh weight of root remained unaffected. The cumulative effects of PGRs included reduction of soil salinity and improvement of soil fertility and increase in chickpea cv. Chaffa yield.

Meena *et al.* (2005) applied 40 kg S/ha and 5 kg Zn/ha and reported the significant increase in growth, yield, protein content,

nutrient content and nutrient uptake. Patil *et al.* (2011) studied the effect of organic manures and rock phosphate on growth and yield of chickpea and significantly higher grain yield is recorded with rock phosphate application of 200 kg/ha (2140 kg/ha) over 50 kg and 1000 kg of rock phosphate/ha except rock phosphate 150 kg/ha (2069 kg/ha). Increase in N uptake due to S application has been reported by Scherer *et al.* (2006). S can readily alter primary and lateral root growth, modifying the overall root architecture. Increased N uptake may also be argued that increased S availability resulted in better root and shoot growth and ultimately increased N uptake due to increased dry matter production. Application of 50 ppm mepiquat chloride, 1.25 ppm triacontanol, 0.2% borax and 1% potassium nitrate resulted in the height flowers setting, 100-seed weight, biomass at harvest, seed yield and harvest index and lowest number of aborted flowers.

Furthermore, GA treatment is useful to increase shoot length, mobilization efficiency, emergence index, speed of germination and co-efficiency of germination while oxygenated peptone showed an upper hand in root length, shoot/root ratio, biomass and vigour index. Application of S with or without P recorded significantly higher seed yield showed significantly higher seed yield than saline in chickpea cv. BG-209 on application of P and S (0, 40 and 80 kg/ha) and P (40 kg S + 40 kg P$_2$O$_5$ and 80 kg S + 40 kg P$_2$O$_5$/ha). Sher *et al.* (2004) reported that 40 kg S/ha resulted in better growth, yield attributes, consumptive use, water use efficiency and S uptake than no S and 20 kg S/ha.

Synergistic Effect of PGRs and Sulphur on Physiological Characteristics

a. Chlorophyll: Chlorophyll content of plants is observed to be invariably influenced with the application of growth substances and supplementation of minerals. Tripathi *et al.*

(2003) reported that chlorophyll content is highest in chickpea cv. Avoradhi, with 20 ppm TIBA treatment at present and past anthesis respectively among the treatment including ALAR (dominozide), Miraculam, GA_3, NAO and Plaofix, cytokinin, triacontanol and CCC (chlormequat). The chlorophyll content of the leaf is influenced by optimum dose of S nutrition and it significantly increased in case of soyabean leaves (Gameshamurthy and Reedy, 2000) but at higher rate applied S does not further increase the chlorophyll content of leaves and significantly reduced. Chlorosis is a common symptom of S deficiency in plant species. Circumstantial evidences indicate that S-deficiency greatly diminishes carbon-fixation of *Medicago sativa*, which is assumed to be caused by the reduction in the synthesis of key carbon metabolic enzymes as a result of reduction in the pods of the free S-containing amino acids. The Chl content is reduced because of a general reduction of PSII and PSI and the associated light-harvesting antenna. The Rubisco content is also significantly reduced in the S-deprived plants. The imbalances between PSII and PSI, and between photosynthesis and carbon fixation led to a general over-reduction of the photosynthetic electron carriers. Moreover, chromatographic analysis showed that the level of monosaccharides is lower and starch content is higher in the S-deprived plants. While no change in metabolite levels is found in the TCA or Calvin cycle, Hajouj *et al.*, (2000) reported the CK delay of the initiation of leaf senescence and bring about the promotion of photosynthetic activity mainly by increasing the chlorophyll content. Moreover, Chaloupkova and Smart (1994) reported the application of ABA significantly decreased chlorophyll content. ABA application enhances senescence more in old leaves as reported by, whereas young leaves are less affected by ABA.

Moreover, result of Karim and Fattah (2007) indicated that 1500 ppm potassium naphthenate spray on chickpea plants at first flowering stage (45 days) could be positively effective for growth and development of plants with higher values of physiological characteristics.

b. **Photosynthesis:** Under the condition of effect of S limitation, the pulse crops showed reduced growth and photosynthetic rates. S^{2-} a major form of sulphate in aqueous phase of apoplast, may reduce photosynthetic rate and thereby crop yield through inducing ROS, involved in S^{2-}-induced stress. A decrease in the yield of some crops due to decreased atmospheric S input has been reported for northern Europe. General responses to S limitation are reduced growth and photosynthesis, and strong reduction in photosynthesis under S-limited growth correlates with a substantial decline of Rubisco and chlorophyll a/b binding protein. According to Sexton *et al.*, (1997), S deficiency at first influences the protein synthesis and later on photosynthesis. The photosynthetic apparatus is severely affected under S deficiency. However, as with N deficiency under S deficiency, shoot growth is more depressed than root growth.

Moreover, a strong inhibition of shoot growth but continuation of root growth under nutrient deficiency might mainly reflect alteration in photosynthate allocation. Grewal *et al.* (1992) observed indirect evidence of improved photosynthetic activities in chickpea by enhancing chlorophyll content and retaining higher LAI with N (50 and 100 kg/ha), spray of CCC (250 and 500 ppm) and ethrel (500 ppm). The kinetin application maximizes the shoot/root weight which could be attributed to CK regulation of photosynthetic capacity due to kinetin treatment is related with increase in total biomass due to kinetin treatment is related with increase in photosynthetic activity. Cares and Vendrig (1986) reported that application of CKs promotes photosynthetic activity mainly by means of increase in leaf chlorophyll content. Hardy and Havelk (1975) and Bethlenfalvay and Phillips (1978) reported the pivotal role of photosynthesis in N-fixation.

c. **Protein content:** It is assumed that yield depression under S deficiency conditions is the result of a limiting protein synthesis. Protein content of chickpea seeds is observed to be invariably influenced with the application of growth substances and supplementation of nutrients. Gupta *et al.* (2007) reported the favourable effect of PGRs on the protein content in chickpea also. Kumar *et al.* (2003) suggested the cumulative effects of PGRs plus S on increasing content of protein in chickpea also as reported by Yadav and Bharud (2006) through combined foliar application of GA_3, NAA and cycoel, benzyladenine, biforce and biopower. In addition, foliar applications of SA and brassinolide also have enhancing effect on protein content of chickpea seeds cv. GG1. Increase in protein and sugars content of leaves related with the increase in nodule activity at the flowering and early pod filling stages, thereafter, degradation of chlorophyll and protein contents become more pronoununced in old leaves as compared to young leaves. Single super phosphate, gypsum and elemental S provide S nutrition during seed development in chickpea cultivars (PBG1 and BG 1053), and Jyoti *et al.*, (2007) also reported the significant increase in the biomass content, seed-S containing amino acids as well as several biochemical parameters responsible for enhancement seed protein quality.

S is a constituent of Met (21%), the first amino acid incorporated during protein synthesis and it also linked to proper functioning of NR, the enzyme regulating the flow of NO_3-N into the amino acid and subsequently into protein (Mazid *et al.*, 2012a). Moreover, arginine response to S deficiency used as an indicator in field conditions. With S deficiency, amino acids accumulate and protein cannot be synthesized which may inhibit N-fixation. S increased nitrogenase activity because of higher ferredoxin and ATP concentration in bacteroid of root nodules of legumes. However, under condition of reduced S supply, arginine contributed 23 and 36% of total free amino acids at 0.125 and 0.075 mM S respectively. The potential of using biochemical indicator such as arginine response to S deficiency prior to changes in growth for the prediction of S deficiency in a large number of crops needs further research. If arginine responds early enough, its use as an S deficiency indicator will be greatly enhanced.

Moreover, Wollaston (1997) suggested that proteins content in leaves can be rapidly degraded according to the need by other plant tissue. Kinetin may recover the decline of protein during senescence. It is proposed that kinetin might have been implicated directly in the process of regulating protein transcription and translation (Brinegar, 1994). S application increased rate of potassium due to an increment in protein synthesis and maintenance of high chlorophyll content. Similarly, results of increased seed yield due to application of S are found by Raina and Tanawade (2005). Besides this, application of S also improves the status of S-containing amino acids in the seed protein of chickpea because seeds have some capacity to increase their rate of S assimilation and S amino acids biosynthesis in response to an added demand.

Furthermore, evaluation of amino acid profile under S-starvation conditions showed two-to-four fold enhancement in the contents of arginine, asparagine and OAS, whereas the contents of Cys and Met are reduced heavily. Exogenous supply of metabolites (arginine, asparagine, Cys, glutamine, OAS and Met) also affected the uptake and assimilation of NO_3^{2-}, with a maximum for OAS. Therefore, this tight interconnection of S-nutrition with NO_3^{2-} assimilation and that OAS plays a major role in this regulation and must be helpful in developing a nutrient-management technology for optimization of crop productivity in future. Moreover, S deficiency resulted in lower N concentration of nodules. Furthermore, the decrease in N concentration under S deficiency implies a parallel decrease in N fixation, which may be indicative of an S limitation on protein synthesis.

d. **Carbohydrate content:** Carbohydrate content of chickpea seeds is observed to be invariably influenced with the application of growth substances and supplementation of S-fertilizer. GA_3, kinetin and IAA are found to be highly effective PGR for carbohydrate metabolism in chickpea. Kaur et al. (2005) reported that amylase activity in cotyledons decreased by drought stress but increased by GA_3 and kinetin after sowing while IAA reduced root amylase activity and neither GA_3 or nor kinetin increased the amylase activity of roots. The higher level of reducing sugars in the shoot of GA_3 and kinetin-treated stressed seedlings could be due to the high activity of sugar phosphatase synthase (SPS) in shoot tissue. Moreover, reducing the acid and alkaline invertase activity in shoots of stressed seedlings is enhanced by GA_3 and kinetin.

It may be assumed that photosynthate translocation to root and nodules may also become a limiting factor in N fixation of S-starved leguminous plants. N fixation is a quite sensitive process to supply of

photosynthetic assimilates (Scherer et al., 2001), and the decline in nodule activity is associated with the development of the pods as a competing assimilate sink, since the decline in nodule activity coincided with the tip when pod growth rate first exceeded total CGR. Modification of soil with glucose, arabinose, sucrose and xylose has increased the rhizobium population significantly compared to unmodified soil. The high demand of available carbohydrates for N fixation under optimum conditions is reflected in the amounts of glucose and sucrose in the nodules provided by the shoots. After the transport of carbohydrates in the nodules, they are metabolized to form organic acids to covert the energy demand of nitrogenase (Scherer et al., 2006).

Moreover, under S-deficient conditions, the amounts of glucose and fructose stayed on the same level, indicating that vegetative and reproductive growth of the plant have preference. Furthermore, the observations of Scherer et al. (2006) also observed that under S deficiency conditions, S and N concentration as well as the amounts of glucose and sucrose in shoots and nodules are significantly reduced. Increased accumulation of carbohydrates observed under S deficiency stress. Kinetin treatment significantly increased the sugar content of leaves at all stages more so at late pod fully stage. The effect of kinetin is greater in old leaves as compared to young leaves. The decrease in sugar content in kinetin treatment at flowering stage is greater in the old leaves as compared to the young leaves. Furthermore, Erwin (1996) reported the CK balances the disproportionate distribution of assimilates in favour of the CK-enriched shoot.

Nitrate Reductase Activity and NO_3 Content

Grain legumes can benefit cereal production systems through enhanced soil N-fertility associated with N fixation. The origin of nitrate is contentious. Unkovich and Pate (2000) suggested that the nitrate most likely originates from mineralized rhizodeposits, legume roots and nodules. N fixing legumes use less soil nitrate than an adjacent non-N-fixing crop resulting in nitrate concentration or sparing. ATP sulphurylase, is the first enzyme of the S assimilation pathway and NR plays a key regulatory role in the NO_3^{2-} assimilation, is to be exploited that the activities of these enzymes are related to root, growth and yield. Chlorophyll content, ATP sulphurylase activity and protein content are also higher in transgenic plants than untransformed plants under S-insufficient conditions (Abdin *et al.*, 2011). In general, high concentration of Cys and GSH represses S assimilation activities, while S starvation results in increased activities of key enzymes in the assimilatory pathway. Administration of high concentration of Cys and GSH to plant's roots leads to lowered steady state levels of mRNAs for the ATP sulphurylase and APS reductasee. Plant's root subjected to exogenous OAS exhibit an increase in accumulation of mRNA encoding the APS reductase. Moreover, deficiency of S in plants results in a reduction of NR activity and an accumulation of amino acids or soluble protein in chickpea seedlings of non-nodulating genotypes than nodulating genotypes and these results hint to a genetic variability of NR activity. Earlier, it is reported that NR is genetically controlled. However, the reduction of NR activity and mRNA level seem to be a relatively late process in plant adaptation to S limiting conditions.

Moreover, N-metabolism is strongly affected by the S-status of the plant. S-deficiency decreases the concentration of N in the shoot of legumes. NO_3^{2-} dramatically increased in S limited cells, probably as a consequence of the lowered activity of NR. For higher plants, it has been suggested that the downregulation of NR is mediated by products of N-accumulation like Gln, Asn and Arg. Furthermore, it has been reported that the NR is extremely susceptible to ammonium rather than to its metabolic products. The increased accumulation of NO_3^{2-} may be correlated with a reduced synthesis of soluble protein due to the reduced availability of SO_4^{2-}.

Carbonic Anhydrase Activity, Leghaemoglobin Content and Nodule Formation

Since under S-deficiency conditions, plant growth reduced the demand for N is lower too, and as a result in the decrease in nodule formation (Scherer and Lange, 1996) may be viewed as an adjustment to a low demand for symbiotically fixed N. The lower nodule yield is not only the results of smaller and fewer nodules per unit length of roots but also of a reduced root growth (Scherer *et al.* 2008). Independent of the S supply, Scherer *et al.* (2006) observed the highest S concentrations in root nodules. According to Zhao *et al.*, (1999), the high S concentrations in nodules as compared to roots and especially to shoots probably reflect the high S demand for the functioning of nodules. Nodules, therefore, provide a strong sink for S. On the other hand, ferredoxins are acidic, low molecular weight, soluble Fe-S proteins. In most instances, the Fe is bound via, SH–groups of cysteine residues and also to inorganic S in Fe-S clusters.

The main role of the Fe cluster is to facilitate electron transfer. Root nodule bacteria require access to adequate concentrations of S in their symbiotic relationship with legumes and S deprivation may bias N fixation by affecting nodule development and function (Scherer *et al.*, 2006). While, it is well-established that nitrogenase activity is reduced under S deficiency conditions while Scherer *et al.* (2008) found no report on the influence of S nutrition of legumes on the energy supply of nodules as well as their ferredoxin concentration. Jain *et al.* (2008) studied the effect of

PGRs (IAA, GA$_3$ and kinetin) on haemoglobin biosynthesis in chickpea nodules and observed that almost all growth regulators showed a general promotory effect on its biosynthesis of haemoglobin. Kinetin being a growth-promoting hormone increased the nitrogenase activity of root nodules of chickpea and by increasing in the volume of pink bacteroid tissue, it also increased in leghaemoglobin contents and nodule bacteroid regions over control. Kinetin caused increase in leg-haemoglobin content and nodule bacteroid region over the control. N fixation is drastically reduced in S-deficient plants as a consequence of a low nodule development, but also due to low nitrogenase and leghaemoglobin pro-duction (Scherer *et al.* 2008).

Interaction Effect on N-fixation and Nutrient Use Efficiency (NUE)

The process of S acquisition and assimilation plays an integral role in plant metabolism and response to S-deficiency involves a large number of plant constituents. The results of Iacuzzo *et al.* (2011) showed that an increase in S availability enhanced nitrate (NO$_3$) uptake and assimilation, which in turn, increased biomass production of leaves with lower NO$_3$ content. In particular, high S availability exerted a positive effect (gene expression and functionality) on the uptake and metabolism of N and Fe acquisition mechanisms and their data show close interactions between N, S and Fe, highlighting that relevant improvements in yield and quality from soilless culture might also be obtained through appropriate adjust-ments of nutrient availability. In this respect, concerning the role of S in the acquisition mechanisms of N and Fe metabolism, its level of availability should be taken into high consideration for equilibrated plant growth.

S-deficiency in legume crops affects yield, quality and nutritional value of seeds, because Met is usually the most limiting essential amino acid in pulse seeds. In chickpea, S application (80 kg/ha) increases seed yield. Application of S containing fertilizers can result in soil acidification which may influence nutrient uptake. The yield response to optimum S application, however, differs among the various crop species, being lower in *Medicago sativa* and *Pisum sativum* as compared to *Trifolium pratense* and *Vicia fava*, suggesting that legumes differ in their S-requirement. Moreover, adverse effect of S-deficiency on inorganic nutrition and biochemical processes might lead to the observed decrease in growth and finally may result in a decrease yield of chickpea. Since, the yield and quality of legume seeds are limited by the amount of S partitioned to the seeds. Moreover, the amino acid S-methylMet (SMM), a Met derivative and a long-distance transport form of reduced S and whether SMM phloem loading and source-sink translocation are important for the metabolism and growth of pea plants. The changes in SMM phloem loading affected plant growth and seed number, leading to an overall increase in seed S, N and protein content. The phloem loading and source-sink partitioning of SMM are important for plant S and N metabolism and transport as well as seed set.

Symbiotic N fixation impaired under S-deficiency conditions and calculated N fixation assuming that all N applied at planting are taken up completely under S-deficiency conditions. S-deficiency may affect N fixation of legumes by causing unfavourable conditions for N fixation in the host or because of the relatively high S content of nitrogenase, and of ferredoxin (Fukuyama, 2004). The chief role of the Fe-S cluster of ferredoxin is to facilitate electron transfer and, therefore, ferredoxin plays a vital role in N fixation. A relationship between ferredoxin concentration and nitrogenase activity shown by Carter *et al.* (1980). Scherer *et al.* (2008) also investigated that the ferredoxin concentration of the bacteroids is significantly reduced under S deficiency conditions.

Varin *et al.* (2010) examined whether the effect of SO_4^{2-} addition on N fixation resulted from a stimulation of host plant growth, a specific effect of S on nodulation, or a specific effect of S on nodule metabolism. The application of SO_4^{2-} increased whole plant dry mass, root length, and nodule biomass, expressed on a root-length basis. Nevertheless, N uptake proved less sensitive than N fixation to the effects of S-deficiency, and decreased as a consequence of the lower root length observed in S-deficient plants. This effect is likely to be due to downregulation by a N-feedback mechanism as under severe S-deficiency, the high concentration of whole plant N and the accumulation of N-rich amino acids indicated that the assimilation of N exceeded the amount required for plant growth. As compared to subterranean clover supplied with S nodulation is markedly decreased in S-deficient clover. This is attributed to the decline in the requirement for N with reduced S supply. However, the observed increase in the number of nodules by S-fertilization of legumes is not the result of increased nodulation per unit length of roots, but rather due to enhanced root growth (Scherer and Lang, 1996).

Moreover, S is a bioelement; its superimposition increases the easy available carbon content of the soil because of a surge in the immobilization-mineralizatiom activity. Thus the environment created is found favourable for rhizobium activity. Hence the number of nodules and their activity increased following the application of S. Although the dry weight content of the nodules at higher level of applied S showed a tendency to increase, but it is not significant beyond 20 kg S ha^{-1}. A response to applied S is observed to 20 kg S ha^{-1} with respect to dry matter production but up to 40 kg S ha^{-1} with respect to seed yield.

Moreover, the dry weight content of the nodules at higher levels of applied S showed a tendency to increase also. Moreover, pulse crop obtain N mainly from symbiotic N-fixation which may be affected by S deprivation, and it is quite sensitive to supply of photosynthetic assimilates which indicate that decline in nodule activity under S deprivation is associated with development of pods. Nitrogenase and ferredoxin which play vital roles in N_2-fixation are rich in S and contain Fe-S clusters. Furthermore, with S-deficiency, amino acids and other N forms accumulate due to the impaired protein synthesis. This could be due to the feedback repression of N-fixation (Scherer *et al.* 2006). Meanwhile, Lang (1998) suggested that S affects leguminous species through its influence on N-fixation by rhizobium species. If symbiotic N-fixation has a greater requirement for a nutrient than the growth of host plants, a negative interaction between the addition of that nutrient and inorganic N on plant growth is expected.

Gupta *et al.* (2007) investigated the effect of growth regulators on the nutrient uptake and protein yield of chickpea cv. JG-74. Moreover, they also reported that application of cytokinin showed higher contents of N, P and K in seed compared to all the other treatments. The maximum N, P and K uptakes are observed in chickpea treated with CK, a multifaceted plant hormone (Mazid *et al.* 2011a). Chaurasia and Chaurasia (2008) studied the effect of fertility levels and PGRs on nutrient contents and uptake in chickpea cv. JG-322 and reported that the increasing levels of fertilizers up to P50S20 with FYM increased the contents and uptake of N, P, K and S almost significantly. Triacontanol (vipul) brought about the maximum uptake of NPK and S. Deo and Khaldelwal (2009) studied the S interaction with P and indicated that grain and straw yield; content of N, P and S; uptake of P and S increased with increase in the rate of application of P and S individually as well as in various combinations. Applied S increased the number of nodules per plant and protein contents in grain of chickpea. Also, Meena *et* al. (2005) reported that application of all levels of S and Zn progressively increased in grain yield, protein content, nutrient content and uptake by chickpea. S has become a major limiting factor for plant production in industrial as well as in remote industrial rural areas. Limitation of S can reduce legume N fixation by affecting nodule development and function. The effects of S-deficiency on N fixation are likely to be caused by the shortage of ferredoxin and ATP. There is a little concern for S-deficiency even though the ability of the soil to retain and release it to crops is small. However, since the last two decades, the declining use of high-analysis low-S containing fertilizers and the reduction of SO_2 emission from industrial sources are resulting in S-deficiency of different crops.

Interaction Effect on Quality Parameters

S-deficient plants generate a lower yield and have a reduced nutritional value (Lunde et al., 2008). S is considered as important nutrient for its role in the production of amino acids Cys and Met as well as antioxidant GSH (glutathione). Reproductive growth and the proportion of the reproductive tissues in total dry matter are significantly increased by the application of S during pod development. Increase in dry weight with reduced S input can be described by the Piper-Steen-bjerg effect. Positive effect of S on seed yield and its quality is visible and significant when S content in soil is low. Analogically, S fertilization does not influence the yield when S content in soil is quite high. S-supply only increases the S-concentration of the plants without enhancing the yield. Mandavia et al. (2006) reported a yield enhancement of methionine and carbohydrate content in chickpea seed cv. GG1 as well as quality improvement in chickpea seeds in terms of increased content of metabolite studied compared with higher seed yield pointout

to the beneficial effect of salicylic acid at vegetative as well as reproductive stages. GA_3 led to comparatively more synthesis of nucleic acid while oxygenated peptone showed more increase in total carbohydrate and soluble protein contents in chickpea.

Interaction Effect on Nodule Characteristics

Under S limiting conditions, in pot experiments with different legumes, a lower N accumulation and a yield reduction are found (Scherer and Lange, 1996). S also affects leguminous plant species growth through its effect upon N-fixation by rhizobium microorganisms because of the relatively high S content of nitrogenase and ferredoxin. S is an essential macronutrient and at an optimum concentration accelerates the plant growth. Lawn and Brun (1974) indicated that decline in nodule activity coincided with the time when pod growth rate first exceeded total crop growth rate. Moreover, S has profound effect on creating assimilation area absorbing PAR (photosynthetically active radiation) and as a consequence on yield of crops (Scherer, 2001). Also, Scherer et al. (2006) assumed that reduced amount of available photosynthate with suboptimal S-supply could become limiting to energy production and as a carbon skeleton for ammonia assimilation and, therefore, cause a lower N-fixation and the reduced yield formation.

Furthermore, Fatima et al. (2008) reported that both the efficiency and the longevity of nodules seem to be favourably affected by kinetin application. Garg et al. (1995) also observed kinetin induced increase in nodule dry weight as well as in the nitrogenase activity. Research work of Fatima et al. (1998) demonstrated the positive role of CKs in nodulation. The nitrogenase activity of nodules is high at flowering stage as compared to pod filling stage. Singh (1993) observed that PGRs like IAA, NAA and 2,4-D, GA and kinetin used as foliar spray brought considerable variations in nodulation.

Moreover, the ABA seed soaking as well as foliar spray treatments significantly decreased nodule weight, nitrogenase activity of nodules, etc. Kinetin and ABA have profound enhancing effect on leaf and nodule senescence in chickpea cv. CM88. Kinetin at 10^{-8} M is found more effective than kinetin at 10^{-6} M which is responsible for delaying the nodule senescence. Islam and Ali (2009) assessed the effect of S (0, 15 and 39 kg/ha) and P (0, 40 and 80 kg/ha) on nodulation, N-fixation and nutrient uptake by chickpea and reported that application of P and S significantly increased all these parameters as well as yield. P and S uptake correlated positively with N-fixation.

Conclusion and Future Guidelines

A survey of foregoing literature reveals that the cultivars of chickpea perform variably under or even the same agro-climatic conditions. Their response to nutrients and PGRs alone or in combination is variable. The survey also reveals that much work has been done on chickpea cultivars in respect of nutrient application, but meagre information is available regarding the effect of pre-sowing seed treatment with PGRs or foliar spray of PGRs. Moreover, the research work on the foliar application of nutrient(s) alone or in combination with PGRs is also scanty. It is therefore, considered justified to undertake an indepth study on the newly released cultivars of chickpea in respect of the effect of various PGRs and their doses applied partly through seed-soaking and partly through foliar spray under the agro-climatic conditions of the western Uttar Pradesh. Furthermore, the study of effect of foliar application of a small quantity of mineral elements particularly in the presence of PGRs is desirable.

REFERENCES

Abdin MZ, Akmal M, Ram M, Nafis T, Alam P, Nadeem M, Khan MA and Ahmad A (2011). Constitutive expression of high-affinity sulphate transporter (HAST) gene in Indian mustard showed enhanced sulphur uptake and assimilation. *Protoplasma*, **248(3)**: 591–600.

Carter KR, Rawlings J, Orme-Johnson WH, Becker RR and Evan HJ (1980). Purification and characterization of ferredoxin from *Rhizobium japonicum* bacteroids. *Journal of Biological Chemistry*, **255**: 4213–4223.

Chaurasia S and Chaurasia AK (2008). Effect of fertility levels and growth regulators on nutrient contents and uptake of chickpea (*Cicer arietinum* L). *Crop Research*, **3691/3**: 76–80.

Choi YE, Harada E, Wada M, Tsuboi H, Morita Y, Kusano T and Sano H (2001). Detoxification of cadmium in tobacco plants: formation and active excretion of crystals containing cadmium and calcium through trichomes. *Planta*, **213**: 45–50.

Clarke EJ and Wiseman J (2000). Developments in plant breeding for improved nutrition quality of soya beans II. Antinutritional factors. *Journal of Agricultural Science*, **134**: 125–136.

Clarkson DT and Luttge U (1989). Mineral nutrition: Divalent cations, transport and compartmentalization. *Progressive Botany*, **51**: 93–112.

Crawford NM, Kahn ML, Leustek T and Long SR (2000). Nitrogen and sulphur. In: Buchanan BB, Gruissem W, and Jones RL (eds), Biochemistry and Molecular Biology of Plants, Rockville, MD: American Society of Plant Biologists, pp 824–849.

Davies PJ (1995). The Plant hormones. Their nature, occurrence and functions. In: Davies PJ (eds), Plant hormones, physiology, physiology biochemistry and molecular biology, 2nd edition. Dordrecht, Kluwer Academic Publishers, pp 1–12.

Deo C and Khaldelwal RB (2009). Effect of P and S nutrition on yield and quality of chickpea (*Cicerarietinum* L.). *Journal of the Society of soil science*, **57(3)**: 352–356.

Despande SS (1992). Food legumes in human nutrition: A personal perspective. *Reviews in food Science and Nutrition*, **32**: 333–363.

Duke SH and Reisenauer HM (1986). Roles and requirements of sulphur in plant nutrition. In: Tabatabai MA (ed.): Sulphur in agriculture. Agronomy Monograph No. 27, American Society of Agronomy, Madison, Wisconsin, USA, 123–168.

Dutta D and Bandyopadhyay P (2009). Performance of chickpea (*Cicer arietinum* L.) to application of phosphorous and biofertilizer in laterite soil. *Archieves of Agronomy and Soil Science*, **55**: 147–155.

Fatima Z, Bano A and Aslam M (1998). Effect of plant growth regulators and rhizobium inoculum on N_2 fixation and yield of chickpea. Proceeding of the 7th international symposium of Nitrogen Fixation with Non-legume. Kluwer Academic Publisher, pp 103–106, Great Britain.

Fatima Z and Bano A (1998). Effects of seed treatment with growth hormones and rhizobium on the oil contents, nitrogen fixation and yield of soya bean. *Pakistan Journal of Botany*, **30(1)**: 83–86.

Fatima Z, Bano S, Sial R and Aslam M (2008). Response of chickpea to plant growth regulators on nitrogen fixation and yield. *Pakistan Journal of Botany*, **40(5)**: 2005–2013.

Fattah QA and Wort DJ (1970). Effect of light and temperature on stimulation of vegetative and reproductive growth of bean plants by naphthenates. *Agronomy Journal*, **62**: 576–577.

Fukuyama K (2004). Structure and function of plant type ferredoxin. *Photosynthetic Research*, **81**: 291–301.

Ganeshamurthy AN and Reddy KS (2000). Effect of integrated use of farmyard manure and sulphur in a soya bean and wheat cropping system on nodulation/dry matter production and chlorophyll content of soya bean on swell shrink soils in central India. *Journal of Agronomy and Crop science*, **185**: 91–97.

Garg N, Dua IS and Sharma SK (1995). Nitrogen fixation ability and its dependence on the availability of cytokinin in soyabean and chickpea growing under saline conditions. *Plant physiology and Biochemistry, New Delhi*, **22**: 12–16.

Gupta B, Shrivastava GK and Annu V (2007). Response of plant growth regulators on nutrient uptake and protein yield of chickpea under vertisols of Chhattisgarh. *Environment and Ecology*, **25(1)**: 100–102.

Hajouj TR, and Gepstein S (2000). Cloning and characterization of receptor-like protein kinase gene associated with senescence. *Plant Physiology*, **124**: 1305–1314.

Hardy RWF and Havelk UD. (1975). Photosynthate as a major factor limiting N_2 fixation by field grown soya beans. In: Symbiotic nitrogen fixation in plants. Cambridge University Press, pp 421–439, London.

Havlin JL, Beaton JD, Tisdale SL and Nelson WL (2007). Soil fertility and fertilizers, An Introduction to Nutrient Management, 7th edition, Pearson Education Incorporation, pp 221–236, Singapore.

Hawkesford MJ (2003). Transporter gene families in plants: The sulphate transporter gene family: redundancy or specialization? *Physiologia Plantarum*, **117**: 155–163.

Iqbal A, Khalil IA, Nadia A and Khan MS (2006). Nutritional quality of important food legumes. *Food Chemistry*, **97**: 331–335.

Iqbal HF, Tahir MN, I-ul Haq K and Ahmad AN (2001). Response of chickpea (*Cicer arietinum* L.) growth towards the foliar application of gibberellic acid at different growth stages. *Pakistan Journal of Biological Sciences*, **4**: 433–434.

Islam M and Ali S (2009). Effect of integrated application of sulphur and phosphorus on nitrogen fixation and nutrient uptake by chickpea (*Cicer arietinum* L). *Agrociencia*, **43**: 815–826.

Islam MS, Karim MF, Ullah MJ, Fattah QA and Hossain MI (2006). Effect of Knap and NAA on shoot dry matter, yield attributes and yield of lentil (*Lens culinaries*). *Journal of Agriculture and Educational Technology*, **9(1 and 2)**: 55–58.

Jain RK, Jain AK and Gera VK (2008). Effect of growth regulators on leghaemoglobin synthase in chickpea nodules. Legume Research, **31**: 303–305.

Janssen KA and Vitosh ML (1974). Effect of lime, sulphur, and molybdenum on N_2 fixation and yield of dark red kidney beans. *Agronomy Journal*, **56**: 736–740.

Jyoti G, Sital JS and Batta SK (2007). Effect of sulphur nutrition on biochemical parameters in developing chickpea (*Cicerarietinum* L.) seeds. *Indian Journal of Agricultural Biochemistry*, **20(2)**: 59–62.

Karim MF and Fattah QA (2007). Growth analysis of chickpea CV. BAPI Chohla-6 as affected by foliar spray of growth regulators. *Bangladesh Journal of Botany*, **36**: 105–110.

Khan TA and Mazid M (2011). Nutritional significance of sulphur in pulse cropping system. *Biology and Medicine*, **3(2)**: 114–133.

Khan TA, Mazid M and Mohammad F (2011). Sulphur management: An agronomic and transgenic approach. *Journal of Industrial Research and Technology*, **1(2)**: 147–161.

Khan TA, Mazid M and Mohammad F (2012). Climatic change, sustainable agriculture and future needs: A perspective of parallel re-thinking. *Journal of Industrial Research and Technology*, **1**: 1–5.

Kumaravelu G, Livingstone VD and Romanujam MP (2000). Triacontanol-induced changes in the grass, photosynthetic plant, cell metabolites, flowering and yield of green gram. *Biologia Planatarum*, **43**: 287–290.

Lange A (1998). Influence of sulphur supply on N_2-fixation of legumes. [PhD Thesis.] University Bonn, German.

Lunde C, Zygadlo A, Simonsen HT, Nielsen PL, Blennow A and Haldrup A (2008). Sulphur starvation in rice: The effect on photosynthesis, carbohydrate metabolism, and oxidative stress protective pathways. *Physiologia Plantarum*, **134(3)**: 508–521.

Mandavia MK, Karkar C, Mandavia C and Khasiya V (2006). Effect of salicylic acid and brassinolide on yield and quality traits of chickpea seeds. *India Journal of Agricultural Biochemisrty*, **19(1)**: 29–31.

Marschner H (1995). Mineral nutrition of higher plants. Second edition. Academic Press, London, pp 889.

Marschner H (2002). Mineral nutrition of higher plants. 2nd edition. Academic Press, London.

Matsubayashi YM, Ogawa A, Morita Y and Sakagami (2002). An LRR receptor kinase involved in perception of a peptide plant hormone phyto-sulphokine. *Science*, **296**: 1470–1472.

Mazid M, Khan TA and Mohammad F (2011a). Cytokinin: A classical multifaceted hormone in plant systems. *Journal of Stress Physiology and Biochemistry*, **7**: 347–368.

Mazid M, Khan TA and Mohammad F (2012a). Role of NO in H_2O_2 regulating responses against temperature and ultraviolet induced oxidative stress in plants. *Acta Biologica Indica*, **1(1)**: 1–16.

Mazid M, Khan TA and Mohammad F (2012b). Role of nitrate reductase in nitrogen fixation under photosynthetic regulation. *World Journal of Pharmaceutical Research*, **1(1)**: 1–28.

Mazid M, Khan TA and Mohammad F (2012c). Role of nitrate reductase in nitrogen fixation under photosynthetic regulation. *World Journal of Pharmaceutical Research* **1(3)**: 3–28.

Mazid M Khan TA and Mohammad F (2011b). Effect of abiotic stress on synthesis of secondary plant products: A critical review. *Agriculture Reviews*, **32(3)**: 172–182.

Meena SK, Sharma M and Meena HS (2005). Effect of sulphur and zinc fertilization on yield, quality and nutrient content and uptake of chickpea under semi-arid tropics. *Annals of Botany*, **8(2)**: 12–71.

Neelima A, Ranjana R and Kaur J (2006). Alleviation of normal and late sown chickpea (*Cicer arietinum* L.) yield through foliar application of bioregulators. *Environment and Ecology*, **24S** (Special-1): 147–176.

Patil SV, Halikatti SI, Hiremath SM, Babalad HB, Sreenivasa MN, Hebsur NS and Somangouda G (2011). Effect of organic manures and rock phosphate on growth and yield of chickpea (*Cicerarietinum* L.) in vertisols. *Karnataka Journal of Agriculture Science*, **24(5)**: 636–638.

Rao KVM and Sresty TVS (2000). Antioxidative parameters in the seedlings of pigeon pea (*Cajanus cafenis* L Millspaugh) in response to ZnO and Ni stresses. *Plant Science*, **157**: 113–128.

Raut RS and Sabale RN (2003). Studies on the yield maximization of chickpea cv.vijay through fertilizer and growth regulation under irrigated conditions. *Journal of Maharashtra Agricultural Universities*, **28(3):** 311–312.

Rupela OP (1990). A visual rating system for modulation of chickpea. *International Chickpea Newsletter*, **22:** 20–25.

Saito K (2000). Regulation of sulphate transport and synthesis of sulphur containing amino acids. *Current Opinion in Plant Biology*, **3:** 188–195.

Salisbury R and Ross H (1992). Plant Physiology. Fourth edition. Belmont, CA: Wadsworth, Inc.

Saxena KB, Kumar RV and Sultana R (2010). Quality nutrition through pigeonpea—a review. *Health*, **2(11):** 1335–1344.

Scherer HW (2001). Sulphur in crop production-invited paper. *European Journal of Agronomy*, **14:** 81–111.

Scherer HW and Lange A (1996). N_2 fixation and growth of legumes as affected by sulphur fertilization. *Biology and Fertility of Soils*, **23:** 449–453.

MCQs

Q. 1. **In which of the following true statement is/are about Katherine Esau, born in 1898 in Ukraine?**

(1) Reported that early top virus spreads through a plant via phloem

(2) She writes plant Anatomy (1954) and Anatomy of seed Plants (1960)

(3) Sixth women to receive precedent award of National Academy of science and national Medal of Science from Presidential George Bush (1989)

(4) **All are correct statements**

Q. 2. **Which book known as to literally bringing about a revival of the displine-plant anatomy?**

(1) Plant anatomy Dr Katherine Easu

(2) Structural anatomy Dr Fahn

(3) **Anatomy of seed plant Dr Katherine Esau**

(4) Anatomy of flowering plant-Peter Raven

(5) **All are correct statements**

Q. 3. **Which book regarded as Webster's of plant Biology. It is enclopediac?**

(1) Plant anatomy Dr Katherine Easu

(2) Structural Anatomy Dr Fahn

(3) Anatomy of seed plant Dr Katherine Esau

(4) **Anatomy of flowering plant-Peter Raven**

Q. 4. **In which of the following is correctly matched?**

(1) Tap, roots system—Dicot

(2) Fibrous root system—Monocot

(3) Adventitious root system—Grass, monster, Banyan

(4) K Esau—Plant anatomy

(4) **All are correct statements**

Q. 5. **In which of the following true statement is/are?**

(1) Primary root is short-lived and replaced by a large number of roots (monoct), make fibrous root system

(2) Primary root bears lateral roots of several orders that known as secondary tertiary roots make tap roots system (dicot)

(3) Roots arise other parts rather than radical, found in grass monster and banyan tree (mono + dicot)

(4) **All of the above are true**

Q. 6. **In which of the following is a correct match?**

(1) It (a thimble like structure) makes its way through the soil/protect tender apex-Root cap

(2) Cells of this region are very small, thin walled and with dense cytoplasm—Region of meristematic zone

(3) Cells gradually differentiate and mature; undergo rapid elongation and enlargement and responsible for growth of root in length—Region of elongation

(4) Cells from region of maturation, some epidermal cells form very fine, delicate and thread like structure—Root hairs

(5) All are correct statements

Q. 7. In which of the following is/are matched facts as one side (modification of root) and other side is (function for which they modified)?

(1) Support—Banyan

(2) Storage—Turnip, carrot, sweet potato

(3) Respiration—Mangrove (Rhizophora)

(4) Usual function of root—Absorption, conduction of water and minerals

(5) All of the above

Q. 8. Tap roots (dicots) of carrot, turnip and adventitious roots of sweet potato get swollen for:

(1) Respiration

(2) Storage of food

(3) Harbor bacteria

(4) Both 1 and 2

Q. 9. The hanging roots of Banyan to support plants are:

(1) Prop roots

(2) Silt roots

(3) Adventurous roots

(4) Tap roots

Q. 10. Supporting roots of stem of sugarcane and maize coming out from lower nodes of stem called:

(1) Slit roots

(2) Adventurous roots

(3) Tap roots

(4) All of the above

Q. 11. Some plants modify their stems into flatten ended (Opuntia) or flesh cylindrical (euphorbia) structures contain chlorophyll and carry-out photosynthesis. They grow in?

(1) Arid regions

(2) Semi-arid regions

(3) Temperate regions

(4) Tundra regions

Q. 12. Some roots comes out from ground and grow vertically upward in swamp areas for getting O_2 to facilitate respects called:

(1) Pneumatophores

(2) Hydathodes

(3) Stomata

(4) Lenticels

Q. 13. Stem is:

(1) Ascending part of axis being branches leaves flowers and fruits

(2) Develops from plumule of embryo of a germinating seed and bears nodes and internodes and buds

(3) It generally grows when young and later often becomes woody and dark-brown

(4) All of the above

Q. 14. Main function of stem is:

(1) Spreading root branches bearing leaves flowers and fruits

(2) Converts water, minerals and photosynthesis

(3) It performing function of storage of food, support protection and vegetative propagation

(4) All of the above

Q. 15. In which of the following true statement is/are about thorns?

(1) Also, axillary buds produced (modified) woody, straight and pointed structure called thorns

(2) Found in citrus, bougainvillea

(3) Protect plants from browsing animals

(4) **All are correct statements**

Q. 16. **In which of the following true statement is/are about stem tendril?**

(1) They develops from axillary buds

(2) They are slender and spirally coiled

(3) They help plants (guards, like cucumbers, pumpkins, watermelons, grave vines) to climb

(4) **All are correct statements**

Q. 17. **In which of the following is the true statement is/are about underground stem of grass and strawberry?**

(1) **Spread to new reaches and when older parts die new plants are formed**

(2) Very productive

(3) No productive

(4) Moderate productive

Q. 18. **A slender lateral branch arises from the base of main axis and after growing aerially for some time arch downwards to touch the ground. It is true for:**

(1) **Mint and jasmine**

(2) Mango and Citrus

(3) Guava and Lettuce

(4) All are correct statements

Q. 19. **A lateral branch with short internodes and each node bearing a rosette of leaves and a tuft of roots in found in aquatic plants like?**

(1) Pistia

(2) Eichornia

(3) **Both**

(4) Mint

Q. 20. **The lateral branches originate from the basal and underground portion of main stem, grow horizontally beneath the soil and then come out obliquely upward giving rise to leafy shoots. This is concerned with:**

(1) Banana

(2) Pineapple

(3) Chrysanthemum

(4) **All of the above**

Q. 21. **What is true about leaf?**

(1) Lateral, generally flattened structure borne on stem

(2) Develops at the node and bears a bud in its axil

(3) Originate from SAM and arranged in an Acropetal order and most important vegetative organ for photosynthesis

(4) **All of the above**

Q. 22. **Underground stems of potato, ginger, turmeric Zamikand, calocasia modified for:**

(1) Store the food

(2) Act as organ of perennation to tide over unfavourable conditions for growth

(3) **Both 1 and 2**

(4) Reproduction

Q. 23. **True statement is:**

(1) The axillary bud develops into a branch

(2) Typical leaf consists of leaf-base, petiole and lamina

(3) The leaf is attached to stem by leaf base and may bear two lateral small leaf like structure (stipules)

(4) **All of the above are true**

Q. 24. **In monocots, the leaf base expands into a sheath (pulvinus, in case of legumes, dicot) covering the stem:**

(1) Completely

(2) Partially

(3) Not at all

(4) **Both 1 and 2**

Q. 25. Function of petiole is:

(1) Hold the blade to light

(2) Allow leaf blades to flutter in wind

(3) Cooling the leaf and bringing fresh air to leaf surface

(4) All of the above

Q. 26. In which of the following statement is/are true about Lamina (leaf blade)?

(1) It is green expanded part of leaf with veins and vein lets

(2) It usually contains a middle prominent vein (midrib), provide rigidity to leaf blade

(3) Act as channels of transport for water, minerals and food materials

(4) All of the above

Q. 27. In which of the following true statement about venation is/are?

(1) Arrangement of veins and vein lets in lamina of leaf

(2) Reticulate type found in dicot (all) and parallel in monocot (most)

(3) Dicot leaves generally possess reticulate venation while parallel venation is the characters of most monocot

(4) All of the above

Q. 28. In which of the following true statement about types of leaves is/are?

(1) Leaf is simple when lamina is entire or when incised and incisions not touch the mid rib

(2) Leaf is compound when incisions of lamina reach of to midrib breaking it into a number of leaflets

(3) A bud in present in axil of leaflets of compound leaf

(4) All of the above

Q. 29. Matches the correct column (a) position of ovary and (b) Kinds of flowers.

(1) Carpel occupy highest position—Hypogynous flower/superior ovary

(2) Carpel occupy centre—Perigynous/half inferior ovary

(3) Thalamus grow upward enclosing the ovary completely and getting fused with it—Epigynous/inferior ovary

(4) Outer-most whorl of the flower—Calyx

(5) All of the above

Q. 30. In which of the following true statement about compound leaf is/are?

(1) Two types, *viz*. pinnately compound leaf and palmately compound leaf

(2) Number of leaflets are present on a common axis (Rachis) in pinnately compound leaf

(3) In palmately compound leaf, the leaflets are attached at a common point (at tip of petiole), e.g. silk cotton

(4) Rachis represents midrib of the leaf (e.g. Neem)

(5) All are correct statements

Q. 31. In which of the following is a correctly matched between (a) leaf modification and (b) For which function?

(1) Tendril—Climbing

(2) Spines—Defence

(3) Fleshy leaves—Food storage (onion, garlic)

(4) Small and short-lived Australian Acacia

(5) All are true

Q. 32. In which of the following true statement is/are about PHYLLOTAXY?

(1) Arrangement of leaves on stem/branch, *viz*. usually 3 types alternate, opposite and whorled

(2) A single leaf arises at each node in alternate manner (alternate type), e.g. china rose, mustard and sunflower

(3) A pair of leaves arise at each node and lie opposite to each other (opposite type), e.g. calotrophis, guava

(4) If more than two leaves arise at a node and form a whorl (whorled type), e.g. Alistonia

(5) **All are correct statements**

Q. 33. **In which of the following true statement is/are?**

(1) Stamens are mono-delphous (China rose)

(2) Stamens are di-adelphous (Pea)

(3) Stamens are poly-adelphous (Citrus)

(4) **All are correct statements**

Q. 34. **Matches the column A and column-B.**

(1) Flowers can be divided into two equal radial halves in any radial plane passing through centre—actinimorphic/radial (mustard, datura, chilli)

(2) Flower can be divided into two similar halves only in one particular vertical plane—Zygomorphic/Bilateral symmetry (Pea, gulmohar, Bean, Cassia)

(3) A flower cannot be divided into two similar halves by any vertical plane passing through centre—Asymmetric (irregular), e.g. Canna

(4) Bracts—Reduced leaf

(5) **All of the above**

Q. 35. **In which of the following true statement is/are about the inflorescence?**

(1) Arrangement of flower on floral axis called inflorescence

(2) In racemes, type of inflorescence the main axis continues to grow, flowers borne laterally in an acropetal succession

(3) In cymose, type of inflorescence main axis terminates in a flower (limited in growth), flower borne in a basipetal order

(4) **All of the above**

Q. 36. **The condition of petiole in those plants where leaves are modified into tendrils spines fleshy and shortnodes:**

(1) **Expand, green and prepare food**

(2) Expand, yellow and make food

(3) Expand, orange and not prepare food

(4) All of the above

Q. 37. **Inferior ovary is found in:**

(1) Guava

(2) Cucumber

(3) Ray-florets of sunflower

(4) **All of the above**

Q. 38. **In which of the following column is correctly matched?**

(1) Sepals—Calyx

(2) Petals—Corolla

(3) Gamopetalous—Petals united

(4) Polypetalous—Petals free

(5) **All of the above**

Q. 39. **Flowers are the three types, *viz.* Hypogynous, Perigynous and Epigynous, based on:**

(1) **In respect of ovary (carpel), the position of the calyx, corolla and androecium responsible for kinds of flowers**

(2) In respect of bracts, the position of the calyx, corolla and androecium responsible for kinds of flowers

(3) In respect of bracteoles, the position of the calyx, corolla and androecium responsible for kinds of flowers

(4) In respect of receptacles, the position of the calyx, corolla and androecium responsible for kinds of flowers

Q. 40. A flower may be:

(1) Trimerus
(2) Tetramerus
(3) Pentamerus
(4) **All of the above**

Q. 41. In which of the following true statement is/are?

(1) Calyx and corolla are accessory organs while androecium and gynoecium are reproductive organs
(2) When calyx and corolla not distinct called perianth (e.g. Lily)
(3) Flower are of 2 types, *viz.* bisexual (contain both organs; androecium and gynoecium) and contain only stamens/carpel called unisexual
(4) **All are correct statements**

Q. 42. In which of the following true statement is/are?

(1) A flower is a modified shoot in which SAM changes to floral meristems
(2) When a shoot tip transforms into a flower, it is always solitary
(3) Internodes do not elongate and axis gets condensed
(4) **All are correct**

Q. 43. What is true about flower?

(1) Reproductive unit
(2) Meant for sexual reproduction
(3) A typically flower contains 4 kinds of whorls arranged successively on pedicel/thalamus/receptacles
(4) **All of the above**

Q. 44. In which of the following true statement is/are about calyx?

(1) Outer-most whorl
(2) Its members called sepals-green, leaf-like
(3) Protect flowers in bud stage
(4) **All of the above**

Q. 45. What is true about corolla?

(1) Units (members) of its called petals, usually bright coloured and attract insects for pollination (ecological importance)
(2) They may be tubular, bell-shaped, funnel shaped or wheel-shaped
(3) Like sepals, also Gamopetalous/polypetalous
(4) **All of the above**

Q. 46. What is true?

(1) If margin of sepals/petals overlaps that of the next one called twisted (China rose, cotton, ladyfinger)
(2) If margin overlaps one another but not in any particular direction called imbricate (Cassia, Gulmohar)
(3) Among the 5-petals, largest one (standard) overlaps two laterals (wings), which in turn, overlaps the two smallest anterior petals (Keel) called vexiallary (Papilionaceae)
(4) **All of the above**

Q. 47. In which of the following true statement is/are about aestivation?

(1) Mode of arrangement of sepals/petals in floral bud with respect to other members of same whorl
(2) It is of valvate, twisted, imbricate and vexiallary
(3) When sepals/petals in a whorl just touch one another at margin without overlapping (e.g. calotrophis called valvate)
(4) **All of the above**

Q. 48. In which of the following column is correctly matched?

(1) Valvate—Calotrophis
(2) Twisted—Cotton, China rose
(3) Imbricate—Gulmohar and Cassia
(4) Vexillary—Pea-beans
(5) **All of the above are correct**

Q. 49. In which of the following column is correctly matched?

(1) Monoadelphous—China rose

(2) Didelphous—Pea

(3) Polyaelphous—Citrus

(4) Variation in length of filaments within a flower—Salvia and Mustard

(5) All are correctly matched

Q. 50. In which of the following true statement is/are about androecium?

(1) Units called stamens

(2) Sterile stamens called staminode

(3) Stamens may be united into a bench (dia-delphous, e.g. Pea) or into more than two bench (poly-Delphos, e.g. citrus)

(4) All of the above are true

Q. 51. In which of the following true statement is/are about androecium?

(1) Stamens are epipetalous (attached together)—Brinjal

(2) Stamens are epiphyllous (Stamens attached to perianth)—Lily

(3) Stamens in a flower may either remain free (polyandrous) or may be united in varying degree (No term for united stamens)

(4) All of the above are true

Q. 52. One of the following statements given below the true one about monocot seeds?

(1) Generally monocot seeds are endospermic but serve as in orchids are non-endospermic

(2) In maize endosperms is bulky and store food; also here seed coat is membranous and fused with fruit wall generally

(3) Outer covering of endosperm separates the embryo by a proteinous layer (aleurone layer)

(4) All are true

Q. 53. One of the following statements given below the true one:

(1) Embryo is small and situated in a groove at one end of endosperm

(2) Embryo consists of one large and shield shaped cotyledons, scutellum and a short axis bears plumule and radicle

(3) Plumule enclosed in a sheath (coleoptiles) and radical enclosed in a sheath (coleorhizae)

(4) All of the above

Q. 54. Semi-technical description of a typical flowering plant includes:

(1) Morphological features describes a flowering plant

(2) Description presented in a proper sequence-(i) habit (ii) vegetative characters (iii) floral characters (iv) inflorescence (v) flower parts (vi) floral diagram (vii) floral formula

(3) Floral formula is represented by same symbols

(4) All are true

Q. 55. One of the following pairs given below the are truly matched (a) name of placentation; (b) Definition?

(1) Placenta forms a ridge along ventral suture of ovary and ovules borne on this ridge forming two rows—Marginal

(2) When placenta is axial and ovules attached to it in a multi-locular ovary—axile

(3) Ovules develop on inner wall/ peripheral ovary is one chambered and becomes two chambered due to formation of false septum—Parietal

(4) When ovules are borne on central axis and septa are absent—Free central

(5) Placenta develops at base of ovary and a single ovule is attached to it—Basal

(6) All are correctly matched

Q. 56. One of the following statements given below the true one about dicot seeds?

(1) Outermost covering is seed-coat-a two phase layer-outer (testa) and Inner (tegmen)

(2) Hilum is scar on seed coat through which developing seeds attached to fruits

(3) Above hilum, Micropyle is present

(4) All of the above

Q. 57. One of the following statements given below the true for gynoecium?

(1) Made up of one or more carpels

(2) Carpels consists of stigma style and ovary

(3) Stigma is usually at tip of style and receptive surface for pollen grains

(4) All of the above

Q. 58. What facts are true about female reproductive organs (gynoecium) of angiosperms?

(1) Each ovary bears one/more ovules attached to a flattened placenta

(2) When more than one carpels is present and free (apocarpous-lotus, rose) fused (Syncarpous-mustard,tomato)

(3) After fertilization ovule changed into seeds and arrangement of ovules in ovary called placentation

(4) All of the above are true

Q. 59. What is an incorrect symbol for floral diagram

(1) K for calyx

(2) P for perianth

(3) G_ for superior ovary and G⁻ inferior ovary

(4) None of the above

Q. 60. One of the following pairs given below are truly matched (a) name of placentation; (b) Example?

(1) Marginal—Pea

(2) Axile—China rose, Tomato, Lemon

(3) Parietal—Mustard, Argemone

(4) Free-central—Dianthus, Prim-rose

(5) Basal—Sunflower, Marigold

(6) All are correctly matched

Q. 61. One of the following statements given below the true one:

(1) Characteristics feature of angio-sperms. It is ripened ovary, developed after fertilization; for it develops without fertilization called partheocarpic fruits

(2) Generally consists of wall (pericarp) and seeds

(3) Generally pericarp is dry and fleshy but when it is thick and fleshy it differentiated into epicarp, Mesocarp and endocarp

(4) All of the above are true

Q. 62. One of the following statements given below the true one about fruits?

(1) Mango and coconut is drupe, develop from monocarpellary superior ovaries and one seeded

(2) In mango, pericarp is developed into epicarp (thin), Mesocarp (fleshy) and endocarp (stony hard)

(3) In coconut (also, drup), Mesocarp is fibrous

(4) All are true

Q. 63. One of the following statements given below the true one about seed?

(1) Ovules after fertilization called seed

(2) Seed made by seed coat and an embryo

(3) Embryo consists of a radical, an embryonal axis and one (wheat, maize) or two cotyledons (gram and pea)

(4) All of the above are true

Q. 64. One of the following statements given below the true one about dicot seeds?

(1) Castor seeds contain endosperm as result of double fertilization while bean gram pea lack this structure at maturate seeds (non-endospermic)

(2) Embryonal axis has 2 ends, i.e. radical and plumule

(3) Cotyledons often fleshy and full of reserve

(4) All of the above

Q. 65. What is an incorrect symbol for floral diagram:

(1) w, for actinomorphic flower

(2) % zygomorphic flower

(3) Fusion by enclosing figure within bracket and adhesion by a line drawn above the symbols of floral parts

(4) None of the above

Q. 66. Floral diagram provides information about:

(1) Number of parts of a flower

(2) Arrangement of parts

(3) Relationships of parts

(4) All of the above

Q. 67. The position of the mother axis with respect to flower is represented by a:

(1) Dot on top of floral diagram

(2) Dot on the below of floral diagram

(3) Dot on the parallel side of floral diagram

(4) All of the above are true

Q. 68. In which of the following below mentioned statements, one is true?

(1) Floral formula show cohesion within parts of whorls

(2) Floral formula show cohesion within parts of whorls and between whorls

(3) Floral formula show adhesion within parts of whorls and between whorls

(4) All of the above

Q. 69. In which of the following below mentioned statements, one is true about *Fabaceae (Papilionaceae)*?

(1) Non-endospermic seeds; K = 5, C = 5, A = 10

(2) Diadelphous stamens usually aestivation, raceme bisexual and zygomorphic ovary is superior, monocarpellary and uni-locular

(3) Muliathi/Licorice/Colemus (medicine) dye (indigofera) comes under this family

(4) All of the above

Q. 70. In which of the following below mentioned statements, one is true about *Solanaceae*?

(1) Widely distributed in tropics, ex-stipulate leaves

(2) Herbaceous rarely woody

(3) Bisexual actinomorphic C = 5, K = 5; valvate aestivation (A = 5-epipetalous), berry/capsule

(4) Superior bicarpellary and locular, syncarpous and fruits are endospermic

(5) All of the above are true

Q. 71. In which of the following below mentioned statements, one is true about LILY?

(1) It is a characteristic representative of monocot plants

(2) Perennial herbs wit underground bulbs/corms/rhizomes

(3) Ex-stipulate leaves (like *Solanaceae*); perianth tepal sex (3 + 3)

(4) Cymose or umbellate clusters, actinomorphic valvate aestivation; tepels often united and form tube

(5) Ovary superior trilocular and capillary; axile placentation; fruit, capsule and rarely berry

(6) All of the above

Q. 72. *Solanaceae* **includes:**

(1) Belladonna
(2) Ashwagandha
(3) Petunia
(4) **All of the above**

Q. 73. *Liliaceae* **includes:**

(1) Aloe (medicinal and colchicines)
(2) Asparagus (vegetables)
(3) Tulip, Gloriosa (ornamental)
(4) **All of the above are true**

C-3

Q. 1. **Techniques useful for enhancing food production of ever-increasing population of world:**

(1) **Animal husbandry**
(2) Plant breeding
(3) Embryo transfer technique
(4) **All of the above are true**

Q. 2. **Among the above mentioned techniques for enhancing the food production most advanced technique is:**

(1) **Tissue culture**
(2) Plant physiology
(3) Bio-informatics
(4) Biochemistry

Q. 3. **Animal husbandry is vital skill for farmers and is as much science as it is art includes:**

(1) Ag. practice of breeding and raising livestock
(2) Deals with care and breeding of livestock
(3) It includes poultry farming and fisheries
(4) **All of the above are true**

Q. 4. **Fisheries includes:**

(1) Rearing of fish, molluscs (shell fish), crustaceans (prawn and crabs)
(2) Catching of fish, molluscs (shell fish), crustaceans (prawn and crabs)

(3) Selling of fish, molluscs (shell fish), crustaceans (prawn and crabs)
(4) **All of the above are true**

Q. 5. **Correct statement is/are:**

(1) More than 70% of world livestock population is in India
(2) Contribution to the world farm production is only 25%
(3) Dairying is the management of animals for milk and its products for human consumption
(4) **All are correct**

Q. 6. **Correct statement is/are:**

(1) In dairy farm management, we deal with processes and systems that increase yield and improve quality of milk
(2) Milk yield is primarily dependent on quality of breeds in farm
(3) Selection of good breeds having high yielding potential combined with resistance to diseases is very important
(4) **All of the above**

Q. 7. **For yield potential to be realized the cattle have to be well-looked after they have to be:**

(1) House well
(2) Adequate water
(3) Maintained disease free
(4) **All of the above are true**

Q. 8. **The feeding of cattle should be carried out in a specific manner with special emphasis on the which milk in the storage and transport of the milk and its products:**

(1) Quality and quantity of fodder
(2) Stringent cleanliness
(3) Hygiene of both cattle and handlers
(4) **All of the above**

Q. 9. Correct statement is:

(1) In dairy farm management, regular visits by a veterinary doctor would be mandatory

(2) Poultry is class of domesticated fowl (birds) used for food or their eggs

(3) Poultry typically include chicken, ducks sometimes, turkey and geese

(4) All of the above

Q. 10. Important component of poultry farm management:

(1) Selection of disease free and suitable breeds

(2) Proper and safe farm conditions

(3) Proper food and water, hygiene, health care

(4) All of the above

Q. 11. Bird flu viruses drastically affected

(1) Eggs

(2) Chicken consumption

(3) All birds of poultry consumption

(4) Both 1 and 2

Q. 12. What is true about animal breeding?

(1) Breeding of animal is important aspect of animal husbandry

(2) Animal breeding aims at increasing the yield of animals and improving the desirable qualities of produce

(3) Breeding between same breed in inbreeding and between different breeds is out-breeding

(4) A breed is a group of animals related by descent and similar in most characters like general appearance features size, configuration, etc.

(5) All of the above are true

Q. 13. Correct statement is:

(1) Jersay is important breed of cattle

(2) Leghorn is important breed of chickens

(3) Inbreeding is mating of more closely related individuals within the same breed for 4–6 generations

(4) All are correct

Q. 14. The breeding strategy is as follows:

(1) Superior males and super females of same breed are identified and mated in pairs

(2) Progeny obtained from such matings are evaluated and superior males and females among them are indentified for further matings

(3) A superior female in case of cattle is low/buffalo that produces more milk per location; a superior male is bull gives rise to superior progeny than other males

(4) All are correct

Q. 15. In which correct statement is:

(1) Homozygous pure lines developed by Mendel

(2) A similar strategy used for developing pure lines in cattle as was used in case of Peas

(3) Inbreeding increases homozygocity and necessary to evolve a pure line in any animal

(4) All are correct

Q. 16. What is true in case of inbreeding?

(1) Exposes harmful recessive genes which eliminated by selection

(2) Helps in accumulation of superior gens and elimination of less desirable genes

(3) Increase productivity of inbreed population in a approach where selection at each step is must

(4) Continued inbreeding reduces fertility or productivity (inbreeding depression) and increases homozygocity

(5) All are correct

Q. 17. Approach or way to short-out the problem of inbreeding depression to restore fertility and yield (reduction in fertility and productivity):

(1) **Selected (superior) animals of breeding population should be mated with unrelated superior animals of same breed and this restore fertility and yield**

(2) Selected (superior) animals of breeding population should be mated with related superior animals of same breed and this restore fertility and yield

(3) Selected (superior) animals of breeding population should be mated with unrelated inferior animals of same breed and this restore fertility and yield

(4) All of the above are true

Q. 18. What is possible for out-breeding?

(1) Breeding of unrelated animals, i.e. between animals of same breed but having no common ancestors for 4–6 generations (out-crossing)

(2) Breeding between different breeds (cross-breeding)

(3) Breeding between different species (inter-specific hybridization)

(4) **All are possible**

Q. 19. Approach/s of out-breeding may be:

(1) Out-crossing

(2) Cross breeding

(3) Inter-specific hybridization

(4) **All of the above are true**

Q. 20. What is true for out-crossing?

(1) Practice of mating of animals within in same breed but have no common ancestors on either side of their pedigree up to 4–6 generations

(2) Offspring's of out-crossing called out-cross

(3) Best breeding method for animals that are below average in productivity in milk production growth rate in beef cattle

(4) A single out-cross helps to overcome inbreeding depression

(5) **All are correct**

Q. 21. What is true about cross-breeding?

(1) Superior males of one breed are mated with superior females of another breed

(2) Allows desirable qualities of two different breeds to be combined

(3) Progeny (hybrid) used for commercial production

(4) **All are true**

Q. 22. Which is used for commercial (based/used) animal breed production?

(1) Out-breeding

(2) Out-crossing

(3) **Cross-breeding**

(4) Inbreeding depression

Q. 23. Products/progeny/hybrids of cross-breeding may be subjected to some form of:

(1) Inbreeding

(2) Selection to develop new breeds that may be superior to existing breeds

(3) Many new animals breeds have been developed by this approach (e. g. Hisardale)

(4) **All of the above are correct**

Q. 24. Hisardale is:

(1) Developed in Punjab

(2) Cross-breeding products

(3) A breed of sheep developed by crossing between Bikaneri and Marinorams

(4) **All of the above are true**

Q. 25. What is correct about inter-specific hybridization?

(1) Male and female of two different related species are mated

(2) Mule is product of such approaches

(3) Progeny have combine characters of both parents and may be of considerable economic importance

(4) All of the above are correct

Q. 26. What is true for artificial insemination (controlled breeding experiments):

(1) Semen collected from male and chosen as a parent and transfer to selected female by breeder

(2) Semen may be used, immediately or later date or can be frozen; transported as frozen state to where female is housed

(3) Desirable matings is possible, helps us to overcome several problems of normal matings

(4) All of the above are true

Q. 27. What is true about MOET (Multiple Ovulation Embryo Transfer Technology)?

(1) To improve chances of successful production of hybrids, it is a progress for herd improvement

(2) Cow (female) administered for hormonal (like FSH) activities to introduce follicular maturation and super-ovulation (6–8 eggs per cycle) at place of usual one

(3) Animal is either mated with an elite bull or artificially inseminated

(4) The fertilized eggs at 8–32 cells stages recovered non-surgically and transferred to surrogate mothers

(5) All of the above are true

Q. 28. In which a correct statement

(1) Normally one egg yield/cycle

(2) MOET has been durated for cattle, sheep rabbits, buffaloes, mares, etc.

(3) Through MOET, high milk yielding breeds of female and high quality (lean meat with less lipid) meat yielding bulls have been bred successfully to increase herd size in a short period of time

(4) All of the above are correct

Q. 29. In which of the following one have been an age-old-cottage industry?

(1) Apiculture (2) Seri-culture

(3) Pisci-culture (4) Agriculture

Q. 30. What is correct statements about Green Revolution

(1) Traditional farming can yield only to a limited biomass as food for humans and animals

(2) Better management practices and increase in acreage can increase yield only a limited extent

(3) Plant-breeding increase yields to a very large extent by developing high yielding and disease-resistant varieties of wheat, rice, maize, etc.

(4) All of the above are true

Q. 31. What is true for apiculture (Bee-keeping)?

(1) Maintenance of hives of honey-bees for honey production

(2) Practical in any area where there is sufficient bee pastures of some wild shrubs, fruit orchards and cultivated crops

(3) Most common species in *Aps indica*

(4) It is not labour-intensive

(5) All above are correct

Q. 32. True statement is/are:

(1) Beehives can be kept in one's courtyard, on Verandah or even roof

(2) Honey is food of high nutritive value and use in indigenous systems of medicine

(3) Honeybee production beeswax uses in industry in cosmetics, polishes

(4) **All of the above are true**

Q. 33. Bees are the pollinators of many of our crops species is/are:

(1) Sunflower

(2) Brassica

(3) Apple and Pear

(4) **All of the above are true**

Q. 34. Keeping beehives in crop fields during flowering periods:

(1) Increases pollination

(2) Improves yield of honey

(3) Improvement yield of crops

(4) **All of the above are true**

Q. 35. Fisheries are:

(1) **Catching, processing or selling of fish, shellfish or other aquatic animals**

(2) Catching, processing or selling of frog, shellfish or other aquatic animals

(3) Catching, processing or selling of tadpole, shellfish or other aquatic animals

(4) Catching, processing or selling of silverfish, shellfish or other aquatic animals

Q. 36. Common fresh water fish is (CCR):

(1) Catla

(2) Rohu

(3) Common Carp

(4) **All of the above are true**

Q. 37. Eaten marine fisheries are:

(1) Hilsa

(2) Sardines and Mackerel

(3) Pomfrets

(4) **All of the above are true**

Q. 38. Through aqua-culture and pisci-culture we have been able to increase the production of:

(1) Fresh water (aquatic plants) and animals

(2) Fresh water animals

(3) Marine and fresh water plants

(4) **All of the above are true**

Q. 39. What is correct statement about Green Revolution?

(1) Traditional farming can yield only to a limited biomass as food for human and animals

(2) Better management practices and increase in acreage can increase yield only a limited extent

(3) Plant breeding increase yields to a very high extent by developing high yielding and disease-resistant varieties of wheat, rice, maize, etc.

(4) **All of the above are true**

Q. 40. What is correct about plant breeding?

(1) Purposeful manipulation of plant species to create desired plant types better adopted for cultivation, better yield and resistant to disease

(2) Many present day crops are result of domestication in ancient times

(3) Today, all our major food crops are derived from domestication varieties

(4) Classical plant breeding involves crossing or hybridization of pure lines, followed by artificial selection to produce plant with desired traits of higher yield, nutrition and resistance to disease

(5) **All of the above are right**

Q. 41. Plant breeding advanced due to association of which disciplines?

(1) **Genetics-Molecular Biology-Tissue culture**

(2) Cytology-Biochemistry-Morphogenesis

(3) Molecular biology-Anatomy-Plant physiology

(4) Tissue culture-Genetics-Environmental biology

Q. 42. Character (trait) that breeders have tried to incorporate into important plants, the first would be:

(1) Increased yield and quality

(2) Increased tolerance to environmental stress

(3) Resistance to pathogens

(4) All of the above are true

Q. 43. Main steps of a breeding programme carried out in the government institution and commercial companies:

(1) Collection of variability

(2) Cross hybridizations among the elected parents

(3) Selection and testing of superior recombinants

(4) Testing, release and commercialization of new cultivars

(5) All are correct

Q. 44. What is germ-plasm collection?

(1) Entire collection (of plants or seeds) having all diverse alleles for all genes in a given crop

(2) Collection of total RNA and DNA

(3) Collection of only DNA

(4) Collection of only RNA

Q. 45. Root of any breeding programme?

(1) Collection of variability

(2) Collection of similarity

(3) Both 1 and 2

(4) None of the above

Q. 46. The desired characters have very often to be combined from two different plants through

(1) Cross hybridization

(2) Inbreeding

(3) Out-breeding

(4) All of the above are true

Q. 47. What is true for cross-hybridization?

(1) Very time consuming and tedious process

(2) Pollen grains from desirable plant chosen as male parent

(3) It is not necessary that hybrids do combine the desirable characters; usually only one in few hundred to a thousand crosses shows the desirable characters

(4) All of the above are true

Q. 48. What is crucial step to the success of breeding objective and requires careful scientific evolution of progeny?

(1) Selection

(2) Breeding

(3) Out-crossing

(4) All of the above are true

Q. 49. Selection process yields plants that are superior to both of parents; very often more than one superior progeny plant may become available. These plants are:

(1) Self-pollinated and show homozygocity

(2) Cross-pollinated and show heterozygosity

(3) Self-pollinated and show heterozygosity

(4) None of the above

Q. 50. The newly selected lines are evaluated for their yield and other agronomic traits of quality, disease resistance, etc. This evaluation is done by growing for how many generations in research field. Several locations in the country is:

(1) At least two

(2) At least four

(3) At least three

(4) At lest seven

Q. 51. **What is true for Indian Agriculture?**

(1) Approximately 33% of Indian GDP

(2) Employs about 62% of population

(3) India has to strive to increase yields per unit area from existing farm land

(4) All are right

Q. 52. **The development of several high yielding varities of which pair of crops lead to dramatic increase in food production in our country?**

(1) Rice-Maize **(2) Rice-Wheat**

(3) Wheat-Barley (4) Rice-Millets

Q. 53. **High yielding wheat varities 'Sonalika and Kalyan' were introduced all over the wheat-growing belt of India was:**

(1) High yield

(2) Disease resistant

(3) Both 1 and 2

(4) Water-resistant

Q. 54. **What is true for semi-dwarf rice varieties?**

(1) Derived for IR-8 and Taichung-Native-I

(2) IR-8 developed at IRRI, Philippines-and TN-1 from Taiwan

(3) Both 1 and 2

(4) None of the above

Q. 55. **Match the correct columns.**

Col. A	Col. B
A. Better yielding semi-dwarf varieties-Jaya and Ratna developed in India	(i) International Centre for Wheat and Maize improvement (mexico)
B. Semi-dwarf wheat varieties developed	(ii) IRRI, Philippines
C. IR-8	(iii) Taiwan
D. Taichung Native-I	(iv) Rice

(1) A (iv), B (i), C (ii), D (iii)

(2) A (i), B (iv), C (ii), D (iii)

(3) A (iv), B (ii), C (i), D (iii)

(4) A (iv), B (i), C (iii), D (ii)

Q. 56. **Matches the column A and B**

Col. A	Col. B
A. Saccharum barberi	(i) Tropical, south India, thicker stems and high sugar content
B. Saccharum officinarum	(ii) Water stress
C. Hybrid Millet varieties	(iii) Indian hybrid wheat variety
D. HD 1553	(iv) North India, low sugar and yield

(1) A (iv), B (i), C (ii), D (iii)

(2) A (iv), B (ii), C (i), D (iii)

(3) A (iv), B (i), C (iii), D (ii)

(4) A (i), B (iv), C (ii), D (iii)

Q. 57. **Correct statement is/are?**

(1) Pathogens affect the yield of cultivated crops species especially in tropical climates

(2) Often crop losses be significant up to 20–30% or rarely total

(3) Resistance of host plant is ability to prevent pathogens from causing disease and determined by genetic constitution of host

(4) Before breeding, important is know about causative organisms and mode of transmission

(5) All of the above are true

Q. 58. **Matches the column A and B.**

Col. A	Col. B
A. Brown rust of wheat, late blight of potato, red rot of sugarcane	(i) Bacteria

B.	Black rot of crucifers	(ii)	Fungi
C.		(iii)	*Venturia inaequalis*
D.	Apple scab	(iv)	Viruses

(1) **A (ii), B (i), C (iv), D (iii)**
(2) A (i), B (ii), C (iv), D (iii)
(3) A (ii), B (iii), C (iv), D (i)
(4) A (ii), B (i), C (iii), D (iv)

Q. 59. Methods of breeding for disease resistance is carried out by:

(1) Conventional breeding techniques
(2) Mutation breeding techniques
(3) **Both 1 and 2**
(4) None of the above

Q. 60. The conventional method of breeding for disease resistance is that of:

(1) **Hybridization and selection**
(2) Hybridization and recombination
(3) Selection and testing
(4) Evolution and hybridization

Q. 61. Sequential steps of any breeding programme:

(1) **Screening germplasm for resistance sources, hybridization of selected parents, selection, evolution of hybrids, testing and release of new varieties**
(2) Screening germplasm for resistance sources, hybridization of selected parents, selection, testing and release of new varieties, evolution of hybrids
(3) Screening germplasm for resistance sources, hybridization of selected parents, evolution of hybrids, selection, testing and release of new varieties
(4) Screening germplasm for resistance sources, selection, evolution of hybrids, testing and release of new varieties, hybridization of selected parents

Q. 62. What is true for Himgiri?

(1) Wheat variety developed by hybridizations and selection
(2) Resistance to leaf and stripe rust
(3) Resistance to hill bunt
(4) **All of the above**

Q. 63. What is true for PUSA SWANIM?

(1) Commonly called Karan rai
(2) It is a brassica variety developed by hybridizations and selection
(3) Resistance to white rust
(4) **All of the above are true**

Q. 64. What is true for PUSA SHUBDRA, PUSA SNOWBALL K-1?

(1) Variety of cauliflower
(2) Resistance to black rust
(3) Resistance to curl blight, black rot
(4) **All of the above**

Q. 65. What is true for PUSA KOMAL?

(1) Variety of cowpea
(2) Resistant to bacterial blight
(3) Both 1 and 2
(4) **None of the above**

Q. 66. What is correct for PUSA SADABHAR?

(1) Chilli variety
(2) Resistance to diseases caused by chilli mosaic viruses, TMV and leaf curl
(3) **Both 1 and 2**
(4) None of the above

Q. 67. Conventional breeding is often constrained by the:

(1) **Availability of limited number of disease resistance genes that are present and identified in various crop varieties or wild relatives**
(2) Availability of limited number of disease resistance genes that are present and identified in various crop varieties only
(3) Availability of limited number of disease resistance genes that are

present and identified in various wild relatives only

(4) Availability of limited number of disease resistance genes that are present and identified in various synthetic crops

Q. 68. Correct statement is/are:

(1) Instead conventional breeding method, selection is other breeding method among the somaclonal varieties and genetic engineering

(2) Induce mutation artificially by chemicals/radiations and selecting and using plants that have the desirable characters as source of breeding, called mutation breeding

(3) In moongbean, resistance to yellow mosaic virus and powdery Mildew induced by mutation

(4) Resistance to yellow mosaic virus in Bhindi transferred from a wild species and created a new variety called Parbhani Kranti

(5) All are right

Q. 69. Correct statement is/are:

(1) Transfer of resistance genes is achieved by sexual hybridization between target and source plant followed by selection

(2) Insect resistance in host crop is due to morphological, biochemical or physiological characters

(3) Hairy leaves associated with insect pests, e.g. resistance to jassids in cotton and cereal leaf beetle in wheat

(4) All of the above are right

Q. 70. Matches the column A and B:.

Col. A		Col. B
A. Jassids	(i)	Maize stem borer
B. Cereal leaf beetle	(ii)	Cotton
C. High aspartic acid, low N and sugar content	(iii)	Bollworms

D. Smooth leaved (iv) Wheat and nectar less cotton varieties

(1) **A (ii), B (iv), C (iii), D (i)**
(2) A (i), B (iv), C (iii), D (ii)
(3) A (ii), B (iv), C (i), D (iii)
(4) A (ii), B (i), C (iii), D (iv)

Q. 71. Breeding methods for insect pest resistance involve the same step as those for:

(1) Yield
(2) Quality
(3) Abiotic stress (drought, salinity, heavy metal stress)
(4) All of the above are true

Q. 72. Sources of resistance genes may be:

(1) Cultivated varieties
(2) Germplasm collections of crops
(3) Germplasm collection of wild relatives
(4) All of the above are true

Q. 73. Matches the column A and B.

Col. A		Col. B
(1) Brassica–Pusa Gaurav	(i)	Aphids
(2) Flat Bean: Pusa sem 2/3	(ii)	Jassids, Aphids and Fruit borer
(3) Bhindi	(iii)	Pusa swami and Pusa A-4
(4) All are correctly matched pairs		

Q. 74. Hidden higher is deficiency of which nutrient because they cannot afford to buy enough fruits, vegetables legumes, fish and meat:

(1) Micronutrients
(2) Proteins
(3) Vitamins
(4) All of the above are true

Q. 75. Diet lacking essential micronutrient particularly Fe,Vitamin A, I2 and Zn affected with?

(1) Increase the risk of disease

(2) Reduce life-span

(3) Reduce nutrient ability

(4) **All of the above are true**

Q. 76. What is true for biofortification?

(1) Most practical means to improve public health

(2) Breeding of crops with higher levels of vitamins, minerals

(3) Breeding of crops with higher levels of proteins and heal their fats

(4) **All of the above are true**

Q. 77. Breeding for improved nutritional quality is undertaken with the objectives of improving?

(1) Protein, oil content and quality

(2) Vitamins content

(3) Micronutrient and mineral content

(4) **All of the above are true**

Q. 78. 'Atlas 66' is:

(1) Variety of wheat

(2) Has high protein content

(3) Used as donor for improving cultivated wheat

(4) **All of the above are true**

Q. 79. Maize hybrid prepared by bio-fortification contain:

(1) **Twice amount of lysine and tryptophan**

(2) Thrice amount of tyrosine

(3) More glycine

(4) Less phenylalanine

Q. 80. Rice fortified for enrichment of which micronutrient:

(1) Mn

(2) **Fe**

(3) P

(4) Mg

Q. 81. Matches the column A and B.

Col. A	Col. B
A. Carrot, Spinach, Pumpkin	(i) Protein
B. Bittergourd, Bathua, Mustard, Tomato	(ii) Vitamin A
C. Spinach Bathua	(iii) Vitamin C
D. Beans	(iv) Fe and Ca

(1) **A (ii), B (iii), C (iv), D (i)**

(2) A (i), B (iii), C (iv), D (ii)

(3) A (ii), B (iii), C (i), D (iv)

(4) A (iii), B (ii), C (iv), D (i)

Q. 82. What is correct for SCP?

(1) Conventional methods of agricultural production not able to meet the demand of food at rate at which human and animal population is increasing

(2) Shift from grain to meet diets also create more demand for cereals 3.3–10 kg of grain to produce 1 kg of meat by animal farming 4.25% human-population suffering from hunger and malnutrition, SCP is an alternate source of protein

(3) **All of the above are correct**

Q. 83. True statements are in reference of SCP?

(1) Microbes grown on an industrial scale as source of good protein

(2) Spirulina grown easily on materials like waste water from potato processessing plants (contain starch), straw, molasses, animal manure and even sewage to produce large amount of and can serve as food rich in protein, minerals fats, carbohydrates and vitamins

(3) SCP reduces environmental pollution

(4) **All of the above are correct**

Q. 84. True statement is/are:

(1) 250 Kg cow produces 200 g protein/day

(2) 250 Kg microorganism produces 25 tonnes protein/day

(3) *Methyophilus methylotrophus* has fifth rate of biomass production and growth

(4) **All of the above are correct**

Q. 85. What is true for tissue culture?

(1) Whole plant could be regenerated from explants

(2) Ex-plant is any part of a plant taken out and grown in test tube under sterile conditions in a special nutrient media

(3) This capacity to generate a whole plant from among cell/explants called totipotency

(4) Media used contain sucrose, inorganic salts, vitamins, amino acids and growth regulators (CK-auxin)

(5) **All of the above are true**

Q. 86. True statement is/are

(1) Methods of producing thousands of plants in short time by tissue culture called micro-propagation

(2) Plants produced from above methods called soma clones

(3) Commonly by this method, tomato, banana and apple have been produced

(4) Recovery of healthy plants from diseased plants also made by this approach

(5) **All of the above are true**

Q. 87. The plant is infected with a virus which meristems are true of virus infection?

(1) Apical

(2) Axillary

(3) Intercalary

(4) **Both 1 and 2**

Q. 88. One can obtain virus free plants from growing which part of plant in *in vitro* culture:

(1) Apical meristems

(2) Axillary meristems

(3) Lateral meristems

(4) **Both 1 and 2**

Q. 89. What are somatic hybrids or somatic hybridization?

(1) **Isolated protoplast from two different varieties of plants each having a desirable character can be used to get hybrid protoplasts called somatic hybrids which further grown to form a new plant**

(2) Isolated protoplast from three different varieties of plants each having a desirable character can be used to get hybrid protoplasts called somatic hybrids which further grown to form a new plant

(3) Isolated protoplast from four different varieties of plants each having a desirable character can be used to get hybrid protoplasts called somatic hybrids which further grown to form a new plant

(4) Isolated protoplast from ten different varieties of plants each having a desirable character can be used to get hybrid protoplasts called somatic hybrids which further grown to form a new plant

---

C-4

Q. 1. In which of the following below mentioned statements, one is true about Biotechnology?

(1) Making curd bread or wine is all microbe-mediated process is a form of biotechnology

(2) Processes which use genetically modified organisms to achieve the same on a large scale

(3) *In vitro* fertilization (test tube baby), syntenic gene and using it developing a DNA vaccine or connecting a defective gene

(4) According the EFB (European Federation of Biotechnology) the integration of natural science and organisms cells, parts there off and molecular analogies

(5) All of the above are true statements

Q. 2. Rene Descartes was:

(1) The French Philosopher, Mathematician, the French biologist of 17 the century

(2) The major utility of biological world is a source of food

(3) Biotechnology, the 20 the century off shoot of modern biology, changes our daily life as its products brought qualitative important in health and food production

(4) All of the above are true

Q. 3. Area of studies of Herbert Boyer (1936 till date):

(1) Couple of restriction enzyme of *E. coli* bacteria with especially useful properties

(2) Useful properties of ribose units

(3) Harmful properties of nucleases

(4) All of the above are true

Q. 4. In which of the following below mentioned statements, one is true about Stanley Cohen (Stanford Scientist) achievements are?

(1) Study plasmid (found freely in certain bacterial cells) and replicate independently from coding strand of DNA

(2) Dispersed method to separate plasmid from bacterial cells and re-inserting in other cells

(3) Along with Boyer, he recognize segments of DNA in desired configurations and insert DNA in bacterial cells act as manufacturing plants for specific proteins

(4) All of the above are true statements

Q. 5. Herbert Boyer (California University, San Francisco) discoveries are/is:

(1) Restriction endonuclease has the capability of cutting DNA strands in a particular fashion

(2) Restriction endonuclease left what has become known as 'Sticky ends' on the strands

(3) Clipped ends of RE made pasting together pieces of DNA—a precise exercise

(4) All of the above

Q. 6. In which of the following below mentioned statements, one is true about Genetic engineering is?

(1) Techniques to alter the chemistry of GM (DNA/RNA) to introduce these into host organism and this change the phenotype of host organism

(2) Techniques to alter the chemistry of GM (DNA only) to introduce these into host plant and this change the genotype of host organism

(3) Techniques useful for production of bees, wine, curd, acids from organism

(4) All of the above are true statements

Q. 7. Principles or core techniques that enabled birth of modern biotechnology are:

(1) Genetic engineering

(2) Maintenance of sterile ambience

(3) Plant morphogenesis

(4) Both 1 and 2

Q. 8. In which of the following below mentioned statements, one is true for reproduction?

(1) Sexual-reproduction-provides opportunities for varities and formulations of unique combinations of genetic set-up beneficial to organisms and population

(2) Asexual reproduction preserves genetic information

(3) Sexual reproduction permits variations

(4) **All of the above are true statements**

Q. 9. Traditional hybridization processes used in plant and animal breeding very often lead to:

(1) Inclusion

(2) Multiplication of undesirable genes

(3) Multiplication of desirable genes

(4) **All of the above are true**

Q. 10. Techniques of genetic engineering include:

(1) Creation of Rec DNA

(2) Use of gene cloning

(3) Use of gene transfer

(4) Isolate and introduce only one or a set of desirable genes without introducing undesirable genes into target organism

(5) **All of the above is true**

Q. 11. What is true about 'Ori':

(1) Responsible for initiating replication

(2) For multiplication of any alien pieces of DNA in an organism it needs to be a part of a chromosome which has a specific sequence known as ori

(3) An alien DNA is linked with ori so that this alien piece of DNA can replicate and multiply the many copies of any template DNA

(4) **All of the above**

Q. 12. In which of the following below mentioned statements, one is true about construction of an artificial rec. DNA molecule?

(1) The construction of first rec. DNA emerged from possibility of linking a gene encoding antibiotic resistance with a native plasmid of *S. typhimurium*

(2) S. Cohen and H. Boyer accomplished this in 1992 by isolating the antibiotic resistance gene by cutting out a piece of DNA from a plasmid which was responsible for conferring antibiotic resistance

(3) The cutting of DNA at specific locations become possible with discovery of so-called molecular scissors restriction endonucleases act on complete DNA molecules

(4) **All of the above are true statements**

Q. 13. Restriction endonuclease used in genetic engineering?

(1) **To form recombinant molecules of DNA composed of DNA from different sources/genomes**

(2) To form recombinant molecules of DNA composed of DNA from a single sources/genomes

(3) To form recombinant molecules of DNA composed of DNA from two sources

(4) None of the above is true statements

Q. 14. Who act as vectors to transfer the piece of DNA attached to it?

(1) **Plasmid DNA**

(2) Cosmid DNA

(3) Both 1 and 2

(4) Bacteriophage

Q. 15. What is correctly matched pair is?

(1) Cut other DNA-Restriction endonuclease

(2) Added $-CH_3$ group to DNA-Restriction exonuclease

(3) First restriction endonuclease-Hind II

(4) Stickiness of ends-DNA ligase

(5) All of the above are correctly matched

Q. 16. Basic steps in genetically modifications of an organisms:

(1) Identification of DNA with desirable genes

(2) Introduction of the identified DNA into host

(3) Maintenance of introduced DNA into host and transfer of DNA to its progeny

(4) All of the above

Q. 17. Key tools of genetic engineering or recombinant DNA technology:

(1) Restriction enzymes

(2) Polymerase enzymes

(3) Ligase

(4) Vectors and host organism

(5) All of the above are true

Q. 18. Overhanging stretches (single stranded portion at the ends) after restriction endonuclease processes called sticky ends because:

(1) They form hydrogen bonds with their complementary cut counterparts

(2) They form ionic bonds with their complementary cut counterparts

(3) They form peptide bonds with their complementary cut counterparts

(4) None of the above are true statements

Q. 19. Enzymes responsible for restricting the growth of bacteriophage in *E. coli*:

(1) Hind II-always cut DNA molecules at a particular point by recognizing a specific sequence of 6 base pairs

(2) ECO-RI-isolated from *E. coli* RY13

(3) Bam-III

(4) Both 1 and 2

Q. 20. In which of the following below mentioned statements, one is true for restriction enzymes?

(1) Eco RI comes from *E. coli* RY13

(2) R derived from name of strain

(3) Each R. endonulease functions by inspecting the length of a DNA sequence and each recognizes a specific palindromic nucleotide sequences in DNA

(4) Restriction endonuclease cut each of the two strands of the double helix at specific points in their sugar-phoaphate backbones

(5) All of the above are true statements

Q. 21. What is indicated by roman numbers associated with restriction enzymes?

(1) Order in which the enzymes were isolated from that strain of bacteria

(2) Order in which the enzymes were isolated from that strain of virus

(3) Order in which the enzymes were isolated from that strain of fungi

(4) Order in which the enzymes were isolated from that strain of both fungi and bacteria

Q. 22. In which of the following below mentioned statements, one is true?

(1) Mosquitoes act as an insect vector to transfer the malaria parasite into human body

(2) A plasmid can be used as vector to deliver an alien piece of DNA into host organism

(3) The liking of antibiotic resistance gene with plasmid vector became possible with enzyme DNA ligase act on cut down DNA molecules and joins their ends

(4) DNA ligase makes a new combinations of circular automatically replicating DNA created *in vitro* and known as Rec.DNA when

transferred to *E. coli*, it could replicating using a new host's DNA polymerase make multiple copies

(5) All of the above are true statements

Q. 23. Features required to facilitate cloning into a vector:

(1) ori-point of replication staring
(2) Selectable marker
(3) Cloning sites
(4) All of the above

Q. 24. Name of method in which Rec-DNA is bombarded with high velocity microparticles of gold/tungsten coated:

(1) Biolistics
(2) Gene gun
(3) Heat shock
(4) Both 1 and 2

Q. 25. In which of the following below mentioned statements, one is true?

(1) The separated DNA fragments can be visualized only after staining DNA with a compound known as ethidium bromide followed by exposure to UV radiation
(2) Pure DNA fragments see in the visible light and without staining
(3) We see bright orange coloured bands of DNA in an ethidium stained gel exposed to UV light
(4) Elution is a process in which the separated bands of DNA are cut out from gel piece
(5) All of the above are true statements

Q. 26. Elution is concerned with

(1) Gel electrophoresis
(2) PCR
(3) Cosmid hybridization
(4) Bacterial transformation

Q. 27. The aim of engineering of vectors during a genetic engineering process

(1) Easy linking of foreign DNA
(2) Selection of recombinants from non-recombinants
(3) To produce selectable marker
(4) Both 1 and 2

Q. 28. In which of the following below mentioned statements, one is true?

(1) Plasmids and bacteriophage have the ability to replicate within bacterial cells independently control of chromosomal DNA
(2) Owing to very high number per cell bacteriophage have very high copy number of their genome with a bacterial cells
(3) Other plasmids may have only one/two copies /cell while others may have 15–100 copies per cells
(4) If we link an alien DNA to plasmid DNA/bacteriophage we can multiply its number equal to copy number of plasmid or bacteriophage
(5) All of the above are true statements

Q. 29. The resultant DNA fragments have the same kind of sticky ends and these can be joined together end to end using DNA ligase; it can cut possible they used of:

(1) DNA cut by same kind of Restriction endonuclease
(2) DNA cut by two different kind of restriction endonucleases
(3) DNA cut by three different kind of restriction endonucleases
(4) DNA cut by various kind of restriction endonucleases

Q. 30. Recognition sequence for Hind II consists of:

(1) Six base pairs
(2) 4 base pairs
(3) 5 base pairs
(4) 7 base pairs

Q. 31. Role of selectable marker in cloning rather than 'ori':

(1) Helps in identifying nontransformant

(2) Eliminating nontransformant

(3) Selectively permitting the growth of transformants

(4) All of the above are true

Q. 32. In which of the following below mentioned statements, one is true?

(1) DNA fragments can be separated by gel electrophoresis which produced by restriction endonucleases

(2) DNA fragments are negatively charged molecules can be separated by forcing them to more towards anode (+) under electric field by a medium/matrix agrose, most common used matrix taken from sea weeds

(3) DNA fragments separate according to their size by sieving effect provided by agrose gel

(4) All of the above are true statements

Q. 33. In order to link the alien DNA, the vector needs to have very few preferably ..... recognition sites for the commonly used restriction enzymes:

(1) Single

(2) Double

(3) Three

(4) Four

Q. 34. A breeding do not want complication of gene cloning what approach he adopt:

(1) Prevent the presence of more than one recognition sites within the vector which produce several fragments

(2) Prevent the presence of more than one recognition sites within the vector which produce single fragments

(3) Prevent the presence of more than two recognition sites within the vector which produce two fragments

(4) None of the above are true

Q. 35. In which of the following below mentioned statements, one is true?

(1) We can legate a foreign DNA at Bam HI site of tetracycline resistance gene in vector pBR322

(2) Rec plasmid will lose tetracycline resistance due to insertion of foreign DNA but can still be selected out from non-recombinant ones by plating the transformants on ampicillin containing medium

(3) Recombinants will grow in ampicillin containing medium but not on a medium in tetracycline

(4) All of the above are true statements

Q. 36. The correct sequence of processes involved in the Rec-DNA technology?

1. Isolation of DNA
2. Fragmentation of DNA by restriction endonuclease
3. Isolation of desired DNA fragment
4. Ligation of DNA fragment into vector
5. Transferring the rec. DNA into host
6. Culturing the host cells in a medium at large scale
7. Extraction of desired product

(1) 1, 2, 3, 4, 5, 6, 7

(2) 1, 3, 2, 4, 5, 6, 7

(3) 3, 2, 1, 4, 5, 6, 7

(4) All of the above are true statements

Q. 37. DNA is enclosed within membranes we have to break the cell open to release DNA, achieved by:

(1) Lysozyme

(2) Cellulase

(3) Chitinase

(4) All of the above

Q. 38. Inside the cells, DNA contained along with?

(1) **RNA-protein-polysaccharide-lipid**

(2) RNA-lipid only

(3) Polysaccharide-protein-lipids

(4) Vitamin-proteins-mineral-lipids

Q. 39. In which of the following below mentioned statements, one is true about 'ORI'?

(1) Sequence from where replication starts and any piece of DNA when linked to this can be replicate within host

(2) Control copy number of linked DNA

(3) If one wants to recover more copies of target DNA it should be cloned in a vector whose origin support high copy number

(4) **All of the above are true statements**

Q. 40. *E. coli* **cloning vector pBR322 showing restriction sites is/are:**

(1) Hind III-Eco RI, Ori

(2) Bam HI, sai I, antibiotic resistance genes amp-R and Tet-R

(3) PvuII-Pst I-Cla I

(4) **All of the above**

Q. 41. In which of the following below mentioned statements, one is true?

(1) Transformations is a procedure by which a piece of DNA is introduced in a host bacterium

(2) Normally the genes encoding resistance to antibiotics like ampicillin chloramphenicol tetra-cyclins or kanamycin (useful selectable marker for *E. coli*)

(3) Normally, *E. coli* cells do not carry resistatance against any of these antibiotics

(4) **All of the above are true statements**

Q. 42. Restriction enzymes cut the strand of DNA:

(1) A little away from the centre of palindrome sites

(2) Between the same two bases on the opposite strands

(3) Leaves single stranded portion at the ends

(4) **All of the above**

Q. 43. What is codes through 'Rop Codes'?

(1) **Proteins (genes) involved in the replication of the plasmid**

(2) Proteins (genes) involved in the translation of the plasmid

(3) Proteins (genes) involved in the transcription of the plasmid

(4) None of the above are true

Q. 44. In which of the following below mentioned statements, one is true about antibiotic resistance gene?

(1) Helps in selecting the transformants

(2) They activated due to insertion of alien DNA

(3) Helps in selection of recombinants

(4) **All of the above are true statements**

Q. 45. Selection of recombinants due to inactivation of antibiotics is a cumbersome procedure because it requires:

(1) **Simultaneous plating on two plates having different antibiotics**

(2) Simultaneous plating on two plates having same antibiotics

(3) Simultaneous plating on four plates having same antibiotics

(4) Simultaneous plating on three plates having different antibiotics

Q. 46. Selective markers developed which differentiate recombinants from non-recombinants on basis of their:

(1) Weight

(2) Ability to produce colour in presence of a chromogenic substrate

(3) Ability to produce based with reaction on antibodies

(4) All of the above are true

Q. 47. In which of the following below mentioned statements, one is not true?

(1) Nucleic acid is genetic material of all organisms without exception

(2) In majority of organisms DNA is genetic material

(3) In order to cut the DNA with RE it needs to be in pure form and free from other macromolecules

(4) None of the above

Q. 48. What are true statements is/are?

(1) Genes located on long molecules of DNA inter-winged with proteins such as Histones

(2) RNA removed by ribonuclease and proteins by protease

(3) Purified DNA ultimately pre-cipitated out after the addition of chilled ethanol

(4) Isolated DNA can be seen as colle-ction of fine threats in suspension

(5) All of the above

Q. 49. Steps involved in the cutting of DNA at specific location?

(1) Digestion of DNA performed by incubating purified DNA molecules with restriction enzyme

(2) Agrose gel electrophoresis is employed to check progression of a RE digestion

(3) Negatively charged DNA moves towards the positive elected (anode) and process repeated with vector DNA also

(4) All of the above are true statements

Q. 50. Agrose gel electrophoresis is employed to:

(1) Check the progression of a re-striction enzyme digestion during cutting of DNA molecules with RE

(2) Check the progression of a restriction enzyme digestion during cutting of RNA molecules with RE

(3) Check the progression of a Hydrolase enzyme digestion during cutting of RNA molecules with Eco. R1 (3)

(4) None of the above true

Q. 51. During preparation of Rec. DNA the gene of interest is cut from the:

(1) Source DNA

(2) Vector DNA

(3) Both 1 and 2

(4) None

Q. 52. A thermostable DNA used is repeated amplification is a achieved, isolated from:

(1) *Thermus aquaticus*

(2) Thermus thurigenesis

(3) Both 1 and 2

(4) None of the above are true state-ments

Q. 53. Primers are:

(1) Small chemically synthesized oligo-nucleotides that is com-plementary to the regions of DNA

(2) Small chemically synthesized oligo-nucleotides that is com-plementary to the regions of RNA

(3) Long chemically synthesized oligo-nucleotides that is com-plementary to the regions of DNA and RNA both

(4) Long chemically synthesized oligonucleotides that is com-plementary to the regions of DNA

Q. 54. Function of enzyme DNA polymerase:

(1) Extends the primers using the nucleotides provided in the reaction and the genomic DNA as template

(2) Extends the primers using the nucleotides provided in the reaction and the genomic DNA as primers

(3) Extends the primers using the nucleotides provided in the reaction and the genomic DNA as template and primers both

(4) None of the above are true

Q. 55. Which enzyme is used in cloning of vector in genetic engineering?

(1) Permease

(2) β-galactosidase

(3) Both 1 and 2

(4) Lactose

Q. 56. If the process of replication of DNA is repeated many times, the segment of DNA can be amplified to approximately?

(1) Billions times

(2) Million times

(3) Lakh times

(4) Thousand times

Q. 57. What is insertional inactivation?

(1) Rec. DNA inserted in the coding sequence of enzyme (beta-galactosidase)

(2) Rec. DNA inserted in the non-coding sequence of enzyme (peroxidase)

(3) Rec. DNA inserted in the non-coding sequence of enzyme (beta-galactosidase)

(4) Rec. DNA inserted in the coding sequence of enzyme (peroxidase)

Q. 58. Repeated amplification is achieved by the use of a?

(1) Thermostable DNA polymerase

(2) Thermostable RNA polymerase

(3) Both 1 and 2

(4) Heat stable RNA polymerase

Q. 59. In which of the following below mentioned statements, one is true for competent host?

(1) DNA is hydrophilic molecule and cannot pass by cell membrane

(2) To make rec. bacterial cell must first be made competent to take up DNA

(3) Bacterial cell make competent by treating it with a specific concentration of a divalent cation (Ca^{2+}) to increase efficiency with which DNA enter the bacterium by pores in its cell wall

(4) All of the above

Q. 60. What is true about Agrobacterium tumifaciens?

(1) A pathogen of several dicot plants is able to deliver a piece of DNA (T-DNA) to transform normal plant cells into a tumour cell

(2) The tumour inducing (Ti) plasmid of A tumifaciens modified into a cloning vector which is number more pathogenic to plants but still able to use the mechanism to deliver genes of our interest into a variety of plants

(3) Both 1 and 2

(4) None

Q. 61. Similarly to *A. tumifaciens* in animals retrovirus have the ability to transform:

(1) Normal cells into cancerous cells

(2) Retrovirus have also been a disarmed

(3) Retrovirus used to deliver desirable genes into cancerous cells

(4) All of the above

Q. 62. Once a gene or a DNA fragment has been ligated into a suitable vector it is transformed into a:

(1) Bacterial host

(2) Plant host

(3) Animal host

(4) **All of the above**

Q. 63. Sampling ports present in the bio-rector facilitates the:

(1) **Small volumes of the culture can be withdrawn periodically**

(2) Small volumes of the culture can be withdrawn regularly

(3) Small volumes of the culture can be withdrawn periodically and regularly both

(4) None of the above are true

Q. 64. How we produce rec. DNA, the correct sequence of steps is/are:

a. Incubating the cells with rec. DNA on ice

b. Cells followed briefly with 42C heat shock

c. Cells putting them on ice

d. Cells putting them on hot coak

(1) **A, B, C**   (2) A, C, B

(3) A, D, B   (4) B, D, A

Q. 65. In which of the following below mentioned statements, one is true for insertion of recombinant DNA into the host cell/organisms?

(1) Several methods of introducing the liagted DNA into recipient cells

(2) Recipient cells after making them competent to receive take up DNA present in its surroundings

(3) If we spread the transferred cells on Ager plates coating ampicillin only transformants will grow untransformed recipient cells will die

(4) **All of the above are true statements**

Q. 66. Recombinant colonial gives which kind of colour in cloning process:

(1) Blue

(2) Black

(3) Yellow

(4) **No any kind of colour**

Q. 67. In cloning process, if the plasmid in bacteria does not have an insert (non-recombinant) then colour:

(1) **Blue**   (2) Black

(3) Yellow   (4) None

Q. 68. In which of the following below mentioned statements, one is true about bioreactors?

(1) To produce large amount of (100–1000 L) of culture

(2) They are vessel in which raw materials are biologically converted into specific products individual's enzymes using microbial plant or animals or human cells

(3) Provides optimal conditions for achieving the desired product of providing optimum growth conditions (temp, pH, substrate, salts, vitamins and O_2)

(4) **All of the above are true statements**

Q. 69. In which a matched column is/are?

(1) Micro-injection-Animal cells

(2) Biolistics (gene gun)-Plant cells

(3) Dis-armed pathogen (vector)-Both animals/plant

(4) A. tumifaciens-T-DNA

(5) **All of the above**

Q. 70. The DNA that separates out can be removed by:

(1) **Spooling**

(2) Hybridization

(3) Mutation

(4) Micropropagation

Q. 71. Rec.DNA is directly injected into nucleus of a animal cell, method called:

(1) **Micro-injection**

(2) Micropropagation

(3) Hybridization

(4) Both 1 and 3

Q. 72. The ultimate aim of almost all recombinant DNA technologies is:

(1) **Produce a desirable protein**
(2) Produce a high quality protein
(3) Produce a low quality protein
(4) Produce distorted proteins

Q. 73. Why protein produced through the genetic engineering called recombinant protein?

(1) **Gene is expressed in a heterologous host**
(2) Gene is expressed in a homologous host
(3) Gene is non-expressing in any host
(4) Consisting of a single kind of amino acids

Q. 74. What is true?

(1) Cells harbouring cloned genes of interest may be grown on a small scale in the Lab
(2) The cultures may be used for extracting the desired protein and then purifying it by using different separation technologies
(3) Cells can also be multiplied in a continuous culture system-medium drained out from one side and fresh medium added to other to maintain the cells in their physiologically most active log/exponential phase
(4) **All are correct**

Q. 75. Which culture medium used for producing large biomass/higher yield of desired protein:

(1) **Continuous culture system**
(2) Batch culture system
(3) Half-Batch culture system
(4) All of the above

Q. 76. The most commonly used bioreactors are:

(1) **Stirring type**
(2) Curved type

(3) Both 1 and 2
(4) Non-stirring type

Q. 77. Select the correct matches about stirring type bioreactors:

(1) Increase surface area-O_2 transfer
(2) Steam-sterilization
(3) Bubbles-increase O_2 transfer area
(4) Acid-base-pH controller
(5) **All of the above**

Q. 78. A stirred tank reactor is usually cylindrical or with a curved base to:

(1) **Facilitate the mixing of reactor content**
(2) Maximum production of CO_2
(3) Maximum production of methane
(4) Minimum production of hydrogen

Q. 79. The Stirrer facilitates the:

(1) Mixing throughout the biorectoter
(2) Oxygen availability throughout the bioreactor
(3) **Both 1 and 2**
(4) Temperature constancy

Q. 80. Bioreactor has

(1) Agitator system-O_2 delivery system
(2) A foam control system-Temperature control system
(3) pH-control system-Sampling ports
(4) **All of the above**

Q. 81. The product in a bioreactor has to be subjected though a series of processes before it is ready for marketing as a finished product, after completion of which phase:

(1) **Biosynthetic phase**
(2) Purification phase
(3) Delivery phase
(4) Separation phase

Q. 82. Downstream processing possess:

(1) Separation
(2) Purification

(3) Biosynthetic phase

(4) Both 1 and 2

Q. 83. What stage will be vary for a recombinant product formulation:

(1) Downstream processing

(2) Quality control testing

(3) Both 1 and 2

(4) Purification

Q. 84. Downstream processing contain clinical trials in case of:

(1) Drugs

(2) Bakery products

(3) Milk products

(4) All of the above

C-5

Q. 1. The principles of photosynthesis are established by:

(1) Melvin Calvin

(2) Hatch-Slack cycle

(3) Both 1 and 2

(4) TCA

Q. 2. Melvin Calvin established the principles of photosynthesis being used in studies on which kind of resource for energy and materials and basic studies in solar energy research:

(1) Renewable resources

(2) Nonrenewable resources

(3) Both 1 and 2

(4) None

Q. 3. Melvin Calvin along with JA Bassham studied reactions in green plants forming sugar and other substances from raw materials like CO_2, H_2O and minerals by labelling the CO_2 with?

(1) C^{12}

(2) C^{14}

(3) P^{15}

(4) S^{32}

Q. 4. Just after World War II, when the world was under shock after the Hiroshima-Nagasaki bombings and seeing the ill effects of radioactivity who put radioactivity to beneficial use?

(1) Calvin and coworkers

(2) Bashaam and coworkers

(3) Hatch-Slack and Calvin

(4) Joseph-Priestly

Q. 5. Who is and who got Nobel Prize (1961), (a) proposed that plants change light energy to chemical energy by transferring an electron in an organized array of pigment molecules and other substances (b) The mapping of pathway of carbon assimilation in photosynthesis?

(1) Malvin-Calvin

(2) Hatch-Slack and Calvin

(3) Calvin and Basham

(4) Basham and Hatch-slack

Q. 6. True statement is/are

(1) Plants need to move molecules over very long distances much more than animals do

(2) In a flowering plant the substances that would need to be transported are water, minerals nutrients, organic nutrients and PGR

(3) Over small distances substances move by diffusion and by cytoplasmic streaming supplemented by active transport

(4) Transport over long distances proceeds through the vascular system (xylem and phloem) called translocation

(5) All are true

Q. 7. True statement is:

(1) In rooted plants, transported in xylem (water plus minerals) is essentially unidirectional from roots to stems

(2) Organic and minerals nutrients undergo multidirectional transport

(3) When any plant part undergoes senescence, nutrient may be withdrawn from such regions and moved to growing parts

(4) PGRs and other chemical stimuli are also transported in a strictly polarize (sometimes) or unidirectional manner from where they are synthesized to other parts

(5) All are true

Q. 8. **Movement of diffusion is passive and may be exemplified through:**

(1) From one part of the cell to the other

(2) From cell to cell

(3) Over short distances (i.e. from the intercellular spaces of the leaf to the outside)

(4) All of the above

Q. 9. **What is a true fact about diffusion?**

(1) Passive process, i.e. no energy expenditure

(2) Molecules move in random fashion

(3) It is slow process and not dependent on living system

(4) Only means for gaseous movement within plant body

(5) All are true

Q. 10. **True facts is/are:**

(1) Rates of diffusion affected by concentrated gradient, membrane permeability, temperature and pressure

(2) Most obvious in gaseous and liquids than solids

(3) Net result of diffusion is substances moving from regions of higher concentration to regions of lower concentration

(4) All are true

Q. 11. **Why substances soluble in lipids diffuse through the membrane faster:**

(1) Lipids is a major part of membrane

(2) Lipids do set a concentration gradient necessary for passing

(3) Membrane lipids provides sites at which such molecules cross membrane

(4) None of the above

Q. 12. **Osmosis is the movement of which molecules?**

(1) Oxygen   (2) Hydrogen

(3) Any   **(4) Water**

Q. 13. **True facts about facilitated diffusion:**

(1) Special proteins help move substances across membrane without expenditure of ATP energy

(2) It would require input of energy

(3) It cannot cause net transport of molecules from a low to a high concentration

(4) All are true

Q. 14. **True facts is/are:**

(1) Transport rate reaches a maximum when all of protein transporters are being used

(2) FD is very specific; it allows cell to select substances for uptake

(3) FD is sensitive to inhibitors reacts with protein side chains

(4) All of the above

Q. 15. **True statement about 'PORINS' is/are:**

(1) Proteins that form huge pores in outer membrane of plastids mitochondria and same bacteria

(2) Proteins form pores allowing molecules up to the size of small proteins to pass through

(3) The transport protein (porins) rotates and releases the molecules inside the cell

(4) All of the above are true

Q. 16. **Number of aquaporins constitutes the water channels in membrane:**
(1) 4
(2) 3
(3) 8
(4) 10

Q. 17. **Matches the column A and Column B**

Col. A		Col. B
A.	Aquaporins	(i) Movement in one direction
B.	Symport	(ii) Movement in both directions
C.	Anti-port	(iii) Water channels
D.	Uni-port	(iv) Both molecules cross membrane in one direction

(1) A (iii), B (iv), C (ii), D (i)
(2) A (ii), B (iii), A (i), D (iv)
(3) A (iii), D (iv), C (ii), B (i)
(4) A (i), B (iv), C (iii), D (ii)

Q. 18. **What is true for active transport?**
(1) Use energy to pump molecules against a concentration gradient
(2) It carried out by membrane proteins
(3) Like enzymes these (carriers) proteins are sensitive to inhibitors that react with protein side chains
(4) All of the above

Q. 19. **What is true about pump (proteins)?**
(1) Pumps are proteins use energy to carry substances across the cell membrane
(2) They can transport substances from a high concentration to a low concentration (uphill transport)
(3) Transport rate reaches a maximum when all the proteins transporters are being used or are saturated
(4) All of the above are true

Q. 20. **Membrane proteins play role in:**
(1) Active transport
(2) Passive transport
(3) Facilitated diffusion
(4) All of the above

Q. 21. **Proteins in membrane are responsible for facilitated diffusion and active transport and hence show common characteristics:**
(1) Highly selective
(2) Liable to saturate
(3) Respond to inhibitors
(4) Hormonal control
(5) All of the above

Q. 22. **What is similarity between diffusion and facilitated diffusion?**
(1) Both takes place only along gradient
(2) Both carried out without energy expenditure
(3) Both are important for plant growth
(4) All are true

Q. 23. **Inhibitors of following mechanisms is not highly selective**
(1) Simple diffusion
(2) Facilitated transport
(3) Active transport
(4) All of the above

Q. 24. **Transport saturates occur in which of the following processes:**
(1) Simple diffusion
(2) Facilitated diffusion
(3) Active transport
(4) All of the above

Q. 25. **In which of the following is a uphill transport and need ATP energy**
(1) Simple diffusion
(2) Facilitated transport
(3) Active transport
(4) All of the above

Q. 26. **What are true facts?**

(1) Protoplasm of cells is nothing but water in which different molecules are dissolved and suspended

(2) Watermelon has 95% water; herbaceous plants contain 10–15% of its fresh weight as dry matter

(3) A seed may appear dry but it still has water-otherwise it would not be alive and respiring

(4) A mature corn plant absorbs almost three liters of water in a day while mustard absorbs water equal to its own weight in about 8 hours

(5) All are true

Q. 27. **True statement is:**

(1) Terrestrial plants take up huge amount of water daily but most of it lost as transpiration

(2) Transpiration is loss of water to air through evaporation from leaves

(3) Water potential (φw) is a concept fundamental to understanding water movement

(4) Solute potential (φs) and pressure potential (φp) are two main components that determine water potential

(5) All are true

Q. 28. **True facts about water potential?**

1. Denoted by Greek symbol Psi/φ and expressed as pressure units like pascals (Pa); affected by both $\varphi S + \varphi P$, $\varphi W = \varphi S + \varphi P$

(2) Pure water has greatest water potential (zero) at standard temperature, which is not under any pressure

(3) The greater the concentration of water in a system, greater is its kinetic energy (water potential)

(4) Water move from a system of higher φw.

(5) All are true

Q. 29. **True statement is:**

(1) Water contains kinetic energy. In liquids and gaseous form they are in random motion (rapid and constant)

(2) If some solute is dissolved in pure water, the concentration of water decreases (φw reduces)

(3) All solution has low φw than pure water

(4) Solute potential (φs) is always negative

(5) All of the above

Q. 30. **The φw of solution will be ....
than solvent or pure water:**

(1) Low   (2) High

(3) Equal   (4) Zero

Q. 31. **What is solute potential?**

(1) The magnitude of lowering due to dissolution of a solute to solvent produce solution and resulting the reduction of φw of solution as compare to solvent

(2) The magnitude of lowering due to dissolution of a solute to solvent produce solution and resulting the enhancing of φw of solution as compare to solvent

(3) The magnitude of lowering due to dissolution of a solvent to solute produce solution and resulting the reduction of φw of solution as compare to solvent

(4) All of the above

Q. 32. **True for solute potential?**

(1) More solute in solution, more negative value of φs.

(2) At atmospheric pressure, for a solution, water potential is equal to solute potential ($\varphi w = \varphi s$)

(3) If a pressure greater than atmospheric pressure is applied to pure water (a solution), its φw increases.

(4) All are true

Q. 33. True statement is

(1) Pressure can build up in a plant system when water enters a plant cell due to diffusion causing a pressure built-up against the cell wall, it makes in cell turgid

(2) When cell turgid then pressure potential increases, i.e. when water enters the cell through diffusion produce pressure potential (φp)

(3) φp is usually positive while negative φp in water column inside xylem plays a major role in water transport in upper side of stem ($\varphi w = \varphi s + \varphi p$)

(4) All are true

Q. 34. The cell wall of the plant cell in solution is permeable to:

(1) Solvent (water)

(2) Solutes (substances)

(3) Both

(4) None

Q. 35. True statement is:

(1) Cell wall is not a barrier of movement of solvent a solute

(2) Pulses are rare known rotational crops

(3) Chickpea does not need any nutrition and usually grow it on the marginal lands

(4) Chickpea is not a good source of green manure

Q. 36. In plant, vacuole/vascular sap contribute to:

(1) φs

(2) φw

(3) φp

(4) All of the above

Q. 37. In plant cells, which are important determinant of movement of molecules in/out of the cell:

(1) The cell membrane-Tonoplast

(2) Cell-wall-Tonoplast

(3) Cell membrane-nuclear membrane

Q. 38. What is true about osmosis?

(1) Term used specifically to diffusion of water across a differentially or semipermeably membrane

(2) Occurs spontaneously in response to a driving force

(3) Net direction and rate depends on booth pressure gradient (φp) and concentration gradient (φs)

(4) Filling of water in potato osmometer in due to osmosis

(5) All of the above

Q. 39. Above figure where two chambers A and B containing solutions separated by a semipermeable membrane. Give the answer of following questions:

(1) Solution of which chamber has a lower water potential B

(2) Solution of which chamber has a lower solute potential A

(3) In which direction will osmosis occur (A → B)

(4) At equilibrium which chamber will have lower water potential-none of both?

(5) If one chamber has a w, of –2000 K.Pa, and the other –1000 K.Pa. Which is the chamber that has the higher φ? And chamber B (other, which has –100 K.Pa.)

Q. 40. If we remove yolk and albumin through a small hole at one end of the egg and place the shell in dilute solution of HCl for a few hours, we find which type of membrane after shell dissolution?

(1) **Semipermeable membrane**
(2) Permeable membrane
(3) Both 1 and 2
(4) None of the above

Q. 41. A thistle funnel is filled with sucrose solution and kept inverted in a beaker containing water, first we find that water will diffuse across the membrane to raise the level of solution in funnel; secondly, pressure can be applied to stop the water movement into funnel. This description is about which process?

(1) **Osmosis**   (2) Hydrolysis
(3) Both 1 and 2 (4) Diffusion

Q. 42. True statement is/are:

(1) Numerically osmotic pressure is equivalent to the osmotic potential
(2) Sign of osmotic pressure is reverse to osmotic potential
(3) Osmotic pressure is posssitive pressure applied while osmotic potential is negative
(4) **All of the above is true**

Q. 43. The behavior of the plant cells (tissues) with regard to water movement depends on the:

(1) Solute concentration
(2) Solved concentration
(3) **Surrounding solution**
(4) All of the above are true

Q. 44. True statements is/are

(1) If the external solution balances the osmotic pressure of the cytoplasm, called isotonic
(2) If external solution, is more dilute than cytoplasm called hypotonic

(3) If the external solution is more concentrated, if is called hypertonic solution
(4) **All are true**

Q. 45. Cell swell and shrink respectively in

(1) **Hypotonic and hypertonic solution**
(2) Hypertonic and hypotonic solution
(3) Hypertonic and isotonic solution
(4) Isotonic and hypotonic solution

Q. 46. Plasmolysis of cell occurs when

(1) Water moves out of the cell
(2) The cell membrane of a plant cell shrinking away from its cell-wall
(3) Cell is placid in a solution that is hypertonic (more solutes) than cell's protoplasm
(4) **All are true**

Q. 47. When plasmolysis occurs, water moves out and it is first lost from?

(1) Protoplasm and then mitochondria
(2) **Cytoplasm and then vacuole**
(3) Cytoplasm and then nucleoplast
(4) Cytoplasm and then protoplasm

Q. 48. During plasmolysis, water is drawn out of the cell through:

(1) Osmosis
(2) **Diffusion**
(3) Both 1 and 2
(4) Facilitated diffusion

Q. 49. In plasmolysis, water moves:

(1) **From area of the high water potential (the cell) to lower water potential (outside the cell)**
(2) From area of the low water potential (the cell) to high water potential (outside the cell)
(3) Both 1 and 2
(4) None of the above

Q. 50. The cells are said to be flaccid when?

(1) Water flows into the cell
(2) Water flows out of the cell

(3) Water movement are in equilibrium

(4) **All are correct**

Q. 51. True statement is/are:

(1) Plasmolysis is usually reversible

(2) Turgor pressure created (produced) when cells put in the hypotonic solution

(3) Turgor pressure is similar to pressure potential (φp) both exerted pressure against cell wall due to entry of water inside the cell

(4) Turgor pressure is ultimately responsible for enlargement and extension growth of cells

(5) All of the above are true

Q. 52. φp of flaccid cell will be:

(1) Zero   (2) One

(3) Two   (4) Three

Q. 53. Turgor pressure (pressure gradient against cell wall) is cell:

(1) When cell placed in hypotonic solution (high φw or low φs or dilute solution as compared to cytoplasm) water diffuses (diffusion) into cells causing the cytoplasm to build up a pressure against the cell wall

(2) Responsible for the germination of seed

(3) It maintain the cytoplasm in a gel condition

(4) All are true

Q. 54. Which process involved in induction of turgor pressure in cell?

(1) Osmosis

(2) Diffusion

(3) Both 1 and 2

(4) Active transport

Q. 55. What is true about imbibition?

(1) Special type diffusion where water absorbed by solid (collides) cause increase in volume

(2) Absorption of water by seeds and dry seeds are classical examples

(3) Prehistoric man used imbibitions to spilt rocks and boulders

(4) All are true

Q. 56. Inhibition is also diffusion because:

(1) Water movement is along a concentration gradient

(2) Water movement is parallel a concentration gradient

(3) Water movement is opposite a concentration gradient

(4) All of the above

Q. 57. True facts about imbibition

(1) The seeds and other such materials have almost no water hence they absorb water easily

(2) Water potential gradient between the absorbent and the liquid imbibed is essential for imbibition

(3) For any substances to imbibe any liquid, affinity between the adsorbent and the liquid is also a prerequisite

(4) All of the above

Q. 58. True facts about imbibition.

(1) The seeds and other such materials have almost no water hence they absorb water easily

(2) Water potential gradient between the absorbent and the liquid imbibed is essential for imbibition

(3) For any substances to imbibe any liquid affinity between the adsorbent and the liquid is also a prerequisite

(4) All of the above are true

Q. 59. Experiment twig bearing white flowers is coloured water and had watched it turn colour. Show what tissue mainly involved for above mentioned change:

(1) Xylem

(2) Phloem

(3) Xylem tracheids

(4) Xylem vessels

Q. 60. True statement is:

(1) Long distance transport of substances within a plant cannot be by diffusion alone

(2) Diffusion can account for only short distances movement of molecular, e.g. About 50 μm take app. 2.5 second

(3) Diffusion or active transport would not suffice for transport of substances across very large distances

(4) All are true

Q. 61. What is true for Mass or Bulk Flow?

(1) Water and minerals and food are generally moved by a mass /bulk flow system

(2) It carried out as a result of pressure difference between the two points

(3) The characteristics of mass flow is that substances whether in solution/suspension are swept along at the same place as in a flowing river.

(4) Mass flow is differ from diffusion-different substances move independently depending on their concentration gradient

(5) All are true

Q. 62. Bulk flow can be achieved either through

(1) A positive hydrostatic pressure (e.g. garden house)

(2) A negative hydrostatic pressure (e.g. suction through a straw)

(3) Both 1 and 2

(4) None of the above

Q. 63. A variety of the BT used in the control of the black cut worms called:

(1) BT 1

(2) BT II

(3) BT III

(4) BT IV

Q. 64. Translocation is:

(1) Bulk movement of substances through the conducting by vascular tissues of plants

(2) Bulk movement of substances through the conducting by tracheids of plant

(3) Bulk movement of substances through the conducting by vessels of plant

(4) All of the above

Q. 65. Xylem is associated with translocation of which substances from root to aerial parts of plants mainly:

(1) Water

(2) Mineral salts

(3) Some organic-N and hormones

(4) All of the above

Q. 66. Dilute means....

(1) A little solute and a lot of water

(2) A lot of solute and little water

(3) Concentrated

(4) The same

Q. 67. Why we apply water to the soil and not to the leaves while main site of water utilization is leaf?

(1) Roots absorb most of water that goes into plants

(2) Roots absorb less of water that goes into plants

(3) Both 1 and 2

(4) None of the above are true

Q. 68. True statement is/are:

(1) More specifically the function of root hairs (million) is responsibility of absorption of water and minerals

(2) Root hairs are thin walled slender extensions of root epidermal cells, increase surface area for absorption

(3) Water is absorbed along with mineral solutes by root hairs purely by diffusion

(4) All are true

Q. 69. Once water is absorbed by root hairs, it can move deeper into root layers by which pathway(s):

(1) Apoplast   (2) Symplast
(3) Both 1 and 2 (4) None

Q. 70. Apoplast is system of adjacent cell walls that is continues throughout the plant except Casparian stripes of endodermis in roots. What is true facts about apoplastic is/are:

(1) Apoplastic movement of water occurs exclusively through intercellular spaces and walls of cells
(2) Apoplastic movement does not involve crossing the cell membrane
(3) Apoplastic movement is gradient-dependent and do not provide any barrier to movement and is mass flow type
(4) All are true

Q. 71. Mass flow of water during the apoplastic movement occurs due to:

(1) Adhesive properties of water
(2) Cohesive properties of water
(3) Both 1 and 2
(4) None of the above

Q. 72. Symplastic system is:

(1) System of interconnected protoplast through cytoplasmic strands that extends through plasmodesmata
(2) System of interconnected membranes through cytoplasmic strands that extends through plasmodesmata
(3) System of interconnected plasmodesmata through cytoplasmic strands that extends through plasmodesmata
(4) None of the above are true

Q. 73. During the symplastic movement, the water travels through the:

(1) Intercellularly (by cytoplasm)
(2) Intracellularly (by plasmodesmata)

(3) Both 1 and 2
(4) None of the above

Q. 74. True statement is/are:

(1) It is slower than apoplastic movement because water enters the cells through the cell membrane
(2) It again down a potential gradient
(3) It may be aided by cytoplasmic streaming
(4) All of the above are true

Q. 75. Examples of cytoplasmic streaming include:

(1) In cells of Hydrilla leaf
(2) Movement of chloroplast
(3) Cyclosis in paramecium
(4) All of the above are true

Q. 76. Most of the water flow in the roots is type of:

(1) Apoplastic
(2) Symplastic
(3) Both 1 and 2
(4) None of the above

Q. 77. Most of water flow in the roots is type of apoplastic. Why?

(1) Cortical cells are loosely packed so no resistance to water movement
(2) Cortical cells are tightly packed so no resistance to water movement
(3) Both 1 and 2
(4) None of the above

Q. 78. True statement is/are:

(1) Inner boundary of cortex-endodermis
(2) Casparian strip-made by Suberin, impervious to water
(3) Water enter the cells by cell membrane because water molecules are unable to penetrate the layer (due to Suberin deposition) so they are directed to wall regions that are not suberized into cells proper by membranes
(4) All of the above are true

Q. 79. The movement of water through the root layers in the endodermis is:

(1) Symplastic
(2) Apoplastic
(3) Both 1 and 2
(4) None of the above

Q. 80. Symplastic movement of water is only way of water and other solutes enter the:

(1) **Vascular cylinder**
(2) Procambium
(3) Cambium
(4) Lenticels

Q. 81. Inside the xylem, water is free to move:

(1) Between the cells (Intercellularly)
(2) Inside the cells (Intracellularly)
(3) **Both 1 and 2**
(4) None of the above

Q. 82. In young roots, water enters directly into the:

(1) **Xylem vessels and or tracheids**
(2) Xylem parenchyma
(3) Xylem fibres
(4) All of the above

Q. 83. Xylem vessels or tracheids are non-living conduits so they make the parts of which pathway:

(1) **Apoplast**
(2) Symplast
(3) Both 1 and 2
(4) None of the above

Q. 84. True statement is/are:

(1) Mycorrhizza is an associated structure help in water and mineral absorption along with apoplastic or symplastic pathway
(2) Mycorrhizal present around the root/penetrate the root
(3) Hyphae of mycorrhizae have large surface area, absorb minerals water from soil at a much larger volume of soil that a root cannot do
(4) **All are true**

Q. 85. Mycorrhizal association of plants is type of:

(1) Obligate
(2) Facilitative
(3) **Both 1 and 2**
(4) None

Q. 86. Mycorrhizal mostly is type of:

(1) **Facultative type association**
(2) Symbiosis type
(3) Protocoperation
(4) Lichen type

Q. 87. Pinus seeds cannot germinate and establish without the formation or presence of mycorrhizal. This show which type of mycorrhizal association:

(1) **Obligate**
(2) Protocoperation
(3) Facultative
(4) Symbisis

Q. 88. In mycorrhizae, fungus provides minerals and water to roots, in expense roots give to fungus:

(1) **Sugar and N-containing compounds**
(2) Only N-containing compounds
(3) Only sugar
(4) All of the above are true

Q. 89. What is true for root pressure?

(1) **It is a positive pressure**
(2) It is found in xylem
(3) Pushing water to small height
(4) All of the above are true

Q. 90. True statement is/are:

(1) Various ions from soil actively transported into vascular tissues of the roots, water follows (its potential gradient) and increases the pressure inside the xylem (Root pressure)
(2) Choose a small soft-stemmed plant and on a day, when there is plenty of atmospheric moisture cut he stem horizontally near the

base with a sharp blade early in morning you will soon see

(3) Drops of solution ooze out of the cut stem; due to positive root pressure

(4) If you fix a rubber tube to cut downstem as a sleeve you can actually collect and measure the rate of exudation and also determine the composition of exudates

(5) Effects of root pressure is also observable at night and early morning when evaporation is low and excess water collects as droplets around special opening of veins near the tip of grasses blades and leaves of many herbaceous parts. Such water loss in its liquid phase called guttation

(6) **All are true**

Q. 91. True statement is:

(1) Root pressure provides only a modest push in overall process of water-transport

(2) Root pressure not plays a major role in tall trees

(3) The greatest contribution of root pressure maybe to re-establish the continuous chains of water molecules in xylem which after break under enormous tensions creates by transpiration

(4) **All of the above**

Q. 92. What is true for transpiration pull?

(1) It account for majority of water transport in tall trees through xylem at high rates (15 m/h)

(2) Water is mainly pulled through plant and driving force for this is transpiration from leaves (cohesion-tension transpiration pull model)

(3) Water is transient in plants; less than 1% of water reaching the leaves is used in photosynthesis and plant growth

(4) Most water is lost by stomata in leaves called transpiration

(5) **All of the above are true**

Q. 93. Cobalt-chloride paper is used to study the where it turns its colour after absorbing water?

(1) **Water loss through transpirations**

(2) Water loss through osmosis

(3) Water loss through guttation

(4) Water loss through imbibition

Q. 94. What is true facts about water loss (transpiration)

(1) It is evaporative loss of water mainly by stomata

(2) Immediate cause of opening or closing of stomata is a change in turgidity of guard cells; opening and closing also added due to orientation of radically arranged microfibrils in the wall of guard cell

(3) When guard cells lose turgor due to water stress, the elastic inner walls regain their original shape cells flaccid and stomata closed

(4) **All are true**

Q. 95. True statement is:

(1) Radial orientation of microfibrils is easier to open the stomata

(2) Wall (inner) towards the stomatal aperture is thick and elastic

(3) When turgidity increases, inner walls of guard cells produce crescent shape

(4) **All of the above are true**

Q. 96. Transpiration process is affected by:

(1) Temperature

(2) Light

(3) Humidity

(4) Wind-speed

(5) **All of the above**

Q. 97. Transpiration process is affected (plant factors) by:

(1) Number and distribution of stomata
(2) Percent of open stomata
(3) Water-states of plant
(4) Canopy structure
(5) All of the above

Q. 98. True statement is:

(1) Usually the lower surface of dicot leaf has greater number of stomata while in monocot both have equal stomata
(2) Transpiration drives ascent of xylem sap depends mainly on physical properties cohesion, adhesion and surface tension of water
(3) Cohesion, adhesion and surface tension give high tensile strength and high capillarity
(4) All of the above are true

Q. 99. Polar surface is concerned with:

(1) Vessels and tracheids
(2) Only vessels
(3) Only tracheids
(4) All of the above

Q. 100. Adhesion of water molecules is concerned with:

(1) Polar surface of treachery elements
(2) Polar surface of companion cells
(3) Polar surface of sive tube elements
(4) All of the above

Q. 101. Matches the col. A and Col. B

Col. A	Col. B
A. Adhesion	(i) Water molecules attracted to each other in the liquid phase more than to water in the gas phase
B. Surface Tension	(ii) Root to leaf vein can supply needed water
C. System of xylem	(iii) Attraction of water molecules to polar surfaces (like treachery elements)
D. Force of transpiration	(iv) Creates pressures sufficient to lift a xylem sized column of water over 130 m high

(1) A (iii), B (i), C (ii), D (iv)
(2) A (i), B (iii), C (ii), D (iv)
(3) A (iii), B (ii), C (i), D (iv)
(4) A (ii), B (i), C (iii), D (iv)

Q. 102. Fact true in reference of transpiration:

(1) Transpiration creates trans-piration pull for absorption and transport of water in plants
(2) Supplies water for photosynthesis and maintains shape and structure of plants by keepings cells turgid
(3) Transports minerals from soil to all parts of plants
(4) Cools leaf surfaces (10–15 C) by evaporative cooling
(5) All are true

Q. 103. Matches the col.A and column-B.

Col. A	Col. B
A. Tensile strength	(i) Tracheids and vessels elements
(B). Capillarity	(ii) Mutual attraction between water molecules
(C) Treachery elements	(iii) Ability to resist a pulling force
(D). Cohesion	(iv) Ability to rise in thin tubes

(1) A (iii), B (iv), C (i), D (ii)
(2) A (iii), B (iv), C (ii), D (i)
(3) A (ii), B (iv), C (i), D (iii)
(4) A (i), B (iv), C (iii), D (ii)

Q. 104. In below mentioned properties, one is not a physical properties of water

(1) Cohesion
(2) Adhesion
(3) Surface tension
(4) **Turgidity**

Q. 105. Reason of humidity of rainforests is largely due to:

(1) **Cycling of water from root to leaf to atmosphere and back to soil**
(2) Cycling of water from leaf to root to atmosphere and back to soil
(3) Both 1 and 2
(4) All of the above

Q. 106. True statement is:

(1) Photosynthesis is limited by available water which can be swiftly depleted by transpiration
(2) Evolution of C4 photosynthetic system is one of the strategies for maximum the availability of CO_2 while minimizing water loss
(3) C4 plants are twice as efficient as C3 plants in terms of fixing C (making sugar)
(4) A C4 plants loses only half as much as water as a C3 plant for same amount of CO_2 fixed
(5) **All are true**

Q. 107. True facts for 'uptake of minerals ion':

(1) Unlike water all minerals cannot be passively absorbed by roots
(2) Most minerals enter by AT in roots by epidermal cells
(3) AT is due to water potential gradient in roots and by so osmosis
(4) Some ions also enter passively
(5) **All are true**

Q. 108. Why most minerals absorbed by roots through active transport?

(1) They present as charged particles ions which cannot move across cell membranes

(2) The conc. of minerals in soil is usually lower than concentration of minerals in roots
(3) **Both 1 and 2**
(4) They are small in size and unable to enter in pores of root hairs

Q. 109. Role of endodermal transport protein in ion transportation?

(1) **Act as check points where a plant adjust the quantity and types of solutes that reach the xylem**
(2) Act as check points where a plant adjust the quality and orientation of solutes that reach the xylem
(3) Both 1 and 2
(4) All of the above

Q. 110. Which layer of plant body has the ability to actively transport ions in one direction only:

(1) **Root endodermis because layer of Suberin**
(2) Root endodermis because layer of lignin
(3) Root endodermis because layer of callose
(4) All of the above

Q. 111. True statement is/are:

(1) Ions are absorbed from soil by both passive and active transport
(2) Specific protein in membranes of root hairs cells actively pump ions from soil into cytoplasm of epidermal cells
(3) Like all cells endoderm cells have many transport proteins embedded in their PM, they let some solutes cross the membrane
(4) **All are true**

Q. 112. Ions reached xylem through:

(1) Active transport
(2) Passive transport
(3) Combination of both
(4) **All of the above**

Q. 113. The chief sinks for mineral elements include:

(1) Growing regions of plant like (RAM and SAM)
(2) Apical and lateral meristems
(3) Young leaves-storage organs
(4) Developing flowers
(5) Fruits and seeds
(6) All of the above are true

Q. 114. Unloading of minerals ions occurs at the fine vein endings through:

(1) Diffusion
(2) Active uptake
(3) Facilitated diffusion
(4) Both 1 and 2

Q. 115. Minerals ions are frequently remobilized particularly from:

(1) Older and senescent parts
(2) Only senescent parts
(3) Only older parts
(4) Young and senescing part

Q. 116. In which category of plants, before leaf fall minerals are removed to other parts?

(1) Evergreen parts
(2) Deciduous parts
(3) Tropical rainforest
(4) Both 1 and 2

Q. 117. An analysis of the xylem exudates shows:

(1) Small amount of material exchange takes place between xylem and phloem
(2) Some of N travels as inorganic ions, and much of it carried in organic form (amino acids and related compounds)
(3) Small amount of material exchanges take place between the xylem and phloem
(4) Both
(5) None of the above

Q. 118. Traditionally believe about xylem and phloem transport is:

(1) Xylem transports only inorganic while P transports only organic
(2) Xylem transports only organic while phloem transports only inorganic
(3) Both of the above are true
(4) All of the above are true

Q. 119. What is true about phloem transport?

(1) Food primarily sucrose is transported by vascular tissues (phloem) from a source to a sink
(2) Source is part of plant synthesis is food, e.g. leaf
(3) Sink is part of plant needs/stores the food
(4) All of the above are true

Q. 120. What is true about source-sink relationship?

(1) Source and sink may be reversed depending on season or plant needs (variable)
(2) Direction of movement in phloem can be upward or downward (bidirectional)
(3) Direction of movement in xylem can be upward (unidirectional)
(4) All are true

Q. 121. True statement is:

(1) In transpiration, water movement is one-way
(2) Flow of food in phloem can be any required direction so long as there is a source of sugar and sink able to use sore or remove the sugar
(3) Sugar stored in roots may be mobilized to become a source of food in early spring when buds of trees acts as a sink; they need ATP for growth and development of photosynthetic apparatus
(4) All of the above are true

Q. 122. Phloem sap is mainly

(1) **Water-sucrose**
(2) Water-glucose
(3) Water-polysaccharides
(4) Water only-PGRs

Q. 123. Most readily microbial elements are:

(1) P
(2) S
(3) N
(4) K
(5) **All of the above**

Q. 124. Phloem sap transported by phloem contain:

(1) Water
(2) Sucrose
(3) Other sugars–hormones-amino acid
(4) **All of the above**

Q. 125. Pressure flow or mass flow hypothesis is:

(1) **Accepted mechanism used for translocation of sugars from source to sink**
(2) Accepted mechanism used for translocation of inorganic substances from source to sink
(3) Accepted mechanism used for translocation of sugars from phloem to xylem
(4) All of the above are true

Q. 126. True statement is:

(1) Accepted mechanism used for translocation of sugars from sources to sink
(2) Accepted mechanism used for translocation of sugars from sink to sources
(3) Both 1 and 2
(4) All of the above are true

Q. 127. True statement is:

(1) Glucose is prepared at source by photosynthesis and converted to sucrose

(2) Sugar moved as sucrose into comparison cells and then into living phloem sieve tube cells by AT
(3) The process of loading (comparison cells to sieve-tube) at source produces hypertonic condition in phloem
(4) Water from xylem moves into phloem by osmosis
(5) **All of the above**

Q. 128. Process necessary to move the sucrose out of phloem sap and into cells which will use the sugar converting it into energy, starch or cellulose:

(1) **Active transport**
(2) Passive transport
(3) Faciliated diffusion
(4) All of the above are true

Q. 129. The movement of sugar in phloem begins at sucrose where sugars are loaded into sieve tube by:

(1) **Active transport**
(2) Passive transport
(3) Faciliated diffusion
(4) Osmosis

Q. 130. True statement is:

(1) Loading of phloem sets up a water potential gradient that facilities mass movement in phloem
(2) Phloem tissue is composed of sieve tube cells, form log columns with holes in their end walls called sieve plates
(3) Cytoplasmic strands pass through holes in sieve plates forming continuous filaments
(4) As hydrostatic pressure in phloem sieve tube increase, pressure flow begins and sap moves through phloem
(5) **All of the above**

Q. 131. Significance of girdling experiment:

(1) Used to identify the tissues through which food is transported

(2) It shows that phloem is the tissue responsible for translocation of food

(3) Transport of food takes place in one direction, i.e. towards the roots

(4) All of the above

Q. 132. Which one is most readily mobilized?

(1) P   (2) N

(3) Ca   (4) S

Q. 133. Which one is not remobilized and a structural element:

(1) Ca   (2) Mg

(3) K   (4) P

Q. 134. An analysis of the xylem exudates shows:

(1) Some N travels as inorganic ions and much of it carried in organic form (amino acids and related compounds)

(2) Some N travels as organic ions and much of it carried in inorganic forms (amino acids and related compounds)

(3) Some N travels as salt form and much of it carried in inorganic forms (amino acids and related compounds)

(4) All of the above are true

C-5

Q. 1. In which of the following true statement is/are for photosynthesis?

(1) Green plants carryout photosynthesis, a physicochemical process by which they use light energy to drive the synthesis of organic compounds

(2) Ultimately all living forms on earth depends on sunlight for energy

(3) The use of energy from sunlight by plays doing photosynthesis is basis of life on earth

(4) Photosynthesis is important for two reasons, *viz.* primary some of food on this planet and responsible for release of O_2

(5) All are true facts

Q. 2. In which of the following true statement is/are for half-leaf experiment?

(1) Showed that CO_2 was required for photosynthesis

(2) There a part of leaf enclosed in test tube containing some KOH soaked cotton (G. hirusutum) while other half exposed to air

(3) Complete experiment set-up placed in light for sometimes

(4) All are true facts

Q. 3. In which of the following true statement is/are for Priestly?

(1) Discovered O_2

(2) Revealed role of air in growth of green plants

(3) A burning candle an animal that breathe the air, both somehow damage the air

(4) Plants restore to the air whatever breathing animals and burning candles remove

(5) All of the above

Q. 4. Concluding point of half-leaf–experiment is:

(1) Exposed part of leaf tested positive for starch while portion that was in tube tested negative

(2) Reverse of above statement

(3) Both 1 and 2

(4) None of the above

Q. 5. On testing leaves for starch explains/suggests that the:

(1) Photosynthesis occurred only in green parts of leaves

(2) Photosynthesis occur in sunlight

(3) Photosynthesis occurs in green parts in presence of sunlight

(4) None

Q. 6. **In which of the following true statement is/are for Ingenhousz?**

(1) Used aquatic plants

(2) Showed that in bright sunlight small bubbles were formed around green parts while in dark they did not

(3) Only green parts of the plants that could release O_2

(4) All are true facts

Q. 7. **In which of the following true statement is/are about splitting of water during photosynthesis?**

(1) PS-II supply electron continuously

(2) Water is split into H+, [O] and electron

(3) PS-II (water photolyse) itself is physically located on inner-side of membrane of thylakoids.

(4) All of the above

Q. 8. **The electron that were moved from PS-II must be replaced by electron available due to:**

(1) PS II

(2) PS I

(3) Both 1 and 2

(4) ETS

Q. 9. **What is difference between experiment setup of Priestly and Ingenhouse?**

(1) Ighenhouse used same set-up but difference is that he placing it once in dark and once in sunlight

(2) Ighenhouse used same set-up but difference is that he placing it in dark throughout

(3) Ighenhouse used same set-up but difference is that he placing in sunlight throughout

(4) All of the true

Q. 10. **In which of the following true statement is/are for Priestly experiment?**

(1) Priestly would have conducted the experiment using a candle and a plant

(2) When he placed a mint plant in the same bell jar, he found that mouse stayed alive and candle continued to burn

(3) A somewhat similar step of experiment used by Ingenhouse (1730–1799)

(4) All are true facts

Q. 11. **In which of the following true statement is/are about Julius Von Sachs (1954)?**

(1) Provide evidence about production of glucose when plant grow; glucose stored as starch

(2) Chlorophyll in plants located in chloroplasts

(3) Green parts in plants is where glucose is made and usually stored as starch

(4) All are true facts

Q. 12. **Joseph Priestely (1733–1804), first person in history of photosynthesis experimentation, in 1770, performed a series of experiment related to photosynthesis that reveals the:**

(1) Essential role of air in growth of green plants

(2) Essential role of CO_2 in growth of green plants

(3) Both 1 and 2

(4) None

Q. 13. **In which of the following true statement is/are for Cornelius Van Niel (1897–1985)?**

(1) He is a microbiologist whose contribution is based on his studies of purple and green bacteria

(2) He demonstrated that photosynthesis is especially a light

dependent reaction in which hydrogen from a suitable oxidisable compound reduces CO_2 to carbohydrate

(3) He proves that O_2 evolved by green plants comes from H_2O not from CO_2 (Later this proves by radio-isotopic technique)

(4) All of the above are true

Q. 14. **In which of the following a correct sequence of scientists who work according to the time in dependent of photosynthesis is correct:**

(1) **Priestly, Igenhousze, von Sachs, Engelmann and von Niel**

(2) Igenhousze, von Sachs, Engelmann and von Niel, Priestly

(3) Priestly, Igenhousze, von Neil, Engelmann and von Sachs

(4) Priestly, von Sachs, Engelmann and von Niel, Igenhousz

Q. 15. **In which of the following true statement is/are?**

(1) Photosynthesis occur in green leaf of plant/chloroplast

(2) Mesophyll cells have large number of chloroplasts

(3) Usually chloroplast aligns themselves along wall of mesophyll cells to get optimum quantity of incident light.

(4) **All are true facts**

Q. 16. **Chloroplast contain:**

(1) A membranous system consisting of grana, the

(2) Stroma

(3) Fluid stroma

(4) **All are true facts**

Q. 17. **In which of the following true statement is/are?**

(1) There is a clear division of labour within chloroplast

(2) Membranous system (grana) is responsible for trapping the light energy and also for synthesis of ATP and NADPH

(3) In stroma (liquid) enzymatic reactions incorpororate CO_2 into plant leading to starch/sugar

(4) All are true facts

Q. 18. **True statement is:**

(1) **Light reaction depend on ATP and NADPH**

(2) Light reaction depend on ATP and FADP

(3) Light reaction depend on NADPH

(4) Light reaction depend on ATP

Q. 19. **In which of the following true statement is/are for T.W. Engelmann (1843–1909)?**

(1) Use a prism to split light into spectral components and illuminated a green algae-Cladophora placed in suspension of aerobic bacteria

(2) Bacteria used to detected the site of O_2 evolution

(3) Bacteria accumulated mainly in region of blue and red light of split spectrum

(4) He described first action spectrum of photosynthesis similar the absorption spectrum of Chl-a/b

(5) **All are true facts**

Q. 20. **The separation of leaf pigments of any green plant can be done through:**

(1) **Paper chromatography**

(2) Thin layer

(3) Both 1 and 2

(4) None

Q. 21. **True statements are:**

(1) Process by which ATP synthesized by cells (in mitochondria and chloroplast) is called phosphorylation

(2) Photophosphorylation is synthesis of ATP from ADP and IP in presence of light

(3) When both PS work in a series, first PS-II and PS-I, process called non-cyclic Photophosphorylation. Both PS is connected by Z-scheme and both ATP and NADPH2 found here.

(4) **All are true facts**

Q. 22. What is true about electron transport system (ETS) of photosynthesis?

(1) Consists of cytochromes

(2) In ETS, the movement of electrons is downhill in terms of an oxidation-reduction or redox-potential scale

(3) In ETS electrons not used up as they pass through ETC but passed onto the pigments of PS I

(4) **All of the above**

Q. 23. In which of the following true statement is/are?

(1) A chromatographic separation of leaf pigments shows that the colour that we see in leaves is not due to a single pigment but due to four pigments- a, b xanthophylls and carotenoids

(2) Chl-a-broght/blue green in chromatogram; Chl-b-yellow green; xanthophylls-yellow and arotenoids-yellow to yellow orange

(3) Pigments are substances that have an ability to absorb light at specific wavelength

(4) **All are true**

Q. 24. Light reaction or photochemical phase of photosynthesis include:

(1) Light absorption

(2) Water splitting

(3) O_2-release and synthesis of chemical intermediates (ATP, NADPH) and several complexes

(4) **All of the above**

Q. 25. True statements is/are:

(1) Living organisms extract energy from oxidizable substances and store this as bond energy

(2) ATP carry this energy in their chemical bonds

(3) When only PS is functional the electron is circulated within photosynthesis and phosphorylation occurs due to cyclic flow of electrons in stroma lamellae

(4) **All of the above**

Q. 26. In which of the following true statement is/are?

(1) The wavelength at which maximum photosynthesis occurs that is maximum absorption by Chl-a, blue and red region.

(2) Blue and red regions shows higher rate of photosynthesis

(3) Chl-a is a chief pigment associated with photosynthesis

(4) A complete one to one overlap between the absorption spectrum of Chl-a and action spectrum of photosynthesis

(5) **All are true facts**

Q. 27. In which of the following true statement is/are about photosystems?

(1) Number is two

(2) They named in sequence of their discovery and not in the sequence in which they function during the light reaction

(3) Each has all the pigment (except one molecule of Chl-C) forming a light harvesting system (LHS) called antennae make photosynthesis efficient by absorbing different wavelength of light

(4) PS I has absorption peak at 700 nm and PS II at 680

(5) **All are true facts**

Q. 28. In which of the following true statement is/are?

(1) Electrons in Reaction centre of PS I are also excited when they receive red-light of 700 nm and transferred to another accept of molecule that has a greater redox-potential

(2) These electrons moved downhill again to a energy rich molecule NADP+ and reduced NADPH2.

(3) ETS, scheme of transfer of electrons, starting from PS II up-hill to acceptor, downhill the ETC to PS I, excitation of electrons, transfer another acceptor and finally downhill to NADP+ causing it to be reduced to NADPH2, called Z-scheme due to its characteristic shape

(4) Z-scheme produced when all the carriers are placed in a sequence on a redox-potential scale

(4) All of the above

Q. 29. True statements is/are:

(1) Membrane of lamellae of grana have both PS I and PS II

(2) Stroma (liquid) of lamellae membrane lack PS II and NADP reductase enzyme

(3) In cyclic photophosphorylation electron does not pass onto NADP+ but cycled back to PS I complex by ETC. Here only ATP is produced

(4) All of the above

Q. 30. In which of the following true statement is/are?

(1) Action spectrum and absorption spectrum show that most of photosynthesis takes place in blue and red-regions of spectrum

(2) Some photosynthesis does take place at outer wavelengths of visible spectrum

(3) Chl-a is major pigment responsible for trapping light other thylakoids pigments like Chl-a, xanthophylls and carotenoids called accessory pigments also absorb light and transfer the energy to chl-a

(4) Chl-a, xanthophylls and carotenoids not only enable a wide range of wavelength of incoming light to be utilized for photosynthesis but also protect Chl-a from photo oxidation

(5) All of the above are true

Q. 31. In which of the following true statement is/are about LHC ?

(1) These are discrete photochemical units in which pigments are organized

(2) Made-up of hundreds of pigments molecules bound to proteins

(3) Both 1 and 2

(4) None

Q. 32. Which kind of photophosphorylation occurs (also) when only light of wavelengths beyond 680 nm is available for excitation?

(1) Cyclic

(2) Noncylic

(3) Both 1 and 2

(4) None

Q. 33. What is true about chemio-osmotic hypothesis?

(1) It put forward to explain the mechanism how actually ATP is synthesized in chloroplast

(2) Like in respiration, photosynthesis too, ATP synthesis is linked to development of a H^+-gradient across a membrane-thylakoids membrane

(3) There is a difference between ATP synthesis in respiration and photosynthesis is that in photosynthesis + accumulation is

towards the inside the membrane (lumen) while in respiration H^+ accumulates in the inter-membrane space of mitochondria when electron move through ETS

(4) All of the above

Q. 34. What causes H^+ gradient across the membrane?

(1) Process that take place during the activation of electrons and their transport to determine the steps that cause a H^+ gradient to develop.

(2) Process that take place during the activation of hydrolysis of membrane lipids and their transport to determine the steps that cause a H^+ gradient to develop.

(3) Both 1 and 2

(4) None

Q. 35. In which of the following steps involving the H^+ gradient?

(1) H_2O splits in inner-side of membrane and results that H^+ accumulate within lumen of thylakoids

(2) As electrons moves through photo systems, H^+ are transported across the membrane because primary acceptor of electron located towards outside the membrane transfers its electron not a electron came but to an H carrier

(3) The NADP reductase enzyme located on stroma side of membrane

(4) All of the above

Q. 36. When in the lumen of the thylakoids membrane, H^+ accumulates during ATP synthesis?

(1) H^+ number decrease in stroma

(2) H^+ gradient across the thylakoids membrane as well as a measurable decrease in PH in lumen

(3) Both 1 and 2

(4) None

Q. 37. H^+ **gradient-important in photo-phosphorylation?**

(1) Its breakdown leads to release of energy

(2) It blocked due to movement of H^+ across the mitochondria to the stroma through the transmembrane channel of the F0 of the ATP-ase

3. ATP-ase enzyme contain two parts; (1) F0 and F0 embedded in membrane and forms a trans-membrane channel that carries out facilities diffusion of the H^+ across the membrane

(4) All of the above

Q. 38. What is true about F1 of the ATP-ase?

(1) It represents outer portion of ATPase

(2) It protrudes on outer surface of the thylakoids membrane on side that faces the stroma

(3) Breakdown of gradient provides energy to cause conformational change in this part

(4) All of the above

Q. 39. Chemiosmosis needs:

(1) A membrane

(2) A proton pump

(3) A H^+ gradient and ATPase

(4) All of the above

Q. 40. Energy produced through chemio-osmosis used in:

(1) To pump H^+ across a membrane

(2) To create a gradient

(3) To maintain a high concentration of H^+ within thylakoids membrane

(4) All of the above

Q. 41. Significance of ATPase include:

(1) Part of chemiosmotic hypothesis

(2) It has a channel that allows diffusion of H^+ back across the

membrane release enough energy to activate ATP ase for ATP formation

(3) Both 1 and 2

(4) None

Q. 42. What is true about the Calvin-cycle?

(1) Occurs in all photosynthetic plants; it does not matter whether they have C3/C4 or any other pathways

(2) It includes 3 steps carboxylation reduction and regeneration

(3) To make one molecule of glucose 6 turns of cycle are required

(4) All of the above

Q. 43. ATP produced along with NADPH by movement of electrons during chemio-osmosis used immediately in:

(1) Biosynthetic reaction taking place

(2) Fixing CO_2

(3) Synthesis of sugars

(4) All of the above

Q. 44. Product of light reaction are

(1) ATP

(2) NADPH

(3) IP

(4) O_2

(5) 1, 2 and 4

Q. 45. Biosynthetic phase of photosynthesis depends on:

(1) Products of light reaction (ATP, NADPH)

(2) CO_2

(3) H_2O

(4) All

Q. 46. What is true about biosynthetic phase of photosynthesis?

(1) It does not directly depend on presence of light

(2) After light becomes unavailable the biosynthetic process continue for some time and then stops

(3) If then light is made available the synthesis starts again

(4) All of the above

Q. 47. What is true about the Melvin-calvin?

(1) Their discovery concerned just after World War II

(2) They effort in field of beneficial use of 14C (radio-isotope) the 14C (radioactive) by him in algal photosynthesis studies lead to discovery that first CO_2 fixation product was a 3C organic acid

(3) They working out the complete biosynthetic pathway so-called Calvin cycle and first product is PGA

(4) All of the above

Q. 48. True statements is/are:

(1) CO_2 fixation product always an organic acid (PGA/OAA)

(2) C3 pathway produce PGA and C4 pathway produce OAA

(3) RUBP is a ketose (5C) sugar, a CO_2 acceptor molecule

(4) All of the above

Q. 49. In which of the following true statement is/are?

(1) Carboxylation is most crucial step of Calvin cycle

(2) RUBP carboxylase (more appropriately called RuBP carboxylase-oxygenase-RuBis-Co) has both activity of oxygenation and Carboxylation

(3) It produce 2 molecules of 3-PGA

(4) All of the above

Q. 50. What is the true about reduction of Calvin-cycle?

(1) It leads formation of glucose/carbohydrate at presence of ATP and NADPH

(2) Used 2 ATP and 12 NADPH (2 ATP for phosphorylation and

2 NADPH for reduction per CO_2 molecule fixed)

(3) Fixation of 6 molecules of CO_2 and 6 turns of cycle required for removal of one molecule of glucose from pathway

(4) **All of the above are true statements**

Q. 51. **In which of the following true statement is/are for regeneration?**

(1) Like carboxylation, it also crucial for Calvin cycle

(2) RUBP is regenerated to continue cycle un-interrupted

(3) Regeneration step requires one ATP for phosphorylation to form RuBP

(4) **All of the above**

Q. 52. **True statement is:**

(1) For every CO_2 molecule entering the Calvin cycle; 3 ATP + 2NADPH required. (different in dark reaction where cyclic photophosphorylation)

(2) One molecule of glucose, 6 turns of the cycle are required

(3) ATP makes one molecule of glucose through Calvin cycle, 18 ATP and 12 NADPH required

(4) **All of the above are true statements**

Q. 53. **Law of limiting factors explain:**

(1) Though several factor interact and simultaneously affect the rate of CO_2 **fixation (photosynthesis), usually one factor is major cause/ one factor that limits the rate**

(2) At any point the rate of reaction will be determined by factor available at suboptimal levels

(3) If a chemical process is affected by more than one favor the its rate will be determined by factor which is nearest or tits minimal

value; it is factor which directly affects the process of its quality is changed

(4) **All of the above are true statements**

Q. 54. **What is true about effect of light on photosynthesis?**

(1) Linear relationship between incident light and CO_2 fixation rate at low light intensities

(2) At higher light intensities gradually the rate does not show further increase as other factors become limiting

(3) Light saturation occurs at 10% of full sunlight

(4) **All of the above**

Q. 55. **Light is rarely a limiting factor in nature for the rate of photosynthesis** *except*:

(1) Plants in shade

(2) Plants in dense forest

(3) **Both 1 and 2**

(4) None

Q. 56. **In which of the following true statement is/are?**

(1) C3 cycle is common to all plants

(2) Bundle sheath cells rich in Rubisco but lack PEP case while in mesophyll Rubis-CO is absent and PEP case present

(3) Basic pathway (C3 cycle) represent a function of sugars. It occurs in all mesophyll cells of C3 plants (not in C4 plants). In C4 plants it occurs in only in bundle sheath cells

(4) **All of the above**

Q. 57. **What is true about photorespiration?**

(1) A process (wasteful) creates difference between C3 and C4 plants

(2) Rubisco is most abundant enzyme in world and characterized that

its active sites can bind to both CO_2 and O_2. It has much greater affinity for CO_2 that for O_2 and this binding is competivitive

(3) In C3 plants some O_2 bind to Ru Bisco and hence CO_2 fixation is decreased. Here RuBP instead of being converted to 2 molecules of PGA, binds with O_2 to form one molecule of phosphoglycerate and phosphoglycolate in a pathway called photorespiration. No sugars, NADPH, ATP synthesis. Rather, it results in the release of CO_2 with utilization of ATP

(4) **All of the above are true statements**

Q. 58. What is true about Hatch-Slack pathway/C4 pathway?

(1) Here primary CO_2 acceptor is 3C a compound, PEP present in mesophyll

(2) Enzyme responsible for fixation is PEP Carboxylation (PEP case)

(3) C4 acid OAA (it forms MA and A. A, transport to bundle sheath cells) first stable CO_2 fixation product (it breakdown a 3C compound into 3C compound and CO_2 back to mesophyll further changed into PEP and complete the cycle. CO_2 released in bundle cells enter the C3 pathway), here found in mesophyll cells

(4) **All of the above**

Q. 59. True statement is:

(1) Particularly large cells around the vascular bundles of C4 pathway plants called Bundle sheath cells and anatomy called Kranz anatomy

(2) Kranz means wreath and is a reflection of the arrangement of cells

(3) The bundle sheath cells may form several layers around vascular bundles

(4) Bundle sheath cells (would help you identify the C4 plants) contain large number of chloroplast thick walls impervious to gaseous exchange and no intercellular spaces

(4) **All of the above**

Q. 60. In which of the following true statement is/are for C4 pathway?

(1) Plants show this cycle, adapted to dry tropical regions a special leaf anatomy tolerate high temperature show response to high light intensities

(2) Lack photorespiration and have greater productivity of biomass

(3) Main biosynthetic pathway also here is Calvin (C3) cycle and first stable CO_2 fixation product is OAA

(4) **All of the above**

Q. 61. In which of the following true statement is/are about the effects of CO_2 concentration on photosynthesis?

(1) CO_2 concentration in atmosphere is very low (0, 03 to 0.04%). Increase in concentration (up to 0.05%) can cause an increase in CO_2 fixation rates; beyond this level CO_2 can become damaging over a long period

(2) C3 and C4 respond differentially to CO_2 concentration. C4 shows saturation at 360 micro litre/L. Thus current availability of CO_2 levels is limiting to C3 plants. So C4 are better adopted and give higher production than C3.

(3) Fact that C3 plans respond to higher CO_2 concentration by showing increased rate of photosynthesis leading to higher productivity has been used for some green house crops (C4

plants, e.g. tomato bell pepper). They allowed in CO_2 enriched atmospheric leads to higher yield

(4) **All of the above are true statements**

Q. 62. **In which of the following true statement is/are about temperature and photosynthesis?**

(1) Temperature need of plants for photosynthesis depend on their habitat

(2) So tropical need more temperature than temperate

(3) Dark reaction is temperature dependent because it is enzymatic rather light reaction is just sensitive (non-enzymatic)

(4) The C4 plants respond to higher temperature than C3

(5) **All of the above**

Q. 63. **Why photorespiration does not occurs in C4 plants?**

(1) **Because they have a mechanism that increases the concentration of CO_2 at the enzyme site**

(2) Lack of C4-machinery

(3) Lack of the chloroplast

(4) Lack of the mitochondria

Q. 64. **What approach/adaptation of C4 plants make them to lacking the process of photorespiration?**

(1) **OAA acid from mesophyll is broken down in bundle sheath cells to release CO-results increasing the intracellular concentration of CO_2 and in turn ensures that Rubisco present in as carboxylase and minimizing the oxygenase activity**

(2) Genetic defect

(3) It has no requirement of CO_2 maintenance

(4) All of the above

Q. 65. **In which of the following true statement is/are about C4 plants?**

(1) They have better productivity and yield

(2) Show tolerance to higher temperature

(3) **Both 1 and 2**

(4) None of the above is true statements

Q. 66. **What is true factors affecting photosynthesis?**

(1) Rate of photosynthesis is important in detecting the yield of plants increasing crop plants

(2) Number, size, age, and orientation of leaves mesophyll cells and chloroplast internal CO_2 and amount of chloroplast

(3) Internal factors affecting photosynthesis dependent on genetic constitution and growth of the plants

(4) **All of the above**

Q. 67. **Blackman's law of limiting factors (1905) comes into effect:**

(1) **When several factors affect any biochemical process**

(2) When only one factor affect biochemical reaction

(3) Both 1 and 2

(4) All of the above are true statements

Q. 68. **In which of the following true statement is/are about the water and photosynthesis?**

(1) Water is one reactant of light reaction

(2) Effect of water as a factor is more through its effect on plant (rather than directly on photosynthesis)

(3) Water stress causes reducing in CO_2 availability by closing stomata and metabolic activity too

(4) **All of the above**

Q. 69. External factors affects photosynthesis include:

(1) Availability of sunlight
(2) Availability of temperature
(3) CO_2 concentration and water
(4) **All of the above are true statements**

C-6

Q. 1. What is true about pollution:

(1) Any undesirable change in physical chemical or biological characteristics of air and water or soilds called pollution
(2) To control environmental pollution GOI has passed the Environment protection Act (1986) to protect and improve the quality of our environment (air water and soil)
(3) Agents that bring about an undesirable change called pollutants
(4) **All of the above are true**

Q. 2. Harm full effects of air pollutants depends on:

(1) Concentration of pollutants
(2) Duration of exposure
(3) Organisms
(4) **All of the above**

Q. 3. One of the following statements given below the true one is for electrostatic precipitation?

(1) Contain scrubber lime spray discharged corona, negatively charged wire and collection plate grounded
(2) Used in smokestacks of thermal power plants smelters and other industries release (SPM) particulate
(3) Most widely used way to removing particulate matter is electrostatic precipitator remove 99%. Plamsma membrane present in exhaust from a thermal power plant
(4) **All of the above**

Q. 4. In which of the following is a matched column?

(1) Electrode wires: Produce several thousand voltage produce corona which release electron attach to dust particle and gave net negative charge
(2) Collecting plates: Attract charged dust particles
(3) Scrubber: Remove gas like SO_2
(4) Catalytic convertors (Pt-Pd and Rd): Reduce emission of poisonous gases
(5) **All of the above**

Q. 5. Examples of accidental leakage of radioactive wastes is/are:

(1) Three Mile Islands
(2) Chernobyl Incidents
(3) MIC Bhopal
(4) **Both 1 and 2 are correct**

Q. 6. One of the following statements given below the true one is?

(1) Noise is un-desired high level of sound
(2) Extensively higher sound level 150 MB or more generated by takeoff of a jet plane or rocket may damage ear drums and permanently impairing hearing ability
(3) Noise causes and sleepness increased heat beat altered breathing pattern and stressing human
(4) Reduction of noise dense by absorbed materials or by muffling noise
(5) **All are correct statements**

Q. 7. The main problems with switching over to CNG is:

(1) Difficulty of laying down pipelines to deliver CNG through distribution points/pumps
(2) Ensuring un-interrupted supply

(3) Both 1 and 2

(4) None of the above

Q. 8. Why CNG is better than diesel?

(1) Burns most efficiently (unlike petrol or diesel) in automobiles

(2) Little residue of it is left unburnt

(3) Cheaper

(4) CNG cannot be siphoned off by thieves and adulterated like petrol and diesel

(5) All of the above are true

Q. 9. Which gas can be remove by scrubber?

(1) N_2 (2) CO_2

(3) SO_2   (4) CH_4

Q. 10. One of the following statements given below the true one is?

(1) A public interest litigating (PIL) was titled in Supreme Court of India in case of Delhi

(2) All buses of Delhi were converted to turn on CNG by end of 2002

(3) Both 1 and 2

(4) None

Q. 11. Function of corona produce by electrode wires:

(1) Release electrons

(2) Release protons

(3) Release SPM

(4) All of the above

Q. 12. Function of collecting plates, a part of electrostatic precipitator

(1) Attract charged dust particles

(2) Not attract the charged dust particles

(3) Attract only to solid materials

(4) All of the above are correct

Q. 13. Why velocity of air between plates must be low enough

(1) To allow the dust to fall

(2) To allow the SPM to enter

(3) Both

(4) None are correct statements

Q. 14. One of the following statements given below the true one is for radioactive wastes?

(1) Radiation from radioactive wastes is extremely damaging to organism cause mutation (cancer)

(2) Nuclear waste is an extremely potent pollutant

(3) Storage of nuclear waste after pretreated should be done in suitably shielded containers in rocks about 500 m

(4) All are correct statements

Q. 15. According to CPCB (Central Pollution Control Board), size of particulate size which are responsible for causing the greatest harm to human health:

(1) 2.5 micro-metre or less in diameter (PM 2.5) because inhaled deep into lungs cause inflammation, irritation and premature death

(2) 3.5 micro-metre or less in diameter (PM 4.5) because inhaled deep into lungs cause inflammation, irritation and premature death

(3) 4.5 micro-metre or less in diameter (PM 4.5) because inhaled deep into lungs cause inflammation, irritation and premature death

(4) All of the above are true

Q. 16. Role of Lead free petrol/diesel can:

(1) Pollutants from automobiles they emit

(2) Pollutants from brick industry they emit

(3) Pollutants from thermal power plants they emit

(4) Pollutants from sound recorders they emit

Q. 17. Stringent norms for fuels means?

(1) Steadily reducing the S and aromatic content in petrol and diesel fuels

(2) Steadily reducing the Hg and aromatic content in petrol and diesel fuels

(3) Steadily reducing the P and aromatic content in petrol and diesel fuels

(4) All are correct statements

Q. 18. One of the following statements given below the true one is for greenhouse effect?

(1) It is a naturally occurring pheno-menon responsible for heating of Earth's surface and atmosphere

(2) Without greenhouse effect, the average temperature at surface of Earth would have been a chilly-18C rather than the present average of 15C

(3) To understand greenhouse effect, it is necessary to know the fate of energy of sunlight that reaches outermost atmosphere

(4) All are correct statements

Q. 19. In India, the air (prevention and control of pollution) Act comes into force (1981) but was amended in:

(1) 1987 to include noise as an air pollutant

(2) 1986 to include noise as an air pollutant

(3) 1990 to include noise as an air pollutant

(4) 1994 to include noise as an air pollutant

Q. 20. Bonder use of CNG in Delhi, parallel steps taken in Delhi for reducing vehicular pollution include:

(1) Application of stringent pollution level norms for vehicles

(2) Phasing out of old vehicles

(3) Use of unleaded petrol, low-S petrol and diesel and catalytic converter in vehicles

(4) All of the above are true

Q. 21. One of the following statements given below the true one is for greenhouse?

(1) Small gas house and is used for growing plants especially during winter

(2) Ina greenhouse, the glass panel lets the light in very much like inside a car that has been parked in sun for a few hours

(3) Greenhouse effect a phenomenon that occurs in a greenhouse

(4) All are correct statements

Q. 22. In scrubber, exhaust is passed through a spray of:

(1) Water　　　　(2) Lime

(3) CH_4　　　　**(4) Both 1 and 2**

Q. 23. Catalytic convertors are fitted into automobiles fur reducing emission of poisonous gases, consists of:

(1) Expensive metals act as catalyst like Platinum-Palladium and Rhodium

(2) Expensive metals act as catalyst like Platinum-Mercury and Rhodium

(3) Expensive metals act as catalyst like Platinum-Palladium and Uranium

(4) Expensive metals act as catalyst like Iron-Palladium and Rhodium

Q. 24. An exhaust passes through catalytic convertor un-burnt hydrocarbons are converted into CO_2 and H_2O and $CO-HNO_3$ are changed to:

(1) CO_2 and N_2 respectively

(2) SO_2 and N_2 respectively

(3) NO_2 and N_2 respectively

(4) KO_2 and N_2 respectively

Q. 25. Motor vehicles equipped with catalytic converter should use non-lead petrol because lead (Pb) in the petrol:

(1) Inactivates the catalyst

(2) Activates the catalyst

(3) Both 1 and 2

(4) None of the above are correct

Q. 26. Correct match is:

(1) Euro-II Norms (Bharat Stage II)-reduce 350 ppm S in diesel and 150 ppm in petrol

(2) Road Map-Reduce 50 ppm in petrol and diesel

(3) Euro-III-1 April, 2005

(4) Euro-IV-1 April, 2010

(5) All of the above

Q. 27. What is Bharat Stage II true?

(1) It is equivalent to Euro-II norms

(2) It current in place of Delhi, Mumbai Kolkata, Chennai, Bangalore, Hyderabad, Ahmadabad, Pune Surat, Kanpur and Agra (11 cities)

(3) It will be applicable to all automobiles throughout the country from 1 April 2005

(4) All are true

Q. 28. One of the following statements given below the true one is for domestic sewage and industrial effluents?

(1) A mere 0.1% impurities make domestic sewage unfit for human use

(2) Solid are relatively easy to remove and most difficult is dissolved salts (NO_3, PO_4 and other nutrients and toxic metals ions and organic compounds)

(3) Domestic sewage primarily contain bi-degradable on substarte for microorganism multiplication using organic substances

(4) All are correct

Q. 29. Biochemical oxygen demand (BOD) in sewage water measuring:

(1) Estimate the amount of bio-degradable organic matter

(2) Estimate the amount of non-biodegradable organic matter

(3) Estimate the amount of both biodegradable and nonbio-degradable organic matter

(4) None of the above are true

Q. 30. What is true for Eichornia crassipes?

(1) Commonly called water-hyacinth/Terror of Bengal

(2) Recognized as World's most problematic aquatic weed

(3) Grow abundantly in eutrophic water bodies and lead imbalance in ecosystem dynamics of water bodies

(4) All of the above

Q. 31. Clouds and gases reflect about ¼ of the incoming solar radiations and absorb some of it but almost which amount of incoming solar radiations falls on Earth's surface heating it, while?

(1) Half a small portion is reflected back

(2) Full portion is reflected back

(3) 1/4 portions is reflected back

(4) All are correct statements

Q. 32. After filing of PIL use of CNG, applying Euro II, III and IV norms what happened in Delhi

(1) Substantial fall in CO_2 and SO_2 between 1997–2005

(2) Substantial fall in CO_2 and NO_2 between 1997–2007

(3) Substantial fall in SO_2 and KO_2 between 1997–2008

(4) Substantial fall in O_3 and SO_2 between 1999–2010

Q. 33. What mean of Euro II norms stipulate that?

(1) S be controlled at 350 ppm in diesel to 150 ppm in petrol

(2) Aromatic hydrocarbons are to be contained at 42% of concerned fuel

(3) Both 1 and 2

(4) None of the above

Q. 34. Correct match between the Act and Amended dates is:

(1) National Forest Policy—1988
(2) Water Act—1974
(3) Air Act—1987
(4) Montreal Protocol—1989
(5) All are correct

Q. 35. According to Roadmap, the goal is:

(1) To reduce S to 50 ppm in petrol and diesel and bring down the level to 35%
(2) Vehicles engines will also need to be upgraded
(3) Both 1 and 2
(4) None of the above

Q. 36. Microorganisms involved in biodegradable of organic matter in receiving water body what happens:

(1) Consume a lot of O_2
(2) Sharp decline in dissolved O_2 downstream from the point of seaware discharge
(3) Mortality of fish and other aquatic creatures
(4) All of the above

Q. 37. What is true about 'Excessive growth of free floating algae (planktonic)'?

(1) Called algae bloom, provide distinct colour to water bodies
(2) Causes deterioration of water quality and fish mortality
(3) Some are extremely toxic to human beings and animals
(4) All of the above

Q. 38. Sewage from our homes and hospitals causes put break of:

(1) Dysentery-typhoid-jaundice-cholera
(2) Dysentery-polio-jaundice-cholera
(3) Diphtheria-mumps-jaundice-cholera
(4) Plague-polio-jaundice-cholera

Q. 39. Heavy metals definitely are:

(1) Elements with density 75 g/cm³
(2) Elements with density 95 g/cm³
(3) Elements with density 105 g/cm³
(4) Elements with density 125 g/cm³

Q. 40. One of the following statements given below the true one is for Eutrophication?

(1) Natural aging of lake by nutrient enrichment of its water
(2) Stream drain into lake introduce nutrients like N and P encourage growth of aquatic organism
(3) As Lake's fertility increases plant and animals life burgeons and organic remains begin to be deposited on lake bottom
(4) All are correct statements
(5) All of the above

Q. 41. 'BOG' is:

(1) Large masses of floating plants
(2) Large masses of aerial plants
(3) Large masses of pteridophytes
(4) Large masses of gymnosperms

Q. 42. When Eutrophication happened through pollutants from man's activities like effluents from industries and homes can radically accelerated the aging process?

(1) Culturally or accelerated eutrophication
(2) Traditional eutrophication
(3) Modern eutrophication
(4) Industrial eutrophication

Q. 43. Commonly known greenhouse gases are:

(1) CO_2–CH_4
(2) CH_4–H_2O
(3) CO_2–H_2O
(4) $CFCs$–CO_2

Q. 44. You may have seen the beautiful mauve coloured flowers found on very appealingly-shaped floating plants in water bodies. These plants (water-hyacinth) which were introduced into India for their ... they caused havoc by their excessive growth by causing blocks our ability to remove them:

(1) Lovely flowers
(2) Medicinal value
(3) Both 1 and 2
(4) Attractive odour

Q. 45. Unlike domestic sewage, waste water from industries after contain:

(1) **Heavy metals (Hg, Cd, Cu, Pb) and organic compounds**
(2) Heavy metals
(3) Organic impurities
(4) Fertilizer elements

Q. 46. What is true about biomagnification?

(1) This happens because a toxic substances accumulated by an organisms cannot be metabolized/excreted and passed to next trophic level
(2) It is well known for Hg and DDT
(3) Few toxic substances in industrial waste waters go in the biological magnification in aquatic food chains
(4) **All of the above are true**

Q. 47. Cultural aging (depleting on climate, size of lake and other factors) of a lake may span:

(1) **Thousands of year**
(2) Hundreds of year
(3) Few months
(4) Few years

Q. 48. Cultural or accelerated eutrophication is:

(1) **Radically accelerated**
(2) Parallel accelerated
(3) Laterally accelerated
(4) Vertically accelerated

Q. 49. During the past century, lakes in many parts of the earth have been severally eutrophied by sewage and agricultural and industrial wastes. The prime contaminants responsible for this is:

(1) **Nitrates and phosphates**
(2) Nitrates and sulphate
(3) Nitrates only
(4) Phosphates only

Q. 50. Plant nutrients responsible for eutrophication?

(1) NO_3 and PO_4
(2) CO_2 and SO_4
(3) CO_2 and SO_4
(4) NO and SO_4

Q. 51. Unslightly scum, unpleasant odours and robbing of dissolved O_2 vital to other aquatic life is due to:

(1) **NO_3 and PO_4** (2) SO_2
(3) NO_2 (4) H_2SO_4

Q. 52. What is true for heated (thermal) waste waters flowing out of electricity-generating units?

(1) **Thermal waste water eliminate or reduces the number of organisms sensitive to high temperature and energy enhance the growth of plants and fish is extremely cold areas but only after causing damage to indigenous flora and fauna**
(2) Thermal waste water eliminate or increases the number of organisms sensitive to high temperature and energy enhance the growth of plants and fish is extremely cold areas but only after causing damage to indigenous flora and fauna
(3) Both 1 and 2
(4) None of the above

Q. 53. **Case study of arteca (integrated waste water treatment) was:**

(1) Conventional sedimentation filtering and chlorine treatment lots of dangerous pollutants like dissolved heavy metals still remains

(2) A series of six connected marshes over 60 hectares of marshland

(3) FOAM (friends of the Arteca Marsh) a citizen group responsible for upkeep and safe guarding this wonderful project

(4) **All of the true**

Q. 54. **One of the following statements given below the true one is for agrochemicals?**

(1) In green revolutions, use of inorganic fertilizers and pesticides has increased manifold for enhancing crop production

(2) These agrochemicals are also toxic to nontarget organisms that are important complements of soil ecosystems

(3) Use of increased amount of them can do to aquatic ecosystem vis-à-vis eutrophication

(4) **All of the above**

Q. 55. **What is true for plastic waste?**

(1) Polyblend, a fine powder of recycled modified plastic

(2) The mixture of polyblend and bitumen used to lay roads enhances the bitumen's water repellent properties

(3) The mixture of polyblend-bitumen helped to increase road life by a factor of three

(4) The raw-material for creating polyblend is any plastic film waste

(5) **All of them are true**

Q. 56. **One of the following statements given below the true one is e-wastes?**

(1) Irreversible components and other electronic goods

(2) Over-half of e-wastes generated in developed world and exported to developing countries mainly to China India are recovered during recycling processes

(3) Recycling is only solutions for treatments of e-wates in an environmental friendly manner

(4) **All are correct statements**

Q. 57. **Where 'EcoSan toilets' used?**

(1) Kerala

(2) Sri Lanka

(3) Maldeep

(4) **Both 1 and 2**

Q. 58. **What is true statements about solid waste is:**

(1) Everything that goes out in trash

(2) A solution to all (solid waste, MSW and sanitary land fill) can only be in human being becoming more sensitive to these environmental issues

(3) State governments across countries are trying to push for reduction in use of plastics and use of ecofriendly packaging

(4) **All of the above**

Q. 59. **MSW (Municipal Solid Waste) is:**

(1) Wastes from homes offices stores school hospitals, etc. collected and disposed by the municipalities

(2) It generally comprises paper food waste plastics glass metals rubbers leather textiles, etc.

(3) Our Kabadi Wallalis and rag-pickers has a great job of materials recycling

(4) **All are correct statements**

Q. 60. What is true for ecological sanitation?

(1) A sustainable system for handling human excreta using dry composting toilets

(2) A practical hygienic efficient and cost effective solution to human waste disposal

(3) In this human excreta can be recycled into a resource (natural fertilizers) reduces the need for chemical fertilizers

(4) All of the true

Q. 61. Hospitals generate hazardous wastes that contain:

(1) Disinfectants

(2) Other harmful chemicals

(3) Pathogenic mimicry

(4) All of the above

Q. 62. All waste that we generate can be categorized into:

(1) Biodegradable and recyclable

(2) Recyclable and nonbiodegradable

(3) Biodegradable and nonbiodegradable

(4) Biodegradable, nonbiodegradable and recycle

Q. 63. One of the following statements given below the true one is?

(1) Sanitary landfills were adopted as substitute for open-burning dumps

(2) In SLF water are dumped in a depression or trench after compaction and covered with dirt everyday

(3) Landfills are also not really much of a solution of present day and a danger of seepage of chemicals from these landfills polluting the underground water resources

(4) All of the above are true

Q. 64. One of the following is a matched column for GHG and per cent age?

(1) N_2O 6%

(2) CFCs 14%

(3) CH_4 20%

(4) CO_2 60%

(5) All of the above

Q. 65. What is true for organic farming?

(1) Integrated organic farming is a cyclical Zero waste procedure

(2) Allow maximum utilization of resources

(3) Increase efficiency of production

(4) Ramesh Chandra Dagow of Sonipat Haryana doing the

(5) All of the above are true

Q. 66. Organic farming includes

(1) Bee-keeping

(2) Dairy management

(3) Water harvesting

(4) Composting and agriculture in a chain of processes support and other and allow an extremely economical and suitable venture

(5) All of the above

Q. 67. Harayana Kisan Welfare Club is linked to:

(1) Spreading information about organic farming

(2) To help on practice of internal organic farming

(3) Both 1 and 2

(4) To remove reduction wastes from field

Q. 68. The use of incinerators is crucial for disposal of:

(1) Solid waste

(2) MSW

(3) Hospitals waste

(4) All of the true

Q. 69. Nuclear energy was hailed as a non-polluting way for generating electivity but its use of nuclear energy has two very serious inherent problems:

(1) **Accidental leakage and safe disposal of radioactive wastes**

(2) Safe disposal and high cost

(3) High cost and not easy to use

(4) Typical use and accidental leakage

Q. 70. True statements is/are:

(1) During past century, temperature of earth has increased by 0.6C most of it doing last 3 decades

(2) Rise in temperature leading El-Nino effect (odd climatic conditions) increased melting of polar ice caps and Himalayan snow caps, results in rise of sea level in coastal areas

(3) Measures to control global warming is cutting down use of fossil fuel, improving efficiency of energy usage reducing deforestation, plating tress and showing down the growth of human populations

(4) **All of the above are true**

Q. 71. When 'Bad Zone' is formed?

(1) **In lower atmosphere (troposphere) that harms animals and plants**

(2) Stratosphere

(3) Mesosphere

(4) All of the above

Q. 72. Where good zone is located?

(1) **Upper part of atmosphere (Stratosphere) act as shield absorbing UV radiation from sun**

(2) Lower part of atmosphere (Stratosphere) act as shield absorbing UV radiation from sun

(3) Both lower and upper part of atmosphere (Stratosphere) act as shield absorbing UV radiation from sun

(4) All of the above are true

Q. 73. Dobson units (DU) is:

(1) **Measure to thickness of ozone in a column of air from ground to top of atmosphere (troposphere to stratosphere)**

(2) Measure to thin-ness of ozone in a column of air from ground to top of atmosphere (troposphere to stratosphere)

(3) Measure to thickness of ozone in a column of air from ground to bottom of atmosphere (troposphere to stratosphere)

(4) Measure to thickness of ozone in a column of water from ground to top of atmosphere (troposphere to stratosphere)

Q. 74. Match the column is correct matchable:

(1) Bad Zone—Troposphere

(2) Good Zone—Stratosphere

(3) Dobson Unit—Ozone concentration in atmosphere from low to top

(4) UV radiations—Chemical bounds in DNA and Protein

(5) **All of the above are correct**

Q. 75. One of the following statements given below the true one is?

(1) O_3 continuously formed by action of UV rays on molecular oxygen and degraded into molecular O_2 in stratosphere

(2) Above balance in stratosphere is disturbed by breaking of CFCs – use in refrigerators discharged in troposphere more upward and reach stratosphere

(3) In stratosphere UV rays act on the releasing Cl atoms in degrades O_3 release O_2 and O and Cl act as catalyzers

(4) **All are true facts**

Q. 76. Why Amrita Devi is famous?

(1) Exemplary course by hugging a tree and daring king's men to cut her first before cutting in tree

(2) Amrita Devi Bishnoi wild life protection Award for Individuals or communities from rural areas that have known extraordinary courage and dedication in protecting wildlife by announced by GOI

(3) Bishnoi community recognized for its peaceful coexistence with nature

(4) **All are true facts**

Q. 77. What is true for Joint Forest Management (JFM)?

(1) It is GOI initiative to show significance of participation by local communities in 1980

(2) JFM concept is to work closely with local communities for protecting and managing forests

(3) As JFM locals get benefits of various forest products and thus forest can sure in a sustainable manner

(4) **All of the above**

Q. 78. One of the following statements given below the true one is?

(1) Ozone whole is area above Antarctica, where ozone layer is the thinnest; it develops each year between Late August and early October

(2) CFCs have permanent and continuing affects on ozone levels

(3) UV radiations of wavelength shorter than UV–B almost completely absorbed by Earth. Only UV–B damages DNA and mutation may occur

(4) UV causes inflammation of cornea (snow-blindness) and cataract due to permanently exposure to cornea

(4) **All are true facts**

Q. 79. One of the following statements given below the true one is for Montreal Protocol?

(1) It is an international treaty signal at Montreal Canada in 1987

(2) Aim of this is to control the emission of ozone depleting substances and others

(3) It is effective in 1989

(4) **All are true facts**

Q. 80. One of the following statements given below the true one is for Slash and Burn Agriculture (Jhum cultivation) is:

(1) Practiced in North-Eastern states of India

(2) Contributed to deforestation

(3) Farmers cut-down forest and burn the plant remains; ash used as a fertilizer and land for farming or cattle grazing

(4) **All are true facts**

Q. 81. One of the following statements given below the true one is?

(1) Almost 40% forests have been lost in tropics; 1% in temperate region

(2) In beginning of 20th century, forests covered about 30% of land of India. At end of century it reduces up to 19.4%

(3) National Forest Policy (1988) of India, has recommended 33% forest cover for plant and 67% for hills

(4) **All of the true statements**

Q. 82. One of the following statements given below the true one is for waterlogging and soil salinity?

(1) Both are problems that have come in wake of Green Revolution

(2) Water logging occur due to without proper drainage of water, deposited on land surface or roots of plants

(3) Increased salt concentration is inimical to crop growth and agriculture

(4) **All of the true statements**

Q. 83. True in case of reforestation:

(1) Restoring a forest that once existed but removal at some point of time in past

(2) It may occur naturally in a deforested area tress with

(3) We can spread it up planting due consideration to biodiversity that earlier existed in that area

(4) **All of the above**

Q. 84. Causes of deforestation:

(1) Major cause is enhanced CO_2 concentration in atmosphere because trees that could hold a lot of carbon in their biomass are lost with deforestation

(2) Loss of biodiversity due to habitat distribution, disturb hydrologic cycle soil erosion

(3) In extreme cases it causes desertification

(4) **All of the above**

Q. 85. Major reason for deforestation:

(1) **Conversion of forest to agricultural land as to feed the growing human population**

(2) Urbanization

(3) Industrialization

(4) Silvi-culture

Q. 86. One of the following statements given below the true one is for axed for mainly?

(1) **Timber**

(2) Fire wood

(3) Cattle ranching

(4) None of the above

Q. 87. The degradation of natural resources can occur:

(1) Action of pollutants; soil erosion desertification water-logging and soil salinity

(2) Importer utilization practices

(3) **Both 1 and 2**

(4) None

Q. 88. The reasons (Human activities) responsible for removal of fertile top soil (takes centuries) resulting marid patches of land:

(1) Overcultivation

(2) Unrestricted grazing

(3) Deforestation

(4) Poor irrigation practices

(5) **All of the above**

Q. 89. In above, a principle region for removal of fertile top soil is:

(1) **Desertification due to increased urbanization**

(2) Desertification due to decreased urbanization

(3) Industrialization due to increased urbanization

(4) Deforestation due to increased urbanization

Selected Readings

1. PHOTOPERIODISM

Photoperiodism is the response of the plant to the relative length and timings of light and dark condition. Photoperiodism influences many aspects of plant development such as leaf fall dormancy and tuber development, but its major effect in on control of flowering. Gaener and Allard were the first to use term photoperiodism. They observed that Maryland mammoth variety of tobacco failed to produce flower during summer but when grown in greenhouse during winter the plant flowered profusely. They further subjected Maryland mammoth tobacco plant to short-day lengths during summer by placing the plant in darkness after exposure to that would be equivalent to a winter day. Plants treated in this way produced flowers. Furthermore they found that the plant can be kept in vegetative state during winter months by lengthening the days with artificial additional light. This variety of tobacco was called short day plants because its flowers only under short days. The plants fall into the following photoperiodic classes with respect to their flowering behaviour. The classification given below is based on 24-hour cycle of light and darkness.

Long-day Plants

Long-day plants flower when the night length falls below their critical photoperiod. These plants typically flower the during late spring or early summer as days are getting longer. In the northern hemisphere, northern hemisphere the longest day of the year (summer solstice) is on or about 21 June. After that date, days grow shorter (i.e. nights grow longer) until 21 December (the winter solstice). This situation is reversed in the southern hemisphere (i.e. longest day is 21 December and shortest day is 21 June).

Some Long-day Obligate Plants

- Carnation (dianthus)
- Henbane (*Hyoscyamus*)
- Oat (*Avena*).

Some Long-day Facultative Plants

- Pea (*Pisum sativum*)
- Barley (*Hordeum vulgare*)
- Lettuce (*Lactuca sativa*)
- Wheat (*Triticum aestivums*)

Short-Day Plants

Short-day plants flower when the night lengths exceed their critical photoperiod. They cannot flower under short-nights or if a pulse of artificial light is shone on the plant for several minutes during the night; they require a continuous period of darkness before floral development can begin. Natural nighttime light, such as moonlight or lightning, is not of sufficient brightness or duration to interrupt flowering. In general, short-day plants flower as days grow shorter (and nights grow longer) after 21 June in the northern hemisphere, which is during summer or fall. The length of the dark period required to induce flowering differs among species and varieties of a species. Photoperiodism affects flowering by inducing the shoot to produce floral buds instead of leaves and lateral buds.

Some Short-day Facultative Plants

Marijuana (*Cannabis*), Cotton (*Gossypium*), Rice (*Oryza*), Jowar (*Sorghum bicolor*), Green Gram (Mung bean, *Vigna radiata*), Soya beans (*Glycine max*).

Day Neutral Plants

Day-neutral plants, such as cucumbers, roses, and tomatoes, do not initiate flowering based on photoperiodism. Instead, they may initiate flowering after attaining a certain overall developmental stage or age, or in response to alternative environmental stimuli, such as vernalisation (a period of low temperatures).

Importance

i. The knowledge of the phenomenon of photoperiodism has been of great practical importance in hybridization experiments.

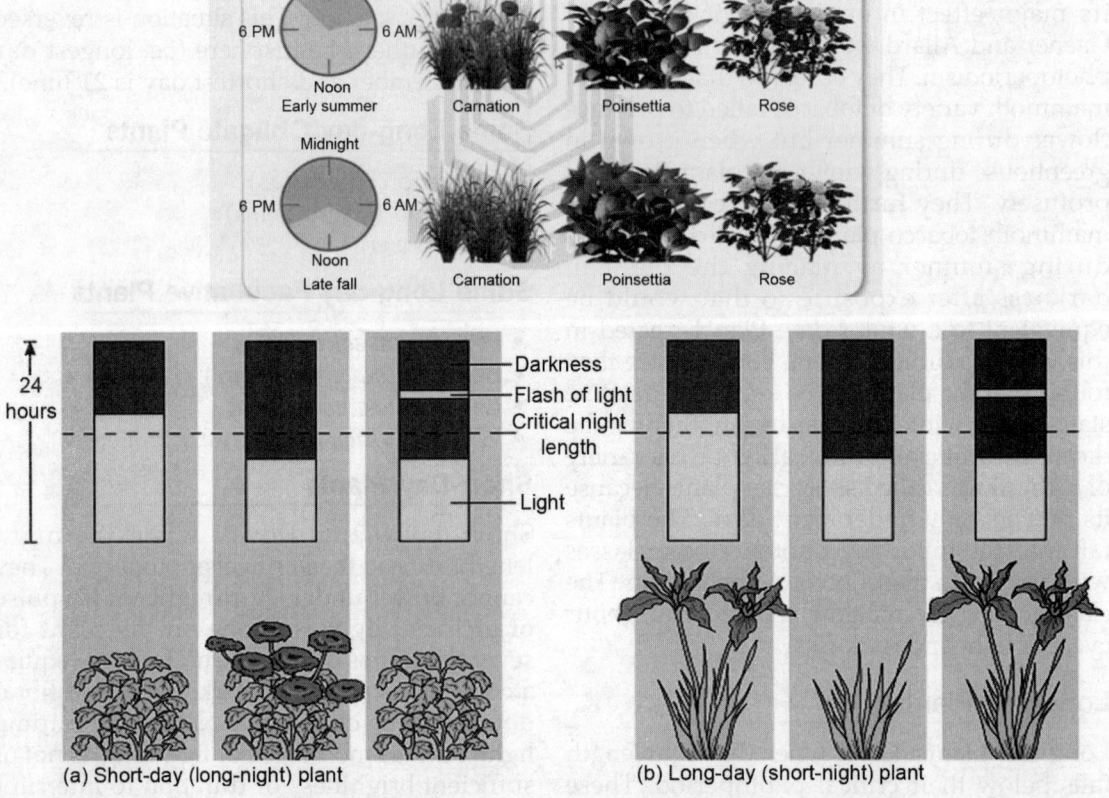

Fig. 1: Photoperiodic categories of plants

ii. Although the floral hormone 'florigen' has not yet been isolated, the isolation and characterization of this hormone will be of utmost economic importance.

iii. The phenomenon of photoperiodism is an excellent example of physiological preconditioning where an external factor induces some physiological changes in the plant the effect of which is not immediately visible. It lingers on in the plant and prepares the latter for a certain process which takes place at a considerably later stage during the life history of the plant. Some Phytochrome Mediated Photoresponses in Plants are:

1. Photoperiodism
2. Seed germination
3. Elongation of leaf, petiole, stem
4. Hypocotyl hook unfolding
5. Unfolding of grass leaf
6. Sex expression
7. Bud dormancy
8. Plastid morphology
9. Plastid orientation
10. Lipoxygenase metabolism
11. Rhizome formation
12. Bulb formation
13. Leaf abscission
14. Epinasty
15. Succulency
16. Enlargement of cotyledons
17. Hair formation along cotyledons
18. Formation of leaf primordia
19. Flower induction
20. Differentiation of primary leaves.
21. Formation of tracheary elements
22. Differentiation of stomata
23. Change in rate of cell respiration
24. Formation of phenylalanine deaminase
25. Synthesis of anthocyanins
26. Increases in protein synthesis
27. Increase in RNA synthesis
28. Changes in the rate of fat degradation
29. Changes in the rate of degradation of reserve proteins
30. Auxin catabolism
31. Incorporation of sucrose into plumular tissue
32. Permeability of cell membranes.

Photoreaction and Flower Formation

The question whether a plant will flower or not depend for both short-day and long-day plants not so much on actual length of the day as on the length of the period of darkness. We should really speak of long-night plants instead of short-day plant and of short-night plants instead of long-day plants. To neutralize the effect of long-night one can give a few hours of weak light following on a short period of strong light. The same effect can also be obtained by giving light for a short-time in the middle of dark period. Such night break light divides the dark period into two shorter periods which are actually too short to initiate flowering in short-day plants whereas in the case of long-day plants this treatment does encourage flowering. The same amount of light given at the commencement or end of the dark period in much less effective or has no effect at all.

Photoperiodic Induction

Plants may require one or more inductive cycles for flowering. An appropriate photo-period in 24 hours cycle constitutes one inductive cycle. If a plant which has received sufficient inductive cycles is subsequently placed under unfavourable photoperiods, it will still flower. Flowering will also occur if a plant receives inductive cycles after intervals of unfavourable photoperiods (discontinuous inductive cycles). This persistence of photo-periodic after effect is called as photoperiodic induction.

1. An increase in the number of inductive cycles results in early flowering of the plant. For instance Xanthium (a short-day plant) requires only one inductive cycle and

normally flowers after about 64 days. It can be made to flower even after 13 days if it has received 4–8 inductive cycles. In such cases the number of flowers is also increased.

2. Continuous inductive cycles promote early flowering than discontinuous inductive cycles.

Some of the example of plants which require more than one inductive cycles for subsequent flowering are Biloxi soya bean (SDP)-2 inductive cycles; *Salvia occidentalis* (SDP)-17 inductive cycles; *Plantago lanceolata* (LDP)-25 inductive cycles.

The Mechanism of Photoperiodism

Perception and translocation of photoperiodic stimulants. It is now well-established that the photoperiodic stimulus is perceived by the leaves. As a result, a floral hormone is produced in the leaves which is then translocated to the apical tip, subsequently causing the initiation of floral primordia. That the photoperiodic stimulus is perceived by the leaves can be shown by simple experiments on cocklebur (*Xanthium pennsylvanicum*), a short-day plant. Cocklebur plant will flower if it has previously been kept under short-day conditions. If the plant is defoliated and then kept under short-day condition, it will not flower. Flowering will also occur even if all the leaves of the plant except one leaf have been removed. If a cocklebur plant whether intact of defoliated, is kept under long-day conditions it will not flower. But, if even one of its leaves is exposed to short-day condition and the rest are under long-day photoperiods, flowering will occur. The photoperiodic stimulus can be transmitted from one branch of the plant to another branch. For example, if in a two branched cocklebur plant one branch is exposed to short-day and other to long-day photo period, flowering occurs on both the branches. Flowering also occurs if one branch is kept under long-day conditions and other branch from which all the leaves except one have been removed is exposed to short-day condition. However, if one branch is exposed to long-photoperiod and the other has been defoliated under short-day condition, flowering will not occur in any of the branches florigen complex (flowering hormone).

Nature of the Floral Hormone

Although there are firm evidences for the existence of a floral hormone but it has not

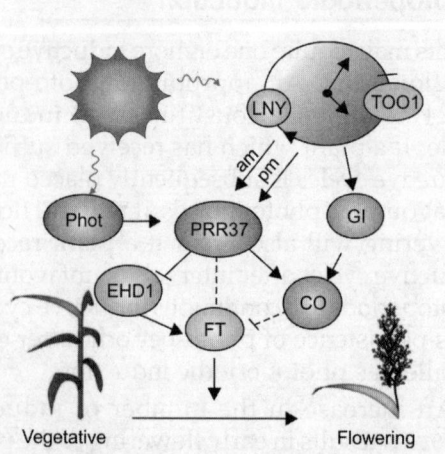

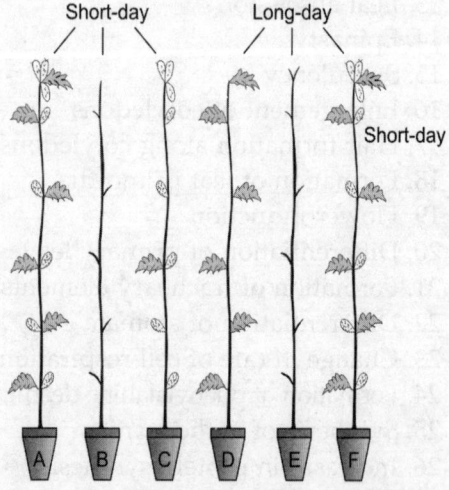

Fig. 2: Experiment on coklebur plants to show that photoperiodic stimulus is perceived by the leaves. Flowering occurs even if a single leaf is exposed to appropriate photoperiod. *See* text

yet been isolated. Therefore, the nature of this hormone which has been named florigen is not very clear. But it is quite evident that this hormone is a material substance which can be translocated from leaves to the apical tips situated at other parts of the plant resulting in flowering. Recent researches are indicative of 'florigen' to be a macromolecule unlike other plant growth hormones which are rather small molecules. This macromolecule may possibly be RNA or protein molecule which is translocated from the leaf to the apical tips (or meristems) via phloem in photo-induced plants (Corbesier and Coupland, 2005). Grafting experiments in cocklebur plants have even proved that the floral hormone can be translocated from one plant to another. For example, if one branched cocklebur plant (Fig. 3A) which has been exposed to short-day conditions is grafted to another cocklebur plant kept under long-day conditions, flowering occurs on both the plants.

This is a question plant biologists have been wondering about for decades! Many models have been suggested over the years, but today, most biologists think photoperiodism at least, in many species is the result of interactions between a plant's 'body clock' and light cues from its environment. Only when the light cues and the body clock line up in the right

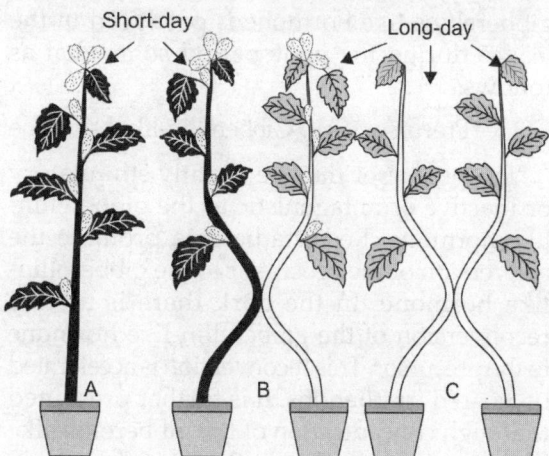

Fig. 4: Grafting experiments in cocklebur plants to show the translocation of floral hormone from one plant to another through graft union

way will the plant flower. This model is called the **external coincidence model** of photoperiodism. Its name highlights that an external cue-day length has to coincide in a certain way with the plant's internal rhythms in order to trigger flowering. These rhythms are **circadian rhythms**, patterns in gene expression or physiology that repeat on a 24-hour cycle and are driven by the plant's internal body clock. It has also been indicated that the floral hormone may be identical in short-day and long-day plants. For example, grafting experiments between certain long-day plants and short-day plants have shown that flowering occurs on both the plants even if one of them has been kept under non-inductive photoperiods.

Gibberellins and the Flowering Response

It is now well known that the gibberellins can induce flowering in long-day plants even under non-inductive short-days. It is also definite that the gibberellins alone do not constitute the 'florigen', but it is usually held that the gibberellins are in someway connected with the overall process of flowering. According to a scheme proposed by Brian (1958), a

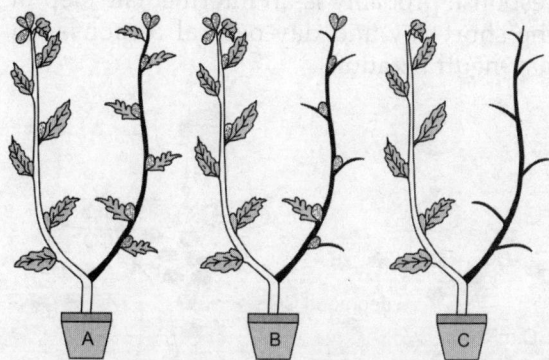

Fig. 3: Experiments on cocklebur plants to show that the photoperiodic stimulus can be transmitted from one branch of the plant to another

gibberellins like hormone is produced in the leaves during the photoperiod somewhat as follows:

$$CO_2 \rightarrow Precursor\ (P) \rightarrow Gibberellin\text{-like hormone}$$

The precursor may be slightly stimulatory or inactive or antagonistic to the gibberellin-like hormone. Red irradiations promote the conversion of the precursor to the gibberellin-like hormone. In the dark there is a slow reconversion of the gibberellin-like hormone to the precursor. This reconversion is accelerated by far-red irradiations. It is further presumed that high concentration of the gibberellin-like hormone leads to the synthesis of florigen in long-day plants. In short-day plants the synthesis of florigen takes place when the level of gibberellin-like hormone is low. But, flowering eventually follows once the florigen synthesis has taken place in both the cases.

The whole Scheme is Diagrammatically shown below

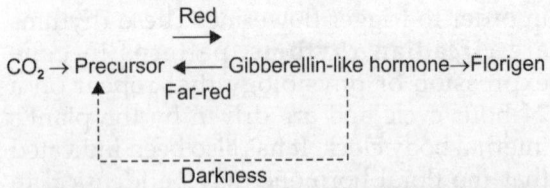

Quality of Light in Relation to Photoperiodism

The effect of the quality of light on the photoperiodic flowering response in four latitudinal ecotypes of *Chenopodium rubrum* was examined. Two southern ecotypes, Sel-184 (50°10′ N) and Sel-194 (34°20′ N), displayed an obligate short-day plant under white (W), red (R) and blue (B) light. Sel-372 (62°46′ N), the most northern ecotype, was day-neutral in B and W light and had an ambiphotoperiodic response in R light. Sel-374 (60°47′ N) was an ambiphotoperiodic in B light and had a short-day response in W and R light. In the B light regimens, the flowering of Sel-374 was modified from a typical ambiphotoperiodic to day-neutral response by changing the temperature from 20°C to 12°C. The photopriodic flowering response in the 8–16 hours photoperiod was suppressed severely by the reducing light intensity from 3,000 to 1,500 ergs.cm^{-2}.sec^{-1}, but that in continuous illumination was lowered only slightly by decreasing the light intensity. The ambiphotoperiodic flowering response differed in its reaction to light; flowering in the 8–18 hours photoperiod required a high intensity light independent of the quality of light, and flowering in the 24 hours photoperiod was promoted by B light. We considered the ambiphotoperiodic flowering response to be a combination of the obligate short-day flowering response and the flowering response for an extreme long-day condition, which is favored by B light. Therefore, this photoperiodic response probably is an intermediate step in the short-day and day-neutral responses in day-neutralization.

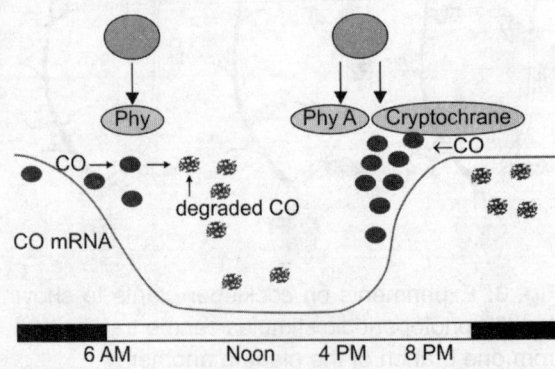

Vernalization

Vernalization is the low temperature treatment given to water soaked seeds, slightly germinated seed or seedling to hasten the time of flowing of plants that will develop from them. Chouard (1960) has defined vernalization as the "acquisition or acceleration of the ability to flower by a chilling treatment." The term was first formulated by T.D. Lysenko (1928) as 'springization'. The implication is not that genetics of the variety is changed to the summer or spring form but only that the variety is made to act like the summer or spring form in response to an artificial cold treatment. In colder countries like that of Europe there are cereals of two physiological kinds', viz. winter cereals and spring cereals. The winter varities are sown in September or October come out about 6" from the ground and then remain dormant throughout the winter months. During spring they again burst forth into activity. The person varieties of wheat are sown after the winter and they flower and fruit the same year on the other hand when winter wheat are sown in springs the conditions are unfavourable for the completion of certain stages of their development which are thus inhibited and the plants appear to remain for an indefinite period at the stage of tellering, i.e. their growth continues but their development is arrested by exposing

Light
FRI
VIN3
VIN1
Cold
VIN2
FLC
Circadian clock
FT, SOC1
Gibberellic acid
AP1, LFY
Flowering

slightly germinated seeds to low temperature, for some periods it is possible to shift the date of sowing of winter variety so as to make it behave like the spring variety without greatly altering the harvesting time.

Spring varieties of wheat are mostly low yielding while winter varieties give high yields. Hence workers attempted to shorten the flowering time of winter wheats to endow them with the same powers of flowering as spring wheats, while preserving their high yielding power. Gassner carried out experiments in petkus rye to determine the effect of exposure to low temperature at early stages of development on subsequent flowering in winter. He found that by germinating the grains at 1C to 2C prior to planting out in spring, the time to flower could be reduced by as much as six weeks compared with that of the grain germinated at 24C. In contrast he observed that temperature during germination has no influence on the flowering time of spring rye, so that when untreated spring rye and treated winter rye were sown together in the spring they came into flower at about the same time. Subsequently similar experiments were initiated in Russia which led to the system of pre treating partially germinated grains on a large scale. The chilling technique was modified to arrest the progress of growth during germination, so that for the first time partially germinated seeds could be stored for long periods without damage to growing points. The method of treating seeds becomes known as vernalization.

The Vernalization Process

In winter cereals the process consists of adding water to the seed in an amount that will produce visible germination. They require a period of 1–2 days in the processing chamber with temperatures at 10C–12C. The seed are then transferred to a temperature of 3C–5C, stirred frequently and their moisture content kept constant by addition of water. The time required in the cold room will vary depending upon the temperature and variety of the speed. Minimum length for any observable effect varies from 8 days to 8 weeks, depending on species. Saturation time vary from 3 weeks for winter wheat to 3 months in henbane. Hansel studied the vernalizing effect of a wide range temperature on petkus winter rye. He found that vernalization fails at temperatures below –4C, but from this temperation to 14C venalization is observed. Temperature from 1 to 7C are equally efficient in shortening the number of days to flowering. There is a rapid fall in the rate of vernalization when temperatures are increased form 7C to 15C. Lysenko stated that vernalization at least for some plants should be completed in darkness. After the seeds have been treated in this manner, they may be planted immediately or dried and kept for later planning. The low temperature effects may be obtained in some species when the moistened seeds are chilled (wheat). In other species, it may be obtained only when growing plants are chilled (Hyocyamus). Some species respond

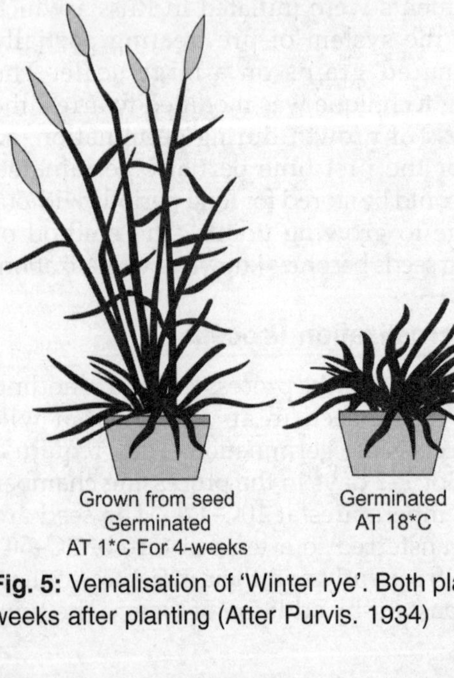

Grown from seed Germinated AT 1*C For 4-weeks

Germinated AT 18*C

Fig. 5: Vemalisation of 'Winter rye'. Both plants 11 weeks after planting (After Purvis. 1934)

readily to chilling at either stage. Proper hydration is necessary for vernalization. As vernalization is aerobic process, so it requires oxygen.

Theories of Flower Induction

Considering the enormous diversity of plant responses to day length and temperature, a number of theories have been proposed to explain the phenomenon of flowering.

C/N Relationship Theory

Before the discovery of photoperiodism and vernalization, a general observation made early in this century was like this: luxuriant vegetative growth is usually antagonistic to flowering. Practices like pruning, girdling that reduce vegetative growth often promote flowering. On the other hand maintenance of a high nutritional status especially as nitrogen supply will favour vegetative growth and incidentally the reproductive development will be delayed. From these observation, klebs in 1913 concluded that flowering is controlled by the nutritional status of the plant. He enunciated the relationship theory which indicates that a high endogenous C/N ratio is essential for flowering and vis, versa. However the later worker believed that klebs theory was too simple to explain the complexity of the flowering process and many subsequent observations have failed to confirm klebs theory which was soon discarded.

Trace Element Nutrition Theory

Trace element, particularly copper and iron is critically involved in photoperiodic induction in duckweed and other plants. Hillman studied the flowering behavior of lemna species and proved that the plants behave as SDP when copper is eliminated from the growing medium. Likewise addition of copper to the medium leads to the loss of SD requirement and the plants behave as DNA. Hillman postulated that Cu acting as

SH-inhibitor interferes with Phytochrome action, possibly by influencing some metal-sensitive membrane system. Iron is also involved in photoperiodic induction. Hillman pointed out that flowering in lemna is inhibited by reducing the iron supply. The role of iron deficiency in the inhibition of flowering process may be related to the role of iron in general metabolism.

Water Stress Theory

In an experiment on *geophila renaris* a perennial herbaceous plant of the tropical rain forest brenchart demonstrated that a period of water shortage is absolutely required for flower ignition. This observation suggests that limitation of water supply during certain development period may have a direct action on flower formation. This phenomenon of xeroduction has also been shown in *cichorium intybus* and *chenopodium polyspermum* in which application of excess water promotes regeneration of vegetative buds but proves to be inhibitory to flowering. Quite an opposite effect of water stress has been observed in the SDP pharbitis and xanthium and the LDP lolium. In these plants water storage prevents flower formation which is due to stress-inhibtion of translocation of floral stimulus from the induced leaves.

Perception and Transmission of Stimulus

Which organ of the plants is involved in vernalization? To get an answer to the above question the method employed is to cool only a certain portion of the plant while leaving the rest at normal temperature. It was discovered that cooling of the apical meristems of root gives the desired result. With the cereal seedling, the embryo itself perceives the cold stimuli are not endosperm. Thus it has been gernalised that it is always the meristems that responds to vernalization. But wellensick reported that young expanding leaves of *lunaria biensis* could perceive the vernalization stimulus only, if they were experiencing active cell division. Thus more specific vernalization seems to be that dividing cells are side to perceive vernalization stimulus and the meristems are well-qualified in that respect (Fig. 6).

Melchers has demonstrated that in hyoscyamus the translocation of vernalization stimulus

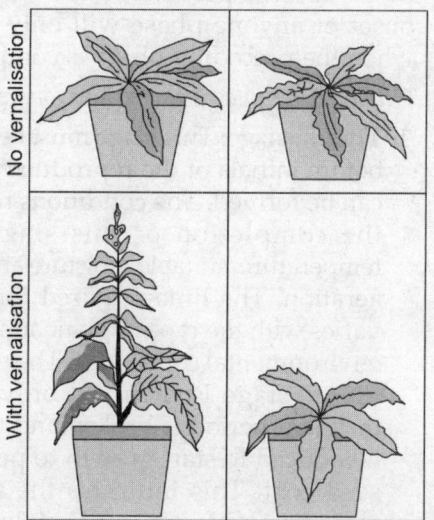
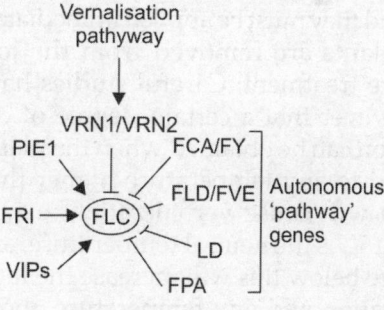

Fig. 6: The requirement of vernisation and long-day treatment for flowering in a blennial variety of hyoscyamus niger

takes place through a graft union. When the stem of vernalized plant is grafted to a universalized henbene stem, the latter with flower. The stimulus is not specific, i.e. can pass across a graft between plants from different species. Melchers suggested that a substance which he called vernalin was produced in the process of vernalization. Attempts to isolate and identify vernalin have not succeeded as yet. Anton Lang found that the low temperature requirements of some long-day plants can be satisfied by treating the apical meristems with gibberellins. Gibberellin promotes cell division under some conditions, perhaps this is its role in the vernalization process. Vernalization is believed to overcome inhibitors and induce the synthesis of growth hormones like gibberellins.

Stability of Vernalization Effect and Devernalization

Chroboezek while working with garden beet and Lang and Melchers with henbane reported that if the requisite period of low temperature treatment is followed period of high temperature, the expected acceleration of flowering did not occur. This phenomenon is referred to as de-vernalization. Such effect was also found in wheat and rye. To be really effective, de-vernalizing temperature much is about 30C or higher and they must be applied immediately after the plants are removed from the low temperature treatment. Careful studies have shown however that a certain degree of de-vernalization can be obtained when the plants are exposed to any temperature higher than that which will cause vernalization, e.g. in winter rye 15C is the neutral temperature, any temperature below this will increase the level of vernalization and any temperature above this applied immediately following low temperature treatment will cause some reduction in the level of vernalization. Anaerobic conditions given just after vernalization also cause de-vernalization usually a period of 3–5 days is

sufficient to stabilize the vernalized condition so that devernalization fails, the vernalized condition becomes stabilized at the natural temperature. After vernalization, most species can be revernalized with another cold treatment.

Mechanism of Vernalization

Three different views have been put forward to explain the mechanism of vernalization in physiological terms; The antagonism between vegetative and reproductive growth: this theory is based upon the concept that vegetative growth and flowering are antagonistic to each other. It is deducted that any means of repressing vegetative growth would result in flowering. The inhibition of vegetative growth by cold treatment allowed reproductive growth to gain the upper-hand. However this concept is over simplified.

1 the hypothesis of phasic development: Lysenko 1932, stress the distinction between growth and development and advocated what has become known as the theory of phasic development. This theory asserts that the process of the development of an annual seed plant consists of a series of phases which must occur in some predetermined sequence. The onset of anyone phase will only take place when the preceding phase is completed.

Outstanding phases in the development are:

1. **Thermostage:** This stage must be completed before initials of the reproductive's organs can be formed. The conditions required for the completion of this stage are low temperature, suitable moisture and adequate aeration. The time required for this stage varies with the type of plant and prevailing environmental conditions. The effect on the thermostage is incurred only when the dormant period is broken and the embryo is induced to start growth to penetrate the seed coat. This indicates the seeds have ceased to be seeds in physiological sense and have become equivalent to growing plants. To all winter wheat fail to head when

sown in spring because the temperatures are too high for accomplishment of the thermostage. Once this stage has been completed the other stages in the cycle of development can normally occur.

Draghetti in 1933, used the term 'crypto-vegetation' to signify state of vegetation maintained by certain plants under low temperature conditions of winter.

2. **Photostage:** The changes involve in the thermostage are not capable of initiating reproduction. A photostage is necessary and it can only become effective after thermostage is completed. Light and darkness play no part in the thermostage. The photostage requires high temperature and can be affected only under conditions of long-day or under continues illumination. This long-day requirement does not hold for the entire cycle of development of plants but only during this one particular stage through which they must pass immediately after thermostage.

Most spring wheat complete their life cycle quietly when given a long-day and temperature at 70°F or above throughout the life cycle on the other hand winter wheat complete their life cycle most rapidly when given a short-day and low temperature during the earlier stages of growth and a long-day and high temperature during later stages of development.

3. **The hypothesis of flower producing substance:** Purvis (1961) has given the following scheme regarding the role of

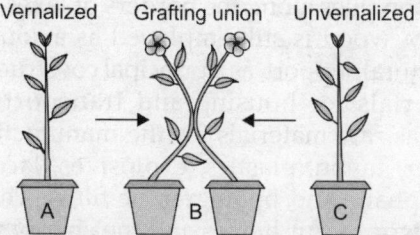

Vernalized   Grafting union   Unvernalized

A   B   C

Fig. 7: Experiments to demonstrate that floweing stimulus can translocate from vernalized plant to unvernalized plant through graft union

flower producing substances during vernalization in cereal plants. According to her scheme. B is some compound that is a part of reaction system-leading to flowering. This reaction system from B to D is under photoperiodic control and possibly leads to the synthesis of flowering hormone. In spring rye B is either present in the embryo or produced from A at normal temperature.

However in winter rye the production of B is retarded although not completely inhibited accumulates at a slow rate with the growth of plant. Exposure to low temperature accelerates the production of B in winter rye. The reaction between B to C to D is under photoperiodic control. The reaction from B to E is day neutral and occurs at optimal rates when the reaction for B to C is blocked. In the scheme D represents flowering hormone and C is an intermediate capable of initiating early stage in flower induction. In spring rye or vernalized winter rye there is a high accumulation of B. under continuous light; B is only slowly converted to C which in turn is rapidly converted to D the flowering hormone. The continual drain of C to from D keeps the reaction B to C to D going despite the unfavourable presence of continuous light on the reaction B to C. Eventually D reaches a critical level and flowering ensues. Under short-day condition, the reaction C to D is inhabited thus forcing the back reaction C to B to E to occur keeping the plant in vegetative state. This state will persist until the inhabited reaction C to D finally produces the critical amount of D need for floral initiation. Vernalization has great physiological significance. Plant can be grown is such regions when normally they do not grow. Crops can be grown earlier. Moreover plants become more resistant to cold and frost condition and fungal diseases. The yield of the crop is also increased. Though in recent years, plant breeders and genetists have developed resistant varieties of various plants through hybridization so that it is no longer necessary to use vernalization treatments.

2. PLANT AND HEALTH

The land and waters of the earth sustain a vast of assemblage of plants upon which all other living forms are directly or indirectly dependent. These Autotrophs have the remarkable property of capturing the inexhaustible energy of the sun to synthesize organic compounds which are vital for the existence of all life on earth. Organic deposits such as coal, lignite, peat and petroleum, are evidence of the photosynthetic activity of plants in the geological activity of plants in the geological past. In addition, plants stabilize soil, conserve moisture and preserve an equable climate. After violent disturbances of the earth such as volcanic eruptions and upheaval of mountains, plants cover the denuded ground with a carpet which protects the surface from being washed away. During the earliest and longest period of human history often called the Paleolithic or 'old stone age', which began one and three quarter million years ago, farming as such did not exist, nor did domestic animals. The people of this age were able to use fire and chipped pieces of hard stone (flint) into rough implements (such as crude hand axes and scrapers), which were used to remove flesh from animals hides. During this period, population was restricted to Africa, with a density of probably only 0.00425 persons per square kilometers and a total population of only about 125000. There are now 16.4 persons per square kilometers of earth's land surface. The stone-age passed into the bronze-age and the latter into the iron age, as man's agricultural needs demanded increasingly better tools. At present, we are living in the 'space age'.

Energy-giving Foods and Flavourings

The three daily meals consist either of plants products, such as cereals vegetables and fruits or products of animals (meat, cheese, butter, milk, and eggs) that have been fed on plants. The direct food value of the lower plants is small although man uses in his diet a number of mushrooms, morels and puffballs. Only a few species of green algae are utilized in Europe and America for food purposes. In China, Japan and the pacific Islands, however, algae are one of the major articles of diet. In a dried and powdered form, Irish moss, *Chondrus crispus* (L.) Stackh., is made into a desert, the well-known 'sea moss farina' as well as other puddings. The food value of angiosperms is correspondingly very high. The three main classes of food materials, namely carbohydrates, fats and proteins as well as important nutrients such as vitamins and minerals are all the obtained from the flowering plants. The bulk of the world's food supply comes from; rice, wheat, maize, sorghum, barley; sugarcane and sugar-beet; potato, sweet potato and cassava; beans, soya beans and groundnuts; coconut and banana. Valuable edible oils are extracted from cottonseed, olive, maize, coconut, soya bean and groundnuts. Large quantities of cottonseed and soya bean oils are converted into solid fats by hydrogenation. Other vegetables oils such as tung, linseed and castor oil are widely used in industry.

Plants and the Home

Prehistoric man used many different kinds of plants for constructing his means of transport and dwellings, such as wattle and daub huts and the more elaborate swiss lake dwelling built on piles along the borders of lakes. Even today, wood is still employed as a source of structural support, as a principal constructional materials for housing and transportation, and as raw materials for the manufacture of paper, rayon, plastics, explosives, lacquers, cellophane and photographic films. The fuel that worms our homes and the energy which operates most of our industry comes directly or indirectly from plants. The paper industry depends largely upon wood pulp. Thus, plants are the carriers of written words, ideas and information, and have been referred to as 'the medium of thought'.

Plants Fibres and Fabrics

From the earliest times, man has used fabrics of many kinds of protection, warmth, personal adornment and even to display personal wealth. Even today, fabrics are being used for these purposes. Besides clothing, plant fibers are used in the manufacture of rope and string, brushes and brooms, paper and paper products, upholstery work (filling mattresses, cushions, etc.) and life belts. Fibers of commercial importance, however are relatively few, the most important which are; cotton and kapok (surface fibers), flax, jute, hemp, Roselle and ramie (soft fibers). Cotton is still the world's most important natural fibre.

Plants and Drugs

Primitive people, the world over, have always used many different kinds of plants as cures for various ailments. Quinine obtained from the bark of several species of Cinchona has long been used as an anti-malarial drug. The leaves of European foxglove (Digitalis purpurea) provide digitalis-a valuable heart stimulant. Opium and its derivatives, obtained from Papaver somniferum, are used to relieve pain and induce sleep. Numerous other drugs of plant origin have been found to be useful in the treatment of various disorders. Among these are Rauwolffia, belladonna, nux-vomica, ephedrine, ergot, aconite, podo-phyllum, ginseng, cascara and curare. Quite recently, a fungus, *Psilocybe mexicana* Heim, used by Mexican Indians in their religious rituals, has been reported to possess psychotherapeutic properties. Antibiotics have the property of preventing the growth and development of pathogens. Since 1928, when the first of them, 'penicillin' was discovered by Sir Alexander Fleming, many other antibiotics have been isolated from bacteria, actinomycetes and moulds. Many more have been extracted from other group of fungi, including yeast, and from algae, lichens, and seed plants. Their use has contributed greatly to a lengthening of the average human lifespan. Man also uses a number of vegetable products for their stimulating and narcotic effect. These include opium and its derivates, marijuana betel nut, coca and tobacco, of which the first two especially are habit-forming drugs, cola.

Plants as Colouring Materials

Vegetable tannins dyes have been used by man since ancient times for the colouring of fabrics, animal's hiders and for personal adornment. Madder, *Rubia tinctorum*, was perhaps the first camouflage to be used in war. Tannins are organic compounds with a bitter (astringent) taste and tend to accumulate in physiologically inactive tissues, such as heartwood, cork and old foliage. They are extracted from- bark (hemlock, chestnut oak, mangrove), wood (quebracho), leaves (sumac), fruits (divi-divi) and from other plant. Tannins combine with proteins in animals hides to form soft and pliable leather. They are also used for the manufacture of inks. Plants dyestuffs were used by primitive man for colouring animal skins and also his own skin during religious festivals and in war time. The use of natural dyes has diminished with the synthetics such as aniline and alizarin derivatives. However, a number of them are still prized, e.g. indigo, logwood, wood, safflower, saffron and annatto. They are used for dyeing textiles, leather, paints, varnishes, paper and ink and also for colouring food, beverages and medicines.

Plants and Beauty

Plants add beauty to the earth's surface and contribute a great deal to man's pleasure. The fields and forests provide retreats where millions of people can enjoy peace and contentment. Artists and poets alike derive inspiration from the detail and beauty of plants. Plants are the ornaments of our gardens and houses. Through planned panting, our environment has been made still more pleasing by the efforts of florists, landscape gardeners and nurserymen. In addition, flowers are the medium through which many varying emotions such as love, worship and sorrow can be conveyed, often more effectively than through words.

Plants and the Atmosphere

From the earliest times, plants have been purifying the atmosphere by assimilating carbon dioxide. By increasing the number of trees in a city its supply of oxygen can be augmented by photosynthetic activity. Trees in regions of low rainfall absorb water from considerable depths and release it into the atmosphere, thereby improving the climate.

Plants and Perfume

Chemically, essential oils are mostly derivatives of terpenes or benzene. Despite having an oily texture, they are not true oils, evaporating rapidly when they come into contact with air. Essential oils were used by the early Egyptians for mummification (persevering the dead). Today, essential oils from the flowers of jasmine, carnation, lavender, champaca, rose and many other plants give a pleasant odour to perfumes, soaps deodorants, cosmetics and incense. Oil of citronella, derived from *Cymbopogon nardus,* is a common ingredient of cheap soaps, perfumes and insects repellents. Camphor, obtained from the distillation of wood of the camphor tree, *Cinnamomum camphora,* is used in the manufacture of celluloid, various nitrocellulose compounds, in medicines and in cosmetics. Wood turpentines derived from the softwood distillation of conifers are used as solvents for paints.

Miscellaneous Products

A variety of other plant products in use today include pectins, gums, resins, latex products, waxes and insecticides.

Pectins

These are found in nearly all plants as the cementing material in the cell wall, but are usually obtained from citrus rind and green apple residue (pomace). They are used in the manufacture of jellies and candies, to increase viscosity in tomato juice, in the tobacco industry and for pharmaceuticals.

Gums

These are mostly amorphous colloids and consist largely of degradation products of cellulose or other carbohydrates. They are hydrophilic forming viscous liquids. They are used in industry as sizing, stiffening agents in ice cream and stabilizers and binders in medicinal pills. Many cough drops and syrups contain plant gums. The most common plant gums are: gum Arabic, gum tragacanth, gum karaya and cheery gum.

Resins

Although resembling gums in superficial appearance, resins differ in their origin and chemical compositions. Some resins are sticky, viscous liquids, while others are hard , brittle solids, generally clear but sometimes opaque. They seem to be oxidative products of essential oils, occurring as secretions in special ducts, often mixed with other substances such as latex, essential oils or gums. Unlike gums, resins are insoluble in water but dissolve readily in alcohol and other organic solvents to form 'varnishes'. When applied in this films, the solvent evaporates leaving behind a hard waterproof layer of resin. Commercial supplies are obtained from plant families such as the Fabaceae (Congo copal, copaiba balsam, balsam of Peru), Dipterocarpaceae (damars) and Pinaceae (Canada balsam). Amber is a fossil resin, occurring chiefly along the shores of the Baltic Sea. It is an exudates from the extinct pine, *Pinus succinifera* (Goppert) Conw. Nowadays it is used mainly for mouthpieces of pipes and holders for cigars and cigarettes.

Resins are used in a great variety of ways, as perfume fixatives, ingredients in incense and tobacco flavourings, in the manufacture of linoleum, oil cloth, printer's ink, roofing compounds, soaps, adhesives and paper size.

Latex Products

Latex is a milky, viscous, colloidal secretion, occurring in specialized laticiferous ducts. Some of the more important products derived from latex are rubber, gutta-percha, balata and chicle. Of these rubber is the most familiar and the valuable, chiefly obtained from the Para-rubber tree, *Hevea brasiliensis* of the family Euphorbiaceae. Because of its elasticity, pliability, and resilience, rubber is used in hundreds of products, such as tyres, tubes, hoses, etc. On the other hand, gutta-percha is non-elastic but is resilient and pliable, and finds wider application in the manufacture of marine cables, golf balls, telephone receivers, waterproofing's, adhesives, surgical apparatus, and in dentistry for temporary fillings. Balata is also used in much the same way as gutta-percha, but particularly well-suited for machine beltings. Chicle is the basis of the chewing-gum industry.

Waxes

They are usually fatty acid esters of mono-hydroxy alcohols such as cetyl alcohol and myricyl alcohol and are found mostly as protective coverings on the epidermis of leaves, stems and fruits to retard water loss. Carnauba, *Copernicia cerifera* of the family Arecaceae, is the world's most important wax plant. The wax derived from the leaves is widely used in the manufacture of candles and polishes. Candelilla wax, obtained from the stem of *Euphoria antisyphilitica* is often mixed with paraffin to make candles.

Insecticides

Many species of plants seem to be possess insecticidal properties. Two of the most potent insecticides of plant origin are rotenone and pyrethrum. Rotenone is extracted from the root of two members of the family fabaceae, *Derris elliptica and lonchocarpus nicou*. Unlike synthetic insecticides such as dichloro-diphenyltrichloroethane (DDT), chlordane, arsenic and copper compounds, natural insecticides are relatively harmless to man and higher animals and are thus safer to use.

Miscellaneous Products

Besides, the non-green plants are also of great economic importance to mankind. The manufacture of vinegar, cheese, and butter sauerkraut; the tanning of leather; the curing of tea, coffee, cacao beans and vanilla pods; the production of silage; and the extraction of fibres of flax, hemp, and the jute, are all the examples of the beneficial activities of bacteria. Yeasts are used in baking and in the fermentation process involved in the manufacture of beer, wine, whisky, and other liquors. Yeast are also important source of vitamin B and D groups. Bacteria and fungi also act as natural scavengers, decomposing the dead bodies and organic waste of plants and animals into simpler units that can be readily taken up by plants, and thereby maintaining soil fertility.

3. THE ORIGIN OF CULTIVATED PLANTS

The cultivation of plants is one of the man's oldest occupations and probably began when he discovered that certain seeds spilled on disturbed ground grew in some mysterious way into new plants. It now appears certain that early domestication were made more or less concurrently and independently on the lower slopes of the Zagros mountains and the 'fertile crescent' of the Tigris and Euphrates valley in northern Iraq and in the Tehuacan valley of mexico. For the discovery of many of these economic plants, their migrations from one continent to another, and knowledge of their properties and cultivation, we are indebted to the scholars of antiquity, the ancient conquerors, the medieval merchant princes, the Spanish conquistadores and the mariners and the explores of many lands. They all took with them seeds of their native plants and in return, brought home for transplantation whatever they found fit. Darwin (1868) considered that the cultivated plants arose by profound modifications in the wild plants under cultivation.

Mendel's work, first published in 1865, remained obscure until 1900. He formulated the laws of inheritance and attributed the origin of cultivated plants to natural selection and hybridization.

In his origin of cultivated plants, Alphonse Decandolle (1883) studied 247 species of cultivated plants and attempted to solve the mystery about the ancestral form, region of domestication and history of most of our important cultivated plants.

The Work of Vavilov

The direction of Nikolai Ivanovich Vavilov, one of the greatest investigators in crop geography and genetics, extensive collections of cultivated plants and their wild relatives were made by sending expeditions all over the world. His deductions were based on a variety of facts, obtained from the sources different from those of his predecessors, such as morphology, anatomy, cytology, genetics, distribution and reaction to diseases. He observed that distribution of plants is not uniform. In some restricted areas, a wild range of genetic variability is encountered. Over 50% of the diversity found in the world was present in these regions. There are few regions and the generally they are small areas confined to the mountains or foothills of the tropics and the subtropics. Vavilov calls these regions with the greatest wealth of forms, 'gene for diversity center' and further suggested that these are regions of origin as well as dispersal.

World Centres of Origin of Cultivated Plants

1. *Chinese Centre*

This is the earliest and the largest independent centre for the origin of cultivated plants. It includes the mountainous regions of central and western China and the adjacent lowlands.

2. *Indian Centre*

A. The main centre includes Assam and Burma. 117 plants are considered to be endemic, including rice, sugarcane, many legumes, mango, orange, and tangerine, jute, coconut palm, oriental cotton, black peeper, cinnamon tree, eggplant, yam, etc.

B. The Indo-Malayan centre includes Indo-China and the Malay Archipelago. 55 plants listed, including banana, coconut, sugarcane, clove, nutmeg, black peeper, Manila hemp, Mangosteen, etc.

3. *Central Asiatic Centre*

This region includes northwest India Afghanistan, Tadjikistan, and Uzbekistan and western Tian-shan. 43 plants are listed, prominent among which are common wheat, pea, beans, lentil, hemp, cotton, carrot, garlic, spinach, pistachio, apricot, almonds, apple and pear.

4. *Near Eastern Centre*

This region includes the interior of Asia Minor, all of Transcaucasia, Iran and the highlands of Turkmenistan. 83 species are included in this region. At least 9 species of wheat as well as rye are indigenous to this centre. Many of our subtropical and temperate fruits and several forage crops such as alfalfa, Persian clover and vetch are also native to this region.

5. *Mediterranean Centre*

This region includes the boarders of the Mediterranean Sea. 84 plants are known to have originated here including olives and many cultivated vegetables; forage plants; oil yielding; wheat; and ethereal oil and spice plants.

6. *Abyssinian Centre*

Comprises Abyssinia, Eritrea and parts of Somalia. 38 species are natives to this region. Wheat and Barley are especially rich in diversity and others includes sesame, castor, bean, coffee and okra.

7. *South-Mexican and Central American Centre*

This centre includes the southern parts of Mexico, Guatemala, Honduras and Costa Rica. Plants native to this region are extremely varied, and include maize, bean, squash, chayote, sweet potato, red peeper, upland cotton, sisal, papaya, guava, cacao, and tobacco.

8. *South American Centre*

1. The Peruvian-Ecuadorean-Bolivian centre consisting mainly of high mountainous area represents the centre of pre-Inca civilization. Plants native to the Puna and Sierra uplands are also included. This centre known to be the original home of many potato species, tomato, lima bean, pumpkins, red peeper, coca, cotton and tobacco.

2. The Chiloe centre, an island near the coast of southern Chile, is thought to be region of origin of the common potato.

3. The Brazilian-Paraguayan centre is believed to be the region of origin of groundnut, cassava, pineapple, rubber tree, and cashew-nut. These areas of diversity constitute only a small proportion of the total land area of the earth, and are geographically distinct, being isolated by deserts or mountain ranges. 85% of the 640 species listed by Vavilov originated in the old world and the remainder from the new world. Vavilov further distinguished between primary and secondary or 'accumulation' gene centres, he suggested that in the primary gene centre, the process of domestication from the native wild relatives began and those are characterized by dominant genes. As the cultivated plants later migrated to another gene centre they were subjected to same natural force which again led to a considerable increase in the diversity of the cultivated plants that came into this region. In this way, a new or secondary gene centre develops from the cultivated plants in question, but significantly is characterized by a diversity of recessive characters and is also devoid of wild relatives. He divided the world into regions and implies that there was no centre. This hardly seems to agree with the concept of 'centre' at all. Also, he gave 'micro gene centre' of wild species genetically related to cultivated plants.

The Mega-gene centres are: China, Indochina-Indonesia, Australia-New Zealand, Indian subcontinent, Central Asia, West Asia, Mediterranean coastal and adjacent regions, Africa, Europe-Siberia, Central America, Bolivia-Peru-Chile, North America. Studies since Vavilov's time have shown, however, that history of plant domestication is much more complicated than had been supposed. A pattern that stem rather consistently from geo-botanical and genetic studies is one of which Harlan (1966) had called 'diffuse origin'. Crop origins can be diffuse in both space and time. Thus, according to Harlan, each crop may have been repeatedly domesticated at different times in different locations or may have been brought into cultivation in several regions simultaneously. At least we cannot pinpoint with any precision a single centre of origin for these particular plants. Cultivated plants were not domesticated as the 'crops' we know today. To begin with they were something like their wild ancestors but as they spread out of their area of origin they picked up additional germ-plasm from their wild relatives on the way. In a number of crops, we have evidence of this periodic infusion of germ-plasm from their wild relatives.

The Future Role of Plants in Relation to Mankind

When we look into the distant future, it seems likely that plants will continue to provide the three basic necessities of life as well as other useful items. Nevertheless, the problem of food production is acute and will become more critical with each passing year. Although the world is increasing its food supply, population growth is now outstripping food production in all underdeveloped countries. If the present worldwide population growth rate of about 2% per year continues, there will be more than 7 billion people on our planet by the turn of the century, double what we have today, i.e. 3.7 billions. According to some estimates, about one-half of the world population is either undernourished or actually starving. The 'population explosion' of the last few decades has given rise to two sharply opposites views. Many scientists, demographers and political thinkers are predicting doom for the human race because of the growing imbalance between food production and population growth. They have predicted mass starvation and civil and international disruption. They pointed out that 120 000 people, mostly children, die each day from hunger, malnutrition and related diseases. The prophesy that the greatest food crises in history will occur in the next twenty years. A crash programme for increased food supply is needed forestall mass starvation. But such an effort will succeed only if combined with population control through a worldwide programme of education as to the dangers of a rapidly increasing population. During the past decade an enormous family planning drive has been launched in many countries to slow down population growth. Increasing the world's food supply will involve many different approaches:

1. Bringing more land under cultivation.
2. The production and more effective distribution of chemical fertilizers and insecticides.
3. The introduction of modern agricultural technology to all the underdeveloped of crop.
4. Improvement of crop, plants and animals through genetic engineering.
5. Extension of irrigation projects, including reclamation of sea water.
6. The increasing utilization of marine resources, not only fish and other animals, but also direct use of marine algae as a source of human food.
7. Tapping other underexploited and unidentified food sources.

Hopefully, a massive and under pre-cedented human effort will master the world food problems and produce a world free from hunger. Thus, it could not only avert the predicted famine of 1985, but also has reduced the possibility of any famine for a long-time to come. The predicted widespread famine in several countries for 1975, particularly in India, has been proved wrong. The management of forests in most countries is now recognized as being as important as that of cultivated crops. Currently, man is constantly looking for ways of harnessing solar energy directly as it will remain available to us for millions of years to come.

4. WHAT IS PESTICIDE?

In the agricultural world, there are **pests** of another kind, and they are any unwanted organisms that feed on or harm agricultural crops, ornamental plants or livestock. Pests can often cause harm to livestock or crops by consuming them or using up vital nutrients. To prevent damage, farmers utilize specific methods to remove or eliminate pest problems. **Pesticides**, chemicals that kill or manage the population of pests, are the main combat method used. Pesticides are the substance used for killing animals and plant paste. A pest is an organism that cause an epidemic disease associated with high mortality. Hence, pest are harmful to man physically and also to his crops causing economic losses. Pests therefore include bacteria, fungi, nematode, insects, etc. Each pesticide is given a name starting with the pests that kills and ending 'cide' (killer). Thus a pesticide killing the bacteria is termed bacteriocide, for fungi–fungicide and so on. Since all pest are living organisms therefore, pesticide could be more effectively placed under a broader category 'biocides'—killer of living organisms.

Due to the fact that there are many different types of agricultural pests, there are also many different types of pesticides. Pesticides are often divided into several different categories, including insecticides, fungicides, rodenticides and herbicides. Insecticides are used to kill unwanted insects, and rodenticides are designed to kill rodents, such as rats and mice. Fungicides are used to kill fungal pests, and herbicides are used to kill unwanted plants, commonly referred to as weeds. According to the Environmental Protection Agency (EPA), the government body that regulates pesticides in the US a pesticide is any substance or mixture of substances intended for preventing, destroying, repelling or mitigating any pest. Though often misunderstood to refer only to insecticides, the term pesticide also applies to herbicides, fungicides, and various other substances used to control pests. Pesticides also include plant regulators, defoliants and desiccants.

A pesticide is any substance or mixture of substances used to destroy, suppress or alter the life cycle of any pest. A pesticide can be a naturally derived or synthetically produced substance. A pesticide can also be an organism, for example, the bacterium Bacillus thuringiensis which is used to control a number of insect pests, or even a genetically modified crop. Pesticides include bactericides, baits, fungicides, herbicides, insecticides, lures, rodenticides and repellents. They are used in commercial, domestic, urban and rural environments. According to the Environmental Protection Agency (EPA), the government body that regulates pesticides in the US a pesticide is any substance or mixture of substances intended for preventing, destroying, repelling or mitigating any pest. Though often misunderstood to refer only to insecticides, the term pesticide also applies to herbicides, fungicides, and various other substances used to control pests. Pesticides also include plant regulators, defoliants and desiccants. There are currently thousands of pesticide products registered for use in NSW by the Australian Pesticides and Veterinary Medicines Authority (APVMA).

Pesticides are substance which kills certain living organisms. These are categorized as follows on the basis of organisms killed by them:

1. Bactericides,
2. Fungicides,
3. Herbicides,
4. Weedicides,
5. Insecticide,
6. Nematicides,
7. Rodenticides.

Pesticide is required for protecting the crops and thus reducing commercial and economic losses. About 30% of the agricultural productivity is estimated to have been lost due to pest and disease. Pesticides have been in use in use since long DDT, an important pesticide came into use during World War second. So also 2, 4D (2,4 Dichlorophenoxy acetic acid—a herbicide) was very widely used at the same time. Bordeaux mixture used for controlling fungal disease of plant, is in use for over a century now.

Narrow-Spectrum Pesticides

Pesticides that have a small coverage range are referred to as **narrow-spectrum pesticides**, because they are designed to kill or manage a select group of organisms. Narrow-spectrum pesticides make it possible to target a specific species or group of organisms that are known to cause damage. Many narrow-spectrum pesticides are designed to interact with a characteristic of the pest that is specific to that organism, such as a pheromone, hormone or physical feature.

An example of a narrow-spectrum pesticide is chitin inhibitors, which are chemicals that interact with chitin, a component of the exoskeleton of insects. This pesticide inhibits the development of chitin and will eventually result in the death of the insect. The chitin inhibiting pesticide will only harm insects that have chitin in their exoskeletons and will not affect other insects.

Broad-Spectrum Pesticides

Although sometimes it is desirable to target a specific species or group of organisms, in some situations, it is necessary to eliminate a wider range of pests that are causing harm. **Broad-spectrum pesticides** are pesticides that are designed to kill or manage a wide variety of organisms. Broad-spectrum pesticides are used when many different species of organisms are causing harm or when the specific organism causing harm is unknown. In order to kill or manage such a large variety of organisms, most broad-spectrum pesticides are designed to target a system that is common

in many organisms, such as the nervous system or muscular system.

Different Types of Pesticides?

Some families or groups of chemical products which are considered pesticides:

Bactericides

These destroy, suppress or prevent the spread of bacteria. Examples are swimming pool chemicals containing chlorine, and products used to control black spot (bacterial blight) on garden plants or in orchards. Household disinfectants and some industrial disinfectants are excluded and not considered pesticides.

Baits

These may be 'ready to use' products or products which need to be mixed with a food to control a pest. This category includes baits prepared for the control of large animals, such as foxes, wild dogs and rabbits, and baits for insects (such as cockroaches and ants) and molluscs (snail and slug pellets).

Fungicides

These control, destroy, make harmless or regulate the effect of a fungus. Examples include chemicals used to treat Grey mould on grape vines and fruit trees, or Downy Mildew on cucumbers.

Genetically modified organisms (GMOs)

Agricultural crops can be genetically modified to make them more resistant to pests and diseases, or tolerant to certain herbicides. For example, a gene from the bacterium Bacillus thuringiensis can be incorporated into cotton to provide protection against the larval stages of the cotton bollworm and native bollworm. GMOs are regulated by the Commonwealth Government through the OGT Runder the provisions of the *Gene Technology Act 2000*. Where a genetically modified product is determined to be a pesticide, it is subject to an assessment and registration process in accordance with APVMA requirements.

Herbicides

These destroy, suppress or prevent the spread of a weed or other unwanted vegetation, for example, the herbicide glyphosate is used to control a range of weeds in home gardens, bush land and agricultural situations.

Insecticides

These destroy, suppress, stupefy, inhibit the feeding of, or prevent infestations or attacks by, an insect. Insecticides are used to control a wide variety of insect pests, including thrips, aphids, moths, fruit flies and locusts. In NSW, pesticides include products used on animals to control external parasites if they require dilution or mixing with water. Products applied directly to animals without dilution, injections or other medicines administered internally to treat animals are veterinary medicines and are regulated by the NSW Department of Primary Industries under the *Stock Medicines Act 1989.*

Lures

These are chemicals that attract a pest to a pesticide for the purpose of its destruction. Solely food-based lures, for example, cheese in a mousetrap, are excluded and are not considered pesticides.

Rodenticides

These are chemicals used specifically for controlling rodents such as mice and rats.

Repellents

These repel rather than destroy a pest. Included in this category are personal insect repellents used to repel biting insects. A number of living organisms that can control pests have also been registered as pesticides. Rabbit Haemorrhagic Disease, for example, has been used to control rabbit numbers; and bacteria that act as biological insecticides have

been used to control various insect larvae, such as moths and mosquitoes.

Natural' Pesticides

Many natural substances can be used as pesticides, such as extracts of pyrethrum, garlic, tea-tree oil and eucalyptus oil. When these natural chemicals are used as pesticides they become subject to the same controls as pesticides produced synthetically. Roman and Chinese are known to have used natural insecticide in past. The Chinese are reported to be the first to find out the insecticidal properties of rotenone's present in root of Derris elliptica. Alkaloid like nicotine from tobacco and pyrethrum and cinerinerom pyrethrum inflorescence have been used as plant insecticide. Pyrethrin is an important ingredient of preparation used a wide range of insect pests as mosquito coil, fly spray and aerosols. Neem is considered to be one of the most useful natural insecticide. Biologically active chemical have been isolated from oil, seed, bark and leaves. Azadirachtin and other limonoids such as meliantoil and salanin are very effective against insect even in minute quantities. Azadirachtin repel insect, inhibits their feeding and affect their hormonal balance. It also affect metamorphosis of several insect larvae and thereby, prevent the increase of new insect population. Neem is known as to resist more than 200 species of insect, mites and nematode.

Chemical Classes

Organophosphates

There are many common active ingredients classified as organophosphates (many ending in-phos, -fos, -vos, or -thion). These compounds have a wide range of toxicity levels and are chemically similar to nerve gases developed for human warfare. Organophosphate insecticides inhibit the activity of an enzyme in the nervous system (acetylcholinesterase), leading to overstimulation and dysfunction of the nervous system. Symptoms of organophosphate poisoning in honeybees include loss of activity, abnormal wobbly movements, lying on the back or spinning while beating wings in this position, and/or regurgitation of collected nectar. Damage to brood and queen by exposure to microencapsulated methyl parathion or acephate (acetamidophos) have also been recorded.

Neonicotinoids

Neonicotinoid insecticides target the nervous system of insects, blocking an acetylcholine receptor. They are a class of synthetic compounds based on the naturally occurring compound nicotine, itself used as an agricultural insecticide. They have become one of the most commonly used insecticide classes in recent years, with compounds registered on many major crops for foliar application and/or seed treatment. Active ingredients include imidicloprid, clothiandin, thiamethoxam, acetamiprid, thiacloprid, and dinotefuran. They are sold under a variety of trade names, and all are classified as highly toxic or toxic to honeybees. They are systemic insecticides, meaning that the compounds are present in the plant tissues rather than just on the surface. There is evidence that pollinators may be exposed via the resources they collect, but further research is required to determine the details and how problems might be mitigated. Neonicotinoid compounds may also pose a hazard if used as a seed treatment or sprayed before bloom, as they can be present in dust from seed drills, pollen, nectar, and guttation water. Neonicotinoids are the group of pesticides most commonly implicated as a contributing cause of widespread honeybee losses, both through direct toxic action and chronic effects on the immune system. Research is ongoing into the role of these compounds in honey-bee declines, but it is recommended that their use near bees or blooming crops or wildflowers be avoided. The Xerces Society recently published a **review** of the scientific literature on the effects of neonicotinoids on bees.

Pyrethroids

Pyrethroid insecticides are a class of synthetic compounds based on the naturally occurring compound pyrethrin, which is extracted from chrysanthemum flowers. Pyrethrin is noted for its quick 'knock-down' of insects, but the natural compound is not always lethal, and degrades readily in the environment. Synthetic pyrethroids have been chemically stabilized to increase their persistence in field applications and/or increase toxicity. Pyrethroids are sometimes mixed with other insecticides, either in a brand name product or tank-mixed at the application site. Symptoms of pyrethroid poisoning in honeybees include regurgitation of collected nectar.

N-Methyl Carbamates

N-methyl carbamates, or simply carbamates, are commonly used insecticides. The names of many of these active ingredients end in the suffix-carb, and the class also includes several insecticides that are responsible for many-bee poisonings (carbaryl, carbofuran). Like the organophosphates, they are inhibitors of acetylcholine metabolism in the nervous system, and thus share similar symptoms. Symptoms of carbamate poisoning in honey-bees include an inability to fly in adult bees, dead brood or newly emerged workers, or queen loss. Sublethal effects on the queen have also been recorded, such as poor or erratic egg laying performance.

Organochlorines

Many organochlorine compounds, the most famous of which is DDT, are no longer used in North America. However, insecticides containing the active ingredient endosulfan are still used and sold under the trade name Thionex or Thiodan in Ontario. Symptoms of organochlorine poisoning in honeybees include loss of activity, abnormal wobbly movements, lying on the back or spinning while beating wings in this position.

Insect Growth Regulators

These compounds are analogues of hormones or other compounds that regulate the development of immature insects. Novaluron (the most common active ingredient in this group) has been found to have very low toxicity to adults of several bee species, including honeybees, in laboratory toxicological studies. However, it has been linked to impaired brood development in honeybees in the field.

Triazianes

These are the derivatives of urea they are used as herbicides in the control of weeds in cotton, tea and tobacoo plantation. The common triazines include atrazine, simazine, etc.

What is in a Pesticide Product?

We normally think of a pesticide as the product that can be purchased in the store—the insecticide, the weed killer or the fungicide. But, unfortunately, there is much more to it than that. The product that you buy or are exposed to is actually a pesticide formulation that contains a number of different materials, including active and inert ingredients, as well as contaminants and impurities. In addition, pesticides, when subject to various environmental conditions, breakdown to other materials known as metabolites, which are sometimes more toxic than the parent material.

Active Ingredients

The active ingredient, usually the only component of the formulation listed on the pesticide label, is by nature biologically and chemically active against a target pest, be it an insect, weed or fungus. By definition these chemicals kill living things. Contaminants and Impurities Contaminants and impurities are often a part of the pesticide product and responsible for product hazards. Dioxin and DDT have been identified as contaminants, which have not been purposefully added but are a function of the production process.

Metabolites

Metabolites are breakdown products that form when a pesticide is used in the environment and mixes with air, water, soil or living organisms. Often the metabolite is more hazardous than the parent pesticide.

Inert Ingredients

If you were to go to your local hardware store and take a look at the label on a can of ant and roach killer, the contents might read something like this, '5% permethrin, 95% inert ingredients.' After reading the label, you may wonder what makes up the other 95%. The fact is, the manufacturer does not have to tell you. Currently, under the Federal Insecticide, Fungicide and Rodenticide Act (FIFRA), pesticide manufacturers are only required to list the active ingredients in a pesticide, leaving consumers and applicators unaware of the possible toxics present in the inert ingredients of pesticide products they are using, unless the EPA administrator determines that the chemical possess a public health threat. Pesticide manufacturers argue they cannot release information on inert ingredients because they are trade secrets, and if released, their products could be duplicated. Quite often inert ingredients constitute over 95% of the pesticide product. Inert ingredients are mixed into pesticides products as a carrier or sticking agent, and are often as toxic as the active ingredient.

The Hazards of Inert Ingredients

Despite their name, these ingredients are neither chemically, biologically or toxicologically inert. In general, inert ingredients are minimally tested, however, many are known to state, federal and international agencies to be hazardous to human health. For example, the US government lists creosols as a 'Hazardous Waste' under Superfund regulations, yet allows these chemicals to be listed as inert ingredients in pesticide products. Creosols are known to produce skin and eye irritations, burns, inflammation, blindness, pneumonia, pancreatitis, central nervous system depression and kidney failure. Some inert ingredients are even more toxic than the active ingredients. One of the most hazardous ingredients in the commonly used herbicide Roundup is a surfactant, which is classified as an inert, and therefore not listed on the label. The pesticide naphthalene is an inert ingredient in some products and listed as an active ingredient in others. According a 2000 report produced by the New York State Attorney General, The Secret Ingredients in Pesticides: Reducing the Risk, 72% of pesticide products available to consumers contain over 95% inert ingredients; fewer than 10% of pesticide products list any inert ingredients on their labels; more than 200 chemicals used as inert ingredients are hazardous pollutants in federal environmental statutes governing air and water quality; and, of a 1995 list of inert ingredients, 394 chemicals were listed as active ingredients in other pesticide products.

Biological Pest Control

Chemical used as pesticide often produce harmful effects on living organisms. It is therefore, became necessary to find alternate to these chemicals which do not produce undesirable effect. Biological control by using plant or animal material has been found useful in controlling many harmful pests.

1. Biological Control of Weeds and Bioherbicides

It is practically impossible to manually remove the weeds in crop field. Uses of chemical as weedicides with selective action on unwanted plant alone were itself a great discovery. But this too was not without its harmful effects. Theses chemical if not used in appropriate does may even the crop or many even stimulate the growth of weed themselves. THE insects to be used as bioherbicide must be thoroughly tested for its host specially before being put to commercial use In India and Australia prodigious spread of prickly pear (Opuntia) was controlled by introduction of cochineal insects (*Cactoblastis cactorum*). The first bioherbicides, called de vine, is being commercially used since 1981. It is a myco-herbicide based on fungus *Phytophthora palmivora*. It controls the growth of milkweed veins in citrus orchards. Another myco-herbicide called **collego** has been developed from conidia of fungus *Colletotrichum gloesporioides*. It controls the growth of northern Joint vetch growing in the rice field.

2. Bioinsecticide

The most suitable insecticide should show following characteristics:

1. It should completely control only the specific or target organism.
2. It should must be biodegradable, non-persistent, nontoxic.
3. It should be cost effective.

Integrated Pest Management (IPM)

Integrated Pest Management (IPM) is an effective and environmentally sensitive approach to pest management that relies on a combination of common-sense practices. IPM programs use current, comprehensive information on the life cycles of pests and their interaction with the environment. This information, in combination with available pest control methods, is used to manage pest damage by the most economical means, and with the least possible hazard to people, property, and the environment. The IPM approach can be applied to both agricultural and nonagricultural settings, such as the home, garden, and workplace. IPM takes advantage of all appropriate pest management options including, but not limited to, the judicious use of pesticides. In contrast, *organic* food production applies many of the same concepts as IPM but limits the use of pesticides to those that are produced from natural sources, as opposed to synthetic chemicals.

Table 1: Some microbial insecticides

S. no.	Target insects	Biocontrol agents
	First fungi	*Fungi*
1	Glasshouse white fly (*Trialeurodes vaparaviorum*)	*Aschersonia aleyrodis* (aseranijia)
2	Range of insects	*Beaveria bassiana* (boverin, Boverol)
3	Citrus rust mite	*Hirsutella thompsonii* (Mycar)
4	Range of insect	*Metarhizium anisopliae* (Metaquino, Metabiol)
5	Lepidopteran insects	*Nomura earileyi*
6	Range of insect	*Verticillium lecanii* (Vertalec Mycotal)
	Second bacteria	*Bacteria*
1	Range of insects and mites	*Bacillius thuringiensis*
	Third virus	*Virus*
1	Boll worms	Heliothiis nuclear (Elcar) polyhedrosis virus

Table 2: Some microbal disease prevention

Disease	Pathogen	Biocontrol agent
1. Crown gall of stone fruit	*Agrobacterium tumefaciens*	Agrobacterium radiobactor
2. Wound of fruit trees	*Chondrostereum purpureum*	Trichodermavirdie

How do IPM Programs Work?

IPM is not a single pest control method but, rather, a series of pest management evaluations, decisions and controls. In practicing IPM, growers who are aware of the potential for pest infestation follow a four-tiered approach.

The four steps include:

• **Set-Action-Thresholds:** Before taking any pest control action, IPM first sets an action threshold, a point at which pest populations or environmental conditions indicate that pest control action must be taken. Sighting a single pest does not always mean control is needed. The level at which pests will either become an economic threat is critical to guide future pest control decisions.

• **Monitor-and-Identify-Pests:** Not all insects, weeds, and other living organisms require control. Many organisms are innocuous, and some are even beneficial. IPM programs work to monitor for pests and identify them accurately, so that appropriate control decisions can be made in conjunction with action thresholds. This monitoring and identification removes the possibility that pesticides will be used when they are not really needed or that the wrong kind of pesticide will be used.

• **Prevention:** As a first line of pest control, IPM programs work to manage the crop, lawn, or indoor space to prevent pests from becoming a threat. In an agricultural crop, this may mean using cultural methods, such as rotating between different crops, selecting pest-resistant varieties, and planting pest-free rootstock. These control methods can be very effective and cost-efficient and present little to no risk to people or the environment.

- **Control-Measures:** Once monitoring, identification, and action thresholds indicate that pest control is required, and preventive methods are no longer effective or available, IPM programs then evaluate the proper control method both for effectiveness and risk. Effective, less risky pest controls are chosen first, including highly targeted chemicals, such as pheromones to disrupt pest mating, or mechanical control, such as trapping or weeding. If further monitoring, identifications and action thresholds indicate that less *risky* controls are not working, then additional pest control methods would be employed, such as targeted spraying of pesticides. Broadcast spraying of nonspecific pesticides is a last resort.

Do Most Growers Use IPM?

With these steps, IPM is best described as a continuum. Many, if not most, agricultural growers identify their pests before spraying. A smaller subset of growers uses less risky pesticides such as pheromones. All of these growers are on the IPM continuum. The goal is to move growers further along the continuum to using all appropriate IPM techniques.

How do you Know if the Food you buy is grown using IPM?

In most cases, food grown using IPM practices is not identified in the marketplace like *organic* food. There is no national certification for growers using IPM, as the United States Department of Agriculture has developed for organic foods. Since IPM is a complex pest control process, not merely a series of practices, it is impossible to use one IPM definition for all foods and all areas of the country. Many individual commodity growers, for such crop as potatoes and strawberries, are working to define what IPM means for their crop and region, and IPM-labelled foods are available in limited areas. With definitions, growers could begin to market more of their products as *IPM-Grown*, giving consumers another choice in their food purchases.

Benefits of Integrated Pest Management

IPM offers several benefits. It helps to:

- Reduce the number of pests.
- Reduce the number of pesticide applications.
- Save money while protecting human health. Did you know that children in the United States continue to face serious risks arising from pests and the use of pesticides in certain cases?

Children may:

- Continue to contract diseases carried by biting insects.
- Suffer respiratory attacks from exposure to asthma triggers and allergens attributed to cockroach and rodent infestations.
- Be exposed unnecessarily to pesticides that have been over-applied or misused in settings they frequent, such as schools. In the United States, more than 53 million children and 6 million adults spend a significant portion of their days in more than 120,000 public and private schools. IPM provides an opportunity to create a safer learning environment—to reduce children's exposure to pesticides as well as eliminate pests. A school IPM program prescribes common sense strategies to reduce sources of food, water and shelter for pests in school buildings and grounds. Put simply, IPM is a safer and usually less costly option for effective pest management in the school community.

Health Benefits

Adopting IPM reduces exposure to both pests and pesticides. Two health concerns faced throughout the country by children and adults are:

- Allergies.
- Asthma.

  Rodents, cockroaches, and dust mites are often present in buildings and can cause or inflame serious allergic reactions and asthma attacks.

- Revealed a significant association between the prevalence of asthma among children and adults, and the incidence of pests, allergens (high cockroach and mouse allergen levels) and pesticides found in public housing.
- Demonstrated the effectiveness of IPM in controlling these allergens.

While pesticides can play a key role in IPM programs, by their very nature most pesticides pose some risk. They are powerful tools for controlling pests but need to be used carefully and judiciously.

Economic Considerations

There is cost savings associated with using IPM. IPM may be more labor intensive than conventional pest control and may require more up front resources. However, costs are generally lower over time because the underlying cause of the pest problem has been addressed. IPM practices also provide financial benefits unrelated to pests. For example, weatherization of buildings not only excludes pests but also saves energy and reduces moisture problems.

Development of DDT

DDT (dichloro-diphenyl-trichloroethane) was developed as the first of the modern synthetic insecticides in the 1940s. It was initially used with great effect to combat malaria, typhus, and the other insect-borne human diseases among both military and civilian populations. It also was effective for insect control in crop and livestock production, institutions, homes, and gardens. DDT's quick success as a pesticide and broad use in the United States

and other countries led to the development of resistance by many insect pest species.

Regulation: Environmental Effects

The U.S. Department of Agriculture, the federal agency with responsibility for regulating pesticides before the formation of the U.S. Environmental Protection Agency in 1970, began regulatory actions in the late 1950s and 1960s to prohibit many of DDT's uses because of mounting evidence of the pesticide's declining benefits and environmental and toxicological effects. The publication in 1962 of Rachel Carson's *Silent Spring* stimulated widespread public concern over the dangers of improper pesticide use and the need for better pesticide controls.

In 1972, EPA issued a cancellation order for DDT based on its adverse environmental effects, such as those to wildlife, as well as its potential human health risks. Since then, studies have continued, and a relationship between DDT exposure and reproductive effects in humans is suspected, based on studies in animals. In addition, some animals exposed to DDT in studies developed liver tumors. As a result, today, DDT is classified as a probable human carcinogen by U.S. and international authorities.

DDT is:

- Known to be very persistent in the environment
- Will accumulate in fatty tissues
- Can travel long distances in the upper atmosphere.

One of the new EPA's first acts was to ban DDT, due to both concerns about harm to the environment and the potential for harm to human health. There was also evidence linking DDT with severe declines in bald eagle populations due to thinning eggshells. Since DDT was banned in the U.S., bald eagles have made a dramatic recovery. Attacks on Carson from groups like The Competitive Enterprise Institute and Africa Fighting Malaria portray DDT are the simple solution to malaria, and blame Carson for 'millions of deaths in Africa.' Many of these DDT promoters are also in the business of denying climate change and defended the tobacco industry by denying the health harms of smoking. After the use of DDT was discontinued in the United States, its concentration in the environment and animals has decreased, but because of its persistence, residues of concern from historical use still remain.

Human Health and Pesticides use

The science on DDTs simple solutions has continued to mount over the years, with recent studies showing harm at very low levels of exposure. Studies show a range of human health effects linked to DDT and its breakdown product, DDE:

- Breast and other cancers
- Male infertility
- Miscarriages and low birth weight
- Developmental delay
- Nervous system and liver damage.

Current Status

Since 1996, EPA has been participating in international negotiations to control the use of DDT and other persistent organic pollutants used around the world. Under the auspices of the United Nations Environment Programmes, countries joined together and negotiated a treaty to enact global bans or restrictions on persistent organic pollutants (POP), a group that includes DDT. This treaty is known as the Stockholm Convention on POPs. The Convention includes a limited exemption for the use of DDT to control mosquitoes that transmit the microbe that causes malaria—a disease that still kills millions of people worldwide.

In September 2006, the World Health Organization (WHO) declared its support for the indoor use of DDT in African countries where malaria remains a major health problem, citing that benefits of the pesticide outweigh the health and environmental risks. The WHO position is consistent with the Stockholm Convention on POPs, which bans DDT for all uses except for malaria control.

Pesticide use in Agriculture

What are the Different Chemicals Used in Agriculture?

The different types of chemicals used in agriculture are:

- Herbicides (to kill weeds)
- Insecticides: (to kill bugs)
- Fungicides: (to get rid of disease)
- Soil fumigants, desiccants, harvest aids, and plant growth regulators
- Natural pesticides: Pesticides are not limited to conventional agriculture. Organic farmers also use a wide variety of natural pesticides to control weeds, insects, and disease. The term 'pesticides' means 'to get rid of pests' and refers to all of these groups at once. 80% of pesticides in the U.S. are used on the following crops (in order of use): Corn, soya beans, potatoes, cotton, wheat, sorghum, oranges, peanuts, tomatoes, grapes, rice, apples, sugarcane, lettuce, pears, sweet corn, barley, peaches, grapefruit, pecans and lemons. Pesticide use peaked in 1981 and has been on a slow decline ever since. Reasons for the initial rise include no-till agriculture, herbicide resistant crops, and crops like corn and soya beans being planted over more acres. Reasons for the

decline include more effective pesticides, better application technology, genetic engineering (GMOs) and new production methods like cover crops.

Why do Farmers Use Pesticides?

Benefits: Increases yield potential, allows a farmer to farm more acres, protects the soil through no-till and conservation methods Costs: Weed resistance, greater pesticide use, large companies benefit, environmental concerns conclusion: Farmers (both conventional and organic) must use pesticides in order to produce enough food to feed the world. Pesticide use peaked in the 1980's and will continue to decline as farmers and scientists develop new and more effective methods.

Use of Chemicals as Pesticides in Agriculture Safe or Unsafe?

There are several things to remember when it comes to the safety of chemicals in society: We come into contact with chemicals all of the time. They are not inherently bad. What do you think of when you hear the word 'chemicals?' In today's society the word 'chemicals' has been turned into something we think of as harmful that we should stay away from. Some people are incredibly scared of chemicals and many try to claim they are living a 'chemical free' lifestyle. The truth is, there is no way we can stay away from chemicals, they are everywhere! Chemicals make-up the earth we live on, the air we breathe, the food we eat, and the things we build. Everyday you interact with thousands of chemicals. Even food in its most basic form is full of chemicals, like this banana. Chemicals are not inherently bad. Chemicals can be used to do a lot of good in a lot of different places. In agriculture we have used chemicals to help produce food more efficiently. But how do we know whether a chemical is good or bad for you? The answer is its toxicity.

Toxicity: The dose Makes the Poison

Any substance can be dangerous depending on how much of it you are exposed to or consume. If you ate 100 bananas in one day you would probably get sick. If you drink 10 gallons of water, you will probably die. However, bananas and water are obviously not very dangerous. When it comes to the safety of any particular substance, the way scientists tell how dangerous it is comes from looking at its toxicity. If a substance is more toxic, it takes less exposure to it to be dangerous. If it is less toxic, it takes more exposure to it to be dangerous. The dose makes the poison. The most toxic pesticides are no longer used. Agriculture has transitioned to using safer chemicals. Most used today have very low toxicity. When pesticides were first introduced, farmers were using chemicals that were very toxic. Those pesticides have long since been removed from application and today have been replaced by safer (less toxic) ones like glyphosate. Glyphosate (the most popular herbicide in agriculture) is the least toxic agrochemical on the list. This is one of the reasons farmers have used it so much instead of other chemicals over the years. Another reason is because glyphosate resistant plants (GMOs) were developed so that farmers could control weeds post emergence with a safer chemical like glyphosate. Household items more toxic than glyphosate include baking soda, table salt, Tylenol, and caffeine. 'The science and our understanding of chemical risk evolve and EPA continues to reevaluate each pesticide's safety every 15 years. EPA's continuous reevaluation of registered pesticides, combined with strict FQPA standards, major improvements in science, and an increase in the use of safer, less toxic pesticides, has led to an overall trend of reduced risk from pesticides.'—E.P.A. Insecticides and fungicides have, in general, a higher toxicity than herbicides. This is mainly because herbicides are designed to affect plants, not animals. This is another reason glyphosate is considered a safer chemical, because it is a herbicide. Over the last 50 years, the use of safer herbicides has risen while the use of insecticides and fungicides has declined.

Pesticide Use Over the Years

- **Herbicides in 1960:** 18% of pesticides– 2008: 76% of pesticides
- **Insecticides in 1960:** 58% of pesticides– 2008: 6% of pesticides
- **Fungicides:** Have remained at approximately 7% of pesticides
- (Soil fumigants, desiccants, harvest aids, and plant growth regulators make-up the remaining 11%)

Pesticides (like any substance) are not dangerous if consumed at a low enough rate. Just because a pesticide residue is detected in food, does not mean the food is unsafe. When farmers spray crops the spray is much diluted and only a very small amount of active ingredient is used per acre. Of that amount, most is activated by the plant/soil, does its job, and becomes non-active and unable to do any harm. There is always a possibility that a very small amount will not activate and will persist and could possibly make it into the food supply as a residue. Therefore, it is true that very small amounts of pesticides may remain on fruits, vegetables, grains, and other foods. This is why you see a lot of information on the internet about 'pesticide residues' in our food. However, these residues decrease considerably as crops are harvested, transported, exposed to light, washed, prepared and cooked. Because of this, the amount of pesticides found in the food and water you drink would be (and is) incredibly small. Based on the toxicity chart above, you would have to consume hundreds of pounds of food each day to reach a toxicity level of pesticides that would be dangerous to your health. The

reason for this is because the chemicals would be so incredibly diluted by the time they reach the food supply. The EPA is responsible for managing our exposure to pesticide residues herein the United States. There are specific regulations that have been put in place to keep the level of synthetic pesticides found in food hundreds of times below what could harm you. There are also many natural pesticides consumed by humans each day that are just as toxic or more so to humans, but are still below the rate that would be considered dangerous to our health: 'About 99.9% of the chemicals humans ingest are natural. The amounts of synthetic pesticide residues in plant food are insignificant compared to the amount of natural pesticides produced by plants themselves. Of all dietary pesticides that humans eat, 99.99% are natural: they are chemicals produced by plants to defend themselves against fungi, insects, and other animal predators. We have estimated that on average Americans ingest roughly 5,000 to 10,000 different natural pesticides and their breakdown products. Americans eat about 1,500 mg of natural pesticides per person per day, which is about 10,000 times more than the 0.09 mg they consume of synthetic pesticide residues.'—Dr. Bruce Ames

If synthetic pesticides were truly causing all the things they have been claimed to cause (cancer, disease, etc.), farmers would be having severe health problems. Farmers have been working with synthetic pesticides for the last 50–60 years. Farmers have a much greater risk of skin or lung exposure to pesticide, as it would be much more dangerous because it has not been diluted yet. This is why farmers wear protective gear when applying pesticides. There are no statistics showing farmers are having severe health problems from pesticides more than the general public. Our family even eats our GMO, pesticide-sprayed, corn straight from the field, after washing it of course and we have not had any health issues.

Environmental Concerns

There are many environmental concerns about pesticides and there are many people working on finding solutions to the problems associated with their use. As technology (better application, better chemicals) has developed, pesticide usage has and will decline, which will hopefully reduce some of these issues. Keep in mind that much of human activity has a negative effect on the environment. Industries (exhaust from vehicles, planes, manufacturing plants, etc.), human/animal waste, construction, deforestation, mining, and a growing population in general are all harming the environment more than pesticides are. The best thing we can do is try to find solutions for all these problems and minimize our environmental impact as much as possible while still functioning as a society and minimizing human suffering (providing people with adequate food and shelter). As you can see, there are a lot of misconceptions about chemicals in agriculture and chemicals in general. It is best to talk to experts about these things and not just rely on what you see on the internet. Those experts include scientists,

dietitians, toxicologists, and farmers. There are a lot of things that contribute to the health epidemic in America and around the world. We eat too much sugar. We eat too many bad fats. We eat too much in general. We do not exercise. We are too busy and operate under high stress levels. We eat out and do not cook for ourselves. Chemicals are most likely not what is causing the main health problems. Even if they are, it is much more likely the chemicals we use around the house (cleaners, etc.), the chemicals in the air (pollution), medicines (side effects) and the chemicals we do not think about (caffeine, tobacco, alcohol) that are causing the problems, not the extremely highly diluted pesticide residues you find in food. In conclusion, food is never 100% safe. Neither is life. We must continue to use chemicals to have a functioning society and feed a growing population. It is important that we regulate these chemicals to prevent misuse and abuse. It is also important that we look for ways to use less chemicals and develop chemicals that are less toxic. However, as long as there are weeds, bugs, and diseases, there will be pesticides.

5. AGRICULTURE: AN INTRODUCTION

Word **agriculture** is derived from the Latin term *Ager cultura* (field cultivation) and may be defined as the science, art and business of producing crops and livestock for commerce/economic purposes. It includes crop husbandry, animal husbandry, dairy, soil science, horticulture, fishery, forestry, agricultural engineering, etc.

An activity of man primarily aimed at production of food, fibre and fuel, etc. by optimum use of terrestrial resources is called **agriculture.**

Agriculture is the artificial cultivation and processing of animals, plants, fungi and other life forms for food, fibres and other by products.

Agriculture is the science and art of producing crops or animal under supervision of human in a specific location.

Agriculture helps to meet the basic needs of human and their civilization by providing food, clothing, shelters, medicine and recreation. Hence, agriculture is the most important enterprise in the world. It is a productive unit where the free gifts of nature namely land, light, air, temperature and rain water, etc. are integrated into. Single primary unit indispensable for human beings. Secondary productive units namely animals including livestock, birds and insects, feed on these primary units and provide concentrated products such as meat, milk, wool. Eggs honey, silk and lac. Agriculture provides food, feed, fibre, fuel, furniture, raw materials and materials for and from factories; provides a free fare and fresh environment, abundant food for driving out famine; favours friendship by eliminating fights. Satisfactory agricultural production brings peace, prosperity, harmony, health and wealth to individuals of a nation by driving away distrust, discord and anarchy. Agriculture consists of growing plants and rearing animals in order to yield produce and thus, it helps to maintain a biological equilibrium in nature.

Branches of Agriculture

Agriculture has three main spheres, viz. Geoponic (cultivation in earth-soil), Aeroponic (cultivation in air) and Hydroponic (cultivation in water). Agriculture is the branch of science encompassing the applied aspects of basic sciences. The applied aspects of agricultural science consist of study of field crops and their management (agriculture) including soil management.

CROP Protection

1. Agricultural entomology
2. Plant pathology
3. Nematology

Social Science

1. Agricultural extension
2. Agricultural economics

Allied Disciplines

1. Agricultural statistics
2. English and other regional languages
3. Mathematics
4. Biochemistry, etc.

Importance of Agriculture

Agriculture forms the backbone of the Indian economy and despite concerted industrialization in the last 40 years; agriculture still occupies a place of pride. Agriculture is contributing nearly 30% of the national income, providing employment to about 70% of the working population and accounting for a sizable share of the country's foreign exchange earnings. It provides the food grains to feed the large population of more than one hundred crores. It is also the supplier of raw material to many industries. Thus, the very economic structure of the country rests upon agriculture. The present role of agriculture in the Indian economy is discussed follow.

1. *Share of Agriculture in National Income*

Agriculture has got a prime role in Indian economy. Though the share of agriculture in national income has come down; still it has a substantial share in GDP. The contributory share of agriculture in Gross Domestic Product was 55.4% in 1950–51, 52% in 1960–61 and is reduced to 18.5% only at present. Due to rapid increase in the production of industrial goods and services in the last fifteen years the contribution of agriculture has declined. The share of the agricultural sector's capital formation in GDP. Declined from 2.2% in the late 1999s to 1.9% at present.

2. *Important Contribution to Employment*

Agriculture, directly or indirectly, has continued to be the main source of livelihood for the majority of the population in India. Agriculture sector, at present, provides livelihood 65 to 70% of the total population. Dependence of working population on other fields of agriculture like livestock, fisheries, forest, etc. is less. The sector provides employment to 58.4% of country's work force and is the single largest private sector occupation of wage goods to the industrial sector; thirdly, the supply of basic consumption goods to the agricultural population; and finally, the supply of materials for the building up of economic and social overheads in the agricultural sector. The interdependence between agriculture and industry is becoming stronger as the economy is developing. The application of science and technology in agriculture induces innovations in respect of industrial products, which are used for agricultural production. Agricultural inputs like fertilizers, pesticides, diesel oil, electric motor, diesel engines, pump sets, agricultural tools and implements, tractors, power tillers etc., are supplied by the industry and oil, sugar, jute and cotton textiles and tobacco industries rely heavily on the agricultural sector. Even the processing industries, which are utilizing agricultural raw material, and developing fruit canning, milk products, meat products, etc.

3. *Importance in International Trade*

India's foreign trade is deeply associated with agriculture sector. Agriculture accounts for about 14.7% of the total export earnings. Besides, goods made with the raw material of agriculture sector also contribute about 20% in Indian exports. In other words, agriculture and its related goods contribute about 38% in total exports of the country.

4. *Contribution to Purchasing Power of People*

Agriculture provides purchasing power not only to those directly engaged in it but to others also who are in the industries and services. When farmers earn more they also spend more in the process, they create new markets and new opportunities for hundreds of blacksmiths, carpenters, masons, weavers, potters, leather workers, utensil-makers, tailors, cotton ginners, oil pressures, transporters and countless others. Thus, there are many industries, the prosperity and employment of which are dependent upon the purchasing power of the agricultural population. Hence, it is concluded that besides purchasing food for nonagricultural workers and raw materials for consumer industries, it has created demands for a great many new industries, which, in turn, have provided high and well paid employment. This existing role of agriculture in the Indian economy points out the necessity for the development of Indian agriculture to the fullest extent possible as the prosperity of agriculture largely stands for the prosperity of the economy. The significance of agriculture lies in the fact that the development in agriculture is an essential condition for the development of the national economy.

Importance of Capital Formation

The pace of development is largely determined by the rate at which production assets increase. Before independence, the capital formation in Indian agriculture was of a low order. During this period, agriculture suffered from constant low yield technology, inequitable land tenure system and exploitation of the rural masses. The capital formation includes land development. Construction of houses, etc. Since independence, much more investment both public and private has been made in agriculture.

Food Problem

India's food problem dates back prior to independence. In the beginning, India's food problem was one of scarcity, shortage of rice-after the separation of Myanmar (Burma) from India in 1937 and shortage of wheat, also after the partition of the country in 1947. Initially, the major concern of the Government was to increase the domestic supplies either through increased production or through imports or through both. In the second half of the 1950s and during the 1960s the major concern of the Government shifted to control of food grains prices. The Government of India entered into an agreement in 1956 with the USA known as PL 480 agreement for the import of rice and wheat. The Government found the PL 480 food imports a good tool to stabilize food prices in the country. In fact, PL 480 imports were the basis of our agricultural and industrial development. The Government set-up the Food grains Policy Committee in 1966 to review the food problem afresh. The committee found India's dependence on food imports was not likely to be easy in future. It took serious note of the fact that the food aid was used openly to influence the internal economic policies and foreign affairs policies of the Government. Between 1967–68 and 1989–90, Punjab, Haryana and Uttar Pradesh had recorded annual growth rates of 5.4, 4.0 and

3.4%, respectively in food grains production. These states are the backbone of our public distribution system. These states have insulated the country from a food grains crisis. In the 1970s and particularly after 1974, there has been a growing surplus of stocks from the original target of 5.0 million tonnes; the Government had succeeded in accumulating over 30 million tonnes of buffer stock of food grains during the 1980s. Actually, it was the huge reserves of food grains which were taken revamp the PDS and its reach extended to 1700 blocks in far-flung and disadvantaged areas like economically backward, drought prone, desert and hilly areas. Allocation of rice, wheat, etc. under the PDS should be increased for the lean period. There is need of the hour to strengthen the public distribution system in the country.

Stabilization of Food Grains Prices

The main objective of the food policy in recent years has been to hold the food grains prices in check. The Government has been adopting such short-term measures as the maintenance of stocks at high level, extension of internal procurement, stepping up of government purchase of food grains for release through fair price shops, measures to curb hoarding and profiteering and fixation of maximum control prices. These measures did have some influence in keeping prices in check but past experience shows that price stability has not been fully achieved. The buffer stock operation by the Government is the key to the problem of stabilization not only of food prices but also of general price level in the country. The Government decided to build up a buffer stock of 5 mt of food grains by 1973–74 but the actual stock with the Government from 1979 onwards has been over 20 mt which is a good sign. It is opined that if it is managed with wisdom and flexibility, it would go a long way to protect both the farmer and the consumer against severe fluctuations in prices. The existence of large food stocks creates a feeling of complacency that the food shortage is a thing of the past. There is every possibility of the output becoming larger with the expansion of irrigation facilities, fertilizers availability, rural electrification, etc. But it should be very clearly understood that the highly fluctuating monsoon and the consequent lips and downs in food output can always spell danger. Naturally, efforts should continue to keep the population in check to take full advantage of increase in agricultural production.

1990–1991	176.39
1996–1997	199.30
1997–1998	192.43
2000–2001	195.25
2001–2002	212
2002–2003	173.70
2003–2004	213.50
2004–2005	213.60
2005–2006	204.60
2006–2007	209.30

Environment

Environment is living things and what is around them. It can be living or nonliving things. It includes physical, chemical and other natural forces. Living things do not simply exist in their environment. They constantly interact with it. Organisms change in response to conditions in their environment. In the environment there are interactions between animals, plants, soil, water, temperature, light, and other living and non-living things.

Natural Environment

In biology and ecology, the environment is all of the natural materials and living things, including sunlight. This is also called the natural environment. Some people call themselves environmentalists. They think we must protect the environment, to keep it safe. Things in the natural environment that we value are called natural resources. For example, fish, sunlight, and forests. These are renewable resources because they come back naturally when we use them. Nonrenewable resources are important things in the environment that are limited for example, ores and fossil fuels. Somethings in the natural environment can kill people, such as lightning.

Environment is defined as the total planetary inheritance and the totality of all resources. It includes all the biotic and abiotic factors that influence each other. While all living elements—the birds, animals, plants, fisheries, etc. are biotic elements, abiotic elements include air, water, sunlight, etc. A study of the environment then calls for a study of the inter-relationship between these biotic and abiotic components of the environment.

6. ENVIRONMENTAL SCIENCE

Environmental studies are a multidisciplinary academic field which systematically studies human interaction with the environment in the interests of solving complex problems. Environmental studies bring together the principles of sciences, commerce/economics and social sciences so as to solve contemporary environmental problems. It is a broad field of study that includes the natural environment, built environment, and the sets of relationships between them. The field encompasses study in basic principles of ecology and environmental science, as well as associated subjects such as ethics, geography, policy, politics, law, economics, philosophy, environmental, sociology and environmental justice, planning, pollution control and natural resource management.

Environmental science came alive as a substantive, active field of scientific investigation in the 1960s and 1970s driven by:

a. The need for a multidisciplinary approach to analyses complex environmental problems.
b. The arrival of substantive environmental laws requiring specific environmental protocols of investigation
c. The growing public awareness of a need for action in addressing environmental problems.

In common usage, 'environmental science' and 'ecology' are often used interchangeably, but technically, ecology refers only to the study of organisms and their interactions with each other and their environment. Ecology could be considered a subset of environmental science, which also could involve purely chemical or public health issues for example, ecologists would be unlikely to study.

Scope of Environmental Science

The subject of environmental science covers a very broad field of numerous different subjects like human health, global economies and the impact of technology on the environment. Environmental science is an inter-disciplinary science. Because of this, it covers numerous different fields of science, including biology, chemistry and the Earth sciences. Environmental science is also very concerned with studying bodies and sources of water. Economics is also a very significant aspect to topics within environmental science. Legislation, too, is another interesting dimension to how environmental scientists study the changes happening in the world. People who work in environmental science commonly have to analyse the market forces and political changes that push industries and nations to use certain chemicals and technologies and how those decisions will come to affect the environment. Environmental science is oftentimes focused on analysing the impact of a particular technology on the environment, and how that impact can be either positive or negative. Students and academics who work in the field of environmental science oftentimes focus on a specific area of study within this field, like studying the ecological changes of the environment, examining water quality throughout the world, investigating the kinds of toxins released into the environment as well as the chemistry of how the world changes in response to human technological development and urbanization. Environmental science can even dive into a zoological framework, looking at how the populations of living things are affected by changes in the environment.

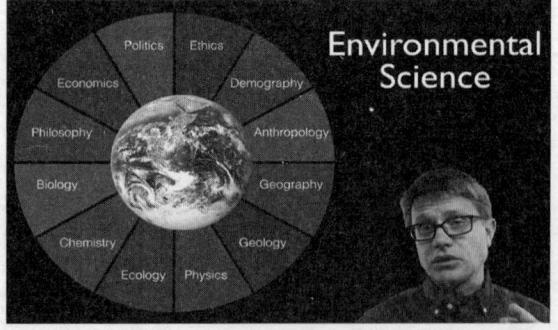

The scope of environmental studies include:

1. Developing an awareness and sensitivity to the total environment and its related problems.
2. Motivating people for active participation in environmental protection and improvement.
3. Developing skills for active identification and development of solutions to environmental problems.
4. Imbibe and inculcate the necessity for conservation of natural resources.
5. Evaluation of environmental programmes in terms of social, economic, ecological and aesthetic factors.

Need of Public Awareness

Increasing population, urbanization and poverty have generated pressure on the natural resources and lead to a degradation of the environment. To prevent the environment from further degradation, the Supreme Court has ordered and initiated environmental protection awareness through government and nongovernment agencies to take part in protecting our environment. Environmental pollution cannot prevent by laws alone. Public participation is equally important with regard to environmental protection. Environmental Education (EE) is a process of learning by giving an overall perspective of knowledge and awareness of the environment. It sensitizes the society about environmental issues and challenges interested individuals to develop skills and expertise thereby providing appropriate solutions. Climate change, loss of biodiversity, declining fisheries, ozone layer depletion, illegal trade of endangered species, destruction of habitats, land degradation, depleting ground water supplies, introduction of alien species, environmental pollution, solid waste disposal, storm water and sewage disposal pose a serious threat to ecosystems in forest, rural, urban and marine ecosystems.

Both formal and informal education on the environment will give the interested individual the knowledge, values, skills and tools needed to face the environmental challenges on a local and global level.

1. Important to understand that natural environment and man-made environment are interdependent.
2. Essential to make the public aware of the formidable consequences of the environmental degradation.
3. Reformative measures if not undertaken, would result in the extinction of life.
4. Environment protection is every individual's obligation and duty.
5. Environmental consciousness needs to be propagated at all levels.

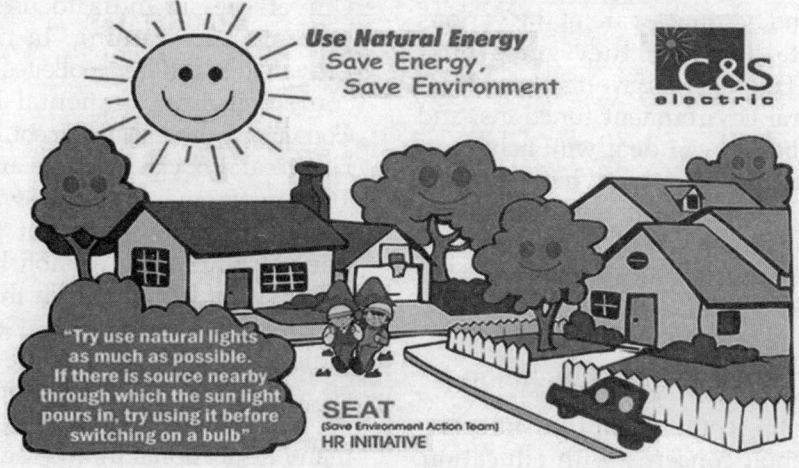

7. ENVIRONMENT EDUCATION

'Environment Education' deals with the need to protect the environment because global warming, pollution and many other issues are ruining our environment badly. We know the importance of healthy environment and we should take all the possible measures to keep our environment healthy. One of the most effective means to promote healthy environment is giving proper education to both new as well as old generations. Environmental education and protection is crucial for the benefit of both the environment and humans. Education has the power to modify the society and present better knowledge to its populace. Education can stand as proper solution to solve different sorts of problems exist in a society and therefore, education has a big role to play to save environment.

Role of Environment Education

The main role of education when it comes to environment protection is offering awareness to everyone in a society. Education can provide better awareness of a variety of environmental issues that take place day by day. Everyone in a society including kids, youths, adults and matured people can understand and become aware of the various environmental issues if they get proper education on it. Education can give right knowledge on how natural environment functions, and how human beings can deal with behaviour and ecosystems for sustainability. In the present day, a lot of people conduct environmental awareness program in schools and societies. It will help people to become aware of environment issues and take actions accordingly.

Necessity of Environment Education

- Every country is putting efforts to integrate environmental concerns with education.

According to these countries, environment education should not only be a part of the education system but also the political system where actions, policies and plans can be formulated and executed at national level.

- Environmental education must be able to assess environmental situation and the conditions leading to the damage of the environment. Environment education must target.
- The routine and how simple changes in a daily life can make a huge difference to the environment.
- Protecting environment is the responsibility of everyone, hence environmental education cannot be confined to one group or society. Every individual must be prepared for saving the environment. It must be a continuous and a lifelong process. Above that environmental education must be practical so that teachings can be implemented directly.
- Conserving nature and environment will be much easier if children are taught about depleting resources, environmental pollution, land sliding and degradation and extinction of plants and animals. Education is a sort of investment that turns into a valuable asset over a period of time.
- Universities in India focus on teaching, research and training. In more than 20 Universities, different colleges and institutes courses in Environmental Engineering, Conservation and Management, Environmental Health and Social Sciences are taught.
- To promote environmental awareness across the Nation, the Centre for Environment Education (CEE) was established in August 1984 with a support from the Ministry of Environment and Forests, Government of India. One of the tasks of the CEE is to put efforts to give due recognition to the role of environmental education. The CEE runs many Educational in this regard.

Because of the societal shifts, today's children are busy playing indoor games and electronic gadgets. They spend most of their time in watching Television, listening to music, playing video games or surfing Internet or using Computer. They have no time to travel around and to explore the natural world around them. This not only impacts the health of children but also detach them from their surroundings and nature. They are grown up into adults who are least bothered about conserving nature. Raising an environmentally educated generation is also necessary because of the depleting of natural resources.

Movements

A movement that has progressed since the relatively recent founding (1960) of environment education in industrial societies has transported the participant from nature appreciation and awareness to education for an ecologically sustainable future. This trend may be viewed as a microcosm to how many environment education program seeks to first engage participation through developing a sense of nature appreciating which then translate into action that affect conservation and sustainability.

Conclusion

Students must be encouraged to understand their surroundings and a framework for action plan must be formulated. Environment education is the need of the day. It must encourage social participation. Hence integrating environment education into a curriculum is a wise option to connect students with the nature right from their childhood.

8. WOMEN EDUCATION

Female education is a catch-all term for a complex set of issues and debates surrounding education (primary education, secondary education, tertiary education, and health education in particular) for girls and women. It includes areas of gender equality and access to education, and its connection to the alleviation of poverty. Also involved are the issues of single-sex education and religious education in that the division of education along gender lines as well as religious teachings on education have been traditionally dominant and are still highly relevant in contemporary discussion.

Meaning of Women Education

Women education refers to every form of education that aims at improving the knowledge, and skill of women and girls. It includes general education at schools and colleges, vocational and technical education, professional education, health education, etc. Women education encompasses both literary and nonliterary education. Educated women are capable of bringing socioeconomic changes. The constitution of almost all democratic countries, including India, guarantees equal rights to both men and women.

Importance of Women Education

The importance of women education are briefly summarized below:

1. **Economic development and prosperity:** Education will empower women to come forward and contribute towards the development and prosperity of the country.

2. **Economic empowerment:** So long as women remain backward and economically dependent on men, the helpless condition of them cannot be changed. Economic empowerment and independence will only come through proper education and employment of women.

3. **Improved life:** Education helps a woman to live a good life. Her identity as an individual would never get lost. She can read and learn about her rights. Her rights would not get trodden down. The life or condition of women would improve a lot, if we take a broad outlook in the field of female education.

4. **Improved health:** Educated girls and women are aware of the importance of health and hygiene. Through health education, they are empowered to lead a healthy lifestyle. Educated mothers can take better care of both herself and her baby.

5. **Dignity and honor:** Educated women are now looked upon with dignity and honor. They become a source of inspiration for millions of young girls who make them their role-models.

6. **Justice:** Educated women are more informed of their rights for justice. It would eventually lead to decline in instances of violence and injustice against women such as dowry, forced-prostitution, child-marriage, female foeticide, etc.

7. **Choice to choose a profession of her choice:** Educated women can prove be highly successful in the fields of life. A girl-child should get equal opportunity for education, so that, she can plan to become a successful doctors, engineers, nurses, air-hostesses, cook, or choose a profession of her choice.

8. **Alleviate poverty:** Women education is a prerequisite to alleviate poverty. Women need to take equal burden of the massive task of eliminating poverty. This would demand massive contribution from educated women. There cannot be much social and economic changes unless girls and women are given their rights for education.

Barriers of Women Education

There is obviously no single good answer, nor is there conclusive data to show us which factors relatively impact girls the most. However we can identify a range of possibilities that could suggest specific reasons for the marginalization of girls from the schooling system.

1. *Expectations of Domesticity*

To start with, girls are expected to contribute to the household far younger than boys are— the implicit understanding being that a girl is being trained for a role as a wife, mother and daughter-in-law, whereas boys are being trained for an occupation. Girls get married younger than boys do a Harvard School of Public Health survey conducted studies in Gujarat looking into rates of child marriage, and found that of girls aged 14–17, 37% were engaged and 12% married. On the other hand, for boys in the same age range, only 27% were engages and 3% married. The same study found strong correlation between marital status and school attendance rates in which marries children were over twice as likely to not attend school than.

2. *Infrastructure Barriers*

The Right to Education bill has set forth some norms and standards in this regard—it codifies single children, but also marriage proved to be worse for the educational prospects of girls than boys. Besides, families often think that the cost of education, both monetary and psychological is wasted on a girl because of her decreased earning potential and this selfsame expectation of domesticity. The economic benefit thereof is not immediately apparent to most families. Overall, the expectation of the girl child's participation in family life seems to be a hindrance in her participation in schooling.

3. *Safety*

Safety of girls travelling alone is a major concern for Indians the prevalent discourse surrounding recent events has brought to the forefront a long-standing problem. We also see a fear that educating girls causes excessive independence, and this is seemingly manifested in the attitude that parents take to a girl's education. In a recent article, the Guardian told the story of a girl in Delhi who was being taunted by boys on the way to school. She was afraid to tell her parents, for she thought that they would prevent her from attending school if she did. She was right, her family was, in the words of the author, 'worried about the effect on their 'honor' if she was sexually assaulted.' These stories are not isolated; rather, this is an endemic and very gendered problem in economically disadvantaged India, be it rural or urban. Expectations and requirements of norms and standards relating inter alia to pupil-teacher ratios buildings and infrastructure, school-working days, teacher-working hours. Therefore we do see legislators are at the very least, considering this area of concern further. It is also one of the easier aspects to tackle, as it falls within the purview of Education Departments in the Centre and in States. However, it is commonly perceived that girls suffer for various reasons from the lack of infrastructure much worse than boys do for instance, as of 2012 40% of all government schools lacked a functioning common toilet, and another 40% lacked a separate toilet for girls. This in fact creates even more reluctance to allow for girls to be educated. Although including girls in the scheme of Indian universalized education, these causes seems to make one thing clear, the causes are ingrained in systems that are larger than education. While temporary solutions are rampant and popular, it will take attention on the long-term scale to ensure that girls across India are able to freely, safely, and consistently attend school and access an education. Government initiatives to improve literacy rate of women in India. The government has initiated many projects to improve the literacy rate of women in India.

Some of them have been discussed below:

National-Policy-on-Education: The national policy on education is a smaller branch or segment of the 'National Education for women'. It has a positive influence in the empowerment of women. It propagates new values through redesigned textbooks, curriculums, and stationery and so on. All these materials have been modeled to suit the needs of women accordingly.

Sakshaar Bharat Mission for Female literacy

This was launched in 2001, to prevent the alarming drop in female education. Its aim was to reduce the illiteracy rate of women by half. In spite of being new in the arena, it has managed to do its share.

Indian Shiksha Karmi Project

This project is all about sharing power through education. This project tries to preach the ignorant Indian population that women too can rise to be on the top after acquiring education. This plan is co-supported by the Swedish Government and it is in vogue in Rajasthan.

Training of Female teachers

Training women to educate the nation is also another forte of the 'Indian Shiksha Karmi Project'. This plan educates them about all the technical know-how's that are required to become a teacher.

Scholarships for Women

The ignorant section of the society always roots for the education of their sons. Due to several biases and superstitions they ignore the education of their daughters. But when questioned they smartly put up answers citing financial difficulties. Several scholarships have been introduced by the central as well as the state government such as the single girl child scholarship for women, scholarship for women scientists and so on. Several scholarships such as the Maulana Azad National Scholarship have been launched to assist meritorious girl students belonging from minority communities. These are an answer to the qualms that were earlier cited by the families of women for not being able to educate them.

Mahila Samakhya Program

This initiative was taken by the government in 1988, in accordance with the New Education Policy of 1968. This group was launched as a rural wing of the Sarva Siksha Abhiyan (SSA). It was launched mainly to help and empower the weaker section of rural women.

Kasturba Gandhi Balika Vidyalaya Scheme

It was launched in the month of July in 2004. Its main aim is to serve girls from backward classes and those having financial difficulties. Nowadays these schools take up about 75% of students from backward classes and 25% from BPL (below poverty level). 54.16% of women from the backward classes are now with education according to the 2001 census report.

National Programme for Education of Girls at Elementary Level

This is also another wing of the SSA. It reaches to the remote places where the SSA cannot reach. This program has uplifted the education standards of several women across the backward provinces of Rajasthan, Gujarat, and Bihar and so on. The female literacy rate grew from 53.67 to 65.46% as per 2011 Census data. The male literacy rate in comparison rose from 75.26% to only 82.14%. So the literacy rate of women is improving at a better rate than for men, thanks to different initiatives by the state governments as well as the central government (Fig. 8).

9. CURRENT ENVIRONMENTAL ISSUES

It is high time for human beings to take the 'right' action towards saving the earth from major environmental issues. If ignored today, these ill effects are sure to curb human existence in the near future. Our planet earth has a natural environment, known as 'Ecosystem' which includes all humans, plant life, mountains, glaciers, atmosphere, rocks, galaxy, massive oceans and seas. It also includes natural resources such as water, electric charge, fire, magnetism, air and climate.

Engineering developments are resulting in resource depletion and environmental destruction. Modern technologies used in the engineering and manufacturing industry have a major impact on our life in past few years. Due to the rapid changes in the engineering and manufacturing industry have been drastic changes in the environment. Learn how going green can help your business, hire the number 1 environmental speaker, Jim Harris. Engineering and manufacturing industry have increased the use of materials like metals, plastic, oil and rubber. These are used in the production of numerous end products which can be associated with different industries such

as Car production units, shipping industries, Cotton mills, plastics industries, Coal mining, heavy machineries and, etc. which are causing numerous arduous effects and are considered to be nonenvironment friendly. Crucial environmental issues are no more a blame game. While most of us crib about dirty air, smelly garbage or polluted water, least do we know it is 'us' who is responsible for this unfavorable circumstances leading to cautionary environmental issues. Here are 10 significant current environmental issues, where human beings play an important role in its cause.

1. **Pollution:** More than half of the human population knows what is pollution, but we are still not ready to face its damaging consequences. Pollution is not only limited to water, soil and noise but has extended to light, visual, point and non-point sources. Human beings and their actions are majorly responsible for causing all types of pollution. Water pollution is essentially cause by oil spills, urban runoff and ocean dumping. Air pollution rises from burning of fossil fuels, hydraulic fracturing and gases emitted by vehicles.

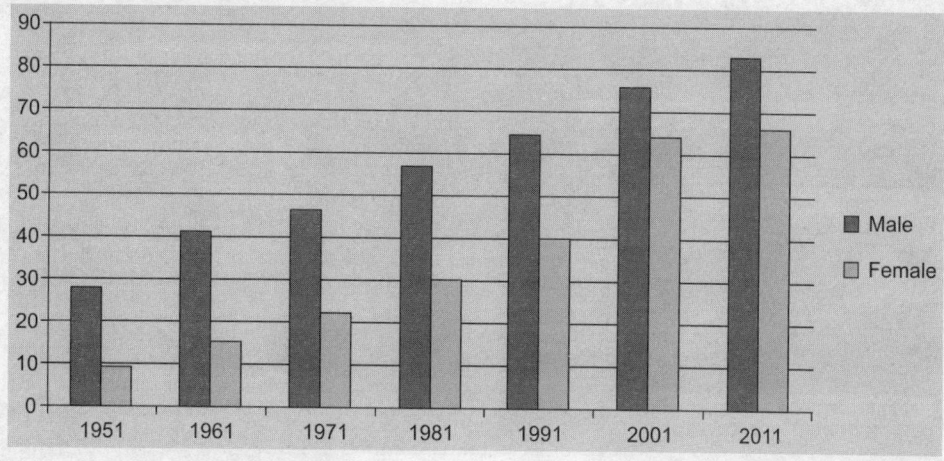

Fig. 8: Literacy rate in India: 1951–2011

Water and soil pollution are majorly cause from industrial waste.

2. **Climate change:** As explain by the U.S agency, the National Oceanic and atmospheric Administration (NOAA), there are 7 indicators that would be expected to inc. in a warming world and indicators would be expected to decline. Climate change today is less of a natural process. It is rapidly occurring due to the ill effects of human actions responsible for disturbing and harmful outcomings such as global warming, greenhouse effect, urban heat, coal industry, etc. Climate change is not only changing the overall weather scenario, but has larger and harmful effects. Some of these include: melting of polar regions, occurrence of new diseases and permanent inhibition in growth of certain plants essential for human survival. Throughout earth history the climate has varied, sometimes considerably. Past warming does not automatically mean that today's warming is therefore also natural. Recent warming has been shown to be due to human industrialization process. John cook, writing the popular skeptical science blog, summarizes the key indicators of a human fingerprint on climate change. This graph based on the camparison of atm. Samples contain in ice course and more recent direct measurement, provides evidence that atm. CO_2 has inc. since the industrial revolution.

3. **Global warming:** Global warming and climate change refer to an increase in average global temperature. This is caused primarily by increase in 'Greenhouse' gases such as carbon dioxide (CO_2).

A warming planet thus leads to a change in climate which can affect weather in various ways, as discussed further below. Global warming is another environmental issue which is increase in earth's temperature due to effect of greenhouse gases called carbon dioxide, methane, water vapor and other gases. These gases possess heat trapping capacities that are needed to create greenhouse effect so that this planet remains warm for people to survive. Without these gases, this planet would turn be cold for life to exist. The

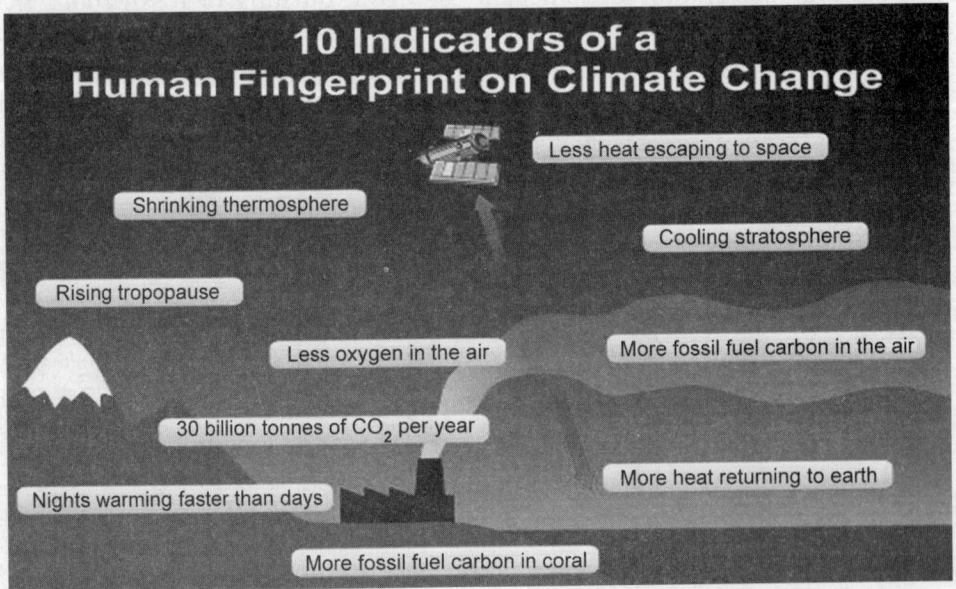

term greenhouse is used in conjunction with the phenomenon known as the greenhouse effect. Six main greenhouses gases are carbon dioxide, methane, and nitrous-oxide plus three fluorinated industrial gases, hydroflurocarbons, perflurocarbon and sulphur hexafluoride.

Water vapour is also considered as a greenhouse effect. Energy from the sun drives the earth's weather and climate, and heat the earth's surface. In turn, the earth radiates energy back into space; Some atm. Gases (water vapor, carbon dioxide and other gases) trap some of the outgoing energy, retaining heat somewhat like the glass panel of a greenhouse. These gases are therefore known as greenhouse gases. The greenhouse effect is the rise in temp. On earth as certain gases in the atmosphere trap energy. For decades, greenhouse gases such as carbon dioxide have been inc. in the atm. To stop but why does that matter? Want warmer weather be nicer to everyone? Inc. greenhouse gases and the greenhouse effect has contributed to an overall warming of the earth's climate, leading to a global warming (even though some regions may experience cooling, or wetter weather, while the temp. of the planet on average would rise).

4. **Greenhouse gases:** During past several decades, the accumulation of greenhouse gases have grown rapidly, which means more heat gets trapped in the atmosphere and few of these gases escapes back into the space. These gases heat up the earth's surface and these results in global warming. According to Environmental Protection Agency (EPA) reports, the earth's temperature has increased by 0.8 degrees Celsius over the past century. Global warming is a serious public health and environmental concern. Global warming can have long-lasting effects which can result in melting of glaciers, climate change, droughts, diseases and increase in hurricanes frequency.

5. **Deforestation:** With population growing at a rapid pace, the demand for food, shelter and cloth has almost tripled in last few decades. To overcome growing demand, a direct action that we have come to recognize as "Deforestation" occurs. Deforestation means, clearing of forests or green cover for means of agriculture, industrial or urban use. It involves permanent end of forest cover to make that land available for residential, commercial or industrial purpose. According to the United Nations Food and Agriculture Organization (FAO), an estimated 18 million acres (7.3 million hectares) of forest are lost each year. The long-term effects of deforestation can be severely devastating and alarming as they may cause floods, soil erosion, increase in global warming, climate imbalance, wildlife extinction and other serious environmental issues.

6. **Overpopulation:** This is a never-ending human tragedy which is responsible for causing all types of environmental issues. Water pollution, resources crisis, gender imbalance, pollution, land pollution, urban sprawling, deforestation, over production are some common examples of dangerous effects cause by overpopulation. Despite efforts taken by the government in terms of family planning in many countries, over population is difficult to control at international level. This has become more like a subjective concern and no method seems to be 100% efficient to resolve the problem of over population.

7. **Industrial and household waste:** At present, tons of garbage is produced by each household each year. Items that can be recycled are sent to local recycling unit while other items become a part of the

landfills or sent to third world countries. Due to increase in demand for food, shelter and house, more goods are produced. This resulted in creation of more waste that needs to be disposed of. Most waste is buried underground in landfill sites. The presence of huge landfills sites across the city pose serious environmental concerns. It affects human health, degrades soil quality, effects wildlife, cause air pollution and results in climate change.

8. **Acid rain:** Acid rain simply means rain that is acidic in nature due to the presence of certain pollutants in the atmosphere. These pollutants come in the atmosphere due to car or industrial processes. Acid rain can occur in form of rain, snow, fog or dry material that settle to earth. Acid rain may cause due to erupting volcanoes, rotting vegetation and sea sprays that produce sulfur dioxide and fires, bacterial decomposition and lightening generate nitrogen dioxide. Acid rain can also be caused due to man-made sources which include combustion of fossil fuels which release sulfur dioxide and nitrogen oxides into the atmosphere. Acid rain can have devastating effects on aquatic life, forests, public health and architecture and buildings.

9. **Ozone layer depletion:** Ozone layer is a layer of gas that sits 25–30 km above earth's surface. It mainly contains ozone which is a naturally occurring molecule containing three oxygen atoms. This layer is present in the stratosphere and prevents too many harmful UV (ultra violet) radiations from entering the earth. Ozone layer is capable of absorbing 97–99% of the harmful ultraviolet radiations that are emitted by sun. However, during last several decades, human and industrial

activity has contributed a lot which has resulted in considerable reduction in the ozone layer of the atmosphere. The main cause of depletion of ozone layer is determined as excessive release of chlorine and bromine from man-made compounds such as chlorofluorocarbons (CFCs). CFCs (chlorofluorocarbons), halons, CH_3CCl_3 (Methyl chloroform), CCl_4 (Carbon tetrachloride), HCFCs (hydrochlorofluoro-carbons), hydrobromofluorocarbons and methyl bromide are found to have direct impact on the depletion of the ozone layers.

10. **Genetic engineering:** Genetic modification of food, human and animal organs seems like the gem of science and technology but this has major harmful effects. Biotechnology is an impressive technology but limiting is use is the need of the hour. Genetic engineering is a controversial subject and has seen more ill impacts than the benefits it brings to mankind. Genetic pollution and alteration of food produce not only have harmful effects on human beings, but are responsible for crucial concern known as 'genetic modification'.

11. **Urban sprawl:** Not only India and China are classic examples of over population and urban sprawl leading to land degradation. Today almost all countries are using the land irresponsibly to meet the ever-growing demand of the greedy human wishes. The expansion of industrial areas has not only led to land degradation and soil pollution, but the habitat destruction is a terrible misery. Natural environment consisting of flora and fauna is indiscriminately destructed and lost completely instead of being replaced. This in the long run has harmful impact for human survival and cause serious environmental issue.

Glossary

Abscisic Acid (ABA): A growth inhibiting hormone enabling perennial plants to tolerate stressful conditions by promoting dormancy, stomatal closure and inhibiting growth.

Abscission Zone: The zone at the base of the flower (pedicel), fruit (peduncle) or leaf (petioles), at which plant cells fray off, thereby facilitating the easy fall of these plant parts.

Absorption Spectrum: Graph indicating the relative abilities of pigments to absorb various wavelengths of light.

Acetyl CoA: Developed as an intermediate of carbohydrate/fat/protein oxidation in the citric acid cycle, acetyle CoA is the acetylated form of coenzyme A.

Achene: A simple, single-seeded, dry, indehiscent fruit comprising one seed attached to only the base of the pericarp.

Active Transport: The forceful movement of molecules from one side of the plasma membrane to the other side against a diffusion gradient, by expenditure of energy.

Adaptive Radiation: Diversification of group of organisms into several new species in order to fit into new environment.

Adenosine Diphosphate (ADP): A nucleotide comprising adenine, two phosphate units and ribose, it is a cofactor contributing either phosphate group or energy or both to a reaction.

Adenosine Triphosphate (ATP): A nucleotide comprising adenine, ribose and three phosphate units, is the major energy currency of the cell. It is a cofactor contributing phosphate group or energy or both to the reaction.

Adhesive Force: It is the force of attraction between dissimilar molecules due to which they stay together. For example, water droplets on a leaf.

Adventitious Roots: The roots that do not originate from primary roots are called adventitious. They generally arise from stems or leaves.

Aerobic Cellular Respiration: Part of cellular respiration, and plays a significant role in producing energy required to carry out different functions of the plant. It requires oxygen for the process.

Aerobic Respiration: Type of respiration requiring free oxygen as the terminal electron acceptor.

Agamospermy: Asexual reproduction methods involving cells of only the ovule to yield seeds and fruit.

Agar: A culture medium used specifically for bacteria. It is produced by some algae (red or brown) and has a gelatinous consistency.

Aggregate Fruit: The conjunction of several small, individual fruits, formed by different ovaries, located within the same flower to form a single fruit like that of raspberry.

Albuminous Seed: Seed containing large amounts of endosperm.

Allele: Gene versions varying from each other in their nucleotide sequence and may or may not result in different phenotypic traits.

Allopatric Speciation: Speciation emerging as the result of physical separation of two or more populations of one species, such that interbreeding is not possible.

Alternation of Generations: Plant life cycle type in sexually reproducing organisms involving alternation of diploid sporophyte phase and haploid gametophyte phase.

Amino Acid: Small molecule comprising nitrogen containing units used to synthesize proteins.

Anabolism: Process of metabolism by which various small molecules are combined to form large ones.

Anaerobic Respiration: Also called fermentation, this type of respiration does not need oxygen as the terminal electron acceptor.

Aneuploid: Anomaly in the usual chromosome number, wherein one or more chromosomes are missing or present as extras.

Angiosperm: Plants with seeds enclosed in ovaries that mature into a fruit.

Annual Ring: The formation of wood in plants on an annual basis comprises two concentric layers of wood: springwood and summerwood.

Anther: Part of the stamen containing sporogenous tissue which produces pollen.

Anthocyanin: Water soluble pigment located in the cell sap, which varies from red to blue in colour. Found in flowers of most plants.

Apical Dominance: Hormones produced at the tip of the shoot cause suppression of lateral bud development in growing plant shoots.

Apical Meristem: Meristem located at the tip of the root, shoot or other organs of the plant.

Archegonium: Female reproductive organ in nonvascular plants like ferns and mosses.

Autotropic: Organisms converting inorganic matter into organic material for the purpose of sustenance.

Auxin: Growth regulating substance involved in apical dominance, cell elongation, rooting, etc.

Axil: Angle formed at the point of attachment between the petiole of a leaf and the upper part of the plant.

Axillary Bud: Bud situated just above the point of attachment of the leaf, i.e. leaf axil. Can be a floral bud or leaf bud.

Bacillus: Rod shaped, spore-producing bacteria belonging to the genus *bacillus*.

Backcross: Cross between a hybrid and one of its parents.

Bacteria: Single celled, omnipresent organisms appearing in spiral, spherical or rod shape.

Bacteriophage: It is an obligate intracellular parasite that breed inside bacteria by using the host's cellular machinery.

Bark: Tissues of the vascular cambium forming tough layer on the outer region of the woody stems and roots.

Base: Substances that reduce the concentration of hydrogen ions.

Basidiocarp: Fruiting body in basidiomycete fungi, such as puffball or mushroom.

Basidiospores: Spores formed on the basidium.

Basidium: The cells in basidiomycete fungi in which fusion of nuclei and meiosis occur to produce basidiospores.

Berry: Simple, thin-skinned fruit comprising a compound ovary with more than one seed, as in the case of gooseberry, grape, tomato, etc.

Biennial: Plants requiring two seasons to complete their life cycle. The first season growth is purely vegetative and the second one bears fruit.

Binary Fission: Process of cell division in prokaryotes, such as yeasts where the cell devides into two daughter cells.

Binomial Classification: System of classification that provides scientific names to organisms. Each name consists of a genus name and a species name.

Biological Controls: Use of natural inhibitors or enemies to combat pests and other damage causing organisms.

Biomass: Total mass of living matter present in a given habitat, expressed as volume of organisms per unit of habitat's volume or weight per unit area.

Biotechnology: Use of living organisms, tissue or cells for the manufacture of drugs or products intended for human benefit.

Blade: The broad, flattened, conspicuous part of the lead called lamina that is distinguished from the petiole or stalk.

Bract: Leaf like structure situated at the base of the flower or inflorescence.

Bryophyte: Phylum comprising non-vascular plants: lacking xylem and phloem. Mosses, liverworts, etc. are bryophytes.

Budding: Type of asexual reproduction involving formation of new cells from protrusions arising from mature cells. Yeast reproduces via budding.

Bundle Sheath: Layer of parenchyma or sclerenchyma cells encircling the vascular bundle in plant leaves and stems.

Callose: A plant polysaccharide composed of glucose residues linked together through α-1, 3-linkages secreted by an enzyme complex (callose synthase), resulting in the hardening or thickening of plant cell walls.

Callus: Tissue formed over damaged areas of the plant in the form of a seal, thereby protecting it from further deterioration, and allowing the wound to heal.

Calvin cycle: Biochemical reactions cycle occurring during photosynthesis in the chloroplasts, wherein carbon dioxide is fixed and 6 carbon sugar is formed.

Calyptra: Small sheath of cells found in non-vascular plants, derived from the archegonium to cover the tip of the capsule partially or completely.

Calyx: Collective terminology for the sepals of a flower.

Cambium: Layer of meristematic tissue (also known as lateral meristems), responsible for secondary growth.

Capillary Water: Water held in the tiny pores between soil particles by the adhesive force: surface tension.

Capsule: Dry, dehiscent fruit consisting of two or more carpels that splits in several ways at maturity to release seeds.

Carpel: Single member of a compound pistil or single pistil unit, bearing the ovule in angiosperms.

Caryopsis: Small, dry, single seeded fruits which do not split at maturity. The pericarp cleaves to the seed coat; typically seen in grains.

Casparian Strip: Band of cell wall material in the radial and transverse walls of the endodermis. It stops the passive flow of materials into the stele.

Cation Exchange: Replacement of an essential element cation released from a soil particle by a proton.

Cavitation: The rupture of the water column in the xylem, when tension surmounts the cohesive nature of water.

Cell: Microscopic structure forming the basic structural and functional unit of living organisms. It encompasses nuclear and cytoplasmic material enclosed by a cell membrane.

Cell Biology: Branch of biology involving the study of cells, their structure, formation, components and functions.

Cell Cycle: Sequence of events occurring during cell division.

Cell Division: Process of division of cell with the purpose of growth or reproduction.

Cell Membrane: The semipermeable membrane sheathing cytoplasmic material of the cell.

Cell Plate: During cell division, the plate formed at the midpoint between two sets of chromosomes, which is involved in the wall formation between two daughter cells.

Cell Sap: Fluid present in the central vacuole of plant cells.

Cell Wall: The rigid boundary forming the outer structure of plant cells.

Cellulose: A complex carbohydrate composed of glucose units, which forms the major constituent of cell wall in plant cells.

Central Cell Nuclei: Mostly two in number nuclei uniting with sperm to form primary endosperm nucleus in embryo sac. It is a membrane enclosed organelle of eukaryotic cells that contains its genetic material in the form of chromosomes.

Centrioles: Small, cylindrical cell organelles found in animals and some algae and fungi. Located near the nucleus in the cytoplasm of most eukaryotic cells each centriole is usually composed of nine triplets of microtubules.

Centromere: Portion of the chromosome holding the two chromatids together before anaphase stage of mitosis or anaphase II stage of meiosis. The spindle fibers are attached to this region and move the chromosomes during cell division.

Chemiosmotic Phosphorylation: Occurring in mitochondria and chloroplasts, this prcoess involves the synthesis of ATP from ADP and phosphate unit.

Chemosynthetic Origin of Life: Theory according to which life began via a series of chemical reactions on primitive earth.

Chiasma: X-shaped structure formed by the attachment of two chromatids of homologous chromosomes to each other during meiosis.

Chitin: Polymer composed of partly amino sugars, it is a semitransparent hard substance forming the outer covering or exoskeleton of crustaceans, arachnoids and insects.

Chlorenchyma: Parenchyma tissues with chlorophyll content.

Chlorophyll: Green pigment found in plants, cyanobacteria and algae, which is involved in capturing light energy required for photosynthesis.

Chloroplast: Plastids opulent in chlorophyll content that carry-out photosynthesis.

Chlorosis: Process of yellowing of leaves, occurring due to lack of chlorophyll.

Chromatid: One of the two identical chromosome strands united by a centromere into which the chromosome longitudinally splits while preparing for cell division.

Chromatin: Found in chromosomes, chromatin is a readily staining substance of a cell nucleus containing DNA, RNA and other proteins that form chromosomes during cell division.

Chromoplast: Plastids containing pigments other than chlorophyll, usually imparting red or yellow colour.

Chromosome: Threadlike bodies made-up of DNA coiled tightly several times around proteins called histones. Its structure consists of chromatids joined together at the centromere.

Chromosome Condensation: Also called pachytene, this process is a part of prophase I, wherein the chromosomes become shorter and thicker.

Cilium: Precisely arranged, short microtubules found mostly in bunches, similar to a flagellum. These may either be sensory or locomotory organelles.

Circadian Rhythm: A rhythmic daily activity cycle exhibited by many organisms in an intervals of 24 hours.

Citric Acid Cycle: In aerobic respiration, the complex series of reactions following glycolysis, which involve mitochondria, ATP and enzymes.

Cladophyll: Also called phylloclade, this is a flattened stem that looks like a leaf.

Class: In classification, the category coming between a division and order.

Cloning Vector: Molecule of DNA that replicates and transfers DNA from one cell to another.

Closed Carpel: It is another phrase used for Angiosperms that are plants with seeds inside the ovary.

Coccus: Sphere shaped bacteria.

Codon: Triplet of adjacent nucleotides in messenger RNA, which specify the amino acid to be incorporated into a protein.

Coenocytic: Large cells containing myriad nuclei. It is formed when the cell nucleus divides multiple times without the actual division of the cell.

Coenzymes: Molecules providing transfer site for biochemical reactions catalyzed by enzymes.

Cohesion-Tension Theory: This theory explains that the upward pull of water takes place by the combination of water molecules cohesion in the vessels and tracheids and tension on the water column caused by transpiration.

Coleoptile: The first leaf above ground level forming a sheath around the tip of the stem, so as to protect the emerging shoot (plumule) of monocotyledons like grasses and oats.

Coleorhiza: Sheath formed around the emerging radicle in plants of the monocotyledons like the grass family.

Collenchyma: Cells containing primary walls thickened at the cells corners, but thin elsewhere.

Companion Cells: Specialized parenchymal cells situated beside sieve tubes in the phloem of angiosperms that regulate flow of nutrients through the sieve tube.

Compost: Combination of several dead and decaying organic substances, such as manure, dead leaves, etc. used for soil fertilization.

Compound Leaf: Leaf blade divided into distinct leaflets attached via a common petiole.

Conidium: Fungal spore formed outside a sporangium and produced asexually.

Conifer: Woody trees or shrubs that are gymnosperms and bear cones.

Conjugation: Process of genetic exchange occurring in bacteria and some green algae, wherein the DNA is passed through a tube connecting adjacent cells.

Cork: Outer tissue layer of an old woody stem produced by cork cambium, whose cells are saturated with suberin at maturity.

Cork Cambium: Lateral meristematic tissue ring found in woody seed plants between the exterior of woody stems or roots and central vascular tissue. It produces cork to its exterior and phellogen to its interior.

Corm: A thick food storing, vertically oriented stem enveloped by some papery nonfunctional leaves.

Corolla: Collective phrase used for the petals of a flower.

Cortex: Generally parenchyma cells forming a tissue extending between the vascular tissue and epidermis.

Cotyledon: A seed leaf or embryo leaf that usually absorbs or stores food.

Crossing-over: The exchange during prophase I in meiosis, between corresponding segments of chromatids of the homologous chromosomes.

Crown Division: Asexual type of reproduction, involving the division of the base of the stem.

Cuticle: Thin hyaline film derived from the exterior surfaces of epidermal cells, covering the surface of plants.

Cutin: Fatty or waxy substance making up the cuticle.

Cutting: Vegetative plant parts used for asexual propagation.

Cyclosis: Flow of cytoplasm with the cell.

Cytochrome: Protein containing iron, acting as small electron carriers by transferring molecules in electron transport system.

Cytogenetics: Study of genetic effects of chromosome behaviour and structure.

Cytokinesis: Cell division followed by mitosis.

Cytokinin: Growth hormone concerned with cell division and other metabolic activities of the cell.

Cytoskeleton: Network of microfilaments and microtubules that protects and maintains cell shape, enables cellular motion and plays important roles in both intracellular transport and cell division. It is present in both prokaryotes and eukaryotes.

Cytosol: Fluid part of the cell into which the organelles are scattered.

Dark Reactions: Stage of photosynthesis which is light independent wherein carbohydrates are synthesized from carbon dioxide.

Day-neutral Plant: Plants independent of specific day lengths for commencement of flowering.

Deciduous: The plants that shed their leaves before a dry season to minimize the transpirational loss of water.

Decomposer: Organism breaking down organic matter into forms suitable for recycling.

Dedifferentiate: Pertaining to cells, dedifferentiate means becoming less specialized.

Deoxyribonucleic acid (DNA): Nucleic acid containing genetic instructions used for the proper functioning and development of all living organisms.

Development: Changes pertaining to the growth and differentiation of plant cells into various tissues and organs.

Diatom: Unicellular, microscopic, freshwater or marine algae belonging to phylum Chrysophyta, which contain two silica shells fitting together like parts of a petri dish.

Dichotomous Branching: Fork resulting into two somewhat equal branches, as in the case of leaf veins or secretory ducts.

Dicotyledon: Angiosperm class whose seeds feature two cotyledons.

Dictyosome: Organelle comprising disc-shaped, mostly branching hollow tubes, which accumulate and pack substances required for the synthesis of various materials in the cell.

Differentially Permeable Membrane: Membrane permitting the diffusion of various substances at different rates.

Differentiation: Conversion of relatively unspecialized cell to a better specialized cell.

Diffusion: Haphazard movement of molecules from regions of high concentration to region of lower concentration, leading to uniform distribution and leveling of the different concentration areas.

Digestion: Conversion of insoluble, complex substances into soluble, simpler substances under the control of enzymes.

Dihybrid Cross: Cross involving heterozygous parents with two different gene pairs.

Dikaryotic: Presence of two nuclei in a cell.

Dioecious: Plants featuring unisexual cones or flowers, with the male cones and flowers belonging to certain plants and the female cones and flowers confining to certain other plants of the same species.

Diploid: Cells comprising two sets of chromosomes in the nucleus. This is denoted by the term '2n', and is a characteristic of the sporophyte generation.

Diuretic: Substances that increase the urine flow.

Divergent Speciation: Emergence of a new species from a part of existent species, with the remnant species continuing as the original species itself, or else transforming into a new species.

Dominance: Phenomenon in which one allele of a gene masks the phenotypic expression of another allele of a gene. The allele masking the other allele is called dominant allele.

Dormancy: The phase of temporary growth cessation in plants, under harsh environmental situations, wherein the regular conditions required for growth cannot be met.

Double Fusion: Phenomenon in which one sperm fertilizes an egg to form a zygote, while another sperm fertilizes the central cell nuclei (polar nuclei) forming a primary endosperm nucleus.

Drupe: Fleshy fruits with one or more seeds enclosed within a hard protective layer called endocarp.

Early Wood: Wood formed during the early part of the growing season, characterized by large, thin walled cells. It features large number of vessels in angiosperms and in gymnosperms, it features wide tracheids.

Ecology: Branch of biology involving study of interactions of organism with the environment and with each other.

Ecosystem: System involving the interactions of living organisms with each other as well as with the non-living environment.

Ectomycorrhiza: One type of mycorrhizal association, wherein the fungi do not invade the cell membrane, instead invade the root cortex cells.

Egg: Nonmotile female gamete.

Elater: Small, twisted, strap-like, elastic filament, usually occurring in pairs that push the spores out of the sporangium, thereby assisting in spore dispersal.

Embryo: The immature sporophyte formed after fertilization from the zygote in the archegonium or ovule.

Enation: Tiny green leaf like structures growing on the stems of whisk ferns and do not have vascular tissue.

Endocarp: The innermost layer of the fruit wall enclosing the seed in fleshy fruits.

Endocytosis: Absorption of solid or liquid material into a cell by means of invagination of the plasma membrane to surround the material and pinching shut to form a vacuole or vesicle around it.

Endodermis: Single layer of specialized parenchyma cells surrounding the vascular tissues in the roots and stems. It forms the inner boundary of the cortex.

Endoplasmic Reticulum: Complex system of narrow tubes and sheets forming a network in the cell's cytoplasm. It divides the cytoplasm into various compartments. The endoplasmic reticulum may or may not have ribosomes attached to them.

Endosperm: Nutritive material derived from the embryo sac in seed plant ovules. It furnishes the developing embryo and seedling with nutrition.

Endosymbiont Hypothesis: According to this hypothesis, mitochondria and plastids were free-living bacteria, which got incorporated into the cells.

Enzyme: A type of complex protein that enhances the rate of a chemical reaction in living cells, without itself being used in the reaction.

Epicotyl: Portion of the seedling above the cotyledon's attachment point.

Epidermis: Single layer of cells, forming the outer tissue of leaves, roots and young stems.

Epigynous: Term used to describe a condition in which the flower parts are attached above the ovary.

Epiphyte: Plants growing above the ground, that attach themselves to other plants without being a parasite. They derive their nutrients and water from air, dust, rain, etc.

Essential Element: Elements which are essential for normal development, growth and reproduction of plants. Nitrogen, calcium, magnesium, phosphorus, etc. are examples of some essential elements.

Etiolation: Term referring to a condition involving poor leaf development, long internodes, pale and weak appearance of the plant due to deprivation of sunlight.

Eukaryotic: Cells comprising nucleus, chromosomes and distinct membrane bound organelles.

Eutrophication: Process of nutrient accumulation in the water bodies resulting in its gradual nutrient enrichment. This entails to increase in the growth of algae and various other organisms.

Exine: Outer coat of a spore or pollen grain.

Exocarp: Outermost layer of the fruit wall.

Explant: Severed portions of the plant; example: leaf or stem tissue that are utilized for tissue culture.

Extranuclear DNA: DNA located outside the nucleus, as seen in mitochondria and plastids.

Eyespot: Tiny reddish sensory organ, which is sensitive to light. It is found within motile unicellular organisms.

Facultative Aerobe (Facultative Anaerobe): Organisms that use oxygen when available, however, can even live without it.

Family: Category of classification above the genus category and below the order category.

Fermentation: Type of respiration involving the process of glycolysis, wherein lactic acid or ethyl alcohol are formed as an end product.

Fertilization: Fusion of two gametes to form a zygote.

Fiber: Cells which are long and thick walled, often containing protoplasm which is dead at maturity.

Fibrous Root System: Cluster of similarly sized roots. It is found in some dicots and most monocots.

Filamentous Body: Usually green algae cells exhibit this kind of body, wherein the cells are held firmly by a middle lamella when they divide transversely.

First Filial Generation: Progeny of an experimental cross between two parent species.

Fission: Cell division of bacterial and other related organisms that results into two new cells.

Flagellum: Multicellular organisms produce threadlike structures, which protrude from the motile cells and assist mainly in locomotion.

Floret: Tiny flowers belonging to the inflorescence of members of the grass family or sunflower family.

Fluid Mosaic Model: A plasma membrane model according to which, the proteins are embedded in the lipids throughout the membrane which gives a mosaic appearance to it. The proteins change their position, hence, it is called a 'fluid' membrane.

Follicle: It is a dry, monocarpellary, unilocular, multi-seeded fruit.

Food Chain: Natural chain of organisms, in which each organism of the chain feeds on members below it in the chain, and is consumed by organisms above it in the chain.

Foot: Attached to the gametophyte, the foot is the basal portion of the embryo of bryophytes and absorbs food from the gametophyte.

Founder: Individuals who are the first to establish a population in a new environment or habitat.

Freely Permeable Membrane: Membranes permitting all kinds of substances to pass through it.

Frond: Usually used for a fern leaf, however, occasionally it is also used to denote palm leaves.

Fruit: In angiosperms, the ripened ovary wall produced from the flower, usually containing seeds.

Gametangium: Cell in which gametes are produced.

Gamete: Haploid sex cells; ovum and sperm which unite to form a zygote.

Gametophore: Leafy stalk on which the gametangium (sex organs) is borne.

Gametophyte: Haploid plant that produces gametes.

Gemma: Cluster of cells that get detached from parent body and possess the ability to develop into a completely new organism or plant. Seen in liverworts and mosses.

Gene: Basic unit of heredity, involving sequence of nucleotide containing necessary information for the structure and metabolism of an organism.

Gene Bank: It is a way of preserving plants and seeds for their germ plasm.

Gene Pool: Total number of all alleles in all the sex cells present in the individuals of a population.

Gene Synthesizer: Machine producing specific DNA sequences.

Genetic Drift: Alteration in the genetic make-up of a particular population, which mostly takes place by chance alone.

Genetic Engineering: Introduction of genes from one DNA form into another, by artificial means is called genetic engineering.

Genetics: Branch of biology involving the study of heredity, which deals with the differences and resemblances of organisms entailing from the interaction of their genes and the habitat.

Genus: Classification category located between a family and species.

Germ-line Mutation: Mutation occurring in the cells from which gametes are derived.

Germ Plasm: Aggregate of all genes of a species or organism groups.

Germination: Commencement or resumption of growth of a spore or seed.

Gibberellin: Group of plant hormones possessing different effects on growth, which are mostly related to enhancement of stem elongation.

Gills: Flattened plates of compact mycelium radiating to the outer region of the stalk on the bottom portion of the mushroom cap.

Girdling: Phenomenon involving the discarding of a band of tissues which extend to the inner side of the vascular cambium on the woody plant stem.

Glycocalyx: Mucilaginous secretion surrounding many prokaryotic cell walls.

Glycolysis: Cycle in which glucose is broken down to form pyruvic acid.

Glycoprotein: Proteins featuring attachment of sugars, which are less than ten sugars long.

Golgi Body: Organelle comprising layers of flattened sacs, which absorbs and processes synthetic and secretory products from the endoplasmic reticulum and then secretes them to the cell's exterior or releases them into different parts of the cell.

Graft: Unification of the scion (shoot) of one plant and stock (root) of another plant.

Granum: The chloroplasts in vascular plants exhibit the presence of a series of stacked thylakoids, called granum.

Gravitational Water: After rain, the water draining into the pores of the soil is called gravitational water.

Ground Meristem: The mersitem producing all the primary tissues of the plant except the epidermis and the stele.

Guard Cell: Pair of specialized cells surrounding the stomata. These help in transpiration.

Guttation: Exudation of water from the leaves in the form of droplets due to root pressure.

Gymnosperm: Type of plants in which the seeds are not enclosed in the ovary during the development.

Habitat: The natural environment in which the plant completes its life cycle.

Haploid: Possessing one set of chromosomes in each cell. Denoted by 'n'.

Hardwood: The wood of both dicot trees and shrubs are termed hardwood. A dicot wood generally contains fibers.

Haustorium: Organ bearing semblance to a root, which is used by a parasite to penetrate into the host plant to absorb nutrients.

Heartwood: Darker coloured non-living wood, whose cells have stopped conducting water.

Herbarium: Collection of plant specimens, which are pressed, dried, mounted on paper, identified and then labelled.

Heterocyst: Thick walled, transparent, slightly enlarged cell located in the filaments of certain cyanobacteria.

Heterokaryosis: Condition pertaining to certain cells in fungi, which feature two or more nuclei of different mating types.

Heterospory: Formation of both megaspores and microspores.

Heterotrophic: Organisms that depend on other organisms for nutrition, as they are incapable of synthesizing their own food.

Heterozygous: Possessing two different alleles of a trait on homologous chromosomes, which are situated at the same locus.

Histones: Basic nuclear proteins forming complexes with DNA to form nucleosomes and then complexing further to form chromosomes.

Hold Fast: Filament like organ of attachment present in algae that holds the algae to the substrate.

Homokaryosis: Condition in fungi, wherein all nuclei in the mycelium are genetically identical.

Homologous Chromosomes: Diploid nucleus comprising a pair of chromosomes, one inherited maternally and the other paternally.

Homozygous: Possessing two identical alleles on a homologous chromosome pair at the same locus.

Hormone: Organic substances produced mostly in small amounts in one part of the organism and then transported to different parts of the organism, where it controls the growth and development of the organism.

Hybrid: Heterozygous progeny of two parents differing in one or more inheritable attributes.

Hybrid Sterility: Post-zygotic isolation process, wherein a hybrid zygote develops into an adult, however, is incapable of forming fertile gametes.

Hydathode: Specialized leaf structure located at the leaf's tip, from which the water is forced out when root pressure increases.

Hygroscopic Water: Water chemically adhering to soil particles due to which they are unavailable to plants.

Hymenium: Layer of fertile cells producing spores in a fungus fruiting body.

Hypha: Threadlike like tubular filaments found in fungi.

Hypocotyl: Portion between the cotyledon and the radicle in a seedling or embryo.

Hypodermis: Cell layer following the epidermal layer and distinct from the cortical parenchyma cells in some plants.

Hypogynous: Condition featuring attachment of flower parts below the ovary.

Immobile Essential Element: Element that cannot be removed from mature tissues. This means if young tissues become deficient in these elements they develop a deficiency, even though this element is present in the older tissues.

Imperfect Flower: Flowers lacking either carpels or stamens or both.

Imperfect Fungi: Those fungi that do not sexually reproduce or their sexual reproduction behavior has never been monitored.

Impermeable Membrane: Membranes that do not permit the passage of any substances across them.

In vitro: Carrying out growth of cells in artificially maintained media, such as test tubes, flasks, etc. instead of inside a living organism.

Inbreeding: Process of individuals with common ancestry mating together.

Inbreeding Depression: Condition in which individuals with common ancestry exhibit low fertility and poor performance.

Incipient Plasmolysis: The point at which the protoplasm just begins to stop exerting pressure on the cell wall, when the plant cell membrane shrinks after losing water.

Indusium: Umbrella shaped membranous tissue covering, located on the fern sorus.

Inferior Ovary: Ovary appearing to have its floral parts like calyx, corolla and stamens attached to the top of it. The appearance is due to the unison of the floral parts.

Inflorescence: Discrete group of flowers attached to a common axis in a specific order.

Integument: Outermost wall of the ovule, which develops into the seed coat. In angiosperms, the ovule has two integuments, while in gymnosperms, a single integument is seen.

Intercellular Space: Space present between two adjacent cells.

Intermediate-day Plant: Plants characterized by two critical photo periods. This means the plant will not flower during too short or too long days.

Internode: Region between two nodes.

Interphase: Phase of cell cycle which is not cell division but encompasses phases such as G1, S, G2. Here, the cell prepares for cell division.

Intrinsic Protein: Protein deeply integrated into the membrane, which cannot be discarded from the membrane easily.

Isogamy: Sexual reproduction taking place between gametes that are similar in size. Seen in certain fungi and algae.

Jungle: A dense growth of various plants where many organism can thrive. Forest is another term used for a jungle.

Junipers: This term refers to members of the Family Cupressaceae, and are characterized needle-like leaves in juveniles and scale-like leaves and cones in the adults.

Jointed Stems: Stems made-up of one jointed, three dimensional and ribbed parts, more like a clump from where branches shoot.

Kinetochore: During late prophase, some specialized protein complexes are developed on the vertical faces of a centromere, and are called kinetochore.

Kingdom: Highest level of classification category.

Knot: Projection of plant tissue in the stem, root, etc. especially when swollen.

Karyogamy: Fusion of two gametes of the nuclei after plasmogamy (protoplasmic fusion).

Karyokinesis: Process of division involving series of active changes in the nucleus of a cell.

Key: Tools used to identify unfamiliar plants. Comprise mainly of pairs of choices.

Lamina: Expanded, flat, broadened portion of the leaf. Lamina is also referred to as leaf blade and does not include the petiole.

Late Wood: Also referred to as summer wood, this is the wood formed late in season, in the secondary xylem. It usually comprises narrow tracheids in gymnosperms and few or no vessels in angiosperms.

Lateral Roots: The scores of tiny roots stemming from the tap root.

Laticifer: Specialized ducts or cells that bear resemblance to vessels. These form a network of cells in the phloem and other plant parts that secrete latex.

Leaf: Expanded, flattened and usually green structures of the plant, arranged in various ways on the stem. If green, they act as sites for photosynthesis.

Leaf Gap: Area above leaf trace, wherein conducting tissues are absent; as seen in fern vascular tissue.

Leaf Scar: Portion of the stem, wherein the leaf was attached, before its abscission.

Leaf Trace: Vascular bundles extending from the stem into the cortex and then protruding their way into the leaf.

Leaflet: Subdivisions of the leaf lamina; as seen in compound leaves.

Legume: Dried fruits comprising seeds adhering to their edges which split along two seams.

Lenticel: Spongy cluster of cells located in the bark of woody plants, which allow gas exchange between the external atmosphere and interior of a plant.

Leucoplast: Colourless plastids that store starch.

Lichen: Fungi living in symbiotic union with algae. They appear either leaf-like, crust-like or in the form of branching trees, rocks, etc.

Light-dependent Reactions: Chain of chemical reactions involving the conversion of light energy into chemical energy with the assistance of chlorophyll pigment.

Light-independent Reactions: Cyclic sequence of chemical reactions utilizing carbon dioxide and energy released during the light-dependent reactions. These reactions are independent of light, and take place in the stroma of chloroplasts.

Lignin: Type of polymer impregnating some cell walls, like those of wood.

Ligule: Small tongue like structures located at the base of the spike moss.

Linked Genes: Genes situated close together on the same chromosome that crosses over only rarely.

Lipid: Hydrophobic and water insoluble compounds, such as waxes, fats, oils, etc.

Locule: Hollow situated within a sporangium or ovary.

Locus: Position of gene on a chromosome, which is determined by the linear order relative to the various other genes situated on the same chromosome.

Long-distance Transport: Transportation of substances from one cell to another cell, which is situated at a far away location.

Long Shoot: These shoots feature tiny papery leaves; as observed in conifers.

Lumen: Inner portion of cell structures such as vacuole, vesicle, resin duct or oil chamber.

Macronutrient: A substance required in large amounts for normal growth of an individual.

Macropore: Larger soil pores from which water drains readily by gravity.

Magnetosome: Small particles of magnetite, which is a compound containing magnesium, present in cells that exhibit magnetotaxis.

Magnetotactic Bacteria: Bacteria that orient themselves according to the earth's magnetic field due to the presence of the magnetosomes.

Manure: Animal excreta, with or without a bedding of litter at various stages of decomposition. It is normally considered to be a good fertilizer.

Mass Flow (nutrient): The movement of solutes in relation to the movement of water.

Medium: A source where microorganisms are grown.

Mesofauna: Animals residing in the soil which are 200 to 1000 microns in length. This group includes nematodes, oligochaete worms, smaller insect larvae, and certain anthropods.

Mesophile: An organism that thrives in temperatures ranging from 15–40° Celsius.

Methanogenesis: The production of methane by biological reactions.

Methanogenic Bacterium: Bacteria that produce methane as a by-product of their chemical reactions.

Methanotroph: An organism capable of oxidizing methane.

Microaerophile: Microorganisms that grow well in relatively low oxygen concentration environment.

Microaggregate: Clusters of clay stabilized by organic matter and precipitated inorganic matter.

Microbial Biomass: Total mass of microorganisms living in a given mass or volume of soil.

Microbial Population: Total number of microorganisms living in a given mass or volume of soil.

Microbiology: The study of microorganisms, often with the aid of a microscope.

Microcosm: A community or any other unit that is representative of a larger community.

Microenvironment: The immediate physical and chemical surroundings of a microorganism.

Microfauna: Protozoa, nematodes, and anthropods that are smaller than 200 microns.

Microflora: This includes bacteria, virus, fungi, and algae.

Micrometer: One millionth of a meter ($10-6$ meters).

Micronutrient: Elements that are required for growth in trace amounts. These include copper, iron, zinc, etc.

Microorganism: An organism that is too small to be seen by the naked eye. Also called microbes, these include bacteria, fungi, protozoans, algae, and viruses.

Micropore: A small-sized soil pore (approximately less than 30 microns in diameter) which is normally found within structural aggregates.

Microsite: A small part of the soil where the biological or chemical processes are different from the rest of the soil.

Mixotroph: Organisms that are capable of assimilating organic compounds as carbon sources, while using inorganic compounds as electron donors.

Mold: A group of saprobic or parasitic fungi causing a cottony growth on organic substances.

Monoclonal Antibody: Antibody produced from a single clone of cells, which has a uniform structure and specificity.

Monokaryon: Fungal hyphae where the compartments contain only nucleus.

Morphometric Characters: These are characteristics regarding the depth, dimension, sediment distribution, water currents, etc.

Motility: The ability of a cell to move from one place to another.

Mucigel: Gelatinous material found on the surface of roots growing in normal soil.

Mucilage: Gelatinous secretions and exudates produced by plant roots and most microorganisms.

Mulch: Materials which are laid down on soil to protect it from rain, crusting, freezing, etc. These materials could be sawdust, plastic, leaves, etc.

Municipal Solid Waste: The total consumer and commercial waste generated in a certain confined and restricted geographic area.

Mycophagous: Organisms that eat fungi.

Mycovirus: Viruses that infect fungi.

Naked DNA: Gene transfer processes such as transformation and transfection involves the passage of nucleosome and histone free DNA. This histone and nucleosome free DNA is called naked DNA.

Nastic Movement: Non-directional movement of flat plant organs such as leaf, petal, etc. irrespective of the stimulus position.

Natural Selection: The process of evolution involving the population rise of organisms which have inherited the traits that enable them to successfully survive in natural conditions and reproduce successfully in comparison to others.

Necrosis: Death of plant cells or tissues, leading to discolouration of leaves and stems. It can even conduce death of the plant.

Necrotroph: Fungus which attacks the host in a virulent manner, and then kills it. They then absorb all the nutrients from the dead organism.

Nitrogen Assimilation: Process of ammonium incorporation into organic compounds present within an organism.

Nitrogen Fixation: Process by which plants convert atmospheric nitrogen into compounds such as nitrate or ammonium, which they can readily use.

Node: Point of attachment of the leaves.

Nucellus: Central region of an ovule, wherein embryo sac development takes place.

Nuclear Envelope: The porous double lipid bilayer sheathing the nucleus.

Nucleic Acid: Macromolecule composed of chains of nucleotides, carrying genetic information.

Nucleolus: Spherical structure which is non-membranous and comprises proteins and nucleic acids. It is present within the nucleus, and each nucleus may contain more than one nucleolus.

Nucleotide: Chain of molecules which make up the structural units of DNA and RNA. Nucleotides comprise a sugar, nitrogenous base and phosphate group.

Nucleus: Largest cell organelle found in most eukaryotic cells. It contains most of the cell's genetic material, thus is involved with inheritance, ribosome synthesis and metabolism control.

Nut: A dry fruit consisting of only one seed and a thick pericarp. Nuts feature a cluster of bracts at their base.

Obligate Aerobe: An organism that requires air for aerobic cellular respiration. They use oxygen in order to oxidize substrates and obtain energy.

Oogamy: It is a kind of sexual reproduction where the female gamete is non motile and larger than the motile male gamete.

Oogonium: It is the term given to the female sex organ of various algae and certain fungi.

Operculum: The covering that protects the peristome of the moss sporangium.

Organelle: The membrane bound cell bodies found in the cytoplasm, e.g. mitochondria.

Osmosis: The differential behaviour of membrane for the purpose of diffusion of water and other solvents. Osmosis always takes place from the region of higher concentration to lower concentration.

Osmotic Potential: This is the minimum pressure required to prevent osmosis from taking place. It is the pressure developed by a solution that is separated from water by a selectively permeable membrane.

Outcrossing: The pollination which takes place between two different flowers which may or may not belong to the same genetic line.

Ovary: That part of the flower which is situated at the base of the pistil and contains an ovule (or ovules) and eventually develops into a fruit.

Overtopping: The ability of a shoot to grow for longer period of time than the other shoot in the same plant, which was a result of branching.

Oxidation Phosphorylation: The energy released during metabolic pathways, which is responsible for the formation of ATP and ADP.

P-protein: This is a fibril protein which is responsible for plugging sieve pores and precludes outflow if sieve elements are damaged.

P-protein Plug: It relates to the obstruction of a sieve region or sieve plate by bast protein.

Palindrome: This term refers to a DNA sequence which can be read forward or backward.

Palisade Mesophyll: It is also known as palisade or palisade parenchyma, and is the upper layer of ground tissue in a plant leaf. It comprises prolonged cells underneath and vertical to the upper cuticle, and constituting the principal area of the photosynthesis process.

Parenchyma: These are cells comprising only thin primary walls. All other features and functions vary from one kind to another.

Parthenocarpy: It is the activity wherein a fruit is produced without egg fertilization in the ovary.

Pedicel: A pedicel is one of the subordinate stems in a ramous inflorescence, bearing a single flower.

Peduncle: It is the stem which holds either a bunch of flowers or a solitary flower.

Perennial: This term refers to the plants which have a life cycle that lasts for over two years.

Pericarp: It relates to the matured and diversely altered walls of a plant ovary.

Pericycle: It is the outermost cell layer of the stele in a plant, which often turns into a zone that is multi-layered.

Periderm: This term pertains to the bark, and comprises cork, cork cambium, and any enclosed tissues like secondary phloem.

Perigynous: This simply means located around the pistil on the edge of a concave receptacle, as stamens or flower petals.

Peristome: The circles of tiny, pointed, odontoid outgrowths around the opening of a capsule or urn of mosses which appear when the lid is removed.

Petals: The coloured segments of the corolla of the flower, which most often are involved in drawing in pollinating agents.

Petiole: The lithesome stem which attaches a leaf to the stem.

Phloem: It is a portion of vascular tissues that comprises sieve tubes, companion cells, parenchyma, and fibers. It forms the food-conducting tissue of a plant.

Photosynthesis: Photosynthesis is a plant activity which includes the synthesis of complex organic substances, peculiarly saccharides, from carbon dioxide, water, and inorganic salts, utilizing sunlight as a source of energy and with the help of chlorophyll and associated pigments.

Photosystem I and II: Photosystem I absorbs light for the transfer of negatron from plastocyanin to ferridoxin. Its reaction center is P700. Photosystem II absorbs light for oxidation of water and reduction of plastoquinone. Its reaction center is P680.

Phytochrome: This term pertains to a plant pigment which is involved in the soaking up of light in the photoperiodic response which modulates various types of growth and development.

Pinna: It is one of the basic divisions of a pinnated leaf.

Pistil: The female organ of a flower which bears ovules or seeds, consisting of a complete ovary, style, and stigma.

Pit: It is concerned with the portion of a sclerenchyma cell, where there is no secondary wall over the primary one, and substances are able to pass into or out of the cell.

Pith: This is a soft and squishy central cylinder of parenchymatous tissues in the stalks of plants having two cotyledons in the seed.

Plant Anatomy: Study of the internal structure of the plant.

Plant Geography: It is also known as phyto-geography, phytochorology, geobotany, geographical botany, or vegetation science; and refers to spatial distribution of plants and vegetation in different environment and regions.

Plant Physiology: The study of plants, which involves processes such as nutrition, reproduction, and other functions.

Plant Taxonomy: The science that refers to the identifications, description, naming, and classification of plants according to their unique characteristics.

Plasmodesmata: It pertains to a narrow hole in the elementary wall, that comprises some cytol, cell membrane, and a desmotubule.

It is a means of communication between cells.

Plasmodium: Body of slime mold, which is a large mass of living substance with hundreds or thousands of karyons. Plasmodium ingest fungal spores, bacteria and other tiny protozoans.

Plasmolysis: It is an activity which relates to the shrinking of the living substances when water is removed by exosmosis.

Plastid: These are major organelles found in plant cells, as well as algal cells. These organelles are sites of manufacture of various essential chemical compounds used by the cell. They often contain chlorophyll, which is used for photosynthesis.

Plumule: It is the bud of the plant axis which moves up while it is still in the embryo.

Pneumatophore: It refers to a differentiated structure that originates from the root in particular plants which spring up in swamplands and fenlands, and act as a respiratory organ, e.g. Mangroove.

Pollen Grains: They relate to microspores in seed plants, that comprise a male gametophyte.

Pollen Tube: The protoplasmic tube which is squeezed out from a spudding pollen grain and develops toward the ovule.

Pollination: This natural process includes the conveyance of pollen from the anther to the stigma.

Pollinium: A cohered mass or body of pollen grains, characteristic of plants which belong to the orchid and milkweed families.

Polymer: It is a big chemical compound that consist of several subunits called monomers.

Pome: It pertains to the characteristic fruit of the apple family such as apple, pear or quince, in which the edible flesh grows from the greatly tumefied receptacle and not from the carpels.

Prickles: These are sharp protuberances of the cortex and cuticle.

Primary Pit Field: It is the region of the primary cell wall which is particularly thin and consists of many plasmodesmata.

Primary Producer: Any green plant which has the ability to convert light energy or chemical energy into organic substance.

Primary Tissue: Any tissue which is directly derived from distinction of an apical meristem or leaf primordium.

Procambium: It is the meristem from which vascular tissues originate.

Prochlorophytes: A class of procaryotes that possess both chlorophyll A and B, and is considered to be nearly associated to the antecedents of plastids in algae and plants.

Producer: A photosynthetic green plant or chemosynthetic bacterium, that comprises the first trophic level in a food chain.

Proembryo: This term relates to the cells which are forced into the endosperm and afterwards become the embryo, in seed bearing plant's embryos.

Prokaryotes: Organisms which do not possess true nucleus or membrane-bounded cell organelles such as eubacteria, cyanobacteria, and archaebacteria.

Promoter Region: The area of a cistron in which control molecules and RNA polymerases bind during the process of cistron activation and transcription.

Prop Root: An adventitious root which holds the plant, as the aerial roots of the Rhizophora mangle tree or of the maize plant.

Prophase: The initial phrase of mitosis or meiosis in eukaryotic cellular division, during which the nuclear envelope breaks down and filaments of chromatin form into chromosomes.

Proplastid: A cytoplasmic cell organelle from which a plastid originates and develops.

Protein: The plant tissue that is rich in organic molecules which are believed as a food source providing necessary amino acids.

Protein Sequencing: This is a process that includes determining the amino acid sequences of its constituent peptides; and also finding out what compliance it follows and if it comprises any non-peptide molecules.

Prothallus: A tiny, flat, and gentle structure developed by a spudding spore, that has sex organs, and is the gametophyte of ferns and some other plants. Its structure resembles a leaf.

Protoderm: A thin outer layer of the meristem in embryos and growing points of roots and stems, which gives rise to the epidermis.

Protonema: A threadlike structure created by sprouting of the spores in small leafy-stemmed flowerless plants and other related plants, and from which the leafy plant, that has the sexual organs, develops as a sidelong or terminal branch.

Protoplast: The living substance of a plant, including the protoplasm and cytomembrane after the cell wall has been removed.

Protoplast Fusion: A method by which two energids are coalesced to create hybrid cells that can develop into mature hybrid organisms; normally performed on plants.

Protostele: The firm stele of most roots, that possesses a central core of xylem enclosed by bast.

Pure-bred Line: The homozygous dominant and homozygous recessive genetic constitution of a line which are selfed and utilized in spawning experiments.

Pyrenoid: A proteinaceous structure that is found within the chloroplast of specific algae and nonvascular plants, which is believed to be related to starch deposition.

Quantitative Trait: These traits are controlled by various genes and environmental factors. They are measured on a continuous scale.

Quiescence: Every plant requires some specific environmental conditions for its proper functioning and rapid growth. The growth or germination of the seeds or plants are hampered if these environmental conditions are not satisfied. This is termed 'quiescence'.

Quiescent Center: Quiescent center is the portion of the root situated at the apex of the plant tissue, i.e. meristem in which cell division does not occur.

Rachis: Rachis is the extension of the axis of petiole or leafstalk in the compound leaf. All leaflets are attached to the rachis.

Radicle: Extension of the axis of petiole or leafstalk in the compound leaf. All leaflets are attached to the rachis.

Ray: Series of parenchyma cells that are radially arranged along the vascular region of the xylem and the phloem. These parenchyma cells transport food, water and other materials laterally in the roots and stems of woody plants.

Reaction Wood: It is formed when a woody plant encounters mechanical stress, as caused by wind exposure, soil movement and excess snow fall.

Receptacle: Expanded portion of the peduncle, wherein various parts of the flower are attached.

Recessive Trait: It is the trait that reflects in the phenotype only when the dominant gene is absent, e.g. colour blindness.

Recombinant DNA: DNA molecule created either by crossing over in meiosis or under laboratory environement (*in vitro*). It is formed when DNA from at least two organisms is taken.

Red Tide: Marine phenomenon in which a reddish tint is formed on the water due to the sudden growth of cells in certain protozoa or red algae.

Reduction Division: Same as meiosis.

Reproduction: It is the birth of a new organism born either by sexual or asexual means.

Resin Canal: Tubular duct present in coniferous trees and seeds, which is lined with resin secreting cells.

Respiration: Cellular breakdown of sugar and other food molecules, in which a part of energy is utilized. If oxygen is utilized during the breakdown, it is known as aerobic respiration or else it is termed anaerobic respiration.

Restriction Enzyme: Also called restriction endonuclease, this enzyme is capable of recognizing specific sequences in DNA at a specific site (restriction site), and then severing it.

Reticulate Venation: Reticulate venation is a thin, flat, laminar like structure of a leaf, featuring a net-like pattern of the veins, structured for the purpose of photosynthesis.

Retrovirus: Common type of plant virus whose genetic material is single-stranded RNA.

Rhizoid: Delicate root like filament that functions as a root in mosses and ferns. It provides support or performs the absorption function in them.

Rhizome: Horizontally oriented, underground root-like stem that has nodes and internodes.

Ribonucleic Acid (RNA): Type of molecule containing large amount of nucleotide units, wherein each nucleotide contains three elements: nitrogenous base, a ribose sugar, and a phosphate. It is involved in protein synthesis.

Ribosome: Cell organelle composed of proteins and ribonucleic acid (RNA), which is responsible for protein synthesis.

Root: Organ of the plant situated below the ground and absorbs water and mineral salts. Buds, leaves or nodes are absent in root.

Root Cap: Thimble-shaped mass of cells that cover and protect the growing tip of the root.

Root Hair: Hairlike outgrowth arising through the epidermal cell of the root. Located just behind the tip of the root, this root hair helps absorb water and nutrients from the soil.

Root Nodule: Plants forming symbiotic associations with nitrogen-fixing bacteria, exhibit swelling in their roots, at the region where the bacteria comes in contact with the root.

Runner: Slender creeping stem that contains long internodes, growing horizontally along the surface of the ground, e.g. strawberry plant.

Saprobe: Saprobes are heterotrophs which contribute to the various nutrient cycles by feeding on decomposing organic matter.

Sapwood: Sapwood is the outer wood which carries water from roots to the leaves in order to facilitate water storage for future use.

Scleroid: Scleroid is a cell, characterized by the presence of a thick secondary wall and absence of a protoplast.

Sclerenchyma: Sclerenchyma is a supportive tissue, found in plants, which is typically composed of hard, thick and dry cells.

Secondary Phloem: Secondary phloem is the phloem which is derived from vascular cambium.

Secondary Tissues: Secondary tissues are the tissues of the secondary plant body which are produced by vascular cambium.

Secondary Xylem: Secondary xylem is the xylem that is derived from vascular cambium.

Seed Coat: Seed coat, also referred to as testa, is the protective outer covering of seeds of various flowering plants.

Selectively Impermeable Membrane: It is a barrier which regulates the movement of substances, allowing some substances to pass rapidly, and others to slow down.

Selectively Permeable Membrane: It is a membrane that facilitates the transmission of certain molecules through it by the process of diffusion.

Selfing: Selfing is a process wherein a plant's stigma is pollinated with pollen either from the same plant, or from a plant of identical genetic constitution.

Sepal: The sepal is the outermost part of a flower, resembling a leaf, which forms the calyx of the flower and surrounds its reproductive organs.

Septum: In botany, septum is a partition wall between two tissues.

Sessile: The term sessile, meaning without a stalk, is most often used in context of plants whose flowers or leaves grow directly from the stem.

Seta: Seta is a botanical term used to refer to the stalk of the capsule, which is located in between the foot and the sporangium.

Sieve Cell: Sieve cells are conducting cells of the secondary phloem, which have a narrow diameter and are more elongated in shape as compared to the sieve tube members.

Sieve Plate: Sieve plates are the pores, in the cell walls of the plant, which facilitate the movement of liquid matter.

Sieve Tube: Sieve tube is a tube formed by cells joined end-to-end in order to facilitate the flow of nutrients in flowering plants.

Simple Cone: A simple cone is a cone featuring only one axis or bearing only sporophylls.

Simple Leaf: A simple leaf is a single leaf blade sporting a bud at the base of the leaf-stem.

Sink: Sink is a botanical term used to refer to any tissue which receives the material that is transported by the phloem.

Siphonostele: Siphonostele is a type of stele, usually characterized by the formation of cylinder surrounding the central pith and possessing leaf gaps.

Softwood: Softwood refers to any of the various varieties of trees, usually coniferous, sporting narrow, needle like leaves.

Species: The term species is used to refer to a taxonomic group of plants or animals whose members can interbreed.

Spermatophytes: Spermatophytes are the plants that reproduce by means of seeds, instead of spores.

Spindle: Spindle is the underlying structure of microtubules which pulls away the chromosomes from the center of the cell, towards the poles during the process of nuclear division.

Spirillum: The term spirillum is used to refer to the spirally twisted bacteria, resembling an elongated rod, which is usually found in stagnant water.

Spongy Mesophyll: Spongy mesophyll are irregularly shaped and distinctly spaced parenchyma cells present in plant leaves.

Sporangium: The term sporangium is used to refer to a plant structure which produces and contains spores.

Spore: A spore is a unicellular asexual reproductive body in several nonflowering plants that facilitates the development of a new individual without sexual fusion.

Sporophyll: A sporophyll is a modified leaf bearing sporangia.

Sporophyte: Sporophytes are those plants which produce spores by the process of meiosis in order to produce gametophytes.

Stamen: The male organ of the flower consisting of the anther and the slender filament meant to hold it in position is known as the stamen.

Start Codon: The term start condon is used to refer to a set of three nucleotides which indicate the initiation of information for the process of protein synthesis.

Stigma: The place at the apex end of the style, where the pollen that's deposited enters the pistil is known as stigma.

Stipules: Stipules are small leafy outgrowths, usually occurring in pairs, observed at the base of a leaf or the stalk.

Stoma: Stoma is a minuscule epidermal pore in the leaf or stem of the plant which allows gases and water vapour to pass through.

Stop Codon: The term stop codon is used to refer to the set of three nucleotides which indicate the termination of information for the process of protein synthesis.

Stroma Reactions: These are the set of reactions which occur in the stroma during the process of photosynthesis, without being directly powered by light.

Stromatolite: The stromatolite is a biological fossil representing colonies of bacteria, usually cyanobacteria, alternating with sediment layers.

Structural Region: It is the part of the gene, comprising nucleotide triplets, that specifies which amino acids are to be incorporated into protein.

Style: In plants, style is a narrow elongated part of the pistil, located between the ovary and the stigma.

Substrate Level Phosphorylation: It is the formation of adenosine triphosphate (ATP) from adenosine diphosphate (ADP) by transferring a phosphate group from a substrate molecule.

Substrate Specificity: In botany, the term substrate specificity is used to refer to the ability of a given enzyme to distinguish one substrate from other similar substrates.

Suspensor: The suspensor is the cell or filament supporting a gamete, most often observed in a zygospore.

Sympatric Speciation: The speciation, i.e. the evolution of a biological species, which occurs within a limited geographical area is known as sympatric speciation.

Symplast: The inner side of the plasma membrane, wherein water and low molecular solutes diffuse freely is known as the symplast of the plant.

Synapsis: The pairing of two homologous chromosomes which occurs during the process of meiosis is known as synapsis.

Syngamy: Syngamy is the process fusion of a sperm and an egg.

Taxis: The movement of a cell that is triggered by external stimulus, towards or away from the stimulus source, is known as taxis.

Tendril: Tendril is a narrow stem-like structure which helps the twining plants in attaching themselves to an object in order to gain support from it.

Test Cross: The test cross is a process wherein a suspected heterozygote is tested by crossing it with a known homozygous recessive.

Thallus: Thallus is a plant which does not feature true stems, roots, leaves or vascular system.

Thorn: Thorns, also referred to as spines, are the leaves of plants which are modified into cylindrical, hard structures featuring sharp ends.

Thylakoid: The thylakoid is a membrane-bound compartment within the chloroplasts and cyanobacteria which is a site for the light-dependent reactions of photosynthesis.

Tinsel Flagellum: A flagellum which is covered with several minuscule hairlike projections is referred to as tinsel flagellum.

Tip Layering: Tip layering is a plant propagation method wherein only the stem tip is buried in order to facilitate the growth of a new plant.

Tissue: A tissue is an ensemble of cells featuring similar structure and performing a specific function.

Tissue Culture: Tissue culture is a process wherein various cells are separated from each other and grown outside the body, on a culture medium.

Tracheid: The elongated cells in the xylem which facilitate the transportation of water and mineral salts within the plants are known as tracheids.

Transcription: A process facilitated by the enzymes to transcribe the information of a DNA strand into a complementary RNA (tRNA) strand is known as transcription.

Transformation: The modification of a cell by the intake and incorporation of an exogenous DNA is known as transformation.

Transgenic Plant: A plant which contains DNA inserted by some form of genetic engineering is known as transgenic plant.

Translation: The term translation is used to refer to a process wherein the sequence of amino acids is facilitated during protein synthesis by the information in an mRNA strand.

Translocation: The process of transportation of dissolved material within a plant is referred to as translocation.

Transpiration: In botanical studies, the process of emission of water vapour from the plant leaves is known as transpiration.

Transposons: The sequences of DNA which can move to different positions within the genome of a single cell through the process of transposition.

Transposition: A form of chromosomal mutation wherein a chromosomal segment is transferred to a new position on the same or some other chromosome.

Trichome: Trichomes are the various extensions developing from the epidermis of the plant which are meant to provide protection to the plant.

Tropism: A biological process, which indicates the growth of a plant, in response to the environmental stimulus is known as tropism.

Tuber: The various types of modified plant structures which are enlarged to store nutrients are known as tubers.

Tubulin: Tubulin is a protein which leads to formation of microtubules on polymerization.

Turgid: In botany, the word turgid is used to refer to a plant with swollen tissues which are filled with moisture.

Turgor Pressure: The outward pressure exerted by the water in the plant cells, which adds to the rigidity of these cells, is known as the turgor pressure.

Tylosis: The tylosis is the process wherein an outgrowth from a parenchyma cell, through the pit cavity into a vessel, leads to the blockage of the vessel.

Unisexual: Flowers that have either the pistil or the stamen are referred to as unisexual flowers.

Uniparental Inheritance: Genetic inheritance obtained from just one parent, and is generally the case for mitochondrial and plastid genes.

Vacuolar Membrane: The membrane sheathing the cell vacuole.

Vacuole: Fluid pocket separated from the cell cytoplasm by a membrane, which mostly occupies about 99% of the cell's volume, and stores dissolved matter.

Vascular Bundle: Column of tissue comprising mostly phloem and xylem, which are usually enveloped by a bundle sheath.

Vascular Cambium: Meristem present in the form of narrow cylindrical sheath, that produces secondary xylem and phloem in the roots and stems.

Vascular Plant: Plants possessing the vascular tissues, i.e. xylem and phloem are termed vascular plants.

Vein: Branching network formed within the leaves by any of the vascular bundles is termed vein.

Velamen Root: Aerial root capable of preventing water loss due to its multilayered epidermis.

Venter: Egg's site in the large basal region of the archegonium.

Vernalization: Cold treatment required to initiate flowering in biennials.

Vessel: Occur in xylem of some vascular plants and most of the angiosperms. They appear as cylindrical tubes, whose cell cytoplasm has been lost. Vessels consist of vessel members that are laid from one end to another.

Vessel Element: Single conducting cells of the xylem featuring a few perforations, which permit flow of water from one vessel to another.

Viability: Seed's or spore's ability to germinate.

Water Potential: Amount of water that can be absorbed or released by a substance with respective to another substance is termed water potential.

Water-splitting (Photolysis): Phenomenon occurring in photosystem II of the process of photosynthesis, wherein water molecules split to release oxygen.

Webbing: According to telome theory of megaphyll origin, the lamina originated from parenchymatic cell production between the telomes.

Whiplash Flagellum: Flagella featuring smooth surfaces are termed whiplash flagellum.

Whorled: Arrangement of three or more leaves, flowers or other plant structures positioned at a node.

Wood: Secondary xylem produced in the stems of trees and other woody plants is called wood. Wood present in living trees perform the function of transferring water and nutrients to growing tissues.

Xylem: The portion of conducting vascular tissue that conducts water and dissolved minerals. It contains several types of cells such as tracheids, vessel elements, parenchyma, sclereids, fibers, etc.

Yeasts: Unicellular ascomycetes which lack mycelium. In yeasts individual cells itself perform the functions of a large mycelium.

Zone of Elongation: Root tip region which lies toward the root apical mersitem, where pronounced elongation of cells takes place.

Zoospore: Motile spore capable of swimming. Occurs in fungi and algae.

Zosterophyllophytes: Bunch of early vascular plants possessing xylem and exarch prostele. They also feature lateral sporangia which open transversely on the top edge.

Zygosporangium: Large multinucleate sporangium produced by the fusion of two compatible hyphae in Zygomycete fungi.

Zygote: Diploid cell conduced by the fusion of two gametes.